Business Communication Design

CREATIVITY,

STRATEGIES,

AND

SOLUTIONS

Pamela Angell
Hudson Valley Community College

With

Teeanna Rizkallah
California State University, Fullerton

 Irwin

Boston   Burr Ridge, IL   Dubuque, IA   Madison, WI   New York   San Francisco   St. Louis
Bangkok   Bogotá   Caracas   Kuala Lumpur   Lisbon   London   Madrid   Mexico City
Milan   Montreal   New Delhi   Santiago   Seoul   Singapore   Sydney   Taipei   Toronto

BUSINESS COMMUNICATION DESIGN:
CREATIVITY, STRATEGIES, AND SOLUTIONS
Published by McGraw-Hill/Irwin, a business unit of The McGraw-Hill Companies, Inc., 1221 Avenue of the Americas,
New York, NY, 10020. Copyright © 2004 by The McGraw-Hill Companies, Inc. All rights reserved. No part of this publication
may be reproduced or distributed in any form or by any means, or stored in a database or retrieval system, without the prior
written consent of The McGraw-Hill Companies, Inc., including, but not limited to, in any network or other electronic storage or
transmission, or broadcast for distance learning.
Some ancillaries, including electronic and print components, may not be available to customers outside the United States.
This book is printed on acid-free paper.

domestic   1 2 3 4 5 6 7 8 9 0 WCK/WCK 0 9 8 7 6 5 4 3
international 1 2 3 4 5 6 7 8 9 0 WCK/WCK 0 9 8 7 6 5 4 3

ISBN   0-07-244128-3

Publisher: *John E. Biernat*
Executive editor: *Andy Winston*
Developmental editor: *Joanne Butler*
Editorial assistant: *Samira Puskar*
Senior marketing manager: *Ellen Cleary*
Media producer: *Mark Molsky*
Project manager: *Jim Labeots*
Senior production supervisor: *Michael R. McCormick*
Lead designer: *Pam Verros*
Photo research coordinator: *Judy Kausal*
Photo researcher: *Robin Sand*
Supplement producer: *Betty Hadala*
Senior digital content specialist: *Brian Nacik*
Cover design: *Pam Verros*
Interior design: *Maureen McCutcheon*
Typeface: *10.5/13 Palatino*
Compositor: *Carlisle Communications, Ltd.*
Printer: *Quebecor World Versailles Inc.*

Library of Congress Cataloging-in-Publication Data
Angell, Pamela.
     Business communication design : creativity, strategies, and solutions
  / Pamela Angell, Teeanna Rizkallah.
        p. cm.
Includes bibliographical references and index.
     ISBN 0-07-244128-3 (alk. paper) -- ISBN 0-07-119921-7 (international :
     alk. paper)
     1. Business communication. I. Rizkallah, Teeanna. II. Title.
HF5718.A746 2004
651.7--dc21
                                                        2003044183

INTERNATIONAL EDITION ISBN 0-07-119921-7
Copyright © 2004. Exclusive rights by The McGraw-Hill Companies, Inc. for manufacture and export. This book cannot be
re-exported from the country to which it is sold by McGraw-Hill. The International Edition is not available in North America.

www.mhhe.com

Preface

Welcome to Business Communication Design

Through a straightforward, eight-step process, *Business Communication Design: Creativity, Strategies, and Solutions* presents a strategic approach to learning the fundamentals of business communication and designing effective business messages.

A Message Designed for Students

Message creation reaches with long arms and touches everything we think, feel, and do as communicators both personally and professionally.

This method-based instruction offers you techniques to design intrapersonal (internal), verbal (speech and writing), nonverbal, interpersonal (interaction), collaborative, and change messages for use in nearly every aspect of business. Through contemporary communication theory, real-world business examples, and practical applications, you will develop the skills necessary to become a successful communication designer. During your career, you will cultivate and use the skills mastered through this text to solve problems, face new challenges and technologies, build relationships, and develop creative communication strategies of your own.

A Message Designed for Instructors, Communication Designers, and Friends

Virtually any student can excel if the instructional design is grounded in both the theoretical and practical applications of communication design.

Business Communication Design focuses on pragmatic design techniques that are easy to use, understand, and teach. This text allows you to integrate your course materials and ideas into flexible and comfortable business communication content. Innovative topics include useful and necessary applications of listening, culture, collaborative, and visual communication. The text presents these topics concisely in its 17 chapters, a manageable number to cover over an average college term.

Skill Building and Creative Challenges, Activities, and Cases

A comprehensive set of creative activities and exercises are included in each chapter to support your course instruction. These features include "In a Nutshell" (introductory examples), "Creative Challenge" (brief critical thinking exercises), "Jump In" (skill-building activities), "Word on the Web" (Web-based exercises and information), "Strategies," "Creative Cases" (situational and topic specific case studies), "Business Communication Projects," and "Discussion Questions." See pages x–xv for detailed descriptions of how these features can enhance the learning experience.

A Message About the Chapters

Chapter 1, *The Basics*, provides the reader with connections to, and applications of, communication skills in 21st century business. This chapter also introduces basic communication principles, the interactive process, and an intrapersonal approach that identifies students as communication designers.

Chapter 2, *How Business Communicates*, offers a brief exploration of directions for 21st century business communications including globalization, management information, technology, and change. This chapter focuses on business messages that flow internally and externally through formal and informal communication networks.

Chapter 3, *Communication Design Strategy*, introduces and describes the heart of communication design—MESSAGES. The acronym MESSAGES spells out the eight steps involved in designing effective business messages. While not every message will require the execution of all eight steps, most business messages do. The steps provide the basis of message construction and a comprehensive strategy for communication designers.

Chapter 4, *Listening: A Silent Hero*, is a comprehensive examination of listening skills, types, and liabilities in business. Because at least 45 percent of a business communicator's time is spent listening, it is a fundamental skill. This chapter explores active, passive, and not listening and offers strategies to listen effectively.

Chapter 5, *Using and Designing Meaning*, explores how meaning is created through perception and is rooted in cultural experience. Meaning is different for each person because perceptions vary. This chapter discusses intended and interpreted meaning, contexts, semantics, and strategies to design messages with clear meaning.

Chapter 6, *Designing Messages with Words*, provides the fundamentals of verbal communication (speaking and writing) and associated speech styles, rules, and limitations. This chapter also focuses on communication apprehension, persuasion and argumentation principals, and design strategies.

Chapter 7, *Designing Oral Presentations*, presents fear factors associated with public speaking and practical anxiety reduction techniques. This chapter also covers topic selection, speech goals, customizing presentations, speech organization, and delivery strategies.

Chapter 8, *Business Writing Design*, is a strategy-based method for written communication. This chapter focuses on business writing including the process, various styles, and using the "you view." Strategies for developing memos, letters, and email messages will help students to construct effective written documents.

Chapter 9, *Direct and Indirect Communication Strategies*, focuses on the use of direct and indirect communication strategies in written business messages. This chapter presents types, goals, and components of positive, negative, neutral, and persuasive messages.

Chapter 10, *The Business of Reports: Informal and Formal Report Writing*, features business writing instruments that are designed to solicit funding, approval, or partnership. This chapter discusses formal and informal styles of reports, research, and techniques for organization and construction.

Chapter 11, *Writing Strategies for Reports and Proposals*, focuses specifically on using direct and indirect strategies in formal and informal reports. Consideration is given to audience, types of reports connected to strategy, and the components.

Chapter 12, *Culture: Inside and Out*, presents a macro view of social culture and diversity, and a micro view of organizational culture. Aspects of both deep and observable organizational culture are provided in this chapter with strategies to understand and work effectively within a diverse organization.

Chapter 13, *Designing Interpersonal and Collaborative Messages*, features interpersonal business relationships, nonverbal, and collaborative group communication. Because most business professionals spend between 80 and 90 percent of their time engaged in interpersonal interaction, readers will understand how relationships evolve in business contexts and what strategies to use to maintain good working interactions. This chapter also examines the development of small groups and teams in business including the four C's of effective small groups, leadership communication, c-commerce technology, and distance meetings.

Chapter 14, *The Business of Change and Conflict*, offers strategies for the business communicator dealing with change. In business transition, messages can become distorted or hidden and communication styles become closed. Resistance and reduction techniques including multidirectional and multimedia communication are examined. This chapter also presents conflict resolution skills to achieve accord through traditional and transformative communication strategies.

Chapter 15, *Creating a Career and Designing Résumés*, features career development strategies, five résumé formats, and the ingredients to construct them. This chapter also provides cover letter design techniques that are ideal for students entering the job market.

Chapter 16, *Interviewing to Get the Job*, features the employment interview process, traditional and behavioral interviews, an overview of interviewer and applicant goals, preparation techniques, and the types of questions asked. This chapter also focuses on strategies for follow-up calls, letters, and negotiating the position package.

Chapter 17, *Creativity and Visual Design*, many business designers will not acquire nor need the necessary skills to become professional graphic designers but most will need some basic knowledge. Because visuals frequently support both written and oral business messages, communication designers need to understand how visuals work to enhance messages. This chapter describes the various types of quantitative and qualitative infographics, and offers strategies to develop effective visual designs and integrate them into documents.

A Message Designed to Express Appreciation

Any creative work of this magnitude requires the expertise and dedication of numerous people to bring it to fruition. This book was a labor of love that included the talents of McGraw-Hill publishing professionals, such as developmental editor Joanne Butler, who went above and beyond to contribute inspiration, insight, and even some visuals and pedagogy to ensure the successful completion of this project. To her I owe the greatest debt of gratitude, and in her I have found lasting friendship. Special thanks also goes to Andy Winston, whose laugh-a-little, fight-a-little approach makes him the champion of all managing editors in my book. Ellen Cleary and Mark Ventra also deserve special appreciation for promoting and carrying the message to so many of my colleagues and their students far and wide.

I would also like to thank three very talented colleagues for their assistance: Teeanna Rizkallah from the State University of California at Fullerton for her contributions on the project and preparation of the Instructor's Manual, B. Barbara Boerner from Brevard College for producing the Test Bank, and Dorinda Clippinger from the University of South Carolina for creating the PowerPoint® package.

I am especially grateful to my colleagues, students, and friends, Tom Niederkorn, Anne Minehan, Carolyn Mackey-Temple, Sherri Wait, Sherry Goldstein, Danielle Blesi, and Mike Lynick, who gave generously of their time and talent with research and visual support.

My heartfelt thanks also go to my mentor and friend Diane Gayeski whose insights more than a decade ago inspired communication design; to Scott Velie whose faith in me never wavered, and to Karen Habel and Lee Aurelia, whose constant support encouraged me to press on.

Faculty and students are encouraged to offer their suggestions, ideas, or comments to Professor Pamela Angell, by e-mail: *pamangell@yahoo.com.*

—Pamela Angell

Designing the Future of Business Communication

creativity, strategy, & solutions

Business Communication Design: Creativity, Strategy, and

Solutions presents a strategic approach to learning the fundamentals of communication and the design of any successful communication. This innovative text focuses on critical and creative thinking as the necessary precursors to designing effective business messages. Thought-provoking pedagogy throughout the text stimulates and enhances these critical, creative thinking skills.

In A Nutshell

Each chapter is briefly introduced with "In a Nutshell." Based on current events and stories from the real world, Nutshells heighten students' awareness of real-life communication issues and underscore how actual business communication practitioners deal with the issues raised within the chapter.

How Business Communicates

IN A NUTSHELL

The recent collapse of Enron offers lessons in communication for everyone. Enron, the Texas-based energy company, capitalized on the volatility of energy prices in the late 1990s. Through its strategic and aggressive marketing of electricity and gas, Enron realized sales of more than $1.1 billion in 2000. The eventual collapse of this energy trader in the largest bankruptcy case in U.S. history is a story of cover-ups and scandals. And it is a story of how organizational messages are sent and received.

The investigation to determine how Enron lost billions of dollars eventually led to Arthur Andersen, Enron's accounting firm. When federal officials approached Andersen, looking for financial documents related to Andersen's audit of Enron, they found many documents crucial to their investigation had been destroyed. Andersen was charged with obstruction of justice for shredding documents.

It was in the fall of 2001 that Andersen managers first got wind that an investigation by the Securities and Exchange Commission (SEC) into their Enron account was likely. In a downward bound structural message, employees of Andersen working on the Enron account were directed by managing partner Thomas Bauer to make sure they complied with the firm's "documentation retention policy." But what, exactly, did Bauer mean when he used the term "document retention"? What message was he sending to the staff accountants working on the Enron audit? Andersen employees apparently understood the message to mean the opposite of document retention—to destroy rather than keep documents. In her testimony, Patrica Sue Grutzmacher, another Andersen manager working with Enron, claimed that when Bauer referred to the firm's document retention policy, it was a policy requiring the destruction of certain records. So, Bauer's message to comply with the policy actually meant employees should destroy documents. Although the verbal message employees received was to comply with the policy of retention, what Bauer ordered and what employees understood was to shred the documents.

CREATIVE CHALLENGE

Break into groups with your class colleagues and consider the following message idea and audience. Then select a source you feel would be credible and would be someone to whom the audience could relate.

Message Main Idea
The main idea of our message involves appropriate behavior and what incarceration will be like in a youth detention center.

Audience
The audience for our message is females from age 12 to 17. These young people have been adjudicated through the court system and will be entering the youth detention center.

Channel
10-minute videotape presentation.

Source
The director of the youth detention center has indicated that although he is open to suggestions, he would like to be the source for this message.

As a team, discuss and describe the characteristics of the source you would select for both the narrative and on-camera talent for this video message.

When to Transmit

Timing is when you transmit your message. Good timing can be critical in determining how welcome your message will be to your audience. Assume you designed a persuasive message to compel your supervisor to grant you a pay raise. You developed a strong argument based on your many accomplishments, extra hours devoted to work tasks, perfect attendance, and superior work performance. However, when you conveyed your carefully designed message, the company was busy preparing to pay taxes. The boss would probably tell you to come back after tax season ends. At Xerox, customers felt that repair representatives arrived too slowly to service machines. To convey the message that its customers' time is valuable, Xerox decided to let customers assess the urgency of their copier machine problems and schedule repairs themselves. Simply having control over the timing of personal contact and service increased Xerox customer satisfaction dramatically.

Many businesses cater to the work schedules of clients, such as FedEx, a package carrier that maintains a "superhub" for cargo planes in Memphis, Tennessee. The last call for package pickup is 11:30 P.M., and the drop-off deadline is midnight at the Memphis FedEx airport terminal. Local computer businesses, repair shops, and aircraft equipment dealers all conduct business and communicate with FedEx employees until about 2 A.M., when the last cargo planes fly in and out of Memphis International Airport.

Creative Challenge

Creative Challenges are flexible critical thinking exercises that challenge students to explore and apply chapter concepts. This material requires students to think strategically. They may be asked to develop a message approach or to prepare a written response to a challenging business situation.

← JUMP IN!

Read the following letter and determine the verbal style(s) used to reach the message goal. Then rewrite the letter using a more appropriate verbal style to make a clear and effective statement. Be prepared to identify what types of verbal style you use and where.

Dear Ms. Swiggins:

Your application for credit has been denied. You have overextended your credit liability so greatly that it is impossible to consider offering you even one of our prefunded cards. Most of our customers have impeccable credit and it is as much for their protection as for our own that high-risk clients are excluded from our prestigious bank.

Perhaps if you practiced better economy in your personal finances you would be in a better position to reduce your debts and eventually build a satisfactory credit history. If this occurs we may consider a new credit application. You would, of course, not be able to avail yourself of our best interest rates and benefits packages, but in time even these restrictions might be lifted, providing your credit situation improves steadily.

If you have any questions, please feel free to call, but only between the hours of 9 A.M. and 5 P.M. Monday through Friday.

Sincerely,
Carle Barrett
New Accounts Manager

descriptor, the concept becomes more abstract. A family tree is not a woody plant; it is a genealogical chart. A phone tree maintains the shape of footwear. Although the concept of a living *tree* still influences perception, the descriptors (*family, phone, shoe*) control the meaning of the term further.

Connotation is less definitive and involves the personal or emotional feelings that we associate with words. Our emotional association with a word or symbol, derived from our personal experiences, becomes its meaning. The word *tree* may bring to mind cool, shady summer evenings sitting on a swing. Or it may also be an object of fear if you've ever fallen out of one and broken your arm. Some may associate the word with a business perspective as in income from the sale of lumber.

We are usually aware of the denotative meaning of words and expect others to view them as we do. But it is important to remember that not all people make the same semantic associations. Imagine being a team leader on a high-priority project. You explain to your two teammates that their components

CREATIVE

CHALLENGE

Think of a situation in which you found communication with someone else dissatisfying or disappointing: an argument with a family member or a missed opportunity to interact with someone you admire, for example. Consider these issues:
• Whom were you interacting with?
• How did you feel about the person you were communicating with?
• What was the purpose of the interaction?
• Where were you?
• What was your mood?
• What was said?
After answering these questions, write a few brief paragraphs about how you could have communicated more effectively and how that interaction could have had a more satisfactory conclusion.

125

Jump In

A Jump In is a skill-based assignment, task, or activity that asks students to design communication strategies. The assignments involve creating or modifying verbal messages and written documents, reacting to specific interactions, or evaluating communication situations.

Word On The Web

A Word on the Web is an interactive Internet activity that offers students an opportunity to access various websites for information pertinent to chapter concepts.

Word on the Web

Many large corporations have diversity programs that help them select their suppliers. These programs give preference to businesses that are owned and run by minorities, women, and people with disabilities, as long as these businesses can offer competitive services. Some of the supplier diversity policies of large companies can be viewed at these websites:

• Quaker Oats: www.quakeroats.com/about/supplier.html
• Boeing: www.boeing.com/companyoffices/doingbiz/terms/sbsdb
• AT&T: www.att.com/hr/life/eoaa/supplier_diversity.html
• Pillsbury: www.pillsbury.com/about/supplierdiv.asp
• Verizon: www.gte.com/Aboutgte/Organization/Supply/supplierguide/supplierdiver.html
• Sun Microsystems: www.iforce.com/aboutsun/coinfo/diversity/index.html

Take a look at some of these sites. Write an e-mail to your instructor in response to the following questions:
1. How do these programs support diversity in the business world?
2. How specific is each program in its definition of minorities?
3. Would you recommend any adjustments or changes in the policies described at these sites, and what would they be?

STRATEGIES

Strategies

Before the Speech

1. Practice and rehearse your speech often. Rehearse with friends or colleagues and ask for constructive criticism and feedback so you can identify and work out any problems before the presentation. Practice and rehearsal will build your confidence. The more familiar you are with the material, the more certain you will feel during delivery.

2. Practice speaking naturally without reading from your notes. Ideally, good speakers know the material they want to present and refer to notes only occasionally.

3. If at all possible, arrange to visit the room in which you will be speaking to check and practice with any equipment and to evaluate room size, acoustics, and seating.

4. Visualize your presentation. Imagine the presentation flowing smoothly and your audience reacting positively. See yourself calmly and confidently presenting the material and effectively engaging the audience.

5. Relax your body and mind. Work out any tension in your body by stretching your arms and legs and breathing deeply in through your nose and out through your mouth. Clear your mind of thoughts by closing your eyes and focusing on your breathing.

6. Use positive self-talk. Tell yourself, "I am relaxed and confident" or "I know my material and I can talk about it easily."

7. Select appropriate dress. A baseball cap, beat-up sneakers, and jeans are probably inappropriate choices for a formal business

Strategies

Chapter strategies highlight skills that students should master once they complete the chapter.

Business Communication Projects

Business Communication Projects are practical exercises and assignments that apply chapter concepts. These projects challenge students to use the communication design skills developed in the chapter. Both group and individual activities are included.

Business Communication Projects

1. Break into small groups with your class colleagues and discuss the following question: How do you ask a business professional of higher rank for a favor? For this project, imagine you want to ask your department director if you can use her for a job reference. Discuss why you might use somewhat vague language in your message to the director and how you would design the request using vague language. Then discuss how to design the same message using specific language. Share your ideas with the class.
2. Ask several people of different ages and backgrounds to define what the following words mean to them:
   - Restructure
   - Term
   - Operative
   - Downsize
   - Change
   - Strategy
   - Code

   Compare the different responses you receive for variations in meaning.
3. Think of a situation in which you have experienced a misunderstanding or miscommunication with another person. Write a short e-mail to your instructor that describes the situation, the reason for the miscommunication, and how it was resolved.
4. Identify each of the following messages as specific or vague.
   _____ Please bring me the proposal from the file.
   _____ It would help if I had the proposal to work with.
   _____ I don't know how I'll get to work, I can't even afford to fix my car.
   _____ I want a raise.

---

as it may seem before the speaker becomes too emotional.
   c. Listening carefully to the speaker and paraphrasing his or her feelings and concerns to gain clarity and provide support.
   d. Telling a similar story so that the speaker won't feel as bad or as alone.
8. During your annual performance evaluation, your manager informed you that he required a higher degree of effort from you and your raise would be less than the company average. On numerous occasions during the year, you had explained to him that you needed additional direction with your work tasks, but he never responded to your requests. Write a letter of complaint to your union representative that discusses your situation and explain that your boss does not listen to you. Back up your concerns with information from the text.

Discussion Questions

1. What business settings require employees to listen actively to learn, critically evaluate, and sensitively support others?
2. How does listening provide you with a better understanding of a business culture?
3. As a business communication designer, explain how you can use what you have learned about listening to increase your audiences' understanding of your messages.
4. How can you demonstrate that you are listening actively to a speaker?
5. What strategies can you think of to reduce or eliminate employee distraction by wireless devices during business meetings?
6. What is the distinction between listening and hearing? Can you name the songs or news reports you heard as you listened to the radio on the way to school or work today? Spend 15 minutes making a list of what you heard. Be prepared to discuss what you remember and why you remember it.
7. What is cultural noise? Come up with some examples.
8. What are the benefits and dangers of passive listening?

Discussion Questions

Discussion Questions are designed to inspire critical and strategic thinking during class discussions.

---

4. What is the importance of the executive summary?
5. Why is it necessary to organize background material according to a specific approach (chronological, situational, or statistical)?
6. Why is it necessary to redefine the problem or topic statement mid-report?
7. What is the purpose of using themes or key words throughout a document?
8. What's wrong with a vague objectives statement?
9. Are there any sections of a report or proposal that could employ an indirect approach, even if a direct approach seems to be the best strategy? Explain.
10. How important is a positive ending to an informational report?

Creative Cases

Creative Cases are examples that describe real-world companies and the communication challenges business professionals face. These studies help students examine and understand communication challenges in business. Creative cases strengthen students' evaluative, problem-solving, and decision-making skills.

CREATIVE CASE

Creative Case

Buying for Baby on the Internet

In 1994, an entrepreneurial group from Carnegie Mellon University approached Lynne Bingham. Bingham owned a successful children's boutique in Pittsburgh, and the group wanted her to participate in an e-commerce project. They wanted her to put her store on the World Wide Web. She agreed.

Sales were slow in the beginning. It was a full year before someone actually ordered anything from her website. But sales improved eventually, and in 2000 she sold her store to focus on web-based sales. Later, a high-tech company in the Netherlands, Stork Group, paid her a six-figure sum to purchase her site's name. This left Bingham with plenty of capital to work with, but no website.

Initially, Bingham solicited bids for a site design. A site built from the ground up, she found, would probably run her $15,000 to $30,000. She also found Yahoo! shopping. On Yahoo! she could build a site herself using Yahoo!'s templates and reporting tools for inventory and site management for $100 a month. A Yahoo! site would be simpler to build and use but would lack the design options and flexibility a brand new site could offer. She just wasn't sure whether the limited capabilities of the Yahoo! service would meet her goals for growth and development of her company, The Stork Delivers.com.

Supplements and Technology

For Instructors

Keep Your Course Current with PowerWeb

The Instructor's Online Learning Center with PowerWeb (OLC) is a website that follows *Business Communication Design* chapter-by-chapter with digital supplementary content germane to the book.

The following supplements are put in digitized format for you on McGraw-Hill's exclusive Instructor's Resource CD (IRCD). Now everything is on one convenient CD:

INSTRUCTORS MANUAL

This manual written by Teeanna Rizkallah, California State University at Fullerton, will save you invaluable time preparing for the course by providing suggestions for heightening your students' interest in the material. There are sections on using the text, organizing course themes, developing a syllabus, creating a schedule, assigning and evaluating writing projects, and suggestions for grading practices.

Each chapter-by-chapter section presents a chapter summary, creative case development, answers to exercises, and suggestions for groupwork.

TEST BANK

Written by the Barbara Boerner, Brevard College, the test bank contains approximately sixty questions per chapter in multiple choice, true/false, and short answer format. Each question is ranked for difficulty level and textbook references are provided for the answers.

POWERPOINT® SLIDES

This PowerPoint presentation includes key points from each chapter, sample figures from the text, and supplemental exhibits that help illustrate the main points of each chapter.

VIDEOS

These videos provide a wonderful jump-start to classroom discussion. The videos include real managers–unscripted–reacting to actors challenging their communication and management skills. The results are authentic dialogues between managers and their employees attempting to resolve challenging situations. Students and professors can discuss the reaction/behaviors of the manager in each particular situation–to weigh the positives and negatives about the way the situation was handled. These videos present situations on topics and skills such as negotiation amidst cultural differences, active listening, and teamwork.

For Students:

BCOMM SKILL BOOSTER

Every new copy of *Business Communication Design* comes with FREE access to the BComm Skill Booster, an Internet-based reinforcement system that delivers fun, interactive lessons on a regular basis directly to the subscriber's computer through push technology. Students get bite-sized lessons that reinforce the main themes of the course lectures and reading assignments. These lessons consist of topical overviews, anecdotes, quiz questions, and other relevant content to reinforce the daily use of business communication skills in real-time, real-life situations.

ONLINE LEARNING CENTER

As students progress through the course and the text, they can access the text's online learning center to take self-grading quizzes, review material, and work through interactive exercises. Thanks to embedded PowerWeb content, students can get quick access to real-world news and essays that pertain to business communication. OLCs can be delivered multiple ways–through the textbook website, through PageOut, or within a course management system such as WebCT or Blackboard.

The student online learning center also provides access to Business Communications Online, where students can stay current and expand their knowledge about the many topics pertinent to business communication. Selecting a topic such as audience analysis, diversity, or résumés accesses two or more online discussion questions or exercises.

Also included in Business Communication Online is "Business Around the World." This link offers an outstanding global resource for researching and exploring business communications online. Business and management news and analysis, country facts, news, and insights about over thirty-five countries are all accessable.

Acknowledgments

I am extremely grateful for the generous and enthusiastic comments, insights, and observations provided by my colleagues and reviewers. So many of the ideas offered helped to form both the text content and pedagogy.

Marilyn Beebe, *Kirkwood Community College*

Suzanne Biedenbach, *The University of Akron*

Karen Bilda, *Cardinal Stritch University*

B. Barbara Boerner, *Brevard College*

Billy Cathings, *University of Indianapolis*

Dorinda Clippinger, *University of South Carolina*

Steven Culbert, *University of Texas, Arlington*

Arnolda Hilgert, *Northern Arizona University*

Glenda Hudson, *California State University, Bakersfield*

Carrolle H. Kamperman, *Baylor University*

Richard Lacy, *California State University, Fresno*

Kathy Lewis, *University of North Alabama*

Jere' W. Littlejohn, *University of Mississippi*

Judy M. O'Neill, *The University of Texas at Austin*

Susan Prenzlow, *Minnesota State University, Mankato*

Terry D. Roach, *Arkansas State University–Jonesboro*

Betty Schroeder, *Northern Illinois University*

Jean Anna Sellers, *Fort Hays State University*

Joyce Monroe Simmons, *Florida State University*

Judy Steiner-Williams, *Indiana University*

Joyce Stroud, *University of Arkansas, Little Rock*

Dana H. Swensen, *Utah State University*

Deborah Valentine, *Emory University*

Randall L. Waller, *Baylor University*

John Waltman, *Eastern Michigan University*

Contents in Brief

Contents

Contents

CHAPTER 3

COMMUNICATION DESIGN STRATEGY   52

CHAPTER 4

LISTENING: A SILENT HERO   76

CHAPTER 5

USING AND DESIGNING MEANING   98

CHAPTER 6
DESIGNING MESSAGES WITH WORDS 120

CHAPTER 7
DESIGNING ORAL PRESENTATIONS 142

CHAPTER 14

THE BUSINESS OF CHANGE AND CONFLICT   332

CHAPTER 15

CREATING A CAREER AND DESIGNING RÉSUMÉS   360

Business Communication Design

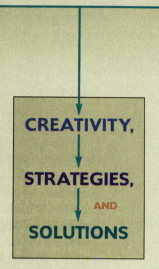

CREATIVITY,

STRATEGIES,

AND

SOLUTIONS

Chapter 1

Chapter 1

The Basics

"You can dream, create, design, and build the most wonderful place in the world . . . but it requires people to make the dream a reality."—Walt Disney

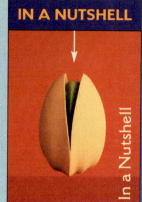

Have you ever considered pursuing a "Ducktorate Degree?" How about a "Mouster's Degree?" That's what you'll earn if you participate in the Disney World College Program. Every year the Disney corporation recruits thousands of college students from around the world to "live, earn, and learn" in the Magic Kingdom. The Disney organization understands that the success of their business is directly related to the communication skills of their cast members (employees). In order for guests to experience the Disney Magic, cast members are trained in the basic skills associated with effective communication. They are directed to:

- Greet every guest (generating a verbal message of welcome).
- Make eye contact and smile (convey a nonverbal message of attention and fun).
- Display cheerful and cordial body language.
- Say thank you (polite messages of gratitude).
- Preserve the "magical" experience (use creativity to entertain and engage guests interpersonally).

Disney is an organization that understands the importance of people to its success as a business. By training cast members to communicate effectively and creatively, Disney presents a magical message that keeps guests coming back.

Does demonstrating cheerful and polite verbal and nonverbal messages encourage positive feedback from message receivers like the guests at Disney? Is communication more appealing when message senders are upbeat and friendly? Could other businesses benefit from the instruction offered at the Disney World College Program?

What Is Communication?

Every business—whether a multibillion-dollar company such as Disney or a small family-owned grocery store—relies on the communication skills of its employees to be successful. But what makes for effective communication? As our "In a Nutshell" discusses, communication involves listening and the exchange of verbal and nonverbal messages. It can be formal or informal. It may involve a large group or just two people. Disney conveys its magical message effectively by educating its cast members about the numerous ways of communicating. To understand the many ways business professionals communicate, it is important to first understand how communication works.

communication is the exchange of message meaning within a person and between people.

Communication is the exchange of message meaning within a person and between people. It is a continuous process that occurs in various contexts and uses cultural symbols. It is a process that purposefully uses spoken, nonverbal, and visual symbols. Communication involves and affects nearly every disciplinary field, including business.

Skills for 21st-Century Business

Modern communication has many applications in the world of business. Virtually all forms of business messages—from simple greetings to customers to formal memos, reports, and presentations—require solid communication skills. Most American businesses (88 percent) currently train their employees in some type of communication skills. Businesses tend to focus on critical thinking and listening skills, interpersonal communication (including interviewing and nonverbal inter-

Twenty-first century business communicators need multiple communication skills.
© JFPI Studios, Inc./CORBIS

actions), collaborative communication involving groups and teams, writing, and oral presentations.

You will need to be skilled in intrapersonal, business, interpersonal, small-group, verbal, and public communication. These categories overlap in a variety of ways.

1. **Intrapersonal** or **internal communication** involves the internal processing of messages. Individuals generate, send, and receive messages. Critical thinking and reasoning, decision making, and message design are all skills that you develop and use by self-communicating. You generate ideas and develop them into messages in thinking and internal dialogue. The messages you create need to be designed in the most effective way to increase mutual understanding and shared meaning with other people. In business, you need to critically think through, evaluate, plan for, and design messages intrapersonally (internally) for eventual delivery to a variety of business audiences. Intrapersonal communication is illustrated in Figure 1.1.

   As an intrapersonal skill, **listening** involves the active mental and cognitive process of attending to and interpreting sounds. Craig Weatherup, chair and chief executive officer (CEO) of Pepsi Bottling Group, believes that listening is one of the most important communication skills. He first had to develop sensitive listening skills (focusing on the feelings and emotions of other people) while working in Japan for Pepsi. Since English was not the native language for his Japanese associates, Weatherup learned to interpret the emotional meaning in messages. The listening skills he developed early in his career have helped him throughout his years at Pepsi. As CEO, he tries

intrapersonal or **internal communication** involves the internal processing of messages.

listening involves the active mental and cognitive process of attending to and interpreting sounds.

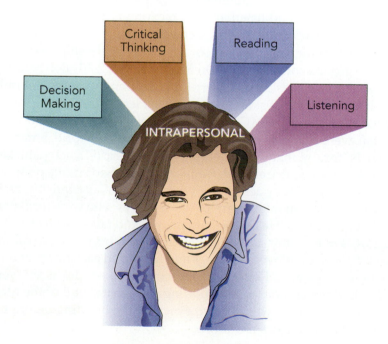

FIGURE 1.1

Intrapersonal Communication

to communicate one-on-one with as many of his 40,000 employees as he can. He listens for their feelings about the business, not just the latest trends. In fact, when he visits the company's 300 sites, he listens actively to the excitement and frustrations expressed in the language his managers use to better gauge how his strategies are working.

In business you will spend nearly half your working day listening. In fact, much of what we know and learn comes from listening. Unfortunately, the skill of listening is underdeveloped in most people. It is estimated that we remember only about 20 percent of what we hear, and fewer than 2 percent of us actually receive formal listening training.

Reading is the intrapersonal process of attending to and interpreting written language. Business professionals spend more time listening and reading than using any other communication skills. Effective reading involves selecting relevant or important points from a document and interpreting those points for meaning.

2. **Business communication** involves the design and exchange of messages between members who work interdependently to accomplish organizational goals. Business communication involves the flow of communication and the structure through which messages are exchanged among an organization's members. The changing nature of business due to technological innovations, ever-evolving corporate structures, and mergers necessitates that business communicators be flexible, knowledgeable, and innovative.

3. **Interpersonal** or **external communication** is the process of interaction and the exchange of messages between at least two people who co-create a relationship. Intrapersonal, spoken, nonverbal, and listening skills are used simultaneously as people communicate. As people think, talk, and listen, they also express themselves nonverbally through various body and facial movements and posture. Interpersonal communication also involves leadership skills in business groups and on teams. On September 11, 2001, Bob Mulholland, senior vice president at Merrill Lynch, demonstrated not only effective interpersonal skills but strong leadership. When terrorists attacked the World Trade Center in New York City, Mulholland and his staff were working across West Street at Two World Financial Center. Naturally, many of the employees at Merrill Lynch panicked and others became frozen with fear as they watched smoke pour out of the building directly across from them. Mulholland quickly gathered information about his employees' relatives who were located in the tower buildings. He listened attentively and talked to each of his employees in a soothing, gentle manner to comfort them. He calmly acknowledged employees' feelings and reassured each one that they had time to escape. Finally, Mulholland walked the employees down the stairs and out of the building. Fortunately, all of the Merrill Lynch employees were able to evacuate the building before the towers collapsed across the street.

reading is the intrapersonal process of attending to and interpreting written language.

business communication involves the design and exchange of messages between and among members to accomplish organizational goals.

interpersonal or **external communication** is the interaction between at least two people who co-create a relationship.

Organizations consist of people, and as a professional you will spend up to 80 percent of your time interacting with others, which is why strong interpersonal skills are a must for any business professional.

4. **Small-group communication** involves two or more people who join together to accomplish specific goals. In the world of business you will almost certainly need to work with other people. Committees, project groups, and problem-solving teams bring different professionals together to plan, develop, and implement company initiatives. Knowing how to participate, cooperate, and collaborate as part of a team is essential. Surmounting and resolving the conflicts that arise as people work together is also a fundamental group communication skill.

5. **Verbal communication** encompasses the use of both *spoken* and *written language* to accomplish message goals. As a business communicator you will use your verbal skills to convey a wide variety of business messages, including formal and informal discussions during meetings, interviews, and presentations. You will also routinely talk to customers and vendors and network with other professionals. While many business professionals prefer spoken communication to written communication, 21st-century business depends on workers who can write well. Virtually all professionals—from executives, engineers, and lawyers to accountants and computer scientists—need to be able to write effective business messages. Entry-level professionals and managers alike prepare written messages (including e-mails, memos, reports, letters, and proposals) every day.

6. **Public communication** refers to public speaking or lectures presented to a group audience. Public speaking is a fact of everyday life for many business professionals. Promotional, sales, proposal, new-product or program, and progress or research presentations are standard in business. Not all presentations are delivered to outside audiences; business communicators also routinely present information informally at meetings and during small group discussions.

small-group communication involves two or more people who join together to accomplish specific goals.

verbal communication is the use of both spoken and written language to accomplish message goals.

public communication refers to public speaking or lectures presented to a group audience.

Basic Communication Principles

Communication Is a Process

The exchange of messages is ongoing and dynamic. Our internal communication and our exchanges with others are always changing and growing. Consider your communication with a hiring manager who is filling a position you are interested in. Your initial contact with the manager will be quite formal—written communication in the form of a résumé. You will then likely have to utilize your oral communication skills in the interview process. Once you get the job, your interaction with the manager will evolve as you become part of a team and a corporate culture. The process of communication is a moving and evolving set of experiences that influence our present and future interactions. Intrapersonal and interpersonal communication are both active and flexible.

Communication Is Contextual

Our interactions with others occur during specific social situations, in different physical environments, and for a variety of purposes. Our communication differs depending on the people involved and the circumstances in which it occurs. Your interactions with co-workers are different from those with family and friends or with other students at school. Our moods, our attitudes, and the roles we play also contribute to changing communication contexts. Each communication experience is unique, because the people, roles, situations, and environments are unique and always changing.

nonverbal communication includes body movements such as gestures, facial expressions, and vocal sounds that do not use words.

Communication Is Continuous

From the moment we are born, we are always communicating. Even if we do not talk, we still communicate nonverbally. **Nonverbal communication** includes body movements such as gestures, facial expressions, and vocal sounds that do not use words. Not all of our communication is intentional: We may not intend to scratch, twitch, or yawn, but some people may still interpret these as nonverbal communication behaviors. If, for example, you inadvertently yawn during a business presentation, the speaker may think you are bored. Even if you really are interested but you got only four hours of sleep last night, the speaker may interpret the yawn as a message you are trying to communicate.

We also continually communicate internally. Intrapersonal communication involves both intentional and unintentional message exchange. Some of our thought processing is unintentional, such as when the body signals thirst to the brain, but our internal critical thinking, listening, and reading are intentional communication. Even during our interactions with other people, we communicate internally as illustrated in Figure 1.2.

CREATIVE

CHALLENGE

Imagine you have decided not to communicate at all for several days. To accomplish your mission, you travel deep into a barren winter desert so that you will not run in to any other people. You bring sufficient water, food, and wood to sustain you for the duration of your isolated adventure. Alone in the desert, you pitch your tent and prepare to start a small campfire.

Now that you are alone in your desert camp, miles away from other people, can you meet your goal? Can you stop communicating completely? Come to class prepared to discuss your conclusion.

Communication Coordinates Our Relationships

Our relationships with other people are coordinated, negotiated, and maintained through communication. For example, your relationships with your co-workers evolve through the varied exchange of verbal and nonverbal communication styles, which involve the selection of words and expressions used by individual communicators. As a rela-

Intrapersonal Communication Is Continuous   FIGURE 1.2

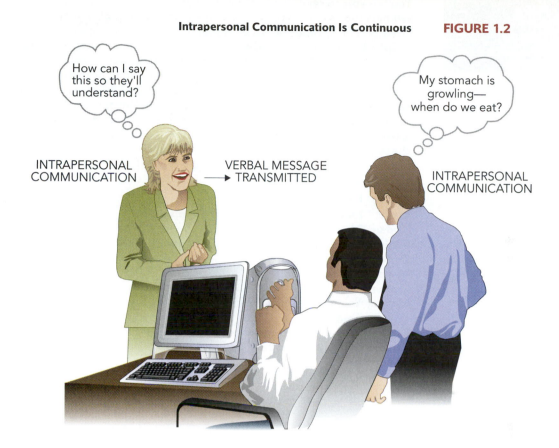

tionship develops, we learn about and adapt to the other person's communication style. While the nature and scope of our social and professional relationships vary, in all of them our listening, verbal, and nonverbal behaviors facilitate the interpersonal interactions through which our relationships develop and grow.

Communication Is Symbolic

When we communicate, we use a series of symbols that comprise our messages and help us to share meaning. A **symbol** is a type of sign that has no natural connection to the idea, word, or object it represents. Symbols are learned codes, such as spoken or written language, that we create and assign to objects or feelings. The word symbol "sun" represents a huge, bright star that illuminates our planet as we orbit around it. While the word *sun* is arbitrary because it has no direct connection to the star it represents, we have learned to associate the word symbol with the object.

Our learned symbols allow us to design messages that others can interpret based on our shared experience with certain verbal and visual symbols. On the other hand, misunderstandings can occur because different people sometimes attach different meanings to the same symbols, especially if they bring different contexts to the symbols. A couple of symbols are illustrated in Figure 1.3.

symbol a type of sign that has no natural connection to the idea, word, or object it represents.

You are able to read this book because you are familiar with the series of symbols that make up the English alphabet. You may also be familiar with other sets of symbols—another verbal language or perhaps computer scripts. Even easily recognizable symbolic systems are often adjusted to suit specific purposes. For example, when conversing with someone else in an Internet application like a message board, chat room, or instant message, people often use abbreviations or odd spellings that imitate oral communication styles instead of typing out entire conventional words. This speeds up the communication, but it can also make it difficult to determine what is being said if one or both parties in the conversation are unfamiliar with the symbolic system being used. Try to decipher the following portion of an instant message conversation. (Hint: Go online for some explanations, read the conversation out loud, and ask friends for help.)

Ogden: Hey Majic! Wassup?
Majic: Hey Og. Just got online. Problems with the puter today.
Ogden: ???
Majic: Keep getting the blue screen of death: fatal disk error.
Ogden: Horrors.
Majic: You're not kidding.
Ogden: BTW, did you hear about the latest virus: Goner?
Majic: Yep, downloaded the medicine for it too, JIC.
Ogden: Smart.
Majic: Can never be too prepared, IMHO.
Ogden: Hang on, my mom's calling me. BRB.
Majic: K

FIGURE 1.3

Common Visual Symbols

Symbols

Peace Infinity

Communication Is Culturally Linked

Our communication style is linked to the culture into which we were born. **Culture** is a socially constructed way of thinking and behaving in the world. We develop culture through symbols that communicate shared perspectives and expectations for behavior. The most obvious cultural aspect of communication is that members of a particular group share the same symbols for language. The most obvious difference between people from other cultures is that they speak another language and share different meanings.

Intercultural communication focuses on the interactions between people from different cultural groups. Because attitudes, perspectives, and communication styles can be different, our verbal and nonverbal business messages need to be designed with an understanding of indi-

culture is a socially constructed way of thinking and behaving in the world.

intercultural communication focuses on the interactions between people from different cultural groups.

10

vidual organizational cultures and other cultural groups. For example, in some Latin American, European, and Arabic cultures, it is natural in conversation to communicate nonverbally by standing very close to others. In American culture, it makes people uncomfortable when someone stands or sits closer than about 18 inches from us.

Communication Is Collaborative

When people work together to accomplish a business goal, they are collaborating. Business communicators may collaborate with many people, both within and outside the organization. While collaborators may have different perspectives, attitudes, skills, and cultural values, they come together to solve problems, make decisions, and work toward the achievement of business goals.

At Nortel Networks, an accounting firm, employees learn to work collaboratively as a team by performing creative improvisation on stage. Through these performances, Nortel accountants learn to work together, think fast on their feet, and adapt to change. Through its innovative training programs the Second City comedy troupe has helped corporate clients such as Nortel Networks, AT&T, Motorola, and Kraft Foods improve their employees' collaborative skills by practicing creative teamwork.

Types of collaborative communication in business include collaborative writing, decision making, problem solving, and presentations.

Collaborative writing	Sharing the planning, analyzing, composing, and editing responsibilities with two or more people is how the process works. Writing as a team or group frequently occurs out of necessity, especially in a business document such as a proposal—which may be too extensive for one person to prepare or require more time than one person can devote to it.
Collaborative decision making and problem solving	In a variety of business situations, more companies are embracing group decision making. Teamwork can enhance decisions because it provides a greater variety of ideas and alternatives. While reaching decisions as a team can be time consuming, it often yields better solutions and alternatives.
Collaborative presentations	Two or more people who integrate material and speak together publicly about a specific topic and make team presentations can gain and maintain audience attention, while each individual speaker's specific skills can enhance the development and content of speech material. While all public speaking requires planning and preparation, a coordinated effort requires a team focus on writing, speech organization, visual aid design, smooth speaker-to-speaker transitions, and coordinated responses to audience questions.

How Does Communication Work?

The process of communication is visually illustrated in Figure 1.4. The primary goal of communication is to achieve mutual understanding of message meanings. When we communicate, we want others to understand what we have in mind and to accept our ideas. Gary Grates,

FIGURE 1.4

Interactive Model of Communication

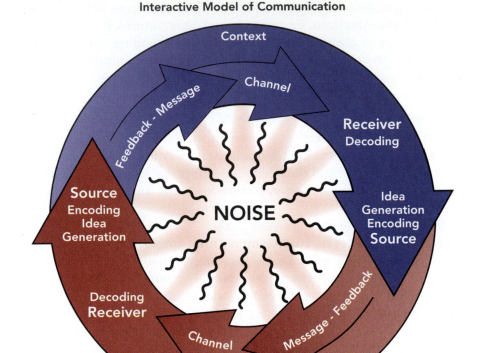

Interactive Model of Communication

executive director of internal communications for General Motors, says, "The biggest issue that leaders face is whether people understand them. Whether you're talking about Wall Street, partners, customers, or employees, people must understand the organization's story . . . Otherwise, you're going to lose valuation, sales, new opportunities, or employees."

Mutual understanding requires that communicators understand message content and emotional meaning. When mutual understanding occurs, we achieve **high fidelity,** which is the ideal communication experience. With high fidelity the meaning the source of the message (the sender) has in mind is exactly the message the receiver understands. As we further explore the various components in the communication process, you'll begin to see how challenging high fidelity can be to achieve.

Is High Fidelity Hard to Achieve?

Noise can make high fidelity hard to achieve and is the primary reason for communication breakdowns. **Noise** is any interference that interrupts or affects the exchange of messages. Noise can be internal, external, or message based.

high fidelity is the achievement of mutual understanding, which is the ideal communication experience.

noise is any interference that interrupts or affects the exchange of messages.

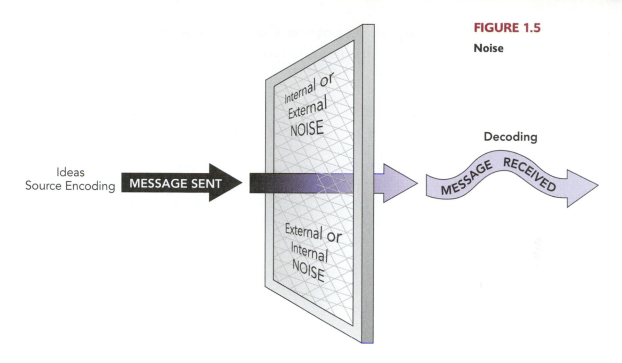

FIGURE 1.5
Noise

Because noise is like a filter, sometimes messages
are distorted or misunderstood.

- *Internal noise* can be any psychological or physio-logical interruption that makes the message diffi-cult to design, receive, or interpret. Emotions, prejudices, or preoccupation with certain thoughts can impede the communication process for both sources and receivers. If, for example, you are thinking about what you want to say at an upcom-ing department meeting, you may not adequately listen to your colleague as she talks to you about a problem with the account tracking system. From a physiological perspective, if you are hungry, tired, or physically ill, the messages you design may be unclear or may become fragmented and jumbled. In that case, the receiver may not interpret your message meaning ef-fectively.

- *External noise* involves any environmental interference—such as loud sounds, strong odors, extreme temperatures, or even lighting conditions—that affects the exchange of messages.

- *Message-based noise* refers to design flaws or differences in meaning that can distort or confuse messages. Emotionally charged words, grammatical or typographical errors, confusing terms, or inappro-priate visuals can create message noise for receivers. Noise is illus-trated in Figure 1.5.

CREATIVE

CHALLENGE

Create an example using each source of noise. Then write a paragraph for each example that describes how the noise interferes with the process of message exchange between communicators. Come to class prepared to discuss your examples.

Components of the Communication Process

The interactive process of communication involves a series of related events that comprise the various components of a communication experience.

1. **Ideas and encoding.**

   Ideas are generated at the point of perception, which occurs when sensory information from the environment or from inside your mind stimulates and arouses your attention. As you initially perceive information, you begin to generate raw thoughts and ideas. In processing the thoughts, you begin to transform them into verbal, nonverbal, or visual symbols. The transformation of ideas into symbols is referred to as **encoding,** which is the design of communication messages. Encoding involves formulating your thoughts into meaningful *symbols* to think about or to share with others. If you intend to share thoughts with others, the encoding process involves determining what symbols will be most appropriate for your receivers and how to transmit the messages to reach high fidelity.

2. **Communication source and receiver.**

   Each person in the communication process is both a message source and a receiver throughout a given interaction. A message **source** is the originator and transmitter of the message. The **receiver** is the recipient of the message, or the destination point. We constantly transmit messages verbally and nonverbally, and we also receive aural and visual messages from others concurrently.

3. **Messages.**

   When ideas are encoded and designed into one or more symbols, they become **messages** used to communicate meaning. We think about these messages internally; formulate them into words, behaviors, or visual images; and send them to other people.

4. **Communication channels.**

   A **channel** is a medium that carries messages within and between people. Thinking is an intrapersonal channel that allows us to send and receive messages within ourselves. Because verbal communication includes both spoken and written messages, the voice is a verbal channel of communication, as is a written memo, business letter, or mission statement. Nonverbal behaviors such as body movements or vocal sounds also carry messages. Channels enable us to transmit messages to other people and to communicate within ourselves.

   Channels can be subdivided into two primary categories: human and technological. **Human channels** include thoughts, verbal communication (speech and writing), nonverbal behaviors (body movements and vocal sounds), sound, sight, and smell. Human channels involve face-to-face interaction and are often better for training,

ideas are generated at the point of perception, when information from the environment or from inside your mind stimulates and arouses your attention.

encoding is the transformation of ideas into symbols to design communication messages.

source the originator and transmitter of the message.

receiver the recipient of the message, or the destination point.

messages ideas encoded and designed into one or more symbols to communicate meaning.

channel a medium that carries messages within and between people.

human channels include thoughts, verbal communication (speech and writing), nonverbal behaviors (body movements and vocal sounds), sound, sight, and smell.

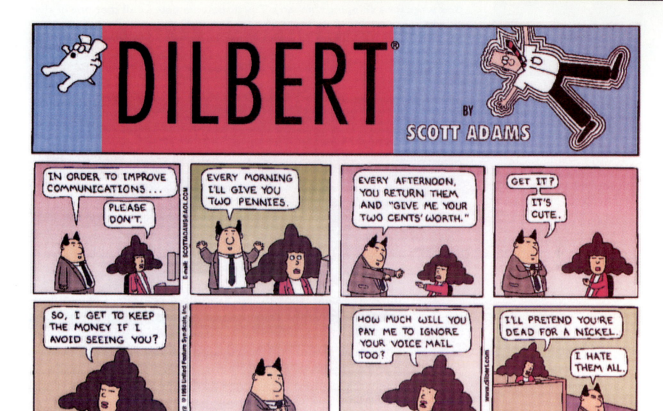

Copyright © 1998 United Feature Syndicate, Inc.

problem solving, decision making, persuading, and working collaboratively in group work.

Technological channels include radio, TV, telephone, fax, video, e-mail, and hand-held devices, among many others. The channel you choose for a given message depends on the speed at which you want it to travel, the cost, the complexity of the message, your reason for communicating, and the receiver you want to reach. Technological channels are convenient for transmitting messages, especially when time and geographic constraints make face-to-face communication difficult.

For example, at NCR, a 120-year-old global technology company, corporate executives from each division all over the country present video quarterly reports to the staff. During the quarterly presentations last fall, one division executive broke with tradition by creating a three-minute action movie instead of using a more conventional video format. This executive used a different channel to present his report because he wanted to demonstrate the division's speed, passion, and energy. Reactions from NCR staffers were very positive.

5. Decoding.

To **decode** means to perceive, translate, and interpret information received in a message. Literally, decoding is listening, reading, or

technological channels include radio, TV, telephone, fax, video, e-mail, and hand-held devices.

decode means to perceive, translate, and interpret information received in a message.

You work for a shipping company. The dispatcher gets a call that one of the trucks has overturned on Route 66 near Flagstaff, Arizona. Part of the shipment may be salvageable (it was mostly pillows and bedding headed for Las Vegas), and you need to get someone out there to assess the damage to the truck, its load, and its driver. You jot yourself a quick note:

Down 66 near Flag. Tell Marc to get T. out there, check tr., load. Joe going to LV hosp. Call CHP, Flag police (report), ins., Joe's wife (#where?).

You need to tell Marc, the company's owner, so after checking the driver's human resources file you sit down to write an e-mail. But now you're not sure that you understand everything you wrote down. For example, "T" could be Tom Johnson, Marc's son and foreman of the warehouse, chief of operations Maria Tannhauser, or business manager Tony Takahatsu. Write an e-mail to Marc Johnson telling him what has occurred and the actions you are taking. Use as much logic as possible to decode your own note.

observing a message transmitted through a channel. Once a message is perceived and the information is translated in the brain, it can be interpreted. The *interpretation* stage of decoding involves attaching meaning to symbols based on the conveyed message content and emotional tone. Interpretation also involves your attitude, level of knowledge, and experience as the message receiver. Thus, not only is the intention of the message source important, but the experience and perspective of the receiver are as well. Because different people may interpret symbols and meaning in slightly different ways, the message received is not necessarily identical to the one transmitted.

6. **Message feedback.**

feedback is a special type of message designed as a response to a received message.

Feedback is a special type of message designed as a response to a received message. Feedback is a critical component in communication because it enables us to gauge how the messages we sent were interpreted and aids in the design of future transmissions.

Communicating Intrapersonally

Intrapersonal communication is the most basic form of communication. It is the cornerstone for all other forms, including interpersonal, group, and business communication. Many forms of communication focus on the number of people in the process, the channels used for message transmittal, and the flow of messages. Intrapersonal communication focuses on the mental processing that occurs within an individual. People design and create messages through their thought processes. To improve the way we design messages, we need to focus on how we think as communicators.

Intrapersonal communication is a private interaction within a single person who is the encoder, decoder, and transmitter of messages. From a cognitive perspective, intrapersonal communication is a mental activity that involves transforming symbols and sensations into meaning. As discussed earlier, symbols are learned codes (such as spoken or written language) that we attach to objects, ideas, or emotions. We mentally process symbols every time we communicate, both within ourselves and with others. While intrapersonal communication does not require interaction with other people, mental activity is obviously not restricted to those moments when we are alone; our thinking minds are operating continuously. When we communicate within ourselves or with other people, we are constantly sending and receiving messages internally through the thinking process.

Encoding and Decoding Messages Intrapersonally

People receive information externally from their environment and internally from within themselves. Information can be anything we see, taste, hear, smell, or feel—including verbal, visual, and nonverbal symbols, which are perceived through our senses. Choosing certain information to focus on is called **selectivity.** We select only some information because we can process only so much at any given time. We also exercise selectivity by choosing information that is consistent with what we already believe. Once perceived, information is decoded mentally, which means it is organized and transformed into linguistic or visual symbols. Decoding also involves attaching meaning to symbols, which become our thoughts and ideas.

selectivity is choosing certain information to focus on.

The encoding process happens when an individual formulates a response to received information. Encoding is not done exclusively during interaction with other people. It also occurs when someone creates and constructs messages for internal analysis or contemplation. For ex-

ample, let's say you observe a co-worker, Kasha, frowning during a company meeting. As you perceive Kasha, you may decide that the frown on her face means she is dissatisfied. In your mind, you think that Kasha probably disagrees with or dislikes the information presented during the meeting. While you may misinterpret Kasha's behavior (her frown may or may not actually be a reaction to the message), you still mentally process the information and construct meanings and messages to communicate with yourself.

The Meaning of Symbols

People create and interpret meaning; symbols do not. While some literal meanings may be synonymous with our individual interpretation, we determine meaning based on intrapersonal, interpersonal, contextual, and social factors.

Intrapersonal factors	Individuals create ideas and meaning associations as they process information internally. Memories, past experiences, and knowledge form the foundation of our interpretation of events and concepts.
Interpersonal factors	Socially constructed or negotiated meanings develop as people interact and build relationships.
Contextual factors	The surrounding environmental, psychological, and social factors help us to shape meaning.
Social factors	Many cultural and familial influences affect our creation of meaning.

Sending Ourselves Messages

Because intrapersonal communication occurs internally, the channels we use to communicate with ourselves are human channels. The three primary channels used in the transmission of intrapersonal communication are self-talk, mental imagery, and nonverbal behaviors.

Self-talk	Self-talk is the internal use of verbal language symbols while thinking.
Mental imagery	Mental imagery refers to the images an individual visualizes without words.
Nonverbal behaviors	Intrapersonal communication involves both intentional and unintentional nonverbal behavior. For example, when you think about ideas, you may also move like Auguste Rodin's famous sculpture "The Thinker," whose head leans forward and presses against his fist. Nonverbal behaviors may or may not be observable by others depending on the situation in which the communication occurs.

The Intrapersonal and Business Communication Connection

In the world of work as in life, the way we have learned to think is central to the way we communicate with others and ourselves. Thinking through the messages we want to communicate can make a big difference in how competently we communicate with other people. Some of our messages are poorly developed and designed because we fail to think through what we want to share. Most of us have transmitted messages that we later wished we had not or have spent considerable time clarifying, explaining, rewriting, and rephrasing. To communicate effectively with other professionals in business, we have to learn how to create clear messages.

To do that, we need to improve our intrapersonal design skills—our ability to conceptualize, generate ideas, combine ideas, plan, evaluate, and use reasoning and logic. In short, business communicators need to become business communication designers.

Designing Business Communication

When we create messages, we communicate with ourselves first. The creation of messages is an intrapersonal encoding process that enables us to plan and design messages that can be understood and accepted by others. The construction of a given message is the domain of the **communication designer,** who skillfully plans and designs effective business messages. To be effective communicators we must all embrace the role of message designers, just as Picasso and Rembrandt were artful designers of visual images and Tommy Hilfiger and Liz Claiborne are designers of clothing. Effective messages are easy to understand. They can inform, build awareness, and influence the behavior and beliefs of other people.

As we communicate with ourselves, we begin to generate thoughts and ideas. While some of these thoughts and ideas will be kept private, others will eventually be transmitted to other people. Those thoughts and ideas that will be shared with others often require solid communication design strategies to achieve organizational goals.

What Is a Communication Design Strategy?

A **design strategy** offers options and techniques that enable a business communicator to design messages more effectively so they will accomplish communication goals. Like a business plan, which guides the development and growth of a business

Auguste Rodin's famous sculpture "The Thinker" demonstrates intrapersonal and nonverbal behavior.
Art Resource, NY

communication designer
someone who skillfully plans and designs effective business messages.

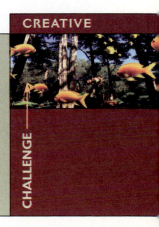

CREATIVE

CHALLENGE

Think of a situation that you experienced when you transmitted a message without thinking about what you wanted to convey. Write two paragraphs that describe what happened and what you needed to do to clarify the message for your receiver.

design strategy a set of techniques that enable a business communicator to design messages more effectively and accomplish communication goals.

enterprise, a communication strategy guides the development of business messages. For example, Southwest Airlines has a customer-friendly, fun, team-based strategy for providing customers with inexpensive, no-frills air travel. The success of the airline's basic strategy (to provide economical air service in a fun and friendly way) has endured for many years. But the company is flexible enough to change with the times while still maintaining a consistent strategic focus.

At Continental Airlines, Bonnie Reitz, senior vice president for sales and distribution, created a new communication strategy after the September 11, 2001, terrorist attacks. To allay passenger concerns about air travel, Reitz and her staff designed a strategy that used various channels—including faxes, flyers, letters, and PowerPoint presentations—to detail the airline's safety and security procedures and the efforts of federal agencies and aircraft manufacturers to prevent future hijackings.

Design strategies may be predesigned or integrated.

CREATIVE

CHALLENGE

Develop and design a strategy to reduce internal noise that interferes with your effective listening during business presentations or lectures. Write an e-mail memo to your instructor that describes what techniques you will use to decrease noise and increase your listening effectiveness and the reasons you chose these techniques.

Predesigned strategies	Predesigned strategies, such as the one outlined in Chapter 3 and throughout this text, involve tactics for communicating in business. Communication strategies can help you design business messages that require public speaking, verbal and nonverbal interaction, written documents, group or teamwork, visuals, and technology. The benefit of predesigned strategies is that they offer tried and tested techniques that can significantly enhance your communication competence. One limitation is that they may not completely fit every unique communication experience. Because no two communication experiences are ever exactly alike, a strategy is only as good as the communicator who uses it, given the specific demands of the communication situation.
Integrated and situational strategies	Integrated strategies involve the modification of predesigned communication formulas to match the situational needs of the communicator. Combining new and existing techniques can be very useful in difficult or complex communication situations.
	Situational strategies are unique and impromptu integrated methods used for specific communication events. For example, there will be times in your career when you will need to communicate in unconventional circumstances that are not outlined in a textbook. Some situations will require that you plan and develop your own strategic formula to communicate successfully with others. Often the foundation for learning how to think strategically is by example, through the practice and use of predesigned strategies.

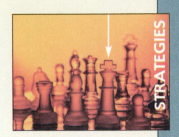

Strategies

1. Once you send a message, particularly in face-to-face interaction, you can't take it back. Once you say something to someone or send a message, you can't erase that experience. Because you can't reverse most communication, it is vitally important that you intrapersonally encode and design your messages effectively before you send them to others. Often just thinking before speaking or writing can help you avoid miscommunication. Thinking about what you want from the receiver and how he or she is likely to respond can also help you crystallize the message. Finally, evaluate how well your receiver is likely to understand the meaning attached to the language or visual symbols you choose when designing the message.

2. It is important for a business communicator to know when to listen. Numerous benefits come from paying attention to co-workers, customers, subordinates, and superiors. Listening to learn and remember new information is a skill that can help you understand others and design better messages.

3. Collaborating with others can be a rich and rewarding experience that offers a chance for you to grow as a business professional. It can also be challenging and frustrating. To work with others productively, you need to listen, offer developed ideas, and accept that people have different perspectives and different ways of approaching work tasks.

4. When you work collaboratively, you may find yourself working with people from other cultural groups. You need to be mindful of the differences between you and others and of what you can do to enhance the communication experience. One way you can learn about other cultural groups is to read documents and literature that describe the business practices, customs, and etiquette of a particular group. You might also talk informally to co-workers who have traveled overseas or to members of the cultural group and ask questions about appropriate social and professional conduct.

5. Communication does not happen in a vacuum. Your interactions with other people occur in a context. You can determine the context by analyzing the physical environment. When, where, and with whom are you communicating? You can also assess your own mood or attitude and the attitudes of the people you are interacting with. Many factors, including the roles of the people involved, contribute to the context in which communication occurs. Being aware of these factors can help you to send and receive messages more effectively.

6. Carefully select channels to carry your messages. To determine the right channel, use your intrapersonal critical thinking skills. Think about the person or persons you want to communicate with, the reason for your message, the speed of the channel, and whether the channel will be appropriate for the receiver.

7. When you interact with other people, remember you are using verbal, nonverbal, and listening skills at the same time. Be sure your gestures and eye behaviors match the verbal statements you make. Excessive or inappropriate nonverbal behaviors are a sure way to create noise for your receiver.

8. Remember that noise is anything that interferes with the communication process. To avoid internal noise, practice listening without judging or planning your next message until the speaker has finished talking. Make sure that you aren't distracted by fatigue or hunger when you communicate with others. While some external noise may be inescapable, you can move to another area that provides a better environment or arrange a different time when your communication won't be interrupted. To prevent message-based noise, evaluate your messages thoroughly. Check written messages for design flaws such as typos and ambiguous meanings.

9. Become aware of your intrapersonal communication process. Think about how you make sense of and interpret information and how you encode messages. Use self-talk to work through and formulate messages that better express your meaning to other people.

Summary

- Communication is the process of creating shared meaning through the internal and external exchange of messages.
- Contemporary business requires communicators who are skilled in intrapersonal, business, interpersonal, small-group, verbal, and public communication.
- The basic principles of communication include the following:
  a. The communication process is the ongoing, changing nature of interactions.
  b. Communication context refers to various environmental, situational, social, role, and psychological factors that affect each communication experience.
  c. Continuous communication means that whether intentionally or not, we are always communicating.
  d. Communication coordinates our relationships because human interaction facilitates and maintains our personal and professional relations with other people.

e. Communication uses symbols, which are arbitrary linguistic or visual codes that we culturally learn to associate with objects, ideas, and feelings.

f. Communication is bound to culture because we learn the symbols, rules, and interaction styles from our group memberships in society.

g. Communication is often a collaborative experience in business, because professionals work together to accomplish organizational goals.

- Ideal communication has high fidelity, which refers to mutual understanding between a message source and receiver. The components of the communication process are ideas and encoding, source and receiver, messages, channels, decoding, feedback, and noise.

- Intrapersonal communication is interaction within an individual, who encodes, decodes, and transmits messages internally. Intrapersonal communication involves mentally processing or decoding received stimuli and constructing or encoding messages. During the process of decoding and encoding, we determine meaning through intrapersonal, interpersonal, contextual, and social factors. Finally, we transmit messages intrapersonally through human channels such as self-talk, mental imagery, and nonverbal behaviors.

- Business communicators need to design effective messages internally before they send them to others. Competent communication designers plan, develop, and design messages thoughtfully in order to inform, increase awareness, and influence receivers. To design effective business messages, communication designers use predesigned, integrated, and situational strategies for a variety of communication purposes.

Business Communication Projects

1. Assess and identify three of your communication skill strengths and two weaknesses. Write a brief paper describing these strengths and weaknesses. Then outline a plan of action that describes how you will improve the weaknesses you identified.

2. Your manager is uncertain about assigning a proposal writing project to more than one person in the department because she thinks a team effort may take too much time. The proposal is due in three weeks. You know that the proposal is a huge undertaking and may take even more time if only one person works on it alone. Write an e-mail to your manager in which you respond to the question "What do we need to complete this project effectively and on time?" Include in your e-mail three primary advantages of collaborative work.

3. Over a period of several weeks, you notice that one of your employees repeatedly comes to work late. You also discover that this employee disappears mysteriously throughout the day without telling anyone where he is going or where he can be reached. You realize that you need to communicate to this employee your concern about his behavior. In two or three paragraphs, explain how you plan to handle this situation and what kind of message (memo, letter, oral, e-mail) should be sent.

4. Think about how internal, external, or message-based noise interfered with a business or school interaction you had. Review the different types of noise in this chapter, and then write a list of the ways this noise could have been avoided or eliminated. Come to class prepared to discuss your conclusions with your colleagues.

5. Think about the components of the communication process. Select the appropriate component for each of the following activities (more than one may apply).
   _____ Deciding what to say in response to a message
   _____ Brainstorming for solutions to a problem
   _____ Laughing at a joke
   _____ Making sense out of a confusing statement
   _____ Sending an e-mail message

6. Work with three of your classmates to think of at least six symbols that you understand without thinking about (consider advertising logos, images related to musicians or bands, and signs you see in public places). Write a paragraph on each symbol, describing any intrapersonal, interpersonal, contextual, and/or social factors that give it meaning for you.

7. You are in a stressful meeting concerning the merger of your company with a large international firm. In the middle of negotiations someone's cell phone goes off, playing a few bars from the *1812 Overture.* Although everyone in the room laughs and releases a little tension, you are embarrassed because it is your assistant's phone. Write a memo to all staffers explaining why cell phones and pagers must be turned off or set on vibrate while they are at the office, especially in meetings.

Discussion Questions

1. Why do businesspeople need to learn about other cultures?
2. What channels of communication do you think are used most frequently in business—human or technological channels? Why?
3. In what ways do you think communication is vital to the success of any business?
4. How is communication used at your college or university? How do you learn about school activities, events, or cancellations?

5. How can effective communication enhance employee morale and productivity?

6. How does feedback improve the communication process and help communicators reach mutual understanding?

7. Why is intrapersonal communication important for a business communicator?

8. Describe business situations that require each of these communication skills:
   a. Intrapersonal communication.
   b. Business communication.
   c. Interpersonal communication.
   d. Small-group and team communication.
   e. Verbal communication.
   f. Public communication.

9. When do you use predesigned communication strategies in your day-to-day life? When do you use integrated or situational strategies?

Creative Case

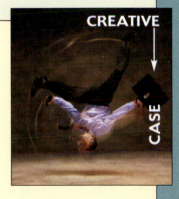

CREATIVE CASE

Wal-Mart Goes to Germany

Wal-Mart, well known as an ultra-American company, is developing itself internationally. It is already a major sales force in Canada and Mexico and is currently expanding into Asian and European markets. Although the stores in the United States currently maintain Wal-Mart's highly successful financial standing, forecasters predict that an international presence will be the primary source of future growth.

In 1997 Wal-Mart bought the German Wertkauf chain, comprised of 21 stores. In 1998 it purchased the 74-store Interspar chain. It upgraded and remodeled these stores using the same pattern used for its stores in the United States, Canada, and Mexico. As of 2001, however, Wal-Mart had lost $200 million on these 95 stores, the result of several problems it hadn't considered at the outset.

Some of the intercultural problems should have been expected: complying with commercial regulations in Germany can delay the opening of a "hypermarket" such as Wal-Mart by as much as five years. In September 2001 the German Cartel Office set standards for the minimum price of some items: a level of government intervention that Wal-Mart officials were unprepared for. Wal-Mart also faced 14 competitive hypermarket chains, all of which are well known already to the German people. Add to that mix a sluggish German market, and it was already apparent that Wal-Mart was facing a major challenge.

In addition to these external factors, Wal-Mart made some internal mistakes. The original managers of the Wertkauf and Interspar chains resented the fact that Americans had come into their stores and were telling them how to do their jobs. The message these managers received was that American methods were better. This tension was increased when they found that the new American bosses didn't speak German and insisted on American marketing practices. And when Wal-Mart tried to impose its own supply system on vendors who were used to doing things differently, the vendors simply refused to stock Wal-Mart warehouses.

Wal-Mart realizes that it didn't strategize its intercultural approach or messages well when it entered the German market. As CEO H. Lee Scott, Jr., said, "We just walked in and said, 'We're going to lower prices, we're going to add people to the stores, we're going to remodel the stores because inherently that's correct,' and it wasn't. We didn't have the infrastructure to support the kind of things we were doing."

What do you think Wal-Mart did to make its stores in Germany more successful?

Some questions to consider:

1. Do you think there are cultural differences between the German market and the American market? What might they be?
2. Why would German managers and vendors revolt against American business practices?
3. Why do you think the Wal-Mart executives didn't intrapersonally think about the context in which they were communicating?
4. What specific communication skills should Wal-Mart managers have used to start off on better terms with the German managers and vendors?
5. How should Wal-Mart address the problems it faces and begin to collaborate productively with the German people?

Source: Zellner, W. "How Well Does Wal-Mart Travel?" *Business Week Online*, Sept. 3, 2001. Retrieved Aug. 27, 2002, from www.businessweek.com/print/magazine/content.

Chapter 2

Chapter 2

How Business Communicates

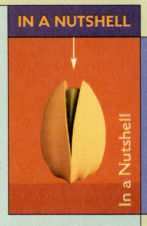

The recent collapse of Enron offers lessons in communication for everyone. Enron, the Texas-based energy company, capitalized on the volatility of energy prices in the late 1990s. Through its strategic and aggressive marketing of electricity and gas, Enron realized sales of more than $1.1 billion in 2000. The eventual collapse of this energy trader in the largest bankruptcy case in U.S. history is a story of cover-ups and scandals. And it is a story of how organizational messages are sent and received.

The investigation to determine how Enron lost billions of dollars eventually led to Arthur Andersen, Enron's accounting firm. When federal officials approached Andersen, looking for financial documents related to Andersen's audit of Enron, they found many documents crucial to their investigation had been destroyed. Andersen was charged with obstruction of justice for shredding documents.

It was in the fall of 2001 that Andersen managers first got wind that an investigation by the Securities and Exchange Commission (SEC) into their Enron account was likely. In a downward bound structural message, employees of Andersen working on the Enron account were directed by managing partner Thomas Bauer to make sure they complied with the firm's "documentation retention policy." But what, exactly, did Bauer mean when he used the term "document retention"? What message was he sending to the staff accountants working on the Enron audit? Anderson employees apparently understood the message to mean the opposite of document retention—to destroy rather than keep documents. In her testimony, Patrica Sue Grutzmacher, another Andersen manager working with Enron, claimed that when Bauer referred to the firm's document retention policy, it was a policy requiring the destruction of certain records. So, Bauer's message to comply with the policy actually meant employees should destroy documents. Although the verbal message employees received was to comply with the policy of retention, what Bauer ordered and what employees understood was to shred the documents.

21st-Century Business Directions

Communicating in business is faster, more convenient, and more accessible, with more technological channels available to carry messages than ever before. More channels and greater accessibility mean that even more information flows between people. Businesses routinely manage information and design messages that flow internally to employees and externally to customers. Employees generate, transmit, and interpret these messages as they did at Arthur Andersen. As discussed in Chapter 1 and in our "In a Nutshell" discussion for this chapter, the meaning of a message depends on the sender and the receiver. In the case of Arthur Andersen, Thomas Bauer (the sender) gave Andersen employees (the receivers) a clear message regarding the Enron audit documents. While a person outside the Andersen organization might interpret a message about document retention as a message to keep documents, the people inside the organization interpreted the message as one to destroy documents. In this chapter we will focus on how and what information flows in and outside organizations.

Globalization

Today's business marketplace is global. It cuts across national borders—not only for exporting and importing products but also for manufacturing contracts and partnerships with foreign firms and franchising. The number of multinational corporations continues to increase as well. Whether an organization conducts international transactions or maintains operations in several countries as do IBM, Exxon, and General Electric, for example, business communicators need more than a cursory understanding of other cultural groups. American business professionals often need to interact with people from other cultures. They need to know the cultural, political, economic, and legal differences among countries. They need a solid understanding of differing interaction styles, social and business customs, perceptions about status, and proper etiquette to achieve effective cross-cultural communication.

The Maze of Information Management

With the explosion of information available to businesses, managers and other staff members must navigate, manage, and analyze enormous amounts of data. **Management information systems (MIS)** are network systems (usually mediated through computers) that enable managers and staff to access ongoing and relevant company information such as sales reports, profit planning data, employee productivity, and customer feedback. The information gleaned from MIS data can help managers and other personnel make decisions and plan for improvements in business performance. Businesses can streamline operations by using advances in information technology, such as the **management decision support system (MDSS).** The MDSS helps

The explosion of information available to businesses has created a maze of data for professionals to manage.
© John Chard/Getty Images

management information systems (MIS) are computer network systems that enable users to access company information.

management decision support system (MDSS) helps users make decisions through coordinated corporate databases that contain important company and industry facts.

managers and other key personnel make decisions through coordinated corporate and user databases that contain important company and industry facts, such as financial and production data.

The number of messages a given business professional receives daily can be mind-boggling. At Intel, a semiconductor company with offices in the United States, Europe, Africa, Asia, and the Middle East, 3 million e-mail messages are received each day. Many of the company's employees each receive up to 300 messages a day. This excess of information could prevent a professional from navigating out of the inbox. In the fight against **information overload** (too much information at once), Intel developed a training program that teaches employees how to frame important messages, categorize pertinent information, and weed out unnecessary filler.

The Way of Technology

Intranets, which are internal company computer networks, allow employees to communicate and share information electronically from wherever they are. Through the **World Wide Web (WWW),** a service provided on the Internet, large and small companies can conduct business domestically and internationally in a fast, economical way. **Wireless hand-held devices** (palm-tops, etc.) offer software features such as spreadsheets, databases, web browsing, and e-mail. To achieve success, business communicators must know how to manage information and send and receive messages through a variety of technological channels.

Change and More Change

Technology, broadening international markets, e-commerce, increased competition, and corporate mergers make changing corporate structures and cultures a reality. As discussed in more detail in Chapter 14, constant change means that the way work is accomplished today will be different from yesterday's business as usual. The trouble is that not everyone in the organization may be willing to accept or make changes. Many midsize firms and one-third of large companies report that employee resistance is a major barrier in the change process. Sometimes the fears associated with change or downsizing overshadow the advantages associated with customer service, process and product improvements, and greater company profits. A primary reason some change efforts falter is a lack of open communication among change makers (agents), management, and employees. Strong business communicators need to know how to design change messages and how to accept and participate in retraining, experimentation, and innovation.

information overload occurs when too much information is received at once.

intranets are internal company computer networks that enable employees to communicate and share information.

World Wide Web (WWW) is a service provided on the Internet to allow large and small companies to conduct business domestically and internationally.

wireless hand-held devices are small instruments that offer software features including spreadsheets, databases, web browsing, and e-mail.

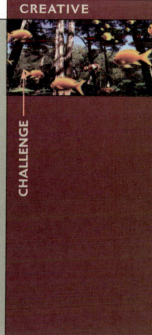

CREATIVE

CHALLENGE

Take a look at one of the latest advances in business-oriented technology: the Palm-Pilot or the Bluetooth chip, for example. Look for information in journals and on the Internet, and don't be afraid to ask people who already use the tool for work. Determine the advantages and disadvantages of the technology you are examining. Be sure to look at ease of use, cost, availability, and features, as well as anything else you can think of. Based on your evaluation, write an e-mail to the company that produces the product recommending ways to improve its design, emphasizing business applications. Be specific in your recommendations.

In the world of business, most jobs are held by professionals who communicate with a variety of people both inside and outside the organization. Communicating effectively in business requires that you understand how work is performed and how people plan, organize, and accomplish simple and complex tasks through human interaction. Companies are made up of people who share information and coordinate their efforts to develop and achieve business goals.

What Is Business Communication?

business communication is a process of creating structure, relationships, and meaning through the design and exchange of business messages.

Business communication is a process of creating structure, relationships, and meaning through the design of messages and their exchange among goal-oriented employees.

Business communication creates *structure* because the way a company organizes, including dividing up work tasks, creating business goals, and establishing levels of authority, is coordinated through human interaction. People build organizational structure by interacting with others and coordinating their mental and physical efforts. Business communicators share information through verbal and nonverbal messages that shape and maintain the organization. *Working relationships* between organizational members and with outsiders such as customers and vendors are also established and negotiated through communication. These relationships vary in their intimacy, formality, and frequency of interaction, depending in part on physical distance and the roles employees play in the organizational hierarchy. For example, employees working in the same office may have interactions that are more intimate, less formal, and more frequent than those with employees who perform their work tasks in different locations. An entry-level manager at a large manufacturing plant may not work in the same physical office as the company CEO. Depending on whether the organizational structure is tall (with many layers of supervision) or flat (with fewer layers), an entry-level manager's interactions with the CEO may be less intimate, more formal, and less frequent as illustrated in Figures 2.1, 2.2, and 2.3.

FIGURE 2.1   **Typical Organizational Structure**

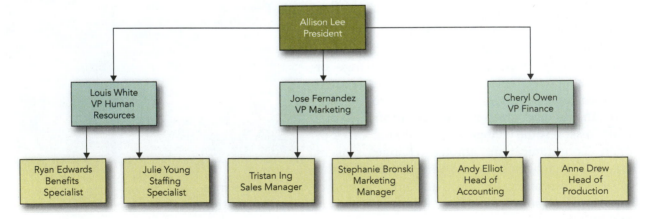

Finally, the ongoing exchange of messages between employees and with outsiders reflects *shared meaning,* a mutual understanding about the organization's mission and the performance of work.

Types of Business Messages

Business messages shape the way the organization functions and maintain the internal relationships among employees and the external relationships with the environment (customers, vendors, business associates). The design effectiveness of these messages is shown in the

Tall Organizational Structure   FIGURE 2.2

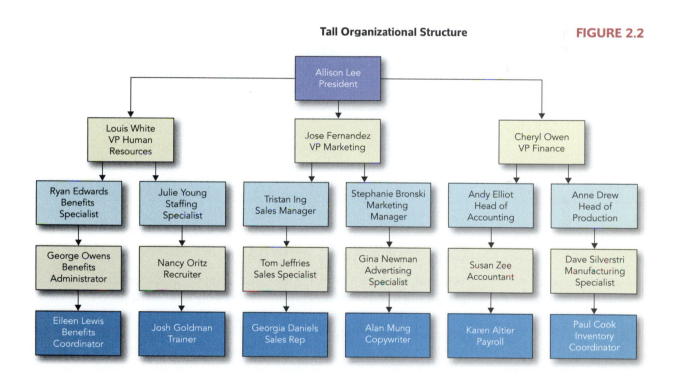

Flat Organizational Structure   FIGURE 2.3

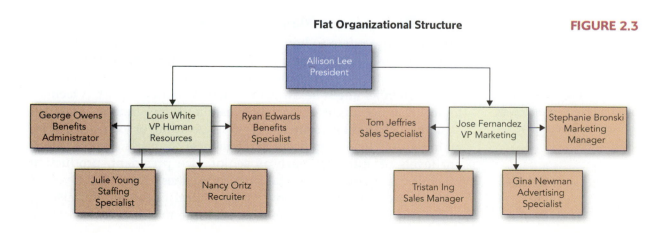

structural messages relate to company operating policies or procedures.

quality of the work produced by the organization and the product or service success achieved in the marketplace. Three primary types of business messages exchanged between organizational members are **structural, relational,** and **change messages.**

Message	Function	Channels
Structural	Structural messages relate to company operating policies or procedures. These messages involve achievement of the organization's goals through the successful production of products or services. Structural messages are directly associated with how the organization functions.	• Employee manuals • Policy statements • Bylaws • Performance evaluations • Task directives • Corporate training
Relational	Relational messages hold an interpersonal function by building rapport between employees and with customers. Relational messages also enable employees to negotiate their roles and aid in the coordination of work performance.	• Conversations • Feedback from employees or customers during promotions, celebrations, and meetings
Change	Change messages help the organization adapt and respond to the environment. They encourage the innovative and exploratory exchange of ideas between employees. Chapter 14 discusses change messages in depth.	• Dialogues and brainstorming sessions that yield experimentation, new techniques, and innovative strategies

Communicating Internally

relational messages are interpersonal in that they build rapport between employees and customers.

change messages help the organization adapt and respond to the environment.

internal communication is the exchange of messages between employees inside the organization.

message flow refers to how communication travels through channels in the organization.

structural channel is related to the role, position, or job occupied by an individual in an organization.

Internal communication is the exchange of messages between employees inside the organization. When you talk, send an e-mail message, or write a memo to co-workers, supervisors, or managers about customer needs, supplier delivery schedules, or project progress, you are communicating internally. Businesses cannot function and employees cannot perform their jobs well without adequate internal communication.

How Do Business Messages Flow?

Message flow refers to how communication travels through channels in the organization. In a business context, channels may be human, technological, or structural. As described in Chapter 1, a human channel might be conversation or a written report. A technological channel might carry messages via phones, fax, or e-mail. A **structural channel** is related to the role, position, or job occupied by an individual in an organization. Structural channels involve different levels of authority, such as senior vice president, production manager, and supervisor. The flow of business messages involves both human communication and structural channels. Because so many employees send and receive multiple messages every day, a

Human Channels

(fax)   (telephone)

(computer)

Technology Channels

FIGURE 2.4

Channels of Communication

Structural Channels

system is needed to manage the flow of communication. Message flows are managed through communication networks. Channels are illustrated in Figure 2.4.

What Is a Communication Network?

The pathways through which messages travel among employees in an organization are **communication networks,** which use a series of human and technological channels to transmit and receive company messages. A communication network can include two people, a group of people, or all company employees. Tall organizational structures with many levels of authority have more links or people in the network chain. Messages must travel through more human and structural channels than they do in flat organizational structures. An employee's role can also determine the channel links to other employees in a formal network.

While many traditional companies maintain tall structures with many links in the communication chain, other new businesses have more open communication structures. In fact, some small emerging businesses practice open-book management. At Wild Planet Toys, a toy design and manufacturing company, all employees have access to

communication networks are the pathways through which messages travel among employees in an organization.

© Wild Planet Toys

formal communication network is an official channel or line of communication.

downward communication is the movement or path of messages from superiors to subordinates.

company financial data such as profit margins, expenses, and even the company bank account. Wild Planet Toys believes that employees need to understand important company information that, in other companies, is reserved for management alone. Similarly, software company MTW has an open-book philosophy. Employees have access to all financial and strategic information. In fact, they own 53.5 percent of the company stock.

Formal Communication Networks

Official channels or the lines of positional authority represent a **formal communication network.** Formal networks move messages through channels that link employees together based on their role in the organization. Business communicators need to know how messages flow in a formal network to design the right types of messages for the right audience. Formal business messages flow in three basic directions: downward, upward, and horizontally as illustrated in Figure 2.5.

Downward Communication

The movement or path of messages from superiors to subordinates in the structural chain of command is called **downward communication.** Downward-bound messages flow through a number of people according to formal network relationships. For example, assume a company's board of directors transmits a message instructing the president to create an employee job-sharing program. The president may send the message to division directors and ask their suggestions for program design and implementation. These directors may inform other person-

FIGURE 2.5   **Flow of Messages**

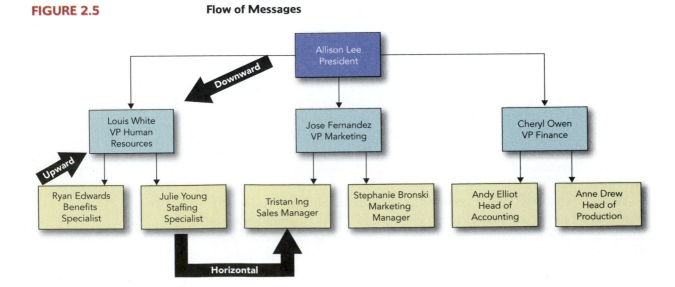

nel and request suggestions. Messages work their way downward to select employees or to all staff.

Downward messages are transmitted through a variety of communication channels, including interpersonal conversations, meetings or evaluations, written memos, reports, training manuals, and newsletters. Usually downward messages are structural and include job-related information such as how to perform tasks. For example, your supervisor may explain your job duties or how certain tasks should be performed so that you know what is expected. Downward messages also comprise information about the company mission, new policies, or human resource benefits that travel to employees from higher-level managers. Finally, downward messages can request employee feedback about job performance or problems in operating procedures.

The advantage of downward messages is that when messages are clear and comprehensive, employees better understand their role in the company, what resources are available, and what is expected from them professionally. The downside of downward messages is noise, as discussed in Chapter 1. Downward noise includes **message filtering and distortion.** Because messages travel through people, their perceptual differences may magnify, minimize, or alter a message as it moves down through the ranks. People perceive messages differently, so they may add, delete, or change information accordingly. For example, a simple memo from the executive vice president requesting new ideas to streamline a procedure may be magnified into a message that requires an immediate change in the way a task should be handled. Message filtering and distortion may occur less frequently when there are fewer people on the message network or fewer levels of authority in the company. Another disadvantage of downward messages is that employees may experience message overload when they receive too much information at one time. Many messages reiterate what employees already know, and other messages do not affect certain employees at all. Overburdened with repeated e-mail, memos, and other messages, employees may react by tuning out or discarding information they feel is unnecessary. Finally, downward messages can be ineffective because they are one-way. **One-way communication** is not interactive; the message source does not expect or encourage a response from the receiver. When opportunities for interaction are limited, employees may feel disconnected and even confused or uncertain about what some downward messages mean.

message filtering and distortion is noise resulting when messages are magnified, minimized, or altered as they travel through people.

CREATIVE

CHALLENGE

Develop a strategy to reduce message filtering and distortion in a downward message about flexible work hours. The message is from the assistant director of human resources in a manufacturing plant. It states that all employees are entitled to flextime, including the 7 A.M. to 3 P.M., 3 P.M. to 11 P.M., and 11 P.M. to 7 A.M. shifts. The memo also states that the flexible hours are at the discretion of the department manager. Write an e-mail to your instructor that describes two different messages: one to employees and one to managers. Include in your e-mail what structural, human, or technological channels you would use to transmit these messages and the words you would use to increase message accuracy and clarity.

one-way communication occurs when a message sender does not expect or encourage a response from the receiver.

Upward Communication

The upward flow of messages from subordinates to higher-ranking employees in the organization is called **upward communication.** Upward messages usually involve project or task progress information; job-related problems; employee needs, attitudes, or morale; and suggestions for improvements. For example, you might talk to your supervisor about the progress you and other team members are making on a particular project or about the overall mood of the team. Upward messages pass through the chain of command. They can include questions, comments, or suggestions. For example, a programmer who had been working at Microsoft for less than a year sent his manager an e-mail that moved up the chain through the network until it finally reached Bill Gates, the chair of Microsoft. Gates replied to the e-mail and offered several comments about the young programmer's ideas. Microsoft product unit manager, Alex Simon, pitched a new idea directly to CEO Steve Ballmer. While he did not accept the idea initially, Ballmer requested that Simon work on it a bit and offered to discuss it again later. Even though not all ideas are used, it is important that many ideas get communicated to top management.

The extensive use of e-mail in organizations has encouraged some employees to disregard levels of authority and send messages upward to top executives. Upward communication of new ideas is so open at Microsoft that no matter what rank an employee holds, he or she can discuss ideas directly with top executives. However, unsolicited upward messages are frowned on in some companies. Find out how your company feels about them before leap-frogging over your boss.

Common communication channels for upward-bound messages include opinion surveys, suggestion boxes, interpersonal conversations and meetings, open-door policies, and informal social gatherings. Many organizations use information gained through upward communication to evaluate the effectiveness of supervisors and managers. In fact, 32 percent of businesses use feedback from workers, known as "subordinate appraisals," to evaluate their managers' performance.

One clear advantage of upward-bound messages to both managers and employees is that they provide feedback about company directives, plans, or procedures. When employees direct messages upward, they can provide valuable information about their understanding of instructions, diagnose problems, and offer vital insights about customers and front-line activities. Employees can also satisfy needs, clarify misunderstandings, and release some emotional tensions by communicating with superiors. Finally, when employees participate in the organizational process by making decisions and solving problems, job satisfaction and productivity tend to increase. Like downward messages, upward messages may have the disadvantage of filtering and distortion, generally because employees don't want superiors to view them unfavorably. Being honest with superiors can be risky if the information involves a problem. Employees may believe they will be blamed. The superior, not wanting to deal with bad news, may dismiss a negative message entirely.

Horizontal Communication

The lateral exchange of messages between people of roughly equal authority is called **horizontal communication.** Messages may be exchanged between members of the same department or members from different departments or teams. Because there are no layers for horizontal messages to pass through, communication moves quickly. The flatter the organizational structure, the more frequently horizontal messages will be exchanged among employees. Horizontal messages include information sharing, problem solving, planning, and project coordination. While the majority of information shared horizontally is business related, some messages involve personal information.

Horizontal communication flows through many channels including interpersonal conversations, interaction on teams and committees, meetings, memos, e-mail, and social activities. Joe Guerra is co-CEO of American Golf, a company that specializes in the operation of more than 300 public and private golf courses. He believes employees at all levels of the organization need to communicate horizontally to share ideas, so he created "workout sessions" that allow rank-and-file employees to develop strategies for improvement on their own, without supervisors and managers being present. Improvement ideas that employees have contributed in these workout sessions have streamlined the business processes and saved hundreds of labor hours.

One advantage of horizontal communication is increased worker productivity through coordination of interpersonal working relationships. Horizontal communication also boosts morale, allows employees to

horizontal communication is the lateral exchange of messages between people of roughly equal authority.

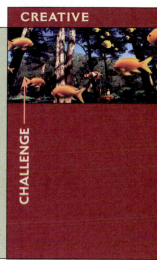

CREATIVE CHALLENGE

Think of a situation in which you communicated horizontally with a co-worker, another student, or someone you worked with in a campus organization. What was the purpose of your communication? Did the communication yield a problem solution or the answer to a question? Write a list of at least five reasons you think horizontal communication can be beneficial and should be encouraged in organizations. Come to class prepared to discuss your ideas.

American Golf operates more than 300 public and private golf courses. Its horizontal communication structure encourages all employees to share their ideas for improving business.
© D2 Productions, Inc. Murphy/Scully

interact and learn from each other, and encourages teamwork and collaboration. The most notable disadvantage of horizontal communication is *professional rivalry*, which is competition between members of different departments. Sometimes employees may be reluctant to share information or collaborate because they feel threatened or jealous. Stiff competition over company resources, choice projects, or new positions can stifle horizontal communication. Finally, *specialization* (expertise or skill in a given field) can also inhibit horizontal communication. Communication can become difficult when employees from different specialties, such as accounting or computer information, use different message symbols. For example, **jargon** (specialized words or language used in a specific field or profession) can complicate communication between employees.

jargon specialized words or language specific to a field or profession.

Informal Communication Networks

An **informal communication network** operates independently from official channels and involves messages that flow in all directions and through all levels of authority. Informal networks are an outgrowth of formal message exchange in that as relationships develop, informal patterns of interactions emerge. These patterns are often based on interpersonal relationships, shared interests, and physical proximity. The most notable informal network is the grapevine as illustrated in Figure 2.6.

informal communication networks involve messages that flow in all directions and through all levels of authority.

Heard It through the Grapevine

The **grapevine** is an informal network of employees who hold various ranks and share information largely through oral communication. Messages travel extremely quickly on the grapevine, which is a shortcut to formal channels. Messages can be dispersed in clusters of three or four people or through serial transmissions from one individual to

grapevine an oral and informal communication network comprised of various employees.

FIGURE 2.6   **The Grapevine**

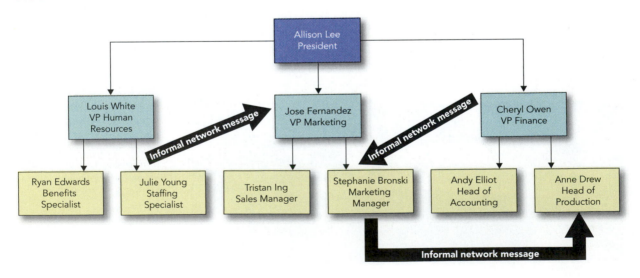

the next. Some employees feel that grapevine information is more detailed and more current or relevant than messages received through formal channels. At Xerox, copier repair technicians (tech reps) were gathering informally at the parts warehouse or the coffeepot to share information and stories about diagnosing and solving copier problems. When upper management at Xerox discovered this informal network of knowledge, it developed Eureka, a database of tips created and shared by the tech reps. Any tech rep can contribute information to the database and everyone has access to the information.

Advantages of the company grapevine include the speed at which messages can travel and the opportunity for management to receive important employee feedback. The grapevine can also carry a good deal more information than is disseminated through formal channels. Finally, the grapevine can explain or confirm confusing or complex formal messages. The downside of the grapevine is that inaccurate rumors can spread that undermine morale or project performance. Message distortion and filtering can also alter messages based on the sender's perspective.

Grapevine versus Gossip

Gossip, false stories, and malicious rumors do travel on the grapevine. But a good 75 to 90 percent of the information flowing on the grapevine is accurate. Factual and even helpful company information routinely travels on the grapevine. For example, some formal downward messages may be designed in an ambiguous or abbreviated manner, which can be difficult for employees to effectively interpret. Information gleaned from the grapevine can often clarify unclear or ambiguous company information.

On the other hand, rumors also travel fast on the vine, and some rumors have little credibility. For example, rumors may abound about

company restructuring or change initiatives, including plans for new hires, job redesign, or layoffs, because not enough formal messages reach employees that specify and explain company initiatives in detail. To fill in the message gaps, employees sometimes invent fictional rumors or gossip. At Charles Schwab, an investment brokerage, employees are routinely informed about company changes such as expense cutbacks through formal network messages so they won't pick up wrong information about changes on the grapevine.

Communicating Externally

external communication is the exchange of messages between the organization and the external environment.

input is all the information the organization receives from the environment.

throughput involves the organization's analysis and evaluation of the input it receives and the transformation of that input into outputs.

output refers to messages the organization transmits to the environment in response to received input.

Messages exchanged between the organization and all aspects of the external environment are referred to as **external communication.** The survival of a business depends on the relationships established between members of the organization and people outside the organization such as customers, stockholders, community members, government agencies, and the media. External communication between the organization and the environment is a process involving input, throughput, and output (the flow of external messages is illustrated in Figure 2.7):

- **Input** is all the information the organization receives from the environment, such as customer perceptions and expectations, product or service problems, economic trends, and new state or federal regulations.
- **Throughput** involves the organization's analysis and evaluation of the input it receives and the transformation of that input into outputs.
- **Output** refers to messages the organization transmits to the environment in response to received input.

FIGURE 2.7

External Communication Process

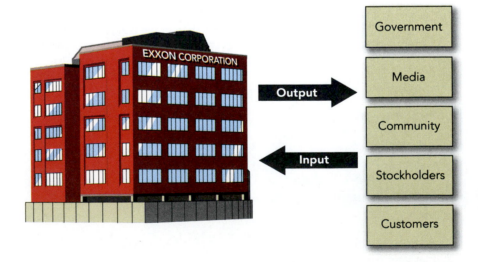

Develop an organization response (output) to the following input received from a patient survey at a busy medical orthopedic office.

A survey distributed to all patients revealed intense customer dissatisfaction with the time management process at the practice. Patients spend an hour and a half to two hours after their scheduled appointment time waiting to see a doctor. The patients surveyed demanded that wait times be significantly decreased. After learning about the overwhelming patient discontent, the doctors, nurses, and staff discussed ways to address the problem. Potential solutions to the wait time problem included:

- Reducing the number of patients scheduled per doctor, per day from 40 to 25.
- Reducing the types of physical problems addressed by doctors, for example, concentrating on knees, wrists, and hips.
- Conducting schedule reviews to match the complexity of the problem with the amount of time allotted for the visit.
- Relying more on physician assistants and nurse practitioners for routine and follow-up patient care.
- Not accepting new patients for three months.

To develop your response, interview an office manager at a medical practice to evaluate each of the discussed alternatives and to gain more insight. Prepare a brief presentation for the class that identifies a solution (your own or one of the alternatives discussed) and the reasons you think the problem can be solved this way to the satisfaction of everyone involved. Include in your presentation a proposed message response for the practice to transmit to patients. Make sure you write a thank-you letter to the person you interview.

For example, an electronics manufacturer may receive information from consumers that its product requires too much time to install. The manufacturer takes that input and decides to redesign the product so that it is easier for customers to install. Then the organization reintroduces the product and promotes the improved installation process to the public. At Nortel and eBay, getting up-to-the-minute information from customers is vitally important, so these companies use Sat-Metrix, a company that gets customer input and responds with output immediately.

The channels used for external communication include annual reports, newsletters, brochures, advertisements, press releases, conferences, and sponsorships of special community events. Many external messages are reviewed or created by company public relations professionals to ensure that they are consistent with the organizations philosophy and policy. The most obvious advantage of external communication is feedback from the environment, which can be vital to the survival of any organization. External information can also help the organization plan, make decisions, avoid problems, and satisfy customer needs.

Strategies

1. As a business communicator, you can manage information better by responding to messages immediately rather than letting your in-box pile up. You may also create specific file folders (either on your computer or as hard copy) in which you categorize and prioritize those messages that require your attention or action. If your job requires you to travel, it is a good idea to inform potential senders of information on your voice mail and e-mail systems that you are out of the office.

2. Think critically about formal and informal messages you receive at work. Consider the perspectives and viewpoints of the people on the network from whom you receive the information. Listen carefully to messages on the grapevine that may clarify or explain ambiguous downward communication. Then cross check the information by asking your superiors for confirmation.

3. Design spoken and written upward messages that clearly describe progress on various tasks. Include in each message the steps you plan to take, any resources that may be required, and expected completion dates.

4. Let superiors know about potential problems before they happen. Formulate clear reasons you think a problem may occur, and be ready to offer ideas and recommendations for prevention. When you do identify a job-related, equipment, or customer problem, make sure to provide as many practical solutions as you can. Problem solving can be an overwhelming responsibility for a manager to tackle alone. Your insights may not only signal process or product deficiencies but help to remedy them.

5. Send upward messages through the chain of command. Avoid communicating problems, doubts, frustrations, or suggestions to superiors who rank above your direct supervisor, unless you indicate your intention to your supervisor first.

6. Select appropriate opportunities to make suggestions or ask questions. Informal conversations during coffee breaks, lunch, or less hectic periods can be good times to approach your superior with helpful ideas.

7. Formulate downward messages that explain why tasks should be performed in a certain way. It is also a good idea to explain how job duties relate to and help accomplish organizational plans and goals. Providing employees with insights into the big picture of the organization can help them understand the importance of their individual work activities in relation to the whole.

8. Make sure you send downward messages about an employee's good performance. Let employees know what aspects of their

performance are outstanding. Single messages such as "Jim, good work on that report" or "Nice job on the newsletter layout" can boost morale and motivate employees to perform their best work.

9. Send downward messages that ask employees for their opinions regarding new projects, initiatives, or decisions that may affect them. Make sure you allow employees enough time to prepare a response.

10. Communicate face-to-face as often as possible when conveying formal information. Face-to-face human channels allow for immediate feedback and follow-up, which can prevent filtering or distortion of messages.

Summary

- Modern business communicates in a global arena and manages information and technology in constantly changing business environments.

- Organizational communication involves the exchange of messages to facilitate structure, working relationships, and shared meaning creation among members.

- The three types of business messages exchanged between employees and with the external environment are structural, relational, and change messages.

- Internal communication refers to the exchange of messages inside an organization. These messages flow through human, technological, and structural channels. Structural channels relate to levels of authority. Internal message flows are often managed by networks, which are pathways through which information travels between employees.

- Formal communication networks are pathways in which information flows through the levels of organizational authority, such as those outlined in an organization chart. In formal networks, messages flow in three directions: downward, upward, and horizontal.

  a. Downward messages move from higher-ranking managers or supervisors to employees at any point lower in the chain of command. Depending on the size of the organization, downward messages may flow through many or only a few human and structural channels. The more channels downward messages travel through, the more message filtering and distortion can occur. Downward messages usually cover such information as how to perform job duties; the company's mission, directives, or new policies; and requests for feedback.

    b. Upward messages flow from subordinates to employees at any point higher in the chain of command. They often involve information about task progress; job-related problems; and employee questions, comments, and suggestions.

    c. Horizontal messages are exchanged between employees of roughly equal authority in the organization. They normally involve information sharing, updates, problem-solving ideas, and coordination of project efforts.

■ Informal communication networks move messages independently of the official levels of authority and involve interaction based on personal relationships between employees. The grapevine is an informal network through which a great deal of company information travels. Information flows much faster on the grapevine than through formal networks and can be dispersed in clusters of three or four people or through serial transmissions, which pass the message from person to person to person. Inaccurate rumors do spread on the grapevine, but 75 to 90 percent of grapevine information is accurate.

■ External communication refers to the exchange of messages between an organization and the environment, including customers, stockholders, the media, and the community. The external communication process consists of message input (all the information received from the environment), throughput (how the organization evaluates and transforms input), and output (the organization's action or response).

Business Communication Projects

1. Some managers believe they can't maintain their authority if their employees feel overly comfortable with them. They fear that if they become friends with employees, a line of authority may be crossed. They think that their role necessitates a professional transformation in both behavior and mental attitude. They send only structural messages, never relational messages, to subordinates. Other managers believe that friendships with their employees can be productive. They think the exchange of relational messages increases morale and motivation and encourages employees to provide productive feedback. Divide into groups of five to prepare a role-play that addresses the following questions:

    a. Can a manager develop friendships with employees and still command respect?

    b. Many employees seem to prefer managers who are sensitive and caring, but still "take care of business." How can this blend of caring and competence be achieved?

    c. Is it necessary to alter your behavior and/or personality to be a successful business manager in today's organizations? Explain your viewpoint.

    d. If some change is necessary to achieve professionalism, what aspects of your behavior and attitude need to be modified? Explain why these changes or new behaviors are necessary.

Potential scenarios for role-play presentations:

- *New manager's training session.* One student plays the role of the trainer and the others play new unit managers. The trainer can ask questions about how managers expect to interact with subordinates and provide them with structural messages about what it takes to achieve professional excellence and solid managerial performance.

- *Company counseling.* A counselor offers guidance to a new department manager who feels her employees are taking advantage and overstepping the boundaries by repeatedly showing up late for work and leaving early. The counselor's mission is to help the manager modify her behavior.

- *Job interview.* An applicant is questioned about his management style and experience with subordinate relationships. The interviewers can react to the applicant's statements and offer ideas about how managers are expected to behave in the company.

2. How, as a department manager, would you encourage employees to communicate upward their honest opinions and comments about policies, procedures, and practices? What steps would you take and what channels would you suggest employees use to transmit their messages? Write an e-mail message directed upward to your division director that outlines your strategy to encourage honest, upward-bound messages from employees.

3. The computer software consulting company you work for has more than 500 employees located in two states. During an afternoon coffee break, you overhear two of your co-workers discussing a rumor that 100 company positions will be slated for layoff in the next few months. You want to know whether this rumor is true. What will you do to find out? Write two paragraphs that detail your strategy to unearth the truth.

4. Employees throughout the accounting department have been complaining that they receive innumerable downward e-mail messages each day. They protest that many of the messages do not pertain to the department, are redundant, and are not related to their job duties. Your department director asks you to develop and present a strategy for the accounting department staff. Prepare a three-minute oral presentation that explains your strategy to reduce the overload of downward e-mails.

5. Your boss places you in charge of selecting a computer dealer, choosing the system, and purchasing the equipment. You research several computer dealers in the local area and select the one that offers the best customer service and competitive prices. You also talk to unit employees to determine their equipment needs, including hard-drive capability, performance speed, and software. Before you place the order, you mention to your boss that you have found a reputable dealer who will also provide system installation, onsite training, and maintenance. Your boss responds that if you do not purchase from the dealer the department used in the past, one employee (his favorite) has threatened to quit. He also tells you to run your dealer selections by two other employees who want to have a voice in the decision. You are angry that the boss has apparently revoked the authority he assigned to you. Design an upward message to your boss that expresses your discouragement in a positive, nonthreatening manner. Explain what channel you will choose to transmit the message.

6. The founder of your company is retiring. Joe King has devoted 52 years of his life to King and Sons Imports, Ltd., and is now moving to the Caymans to enjoy the sun and the sand with his wife. The board of directors is planning a formal banquet to honor Mr. King, complete with entertainment and door prizes. They want to invite family, friends, employees, and customers. You have been asked to design the invitation to the banquet. Design an invitation for a formal dinner that will be appropriate for everyone included, from the janitorial staff to billionaire client Tom Drump.

7. Think about the concept of shared meaning in relation to any current job, activity, hobby, or organization. Make a list of terms you use on a regular basis in that activity that wouldn't make sense to outsiders. Then write a series of definitions for those terms to explain what they mean, how they are used, whom they are used with, whether they are formal or informal, and how they make the company or organization more efficient.

Discussion Questions

1. What are the differences between formal and informal communication networks?

2. How can business professionals better manage the bulk of information they receive each day?

3. What factors contribute to the decrease in speed at which a given message travels to organizational members?

4. Explain why employees are often reluctant to send upward messages to higher-ranking supervisors and managers.

5. What types of messages have you received through the company or school grapevine that were not gossip?

6. Why is the throughput aspect of external communication so important for an organization?

7. As a manager, from what communication network might you expect to find the most honest employee feedback?

8. What aspects of another cultural group should communicators be aware of when they conduct business? How can they avoid cultural miscommunication?

9. Could a negative horizontal message do serious harm to a company? Why or why not?

10. How do formal communications fill in the gaps in information transmitted through the grapevine? For example, if a rumor is circulating that an executive is about to retire and her position has already been promised to another employee, even before the position announcement has gone out, what effect would a formal notice from the CEO's office have on the employees' knowledge of the situation?

Creative Case

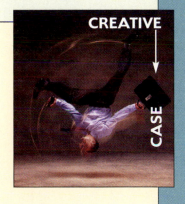

CREATIVE CASE

Standardizing Information at Microsoft

When Robert Herbold became chief operating officer at Microsoft, he faced quite a challenge. It seems the software giant had a very disorganized communication system. Prior to Herbold's arrival, the financial, purchasing, human resources, and sales information systems at Microsoft were mishmashed and incompatible. Many divisions had created their own individual operating practices, making communication between departments difficult. When employees needed supplies or products, they would order them for their individual department from whatever vendor they chose. Problems arose when payments to vendors were delayed or overlooked. There were no discounts for volume purchasing since purchases were made piecemeal and buying patterns were unstructured. Because managers used different practices to suit their needs, Microsoft's informal information practices led to difficulty accessing information and distribution of outdated information. In order to solve these problems, Herbold standardized and formalized company communication practices and implemented a management information system (MIS) with Web-based menus. His system offered employees instant access to information from any department in the company, provided uniformity of operating practices, and saved the company money.

While the new formalized system untangled the way Microsoft employees communicate, it destroyed the creativity, independent thinking, and authority many of the employees enjoyed.

Is some creativity lost when business practices and information become standardized?

Consider the following questions:

1. Can employees be encouraged to develop innovative ideas when standard procedures are in place? If so how?

2. What are the advantages and disadvantages to creating a centralized database of information?

3. What aspects of conducting business are made easier with standard information systems? What aspects suffer when systems are standardized?

4. When communication practices become more formal and standardized does the flow of information through human communication networks become more formal too?

SOURCE: Herbold, R. J. "Inside Microsoft: Balancing Creativity and Discipline." *Harvard Business Review.* Vol 8ß0, no. 1, 2002, pp. 73–79.

Chapter 3

The following themes are explored in this chapter:

MAP OUT MESSAGE GOALS

primary goals / secondary goals / goal feasibility / goal intention / goal response

EVALUATE YOUR AUDIENCE

size / types / demographics / what's known and what's new / what's real and what's right / benefits / what's first and what's last / empathy

SHAPE MESSAGE CONTENT

main idea / theme / designing arguments / framing your content / elements

SELECT CHANNELS

keys to selection / specific channel choices

ACQUIRE RESOURCES

time / personnel / outsourcing / research / money

GENERATE SOURCE CREDIBILITY

competence / reliability / dynamism / similarity

ELIMINATE DESIGN FLAWS

unneeded data/visuals / sensory overload / missing details / hidden agenda / contradictions / cultural inconsistencies / inaccuracy / poor formatting

SEND MESSAGE

timing / location

Communication Design Strategy

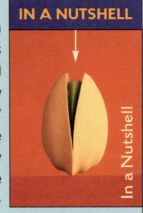

Doctors at a teaching hospital found themselves in a dispute with their hospital administration. The doctors believed their primary goal was to learn, teach, and perform progressive medicine. They realized that new treatments could not only save some of their clients' lives but also lead to new discoveries and research. The administrators were focused on the financial feasibility of new medical procedures, which many insurance companies are reluctant to pay for. The doctors continued to request the tools, operating space, and staff required to perform these new treatments, but the administration continued to deny their requests. The administrators claimed the hospital could not afford to absorb the costs of providing care not covered by insurance. Frustrated, the doctors were determined to develop a strategy to persuade the administration to allow their clients to receive the most technologically advanced treatments available. To create an effective strategy, the doctors knew they had to consider the administrators' perspectives, what they needed to know about the new treatments, and how the hospital could benefit from new medical discoveries. They also needed to select the most appropriate channel to carry their thoughtfully designed message and the best possible person to deliver it. Time was of the essence, and the challenge of creating a solid strategy seemed daunting, but their clients were depending on them. After weeks of feverish activity—including meetings, research, study and cost comparisons—the doctors created a presentation that they believed would convince the administration of the merits of their case. When the chief surgeon returned from her meeting with the administration with a big smile on her face, the doctors knew they were about to start practicing a new kind of medicine.

Communication Design

In the world of business, creating messages is not an arbitrary process. Designing effective messages requires planning and developing strategies to better achieve desired results. Like the strategy created by doctors at the research hospital in our "In a Nutshell" discussion, effective communication design involves clarifying goals, understanding your audience, selecting the right channel, and eliminating noise from your message. While not all of your messages will be persuasive, thorough planning is still necessary for most business messages.

This chapter will provide a framework for how to plan and design messages strategically to increase your chances of achieving high fidelity and reaching your goals.

communication design is the intrapersonal process of planning for and creating meaningful messages.

Communication design is the systematic intrapersonal process of planning for and creating meaningful messages. Depending on the message, goal, and audience, different planning elements are required to communicate our thoughts and ideas effectively. Communication design involves several steps before the designer transmits a message. While not every message requires every step, many business messages require a comprehensive design strategy to reach their goals.

Eight steps comprise this communication strategy (see Figure 3.1). They can be used in the development of various internal and external business messages, including oral presentations, written reports, memos, letters of correspondence, meetings, newsletters, brochures, feature articles, web pages, proposals, and face-to-face human interaction. While some messages require less time to design than others, it is a good idea to think about and practice these design steps in virtually all of your personal and professional communication. You may also plan your message in the order these steps are organized, but

FIGURE 3.1

Eight Steps of Communication Design

Map out message goals

Evaluate your audience

Shape message content

Select channel

Acquire resources

Generate source credibility

Eliminate design flaws

Send message

they can be rearranged or performed in a different order depending on the communication situation or task.

Map Out Message Goals

A **goal** is an outcome that you want to achieve at some future point. From a business communication standpoint, goals are the purpose of and the reason for our communication. Well-defined goals make the process of planning somewhat easier, since the better you understand your goals, the easier it is to set a workable plan in motion. Most messages are created with both primary and secondary goals in mind. **Primary goals** represent the outcome that you want to achieve. **Secondary goals** help you to achieve your primary goals. For example, if your primary goal is to be hired by a *Fortune* 500 company, you must have solid credentials, including academic and professional achievements. To reach your primary goal, you need to accomplish at least one secondary goal, such as graduating in good standing from a top school.

When determining your message goals, consider feasibility, intention, and goal response.

goal an outcome that you want to achieve and the reason you are communicating.

CREATIVE
CHALLENGE

Imagine you are the assistant manager of a marketing department. Write an e-mail message to your manager in response to a companywide request for employee feedback about flexible work schedules. Employees can choose to work 9 A.M. to 5 P.M., 8 A.M. to 4 P.M. or 7 A.M. to 3 P.M. Your e-mail should address the feasibility of flexible work schedules, including the costs involved and how work may be accomplished if too many employees choose the same schedules.

Is the Goal Feasible?

The practicality of your message goals is their **feasibility.** Assessing whether goals are feasible or not involves asking specific questions about them. Is the goal realistic? Can the goal be reasonably managed and attained? Communication designers need to narrow their focus to manageable and realistic goals.

primary goals represent the outcome that you want to achieve.

secondary goals help you to achieve your primary goals.

feasibility refers to the practicality of your message goals.

What Is My Intention?

A **goal intention** is what you specifically want, need, or intend to do. The intention of the message is the reason you are communicating. It is what you want or need from your receiver. Table 3.1 highlights four goal intentions.

goal intention is what you specifically want, need, or intend to do.

What Response Do I Want?

The reaction you want or expect from your receiver is a goal **response,** and it is an important part of your message goal. To satisfy your goal intentions, feedback is necessary. For example, suppose your goal intention is to persuade your fellow students to sign a petition to lower the prices and improve the food in the student center cafeteria. The students' potential reaction to your message is an important aspect of the planning you will need to do to achieve your goal.

response is the reaction you want or expect from your receiver.

TABLE 3.1   **Goal Intention**

Goal	Intention	Response
To inform	To provide specific or general information to increase awareness and understanding	Receivers obtain information that you want them to know.
To persuade	To reach receivers in such a way that they change their behavior or alter their beliefs or views	Receiver is provided with compelling reasons, facts, or evidence to support your position. For example, assume you recently concluded that your campus should have more student parking. Your goal would be to convince administrators to increase the size of the parking facility to better accommodate students who commute to class.
To call to action	To motivate and inspire others to think or act	The receiver is motivated to consider your new idea or proposal, remember important information, or resolve a particular conflict.
To connect	To influence receivers to accept and include us	The goal is acceptance by others, to be included in some activity with another person, or to gain membership in a social or professional group.

Evaluate Your Audience

audience an individual or group who receives a message.

When you plan your design, you need to think about who is going to receive your message. An **audience** is an individual or group who receives a designed message. While the word *audience* has traditionally referred to a mass of people, it can also refer to just one person. The word is often used to describe an interaction with an individual who has authority. You might have an audience with the governor of your state or the president of your college.

Does the Size of the Audience Matter?

While an audience can be comprised of many people or just one individual, you need to approximate how many people will receive your message. Estimate how many people will receive the information, and design your message accordingly. For example, if your audience consists of thousands of people who will potentially log on to your website, chances are your message would be less personal and more eye-catching and clever in its design than a message conveyed to a small group in a meeting.

What Is the Type of Audience?

Groups of people have dynamic personalities, just as individuals do. Different types of audiences have different characteristics, needs, interests, and skill levels that you need to evaluate throughout the communication design process. Traditionally, audiences have been described as either heterogeneous (a mass of diverse and differently lo-

Types of Audiences   **TABLE 3.2**

Business audience	A business audience is made up of either internal or external business professionals and customers. An **internal business audience** is people employed by the same company as you are. An **external business audience** is composed of customers or clients and those who work in other organizations similar to yours. For example, if you work at a restaurant, external business professionals are people who work for other restaurants and who perform the same work you do or people who work for companies that distribute or sell restaurant goods and supplies.
Public audience	A public audience is people in the environment or community with whom you communicate. It can include professionals in other industries, members of the community, neighbors, your student colleagues, the voters who elect you to some public office, and so on.
Intimate audience	An intimate audience consists of people with whom you share a close relationship, such as family, friends, and significant others.

cated people) or homogeneous (a group of people who are considered similar). Furthermore, audiences are often classed as primary and secondary. A primary audience includes those people you want or intend to communicate with. A secondary audience includes people you do not intend to communicate with but who may receive your message, whether you want them to or not. Table 3.2 expands the descriptions to include three basic types that comprise both primary and secondary audiences.

At Pitney Bowes, an integrated mail and document management company, the internal business audience is multigenerational. It includes baby boomers (people born between 1946 and 1964) and generation X (people born between 1965 and 1981) and generation Y employees (born after 1981). The company has developed programs that specifically meet the needs of each generation of employee. For example, online services help boomers find colleges for their children and medical services for their elderly parents, generation X employees receive assistance with child care services, and generation Y employees are connected to housing opportunities and car dealers. The Pitney Bowes programs also link older and younger workers together to share information and build communication networks so they can learn new skills from each other and pool their collective knowledge.

internal business audience refers to people employed by the same company.

external business audience refers to customers or clients and those who work in other similar organizations.

CREATIVE

Select an audience of 10 people you know, and develop a demographic profile to describe them generally. Analyze this audience by looking for patterns that suggest similarity. The categories for analysis can include age, gender, cultural affiliation, profession, education, and so on. Come to class prepared to discuss your analysis.

CHALLENGE

What Do I Need to Know about My Audience?

When you evaluate your audience, think about *demographics*, gathering general statistical information from sources such as the U.S. Census Bureau. You can also administer surveys, hold focus groups, or

FIGURE 3.2   **Audience Demographics**

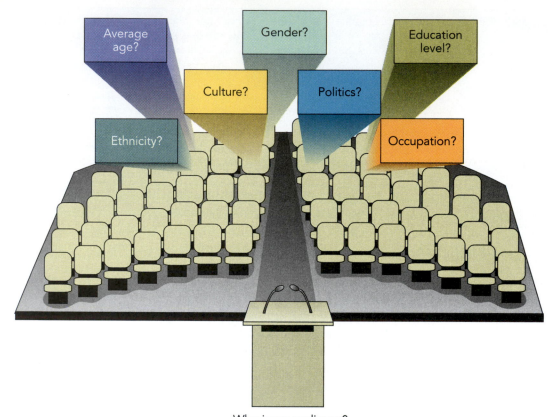

Who is my audience?

conduct personal interviews to gather information. The demographic information you want to collect about your particular audience may include average age, gender, education level, occupation, ethnicity, and sociocultural and political affiliations. By gathering as much general information as you can about your audience, you can tailor your message to fit their business, social, and cultural perspectives. Audience demographics are illustrated in Figure 3.2.

What's Known and What's New

It is a good idea to ascertain what your audience members already know about the information you plan to provide in your message. Do they have general knowledge or advanced understanding about the topic? The answer will shape your message content, language, visuals, and tone.

- *Known information.* An audience that is already familiar with the topic may become bored or disregard the message if there is nothing new or interesting. On the other hand, you can hold an audience's attention on a subject they already know if you suggest new methods of using the information or present it in a new or entertaining way.

- *Blend of known and new information.* It is equally important for you to discover what your audience needs to know about your topic or how new aspects of what they know can benefit them. For example, an audience of aspiring entrepreneurs may know that starting a new business requires capital resources. What they need to know is that a new business can require up to 18 months of liquid capital to remain operational before it turns a profit. Countless new businesses fail because they are undercapitalized and run out of money.

- *New information.* While new information or a new twist on old information can gain audience attention, messages that have too much novelty or are overly complicated can cause the audience to lose interest, become confused, or even tune out in frustration. If you absolutely need to design a complicated message, make the design easier to grasp by including examples to which the audience can relate or visuals that will help them to understand.

What's Real and What's Right

It can be challenging to discover what your audience values and believes, but you need some idea of where your audience stands on the issues or topics you will introduce to avoid offending or irritating them. Background information about their cultural, political, religious, occupational, or group affiliations can provide clues to their beliefs and values. Drawing on examples or current news items that are relevant to the audience can be an effective strategy to gain acceptance.

What Is the Audience Benefit?

When planning your message, think about how the audience expects to benefit from it. Consider spelling out what the reward for attending to the message will be. For example, techniques to save money or methods to advance in the company may be the reward offered.

What's First and What's Last

The first and last things presented in a message are often the most important. The audience will decide whether or not to pay attention to the message based on the introduction. People select what messages they want to listen to—and for varying reasons. In the introduction, give your audience a reason to focus on your message, perhaps by presenting new or interesting information there or explaining how the message is relevant to the audience. You may also decide to ask a question, which can stimulate audience interest. The last aspects of your message should also be interesting because they are what the audience will probably remember best. At Malaysian Airlines, customers' last experience with the company is when baggage is claimed and collected, so airline employees routinely assist customers with baggage collection and even ground transportation to ensure that the last message conveyed is helpful and positive.

Empathy

empathy is sensitivity to someone else's feelings and situation.

Empathy is sensitivity to someone else's feelings and situation. Empathetic people are good at walking in another person's shoes. Demonstrating empathy means designing messages that keep the viewpoints, limitations, and cultural perspectives of your audience in mind. Try to place yourself in their position when you plan and design your messages so you can better gauge how your message will affect them.

Even big toy companies can sometimes forget to keep the audience in mind. Several top toy companies, such as Mattel and Hasbro, have invested billions of dollars on high-tech toys such as children's laptops, digital microscopes, and robotic animals. They forgot that children just want to have fun and technology isn't always as fun as good old-fashioned Play-Doh®, Monopoly®, or crayons. Many companies are learning that children are still more interested in traditionally popular toys such as Hot Wheels®, which were designed for simple fun, than they are in today's high-tech toys. While the wave of technology can offer amazing opportunities for 21st-century companies, they still need to remember their audience.

High-tech toys can enhance children's learning and development during 21st-century playtime.
© Michael J. Doolittle/ The Image Works

Old-fashioned crayons are still a fun way for children to express themselves and communicate lasting messages during play.
© Michael Newman/Photo Edit

Shape Message Content

Main Idea

Your **main idea** is the primary goal you want to accomplish with your message. For example, suppose your message goal is to recruit people to serve by working in one of the helping professions, such as social work. Your main idea involves what working in social service is all about and the many rewards the work offers. To reach the important aspects of your message, brainstorm and write down all your ideas. Then combine some and eliminate others until you have a manageable core of one or two main points.

main idea the goal you want to accomplish with your message.

Theme

The theme of your message should be consistent with your main idea and should carry that idea through the entire message. While you may present secondary points that support your idea, the theme should keep focused on your subject matter. A **theme** is a specific frame of reference or point of view about a given idea or topic. A potential theme for a career in social work might be "improving our quality of life."

theme a specific point of view about an idea or topic.

At Millennium Pharmaceuticals, a new theme is brainstormed by employees every year to guide the organization's culture and innovation. When the company was established in 1994, the theme was "nothing's impossible" to signify all the possibilities for the future. In 1995 the theme was "jammin'" to encourage departmental collaboration, as in a musical jam session. The theme for 2001 was "focused execution." It centered on the creation and achievement of important company goals.

Designing Arguments

While designing arguments will be addressed in Chapter 6, we will briefly discuss the concept here. Many messages with goals to persuade, call to action, and connect require a compelling argument. An **argument** is an appeal set forth to influence behavior or belief through reasoning. To build an argument you must provide reasons or evidence to support your claim or position and show why others should believe or act in a certain way. For our social work example, it would be wise strategically to develop and offer a reasonable argument explaining why social work is a rewarding career.

argument an appeal to influence behavior or belief through reasoning.

Framing Your Content

Framing your message means tailoring it to your specific audience based on such characteristics as education level, occupation, age, sociocultural level, and perspective of your audience. For example, if your audience is prospective social work students who have only general knowledge about the field, then you should frame your message content in a concrete way. Develop clear and concrete ideas for the message, and choose language and visual materials that are appropriate to your audience's level of understanding.

framing tailoring a message to your specific audience.

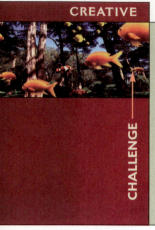

CREATIVE

CHALLENGE

Select the appropriate color element for an informational pamphlet that contains information about prenatal and infant care. The audience for the pamphlet is pregnant, parenting, and at-risk young women ranging in age from 14 to 20. Determine what color or colors the cover of the pamphlet should use and come to class prepared to discuss your choice.

Message Elements

Visual and verbal designs will be covered in later chapters, but for now begin to map out some of the elements you will need to design an effective message. As you think through the message content, you need to consider what language and visual, color, layout, or sound elements to include. For example, in considering the needs of your audience, you may realize that photographs may help the audience to understand key points better than words alone could.

Select Channels

As we discussed in Chapter 1, a channel is a medium that carries messages between people. The two most frequently used channels are sight and sound. Our ability to see objects and people is one of the primary channels through which we receive information. Similarly, sound carries many human speech messages that we receive through listening. Another human channel is face-to-face interaction with others. Sight, sound, smell, taste, and touch also operate as human channels to carry messages. When designing your messages, choose the most effective human or technological channel. Consider Tellme Networks Inc., a company that recognizes that not everyone can surf. This company is using a 125-year-old channel, the telephone, to link people to the Internet through a voice portal. The speech-driven voice portal allows people to dial a phone number and speak to access services and information on the Internet. Clients such as Jiffy Lube use the Tellme system to facilitate customer scheduling and appointments. Figure 3.3 illustrates primary human channels.

FIGURE 3.3

Primary Message Channels

Primary Message Channels

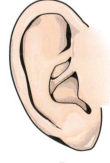

Eyes   Ears

Keys to Channel Selection

All channels have advantages and disadvantages. Table 3.3 shows some keys to your selection process.

Channel Choices

Once you consider the keys to selecting the best channels for your message, you need to evaluate which specific channels meet your requirements (see Table 3.4).

Audience	When you select a channel for your message, think about the information you have already analyzed about your specific audience. For example, if your audience is 50 teenage boys living in a rural community, the channel you select will be quite different than for an audience of 10 corporate executives working on Wall Street.
Message content	In the case of the boys, the depth of their understanding about your message ideas will determine not only how you frame the message content but also what channel you select to reach them. The more complicated the message, the more visual your channel for this audience should be.
Availability	Consider whether the channel will actually reach your audience. For example, if you choose a Web page to sell a product to teenage boys, consider whether they have access to a computer and whether they make purchases on the Web.
Appeal	The channel also has to appeal to your audience. For example, while a journal or newspaper article may have some appeal to the Wall Street executives, it probably will not appeal to teenagers.
Effect	Consider the effect of the channel on your audience. If your goal is to persuade or influence behavior, try a channel that enables you to interact face-to-face with your audience.
Speed	The speed at which a channel can carry a message is important. If you need your audience to receive a message fast, select a face-to-face conversation or a telephone call rather than the U.S. mail.

TABLE 3.3

Channel Keys

TABLE 3.4   **Channels**

Channel	Examples	Advantages	Disadvantages
Intrapersonal interpersonal	• Thoughts or self-dialogue • Sight • Sound (human speech, music, etc.) • Smell • Taste • Telephone • E-mail • Nonverbal body movements	Informative, entertaining, persuasive, educational, can present lengthy or short messages, personal, provides opportunity for feedback, fast, can be less expensive than other technological channels	Sometimes familiarity can produce boredom, can reach only smaller audiences
Print media	• Newspapers • Direct mail • Brochures • Magazines • Newsletters • Flyers • Books • Pamphlets • Letters	Informative, persuasive, can reach large audience, can be cost effective for advertising, fast	Static, with no dynamic movement, requires literacy, may be considered clutter, impersonal, and can require time to produce
Broadcast media	• Television • Radio • Film • Videotape • DVD • Web page	Informative, entertaining, persuasive, educational, can reach large audiences, dynamic and allows flexibility in design; good for brief to moderate messages	Cost, limited exposure time, lengthy messages, impersonal, and can require time to produce
Communications media	• Videoconference • Teleconference • Web conference	Informative, educational, persuasive, differently located people can interact, lengthy and brief messages, personal, moderate to small audiences, opportunity for feedback, fast	Cost, participation must be coordinated, and difficult for large audiences
Outdoor media	• Billboards • Posters • Transportation ads	Informative, persuasive, can reach large audience, can be cost effective, fast	Only brief messages, message size restrictions, impersonal, and requires immediate audience attention
Internal business media	• Memos • Reports • Newsletters • Telephone • E-mail • Teleconferences • Videoconferences • Meetings • Bulletin boards	Informative, educational, persuasive, good for both lengthy and brief messages, can reach both large and small audiences	Some can require time and money to produce, and some do not offer opportunity for feedback

A customer writes a letter to complain about a company product and customer service. Design a strategy to respond to this customer. Include your essential and intended goals, how you will learn more about this customer, the content of your message, and the channel you will choose to communicate with her.

June 19, 2003

Ms. Joan T. Stewart
President
Speedlink.com
Internet Service Provider
606 Sage Drive
Bountiful Falls, ND 50626

Dear Ms. Stewart:

Several weeks ago, I purchased a yearly contract for Internet service through Speedlink.com. When I attempted to connect online to purchase an airline ticket for an emergency trip to care for my ill grandmother, I received a busy signal. After nearly four hours of a steady busy signal, I called your toll-free number for customer assistance.

Navigating through an extensive voice menu finally connected me with a customer service representative. As I explained my dilemma, the rep abruptly interrupted me and said: "Duh, don't you know that peak connection hours are between 6 P.M. and 10 P.M.?" Not accustomed to being berated by someone employed to assist me, I responded, "Excuse me?" The rep then told me to try again later during off-peak hours, such as around 2 A.M. or so. This is a terrible way to conduct business!

The next morning (not 2 A.M.), I obtained a ticket from my travel agent over the phone. Later that week when I returned from my trip, I received a bill from Speedlink.com charging me $25. The reason I agreed to your contract was because yearly subscribers receive 20 percent off the regular $25 charge. When I contacted Speedlink again they maintained that the 20 percent discount was a promotional offer that expired the day before I signed up. I was unaware of any time limitation on the offer advertised in my local newspaper. As a consolation, they promised to send a 10 percent discount coupon for this month, which I never received. Thus, I feel I have no choice but to discontinue service with your company. Please terminate my so-called service agreement.

Sincerely,
Jackie O'Connor
Jackie O'Connor

research is the process of acquiring information to ensure message accuracy, support a claim, or guide decision making.

Acquire Resources

To accomplish your message goals you will need to consider the five resources listed in Table 3.5.

TABLE 3.5   Resources

Time	Consider how much time will be required to produce the message from concept to finished product. It is also a good idea to determine how much time will be required from receivers. Some communication designs are more time consuming than others. Messages that generally require more time are those with extensive text, visual layout, graphics, or videography/photography. Other time-intensive elements include coordination of equipment and participant schedules for meetings, training, teleconferences, videoconferences, and computer conferences.
Personnel	Determine the scope of the work involved and assess the necessary elements to help you decide who will be needed to create the message. For example, if one of your message elements is likely to be graphic designs or printing, consider who can assist you internally or to whom you can outsource the work.
Outsourcing	Outsourcing a service means hiring an outside individual or firm to perform certain work that your business is not equipped to handle. Many small businesses outsource services such as accounting and advertising. Numerous startup companies are emerging to "netsource" technology services that businesses can rent monthly. Application service providers such as Exodus, Oracle, and vJungle.com provide large and small businesses with web-hosting sites, e-mail, accounting, and software over the Internet. Businesses that outsource their websites, such as FTD.com, can farm out a wide variety of their e-business needs to Internet specialists.
Research	We all frequently conduct research. Perhaps you read some consumer magazine or consulted friends or relatives about which CD player or computer to buy. **Research** is the process of acquiring information to ensure message accuracy, support a claim, or guide decision making. Your message may require that you perform certain research, such as interviewing a subject matter expert (SME) who has expertise in a given area or gathering data from journals, magazines, and books.
Money (capital)	Carefully analyze the cost associated with the design, planning, and resource materials needed for your message. If your message content is extensive and aimed at a relatively large audience and you plan to outsource graphic designs, chances are your production costs will be high. If your message is a simple memo aimed at a small internal business audience, your cost will be low.

Generate Source Credibility

source is the live person, narrative voice, business entity, or author from whom the message is transmitted.

A message **source** is the live person, narrative voice, business entity, or author from whom the message is transmitted. The selection of a message source is important because the audience recognizes the source as the sender of the message. The relationship between source and audience is fundamental to the effectiveness and ultimate success of the message. To build a relationship with your audience, you need to establish **credibility,** meaning that you must make your message believ-

credibility is making your message believable.

able or plausible. Aristotle referred to the idea of credibility as "ethos." Two of the primary components of ethos are competence and reliability. **Competence** has to do with the expertise or knowledge that a source is perceived to have in a given area. The source's level of preparation, ability to communicate, and authority also demonstrate competence. **Reliability** is related to the trustworthiness of a message source. Honesty, dependability, and responsibility can demonstrate trustworthiness. For an audience to perceive a message source as credible, they need to trust that the source is up-front and honest. Credibility is illustrated in Figure 3.4.

For example, in the original 1999 *United States* versus *Microsoft* trial, U.S. District Judge Thomas Penfield Jackson indicated in his decision to split the company in two that he believed that Microsoft's case lacked credibility and was not trustworthy. But in the 2001 decision by the U.S. Circuit Court, seven judges reversed Judge Penfield Jackson's remedy to break Microsoft into two companies and sent the case back to the District Court to be handled by a different judge. The Circuit Court found that because Penfield Jackson offered negative comments to the news media after the trial, his decision lacked credibility. It suspected that he may have been biased against Microsoft and founder Bill Gates when he made his original decision.

Two other important aspects of credibility are dynamism and similarity. **Dynamism** refers to a source's demonstrated enthusiasm and passion about the message. Dynamic sources are considered more credible because of the confidence they exhibit and their lively communication style. A dispassionate source can turn an audience off to both the source and the message. **Similarity** is related to the source's connection to his or her audience. Can the audience identify with the source in

competence is expertise or knowledge that a source has in a given area.

reliability is the trustworthiness of a message source.

dynamism refers to the demonstrated enthusiasm the source has about the message.

similarity is the sources' connection to his or her audience.

© AP Photo/Joe Marquette

FIGURE 3.4

Source Credibility

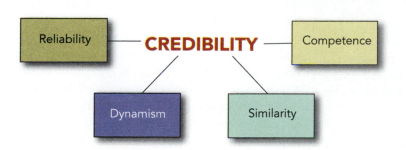

some way? For example, an ad directed at middle-aged women would probably not use Britney Spears as a spokesperson.

Eliminate Design Flaws

Message design flaws include any aspect of your contents or any message element that distracts your audience. Design flaws can be simple mistakes such as spelling errors, typographical errors (typos), color variations, inconsistent theme, or lack of readability, or they can be one of the message flaws discussed in Table 3.6.

Send Message

timing is when you transmit your message.

The final step in communication design is sending the message. This includes when and where to implement or transmit the message.

When to Transmit

Timing is when you transmit your message. Good timing can be critical in determining how welcome your message will be to your audience. Assume you designed a persuasive message to compel your supervisor to grant you a pay raise. You developed a strong argument based on your many accomplishments, extra hours devoted to work tasks, perfect attendance, and superior work performance. However, when you conveyed your carefully designed message, the company was busy preparing to pay taxes. The boss would probably tell you to come back after tax season ends. At Xerox, customers felt that repair representatives arrived too slowly to service machines. To convey the message that its customers' time is valuable, Xerox decided to let customers assess the urgency of their copier machine problems and schedule repairs themselves. Simply having control over the timing of personal contact and service increased Xerox customer satisfaction dramatically.

Many businesses cater to the work schedules of clients, such as FedEx, a package carrier that maintains a "superhub" for cargo planes in Memphis, Tennessee. The last call for package pickup is 11:30 P.M., and the drop-off deadline is midnight at the Memphis FedEx airport terminal. Local computer businesses, repair shops, and aircraft equipment dealers all conduct business and communicate with FedEx employees until about 2 A.M., when the last cargo planes fly in and out of Memphis International Airport.

CREATIVE

CHALLENGE

Break into groups with your class colleagues and consider the following message idea and audience. Then select a source you feel would be credible and would be someone to whom the audience could relate.

Message Main Idea
The main idea of our message involves appropriate behavior and what incarceration will be like in a youth detention center.

Audience
The audience for our message is females from age 12 to 17. These young people have been adjudicated through the court system and will be entering the youth detention center.

Channel
10-minute videotape presentation.

Source
The director of the youth detention center has indicated that although he is open to suggestions, he would like to be the source for this message.

As a team, discuss and describe the characteristics of the source you would select for both the narrative and on-camera talent for this video message.

Design Flaws   **TABLE 3.6**

Unnecessary information or visuals	Edit written work to cut superfluous information, especially redundant words or ideas. Keep visual designs clean and simple to avoid distracting viewers.
Sensory overload	Even relevant information may be overwhelming if there is too much of it. Analyze how much information is really essential to offer in one message. If you determine that a substantial quantity of data is required, you may need to design multiple messages. For example, in your business communication course, extensive material is broken up into chapter or topic segments so you are not bombarded with volumes of material all at once.
Missing details	It is also important to look for what might be missing from your message. If you inadvertently leave out vital information such as directions or solutions to discussed problems, the audience may become confused or frustrated.
Hidden agenda	Sometimes communication designers purposely delete information or hide the real motivation of their message. This is a calculated strategy that can backfire if the audience becomes aware that the message has a hidden motive. While leaving out information that could offend or panic an audience can be prudent, excluding relevant opposing data for ulterior purposes can threaten the message's success.
Contradictions	It is sometimes a good strategy to present opposing views when you persuade an audience to change their beliefs or behaviors, but make sure you lead the audience to a conclusion. Make sure you clarify information so that your audience understands the content, what you want, and where you stand on the issue.
Cultural inconsistencies	Review your message to ensure that the values, beliefs, and overall cultural perspectives you offer are consistent with your audience's.
Content inaccuracies	Analyze the content of your message to make sure the information is accurate. Inaccurate information weakens your credibility with the audience.
Poor formatting	When you design written documents, formatting is very important. Make sure the text font and size are readable. The pages shouldn't look too busy, and any visuals you include should enhance or clarify rather than detract from your message.

Time-related materials have a limited life span. For example, if you developed a message that offered money-saving tax information for businesses but you conveyed the information after the deadline for quarterly or year-end tax returns, the information would be useless for that year.

time-related messages or **materials** have a limited life span.

Where to Transmit

Location is the place from which you transmit your message. Is enough space available? Is the environment in which you convey your message appropriate? If you asked your supervisor for a pay raise on the display floor of the store where you worked while she was busy talking to customers, she would probably tell you it was neither the

location is the place from which you transmit your message.

time nor the place for that message. No matter how skillfully your message content is designed, choosing the wrong place for delivery can spoil your chances. Location as a planning consideration involves cultivating a communication environment that increases the likelihood that your message will be received without noise.

Strategies

1.   **M**ap out message goals: Make sure you know your communication goal—what you want or need before you send a message. Messages that clearly indicate what is required from the audience are more likely to produce desired results.

2.   **E**valuate your audience: Knowing your audience helps you to design messages that are appropriate to their specific needs and viewpoints. When you tailor your message to the characteristics and knowledge level of your audience, your ideas, directions, or requests have a better chance of being understood and accepted.

3.   **S**hape message content: Shaping your message content combines using what you know about your audience to select the best ideas to convey your message. You need to create appropriate themes, argument points, and elements to help you frame the message specifically to the audience.

4.   **S**elect channel: Choose the best channel to carry the message to your audience. Make sure you evaluate channel availability, appeal, and speed, and whether the content of your message is best suited for the channel you choose.

5.   **A**cquire resources: Big and small communication ideas require resources. When you plan your message, you need to determine how long the message will take to produce, whom you will need to create the message, what information will be required, and how much the development of the message will cost. Not all messages require money or materials, but many of them do. All messages require time for design and transmittal as well as time for reception by the audience. Plan ahead for any resources you may need, including the time your audience will need to receive the message.

6.   **G**enerate source credibility: The best source for a message is a person or people the audience perceives as credible. To establish a relationship and build credibility with your audience, you need to select a message source who has subject matter expertise, who is trustworthy, who is dynamic, and with whom the audience can identify.

7.   **E**liminate design flaws: Throughout the process of designing your message, you need to check for flaws and mistakes, which

can distract or confuse the audience. Even typographical errors can become noise, because the audience may detect them and focus their attention on the mistake rather than on the message. Furthermore, design flaws reduce the credibility of your message and the source. Proofread documents for errors and inaccuracies, locate missing details or unnecessary information, and look for formatting flaws that can create noise for your audience.

8. **S**end message: Make sure to determine the best time to send your message. Good timing can make the difference between whether your message is received or not and can determine how it will be perceived by the audience. Assess times when your audience is more likely to be receptive to your message, including their availability, the time of day, and the conditions during which you send the message.

Summary

- The development of message goals involves figuring out what your purpose for communicating is and whether the goal is feasible. Goal intentions cover your wants or needs and what you expect from the message receiver. Goal response is feedback from the message receiver. Messages that specify what is required from the audience are more likely to produce desired results.

- Knowing your audience helps you design messages appropriate to their specific needs and viewpoints. Audience considerations include audience size and demographic analysis (collecting and interpreting relevant statistical information to construct an audience profile). Audience identification also includes what is known about the topic, what the audience may need to know, and what their perspective on the topic is likely to be. Tell the audience what they may gain from your message. Use empathy (sensitivity to others' needs, viewpoints, or situations).

- Message content includes your main idea, theme, argument, message frame, and elements. Present your main ideas consistently with the theme of your message. Your argument is the support or evidence you offer as part of a logical appeal to your audience. Framing your message means designing it in accordance with your audience's characteristics. Message elements include various visual, color, sound, and language choices.

- Select the best channel to carry your message to your audience. Channel selection focuses on audience, content, channel availability, appeal, potential effect, and speed. Channels include intrapersonal, interpersonal, print, broadcast, telecommunication, outdoor, and internal business media.

- Resources are what you will need to accomplish your goals. Resources include time, personnel, outsourcing, research, and money.

- The source is the sender of the message. A preferred source has audience credibility, which encompasses competence, expertise or experience, and reliability (trustworthiness). Two other important source traits are dynamism (the confidence and enthusiasm the source demonstrates) and similarity (the connection the audience feels to the source).

- Design flaws are anything that disorients or distracts an audience. They reduce the credibility of your message and its source.

- Sending a message involves the timing and location of message delivery. Timing and location both affect whether your message is received at all and how it is perceived.

Business Communication Projects

1. Write an e-mail to the director of communication of a real or imagined organization offering your suggestion/recommendation for an internal channel of communication the organization has not used before. Support your position by describing why you think your proposed channel will reach employees and convey the company messages better than the channel the organization has used in the past. Compare and contrast the two channels.

2. Find two similar print documents such as brochures, advertisements, or newsletters. Compare and contrast the two documents for the following: intended goal, audience focus, content, and readability. What do you think the intended goals were? At whom do you think the messages were aimed? How were the messages framed? Did you detect any design flaws in the documents? Which document seemed to work better? Come to class prepared to discuss the written documents you analyzed.

3. From the following list, identify the goal intention of the communication: (a) inform, (b) persuade, (c) call to action, or (d) connect.

   _____ Correspondence from manager to employees regarding a policy about prohibiting company cars for personal use.

   _____ PBS donation drive during the intermission of a popular educational series.

   _____ Radio talk-show host asking listeners to call in with questions and comments.

   _____ Peer-support group member relating a personal experience.

   _____ TV commercial featuring a political source seeking voter support for handgun legislation.

   _____ News broadcast about a significant event of the day.

4. Find a product tailored to a specific audience (for example, a Penn fishing reel or Adobe Photo Shop graphics software program). Discuss the characteristics of the product audience. How do the product's marketing messages connect with this audience? Consider the source of these product messages, the logistics, and channel selections to reach the audience with product information.

5. You are given an assignment from your supervisor to develop a program strategy that will improve communication between the administration and technical staff. The primary obstacle is that the technical staff is intimidated to approach the administration. Write a short description of your strategy to ease tensions and encourage open dialogue. Include the primary goal, goal intention, what the audience may need to know, main ideas, theme, how you would frame the message, the channel for transmission, and the message source.

6. Identify a dynamic message source. Come to class prepared to discuss how this person's dynamism affects both the audience and the messages he or she delivers.

7. Consider the various channels available to reach the audiences listed. Select channels appropriate for each. (More than one may apply.)

All company employees

Men and women between 25 and 40

Women aged 60 to 75

Rush-hour drivers

Voters in a rural town

Your manager

8. Choose a television program to watch. Write down the name, air-date, and time of day. List all the commercials that air during the program. Assess the message content, goal intent, and target audience of each commercial in a presentation to the class. Then answer the following question: Why do you think the sponsors chose to air their commercials at that particular time and on that particular channel?

9. You are the creator of Toothsome, a new cat food that protects cats' teeth from decay. You have been invited to speak about your product at both a local senior center and a day care school. Prepare two messages with similar content suitable for these two very different audiences.

10. Take a look at your classmates. Consider the age, gender, social and/or economic status, and cultural background of each of them. Design a brief presentation about one of the sections in this chapter, delivering the information in a new or surprising way that will appeal to (but not offend) the other members of your class.

Discussion Questions

1. What makes a person dynamic when he or she communicates?
2. If you know specifically what your goals are and your message content is clear, why does the audience matter?
3. Why is the outsourcing of services sometimes necessary?
4. How could a hidden agenda become a problem in a message?
5. What might happen if a message source lost credibility with the audience?
6. Why is it important to frame your message content?
7. Why does the design of a message depend in part on audience size?
8. What kinds of design flaws are distracting and why?
9. How does the theme of a message help convey the message goal?
10. How can you hold an audience's interest if they already know the information you are providing?

CREATIVE → CASE

Creative Case

Show Me the Money

Norma Gutierrez is a freelance writer and editor. She produces company newsletters and edits procedural manuals and corporate reports from her home. Most of her clients are small industrial companies and independent retailers. She takes great pride in her work and is developing a fine reputation in her field.

When Julia Jackson, a financial analyst for a local consulting firm, approaches Norma about editing a statistical report, Norma agrees. Julia states that she needs to outsource the work to Norma because she is currently overloaded with projects. Julia's audience for the report consists of several managers from a state government agency that hired Julia's firm to conduct research. Julia tells Norma that the statistics cited in the report don't confirm the outcomes she had originally projected and that the agency she is working for is a good client. Rather than admit that her original projections were off the mark, Julia wants Norma to revise the report and try to cast the statistics in a more positive light. She also wants Norma to frame the content of the message in a way that will make her projections appear more feasible. Norma explains to Julia that she has two problems with the requests: (1) She doesn't know a lot about statistics, and (2) she's not sure she wants to juggle numbers and write about information in a possibly unethical manner. Julia assures her that the report won't affect anyone financially and that as an experienced business writer she certainly knows enough about statistics to accomplish this task, so Norma decides to do what she can.

Norma works on the report for two weeks and changes as much of the text of the report as she can to make the statistics seem to agree with Julia's projected results. However, when she returns the report to Julia, Julia isn't satisfied. She wants Norma to re-figure the numbers themselves, in other words, shift the values to make the differences between the projections and the actual results smaller. Norma reminds her that she doesn't know enough about statistics to do this, but Julia tells her that she won't pay unless the numbers are re-figured. It's as if Julia doesn't comprehend that Norma is not a financial analyst. Norma wants her $500, but she simply isn't qualified to do what Julia is asking her to do. Furthermore, she feels strongly that her reputation and credibility as a professional writer may be in jeopardy if she produces a document that misrepresents important information.

What should Norma do?

Some questions to consider:

1. Should Norma have accepted the project in the first place? Why or why not?

2. How should Norma create a message that Julia will understand and accept about her inability to re-figure the numbers? What should she say? What channel should she use to communicate with Julia?

3. Should Norma again discuss the problem of misrepresenting information or avoid that topic and focus only on her insufficient statistical skills? Should she bring up the credibility issue?

4. Should Norma attempt to persuade Julia not to present the report to the agency with misleading numbers and deceptive findings? If so, what should the message contain that may convince Julia to be honest with her client?

SOURCE: Angell, P. & Rizkallah, T. (2002).

Chapter 4

Chapter 4

Listening: A Silent Hero

A small technology company in Silicon Valley developed a revolutionary new microchip that could speed up computer performance by 300 percent and increase storage capacity by half. Although response to the prototype chip in the United States was favorable, the company also wanted to test the chip in international markets. The problem was that the company had no experience in getting prototype technology out of the country and didn't understand the complex customs regulations. On a trip to Canada, one of the company's chief researchers was detained for five hours and ultimately was not allowed into the country with the prototype chip. The U.S. Customs Department provided a copy of technology exporting policies. These policies were so detailed and complex that the company CEO couldn't decipher them. In his distress, he contacted the import/export director of a defense contractor he thought could shed some light on the exporting policies. The defense director agreed to give a two-hour presentation on the practical applications of customs export policies regarding prototype technologies. With only two hours of the expert's time, the technology company had to be prepared to listen and listen well. To prepare for the director's visit, the company CEO informed certain staff that they were to come to the presentation well rested and ready to listen actively to the message. Because employees were going to need to use their listening skills to learn and remember important information, they planned to use a quiet conference room to avoid any external distractions. Employees who were invited to attend the presentation planned to bring a pad of paper for notes, and they also knew they should leave behind hand-held devices and cell phones. Just before the presentation started, the CEO leaned over and whispered to the chief researcher, "Make sure you ask questions!"

IN A NUTSHELL

In a Nutshell

Are You Listening?

While speaking and writing are extremely important skills in business, they are not the most often used. We use listening more than virtually any other communication skill, yet we often neglect this important business tool. Like the technology company discussed in the "In a Nutshell" feature, effective listening can make a big difference in gaining new business and profits. Not only do we listen to learn and remember information as the technology company did but we also listen to make decisions and to understand customer and employee needs. In most business situations, we listen more than we read, write, or speak. Managers and employees use their listening or receptive skills to increase productivity and profit, build employee morale, mainstream business procedures and practices, meet changing consumer needs, and improve customer relations. Listening is so important that many contemporary organizations offer extensive listening training programs for employees. Companies such as General Electric, IBM, Xerox, and Ford recognize that listening competence is the keystone to business success in the 21st century. Most company employees spend 40 to 50 percent of their time listening at work. While listening is critical for all employees, the time spent listening increases significantly as a person ascends up the corporate ladder into the executive ranks.

Figure 4.1 illustrates the percentage of time we spend listening, speaking, reading, and writing.

Is Anybody Really Listening?

Because we listen every day, we often assume that we are already competent listeners. Although some people develop and strengthen listen-

Some professionals spend most of their working day listening to customers.

© Lonnie Duka/Index Stock Imagery, Inc.

FIGURE 4.1

Profile of Business Communication Skills

Business professionals spend most of their time using listening skills at work.

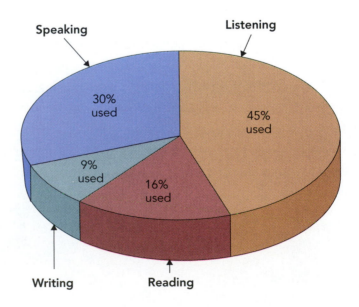

Speaking — 30% used

Listening — 45% used

Writing — 9% used

Reading — 16% used

ing skills, others do not realize that they are mediocre or even poor listeners. Inadequate listening can cost valuable time and money; produce uninformed decisions; cause inaccuracies in shipping, ordering, and other company messages; and threaten customer relations or work performance. Listening requires effort, and we sometimes don't put forth the effort necessary to listen effectively.

Because 85 percent of what we know or learn comes from listening, it is certainly wise to develop this skill so that we may know and learn more. Smart companies listen carefully to both their internal and external environments so that they can improve their processes and their many business relationships. Cynthia Trudell, vice president of General Motors, believes that listening is one of the most fundamental skills of good leadership. Leaders, she believes, understand the importance of listening in facilitating collaboration and valuable partnerships with customers.

At any given time, business managers and employees must listen to customers, colleagues, subordinates, stockholders, and vendors concerning complaints, requests, process or product deficiencies, trends, innovations, needs, and improvements. Listening opportunities in business occur not only during face-to-face conversations, but also during conferences, training seminars, focus groups, interviews, problem-solving forums, and project team meetings.

Hearing is the involuntary physiological process of receiving sound waves through receptors in the ear that transmit them to the brain. We automatically sense and receive various sounds without effort. You can hear sounds, but not be consciously aware that you are hearing them. For example, you may hear the hum of your printer without actually listening to it.

Unlike hearing, listening requires intrapersonal focus and message decoding to attach meaning to the messages we hear. **Listening** is an active process of selecting, attending to, interpreting, and remembering sounds. Figure 4.2 illustrates the listening process. *Selecting* essentially refers to becoming aware of and choosing a given sound among many competing sounds. *Attending* involves consciously focusing on sounds because they are interesting, expected, or surprising. You may also attend to certain sounds because you actively want or need to attend to them. *Interpreting* is the process of decoding sounds to gain understanding and assigning meaning to messages in the context in which they are received. Associating messages with your personal experience or prior knowledge can help you interpret them. *Remembering* involves the storage of received information in short- and long-term memory. We remember information for the purpose of later retrieval and use.

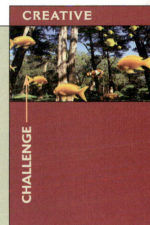

CREATIVE

CHALLENGE

During the 2000 campaign for the U.S. presidency, the Reverend Jesse Jackson used the phrase "Get your soles to the polls and stay out of the bushes." As a communication professional, write an e-mail to your professor that explains how this particular soundbite could affect selecting, attending to, interpreting, and remembering on the part of the listening audience.

hearing is the involuntary physiological process of receiving sound waves through receptors in the ear that transmit them to the brain.

listening is an active process of selecting, attending to, interpreting, and remembering sounds.

FIGURE 4.2

Listening

Listening involves the process of hearing and additional skills including selecting, attending, interpreting, and remembering.

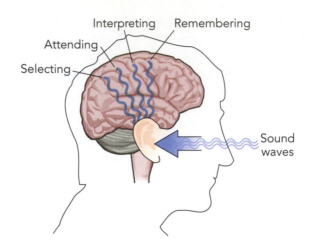

What's the Difference between Hearing and Listening?

Hearing is a precursor to listening. You must be physically able to hear sounds in order to listen to them. Still, listening involves other abilities such as the mental or cognitive processing of received messages, which hearing does not, but hearing and listening are not the same thing. We often confuse both the terms and the processes.

ARE YOU LISTENING DIALOGUE

Consider the following conversation between two co-workers in a busy marketing department. Liza and Jorge are both marketing analysts in adjoining cubicles.

Liza:	"Jorge, make sure you save your documents because the system keeps going down."
Jorge:	Responds absently, "Yeah, okay," and then continues with what he was thinking about.
	"What's up with the focus group data? I really need it for my report analysis. I've got a meeting with Jack Tuesday morning."
Liza:	"I don't know. Have you talked to Frank about it? He was going to put summaries together for us."
Jorge:	"I'll give him a call right now and see if he's finished with the data."
	Ten minutes later Jorge exclaims, "Oh no! The stupid system crashed and I can't retrieve my report file!"
Liza:	"I said the system has been crashing a lot lately."
Jorge:	"Why didn't you tell me?"
Liza:	Replies defensively, "I did tell you!"
Jorge:	"When?"
Liza:	"Just a few minutes ago."
Jorge:	"Oh, I didn't hear you."

It seems clear that Jorge's problem was not related to an inability to hear, but rather to his inadequate listening skills.

Active Listening in Business

Active listening is an intrapersonal and interactive process in which we actively focus on, interpret, and respond verbally and nonverbally to messages. The most significant aspect of active listening is vigorous participation by the listener, demonstrated by his or her full concentration on the message and thoughtful and appropriate feedback to the speaker. To listen actively, you must be alert; control the tendency to become distracted; and fix your attention on the content, context, and emotional tone of the message. You must also provide topic-related, timely feedback to the speaker. Timeliness involves waiting until the speaker is either completely finished talking or is making a transition from one idea to another.

Active listening may be the most important listening skill for business. It provides the foundation for other types of listening such as learning, critiquing what is heard, providing sensitivity or assistance, and participating in open group dialogues.

active listening is an intrapersonal and interactive process in which we actively focus on, interpret, and respond verbally and nonverbally to messages.

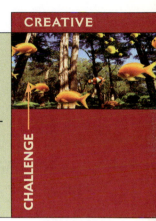

CREATIVE CHALLENGE

Break into groups of two. Brainstorm your personal strategies for listening to learn. Then prepare a brief presentation for the class that describes both of your methods for listening effectively during lectures, discussions, and speeches.

Listening to Learn

We learn a good deal of what we know from listening. As children, we gain the vast majority of our understanding from listening to our parents, teachers, and friends. Listening for information and learning is an active skill that involves understanding and remembering what we hear. Learning in college classes, business seminars, conferences, and meetings often involves listening to learn. At Trilogy University, a large employee orientation program developed by the Trilogy software and e-commerce application company, new employees listen to learn not only about the company but also about each other. Recruits listen to each other's stories about their lives to build relationships that will last throughout their careers. With clients such as Hewlett-Packard, Trilogy wants new hires to learn valuable listening skills needed for innovation, customer services, and relationship building.

WORD ON THE WEB

Listening doesn't always require ears! Find an Internet chat room that discusses business topics like www.mbanet.net; www.caplan.net or www.infinitymerchantservices.hypernart.net. There are a number of other sites. Do some exploring and either enter the chat room or look at transcripts of previous chats. Examine the participant responses. Are they paying attention to what is being said? Is the interchange confusing? Organize and summarize the contents of a particular session and then suggest ways listening techniques could be used during chat-room sessions.

Word on the Web

CREATIVE

CHALLENGE

Break into four or five small groups with your class colleagues. Each group will select one person to be the designated reader/speaker. Each designated speaker will read aloud the vignette. Listeners can take notes during the reading. After the speaker is finished reading, the group members should turn their notes over and answer four questions about what they have heard. After the questions have all been asked and answered, the group members may refer to their notes to aid their memory.

When Janet Rogers returned from the conference room to her office on the 41st floor, she realized that two policy memos concerning new federal safety mandates had not been distributed during the early afternoon board meeting. Frantic with worry since the new safety measures needed to be in place by next January, Janet drafted an e-mail to her colleagues and a letter to the board. After e-mailing five of the key department heads (personnel, finance, marketing, public relations, and administration) to inform them about the oversight, she notified her assistant that 28 memos would need to be copied and mailed to the 14 board members on the next business day. A letter addressed to each board member would be attached to the memos. Janet felt that since the policies outlined in the memos involved her production department, it was her responsibility to write a letter to the board members explaining the oversight. Before the close of business at 5 P.M., three of the department heads responded to Janet's e-mail. David Daly from finance and Chris Crawford from marketing called Janet and Scott McPherson from administration stopped by her office on his way to the elevator. Janet informed Scott that the memos would be sent to board members and should be included on the agenda for the next board meeting scheduled for November 16. Scott told Janet the exclusion of the policy memos was not a big deal. He also said that the agenda for the upcoming board meeting would not be very extensive, since it would be the last meeting before the new year.

Questions
1. During what time of day was the board meeting held?
2. Why did Janet attach a letter to the memos to be mailed?
3. What department was Scott McPherson from?
4. What did Scott McPherson think about the memos not being included at the meeting?

Discuss your group's listening experience with the rest of the class.

---

listening to learn involves focusing on, interpreting, and remembering information.

When you **listen to learn,** you mentally focus on and interpret information that you will later be able to recall and use in your personal or professional life. For example, your office supervisor may explain operating procedures for a new e-mail system that you will be expected to learn in order to perform certain tasks. When you listen to learn, it is a good idea to remain quiet and withhold judgment about the information until the speaker is completely finished. You may also take mental or written notes that can aid your work performance after listening is completed.

You can further support your learning by mentally summarizing the information and then asking the speaker specific questions to make sure you understand the message.

Practice Listening to Learn

Prepare yourself to listen actively.	• Commit to being mentally sharp and alert. • Avoid internal distractions. • Concentrate and remain quiet.
Interpret the message meaning and support memory.	• Relate ideas to your own experience and prior knowledge. • Visualize key aspects of the message in your mind.

Withhold judgment.	• Avoid openly or mentally criticizing the information until you completely understand the message.
Outline the message.	• Mentally outline the message's primary and secondary ideas.
Take notes.	• Take mental or written notes on both main and secondary points to keep focused. • Written notes can also aid retention.
Mentally summarize the information.	• Restate the information and details in your mind.
Ask questions.	• Ask the speaker specific questions to make sure you understand the message.
Practice listening to challenging material.	• Listen to news programs, debates, documentaries, or educational audiotapes and seminars to enhance your listening skills.

Critical Listening

Critical listening requires you to not only exercise skills to comprehend information but also to make assessments and decisions about what you hear. When you listen critically, you evaluate and analyze the credibility, accuracy, and validity of messages. This type of listening usually involves persuasive information. You must recognize fallacies and sort out various facts from opinions. Critical listening also requires critical thinking—you need to balance the argument you hear with your own expectations, beliefs, and viewpoints.

Assume one of your job responsibilities is to hire new employees for the company. To accomplish this task, you will need to review numerous résumés and select certain applicants to interview. During the interview process, you will need to seek information and critically evaluate the responses you receive. Your critical listening skills will help you determine the suitability of each applicant's professional experience and his or her ability to work well with other employees in your company.

While you will sometimes be expected to make snap decisions in business, it is usually wise to listen to all the information you hear before trying to evaluate supporting data and determine the credibility of the message and the speaker's intentions or motives.

critical listening involves making assessments and decisions about what you hear.

Critical listening requires that you evaluate and analyze information in order to make a decision.
© James Pickerell/The Image Works

Sensitive Listening

Sensitive listening is supportive. It demonstrates empathy toward others when they share their thoughts and feelings. Listening sensitively requires orienting your full attention to the other person's point of view and allowing him or her to vent and express feelings without

Your boss is known to have a short temper and a short memory. Often things that she says in the heat of the moment are not what she means in the long run. One morning she calls you into her office and begins to complain about the new policy concerning transportation compensation. The previous policy paid 60 cents per mile for trips in private vehicles for any distance over 10 miles. The new policy (in response to rising gasoline prices) provides only 15 cents per mile for any distance over 7 miles. In reality, the savings to the company are small. Your boss is on the warpath because she travels about 100 miles per week on company business. This means she will receive only $13.95 for travel instead of the $54.00 she got before—a minimal change, but one that irks her. She asks you to write an e-mail message for her review to your co-workers, explaining the change and describing its application. **Write this e-mail,** keeping in mind that although she is upset now, her mood may have quieted down before she reads and sends the message you prepare.

sensitive listening is supportive and nonjudgmental; it demonstrates empathy toward others when they share their thoughts and feelings.

judgment. Sensitive listening is other-focused. You can assist or support others by acting as a sounding board and offering supportive feedback. At MTW Corporation, a software and consulting services business, employer and employees work together to craft an "expectations agreement" that requires sensitive listening and open communication. During the process, a manager must listen carefully and without judgment to an employee's expectations and needs. Once the speaker is finished, the listener paraphrases the speaker's message to make sure he or she heard it correctly. Then both parties jointly develop a flexible working agreement that meets the needs of both the employee and the organization. Ed Ossie, the CEO of MTW, believes that the listening involved in an expectation agreement is vital for real understanding, mutual affirmation, and the accomplishment of personal and professional goals.

In a wide variety of situations, you may need to listen sensitively to everything from co-workers' or subordinates' problems to customers' criticisms and complaints to managers' concerns about troubled initiatives and procedural deficiencies. To listen sensitively, you need to take the time and offer supportive paraphrasing and nonverbal listening cues that reassure, approve, or soothe. For example, during lunch your co-worker Leon says, "I'm so upset about Rena not granting me my raise after all the overtime and extra work I've done for her. I'm mad. But I need to calm down before I do something I'll regret like quit." In response, your supportive paraphrase should not mimic Leon's message. Rather, it should offer a reassuring interpretation of his message formulated in your own words. "I understand the raise situation is really upsetting, and you deserve it more than anyone. Why don't we sit down for a few minutes so you can relax." Telling someone not to be upset about the situation or pointing out that other people have been denied raises or even advising him to talk to the union representative is not supportive. The fact is Leon is upset. He is going through the problem now and may need you to simply listen to his feelings rather than give advice. While in some situations, offering advice or alternative options can be beneficial, you need to consider carefully the speaker's individual situation, his or her need for advice, and the context.

Practice Sensitive Listening

Take time to listen.	• Taking the time to listen attentively to co-workers and customers shows that they are important to you and worth your time.
Empathize with the speaker.	• Try to imagine what the speaker is feeling from his or her point of view. • Focus on the speaker's emotional tone and feelings.
Let the speaker vent.	• Allow the speaker to completely express his or her feelings.
Withhold judgment and criticism. Avoid downgrading.	• Hold back the urge to openly disagree or dispute the speaker's perspective. • Avoid playing devil's advocate or taking an opposite position, even if your intention is to help the speaker to see other points of view. • Don't negate or minimize the speaker's feelings with statements such as "You shouldn't feel that way" or "It isn't *that* bad." • Avoid the "top this" motif ("If you think that's bad, wait until you hear this.") • Avoid a superior attitude or position ("I used to feel that way too, but now I'm more mature.")
Don't offer advice or try to solve the problem.	• Providing the speaker with advice may not be prudent since the advice may not be desired or could increase the speaker's anxiety and irritation. If the person hasn't asked you to fix the problem, don't. • Assist the speaker to explore and work through the problem on his or her own.
Demonstrate supportive verbal and nonverbal feedback.	• Paraphrase what the speaker is saying in your own words so you can better understand his or her intended meaning. • Provide supportive nonverbal feedback such as an open and leaning posture, direct eye contact, and responsive facial expressions and gestures. These nonverbal cues signal your involvement with the speaker and the message.

Dialogue Listening

Dialogue listening is used to identify, share, and explore other people's meaning and perspectives in an open group dialogue. This type of listening is not self-focused or other-focused. It is us-focused communication because it is co-created and collaboratively developed by all the participants. Dialogue listening is like a brainstorming session in that the ideas of all the participants are encouraged. It is also like sensitive listening in that those ideas are not judged or negated. However (unlike sensitive listening), dialogue listening includes and focuses on all the people in the interaction. Furthermore, while assessment and decisions are not usually the primary goal of dialogue listening, solutions and decisions are sometimes outgrowths of these listening experiences. At General Electric, the Corporate Executive Council meets for more than two days of open dialogue. Employees listen to and discuss new ideas, share information, and establish goals. Over the years, initiatives such as "six sigma" quality improvement and the

dialogue listening is used to identify, share, and explore other people's meanings and perspectives in an open group dialogue.

company's e-commerce strategy have emerged from these intensive dialogue sessions.

Dialogue listening is an especially effective tool for business professionals since it combines active listening skills such as learning and sensitivity. Situations that involve conflict or problem identification, idea generation, change initiatives, and strategy sessions can all be enhanced through dialogue listening.

Practice Listening in Business Groups

Prepare for listening in advance	• Gather and familiarize yourself with relevant documents and materials before the meeting. • Write down any questions, ideas, or concerns you have about the topic. • Decide to commit your mental and physical energy to listening actively.
During the meeting	• Remain alert and attentive. • Consciously avoid internal distractions. • Be patient and let speakers complete their statements. • Concentrate on the content and feeling in the messages. • Don't rely on others to listen or respond for you. • Take notes. • Avoid judging or criticizing participants' ideas or comments. • Demonstrate positive nonverbal feedback to speakers, such as head nods and eye contact. • Provide positive verbal feedback to speakers: "Good idea" "Really?" "Tell us more." • Ask questions to clarify messages.

Passive Listening in Business

passive listening is the absorption of sounds without the personal involvement necessary for active attention, interpretation, or feedback.

Passive listening is the absorption of sounds without the personal involvement necessary for active attention, interpretation, or feedback. The difference between passive listening and not listening is that when you listen passively, you listen for enjoyment. Not listening is when you don't pay attention at all to the sounds you hear. While most listening in business requires active skills, sometimes passively listening for simple pleasure can rejuvenate a busy professional during moments of downtime.

Listening for Pleasure

Pleasure listening is a passive activity. It involves enjoying and relaxing to the comforting sounds of ocean waves, rustling leaves, singing birds, or harmonious music. While listening for pleasure does not require specific skills, it can be therapeutic in some business situations. For example, music or calming oceanic sounds can create a relaxing atmosphere for business professionals after long or difficult meetings, during lunch or other breaks, and sometimes while they are composing proposals or other business reports.

It can also be a great way to wind down from a stressful meeting. Pleasure listening can build strong relationships and foster team-work. Ben Zander, conductor of the Boston Philharmonic Orchestra, helps executives at IBM and Goldman Sachs become better team players by singing classical music and listening to each other. As an exercise in creating collaborative harmony, workers learn to listen and harmonize together as they sing, which may also improve their listening skills at work.

Casual Listening

Informal casual listening involves both conversational interaction and polite acknowledgment of the speaker's social message. Casual listening is informal. It usually occurs in informal business settings such as the company cafeteria or break room or during social or entertaining business activities.

Conversational casual listening is interpersonal listening that occurs among two or more people in a social setting. Sometimes conversational casual listening demands active skills, since the interactants may take turns speaking and listening. However, conversational listening does not necessarily require effective listening because listeners may elect not to concentrate on or respond to all the messages they hear while in social groups.

conversational casual listening is interpersonal listening that occurs among two or more people in a social setting.

Polite casual listening is primarily passive in that the listener may not be interested in the topic and does not participate in the interaction. However, the listener may politely nod or smile at the speaker to avoid looking uninterested. It is not advisable to view all social situations in business as fair game for passive listening, since valuable insights can be derived from casual conversations. It is also important for you to know that many important business contacts can be made during social business gatherings. Some of the relationships you develop socially will benefit you both personally and professionally.

polite casual listening is passive because the listener may not be interested in the topic and does not participate in the interaction.

I'm Not Listening

While passive listening can sometimes be beneficial, not listening at all can present serious problems. **Not listening** occurs when we ignore messages. When people think that they don't need to listen actively or respond to messages, they may cross the line from listening passively to tuning out completely.

not listening occurs when we tune messages out.

Some people in business project groups or on committees do not always listen effectively. In an exchange involving only two people, both communicators listen and respond as necessary during the interaction. The demand for effective listening is increased because the listener will likely need to respond to received messages. However, during business group interactions, some listeners may perceive less pressure to listen carefully to all messages because others can be relied on to listen

More and more companies are cracking down on the use of cell phones and hand-held devices, which can distract listeners during meetings.
© Rob Lewine/CORBIS

and respond. Sometimes group participants may simply absorb information as they would a TV program—without personal involvement, concentration, or responsible feedback. The problem begins when careless listeners realize they have missed valuable information.

Assume that during a weekly staff meeting at work, you become distracted from listening by thinking about your plans to pick up your new car from the dealership that evening. You reason that since other employees are listening, it won't be a big deal if you don't pay really close attention. Later in the day, your supervisor informs you that she really likes the idea discussed at the meeting about changing the processing of customer complaints. She asks you to write a plan that would further outline the new process. Suddenly you realize that you don't know anything about this new idea or how to proceed with the plan, because you didn't listen actively at the meeting.

Too Busy with Wireless to Listen

Technology may lead to meeting-time distractions. While the mobility of new hand-held wireless devices such as two-way pagers and palmtops can increase productivity by letting people work from virtually anywhere, it can decrease productivity in a business meeting. Listening may decline because employees are busy attending to their palmtops rather than the speaker. In fact, eTour.com, a website company, now requires participants to place their wireless devices in plain view during business meetings. The restriction began because some employees, with their heads down, appeared to be taking notes and listening earnestly, when in reality they were writing e-mail messages, making hotel reservations, Web surfing, or playing video games.

You have been chosen to represent your public relations company at an international conference on advertising. To make a positive impression (enhancing your company's reputation) on the powerful advertising and promotional executives attending the conference, you want to be prepared with questions and comments on the advertising they have produced on commercial television in the United States. Listen to at least five commercials aired during prime time or during a special event such as the Super Bowl. Take notes on these commercials, detailing not only their content but also their implications and the strategies at work that get consumers' attention. Formulate a series of questions that invite *open-ended responses* from the producers of the commercials. Here are some examples:

- How did you determine who the audience would be for your commercial?
- Why did you choose those particular graphics and/or music for the commercial?
- Whom did you hire to direct this commercial and why?
- Now that the commercial has aired, are there any changes you would make in it?

Listening Liabilities

Poor listening habits can become significant professional liabilities in business. Miscommunication is not only a speaker's shortcoming; receivers also have responsibilities, including listening effectively and seeking clarification if messages are unclear. Sometimes inadequate listening is the cause of miscommunication, limited recall, and performance mistakes. The main liabilities that impede effective listening in business are external, internal, and message noise; channel deficiencies; and cultural barriers.

External Noise

In most busy companies, it is easy to become distracted by external sounds: the buzz of ringing telephones, fax machines, employee chitchat, the constant clicking of computer keyboards. Some employees may also become distracted because they focus on their hand-held devices rather than on the messages presented during business meetings.

Internal Noise

1. Preoccupation with physical, emotional, or professional concerns can inhibit listening.
2. Self-centered listening is another internal form of distraction. The receiver is focused on his or her own ideas or formulating a response instead of attending to the speaker's message. Often self-centered listeners interrupt the speaker, exhibit "hurry up" nonverbal behaviors, or change the subject during interaction.
3. Focusing exclusively on facts and ignoring supporting details, emotional tone, and other information in the message can also lead to

misinterpretation. Yet, attending to the speaker's physical characteristics or delivery style more than to the message can also create distraction. For example, an older employee may have trouble listening to his younger supervisor because he thinks, "She's only 25, so she doesn't know anything." Finally, a speaking delivery style that lacks fluidity or is perceived as dull and uninteresting may divert some listeners from the message.

4. While the average speaker can talk at a rate of 120 to 150 words per minute, the average listener can absorb between 400 and 600 words per minute. Listeners sometimes spend this extra mental time unproductively, perhaps by daydreaming or tuning in to distractions. Or they may jump to conclusions about what a speaker will say next. Sometimes predicting logical thought progressions can be a good way to fill the time gap, especially when listeners wait to see if the speaker's next remarks confirm their prediction. However, predicting can be unproductive when listeners either stop listening or interrupt the speaker.

5. Often in business, listeners fear appearing unknowledgeable or inexperienced, so they resist asking important questions that could clarify the speaker's points.

Message Noise

1. Messages that are perceived as uninteresting or challenging can dispose some listeners to tune out, because the information seems too boring or complex.

2. Emotionally charged words or messages can interfere with listening because the listeners focus on the emotions. For example, a witness who becomes emotional during a trial can distract the jury from the message conveyed.

3. Preconceived ideas and prejudices about a given topic can generate listening resistance if the message contradicts what the listener believes.

Channel Deficiencies

The channel used to transmit a message can also become a source of distraction. Telephones, audiotapes, two-way radios, and teleconferences can make listening more difficult because listeners do not have the benefit of observing the speaker's nonverbal behaviors reinforcing their verbal message. Face-to-face contact enhances listening abilities and improves the chances that the message will be received more accurately.

Cultural Barriers

1. Some foreign-born speakers have accents that may distract listeners from focusing on the content of the message. In some instances, listeners may have so much difficulty understanding the speaker's

words that they give up trying to listen. But it is important to keep trying and to listen harder. For example, a professor at Northern Arizona University related a story about a telephone conversation she had with a prospective student from Brazil. The professor eventually learned that this student wanted a school brochure and program application. During the conversation, the student's accent was very thick, but the professor slowed down her own speech, repeated key sentences back to him to clarify and re-clarify, and also went over the correct spelling of his name and address several times. As a result of this professor's efforts to listen carefully, the Peter F. Drucker Graduate School of Management recruited its first student from Brazil.

2. Some evidence suggests that listening habits are different for men and women. Men may be more inclined to listen for the overt content of a message, whereas women may tend to listen for the emotional tone. The ideal listener picks up on both facts and feelings.

Strategies

1. Mentally and physically prepare for active listening. Active listening can be hindered when you are physically tired or emotionally preoccupied. Fight fatigue and purposely concentrate on being an attentive listener.

2. Attend to both the message content and its emotional tone. If you listen only for facts or concentrate chiefly on feelings, you can miss important details of a message.

3. Focus on the message rather than the physical attributes or delivery style of the speaker. When you become distracted, consciously channel your focus back to the message.

4. Avoid interrupting the speaker. Interruptions can communicate that you think your ideas are superior or that you are impatient, insensitive, or downright rude.

5. Relate message ideas to your own experience or prior knowledge. Associating message ideas can aid your interpretation of meaning, understanding, and memory.

6. Use the difference between speaking and thinking times productively.
   - Organize what you receive mentally by outlining the speaker's message. Listen for the primary purpose. Then mentally highlight the speaker's main ideas, supporting ideas, and any new points.
   - Take mental or written notes. Taking notes can help you focus on the message and can also enhance recall of information for later use.

- Restate ideas, summarize, and mentally review the speaker's arguments and ideas.
- Identify the points in the message that are similar to or different from your own.

7. Listen all the way through the message, until the speaker is completely finished, before responding or before you stop listening.

8. Paraphrase either silently or aloud what the speaker has said. By rephrasing the message in your own words, you can enhance the decoding process and gain a better understanding of it. When you paraphrase, you are not mimicking the sender's statement verbatim. Rather, you are processing and restating information and offering your interpretation to gain clarity. You might say, "So, you feel that " or "What I think you mean is" as feedback; paraphrasing also allows the sender to confirm, expand, or alter the message.

9. Ask questions to clarify the intended meaning of a message. You might ask, "So does that mean?" or "Do you mean?"

10. Provide nonverbal feedback. Active listening behaviors such as head nodding, eye contact, eyebrow movement, appropriate facial expression, and an open posture signal that you are focused, receptive, and involved in the message. Focus too on the speaker's nonverbal behavior to enhance your understanding of the message.

11. Listen critically by evaluating the supporting data and reasons presented. Sort out the facts and opinions offered in the message and think about the speaker's motives and intentions.

Summary

- Listening consumes half our workday and is one of the most important business skills.
- Poor listening can create numerous problems in business, including message misinterpretation as well as shipping, scheduling, ordering, and customer information mistakes.
- Hearing is the physiological reception of sound waves that is necessary for listening.
- Listening is the intrapersonal process of selecting, attending to, interpreting, and remembering the sounds that we hear. Sound selecting means becoming aware of, isolating, and choosing a particular sound. Attending means focusing and concentrating on a sound. Interpreting is decoding the sounds to which we attend to assign meaning and gain understanding. Remembering is storing information in short- and long-term memory.
- Active listening is an important business tool in which you focus, interpret, and respond verbally and nonverbally to the messages

you receive. Active listening skills can be classed into four types: listening to learn, critical listening, sensitive listening, and dialogue listening. Listening to learn means making sense of and remembering the messages we hear. Critical listening involves applying active listening to analyze and make decisions largely about persuasive information. Sensitive listening is the process of demonstrating nonjudgmental support and empathy while others vent their feelings. Dialogue listening means identifying, sharing, and exploring the meanings and viewpoints of others in business groups.

- Passive listening is the absorption of sounds without the personal involvement needed for active attention, interpretation, or feedback.

- Listening for pleasure is an example of passive listening. Pleasure listening can be a soothing way for busy professionals to relax after long meetings or while they are crafting documents.

- Casual listening is the passive reception of messages in an informal business setting.

  a. Conversational casual listening occurs during social and spontaneous interaction with one or more people. It can involve either passive reception of messages or active decoding and responding, depending on the situation.

  b. Polite casual listening is usually passive in that the receiver merely listens cordially without being engrossed in the exchange or participating in the interaction.

- Not listening in meetings, conferences, or other business groups can cost a business precious time and effort because messages may need to be repeated or assignments may need to be revised.

- Poor listening habits can be serious liabilities. The most common listening liabilities in business are external, internal, and message noise; channel deficiencies; and cultural barriers.

Business Communication Projects

1. Write a memo to your instructor that proposes and describes a listening improvement strategy for use in a customer service department. Include at least two techniques that will improve employee listening for each of the following: customer problems and complaints received by phone, by e-mail, and in person.

2. Watch a televised political debate or news program such as *60 Minutes*. Listen critically to the program. Then write a report that evaluates at least one speaker's position based on your analysis of the following:

   - Did the speaker respond with specific answers to direct questions asked or did the speaker generalize or relate the question to some other point he or she wanted to make?

- Were the supporting points the speaker offered logical? Did they further the purpose of the message?
- Could information be obtained that would corroborate or disprove the speaker's statements? For example, if someone said it was raining in Pittsburgh on June 21, 2001, that's verifiable.
- Was the speaker's argument factual or largely opinion based?

3. Break into two groups with your class colleagues. Ask three students to prepare a role-play in which two employees are relating a problem to their manager. Employee A has drafted a proposal for a new sales approach that was accepted by the manager. Employee B complains that it was really his (or her) idea and employee A must have snatched the idea off his (or her) computer. Both employees present their arguments to the manager. During the role-play, the class group must listen and observe the manager's verbal and nonverbal techniques (supportive paraphrasing, eye contact, gestures, and other body movements) as she (or he) listens to the employees. Then the group should formulate feedback about the manager's ability to listen sensitively. The second class group must listen critically to determine the logic and credibility of the arguments provided by the two employees. Both groups should share their findings with the class.

4. Your manager has just requested that you attend a training seminar for three days. Upon your return, you will be expected to share the insights and strategies you learned with the rest of the staff. Prepare a list of actions that you will take to prepare yourself for active listening during the seminar and for your presentation of the information to your co-workers.

5. Break into pairs with your class colleagues and create a brief skit in which you act out a specific type of listening noise. For example, one of you could describe the difference between active and passive listening while the other taps a pencil on the table or pretends to chat on the phone to a friend. (Be creative and think about all five of your senses—sight, hearing, taste, touch, and smell. They can *all* contribute to listening noise.) Perform the skit for the class. Ask your classmates to identify the type of noise you displayed and evaluate its effect on the message you were trying to convey.

6. Identify the following statements as either true or false:

———— In critical listening, you are attempting to evaluate the validity of the message.

———— Passive listening has no place in the business world.

———— Listening is the same as hearing.

———— One step for preparing to listen is to be rested and alert.

———— People always listen actively to good speakers.

———— Listening skills can increase productivity.

———— Listening skills can be developed and improved.

———— Listening becomes less important as people move into higher-level positions.

———— You cannot hear without listening

7. Which of the following statements do you think *best* demonstrates sensitive listening? Come to class prepared to discuss your perspective.

   a. Asking to discuss the issue the speaker has initiated later when you can spend more time.

   b. Interrupting the speaker to point out that the issue is not as bad as it may seem before the speaker becomes too emotional.

   c. Listening carefully to the speaker and paraphrasing his or her feelings and concerns to gain clarity and provide support.

   d. Telling a similar story so that the speaker won't feel as bad or as alone.

8. During your annual performance evaluation, your manager informed you that he required a higher degree of effort from you and your raise would be less than the company average. On numerous occasions during the year, you had explained to him that you needed additional direction with your work tasks, but he never responded to your requests. Write a letter of complaint to your union representative that discusses your situation and explain that your boss does not listen to you. Back up your concerns with information from the text.

Discussion Questions

1. What business settings require employees to listen actively to learn, critically evaluate, and sensitively support others?

2. How does listening provide you with a better understanding of a business culture?

3. As a business communication designer, explain how you can use what you have learned about listening to increase your audiences' understanding of your messages.

4. How can you demonstrate that you are listening actively to a speaker?

5. What strategies can you think of to reduce or eliminate employee distraction by wireless devices during business meetings?

6. What is the distinction between listening and hearing? Can you name the songs or news reports you heard as you listened to the radio on the way to school or work today? Spend 15 minutes making a list of what you heard. Be prepared to discuss what you remember and *why* you remember it.

7. What is cultural noise? Come up with some examples.

8. What are the benefits and dangers of passive listening?

9. How do you feel about people who talk on cell phones while they drive? Do you believe it's possible to listen to someone on the phone and still "listen" competently to the traffic around you?

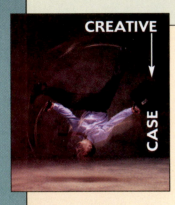

CREATIVE CASE

Creative Case

Standing Room Only on Kawasaki Jet Skis

When searching for innovative product ideas, the questions are as important as the answers. It is important to come up with result-driven questions that explore what customers want products to do for them and not just ask customers how they would improve products. Listening only to new product ideas that address problems can be limiting for companies, especially because many customers don't know what to recommend. Listening to customers with advanced product or service knowledge can also be risky because what they want may not appeal to the average (less technically savvy) customer.

For many years the motorcycle company Kawasaki led the recreational watercrafts market with their Jet Ski ® Watercraft. Kawasaki asked customers what they would recommend to improve the Jet Ski's standing position ride. Customers responded with the suggestion of more padding on each side so standing would be easier and more comfortable. Meanwhile, competitors were asking customers more result-driven questions about what they wanted personal watercrafts for and were listening to their ideas. Competitors such as Yamaha and Sea Doo developed personal watercraft models with seats. Kawasaki's Jet Ski ® quickly lost its leadership position with the introduction of Yamaha's Wave Runner with its seated ride.

Does learning what to listen for come from knowing what to ask?

Some questions to consider:

1. Which of these questions would have helped Kawasaki better meet customer needs? Why?

   "How can we improve the Jet Ski®?" or "What do you want a Jet Ski® for?"

2. What other questions might Kawasaki have asked to find out that sitting was preferred?

3. Do you think asking customers to describe what new products they want can yield useful information? Why or why not?

SOURCE: A. W. Ulwick, "Turn Customer Input into Innovation," *Harvard Business Review* 80, no. 1 (2002).

Chapter 5

The following themes are explored in this chapter:

WHAT *MEANING* MEANS

assuming you know what I mean / the meaning in messages / intended meaning / interpreted meaning

HOW WE CREATE MEANING

perception / organization / interpretation / signs and symbols

THE CONTEXTS OF MEANING

intrapersonal / personal history / cultural / interpersonal / business

THE MEANINGS OF WORDS

concrete words / abstract words

SPECIFIC AND VAGUE MESSAGE MEANINGS

specific meaning / vague meaning / blaming the receiver

Chapter 5

Using and Designing Meaning

At the Midland, Michigan–based Dow Chemical Corporation (the world's fifth largest chemical company), employees have begun to use terms that they believe will generate different meanings in both the minds of the sender and the receiver. For example, employees learn to refer to work tasks from a dollar-value perspective. Imagine the phrase "providing superior customer service" translated to "maintaining millions of business dollars." The trick is to transform the meaning of a phrase into something more financially proactive in an effort to change behavior. Is it possible to affect the behavior of employees by changing the labels under which they operate? Consider what perception and performance changes could occur when a manager is called a leader or a laborer is called a technician. Will employees and customers interpret the meanings of the transformed words or phrases in the way the company intends? Can modifying titles, words, or phrases begin to change deep-seated perceptions, or will people ignore them and focus on old meanings?

What *Meaning* Means

While changing the meaning of abstract and concrete words isn't easy, as discussed in the "In a Nutshell" feature, it is possible. Like Dow Chemical, many companies attempt to transform the way titles or concepts are interpreted by changing or using different words. But when the meaning of a familiar word or idea is modified, do people's intrapersonal and perceived meanings also change? People may understand that the title "Custodial Engineer" refers to a necessary and needed job but still think of it as a janitor. This chapter will explore how we learn and design clear message meaning.

You won't find the definition of *meaning* in this book. You can find definitions of meaning in various dictionaries, but the real definition should come from you. While meaning is a very difficult concept to define or describe, it is worthy of discussion because understanding the way we acquire, make, and interpret meaning can help us communicate more effectively. We need to discuss meaning because differences in interpretation can often lead to miscommunication. If we all shared identical meanings for identical experiences and had the same interpretation of those experiences, there would be no misunderstanding. Yet even with shared, obvious cultural similarities and experiences, people interpret life and the world differently. What people think, how they think, and who they believe they are is socially constructed through learned interaction with other people. We learn much of what we know from each other. People have different experiences in life and their reactions to those experiences are also different. Even in a play with a written script, actors change words or sentences or express words differently, which can change the meaning intended by the scriptwriter. For example, we learn that, in our culture, marriage is a legal and personal bond established between two people. But the meaning of this bond can range from happiness in a committed love relationship to entrapment in the conventions of society. Personal experience often shapes the specific meaning individuals attach to ideas and events.

CREATIVE CHALLENGE

Break into groups with your class colleagues to brainstorm at least three words, concepts, or job titles that you know have been changed to reflect new meaning. Prepare a brief role-play presentation for the class. For this role-play, you are managers informing employees (the class) about modifications in terms or titles. Make sure you explain the reason for the change and what intended perception or behavior change is desired.

Assuming You Know What I Mean

Given our cultural and interpersonal connections to other people, it is quite natural for us to assume that others understand our meaning. Often they do, and our communication flows quite smoothly. Still, situations arise when even the people closest to us don't understand what we mean. Have you ever said to a friend in an important conversation, "Do you know what I mean?" And your friend responds by furrowing her brow, squinting her eyes, and cocking her head to one side, which probably means no. This situation has happened to all of us.

Consider the following assumption as it relates to meaning:

When Scott communicates with Morrie, Scott transfers meaning from his mind to Morrie's mind.

Scott says to Morrie in an office corridor, "You got my e-mail, didn't you?" Morrie confirms by responding "Yes," he did get it. Then Scott looks at Morrie a moment and says expectantly, "Well?" Morrie stares blankly back at Scott and replies, "What?" "I mean did you get it?" Scott remarks, frustrated. To which Morrie snaps, "I said yes." Scott rolls his eyes and walks away.

Can we assume that Scott's meaning was transferred to Morrie? Perhaps what Scott meant by "get it" was "Did you get the meaning of the e-mail message?" not "Did you physically receive it?" What this assumption fails to account for is that people experience the world differently and what means one thing to one person may mean something very different to another person. This flaw in logic is called the **conveyor-belt fallacy.** The conveyor-belt fallacy is illustrated in Figure 5.1. It is the idea that because you transmit a message to another person, he or she will automatically understand your message. We send our messages as if on a conveyor belt that can carry the message directly to our intended receiver. We think physical reception ensures that our meaning will also be received. But the act of transmission does not guarantee that meaning is understood and accepted in the way we intend it to be. While the receiver may physically get your message, he or she may not "get" your meaning. For example, what does *ambition* mean? Think about what this word actually means to you personally. If you asked 10 people to fully and truthfully describe what they think

conveyor-belt fallacy is the assumption that because a message is sent and received, the receiver therefore understands what the message means.

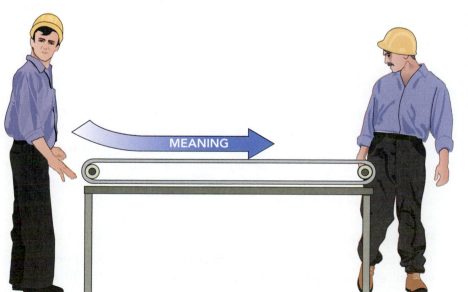

FIGURE 5.1

The Conveyor Belt Fallacy

When we send messages, as if on a conveyor belt, we assume people understand what we mean.

MEANING

ambition means, you would receive 10 different responses. To some, ambition may involve being energetic and enterprising. To others, it may mean that a person is aggressive and cutthroat in moving up the corporate ladder. Even if we understand certain cultural meanings for words, ideas, or phrases, we still interpret them somewhat differently. The differences are based on our personal histories, our sets of experiences, and even the interpersonal contexts through which we first learned certain words, phrases, and ideas.

The Meaning in Messages

Messages are more than words, sentences, or visual images created as content for the purpose of transmission. Messages contain both intended and interpreted meaning. **Intended meaning** is the meaning the sender has in mind when designing his or her message. **Interpreted meaning** is the meaning the receiver interprets from the message. When intended meaning and interpreted meaning match, shared meaning is created.

It is a common misconception that a receiver always interprets meaning in the way intended by the message maker. The connection between the message maker and the message receiver is not simple either. The achievement of shared meaning often requires thoughtful planning and clarity on the part of the sender and clarification seeking on the part of the receiver. Kristen Stanley Milburn, the idea ambassador at 2think Inc., a Web and digital design company, serves as the message meaning interpreter between clients and Web designers. Because customers and designers may use and interpret words differently, Stanley Milburn designs messages that convey the needs and intentions of her clients in a way her designers can understand.

intended meaning is the meaning the sender has in mind when designing his or her message.

interpreted meaning is the meaning the receiver interprets from the message.

CREATIVE CHALLENGE

Divide into small groups with your class colleagues to brainstorm different meanings for the following words:

- Success
- Professional
- Performance

Share your ideas with the rest of the class.

How We Create Meaning

In our everyday lives, we routinely receive more than 10,000 bits of stimuli every second. However, we actually focus on and mentally process only a small amount of the data we receive. This way, we experience selected sensory stimuli (what we hear, see, taste, touch, or smell) and we perceive, organize, and interpret what those stimuli are and what they mean to us.

Perception

The initial act of sensing occurs with perception, which happens when you receive and mentally record sensory information. To mentally

Jump In!

JUMP IN!

React to the following statements by writing what meaning you think may have been interpreted by the receiver. Then rewrite the statements to better reflect the sender's intended meaning.

1. Just before an important business meeting, a colleague who knows you like the comedian Steve Martin remarks loudly enough for others to hear, "Last night on one of those movie channels I was watching *The Jerk*, and I kept thinking about you."

2. In a speech, a politician once said, "I stand by all the misstatements that I've made."

3. This politician also said, "It isn't pollution that's harming the environment. It's the impurities in our air and water that are doing it."

record stimuli means to become aware of what you have received. For example, just after you hand your instructor a report she's been asking for, you perceive her physically turning her body away from you. You perceive this information through visually observing her nonverbal behavior.

Organization

Organizing essentially refers to ordering and categorizing the information you receive like a story and then associating it with knowledge you already have about objects, ideas, and people. You group experiences together when they are similar and separate them into categories when they are different, just as you would put lemons in a different category from people or buildings. When you saw your instructor turn her body away, you associated that behavior with similar experiences and grouped it into a category that you had already mentally constructed for that type of information.

Interpretation

Once you have organized the sensory information, you begin to interpret what the experience may mean. Interpretation refers to analyzing what you are experiencing and what it means from your past experiences with similar behaviors. You may interpret your instructor turning her back on you as meaning that she is upset about your report being a day late. In reality, she may just have accepted your paper and then shifted her attention elsewhere, but you interpret the meaning based on your experience. Figure 5.2 illustrates how we create meaning.

To more fully understand the meaning process, it is important for you to know that perception, organization, and interpretation can happen in a split second. Sometimes the organization of information and interpretation can take a good deal longer, but registering simple or familiar stimulation can happen very quickly.

FIGURE 5.2   **How We Create Meaning**

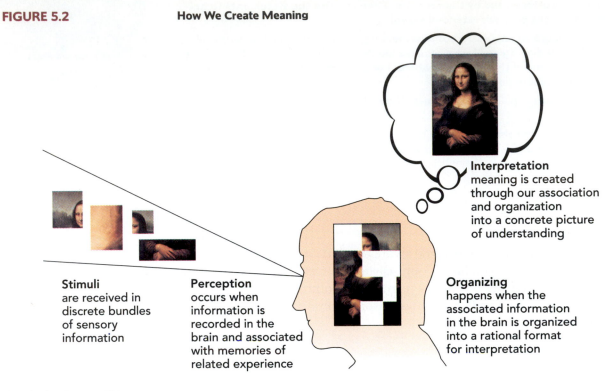

Interpretation
meaning is created
through our association
and organization
into a concrete picture
of understanding

Stimuli
are received in
discrete bundles
of sensory
information

Perception
occurs when
information is
recorded in the
brain and associated
with memories of
related experience

Organizing
happens when the
associated information
in the brain is organized
into a rational format
for interpretation

Giraudon/Art Resource, NY

Signs and Symbols

Meaning is created and interpreted by people. While meaning is an internal process, much of what we perceive things to mean comes from what we have learned from our experiences with family and friends and from our culture. It is important to understand several words that help us to gain insight into the process of how we learn to assign meaning to objects, events, and ideas. A **sign** is something that people agree represents something else. A sign usually is linked with what it represents. For example, if you see dark clouds on the horizon and the wind picks up, you interpret these weather conditions as signs of rain. The weather conditions are signs representing the possibility that rain is coming. Figure 5.3 illustrates signs of a storm.

A **symbol** is a type of sign that has no natural link or has an indirect association to what it represents, like Nike's swoosh logo. In most cases, the connection between the actual symbol and what it represents is random. Nevertheless, symbols are connected to our interpretations of what objects, ideas, and behaviors mean. They can hold deeper meaning than signs. Even spoken and written languages are systems of symbols that use sounds or letters to create meaning. These symbols do not contain innate meaning. Rather, we learn to attach meaning to them. For example, we have learned that the word *book*

sign something that
people agree represents
something else and is
usually linked with what it
represents.

symbol a type of sign that
has an indirect association
to what it represents.

FIGURE 5.3

Storm Sign

Dark, gray clouds are a sign that a storm is approaching.

symbolizes an object that consists of words, pictures, maps, or illustrations that are printed on pages of paper and bound together into a single document.

The Contexts of Meaning

There are many layers involved in the process of constructing meaning. One layer of meaning making is context. How we acquire meaning comes from the contexts in which our experience or our communication occurs. The contexts of meaning are illustrated in Puzzle Figure 5.4.

Context is the physical, social, and psychological situation in which a communication event occurs. Words and behaviors acquire meaning through a specific set of circumstances that are in place as the communication happens. A given context is like a puzzle made up of many individual pieces that, when combined, help us to assemble the whole puzzle. For example, if you walked by two people in a parking lot who were yelling angrily at each other, you would probably have some difficulty interpreting what was causing the trouble between them. Even if you overheard certain key words from their exchange, you might not have enough pieces of the puzzle to interpret their problem accu-

context is the physical, social, and psychological situation in which a communication event occurs.

FIGURE 5.4

The Contexts of Meaning

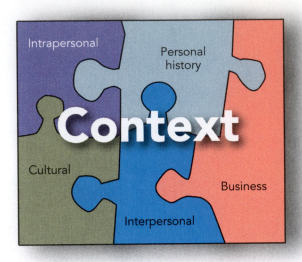

rately. The reason for your confusion would be that the various contexts of their communication were unknown to you. These contexts might include their feelings toward each other, the history they have shared, and other past or present problems they have experienced. These different contexts provide us with valuable sense-making information that we categorize in our minds in an effort to understand events or actions.

Consider the question "Did you see the table?" This question can have different meanings depending on the context in which it occurs, including both the physical environment and the relationship between the sender and the receiver. One researcher may ask it of another regarding a set of numbers in a business report. In a different context, a husband intent on surprising his wife with a candlelight dinner may ask the same question as she arrives home from work. The different contexts that shape our understanding of what an event, action, or idea means are intrapersonal, personal history, cultural, interpersonal, and business.

Intrapersonal Context

Thinking and communicating are a simultaneous interaction. When we think, we communicate with ourselves. However, intrapersonal communication is more than an ongoing dialogue we have with our thinking selves. It is a mental process of decoding and encoding both internal and external stimuli. **Intrapersonal decoding** is a process of receiving data that originate either inside or outside ourselves and then interpreting and assigning meaning to those data. For example, during class you begin to decode the information presented by your instruc-

intrapersonal decoding is a process of receiving data that originate either inside or outside ourselves and then interpreting and assigning meaning to those data.

tor by making sense of both the visual and verbal messages. You would try to determine what ideas your instructor was attempting to convey.

Intrapersonal encoding is the process of organizing the data and translating thoughts into a managed internal response. For example, during class you would probably try to determine whether the information in the presentation was relevant to you or whether you could use the advice. If so, you might react to the messages by becoming more mentally absorbed and asking questions. If not, you might look at your watch or roll your eyes. You might use a combination of responses, which might or might not be observable by others.

The intrapersonal context of meaning occurs within ourselves, but it also involves a variety of other contexts that operate concurrently.

Personal History Context

A personal history context is our memory of past experiences, which we use to make sense and meaning of new experiences. Your memory bank of experiences helps determine how a given perceived event may play out and what it means. For example, your memory of past employment experiences helped to shape your expectation about receiving a paycheck from your current employer. In your past experience, you observed that the boss handed out paychecks every other Friday. Therefore, you reasoned that after you had worked two weeks for the new company, your new boss would also disseminate paychecks.

This particular context provides a historical perspective through which you can attach meaning to new events. Your past experiences leave imprints on your memory that shape the way you assign meaning to and interpret new events or ideas. You process the new information interactively with knowledge already stored in your memory.

Cultural Context

While each of us mentally processes individual experiences in our own way, we are connected by our collective experience in social life. This collective experience is a sociocultural perception, and it provides a framework for how we should behave, think, and feel as members of a society. It teaches us to view the meanings of ideas, objects, motivations, behaviors, and feelings through a cultural lens. The sociocultural influences on meaning making include our family, friends, ethnic groups, level of education, profession, political or religious affiliations, gender, and so on. They help to frame how we view reality and what is meaningful in our lives. Consider these questions:

Do we come from a culture that values freedom?

Does our cultural perspective provide us with a general meaning for freedom, such as the right to speak our minds?

The meaning of words or nonverbal behaviors can be confusing without knowledge of the cultural and interpersonal contexts.
© David Young-Wolff/Photo Edit

intrapersonal encoding is the process of organizing data and translating thoughts into a managed internal response.

CHALLENGE

Consider the following situation:

In an oral agreement, a homeowner agreed to pay $75 per week for housecleaning. At the end of the first week, the homeowner and the cleaner had a disagreement because the bed sheets had not been changed and laundered. The homeowner claimed the house was not clean with dirty sheets. The cleaner maintained that changing sheets was not part of the job and that a housecleaner is different from a housekeeper at a hotel.

Do you think the term "housecleaning" means the same thing to everyone?

Break into two groups with your class colleagues. One group should prepare and present a skit in which the meaning of this cleaning job is misinterpreted. The other group should prepare a second skit in which the meaning of housecleaning is understood by both parties before the job is completed. The second skit should illustrate how this disagreement between the homeowner and the cleaner could have been avoided.

The answer to both is yes, unless you yell "fire" in a crowded theater, since one of our cultural meanings for freedom is the liberty to speak freely unless that speech harms someone or incites violence. Our cultural experience influences our interpretation of what matters to us and guides us to view life in a particular way. Corporate culture is the philosophy of an organization and shapes the meaning of the corporate way of life. At Alberto-Culver, manufacturer of Alberto V05 hair products and Mrs. Dash seasonings and owner of Sally's Beauty Supply stores throughout the United States, shared passion drives the company culture. Employees are encouraged to innovate, become group leaders, and take risks—all of which require great passion and commitment. Passion has helped Alberto-Culver reduce employee turnover, recruit top professionals, and increase sales by more than 18 percent.

Interpersonal Context

Our family, friends, mentors, and co-workers all provide a view of what is meaningful and real in the context of our interpersonal connection. When we interact with others, that interaction itself becomes a context from which we derive meaning. The verbal and nonverbal behaviors transmitted in an interaction contain more than literal meaning. The way we say certain things, our demeanor, our tone, our mood, our relationship to each other, and the roles we play all affect the meaning we get from the interaction. For example, in a conversation between two co-workers one says to the other, "That's brilliant." The literal meaning of *brilliant* is "very intelligent," but if these words are uttered sarcastically, the meaning exchanged is quite different. An interpersonal context is illustrated in Figure 5.5. *Paralanguage*, as we will discuss in Chapter 13, refers to nonverbal vocal sounds, inflection, tone, and volume rather than the actual content of the words spoken. A sarcastic person who said "brilliant" would mean "stupid," which in context might or might not offend the other person. Suppose you notice a group of people talking. One winks at another and they smile at each other. This nonverbal action may signal an inside joke or attraction between the two people. You need to look at the context in which the interaction takes place to understand the meaning of interpersonal messages.

That's brilliant!

FIGURE 5.5

In context, the sarcastic words "That's brilliant" may mean the action is stupid.

Business Context

In the business environment, we learn what is meaningful from our co-workers and from the culture of the organization. We interpret business messages and professional conduct through learned business meanings. We use our skills to interpret our professional experiences from a business perspective.

The software company SAS provides 300 pounds of M&Ms for workers every Wednesday. The company values building employee relationships and sharing knowledge, and the mound of candy provides a way for employees to socialize and weave ties that bind them together in a meaningful way. The nonverbal meaning behind the pile of M&Ms is a commitment to employees that goes beyond the work they perform. If employees feel comfortable, feel valued, and feel a sense of community, they are more likely to stay with the company. The M&Ms, combined with a host of other perks such as a company choir, a recreational center, and two on-site child care facilities, contribute to the company's low (4 percent) employee turnover rate.

In other business contexts, you may frame messages differently than you would at a social gathering with friends and family. Business messages are often more structured and formal in design. Formal messages can be clear and easily interpreted, but some can be vague or confusing. For example, suppose your supervisor assigned a special cost analysis report for you to prepare. After she finished explaining how

Copyright © 2002 United Feature Syndicate, Inc.

important it was that you take time to be thorough in your analysis, she glanced over at one of your co-workers and remarked, "You know Jean works late nearly every night. Her reports are always turned in before deadline." While your supervisor may want you to spend time preparing a comprehensive report, she may also be implying that she wants it fast. Learning what it means to miss a department meeting and how the boss interprets friendly banter can be important survival tools in a business environment.

From an external business perspective, many companies are realizing that their interpretations of what new products and technologies mean for the future need to match their customers more closely. IBM's research division encourages its scientists and mathematicians to go out into the field and talk to customers about problem solutions, innovations, and technologies that could benefit them. The connection between the scientists and customers creates a basis for shared meaning and interpretation that didn't exist before. Each organization and each business situation has a different context that determines what words, behaviors, and even future innovations mean.

The Meanings of Words

semantics is the relationship between words and the meanings we attach to them.

People have different interpretations of the same words, events, or ideas based on their personal experiences. **Semantics** is the relationship between words and the meanings we attach to them. Words do not contain independent meanings. Rather, people attach meanings to symbols and create connections between symbols to generate meaningful concepts and ideas. Many of the most commonly used words have a dozen or more different meanings. The more overlap we have in our experiences together, as with family and friends, the more likely we are to interpret the meanings of words in the same way.

Concrete Words

Concrete words are associated with objects or events that we have experienced through our senses. Message receivers can usually interpret concrete words such as desk, office, or paycheck with greater accuracy. But the context of the communication still contributes to the meaning, as does the message sender's intent. At General Electric, *paperless* is a concrete word that means do the job electronically without using paper products. In an effort to reduce costs, personal fax machines, printers, and even desk copiers were eliminated. In all, 30,000 machines were donated to charities, sent back to vendors, or thrown out to save the company an expected $18 million in paper consumption. Paperless also means that employees need to use computers to save files and use smart phones or other paperless channels to communicate.

concrete words are associated with objects or events that we have experienced through our senses.

Abstract Words

Ideas or concepts that we cannot directly experience through our senses are symbolized by **abstract words.** Words such as *interest, clear, work,* and *absolute* are abstract because they represent intangible ideas and can mean different things to different people.

Abstract words carry a greater risk of message misinterpretation, but examining the physical and relationship context and the sender's tone and attitude can often enhance meaning interpretation.

abstract words refer to ideas or concepts that we cannot directly experience through our senses.

CREATIVE

CHALLENGE

Look up the following abstract words in the dictionary and review the different meanings. From a business perspective, write two different sentences using each word:

- Close
- Trade
- Level
- Make
- Value
- Clear
- Money

Practice Designing and Interpreting Meaning

Designing meaning	• Determine your meaning goal or exactly what you want your message to mean.
	• Select word symbols that focus on the object, event, or idea and can be easily understood by your audience.
	• Frame the message in such a way that the content meaning conveyed to your audience matches your meaning goal.
	• Select message elements, such as visuals, that can simplify or better present your message meaning.
	• Express the intention or purpose of the message.
	• Combine word symbols and nonverbal behaviors to express message content, perspective, and emotion.
	• Convey any action or change desired.
Interpreting meaning	• Listen actively to identify the message focus, including the object, event, or idea.
	• Determine message content, emotional tone, and sender's perspective.
	• Assess the message context (including the environment, the situation, and the relationship) to help you understand the message meaning.
	• Evaluate the message in terms of clarity.
	• Ask for clarification or paraphrase the primary or secondary message ideas if you are uncertain about the meaning.

Specific and Vague Message Meanings

In the messages we send, the message meaning can be either clear or confusing to the receiver. Since receivers interpret the meaning of our messages, it is important to spot and eliminate vagueness in the messages we create.

Specific Meaning in Business Messages

specific business messages are straightforward, explicit, and clear, with nothing hidden.

Specific business messages are straightforward and explicit, with nothing hidden. Intentions are clearly expressed to reveal what the sender wants, feels, and needs. Specific messages are designed to facilitate the receiver's understanding of meaning. However, even in a direct message, brutal honesty is not desirable. While your messages should present a clear representation of what you want or intend, do not abandon diplomacy.

Vague Meaning in Business Messages

vague business messages couch our intentions in ambiguous language or behavior.

Vague business messages couch our intentions in ambiguous language or behavior. A literal interpretation of the words used or behaviors exhibited does not yield a clear meaning. Vague messages are sometimes used when a communicator is uncertain about the receiver's reaction or wants to avoid potential embarrassment. Sometimes the business con-

---

VAGUE MEANING DIALOGUE

The following dialogue illustrates the vague nature of some communication. Discuss with the members of your class what you think the messages mean between these two people. This dialogue took place in a mental health clinic between a therapist and his supervisor. Alfred, the therapist, was called to his supervisor's office to discuss a case. Case histories were reviewed on a pass/fail basis, depending on how complete the information was. The state agency that monitors mental health clinics was going to be conducting a review of this clinic's case files in the near future. At the time of this dialogue, clinic personnel did not routinely meet some of the state requirements for case files, such as obtaining clients' signatures before discharge. In fact, Alfred was not even aware the state was coming for a review until after this conversation.

Alfred:	What's up? You failed me on a signature.
Dr. Detroit:	(deadpan) Yeah.
Alfred:	You made a mistake, right? You failed me on a signature?
Dr. Detroit:	You gotta get the signature.
Alfred:	Nobody fails anybody on a signature. The patient has been discharged and I can't get the signature.
Dr. Detroit:	(smiling) I don't care if you sign it yourself, just get it.
Alfred:	I'm not forging anybody's signature.
Dr. Detroit:	I have to attend to something more important now.

What do you think the source of Alfred's confusion was? Did Dr. Detroit provide enough information in his messages so that Alfred could understand? Reframe Dr. Detroit's message using more specific (direct) language.

text in which the communication occurs can make meaning easier to interpret, and certainly using active listening skills can significantly enhance meaning interpretation. But other times, accurate interpretation can be extremely difficult.

Blaming the Receiver

Even when we are vague, we expect others to understand what we mean and respond in the way we intend. But vague and ambiguous messages are often not interpreted in the way that we want them to be. When our receivers do not respond in the way we intend, we may become annoyed with them. Sometimes we even place blame on receivers by claiming that the misunderstanding is their fault.

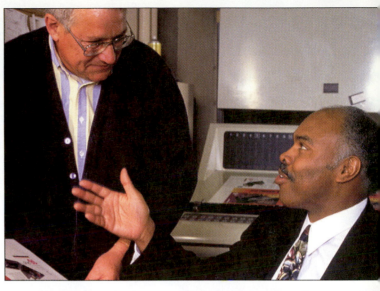

Both the message sender and the receiver have responsibility for effective communication and meaning clarity.
© Michael Newman/Photo Edit

While the receiver does have responsibility in the communication process, the responsibility for clarity of meaning rests on the sender's shoulders. The receiver can and should seek clarification when a message is ambiguous. However, the sender needs to design clear messages so that the receiver will have less difficulty understanding their meaning.

BLAMING THE RECEIVER DIALOGUE

Consider the following conversation between two co-workers: Jamaal, a 27-year-old human resources associate, and Sakina, a 25-year-old human resources associate who has just been promoted to assistant director in the human resources department. Jamaal and Sakina are discussing the promotion.

Jamaal:	Why did they pick you?
Sakina:	Perhaps because they thought I was qualified.
Jamaal:	You know why I think they promoted you? I think they really wanted someone who dresses well in that position.
Sakina:	What do my clothes have to do with anything?
Jamaal:	There's probably an image they want to project.
Sakina:	What image?
Jamaal:	They were probably looking for someone young and well dressed.
Sakina:	What does that mean? Are you saying my qualifications were not important?
Jamaal:	You always misinterpret what I say to you.
Sakina:	How am I supposed to interpret it? It sounds like you're telling me I got promoted because I'm cute or something.
Jamaal:	That's your interpretation. I just won't say anything anymore.

What do you think Jamaal meant by his comments to Sakina? Did he imply another message? What do you think the goal of his message was? Do you think Jamaal held Sakina responsible for the misunderstanding they experienced? Is there anything Sakina, as the message receiver, could do to open the dialogue more with Jamaal so they could share the same meaning?

JUMP IN! ⟶

The following paragraph is part of a bank disclosure statement. The statement involves a specific charge on a personal savings account. Draw a diagram of this statement and then rewrite the information to reflect a clear meaning of what the charge is for.

If the number of checks or debit card transactions payable to third parties exceeds four per monthly period, or if the number of transfers to another account of yours with us and/or payments to third parties exceeds seven per monthly period, or if a combination of checks, debit card transactions, transfers, and payments exceeds a total of seven per monthly period your account will be charged $15 for each transfer or payment over the limits.

Strategies

1. Evaluate what you really feel, want, intend, or need. Thoughts are easier to communicate if *you* fully understand your meaning before designing your message.

2. Define your goal for communicating. Part of defining your goal is to determine what you want. The other part is to determine what you want your audience to do, think, or feel.

3. Do not assume that receivers will automatically know what you mean. Assess your audience's potential interpretation of your message meaning. Use empathy for your receivers to create messages they will likely interpret in the way you intend. Make sure the message content and associated concepts and language fit the receivers' level of understanding.

4. Make sure your intention and motivation are clear. Be as specific as you can about the reason for your message.

5. Stick to the primary point you want to convey. Avoid digressing or focusing on unrelated ideas in a single message. Receivers will have difficulty interpreting your main points if you muddy the message with noise.

6. Lead receivers to your meaning. Provide adequate explanation and description in your message so receivers can interpret your meaning. Choose words, examples, and ideas that will guide receivers to your meaning through a connection to their own contexts. In other words, design your examples to fit each receiver's personal history, cultural or business context, or your shared interpersonal contexts.

7. Avoid information overload. As we discussed in Chapter 3, more information than is needed for full interpretation is not necessary and can become noise for receivers.

8. Make sure your message is complete, and avoid deleting important information. Presenting only part of a message can result in misinterpretation of your meaning.

9. Assess audience receptivity. Good timing, receivers' moods, and the location for transmittal are all important aspects of context for your message meaning.

Summary

- Because we understand ourselves when we communicate intrapersonally, we assume that other people understand us the same way. A common misconception known as the conveyor-belt fallacy is when we assume reception of our message guarantees reception of our meaning. Problems arise if we fail to realize that others interpret the world differently from us and that our meanings for things are not always shared.

- Meaning is a process of perception and interpretation. As individuals, we intrapersonally make meaning according to our social, cultural, historical, interpersonal, and business environments. Shared meaning involves both the message maker and the message receiver. If the sender's intended meaning and the receiver's interpreted meaning are different, misunderstandings result.

- In meaning making, we receive sensory information from our environment through sight, sound, taste, touch, or smell, and we mentally become aware of, or perceive, the stimuli. We organize the stimuli into categories defined by knowledge we already have stored in our memories. These categories help us interpret the data we have perceived. When we interpret information, we are determining both what the information is and what it means.

- Signs that arise in our experience tend to point toward meaning for us. A sign is something that we collectively agree means or suggests something else. We also associate meaning with certain symbols as a type of sign with only an indirect association. Symbols are not directly connected to what they represent. Both signs and symbols are socially created to help us share and communicate meaning.

- Meaning is also derived through the various contexts in which our communication occurs. A context is a physical, social, and psychological situation in which a message is sent. The different contexts that create the conditions for our different interpretations of meaning are intrapersonal, personal history, cultural, interpersonal, and business contexts. Understanding each other's meaning is not always easy because two people rarely see their personal and social worlds in exactly the same way.

■ Semantics includes the meanings of concrete and abstract words. Concrete words are easier to understand because they are associated with objects or events we directly experience through our senses such as *restaurant* or *cat*. Abstract words refer to concepts or ideas that are often less tangible such as *restructure* or *performance.* Depending on the context and the people involved in the interaction, these words can create misunderstanding. Similarly, specific messages are straightforward with meaning that is usually easy to understand. Vague messages are less clear or ambiguous with meaning that is sometimes difficult to interpret.

Business Communication Projects

1. Break into small groups with your class colleagues and discuss the following question: How do you ask a business professional of higher rank for a favor? For this project, imagine you want to ask your department director if you can use her for a job reference. Discuss why you might use somewhat vague language in your message to the director and how you would design the request using vague language. Then discuss how to design the same message using specific language. Share your ideas with the class.

2. Ask several people of different ages and backgrounds to define what the following words mean to them:
    • Restructure
    • Term
    • Operative
    • Downsize
    • Change
    • Strategy
    • Code

    Compare the different responses you receive for variations in meaning.

3. Think of a situation in which you have experienced a misunderstanding or miscommunication with another person. Write a short e-mail to your instructor that describes the situation, the reason for the miscommunication, and how it was resolved.

4. Identify each of the following messages as specific or vague.

    _____ Please bring me the proposal from the file.

    _____ It would help if I had the proposal to work with.

    _____ I don't know how I'll get to work, I can't even afford to fix my car.

    _____ I want a raise.

———— A good worker will go the extra distance to get the job done.

———— I want you to work late and finish the report.

5. Write several paragraphs about two different situations that both use the statement "I'm leaving." How does the meaning of the phrase differ? Be prepared to discuss your ideas with the rest of the class.

6. A contract between a roofing contractor and a homeowner indicated that a new asphalt-shingle roof system would be applied following removal and disposal of the existing shingle roof. The contract specified the product and price and stipulated that the work be completed within a reasonable time. Break into small groups with your class colleagues to answer the following questions: What does "reasonable" mean? If the work was not completed within three months, would the roofer be in violation of the contract? What if there was an unusual amount of rain, threatening damage to the house during the work? Discuss how this contract could have been written in a more specific, concrete way.

7. You are a retail store manager who has received a complaint from a customer about the length of time spent waiting in the checkout line. This customer also complained that there are too few register clerks to accommodate the flow of customers. What issues do you want to communicate to the customer? (Think intended meaning.) Draft a sample letter in which you clearly address these issues.

8. Your company softball team has been the league champion for the last three years. The team started out as a way for co-workers to interact in an informal, team-oriented manner; the weekly games were an opportunity for families to get together and socialize. But now positions on the team are hotly contested, and many employees are complaining that the ultracompetitive behavior of the softball team members make them unwilling to bring their children to the games. Design some strategies to remind the team of the real purpose of the games (to relax) and set some ground rules, complete with consequences, for behavior at all games. Write an e-mail to all employees describing your strategies and rules. Remember your audience: The point of the games is to have fun. Don't be too harsh.

9. Make a list of 10 outdated or wordy business phrases and explain what they are supposed to mean. Here's a few to get you started:
   - Thank you for your cooperation (*do it or else*)
   - At your earliest convenience (*right now, please*)
   - As per your request (*as you asked*)
   - Enclosed please find (*enclosed*)

After you complete your list, write a paragraph about why some people still use such outdated and ineffective phrases and how they undermine message transmission.

Discussion Questions

1. Why do people sometimes take things the wrong way when we communicate with them?

2. How does the context of business influence our interpretation of meaning?

3. In what type of situations are vague messages sometimes preferred over specific messages?

4. In what ways are business messages and social messages the same? In what ways do they differ?

5. What is a meaning context, and why is context important in understanding the meaning expressed in messages?

6. Why do we sometimes blame the receiver when he or she fails to understand what we mean?

7. What is the difference between intrapersonal and interpersonal encoding? Be prepared to give examples of both activities.

8. In what ways might different cultures influence or change the context of meaning?

9. In a business context, which words are more useful when you are encoding a message to an unknown audience: concrete words or abstract words?

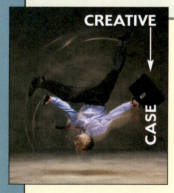

CREATIVE → CASE

Creative Case

A Clean Sweep

Financial documents are typically full of abstract terms and convoluted language. Fred Holden was in charge of the economic awareness program at Adolph Coors Company. But his experience reading and interpreting the meaning of financial data didn't help him when he went to open an account at U.S. Bank. He was stumped by a statement in the disclosure information for his account. It said, in part, "We may divide your checking account into two subaccounts. . . . You cannot directly access the nontransaction subaccount, but you agree that we may automatically, without a specific request from you, initiate individual transfers of funds between subaccounts from time to time at no cost to you."

What the bank intended, but didn't explain the meaning of clearly, was to convert some customers' checking accounts to "sweep" accounts. Such an account allows the lender to periodically "sweep" or move money from a customer's checking account to a savings or money market account. Banks use sweep accounts to lower the cost of interest they have to pay on accounts to the Federal Reserve Bank.

The information from his bank about changing his checking account lacked clarity and an explanation, and Holden wanted both.

Is it the customer's fault if he or she doesn't understand the meaning of a business message?

Some questions to consider:

1. What are the abstract words in the message U.S. Bank included in its disclosure statement?

2. Would you classify the disclosure statement as a direct or a vague message?

3. How could U.S. Bank have designed a more effective message about its use of sweep accounts?

SOURCE: P. Moore, "Demand Rises for Simpler Documents." *Business Journal*, March 11, 2002. Retrieved online June 3, 2002, *http://denverbizjournals.com*.

Chapter 6

Chapter 6

Designing Messages with Words

A small manufacturing company evaluated new hires after three months of employment. Until then they were considered "temporary employees," meaning that they could be terminated if their performance was not up to the company's standards. Myra Burke, customer service manager, usually enjoyed her job, but she never enjoyed evaluating employees. Even when the evaluation was positive, Myra was always careful to prepare her remarks in advance because she understood the importance of her message, not only to the employee she would be talking to but to the company's overall image. This time the news was not good. A young man who had been hired three months earlier was up for review, and she had decided to terminate him. His productivity was satisfactory, but his customer service skills were very weak. After weeks of training, he was polite with customers but projected a cold, inflexible image to which customers couldn't relate. The company believed that building positive relationships with customers was the key to success and worked hard to create a friendly environment for both employees and customers. This new employee's verbal style undermined company goals. Through role-playing, trainers and supervisors practiced appropriate word selection and how to convey expressive verbal messages with this employee but he made little progress. As Myra prepared for the evaluation meeting, she had to consider a variety of factors: company goals, productivity standards, customer service standards, and personality issues. How would she frame her termination notice? What should she emphasize? How could she explain the problem to this employee without offending him or undermining his confidence? Should she be tough or compassionate? Myra knew she needed to consider how he might react.

Can We Talk?

Myra understood the power of her words. She realized words should be carefully chosen to ensure message clarity and to avoid misunderstanding. As discussed in this "In a Nutshell" feature, verbal messages require thoughtful and tactful design skills that virtually every business professional must develop. "Off the top of my head . . ." is an example of an introductory sentence that usually means the sender is probably not thinking about what he or she is about to say. Designing messages with words requires intrapersonal communication skills even in impromptu conversations. Verbal messages include oral communication (listening and speaking) as well as written communication (reading and writing). We choose our words depending on our audience and the situations in which we find ourselves communicating. Most of us have experienced embarrassment after saying something we regret or using an important word incorrectly (usually when we speak before thinking carefully about the audience and current circumstances). We may say later, "The words just flew out of my mouth!" Creating a message, oral or written, before thinking it through completely can create the conditions for misunderstanding of our message, which is why we need to think about the words we use.

verbal communication is the use of any linguistic symbols—spoken, sign, or written language—to accomplish message goals.

Verbal communication is the use of any linguistic symbols—spoken, sign, or written language—to accomplish message goals. Speaking orally to an audience is one form of verbal communication that we will discuss in more detail in Chapter 7. Verbal sounds and writing are human channels of communication that depend on a system of language symbols to communicate meaningful messages. As discussed in Chapter 5, a symbol is a type of sign that has no direct connection to what it represents. We assign meaning to symbols and use them to convey messages. Words are symbols that we use in speech. Groups of sounds combine to form the roots of words. From them phrases are formed, and finally phrases combine to make sentences. People combine and organize word symbols into sentences to form meaningful verbal expressions.

A communicator's effectiveness depends on the appropriate choice of words and their arrangement in a message. Meaning, as you recall from Chapter 5, includes the interaction of perception and interpretation. When we design a message, we must choose language that will enable the receiver to interpret our meaning as closely as possible to what we intend. We must take into account the circumstances surrounding the interaction and the verbal style in which we deliver the message.

Because it uses words, sign language is verbal communication.
© Michael Newman/Photo Edit

The ultimate practitioners of persuasion are public relations professionals. It is their job to make announcements, deliver good news, and put a positive spin on not-so-good news. They have to persuade an audience to attend events or take action. PR people influence the way we perceive a company, an industry, or even a government. It's all about the image. The public relations industry is one of the most communication intensive of all. If you want to know what the PR professionals know, look at the resources they use:

Word on the Web

- www.online-pr.com
- www.prfirms.org
- www.publicrelationsresources.com
- www.public-relations-online.net
- www.publicrelations.about.com

What Is a Verbal Style?

Our particular choice of words, phrase or sentence arrangements, and the formality of expression we use create our **verbal style.** While verbal style is a set of behaviors that reflect aspects of our individual personality, it also varies depending on the context in which the verbal interaction occurs. We adapt it to our purposes and to accommodate other people. If you were explaining savings accounts to a child, for example, you would use simple, vivid words to explain banking transactions and interest. If you were discussing savings accounts with an adult customer, you would use more formal, complex language and ideas to describe different types of savings programs and investments. Learning how to adapt your verbal style for different audiences and to attain specific message goals involves intrapersonally thinking through the communication design.

There are nine primary verbal communication styles, all of which are used for different purposes. Your choice of style depends on how involved you are and the relationship you share with the people with whom you are communicating as well as the responsiveness, attentiveness, and experience of your audience and, of course, the context and purpose of the message. Assess your audience and the situation to determine what verbal style to use.

verbal style is our particular choice of words, phrase or sentence arrangements, and the formality of expression we use.

Types of Verbal Styles

| Expressive and supportive | Generally informal; reveals feelings and thoughts and uses expressive and meaningful language, including metaphors and proverbs. Requires knowledge of the cultural context in which the message is being transmitted since metaphors and proverbs do not always translate well from culture to culture. Also used to praise and encourage. | This style is straightforward. It invites the receiver to respond in an open manner and fosters a comfortable atmosphere to make the audience feel at ease and valued. The message goal is clear and usually apparent early in the message. An expressive style may also emphasize positive aspects of the speaker's personality and performance. |

Dynamic	Formal or informal; attempts to create a lasting image in the mind of the receiver. Uses stories and anecdotes to keep audience interest.	Useful for presenting new or controversial material, this style can also help build rapport between speaker and audience.
Combative	Usually informal; a disputing and challenging style in which the message designer argues with other's position.	Although this style seems negative, constructive argumentation can be positive and even necessary when evaluating choices and making decisions.
Minimalist	Often formal; uses understatement to provide the bare bones of an idea. Gives a minimum of description or explanation.	The receiver of a spoken or written minimalist message needs to know a great deal about the message's context in order to understand it. Otherwise, the receiver must work hard to interpret the message.
Subtextual	Can be formal or informal; delays the message goal and sometimes hides or disguises it. Indirect communication.	In American business, indirection is sometimes used to deliver bad news or try to persuade an audience.
Descriptive	Often formal; provides detail, definition, and description.	The descriptive style demonstrates the communicator 's accuracy and thoroughness. The sender includes enough information and explanation to make the message goal clear to a receiver who may not know much about the subject.
Authoritative	Almost always formal; used by a leader to control an interaction.	This style often provides the organizing and mobilizing aspects of a communication act.
Low key	Formal or informal; used by a speaker to appear unaffected in stressful situations.	In a busy or confusing atmosphere, like a newsroom, seeming relaxed can calm others.
Demonstrative	Formal or informal; uses nonverbal behaviors to express meaning.	Gestures and facial expressions show the communicator's attitude toward the subject and hint at how the receiver should respond.

Talk about Meaning

As discussed in Chapter 5, *semantics* refers to the relationship between words and the meanings we attach to them. Word symbols do not contain independent meaning. We attach meaning; people create and interpret meaning. We attach meaning to symbols and create connections between symbols to generate meaningful concepts and ideas. These connections generally come from our experience, education, and culture. There are two primary types of word meanings: denotative and connotative.

denotation is the literal or common description of a word that can be found in a dictionary.

Denotation is the literal or common description of a word that can be found in a dictionary. For example, the word *tree* is defined as a woody perennial plant with a long stem and few or no branches on its lower part. We all know what a tree is because we have semantically made a connection between the word symbol *tree* and the physical object it represents. Nevertheless, *tree* has a variety of denotative meanings, even in everyday speech. If we augment the word with a

Read the following letter and determine the verbal style(s) used to reach the message goal. Then rewrite the letter using a more appropriate verbal style to make a clear and effective statement. Be prepared to identify what types of verbal style you use and where.

Dear Ms. Swiggins:

Your application for credit has been denied. You have overextended your credit liability so greatly that it is impossible to consider offering you even one of our prefunded cards. Most of our customers have impeccable credit and it is as much for their protection as for our own that high-risk clients are excluded from our prestigious bank.

Perhaps if you practiced better economy in your personal finances you would be in a better position to reduce your debts and eventually build a satisfactory credit history. If this occurs we may consider a new credit application. You would, of course, not be able to avail yourself of our best interest rates and benefits packages, but in time even these restrictions might be lifted, providing your credit situation improves steadily.

If you have any questions, please feel free to call, but only between the hours of 9 A.M. and 5 P.M. Monday through Friday.

Sincerely,
Carole Barnett
New Accounts Manager

descriptor, the concept becomes more abstract. A family tree is not a woody plant; it is a genealogical chart. A phone tree is an organizational plan for communication. A shoe tree maintains the shape of footwear. Although the concept of a living *tree* still influences perception, the descriptors (*family, phone, shoe*) control the meaning of the term further.

Connotation is less definitive and involves the personal or emotional feelings that we associate with words. Our emotional association with a word or symbol, derived from our personal experiences, becomes its meaning. The word *tree* may bring to mind cool, shady summer evenings sitting on a swing. Or it may also be an object of fear if you've ever fallen out of one and broken your arm. Some may associate the word with a business perspective as in income from the sale of lumber.

We are usually aware of the denotative meaning of words and expect others to view them as we do. But it is important to remember that not all people make the same semantic associations. Imagine being a team leader on a high-priority project. You explain to your two teammates that their components

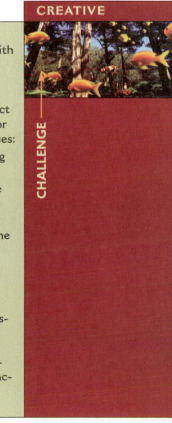

CREATIVE

CHALLENGE

Think of a situation in which you found communication with someone else dissatisfying or disappointing: an argument with a family member or a missed opportunity to interact with someone you admire, for example. Consider these issues:

- Whom were you interacting with?
- How did you feel about the person you were communicating with?
- What was the purpose of the interaction?
- Where were you?
- What was your mood?
- What was said?

After answering these questions, write a few brief paragraphs about how you could have communicated more effectively and how that interaction could have had a more satisfactory conclusion.

connotation involves the personal or emotional feelings that we associate with words.

of the project need to be completed as soon as possible. One team member may put off all other duties and have her portion completed within a week. The other doesn't even begin his until two weeks later, stating that other duties were more pressing. Both team members believed that they were completing their tasks "as soon as possible." Without a clear due date, the team is unable to work as a cohesive whole.

Speaking of Rules

We are born with an ability to learn linguistic rules by observing and listening to the people around us. **Speech rules** are a set of verbal speech conventions in message exchange. They include rules of grammar, interaction, social style, and semantics.

speech rules are verbal rules we use during interaction.

grammatical rules include sentence construction, the arrangement of words, syntax, and language fluidity.

1. **Grammatical rules** include sentence construction, the arrangement of words, syntax, and language fluidity. To be sure that others understand us, we automatically use grammatical rules. If someone called and told you, "Late I will be today," you would understand the meaning of the sentence but would be at least momentarily confused because the syntax of the sentence doesn't follow normal patterns; the words aren't in the correct order. Grammar rules are most rigid in written communications. However, spoken communication must also follow these rules to a degree.

talking and interaction rules involve topic relevance, turn taking, length of talk time, silence, and clarity.

2. **Talking and interaction rules** include topic relevance, turn taking, length of talk time, silence, and clarity. These rules govern ordinary interactions such as conversations. If everyone spoke at once or no one spoke at all, there would be no communication. Instead, we learn how to take turns in a conversation. We also know that we cannot dominate a conversation, nor can we switch topics in mid-sentence without bewildering those who are interacting with us.

social rules refer to greetings, appropriate word usage, style of expression, and ambiguity.

3. **Social rules** include greetings, appropriate word usage, style of expression, and ambiguity. We are trained in politeness early on; we say "please" and "thank you." When we meet someone new, especially a professional acquaintance, we are more respectful in our address than we might be with someone we've known for a long time, and we tend to be more vague or ambiguous when discussing issues that we may disagree on.

semantical rules refer to the denotative and connotative meanings of the words we use.

4. **Semantical rules** include both denotative and connotative meaning. Words that have particular meanings for some individuals have different connotations for others, and many meanings change according to the context in which the words are used. To say that someone "choked" during an interview is very different from saying that someone "choked" on a sandwich.

Communication designers choose from multiple rules to accomplish their communication goals based on their intention, message, audience, and context. While some speech rules are learned and embedded in our everyday communication experience, others are negotiated by the communicators themselves. Rules are not static because the ways we use language and adapt to situations change.

What Are You Talking About?

Sometimes when we talk in conversation, write, or make oral presentations, we assume people will understand the words we use. Education, experience, and culture can help determine what words should and should not be used with different audiences.

Jargon is a specialized language used by members of a specific profession or field, such as physicians, attorneys, engineers, or stockbrokers. Jargon generally relates to specific concepts or tools used in a field that can be referred to as *technical knowledge*. Knowledge of the jargon specific to a field or discipline is necessary to become a member of that trade. You may know what the water pump and the engine are in relation to your car, but if your mechanic tells you need a new right front camber and a realignment of its injection valves, you may have no clue what is actually wrong with the car.

Jargon often operates as verbal shorthand. A computer hacker who says, "This code is crispy!" is referring to a well-written computer program. The word "code" instead of "program" defines the speaker as knowledgeable about computers and refers both to the program itself and to the components that went into building it. "Crispy" is hacker shorthand for "well written," but it also implies excitement and approval.

jargon is a specialized language used by members of a specific profession or field that denotes technical knowledge.

Stockbrokers use jargon to buy, sell, and trade in the market.
© AP Photo/Chicago Mercantile Exchange, David R. Barnes

CREATIVE

CHALLENGE

Listen to your friends or co-workers. Do they use professional jargon or slang? Make a list of unusual terms that you hear during interactions with others. Then write definitions of these terms that someone without technical knowledge in that field would understand.

If you are communicating with a group of people who are technically knowledgeable and will understand, jargon can make the message's meaning clearer and more precise. But, if you are communicating with individuals who do not share your technical knowledge, you need to use more common language or supply simple explanations of important terms.

Slang is an informal set of terms used within a social group or culture. Like jargon, it signifies membership in a group, but unlike jargon, slang is generally used for descriptive purposes or to imply certain meanings about both the term used and the object to which it refers. For example, a slang expression such as "beat around the bush" can be used appropriately in some situations. However, if you are communicating with people whose native language is not English, it is not wise to use even the most common slang expressions.

slang is an informal set of terms used within a social group or culture.

Language Limitations

Occasionally we believe that we are being clear, but our receiver misunderstands our message anyway. This happens when we use language in limiting ways. Our word selection and use of verbal style can undermine our message, especially when we are trying to persuade or argue a point. Sometimes we use words and phrases that negate the very thing we are trying to say. Sometimes it is the result of using inappropriate terms in a given context. The way we use language always has an impact on our audience. By recognizing language limitations, like those listed below, we can design clearer messages that have a greater impact.

Intensifiers	• Intensifiers are one of the most common speech problems. Words such as *very*, *such*, *so*, and *quite* are usually intended to intensify a statement but often act to undermine its strength: "It's *quite* hot outside"; "she's *very* angry at you"; "I'm *so* tired"; "he's *such* a good driver."
Qualifiers	• Qualifiers may make the communicator sound insecure or negative. There are times when it's appropriate to say "I think this is a good plan," but at other times it makes us sound unsure. Verbal qualifiers include *I think, I guess, I believe, you know, sort of, kind of, possibly, perhaps,* and *in my opinion*.
Tag questions	• Tag questions are words and phrases added to the ends of sentences, usually included to elicit some kind of response. But this strategy can backfire. If you say to a co-worker, "This is a good report" and then add the tag "don't you think?" it may convey that you are looking for an opinion rather than stating one.
Adjective cramming	• In an effort to be clear and descriptive, sometimes communicators use far too many adjectives in their messages: "The small, dark, stuffy, crowded, smelly, damp office belonged to Ms. Dread." Instead of clarifying a concept and describing it fully in a succinct way, adjective cramming actually makes the message harder to understand.

Euphemisms	• Euphemisms undermine message goals by minimizing components of the message. They are "positive" terms to describe negative things. When we use the term "downsizing," for example, what we're really talking about is firing employees. Although such terms are common and are used to soften the blow of potentially unpleasant news, euphemisms have a tendency to backfire. They can fail to communicate important, if unwelcome, information. They can also give your audience the impression that you don't appreciate the severity of the problem.

These verbal problems may make your message less powerful and more vague, but the meaning may still be understandable. There are other limitations that can interrupt a verbal interaction in more serious ways and obscure the message.

- **Abstraction** is the use of complicated rather than concrete language. If someone tells you, "The deterioration of the corpus at the margin of the vehicular throughway made a substantive finding as to its original genus difficult to determine," are you likely to realize that the speaker is talking about an unidentifiable dead animal at the side of the road? The clearest language almost always uses the most concrete, recognizable words in the simplest constructions.

  abstraction is using complicated rather than concrete language.

- **Bypassing** happens when different meanings are associated with the same word symbol or when different symbols are used to identify the same idea or object. Sometimes bypassing is a cultural phenomenon. For example, a British person who asks you to get a torch out of the boot is probably asking you to get a flashlight out of the trunk of the car. But bypassing can also occur between people from the same culture. A supervisor may tell her administrative assistant that her mouse is dead. The administrative assistant may wonder whether her supervisor has just lost a beloved pet or if she needs a new mouse for her computer. In this case, the concepts of mouse (animal) and mouse (computer tool), as well as dead (no longer living) or dead (no longer functioning), complicate a seemingly simple message.

  bypassing occurs when different meanings are associated with the same word symbol or different symbols are used to identify the same idea or object.

- **Fact inference** is jumping to conclusions. This problem arises from insufficient information in the original message. If you find your lunch missing from the refrigerator in the employee lounge and are told that the last person seen in the lounge was Sou-Yin, you may want to assume that she was the one who stole your lunch. The trouble is, someone else may have taken it earlier, or the janitor who was cleaning the room mistook it for trash. Until you have adequate information about the circumstances surrounding the situation, you should not come to definite conclusions.

  fact inference is jumping to conclusions.

- **Misused words** can render a message meaningless because words are misapplied. If you transfer schools and send your transcripts to the "Department of Reticulation," they will never arrive because *reticulation* is a network. The correct word is *articulation*, which means to translate or interrelate. In this case, you want your

  misused words means that words are misapplied.

overgeneralization is the use of sweeping statements that do not provide enough information.

extremism means to see the world simplistically, in black and white, rather than in shades of gray.

inflexibility results from rigidity in our awareness of the world around us.

communication apprehension (CA) is the experience of feeling anxious or uneasy about communicating with other people.

courses from your old school to apply (*articulate*) to the course requirements of the new school.

- **Overgeneralization** is similar to stereotyping. Sweeping statements prevent us from providing enough information in our messages. "The fact is, the boss loves me" is one example. The boss may indeed like your work but may not be interested in you as a person at all. Some people might think your statement means that the boss likes you personally and doesn't care whether you do a good job—which could harm your credibility in the company.

- **Extremism** means to see the world simplistically, in black and white, rather than in shades of gray. Extremism fails to allow a range of responses to a statement or action. It is easier to say that an idea is big or small, good or bad, but such a statement doesn't explain the particulars of the idea or all the gray area in between the extremes. For example, if two teams are asked to come up with suggestions for a new promotional campaign, the project leader isn't required to use the concepts from either team. She is free to combine concepts and suggestions from both teams.

- **Inflexibility** results from rigidity in our awareness of the world around us. Even though we are constantly changing, gaining new experiences, and learning new things, we retain perceptions as if nothing has changed. For example, someone who hated broccoli as a child may avoid eating it in his or her adult years. Even though many people eventually develop a taste for certain foods they once disliked as children, some remain inflexible to trying them again. If we are unable to change our environment and ourselves, we may find it difficult to function effectively. For example, airport security across the United States was increased following the September 11, 2001, attacks on the World Trade Center in New York and the Pentagon in Washington, D.C. Because the situation in America had changed, it was necessary to reevaluate security procedures. Retaining the old security protocols may have put travelers in danger.

Must We Talk?

When you pay close attention to the specific words and phrases you use to communicate, you might become self-conscious of your ability (or inability) to convey a coherent message to an audience. In some cases, this may make you nervous or unwilling to initiate communication with other people, especially if they don't know you well. The experience of feeling anxious or uneasy about communicating with other people is called **communication apprehension (CA).** One form of communication apprehension is illustrated in Figure 6.1. CA is an intrapersonal experience that can be very uncomfortable. The most common form of CA is stage fright before an oral presentation in front of a roomful of people. Some people become nervous or panicky, which

FIGURE 6.1

Communication Apprehension

Stage fright is one of the most common forms of communication apprehension.

can cause the mouth to dry up and the heart to pound. However, communication apprehension can take place at any time and in any context, including speaking with a superior, giving bad news to an employee, or writing an important letter. Many people feel anxious when they must speak during meetings, in small groups, or even one on one. Still others become fearful when they speak to strangers, acquaintances, co-workers, or even friends.

Communication apprehension is both natural and widespread. When we communicate with people, we want them to come away with the sense that they have learned something from us. We want them to be impressed with our knowledge and our ability to analyze a problem or situation. If you are aware of your own anxiety and recognize its causes, you can be better prepared for stressful interactions and project a more professional, confident appearance.

Why Are We Scared?

The following factors can contribute to communication apprehension (CA):

Introversion	• Introverted and introspective people may prefer to listen rather than participate in interactions. They can appear timid, quiet, and shy, even if they really are not.
Alienation	• Some individuals have not learned the common speech rules of communication. They may interrupt other speakers, fail to respond to questions, or respond inappropriately. They may not fully understand the natural flow of conversation. Such people often appear to be negative or dismissive of messages, even if they are actually quite interested.

Low self-esteem	• Some individuals' sense of self-worth may suffer if they have had problems with communication in the past, perhaps because they are introverted or alienated. People who don't feel good about themselves probably feel that they have nothing important to say or can't express important ideas well.
Cultural divergence	• Styles of communication appropriate in one culture may not be appropriate in another. In many Asian and Middle Eastern cultures, the direct approach is considered rude. In western Europe ideas should be expressed directly, but the language should be formal and somewhat complex. In the United States both directness and simplicity are considered the best form for most business communications.
Poor communication skills	• Some people know what they want to say but feel they lack the necessary skills (vocabulary, grammar, sufficient awareness of audience) to make their meaning clear. This may or may not be true, but this fear alone may result in a garbled message.
Communication incompetence	• People who doubt their ability to communicate clearly may deliver their messages inappropriately by butting into another's conversation or speaking too quietly.

CA can range from fear in virtually any situation in which you must communicate to fear only in a specific circumstance such as public speaking. The fear may be associated with a particular person, such as the CEO of your company, or a combination of factors may trigger it, such as running into your boss at a party.

Communication apprehension detracts from the purpose of the message and can disrupt communication altogether. Some individuals avoid situations in which they may have to communicate, especially if they must deal with strangers or groups. Some find themselves withdrawing from conversations even if they feel they have something useful to contribute. On the other hand, sometimes when people are uncomfortable communicating with others, they talk too much. All of these behaviors can undermine communication and project an unprofessional or incompetent image of the speaker.

The key to reducing communication apprehension is preparation. Start working well ahead of time and plan for as many aspects of the event as possible. If you will be communicating with another individual who is unknown to you, try to learn something about him or her beforehand. Ask advice from others who have been in situations like the one you are now facing. Try to anticipate a variety of responses from the other person or people you will be communicating with and plan for them. How much do they already know about your subject? Are they colleagues, superiors, or complete strangers? Will they agree with what you are about to say, or will they resist the content of your message? Thinking about these issues may make you even more nervous at first, but considering them beforehand will reduce the amount of fear you have when you actually communicate; you will be reducing your fear of the unknown by making it known. And many of these questions you will have already answered through the process of developing your argument.

Using Persuasion and Building Arguments

Persuasion is the process of attempting to influence people's behavior, attitudes, or beliefs. A communicator uses verbal techniques to try to bring about a desired change in another person. An **argument** attempts to influence behavior, attitudes, and beliefs through reasoning. To build an argument, you must provide oral or written reasons (evidence) that support your position and convince others to think or act in a certain way. An argument is composed of a claim (a statement of fact or opinion) and reasons that back up the claim.

Both persuasion and argumentation come into play often in our roles as business communicators, from refusing credit to customers to creating a proposal for a new entrepreneurial venture. Most business arguments are based on the Toulmin argumentation model. Stephen Toulmin developed an argumentative model that derives its conclusion from specific situations or reasons, using reasoning to describe the result. Such arguments are built by using (1) **grounds,** evidence to support the argument; (2) **warrants,** which are the relationship of the evidence to the claim including common sense, common knowledge, and traditions; and (3) the **claim,** which is the matter that the argument is directed toward: its thesis.

> **persuasion** is the process of attempting to influence people's behavior, attitudes, or beliefs.
>
> **argument** a statement or series of statements aimed at influencing behavior, attitudes, and beliefs through reasoning.
>
> **grounds** are the reasons or evidence used to support an argument.
>
> **warrants** are reasoning; making a relationship of the evidence to the claim.
>
> **claim** a statement of fact or opinion.

$$\text{Grounds} \rightarrow \rightarrow \rightarrow \rightarrow \rightarrow \rightarrow \rightarrow \rightarrow \rightarrow \text{Claim}$$
$$\downarrow$$
$$\text{Warrants}$$

Notice that the claim is the final product in this diagram. When we develop an argument it is usually the claim we begin with, then we search for grounds and warrant. This is the basic structure of an argument. However, most arguments require more development before they can convince an audience. To accomplish this we must add (4) backing to the warrant, additional facts and evidence that support the claim; (5) rebuttal, a recognition of opposing arguments to the claim; and (6) qualifiers, which address the rebuttal and reassert the correctness of the claim.

$$\text{Grounds} \rightarrow \rightarrow \rightarrow \rightarrow \rightarrow \rightarrow \rightarrow \rightarrow \rightarrow \text{Claim} ----- \text{Qualifier}$$
$$\downarrow \qquad\qquad\qquad\qquad |$$
$$\text{Warrant} \qquad\qquad \text{Rebuttal}$$
$$|$$
$$\text{Backing}$$

Here's a high-tech example of argumentation at work. Kepler is a satellite telescope that takes light readings. The team that designed Kepler claims that by examining starlight in a small patch of sky, the telescope can find other planets like Earth. Kepler has been proposed to the National Aeronautics and Space Administration (NASA) Discovery Program three times. Each time it has been refused. First NASA said that the technology didn't exist, then it said that the project would cost too much, and finally it told the Kepler team that the science wasn't sound. After each refusal, the Kepler team put together additional arguments and evidence (including models, test results, opinions from industrial and technological authorities, and theoretical formulas) to prove that the project would work. Although the NASA committee still isn't completely convinced, it has given the Kepler team funds to build prototypes.

Reasons and Reasoning

The goal of argumentation is often to persuade others, but persuasion does not need to offer an argument. A persuasive message such as an ad can influence people's behavior and beliefs without offering any reasons. But an argument must include at least one reason as evidence or support.

reasons are statements of evidence, support, or proof used in an argument.

Reasons (which Toulmin called grounds) are statements of evidence, support, or proof used in an argument to influence others. An argument must contain reasons, or it is not an argument. Popular sources of reasons include quotes and paraphrases from published works and information from subject matter experts (SMEs), but reasons can also come from comparisons of similar situations, explanations of key terms and concepts, and the use of examples. Evidence is usually easier for an audience to understand when accompanied by examples that illustrate the principles being described.

reasoning is the ability to see connections between ideas and evidence and to use reasons as building blocks to support your conclusion.

Reasoning (which is similar to Toulmin's warrants) is the ability to see connections between ideas and evidence and to use reasons as building blocks to support your conclusion. Reasoning can be either deductive or inductive. **Deductive reasoning** moves from general principles to specific instances. When building an argument using deductive reasoning, you make a general claim such as "Computer programmers like Andy are good at math." Then offer more specific reasons to support your claim—for example, "Andy took several algebra and calculus courses in school. These reasons show that Andy is good at math." Causes and analogies are forms of deductive reasoning. To build an argument from cause, you reason from the effect what the cause may be. For example, when you see a co-worker cleaning out her desk, you can reason that she has been fired. After gaining a general concept of how to change printer cartridges, you may infer that by analogy the same process is used to change the cartridge in a specific printer.

deductive reasoning moves from general principles to specific instances.

Inductive reasoning moves in the opposite direction, from specific instances to general conclusions. To build an argument using inductive reasoning, begin with your reasons or evidence and build to a general conclusion or claim. Examples and signs are usually inductive forms of reasoning. You might begin with reasons such as "As a programmer, Andy has a lot of experience analyzing codes and computing complicated math problems, and he has a degree in computer science. Computer programmers need to understand and use the principles of mathematics to do their jobs. Therefore, programmers are good at math." You might observe specific signs, such as several co-workers leaving for lunch and dark clouds forming in the sky and deduct a generalized conclusion: "These employees will be caught in a rainstorm before they return from lunch."

inductive reasoning moves from specific instances to general conclusions.

Appealing to Your Audience

Ethos, pathos, and *logos* are Greek terms that Aristotle used to describe different types of appeals people use to persuade others to agree with them. You can persuade on the basis of credibility (*ethos*—ethics), emotion (*pathos*), or proof (*logos*—logic).

ethos is credibility determined by an audience but established by a speaker.

pathos is the use of emotion to persuade an audience.

- **Ethos** (credibility) is determined by an audience but established by a speaker. If the audience believes that the speaker is a reliable source because of his or her knowledge of the subject or trustworthiness, the audience will be more willing to be persuaded.

- **Pathos** (emotion) can stir an audience into agreeing with a speaker who arouses specific feelings about a topic. Fear, anger, hope, hate, shame, love, and pride are just a few of the emotions that can be sparked by persuasive verbal messages and arguments. Communication designers focus on the audience members' needs and desires to predict how to stir their emotions. Emotional appeals can be very powerful, but their misapplication can undermine an argument's strength if the audience does not already agree with the claim. For example, an emotional appeal requesting football equipment for a dedicated team with few resources will have little effect on listeners who are not football fans.

logos is proof in the form of evidence or reasons.

- **Logos** (proof) is evidence or reasons, which can take the form of authoritative opinion, reports or studies, analogies to similar events, and examples. Evidence serves as a guidepost for making rational decisions. Without evidence, there is no argument. If a chain-store manager demands a larger budget for her store, she must provide evidence that the budget is justified by current sales, potential sales, and individual store needs.

One-Sided and Two-Sided Arguments

one-sided argument involves the presentation of only one point of view or one side of an issue.

A **one-sided argument** involves the presentation of only one point of view or one side of an issue. This type of argument is most effective with an audience that already agrees with the speaker's position. Employees at a company located in a remote area might build an argument along these lines: "Many of our employees like to eat a hot lunch (reason). To get a hot lunch they must travel a distance (reason). So we need a microwave in our lunchroom (claim)."

two-sided argument presents both sides of an issue—not only the speaker's position but also opposing views.

For a potentially hostile or ambivalent audience, however, a **two-sided argument** is better. A two-sided argument presents both sides of an issue—not only the speaker's position but also opposing views. Such an argument relies heavily on rebuttal evidence and reasons to persuade the audience to agree with the speaker. The microwave argument would include opposing ideas: Will enough people actually use the microwave to justify the cost? Who will assume responsibility for the maintenance and cleaning? The speakers could refute these concerns by reasoning that the money could

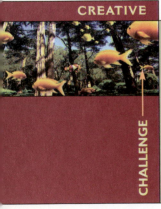

CREATIVE

CHALLENGE

Write a two-sided argument for and against employees participating with management in decision making at all levels in the workplace. Be sure to come up with concrete examples to back up your argument and to refute the opposing side. Come to class prepared to present your argument to the class.

come from the company picnic fund and employees would care for the appliance on a rotating schedule. Further, they could argue that if employees didn't have to drive half an hour to get to the nearest diner, more people would get back from lunch on time.

Strategies

1. Choose your words carefully. You control the words you use when communicating with other people. Use positive and concrete language and common, widely understood words.

2. Be aware of your audience, message timing, and the location of delivery. If your message is written, think about when and who will read it. If it is spoken, think about the situation and mood of your receiver.

3. Consider your relationship to the people with whom you are communicating. Are they good friends? Are they strangers to you? Adapt the formality of your verbal style to how well you know them.

4. Think about the personalities and life experiences of those you talk to. If they are older, supervisors, employees, from another country, or from another social group, adapt your verbal style accordingly.

5. Listen for pauses when others speak, and pay attention to those who do not speak. Those silences may give you clues to what the message goal truly is and how it is being received.

6. Don't hog the conversation! Follow the rules of talking by sharing the floor with other speakers.

7. Keep an open mind. Just because something was once true doesn't mean it hasn't changed with time.

8. Limit the use of jargon when you are not sure whether other people will understand the specific language in your message. Avoid the use of slang in professional situations.

9. The key to reducing communication apprehension is preparation. Start working well ahead of time, and plan as many aspects of the verbal communication event as possible.

10. Practice beginning your argument with a claim statement, as you would in deductive reasoning, and following the claim with viable reasons. Then practice providing reasons first and ending with a claim or conclusion, as you would in inductive reasoning. Use this sample claim: "A workweek of four 10-hour days would improve productivity." Develop the claim statement into an argument by adding clauses using the words *although* and *because*: "Although some may not like working longer hours, a four-day workweek would improve productivity because more could be accomplished in a single day." When you design your argument,

research your reasons fully. The more information you have, the more convincing you can be.

11. Consider opposing views from others' perspectives. You need to understand what you are arguing against as much as what you're advocating for.

12. Be polite, especially when your audience disagrees with you or is hostile.

Summary

- Verbal communication is the use of language symbols to deliver meaningful messages. We use a particular verbal style to convey our meaning to a specific audience and within a specific context. The circumstances surrounding the interaction determine the context of a message.

- Words have both a denotative (literal) meaning and a connotative meaning (the personal association we attach to them).

- Speech rules are a set of oral and written speech conventions in message exchange. They include grammatical, talking and interaction, social, and semantical rules.

- Individuals who are members of a specific community use jargon to describe concepts and tools used in their particular field. Social groups and cultures sometimes use slang to informally describe or imply meaning about a subject.

- If we believe we are communicating clearly but our audience still misunderstands the message goal, we may be using words, phrases, or strategies that limit or undermine our meaning. Language limitations include intensifiers, qualifiers, tag questions, adjective cramming, and euphemisms, as well as abstraction, bypassing, fact inference, misused words, overgeneralization, extremism, and inflexibility.

- Communication apprehension is fear or anxiety we experience when faced with a certain type of communication interaction. CA can come from our personality, anxiety, the context, and/or the situation.

- Persuasion is a process by which a communicator attempts to influence another person's behavior, beliefs, or attitudes. An argument attempts to influence behavior, beliefs, or attitudes through the use of reasons that support a claim. Reasons consist of evidence, support, or proof used in an argument.

- The process of making connections between ideas and evidence is called reasoning. Deductive reasoning moves from general principles to specific instances. Inductive reasoning moves from specific instances to general principles.

- Appeals to an audience can be based on personal credibility, the arousal of an emotional response, and proof.
- A one-sided argument presents information from one side of an issue. It can be effective with an audience that already agrees with the argument's general principles. A two-sided argument presents both sides of an issue and can be more effective with an audience that is hostile or ambivalent toward the message.

Business Communication Projects

1. Choose a common word (*book, chair, dog*) and think about the *exact* picture or sensation that forms in your mind when you hear that word. Ask at least four people what image or feeling the same word evokes in them. Write two or three paragraphs comparing these connotative experiences with the denotative definition in the dictionary.

2. Tape record a conversation with friends (ask their permission first). Listen carefully to the tape, and identify the grammatical, talking and interaction, social, and semantical rules at work. Write a series of examples drawn from the conversation to illustrate each rule.

3. Write a 30-second speech on the topic of your choice composed entirely of slang. Deliver it to the class. Ask your classmates to translate it into standard English.

4. With a partner, write a one- to two-minute skit in which you act out one of the following forms of language limitation: abstraction, bypassing, fact inference, misused words, overgeneralization, extremism, or inflexibility.

5. Recall a communication experience that caused you anxiety: writing an important paper, giving a presentation in class, acting in a play, or the like. Write a one-page analysis of the experience, identifying the type of communication apprehension you experienced and describing a strategy you can use when faced with a similar situation in the future.

6. Break into groups with your class colleagues to examine a feature in the business section of the newspaper or in a business magazine. Identify the argument strategy, reasons, and reasoning at work in the article and outline them. Be prepared to discuss the arguments with the rest of the class.

7. Write three paragraph-long appeals requesting a promotion: one based on your credibility, one based on emotion, and one based on evidence.

8. Using the strategies you've learned about persuasion and argumentation, write an e-mail message to your instructor requesting an extension on the due date for your final class project. Be sure to use logic and support your position with evidence.

Discussion Questions

1. What verbal style would be appropriate for responding to these individuals:
    - An irate customer?
    - A tourist asking for directions?
    - A frazzled mother?
    - A member of your project team?
2. What is the difference between connotative and denotative meaning?
3. After reading the Nutshell at the beginning of the chapter, how do you think Myra should frame her message to the employee? Should she focus on his cold verbal communication style? If so, what should she say?
4. How do speech rules influence communication?
5. When is it appropriate to use jargon?
6. Why is using abstract language aimed at impressing others rather than concrete language that may better express your point a mistake?
7. What are the causes of communication apprehension?
8. What is the primary difference between persuasion and an argument?
9. Why is reasoning necessary in an argument?
10. What strategies can we use to avoid offending a hostile audience?

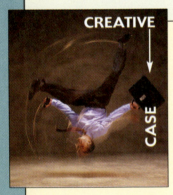

CREATIVE CASE

Creative Case

Talk to Me

In some cases, silence may communicate more effectively than words can. Hesitations and pauses are sometimes signals that reveal what is going on in a person's mind. Silence could mean that the person is thinking about something that has been said or done, or formulating a response. It could mean that he or she is trying to make some kind of decision. If the individual perceives danger, he or she may be afraid of repercussions that might arise from the message or the situation. Also, the individual may be worried or nervous.

Mrs. Whitney checked into University of California Hospital to have surgery on an ulcer. The day after her surgery she rested quietly, requiring little of the hospital staff's attention. The next day, however, she began to issue a never-ending list of verbal demands. She said she needed painkillers, pillows, blankets, and air conditioning, among other things. For the next two days she kept the entire ward's staff running, which meant they couldn't properly attend to the other 30 to 40 people in their care.

By the fourth day the staff were at the end of their rope. They discussed the situation with Dr. Pierre Mornell, the psychiatric resident at University of California Hospital. Dr. Mornell reviewed her case, noticing that she had gone from docile patient to madwoman seemingly overnight. He also noticed that the only time the staff had contact with Mrs. Whitney was when she used her call button.

Dr. Mornell advised the staff to pop into Mrs. Whitney's room more often to visit, but only when she had *not* used her call button. When she did use it, they were still to respond, but only after waiting for an extended length of time.

What do you think happened?

Some questions to consider:

1. What do you make of Mrs. Whitney's initial silence? Was she thinking or deciding something? Did she feel she was in danger, or was she nervous?

2. Why was Mrs. Whitney so verbally demanding on the second, third, and fourth days when she had been so quiet on the first? Did she really need all the things requested or was there another underlying reason for her demands?

3. Why do you think Dr. Mornell asked the staff to visit with Mrs. Whitney, but to respond slowly when she called for assistance?

4. How effective do you believe Dr. Mornell's management strategy was?

SOURCE: P. Mornell, "The Sounds of Silence." *Inc.*, February 2001, pp. 117–18.

Chapter 7

chapter 7

Designing Oral Presentations

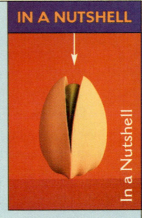

In a Nutshell

Terry Wilson, the owner of a growing commercial janitorial business, planned carefully for a presentation to Alliance Banks South (ABS). He wanted a contract to provide cleaning services for the bank's facilities throughout the state. After researching what janitorial services ABS needed, he wrote a detailed outline, complete with company facts and figures. He gave himself plenty of time to write and bind copies of the proposal and to construct clear electronic slides for the presentation. On the appointed day, he arrived at the ABS conference room 30 minutes early, turned on the computer/projector, placed his speech notes on the lectern, and began checking his slides.

Stunned, then panicked, Terry realized that he had brought the wrong disk. These slides did not include the latest financial updates and would not match the printed documents that he planned to distribute. He flipped to the handouts to check the numbers, only to find that in collating he had reversed several pages. With these mistakes, he had to do some creative thinking to save the presentation and maintain credibility. He also knew that he needed to remain upbeat and confident during the presentation. What would be his best course of action? What could he have done before arriving at the meeting room to minimize these difficulties? What could he say or do after the presentation that would help him to achieve his goal?

Speak Up

While Terry planned some aspects of his speech adequately, he wasn't thorough. Even minor mistakes can upset presenters and fill them with fear. Terry knew he had to prepare in advance to deliver a compelling speech, but he didn't plan for any potential problems with his slides. As discussed in the "In a Nutshell" feature, planning, preparation, and rehearsal are key ingredients to successful oral presentations and reducing anxiety. This chapter will explore how to overcome speech anxiety and strategies to design effective presentations.

The Fear Factor

Your palms are sweaty, your face feels hot, you can't catch your breath, and your heart is beating so loudly they can hear it in Australia. You must be getting ready to deliver a speech. For some people, just the thought of public speaking sends as big a wave of panic as being chased through the jungle by a raging rhino.

Before and during a public speaking experience, many people develop apprehension and anxiety. As we discussed in Chapter 6, *communication apprehension (CA)* usually involves the prospect of embarrassment while on center stage. Manifestations of prespeech fear include preparation procrastination, jitters, sweating, negative self-talk, difficulty breathing, and forgetfulness. Manifestations of delivery fear include loss of memory, fast speech rate, sweating, stiff posture, nervous adaptive behaviors, and difficulty breathing. If you feel anxious about public speaking, the good news is you are not alone and you can overcome your fears. You may be surprised to know that many teachers, politicians, and professional lecturers once shared the same fears about public speaking that you feel now.

It may also ease your mind to know that as a speaker, you are providing skills or information that your audience didn't have before. You are in control of the communication experience, because you decide how the speech is organized and conveyed. You are also the source of information. Even if there are other people in the audience who know about the subject, it is still your moment to shape and share the message from a unique perspective. Finally, you need to know that oral presentations can be extremely rewarding. Giving a good speech can make you feel incredibly energized and on top of the world. Audience members can also feel inspired and motivated, which is why public speaking remains one of the most important communication skills in business and the professions.

How Can I Reduce Speech Anxiety?

One of the best ways to reduce CA is to practice delivering the speech until you know it inside and out. Your assurance as a speaker will increase tremendously when you become comfortable and familiar with your material. Practicing at the site of the speech is helpful because you can check the light and temperature levels of the room, any equipment that will be used, and the audience seating. Getting acquainted with the surroundings can decrease the anxiety of being in an unfamiliar communication situation.

Some people put off practicing their speech because even the experience of rehearsal can produce feelings of anxiety. But rehearsal and practice help you to retrieve information from your memory more easily when you actually deliver the speech. Reducing anxiety also involves relaxing. Learning to relax is not easy when you keep thinking about what your listeners will be thinking about you. The good news is, they will probably never think about you as much as you do. They will be more interested in the material you present. With this in mind, focus on your material and on framing your message in the best way to reach your audience.

Choosing a Speech Topic

A primary speech goal is to select an appropriate topic about which to speak. In some instances, the choice of topic will be made for you. In business, the topic is often spelled out by the context, such as a monthly staff meeting where you need to present progress or performance updates. In other circumstances, you may need to personally select a topic to talk about.

Practicing and rehearsing a speech can help to reduce your anxiety and build your confidence during delivery.
© Frank Siteman /Getty Images

What Should I Talk about?

In considering your topic, you need to determine what you want to communicate. A good place to start is to think about what interests you. If you are interested in the subject matter, you will be more motivated to prepare and deliver an interesting speech. If you are still stumped about a topic, think about what skills or abilities you possess that could become the subject of a discussion. Do you know anything about karate? Dating? The stock market? You might also look through your favorite magazines and books or watch news and issue-oriented TV programs to get ideas.

What about a Really Big Topic?

Whether a topic is chosen for you or you select one of your own, it is a good idea to narrow it down to a manageable core of ideas. A topic such as health care, crime, or business is just too broad. Select the most relevant aspects of the topic that meet your interests, the needs of your audience, and the time or occasion requirements of the speech situation. For example, if your topic is organizational change, you may need to narrow the focus to one or two of the following aspects:

- Developing audience awareness of change urgency.
- Recognizing and handling employee resistance.
- Gaining support for a change effort.
- Communicating through change.

Once you narrow down the topic, focus on one to three main ideas that you want to convey. A **main idea** is a central point you want to make with your audience that will run through the entire message. For example, if you narrow the organizational change topic down to "handling employee resistance through better communication," your main ideas may be that (1) employee resistance is often the result of inadequate change communication and (2) implementing strategic communication techniques can reduce fear and resistance.

main idea a central point you want to make with your audience that will run through the entire message.

It is important for you to know that no matter how interesting your speech is, *most listeners will not remember more than three of your main points.*

To share the company vision and encourage employees to discuss ideas, Joe Liemandt, CEO of the software manufacturer Trilogy, developed a platform called Leadership.com through which employees can post video presentations to talk about the company vision, changes, business strategies, and departmental issues. These online video presentations are accompanied by a list of the speaker's main ideas, which are open for discussion and evaluation. Employees can evaluate each speaker's delivery performance as well as the content of the speech. The result? More Trilogy employees throughout the organization are learning about and discussing business strategies, values, and goals, and relationships among employees have developed and grown stronger. Furthermore, many of the video presenters have become teachers and mentors at the company's orientation program for new recruits.

CREATIVE **CHALLENGE**

Imagine that you are a project manager in a large research and development department. One of your responsibilities is to talk to new department personnel about working in project groups. Narrow the topic "the importance of employee team building" to three main ideas that you want to discuss with new employees. Then write two or three full sentences to describe each idea. Come to class prepared to discuss your ideas and why you selected them.

Speech Goals

After you have narrowed your topic and developed a main idea, you need to think about what you want or need from your audience and why you intend to communicate.

Your speech goal is why you are communicating and what you want to accomplish through your speech. There are four speech goals: informative, persuasive, requesting, and entertaining.

Informative speeches	Through informative speeches, you can provide information to build audience awareness, knowledge, and memory about a subject, or you can explain and demonstrate how to develop a particular skill. For example, an informative speech about organizational change may include a definition and description of what organizational change is, how it occurs in organizations, the reasons change is often necessary, and how it can directly affect employees. It may also offer a historical perspective that explains the events leading to change and real-world examples that bring the topic to life for the audience.	• Progress, performance, or research reports • Situation or event briefings • Training and seminars • New-product or policy introductions • Equipment demonstrations
Persuasive speeches	The intention of persuasive speeches is to influence a change in audience attitude, behavior, or belief. Since successful persuasion depends greatly on audience response, it is important to keep your listeners' point of view in mind and tailor your message accordingly. For example, to gain support for an organizational change effort, you need to relate the reason for and the outcomes of change clearly and directly to the audience. Making the appeal personal can increase audience acceptance. Building a solid argument that provides evidence to support your position, and establishing your credibility as a speaker, can also lead to positive audience response. It is critical for experienced and inexperienced speakers alike to understand that changes in behavior, attitude, and belief are often incremental. While a successful persuasive speaker can sometimes influence beliefs, radical changes in behavior do not usually happen overnight. A persuasive speech may plant powerful seeds in the hearts and minds of the audience, but time may be needed for those seeds of change to grow into observable action.	• Performance and motivational appeals • New policy and procedure initiatives • Political or union choices • Organizational change efforts
Requesting speeches	Business speeches that make requests are a type of persuasive presentation. The difference is that a requesting speech aims to gain funding or approval for a specific product, program, process, or charitable proposal. You are proposing a new initiative or program that will benefit the audience and are trying to convince them to provide funding or support.	• Report or proposal bids • Research funding requests • Product or service sales
Entertaining and special occasion speeches	Speeches to entertain or mark special occasions arouse emotion through celebration and an exchange of goodwill. For example, once an organizational change initiative is well under way, a quality improvement ceremony can be held to recognize employee achievements. During this event, a celebratory speech can further build momentum for the change effort by raising morale and encouraging employee commitment.	• Retirement dinners • Awards and honors ceremonies • Achievement and recognition celebrations • Tributes and roasts

Doing Your Homework

Preparing for a presentation means investigating your audience and the occasion, gathering the information you'll need, choosing the language you will use, and determining time and location. Doing your homework can enable you to plan, organize, and write a solid, successful speech.

Who Is My Audience?

While it is virtually impossible to know everything about a given audience (as discussed in Chapter 3), you need to gather as much information as possible about the audience with whom you plan to speak. Understanding your audience helps you to plan and develop a **customized presentation,** a carefully planned speech that is tailored to their specific needs, knowledge, perspectives, and background.

If you are not interested in the topic for your speech, your lack of interest may spread to your audience. Likewise, your enthusiasm and energy about a topic can inspire excitement in your audience. In Chapter 3, we discussed dynamism as a powerful determinant of credibility and appeal. Your audience will be more likely to pay close attention to your speech if you demonstrate confidence and enthusiasm. Think of public speaking as developing a personal relationship with some good people whom you really like. Talk to them as you would someone who is important to you, and they may well respond to your warmth in a positive way.

Alberto-Culver manufactures Alberto VO5 hair products, Static Guard, and Mrs. Dash spices. Carol Lavin Bernick, the company's president, invited all of her employees to a "state of the company" address. She sprinkled pennies throughout the auditorium beforehand. To start her speech, she sparked employees' attention by asking a direct question: "Where do our profits come from?" As they paused to consider the question, Lavin Bernick asked them to look at the pennies she had strategically placed on the floor. She went on to explain that those pennies represented the profits the company makes on a bottle of shampoo. Having gained the interest of her listeners, Lavin Bernick delivered a speech that focused their attention on the business and included them as partners in the process of building a more profitable company.

Another technique to gain the interest of audience members is to make the subject matter relevant. Focus on aspects of the topic that relate to their situation, field, position, or experience. Provide the audience with helpful facts, tips, or strategies they can use in their personal and professional lives.

Every audience is different and has a unique personality just as each person does. Still, you can acquire some information about audience members: their job titles, their fields of expertise or specialty, and the reason for their attendance at your presentation. You may recall from Chapter 3 that it is a good idea to find out if the audience is composed of internal professionals, external professionals, customers, or

---

customized presentation
a carefully planned speech that is tailored to the specific needs, knowledge, perspectives, and background of an audience.

The program chair of a local chapter of Junior Civitan, a service organization for teens, knows you have some knowledge of Stephen Covey's 7 *Habits of Highly Effective People* and has asked you to present a 20-minute informative speech about the fifth habit, "Seek to understand, then be understood." The fifth habit focuses on sensitive listening skills as applied to understanding other people. This habit emphasizes orienting our listening to the perceptions of others. When we respect other people's points of view, we can communicate from a position of alignment.

In small groups, brainstorm the following with your class colleagues:

1. Potential interests and concerns of the audience.

2. Attention-getters that would introduce the topic and address audience concerns.

3. Visual aids that might promote a better understanding of the concept.

some combination of these three types. While it can be difficult to determine your listeners' exact attitudes and beliefs, you can gain insight by understanding what the organization values and by asking potential audience members questions before your presentation. In this way, you can explore your main ideas with department managers and other employees so you can better customize your speech to meet their needs, preferences, and interests.

What's the Occasion?

It is important to have some idea about why people will be gathering to hear your speech. Is the occasion festive or strictly business? Is the speech part of a series of conference presentations, or are you the only presenter? Is attendance mandatory (as with required training) or optional? Audiences also want to know why you were selected to address them. Make the connection in your speech among you, the occasion, and the audience.

Where Do I Look for Information?

If you don't know what you are talking about or you haven't researched relevant facts, statistics, or data, it will show. Even if you have extensive experience to draw from, it is difficult to wing a presentation without doing some research. For example, if you plan to conduct a product comparison or discuss a marketing strategy, you really need to do some investigating to make sure your information is accurate.

There are countless sources of information on any given topic, including the Internet, online databases, CD-ROMs, and other computer-search services. Conventional sources such as books, magazines, periodicals, journals, almanacs, and government financial or statistical reports are also useful. The public library is an incredible repository of these information sources. Another good source for data is a subject matter expert (SME), a specialist in a particular area of expertise. Interviewing an SME is a good way to obtain answers to questions you have after reviewing certain statistics or other materials.

Using the Right Language

When you are preparing your speech, remember that written language is structured differently than oral language. Most writing is impersonal, grammatically correct, and composed of varied sentence lengths. The spoken word, on the other hand, should be personal, grammatically adaptable, and filled with short statements. When you speak, personalize the relationship you are developing with your audience by using personal pronouns: "I have concluded," "you may know," or "we often use" (not "our study concluded," "one may know," or "people often use"). While correct grammar is vital in written language, it can stiffen your speaking. Don't sound too formal; use contractions and address the audience directly: "You won't believe it if you don't see it for yourself." Finally, use short statements, or "voice bites," that you can say in one breath. Long sentences can be acceptable in writing since readers can reread them to better interpret their meaning, but your listeners need brief, idea-focused statements.

Practice Your Spoken Language

Be clear	• Use direct, conversational language that is easy to understand.
Personalize language	• Use personal pronouns (such as *I*, *you*, and *us*) that build a relationship with your audience.
Adapt sentence grammar	• Use contractions (such as *let's*, *don't*, and *we've*) that relax verbal statements.
Decrease sentence length	• Keep statements short and concise so you can say them in one breath and your audience can grasp what you are saying.
Avoid jargon	• Avoid technical jargon unless you are certain the audience will understand it.
Active voice	• Say "we determined," not "it has been determined."

Timing and Location

In Chapter 3, we discussed timing and location for message delivery. Both timing and location are also important considerations for successful oral presentations. Knowing what time of day you will be presenting is especially important. Many audiences are more alert and ready to go in the morning. Nevertheless, if your speech will take place in the evening, keep it concise and interesting so you can hold your weary audience's attention. Find out how long your speech is expected to be. Stick to that time frame, since your audience may become restless if you talk too long or feel cheated if you conclude prematurely. Finally, timing can involve current trends and events that are relevant to your speech. Explore the physical setting of your presentation ahead of time. Check out the size of the room, seating arrangements, acoustics, lighting, and equipment availability so you can plan your presentation activities accordingly. A room for presentations is illustrated in Figure 7.1.

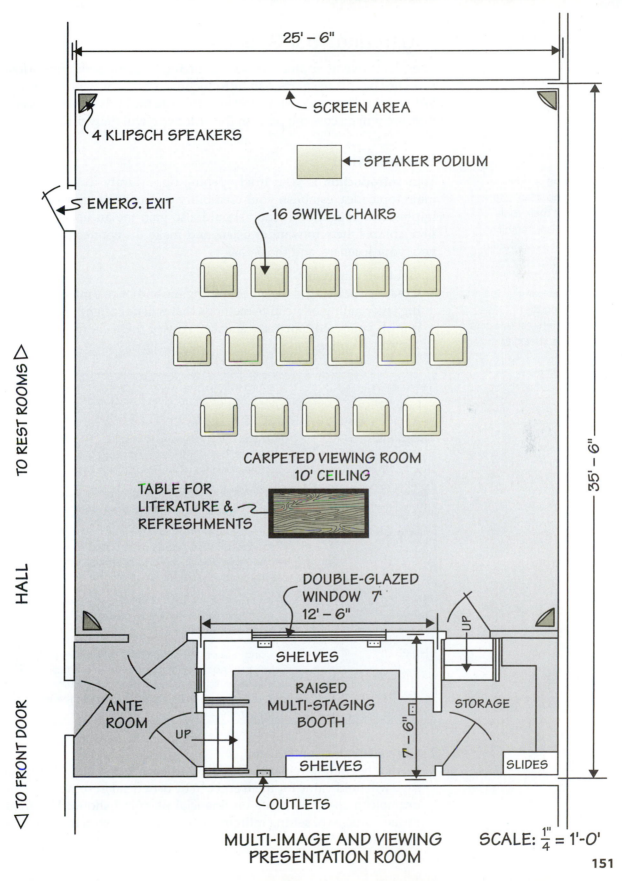

MULTI-IMAGE AND VIEWING PRESENTATION ROOM

SCALE: $\frac{1"}{4}$ = 1'-0'

Organizing Your Speech

There are several approaches to organizing your presentation. Most speeches have three parts—an introduction, a body, and a conclusion. While it can sometimes be a good idea to write the body of your speech first, we will discuss the parts in the order you will deliver them.

Introduction

introduction a brief opening opportunity to preview the main topic idea, establish credibility, and present a positive first impression.

creative speaking is the art of gaining the audience's interest by using entertaining speaking methods.

Your **introduction** is your brief opening opportunity to preview the main topic idea, establish your credibility, and present a positive first impression. Your introduction should also gain the audience's attention; compel them to want to listen; and make the connection among you, your listeners, and the occasion.

1. **Get their attention.**

   Creative speaking is the art of gaining the audience's interest by using entertaining or creative methods that will not offend them or diminish your credibility as a speaker. Any of these six methods will capture attention.

Anecdote	• An anecdote is a catchy story that draws from common experience with which the audience can relate. Choose one that leads in to your topic.
Ask a question	• Asking the audience a straight or rhetorical question can foster interest by getting them involved and making them think about a potential answer.
Examples	• Offering a personal or topic-connected example can illustrate an idea or establish your credibility.
Use a quotation	• A clever statement or phrase from a notable source can be a good springboard to your opening ideas. It can also briefly divert the spotlight from you to the source of the quote.
Startling or surprising remarks	• Surprising the audience with facts, statistics, or events can create a *whoa* reaction, which arouses attention.
Humor	• Using humor can sometimes be a tricky tactic because not everything you think is amusing will amuse your listeners. Nevertheless, humor that is appropriate to the topic can break the ice and build rapport with the audience.

2. **Give them a reason to listen.**

   In your beginning remarks, let your audience know that your message will hold value for them and can be beneficial in some way. For example, a speech focused on financial planning should highlight the advantages of setting retirement goals and investment strategies aimed at growing money.

Late night talk show host David Letterman routinely uses humor to capture his audience's attention. As a professional comic, Letterman finds humor an ideal attention getter. But other techniques may be more appropriate for your particular audience.
© David Young-Wolff/Photo Edit

In American business, creativity is in demand, and new creative ways to conduct business give many people a reason to listen. Creativity guru Doug Hall helps clients such as Chrysler and Coca-Cola generate innovative ideas for goods and services. Hall's speeches give his audience a reason to listen because his message helps them create new products and better marketing strategies. For a chance to learn about strategies such as "capitalist creativity" or "marketing physics," some clients pay as much as $150,000. Through Hall's Eureka creativity sessions, trailblazer training, and new online Merwyn idea evaluator, large and small companies find inventive strategies to grow their businesses and communicate more creatively.

3. **Establish credibility.**

As discussed in Chapter 3, *credibility* (ethos) involves showing an audience that both you and your message are believable and trustworthy. Speakers who have academic or work-related knowledge of the topic, experience performing certain work, or a track record in certain activities can establish credibility because they know their subject. Good preparation, topic research, honesty, and a fluid, confident speaking style also demonstrate credibility.

Ted Matsumoto, CEO of Qualcomm's Japanese division, presented a controversial speech to various software program analysts and customers. Many of the people in attendance were not in favor of Matsumoto's position on third-generation wireless phone principles. To gain their trust, he conveyed great enthusiasm about the subject and used gestures, postures, and eye behavior to reach out to the listeners. As he discussed his ideas, Matsumoto leaned toward audience members and maintained eye contact with as many people as he could. While his persuasive speech may not have converted everyone to his point of view, Matsumoto established credibility as a speaker and won the audience's respect.

4. **Relate to the audience and the occasion.**

You might refer to the occasion by saying, "We're here today to celebrate our success." To connect to the audience, you might say, "We share a common goal and we'll reach that goal together."

There are various websites that can help you to develop better speeches and deliver more successful presentations. Check out the following site:

- http://www.presentingsolutions.com/effectivepresentations.html.

Find three more websites designed to assist you as an informative or persuasive speaker.

Body

body the substance of a speech that explains main ideas and backs them up with supporting details.

secondary ideas support your main ideas.

The main substance of a speech is the **body,** which explains your main ideas and backs them up with supporting details, or **secondary ideas,** that serve to support your main ideas. Strategically, it is wise to set a limit of three to four main points, since you don't want to present more than your audience can remember from a single speech. You will likely have more secondary points because they expand on each main idea.

To arrange the material you have collected and want to share, select a pattern of organization that will help you achieve your speech goal and your audience to understand and follow what you are saying. Select the best of the following speech organization patterns for the needs of your audience and your message.

Chronological	A chronological speech pattern arranges material in a time sequence. This approach is effective for explaining historical developments or describing a process to be followed in order. Informative speeches that present information by moving forward or backward in time work best with a chronological pattern.
Topical	A topical pattern groups your subject logically into major categories. For example, a speech about the three most effective ways to invest in the stock market or the four available health insurance options and their advantages would work well in a topical arrangement.
Spatial	Spatial speech organization describes physical layout, location, or space. For example, a speech about interior decorating might use a spatial arrangement to describe the aspects of different rooms and the appropriate décor for each. Another spatial arrangement might be to compare the various field locations of an organization with different offices located in regional areas across the country.
Cause and effect	A cause and effect pattern shows a relationship between an event and a circumstance or result that may happen. Examples are a speech about the causes of organizational change, such as increased competition, and a speech about air bags that may decrease car accident fatalities. You can present the cause first and then discuss the effect or vice versa, as long as you clearly convey the relationship between the two. Persuasive presentations work best using a cause and effect pattern.
Problem and solution	Problem and solution speeches present an existing or potential problem and then suggest a course of action to solve it. Persuasive speeches that use this pattern can promote change—for example, a presentation about low employee productivity and a plan to boost morale and increase productivity.

Conclusion

The **conclusion** of your speech should do three things—tie together your main points, inspire a next step, and provide a strong sense of closure.

conclusion ties together main points, inspires a next step, and provides a strong sense of closure.

Connect your main points	• Summarize and reemphasize your primary points.
Inspire a next step	• Tell your listeners what you want them to do, think, or feel. Offer them guidance about where to go from here and what they need to do to get there.
Give a sense of closure	• End with a bang. Closing a speech in a dull manner can leave your audience with a "ho-hum" impression of both you and the experience. So end as you began, with a powerful statement, question, or quotation that you really want people to remember and think about later. Don't tease your audience with a false ending. If you say you are concluding your speech but keep adding "oh, one more thing" statements, your audience will become restless and annoyed (which is exactly what you want to avoid).

Don't Forget Transitions

Transitions are key words or short sentences that bridge one idea to another, the speech's introduction to the body and the conclusion, or one speaker to the next. Transitions help your audience move with you smoothly from one point to another. Have you ever noticed an awkward transition during a presentation? Perhaps one speaker didn't introduce the next but merely said, "Uh, and I guess that's it for me." Did it distract you from the content of the speech?

transitions are key words or short sentences that bridge one idea to another, the speech's introduction to the body and the conclusion, or one speaker to the next.

Ideas	• The next thing is • First, second, last • In addition • Moving to the next point • Moreover • Now, let's look at • Let's also consider • Another idea is
Introduction of next speaker	• Now I'd like to introduce you to • Our next speaker, Bill Jones, will talk to you about • At this point, I'd like to turn the microphone over to
Contrasts and comparisons	• However • But • Rather • Nevertheless • To look at it in another way • On the other hand • At the same time

Conclusion	• Finally
	• In wrapping up
	• Therefore
	• In conclusion
	• In summary

Visual Aids

Appropriate visual aids for your presentation can do the following:

- Increase message clarity.
- Visually demonstrate and explain more than words.
- Increase audience interest.
- Dramatically extend audience recall of speech information.

Well-designed visual aids such as tables, charts, transparencies, diagrams, videos, posters, and handouts can strengthen a speech, but you need to determine which visual channel is the most appropriate for your message and your audience. (See Chapter 17 for more details on designing visual messages.)

Types of Speech Delivery

There are four types of speech delivery: impromptu, manuscript, extemporaneous, and memorized. Each approach requires more preparation than the one before it. Which type you use will be determined by the circumstances, the topic, and your comfort level.

Impromptu speeches are unexpected and off the cuff. Inexperienced or fearful speakers should probably avoid them. Impromptu delivery is usually brief and about a familiar subject and does not require polished speech perfection. For example, you may be asked to say a few words at a celebration or a staff meeting. No one will expect you to speak for long or present an in-depth analysis, since the obvious drawback to impromptu speaking is little or no preparation.

A **manuscript** speech is written word for word and read aloud. An advantage of a manuscript speech is that it can be tailored to fit in a given timeframe. When exact wording is necessary (as when a judge reads a court decision), manuscript delivery may be the best choice. On the other hand, because oral and written language differ, a manuscript speech can sound mechanical and flat when the speaker is untrained in reading aloud. The result is a bored and uninterested audience.

Extemporaneous speaking is planned and rehearsed but not memorized. The prepared notes outline only key ideas. The advantage of extemporaneous presentations is that the speaker has flexibility to explain points and respond to verbal and nonverbal feedback from the audience. Extemporaneous presentations are also more conversational and can flow more naturally than any other presentation style.

impromptu speeches are unexpected and off the cuff.

manuscript speech is written word for word and read aloud.

extemporaneous speaking is planned and rehearsed but not memorized.

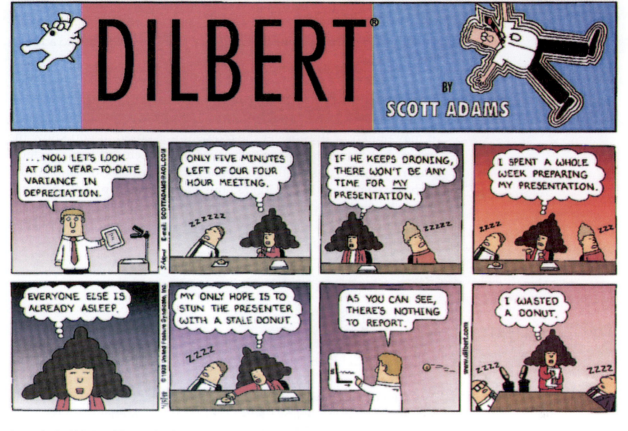

Copyright © 1998 United Feature Syndicate, Inc.

With a **memorized** speech, the text is written word for word and committed to memory. The good news about memorizing is that speakers know their speech inside and out. The bad news is they may forget it. Even if they don't forget anything, the speech may come across as stiff and programmed.

memorized speech involves memorizing a speech word for word.

After the Speech

You've just finished delivering your speech. The hard part is over, right? What can go wrong at this point?

What If the Audience Disagrees with Me?

This is why you researched not only your topic but also your listeners' perspective before your presentation. If you knew the audience was likely to disagree with your point of view, you framed the message to be persuasive but not threatening. You also provided a compelling argument with credible reasons that supported your position and addressed listeners' potential concerns. If the audience still disagrees with you by the end of your speech, ask for volunteers to explain their points of view. Then address each issue as it is raised. You may not convince everyone in the audience, but you can win many of them over by listening to their viewpoint and using solid argument points to address their objections.

What If I Can't Answer a Question?

Even experienced speakers sometimes go blank when asked a question or may not know the answer the moment it is posed. If you know the answer but momentarily can't retrieve it from memory, you can delay your response by asking the questioner to rephrase the question or rephrasing it yourself. If you don't know the answer, simply tell the questioner honestly that you don't know but you will research the information and get back to him or her with a response later. Then make sure you do so.

STRATEGIES

Strategies

Before the Speech

1. Practice and rehearse your speech often. Rehearse with friends or colleagues and ask for constructive criticism and feedback so you can identify and work out any problems before the presentation. Practice and rehearsal will build your confidence. The more familiar you are with the material, the more certain you will feel during delivery.

2. Practice speaking naturally without reading from your notes. Ideally, good speakers know the material they want to present and refer to notes only occasionally.

3. If at all possible, arrange to visit the room in which you will be speaking to check and practice with any equipment and to evaluate room size, acoustics, and seating.

4. Visualize your presentation. Imagine the presentation flowing smoothly and your audience reacting positively. See yourself calmly and confidently presenting the material and effectively engaging the audience.

5. Relax your body and mind. Work out any tension in your body by stretching your arms and legs and breathing deeply in through your nose and out through your mouth. Clear your mind of thoughts by closing your eyes and focusing on your breathing.

6. Use positive self-talk. Tell yourself, "I am relaxed and confident" or "I know my material and I can talk about it easily."

7. Select appropriate dress. A baseball cap, beat-up sneakers, and jeans are probably inappropriate choices for a formal business

presentation. However, depending on the audience and the subject matter, somewhat casual dress may be a good idea. Find out in advance what attire will be most appropriate for your audience and the occasion.

Delivering the Speech

8. Speak up! Make sure everyone in the room can hear you when you speak and none of your pearls of wisdom are lost to listeners. In a large room, you may need to increase your volume beyond that of a normal speaking voice. If the speech will be amplified, be sure to talk into the microphone. But don't lean into it or bend down to speak; stand naturally.

9. Focus on your audience. Talk directly to them and make eye contact with at least a few people located throughout the room. It will help them concentrate on your speech because they'll feel as if you're talking directly to them.

10. Refer to your notes just often enough to stay on track and remember key points.

11. Pace yourself. If you are nervous, you may speak too rapidly, which can distract the audience and make you hard to understand. If you speak too slowly, listeners can become bored or frustrated. Aim for a conversational pace of around 140 to 150 words per minute. Speak as if you are talking to co-workers or friends. You might want to slow down to convey instructional material and speed up to emphasize an emotional point.

12. Avoid vocal interferences, which are nonverbal sounds that fill dead air, such as "uh," "er," and "um." These interferences can distract your audience and convey the message that you are not fully prepared.

13. Try to avoid nervous adaptive behaviors such as tapping a pen or repeatedly twisting jewelry during your presentation. On the other hand, little or no movement can appear stiff and unnatural during a presentation. Use hand gestures and facial expressions that correspond to your message. Natural movements can be very useful to emphasize or even describe certain points.

14. Remember that nervousness is natural. Nearly everyone has experienced feelings of anxiety in communication situations at some point, so your listeners can empathize with you. Furthermore, most people never see the extent of what you feel. You may say to a colleague after your presentation, "Did you see my heart beat out of my skin?" She may respond, "No. You didn't look nervous at all." Even if people do detect some nervousness or a mistake, they will generally understand and overlook it. They'll be rooting for you to succeed.

Summary

- Sometimes a speech topic is predetermined and other times you will need to select one. Select a topic based on your interests, your skills, or current events. Narrow it down to three or four main ideas (based on the audience and the occasion requirements).

- There are four speech goal intentions: informative, persuasive, requesting, and entertaining.

- Analyze your audience to customize your presentation to meet their information, point of view, and background needs. Find out why people will gather to hear your speech, the physical location at which it will be delivered, and the time constraints involved.

- Gather pertinent topic information by exploring a wide variety of sources, including the Internet, books, articles, reports, and interviews of subject matter experts.

- Written language is different from the language used in oral presentations. A speech should be clear and conversational. It should use personal pronouns, contractions, short sentences, active voice, and jargon-free language.

- A speech should have an introduction, a body, and a conclusion. The introduction should preview the main idea; establish your credibility; get the audience's attention; and make a connection among you, the audience, and the occasion. The body of the speech should describe, explain, or demonstrate the main ideas through supportive secondary ideas. It should use one of the five primary speech organization patterns: chronological, topical, spatial, cause and effect, or problem and solution. The conclusion should summarize and connect main points, provide future direction, and close in a meaningful and memorable way. Use transitions to bridge ideas and bring the introduction, body, and conclusion together.

- The four types of speech delivery are impromptu, manuscript, extemporaneous, and memorized.

- If your listeners disagree with you, ask them to explain their point of view and address each issue as it is raised. If you know the answer to a question but can't remember it, stall by rephrasing the question. If you don't know an answer, say so. Promise to find out.

Business Communication Projects

1. Stand and deliver a 30-second to one-minute impromptu speech about one of the most embarrassing moments of your life (it can be this one if you like).

2. Observe a speaker at your school or in the community. Write a brief analysis about the strengths and weaknesses you observed about this speaker's delivery. Focus on the speaker's attention-getting techniques, use of spoken language and visual aids, and type of speech delivery.

3. Watch a speech on TV or find one on the Internet. Write a one-page essay that identifies the speech goal, the organization pattern (chronological, spatial, etc.), and the main and secondary ideas.

4. Outline a two-minute speech about one of the following topics:
   - If I received a million dollars, I would . . .
   - If I could live during any time in history, it would be . . .
   - If I could solve any problem in the world, I would . . .

   Then practice delivering this speech extemporaneously to friends or family.

5. Select two long paragraphs of text from a book or an article. Replace words in the paragraphs with personal pronouns and contractions to transform the text into more accessible spoken language. Practice reading the paragraphs aloud, making sure you vary your speech rate, volume, and inflection. Also practice looking up at key points during delivery to make eye contact.

6. Your local TV news is a series of different oral presentations about the day's major events. Watch tonight's news and observe how the newscasters transition from one speaker to the next. In a brief speech to the class, describe the transitions and tell whether you think they were effective.

7. If you were a participant at a business meeting, what would you want the presenter to know about you so that he or she could hold your attention and inform you effectively? Consider things such as your interests, your family relationships, your values, your financial needs, and your attitudes. List your answers. Then choose *the most important* piece of information that would help the speaker to reach you. Explain your choice.

8. Experiment with your voice by selecting an interesting paragraph from any source to read to a small group in class. Change your pitch, tone, rate, and volume. Listen to yourself and watch others' reactions. Try this in the privacy of your home as well.

Discussion Questions

1. Why is it necessary to narrow some topics down to three or four main ideas?

2. What does the occasion or event matter as long as the speech is well organized?

3. How can you get an audience involved in your speech?

4.   Why is it necessary to develop a jazzy introduction and conclusion?

5.   What are the advantages of extemporaneous speech delivery over all the other types of delivery?

6.   How might an audience required to attend a speech respond differently from an audience whose attendance was optional?

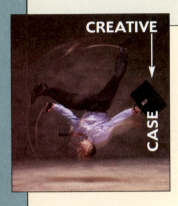

CREATIVE → CASE

Creative Case

Speaking of Health Care

PacifiCare Health Systems is one of the country's largest managed health care providers. The company provides health care for Medicare patients and various employer groups. It serves 4 million members in eight states and Guam. After careful consideration of long-range financial goals, corporate leaders decided in June 2000 that the company would close its operations in Ohio and Kentucky at the end of the year. This decision affected 54,400 members in its commercial HMO and self-funded programs, as well as 6,300 members of Secure Horizons, the company's Medicare+Choice plan. To facilitate the closing, PacifiCare entered into a transition agreement with another health care company, Anthem Blue Cross and Blue Shield. The agreement was established to ensure comparable health care coverage for those members affected by the PacifiCare departure. In an effort to ease the transition, many of the 49 PacifiCare employees in the Cincinnati, Ohio, branch would be hired by Anthem. However, realizing that the closings would affect many other constituents, PacifiCare prepared a number of written and public presentations. Hospitals, health practitioners, customers, employees, stockholders, and brokers all deserved an explanation about the closings and the transition to Anthem.

What speech would you deliver about the closing and to whom?

Consider the following questions:

1.   To which of these groups would you deliver an oral presentation? To which would you provide a written explanation?

2.   What would your speech goal be? Describe three of the most pressing concerns for each group.

3.   How would you frame the message for each group?

4.   What strategy or strategies would you use to get your desired response from each group?

SOURCE: "Pacificare Health Systems Announces Exit from Ohio and Kentucky Markets." Retrieved online (June 14, 2000). http://www.pacificare.com/corporate/news/pressrel/.

Chapter 8

Business Writing Design

Some people call Warren Buffet (a.k.a. The Sage of Omaha) a financial genius. His holding firm, Berkshire Hathaway Inc., owns large blocks of stock in many major companies, including Disney, Amazon, Coca-Cola, American Express, and the Washington Post, not to mention dozens of lesser-known businesses. His estimated personal worth is $34 billion. Buffet runs this huge enterprise with a staff of only 13.8 people (one works only four days a week). He drives his own car and has lived in the same house for decades (he purchased it for a little more than $30,000). Buffet is a strange mix of corporate mastermind and regular guy, so when he needs to communicate with his shareholders it is expected that his communication style will be equally unique. When Buffet writes Berkshire Hathaway's annual report, he starts by taking a yellow legal pad and a black felt pen and imagines one of his siblings. He knows his sibling is an intelligent, educated person who, like many, doesn't always understand the technical aspects of high-level financial dealings. He begins writing the annual report as if he were writing a letter to his sibling, explaining in simple and clear terms what the company has accomplished in the past year. He uses wit to keep readers interested: "I will tell you now that we have embraced the 21st century by entering such cutting-edge industries as brick, carpet, insulation, and paint. Try to control your excitement." He includes the reader personally in his message by referring to the captains of industry he deals with by their first names: "Ed and Jon are fourth-generation owner-managers of a business started 89 years ago in Seattle." He is also very direct when he discusses his reasons for acquiring new businesses: "We liked them; we liked the business; and we made a $1 billion cash offer on the spot." Buffet's active style and concrete descriptions draw intriguing and amusing pictures in the minds of his readers. No wonder his shareholders look forward to their Berkshire Hathaway annual report.

In a Nutshell

Thinking through the Written Design

To get a good job, get people to pay attention to your ideas, and to make an impact in your field (as Warren Buffet does), you must start working on your business writing. Employers are always looking for individuals who have excellent writing skills. Even if you get a job in finance, you will probably still be required to write well. Some companies even require applicants to supply a writing sample or ask interviewees to take a writing test. As discussed in the "In a Nutshell" feature, using the formats and stylistic devices that are common in business makes the written communication process smoother and even more impressive. It isn't just a fluke that Buffet has superior writing skills and also happens to be successful. His ability to write well has contributed significantly to the good rapport he maintains with shareholders and his overall business success. The ability to write clearly and use the tools and formats appropriate to your audience will significantly increase your chance of moving up the corporate ladder.

Warren Buffet uses a clear and down-to-earth writing style that really engages readers of his Berkshire Hathaway's annual report.
© Eric Francis/Getty Images

As discussed in Chapter 6, *verbal communication* is any communication act that includes the use of words. Written language is an important form of verbal communication because it forms a communication act that lasts. You can access and read a written document over time, which is not the case with spoken verbal communication (unless it has been recorded). For example, you may discuss the concept for a new advertising plan with your marketing team, but until the plan is memorialized in a written document, the various members of the team may remember the plan differently. The written plan helps the team execute a united marketing effort. A written document is a tangible artifact that can be referenced at any time.

Because of its more lasting nature, written communication requires both the strategies used for spoken verbal communication and additional rules. In addition to concerns such as communication style, connotative and denotative meaning, speech rules, rules concerning the use of jargon and slang, and language limitations, written communication incorporates a development process and final product that is unique.

In business, writing accounts for most of the material that memorializes actions, ideas, and contacts. Typical written documents include e-mails, memos, letters, reports, proposals, contracts, forms, manuals, and websites. Business writing should be concise, precise, and clear. A written document should strive to avoid as much communication noise as possible. Written communication noise includes mechanical mistakes in grammar, spelling, and punctuation, as well as conceptual noise, such as vagueness and unfamiliar language.

The Writing Process

1. Generating ideas and prewriting.

Before you can actually write anything, you must generate some ideas. Several options are available to help you develop your ideas, including freewriting, listing, and clustering. For each of these prewriting strategies you must determine the specific message goal required. Ask yourself these questions: What is the purpose of my message? What points should I communicate? Who is the audience? What do they already know about the subject? These questions give you a place to start prewriting.

- **Freewriting** is the process of writing all the message ideas that come into your mind nonstop without lifting your pen or pausing at the computer. When you practice freewriting, you need to write for at least 15 minutes. Write down every idea and don't worry about spelling, punctuation, or grammar—the idea is to get the ideas and thoughts out onto paper. When you finish, go over what you have written and highlight the most important and useful ideas.

- **Listing** is composing a list of all the things that need to go into the document you plan to write. You can revise this list and rearrange its order later. Listing is similar to outlining, but it is less formal and can help you generate new ideas without worrying about their hierarchy in the message. This method of prewriting is most useful when you have a series of explanations or actions to communicate.

- **Clustering** involves determining the relationships among the facets of a message. Write the primary message goal in the center of a page. Then write other ideas connected to the message goal around it and draw lines between the original idea and the new ones. Clustering is illustrated in Figure 8.1.

  To develop the ideas even further, continue this process with each of the new ideas you've written.

  You can combine all of these prewriting strategies by freewriting to generate ideas, selecting among the ideas to form a list, and then clustering certain ideas to develop connections between them.

freewriting is the process of writing all the message ideas that come into your mind nonstop without lifting your pen or pausing at the computer.

listing is composing a list of all the things that need to go into the document you plan to write.

clustering involves determining the relationships among the ideas of a message.

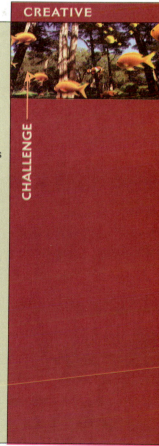

CREATIVE

CHALLENGE

What is your writing process? Some people like to read other documents before they start to write. Others require a physical workout or a particular snack to sustain them during the writing process. The elements that help to generate and support the writing process are often as important to the writer as the task at hand.

When you write a paper, what do you do to prepare yourself and generate Ideas? Do you read, do you play music, or do you prefer complete silence? Do you like to work at home, school, or at the library? Think about what makes you most comfortable when you write. Then think about why these things make you comfortable. Interview a friend and ask when, where, and how he or she writes best. Be prepared to discuss your preferences, as well as your friend's, in class.

FIGURE 8.1

Clustering

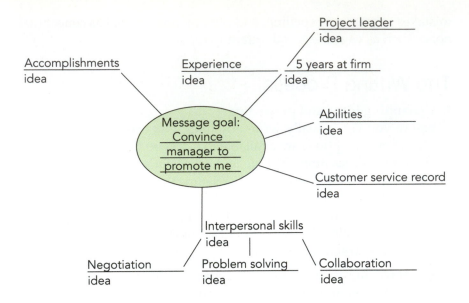

2. **Writing.**

- *Gathering information.* Once you've generated the ideas needed to communicate your message, you need to gather the information to explain and support your message goal. Sometimes the information is in the form of research, gathering data from library literature, surveys, or interviews. Often it is simply relevant phone numbers, dates, locations, or policy details. While gathering your information, keep the audience's needs in mind. Focus on specific details rather than vague assertions. The purpose of a written document is to draw a mental picture for your audience, so if you give your readers concrete data to work from, your message will be much clearer.

- *Considering strategy.* The next step is to consider your purpose: What should the message communicate and what do you want the result to be? The primary consideration is your audience: What do they *want* to know, and what do they *need* to know? These aren't always the same goals. Perhaps your manager wants to know that a project will be completed by a certain deadline, but you must respond that the necessary equipment won't arrive until three days after the deadline, delaying manufacturing by at least two weeks. The challenge of constructing the written message that will communicate this delay is to not only tell the manager that the delay is unavoidable (needs to know) but also to reassure him or her the project will be completed within a short period of time (wants to know).

  To accomplish this task, business writers have two strategies at their disposal. In the **direct strategy,** the message goal is the

direct strategy states the message goal first.

Copyright © 1998 United Feature Syndicate, Inc.

first piece of data stated. It gets right to the point. Documents that employ the direct strategy include transmissions of information, orders, claims, adjustments, replies, and recommendations. The **indirect strategy** warms up the audience with information and goodwill before delivering the message goal. An indirect strategy is used to transmit persuasive messages or relate information to which the receiver may respond ambivalently or negatively. These strategies and their applications will be described in Chapter 9.

indirect strategy warms up the audience with information and goodwill before delivering the message goal.

- *Outlining and drafting.* After you have determined which strategy is most appropriate for your message, you are ready to begin writing a first draft of the document. Don't expect perfection in your first draft; just try to include the important points and details necessary for message clarity. You can refine your ideas and language during the revision process. To create an outline from freewriting, listing, or clustering, number the sentences, listed items, or clustered ideas.

  Outlining is a useful tool to organize the ideas you generated during the brainstorming stage and incorporate them into the

What's wrong with the organizational strategy in this outline? Create a new outline that provides a more logical delivery of information and add more detail.

Writing a Report
1. Research
   a. Internet
   b. Library
2. Brainstorm
3. Freewrite
4. Create introductory materials
   a. Cover page
   b. Write letter
   c. Write summary
5. Bibliography
6. Draft
   a. Proofread each paragraph
   b. Assemble notes
   c. Choose appropriate format
7. Revise
   a. Edit
   b. Check facts and figures
   c. Add citations to text
8. Submit report.

outline a structured list of the information to be included in the message.

drafting writing the first version of text on paper or computer screen.

information you have gathered. An **outline** is a structured list of the information to be included in the message. Using the strategy you've chosen to relate the message goal, begin to form a hierarchy that conforms to the type of document you are writing: an e-mail, memo, letter, or whatever. Usual components include the introduction of an idea, clarification and explanation of the idea, supporting evidence for the idea, and the desired response of the audience to the idea.

Drafting is getting the text down on paper or computer screen in its first, bumpy version. The development of the outline helps you develop individual paragraphs. Each paragraph should contain only one idea or aspect of an idea and should be fairly short. Long paragraphs tire the eye and bore the reader. Incorporate key words from the message goal within the paragraphs to keep readers focused on the purpose of the message. Individual paragraphs should be linked by transition words or phrases that show the sequence of ideas. Transitions bridge ideas and sentences. They can be accumulative (*in addition, also, furthermore*) or relational (*on the other hand, however, in opposition*). Transitions make the document easier for readers to follow and they help you make sure that the ideas you are relating follow a logical sequence.

Accumulative	• in addition • also • furthermore • moreover • consequently • accordingly • besides • similarly • for example • therefore • thus • finally • specifically
Relational	• on the other hand • however • in opposition • in contrast • comparatively • alternatively

3. **Revising and redrafting.**

- **Revising** means *re-vision*, looking at the document as if you had never seen it before, as if you were an audience member instead of a writer. When you revise a document, check to make sure you have covered the message goal, its explanation and development, and desired response in enough detail to make it clear to your readers. Sometimes revision simply requires cutting and pasting sections or sentences to put them in a more logical order, but be prepared to delete material and write new material to fill in gaps, clarify meaning, and create a logical sequence of ideas.

  > **revising** means re-vision, looking at the document as if you had never seen it before,

  The ideal revision strategy is to set the document aside for a day or two and then read it again. If this isn't possible you may want to use one of these suggested revision strategies:

- **Re-outlining** involves writing a new outline based on the document you wrote. Compare the new outline with the old one: Have you missed any key points? Have you included information that wasn't in the original outline? Is that information necessary? Are the transitions between ideas clear? Use the comparison to refine your draft of the document.

  > **re-outlining** involves writing a new outline based on the original document you wrote.

- **Slash and burn** is a total revision tool that can save a document you are completely dissatisfied with. Take the draft and highlight in another color specific points that are the most important to the message goal. Then delete everything else and rewrite the draft using only the details you have highlighted. This is a difficult revision tool to use, but it almost always results in an extremely clear, information-packed message. The slash and burn process is illustrated in Figure 8.2.

  > **slash and burn** is a total revision strategy in which you select certain points of a document and then rewrite it using only those points from the original work.

4. **Editing and proofreading.**

   Once you are satisfied with your draft, you are ready to prepare its final version. During the editing process, look at the language and style you have chosen. Delete unnecessary words and phrases, especially excess descriptors such as *"perfectly* clear" (what would *imperfectly* clear be?) and *"end* result" (don't all results come at the end?). Make sure that you use active sentence constructions with strong verbs and concrete nouns. Look for negative words and when possible replace them with positive expressions. Examine the draft for tone, including courtesy.

FIGURE 8.2

Slash and Burn

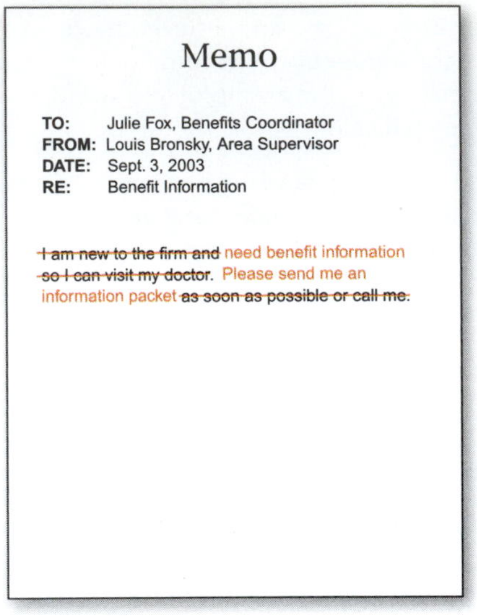

Memo

TO: Julie Fox, Benefits Coordinator
FROM: Louis Bronsky, Area Supervisor
DATE: Sept. 3, 2003
RE: Benefit Information

~~I am new to the firm and~~ need benefit information ~~so I can visit my doctor.~~ Please send me an information packet ~~as soon as possible or call me.~~

WORD ON THE WEB

Word on the Web

A good way to improve your writing is to expand your vocabulary and understand the nuances in meaning that different words have. To improve your own vocabulary, visit these websites, and select 5 new words each week. Practice using one of the words each day in your writing and speaking.

- www.better-english.com/vocabulary.htm
- www.homepages.tesco.net/~albatraining/game.htm
- www.wordexplorations.com
- www.m-w.com (Merriam-Webster site)
- www.vocabulary.com
- www.sec.gov (look for the link to the Plain English Handbook).

Proofreading presents a challenge because by this point in your writing process you are so familiar with the text that it is difficult to see errors. Use the spell-check and grammar-check features of your word-processing program, but don't rely on these tools alone. Ask another person to read over the draft to look for mistyped and misused words. Read the document aloud, and in every place you stumble, place a mark: there's probably an error there. Read it backward, because to do so enables you to look at every word. Finally, double-check figures and the spelling of names.

Business Writing Style

Most of us are trained to think of writing as an exercise in personal expression. While this is true for many disciplines, in business environments, writing is a communication act that is performed for the benefit

Business writing focuses on the audience and how they will interpret and respond to the message.
© Kaz Mori /Getty Images

of the audience. The tone of the message is audience-focused, but a message that accomplishes what is intended also benefits the writer. Before the first word is typed, the writer has to consider what the message will mean to the audience, how they may interpret it, and how they will respond. Business messages not only provide information, they also promote goodwill. Even when the message is negative, the reader should feel that the company cares about and values him or her. To accomplish this, specific business writing styles have evolved to help the writer refocus the purpose of the writing act from self-expression to public expression. Among them are the "you view," positive expression and reader benefits, active sentences and concrete language, and grammatical correctness.

The "You" View

Your document is the voice of the business for which you are writing. It is not about "I" or "me" but about your audience, the "you" addressed in the document. Think of the business document as an explanation, rather than as an expression of personal opinion. To write from a **"you" view,** focus on the interests of your readers. For example, rather than saying, "We are pleased to welcome you to our firm," you can refocus the message on the audience by cutting "we": "Welcome to our firm." People are most interested in messages that refer to them directly. Avoid first-person pronouns (*I, me, my*) as much as possible, and stress words that highlight the message's importance: what your audience will receive or what they need to do. Remember that the audience is the most important consideration in

"you" view is writing that is focused on the interests of readers.

business communication. A reader who does not perceive personal involvement with the issue clearly may not consider it worth reading or remembering.

On the other hand, when noting a mistake the reader has made or delivering any kind of negative message that might make the reader seem at fault, avoid using "you"; try to minimize the negative message using neutral language, even using passive sentence constructions if necessary (but use them sparingly).

Not "You" View	"You" View
All of our new customers will receive a 10 percent introductory discount on every item we carry.	You will receive a 10 percent introductory discount on every item in the store.
We'd like to say thanks for your generous contribution to the Sheriff's Teen Relief Fund.	Thank you for your generous contribution to the Sheriff's Teen Relief Fund.
Our operators are standing by.	Call now!
Your shipment will be sent as soon as your amended payment is received.	The order will be sent when the amended payment is received.

Positive Expression and Reader Benefits

Always emphasize what you can do over what you can't do. Instead of telling a loan applicant, "We cannot process your loan application until we receive your mother's maiden name," you can focus on the positive aspect of the message by saying, "Your loan application will be processed as soon as we receive your mother's maiden name." Search out and replace negative words such as *can't, won't, unfortunately, reject, bad, boring, unacceptable,* and *poor.* Occasionally you'll need to use a negative word. Just be sure that it doesn't dominate the message.

Notice that this strategy also features the readers' benefit. Even if the document is more for the company's benefit than the audience's (for example, gathering e-mail addresses for a company newsletter), always find a way to locate and highlight the benefits to the readers (the newsletter will keep readers informed about company policy changes and social activities).

Active Sentences and Concrete Language

Keep your reader interested by using vivid language and active sentence constructions. Although passive constructions are useful in some business writing situations, usually they slow down the reader and obscure the message. An active sentence construction makes the verb work harder. Active sentences express ideas more directly and emphatically and are less wordy. Passive sentences are less decisive, more vague, and long winded. Passive sentences often begin with phrases such as "there is," or "there are," and incorporate more *to be* verbs in them. Active sentences emphasize the person and the subject carrying out an action. In passive sentences the subject receives or is granted the action.

Passive Sentences	Active Sentences
• This policy is for the benefit of all employees.	• This policy will benefit all employees.
• The proposal is scheduled to be submitted sometime this week.	• I will submit the proposal this week.
• Smoking in the office would be in violation of company policy.	• Smoking in the office violates company policy.
• The memo was written by Dylan.	• Dylan wrote the memo.
• There are many payment options available to our clients.	• You have several payment options available.

You also need to avoid passive verb structures. Often, verbs are weakened when they are used as nouns. When a verb is used in a noun form, several other words have to be added as well, which makes the sentence longer, bulkier, and harder to read. For example, the sentence "The implementation of the new procedures led to increased production" is difficult to read and understand. The sentence "Production increased when the new procedures were implemented" is much easier to comprehend.

Passive Verb Structures	Active Verb Structures
• These concerns should be taken into consideration.	• Please consider these concerns.
• The elimination of the primary debt is our most important priority.	• Our first concern is to eliminate the primary debt.
• All winners will receive notification through the mail.	• All winners will be notified by mail.
• Several celebrities will make an appearance at the gala.	• Several celebrities will appear at the gala.
• We will hold a discussion of the new bylaws at the next stockholders' meeting.	• We will discuss the new bylaws at the next stockholders' meeting.
• Our sales staff will do everything they can to provide customers with the ultimate in accommodation.	• Our sales staff will do everything possible to accommodate customers.

CREATIVE

CHALLENGE

Go to an office or other place of business and observe the physical environment (office furniture, position of desks, number of private offices) and the people in it (number of people, their nonverbal gestures, and posture). Then write one page describing that environment and the people you saw, using only *concrete* language.

Use concrete words rather than abstract words. We are used to including vague adjectives to describe objects and situations—the woman was efficient, the building was old—but this type of language doesn't evoke an image for the reader. You want to use concrete language whenever possible, language that shows rather than merely telling. Don't just say the woman was efficient or the building was old. Describe what she did or what is wrong with the building.

Grammatical Correctness

Nothing turns readers off faster than poor grammar and sloppy punctuation. Grammatical errors make it more difficult to grasp your meaning, and make you seem unprofessional. Start by using spell-check and grammar-check, but don't rely on them; they don't catch misused words and homonyms (words that sound alike but are spelled differently), and they don't make exceptions for language style. It is vital to look carefully at the document you have composed. You may even want to read it out loud, marking the places where you stumble. Those are the places where there are probably mistakes in grammar.

Beware of "thesaurus-itis." To avoid repeating words, we often look in a thesaurus for new words to describe a concept. The problem is that each of these words has its own individual connotation. If you don't understand the connotations, you may be including meanings in the message you don't intend. For example, the statement "We pander to our customers" does not express the same meaning as "We cater to our customers." To pander means to provide gratification for vulgar desires, whereas to cater means to provide or accommodate. While you want to emphasize customer gratification, you don't want to imply that your customers are vulgar.

Commonly Misused Words

Words	Meaning	Examples
Accept	• To agree or consent	• We ask the board to *accept* the terms of the contract.
Except	• To exclude; an indication of specific conditional agreement	• We all went to lunch, *except* for Sally, who hadn't finished her report.
Advice	• A suggestion	• My *advice* is to wait until after the holidays.
Advise	• To counsel	• I asked the Senior Vice President to *advise* me.
Affect	• To influence	• The new schedule will *affect* our delivery policy.
Effect	• To cause to happen or create; the consequences of an action.	• The CEO's death had a profound *effect* on every employee in the company.

Words	Meaning	Examples
Among	• To distribute within a group of more than two	• Please distribute these brochures *among* the members of the audience.
Between	• To distribute within a group of two only	• The merger *between* Compaq and Hewlett Packard caused controversy.
Assure	• To promise	• I can *assure* you that all customer information is confidential.
Ensure	• To make certain	• The components of this motor oil will *ensure* the long life of your engine.
Insure	• To make financial guarantees	• We will *insure* the warehouse against fire, flood, and earthquake damage.
Confidant	• A trusted friend	• Mr. Takawa's administrative aide is not only his assistant, but also his *confidant*.
Confident	• Sure of one's own abilities	• I am *confident* that I can have a positive impact in your company.
Conscience	• Knowledge of right and wrong	• Moral judgments are based on the *conscience* of the individual.
Conscious	• Physically and mentally aware of one's surroundings	• She was *conscious* of the many eyes staring at her from the audience.
Elicit	• To draw out	• His questions were designed to *elicit* a strong reaction from the suspect.
Illicit	• Illegal	• The board promised the court to investigate rumors of *illicit* stock dealing.
Envelop	• To wrap around or conceal	• The warmth of their reception seemed to *envelop* the keynote speaker.
Envelope	• Paper packet in which other materials can be enclosed	• He removed the contract from its *envelope* and handed it to the negotiator.
Every day	• Each day (individual days)	• Timecards must be stamped *every day*.
Everyday	• Ordinary, mundane	• Making the bank deposit is an ordinary, *everyday* task.
Formally	• Acting in an established, conventional manner	• We will *formally* accept the proposal at the annual stockholders' meeting.
Formerly	• In the past	• The company was *formerly* known as West Electronics; now it is called Elite Electronics.
Irregardless	• INCORRECT USAGE OF REGARDLESS	• NOT APPLICABLE
Regardless	• Despite other circumstances	• The shipment must arrive by Friday, *regardless* of the union's situation.
It's	• Contraction of 'it is'	• *It's* time to consider the ethical ramifications of our decisions.
Its	• Possessive form of 'it'	• The board made *its* decision during the weekend retreat.
Lays	• To put or place	• Watch the contractor as he *lays* the new foundation of the house.
Lies	• To recline (object already placed)	• The briefcase *lies* on its side.

Words	Meaning	Examples
Loose	• Unfastened, not tightly held	• The tire came off of the car because the lug nuts were *loose*.
Lose	• To mislay	• I hope you didn't *lose* the Maucaulay account!
Manager	• Supervisor or other upper-level employee	• Your *manager* must approve all vacation time.
Manger	• Structure used to hold animal feed	• The farmer poured the cattle feed into the *manger*.
Moral	• Ethical; consideration of right and wrong	• Sometimes the *moral* decision costs businesses money, but improves their public image.
Morale	• Feelings, especially as relates to a group of people	• Employee *morale* is at an all-time high since the introduction of the profit-sharing plan.
Passed	• To move along, circulate	• Gossip is sometimes information that is *passed* along the company grapevine.
Past	• Previously; occurred at an earlier point in time	• Interest rates are lower now than they have been in the *past*.
Personal	• Pertaining to an individual	• Please keep *personal* phone calls to a minimum during working hours.
Personnel	• A member of a body of employees	• This policy change will affect *personnel* in several different departments.
Principal	• Capital sum; head individual of a group	• The *principal* shareholder controls the *principal* of the account.
Principle	• A fundamental belief or primary point	• She then stated her *principle* argument.
Propose	• To submit an idea	• Our team would like to *propose* a new marketing plan.
Purpose	• Reason, desired result	• Our *purpose* is to create more exciting campaign.
Quiet	• Peaceful, not noisy	• The boardroom suddenly became *quiet* when the losses were announced.
Quite	• Completely, totally	• The new equipment has made *quite* an improvement in our productivity.
Raise	• The act of lifting or increasing	• If you have any questions, please *raise* your hand.
Rise	• To move upward or increase in value	• Stocks should *rise* after we announce our restructuring plan.
Receipt	• Evidence of receiving payment or an object	• You may receive cash back when you return merchandise with its original *receipt*.
Recipe	• Formula	• The delicious casserole was made using an old family *recipe*.
Role	• Position within an organization	• Your *role* in the project team will be researching the problem.
Roll	• To turn; a wound object; lists of names	• Please hand me that *roll* of tape. The instructor called *roll* at the beginning of class.

Words	Meaning	Examples
Sew	• To attach using a needle and thread	• All security personnel must *sew* the official company crest onto their blue blazers.
So	• Degree (used like *therefore*)	• Please contact the personnel department *so* that they can update your records.
Sow	• To plant seed	• Before a plant can grow, one must first *sow* its seeds.
Stationary	• Unmoving	• The gym includes a *stationary* bicycle.
Stationery	• Paper writing materials	• Please use the letterhead *stationery* for all official business correspondence.
Their	• That which belongs to a person or people	• All employees must have *their* W-2 forms submitted before the end of the fiscal year.
There	• Location	• You may use the desk over *there*, next to the water cooler.
They're	• Conjunction of "they are"	• Before they can act, *they're* going to need additional funding.
To	• Direction or movement	• The clerk pointed *to* the closed door.
Too	• Also	• Could you put that in the bag, *too*?
Two	• Number	• I can provide *two* copies of all relevant documents.
Weather	• Atmospheric conditions	• The rainy *weather* delayed construction.
Whether	• Alternatives, comparatives	• We weren't sure *whether* to continue the project or not.
Who's	• Contraction of "who is"	• *Who's* going to the company picnic this year?
Whose	• Possessive of "who"	• *Whose* stapler is that?
You're	• Contraction of "you are"	• Whenever *you're* ready, we can begin the meeting.
Your	• Possessive of "you"	• Shall we take *your* car or mine?

Designing Memos and Letters

When choosing the channel for your message, think again about who your audience is. Some channels are more appropriate for particular audiences than others. Consider whether the audience is internal or external. If you are writing to someone who works for the same organization as you do, you may choose a memo or an e-mail. If the reader is someone you don't know, you may write a memo (internal) or a letter (external). In direct communication, e-mail messages are less formal and can be used for internal and external audiences. Memos and letters are more formal. Memos are generally used to communicate with people inside the organization, and letters are used to communicate with external audiences. Although much communication today is conducted through e-mail, many memos and letters still circulate within and outside the office. While these documents require the same writing process described earlier, they also require fairly specific structure. Most word-processing programs have templates for memos and letters, but the text design of a

FIGURE 8.3

**Components of Letters
and Memos**

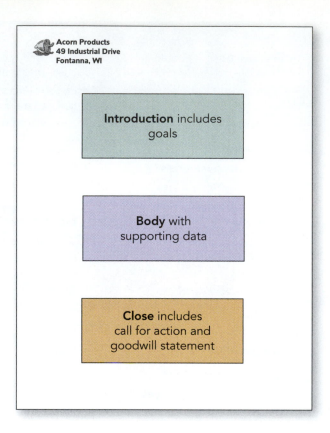

document is still up to you. Furthermore, specific formatting rules are not necessarily followed in a template.

The primary components of both letters and memos are the same: an *introduction*, which usually includes the message goal (specifics for direct and indirect structures will be discussed in Chapter 9), a *body* (supporting data for the message goal), and a *close* that incorporates a call for action with a goodwill statement. At every point in the document you should keep your audience in mind, using positive expressions and highlighting reader benefits whenever possible. Remember the "you" view! The components of letters and memos are illustrated in Figure 8.3.

Introduction

If you have good news or the information you are relating is not likely to produce a negative response from your audience, get to the point right away. In fact, in memos and letters that use a subject line (topic of message stated briefly at the beginning of your message), you can relay the message goal directly in that one phrase. Use the introduction to create a rapport with your audience, detailing the message goal as much as possible to make sure it is clear.

Body

The main body of the document should explain the reasons for the message and offer enough information to clarify its purpose. This supporting information can include rationales, facts, policies, anecdotal evidence, and statistics. Include just enough information to clarify the message goal; don't overwhelm the audience with unnecessary information. To highlight important points, you can use enhancements such as subheadings, special fonts, and bullets—but use them sparingly.

Closing

The close can contain both a call to action and a goodwill statement (a sentence that thanks your reader or demonstrates your appreciation). The call to action tells the audience exactly how to respond to the message. It includes due dates, locations, duties, and materials that the receiver should prepare ahead of time. The goodwill statement reassures the receiver that you care about his or her opinion and often requests feedback.

Formatting

The appearance or "packaging" of your business documents is extremely important. As discussed in Chapter 3, poor formatting can create noise for the reader.

Margins	• Standard margins for any document are 1 inch or 1.25 inches on all four sides. However, some documents should be 2 inches at the top to accommodate letterhead or memo forms.
Font	• Use an easy-to-read font such as Times New Roman, Courier, or Helvetica and a point size of between 10 and 14 (12-point type is the most comfortable for most people to read).
Justification	• A justified text is one in which the text is aligned evenly on left and right, as it is in textbooks or brochures. You can also use a hyphen to minimize right margin raggedness. Justified text can be difficult to read in the common sizes and fonts used in business, however, so make sure you use a ragged right margin when you write letters and memos. Ragged right margins are easier to read because of standard spacing throughout text.

Memos

Memos are an internal channel of communication. They travel within a company between and among employees. On occasion, a memo may be routed to an external recipient. Usually designed to discuss one topic only, memos communicate changes in policy, notifications, brief reports, and queries, among other things. When high-level managers want to communicate a single issue to many employees at the same

memos are an internal, written channel of communication.

Enhancements are used to draw attention to special points. Fonts, like **bold** or *italics*, are used to emphasize important information or key words. Bullets, numbers, or letters are used to present lists or specific points of interest to the reader. Revise the following message using enhancements to clarify the message goal.

MEMORANDUM

TO: All staff

FROM: Irma Brom, CEO, Finn Financial Services IB

DATE: July 27, 2003

SUBJECT: Agenda for Tuesday's staff meeting

Since there are several subjects we will need to cover during Tuesday's staff meeting, I would like everyone to prepare responses for discussion.

The key issues are customer service preparation for the holiday season, advertising campaign suggestions, new retirement plan options, and changes in stocking procedures.

When preparing your responses, try to be as specific and detailed as possible. We can't do it if we can't understand it.

The meeting will be held Tuesday at 3 P.M. in the cafeteria (Building A).

Thank you.

---

time, they often use memos, especially if the information is important or will have a widespread effect on the company. For instance, when Compaq was involved in a computer price war with Dell in 2001, chair and CEO Michael Capellas sent a memo to all employees. The memo described Compaq's plans for restructuring and acquisitions and redirected the company's focus from hardware to services and software.

The design of a memo's "guide" words varies from business to business, but all include the same components: the recipient's name, the sender, the date, and a subject line. Guide words (TO, FROM, DATE, and SUBJECT) should all be written in caps and are often bold:

TO: Marion King, CEO, Industrial Enterprises
FROM: Justin Potter, Marketing Director *JP*
DATE: March 1, 2004
SUBJECT: Productivity statistics for fourth-quarter 2003

Notice that this memo gives the titles of the receiver and sender in addition to their names. This helps the receiver determine the context in which to read the document as well as making it clear who sent it. Also note that the sender has included initials after his name. In a memo, the initials replace the signature at the end of a letter. They show that you have read and approved the contents. The subject line is also very important: It should tell the receiver exactly what to expect in the body of the document. Most people scan the subject line right away to prioritize their reading. If the subject line is unclear, the memo may go right to the bottom of the pile.

Sample Memo

MEMORANDUM

TO: Edmund Fox, Shipping Manager
FROM: Bonilla Orlov, Customer Service Representative *BO*
DATE: June 10, 2003
SUBJECT: Missing Shipment #4205

A customer called today to say that he has not received the Camelot Card series he ordered from us eight weeks ago. I tracked the order (#4205) and found that it was to be included in the UPS shipment on April 29, 2003. However, UPS does not have a tracking record of the shipment.

A reorder has been placed for the customer—#6708. I would appreciate it if you could handle the shipping procedures personally to ensure this customer receives the shipment. To rule out any potential problems within the warehouse, please track the missing order #4205 as well.

I can be reached at ext. 3333, if you need more information.

Thank you.

Letters

In the business world, letters serve a variety of purposes, among them requests, claims, adjustments, rejections, reports, sales, and goodwill responses. **Letters** are typically an external, written channel of communication (although sometimes used internally). The strategies for these types of letters will be covered in Chapter 9.

The tone of letters is usually conversational, but the degree of formality is determined by the relationship between the sender and the audience and by the purpose of the letter. To make a matter "official," information has historically been transmitted through letters. When Shooting Gallery, the independent film company that produced the hit movie *You Can Count on Me*, went bankrupt, its parent company, Itemus, wrote letters to shareholders explaining the situation. When employees

letters are typically an external, written channel of communication.

went on strike, paper manufacturer Finch, Pruyn & Co. Inc. sent letters threatening to replace them with nonunion workers. Entrepreneurs looking for funding often write letters of intent to potential funders.

If a memo or letter is longer than one page, include identifying information at the head of the following pages. Type the recipient's name, the page number, and the date, either along the top line or on consecutive lines along the left margin:

```
Justin Potter            2            March 1, 2003
```

```
Justin Potter
Page 2
March 1, 2003
```

The following table outlines the components of business letters and memos:

Letterhead stationery or sender's address	• Most companies have their own preprinted letterhead that includes all necessary contact information for the sender. If letterhead isn't available, be sure to include full contact information and keep it even with the left margin.
Date	• Type the date the letter was written 2 to 3 lines below the letterhead. Return 4 to 6 times before the recipient's address, depending on the length of the message.
Recipient's address	• Type the name and address of the receiver 4 to 6 returns below the date; enter the recipient's name (line 1), company name or position title (line 2), street address (line 3), and city, state, and zip code (line 4). Don't include the recipient's phone number and e-mail address. Return twice before the salutation (one blank space).
Salutation: terms of address	• Double-spaced below the recipient's address, enter a salutation, usually "Dear Mr. _____" or "Dear Ms. _____" Always try to send a letter to a specific person. If you cannot determine a name, however, refer to the individual's title: "Dear Production Chief" or "Dear Registrar." If there are multiple recipients, use a more general opening like "Members of the Council."
Salutation: mixed/open punctuation styles	• For mixed punctuation style, put a colon after the recipient's name on the salutation line and a comma after the complimentary close. Open punctuation uses no punctuation at all in those positions.
Subject line	• This is an optional component for a letter that helps your receiver understand immediately what the message goal is. The subject line should be typed two returns (one blank line) below the salutation in all caps. Return two times after the subject line (to leave one blank line).
Body	• The body of the message must be single spaced, with two returns (one blank space) between paragraphs. Using spaces, not to mention textual enhancements such as fonts and bullets, will also help clarify your message; keep paragraphs separate. Return two times after the last paragraph.

Complimentary close	• Letters should end with a traditional close such as "Sincerely," or "Cordially yours." Return four times after the complimentary close, leaving three blank spaces between the close and the signature lines. This space below the close allows you to sign the letter.
Addenda	• Reference initials: Return two lines after the signature lines. Use this item only if you have someone preparing your letters for you. That person should key in his or her initials like this: rje. • Enclosure notation: Use this item if you are enclosing something with the letter (receipts, contracts, copies, etc.). Return two times after reference initials. The notation should look like this: Enclosure or Enclosures; Enc. or Encs. • Courtesy copies: If you are sending a courtesy copy of the letter to another person, return two times after enclosure notation, if there is one. Key in "cc" followed by the individual's name: cc Lasha Brown. • Blind copies: Return two times after enclosure notation or cc notation, whichever one is last. Key in blind copy notation like this: bcc Mary Johnson. Use this notation if you are sending a copy to another person but you prefer that the receiver of your letter not know.

There are two common structures for business letters: full block style and modified block style. In full block style, everything in the letter begins at the left margin. In modified block style, the date and the closing lines begin in the middle, while the other components remain at the left margin. The full block example shows mixed punctuation style with a colon after the recipient's name and after the close. Open punctuation, seen in the modified block example, uses no punctuation at all in those positions. Indenting paragraphs is an option in the modified format but is not in the full block format.

Full Block Style

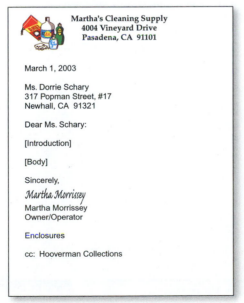

Modified Block Style

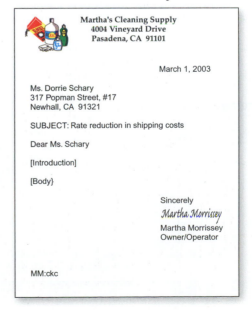

Sample Letter

Maria Lopez
833 Spring Hill Rd.
Orlando, FL 32830
(555) 882-1749

May 24, 2003

Jeffrey Pittman
Director, Orlando Chamber of Commerce
11 Adell Ave.
Orlando, FL 32830

Dear Mr. Pittman:

Like you, I love Orlando. Having lived here well over thirty years, I take pride in the community and support local businesses. It is with regret, therefore, that I must submit the following complaint against a local business.

On April 13, 2003, I brought my car to the Orlando Auto Clinic for repairs. The mechanic diagnosed the problem and recommended replacement of the car's water pump. The water pump plus the labor cost me $617.21. The invoice is attached.

A week or so later my car still leaked, so I took it to another mechanic based on recommendations from friends. When the mechanic at Crescent Street Garage inspected the car, he noticed the water pump was not new. Documentation of this inspection is also attached. The Orlando Auto Clinic clearly charged me for parts and services that I never received.

I tried to contact the owner of the Orlando Auto Clinic, but he would not speak with me on the phone and refused to see me when I visited his garage last week. My desire is to recover the $617.21 from the Orlando Auto Clinic, register a formal complaint against this business, and make sure other citizens of Orlando do not experience the problem I did.

I can be reached at 882-1749 if you have any questions or require additional information.

I appreciate your assistance with this matter.

Sincerely,

Maria Lopez

Maria Lopez

Enc.

Designing E-Mail Messages

Communication Style

Is **e-mail** considered written or oral communication? It is written communication. While e-mail messages combine conversation conventions and written conventions, they are still writing. Although we aren't speaking face-to-face with our receiver, we tend to feel much more comfortable communicating through e-mail. We know the receiver will see the message almost instantaneously and will probably respond much more quickly than he or she would to a letter. Yet you are typing words into a computer that will be read, rather than heard, by a receiver. While some people think the usual style for business e-mail is more relaxed than the style for letters or memos, it is important to remember that your e-mail represents your company electronically the same way letterhead stationery represents your company on paper. The traditional standards for writing correctness and conciseness still apply to e-mail.

Privacy Issues

Did you know that when you delete an e-mail message it isn't really gone? Some companies retain e-mails on their servers for up to 10 years. Companies also have the right to monitor e-mail. In 1997 only 15 percent of American businesses monitored employee e-mail, but by 2001 nearly half (46 percent) reported monitoring it on a regular basis. Employees have been reprimanded, suspended, or even fired for using e-mail inappropriately. In September 2000, Dow Chemical Company fired 24 employees and reprimanded 235 others in Freeport, Texas, for sending offensive e-mails from their office computers. The New York Times Co. fired 20 employees for the same reason, and the investment firm Edward Jones & Co. fired 19 employees, allowed one to resign, and gave warnings to 41 others following an investigation into inappropriate e-mail use at the office. Although questions about privacy issues have been raised, in every case so far the courts have sided with the business over the individual, stating that since the employee's computer is company property, any content on its hard drive or on the server that it is connected to is also company property.

What this means is that you should never send private or confidential information in an e-mail message. Such information includes

e-mail is an internal and external written channel of communication that transmits messages over the Internet.

CREATIVE CHALLENGE

One of the most interesting things about e-mail is that you can contact anyone at anytime, from a mailroom clerk to the CEO of the corporation. This means that the lines of communication that were standard in an old-style hierarchical corporate structure are now considerably more complex, reflecting the flattened corporate structure of many modern businesses.

The next question is, should the lines of communication be completely wide open, or should we consider some contacts inappropriate? Just because you *can* e-mail the president of the company, *should* you? Write an e-mail to your professor that examines this issue.

Take a look at the following e-mail message. The author is writing to another member of a promotional planning committee he has known for a few weeks. The recipient was unable to attend one of the meetings and asked that he send her an update. Look at the list of e-mail do's and don'ts. Has this author committed any netiquette sins? Write a paragraph describing the mistakes you find and explain why you think this writer made them.

Hi,

I just came from the committee meeting, Karen Jones led the discussion. i was excited about finalizing the plan for the new newsletter. Karen is going to submit the first draft next week.

BTW, i also saw Jack Anderson. He kept watching the door expecting u to arrive. Of course he asked about u:). i wished u could'v made it to the meeting. We really could'v benefited from your expertise when we talked about layout and design.

I've attached my notes.

Bob

credit card numbers, home phone numbers and addresses, Social Security numbers, medical information, and anything else you don't want the whole world to know. Avoid sending or forwarding jokes and nonbusiness-related website links, and *never* send an e-mail message that uses obscene language or threatens someone.

Constructing the Message

According to some researchers, people typically spend 30 minutes writing a letter but spend only 5 minutes writing an e-mail message. Since many e-mails are very brief, five minutes may be plenty of time to write a response. E-mail is often used to convey necessary information to people both internal and external to the organization. When this is the case, brief e-mails need to be constructed in a manner that lets recipients understand them quickly and easily.

Finally, always proofread your messages carefully before you send them! E-mail may be an informal communication channel, but it needs to be as correct as any other document. If your readers can't trust your spelling and grammar, they'll wonder whether they can trust the content of your message.

Suggested Format for E-Mail Messages

Subject line	Use the subject line to give the reader a clue about the content of your message. Use key words such as "question about employee survey" or "meeting agenda revisions" to clarify the purpose of your message.
Courtesy copies	To send your message to more than one person, use the "cc" or "copy to" feature of your e-mail software. If you are sending the message to a long list of people you may want to use the "blind courtesy copy" feature. It will send the message to all on the list, but their names and e-mail addresses won't be visible on your readers' screens.
Salutation	Type your addressee's full name and title unless he or she is a friend, contact, or co-worker you know well. If you leave out a salutation, the message may seem cold and impersonal.

Direct and Indirect Communication Strategies

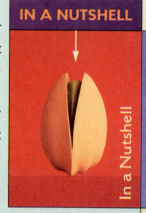

Rosalia Mtumbo has interviewed four candidates for product development manager. Candidate 1 is fresh out of college. He is enthusiastic and gave a wonderful presentation, but he lacks the experience the position requires. Candidate 2 has plenty of experience but is very direct and aggressive. Rosalia knows the vice president for product development quite well: He is an emotional and intuitive person. She suspects that he would be uncomfortable working with her. Candidate 3 may have been a good prospect, but his nervousness during the interview made it hard to determine whether he could do the job or not. Candidate 4 was also nervous, but her low-key manner and the creative ideas she came up with on the spur of the moment make Rosalia feel she's the best one for the job.

Now comes the really hard part. Rosalia has to write letters to each interviewee explaining her company's decision. She thinks about the personality of each candidate carefully and uses those thoughts to plan her strategy for each letter. She decides to use a direct strategy to candidate 4. After all, she got the job! Rosalia makes this letter sound as warm and welcoming as possible; she wants this shy woman to understand how excited the company is about having her on board. Rosalia is also very clear about the details of the employment process. She ends the letter with complete contact information for all the people candidate 4 will need to talk to and reiterates her welcoming message.

The other three letters need to incorporate an indirect strategy. Although the three candidates are being refused, she wants them to retain goodwill toward the company. She begins by thanking them for their interviews and personalizes each letter by adding details from each interview: comments they shared or interesting points in their presentations, for example. She also notes their individual strengths. She moves into a brief discussion of the requirements for the management position and then quickly but clearly tells them that the position has gone to another candidate. She closes the letters by reiterating how impressive all the candidates were and how much she enjoyed the opportunity to meet them all.

Why Use Direct or Indirect Communication Strategies?

Rosalia realized that some messages can get to the point directly like the acceptance letter she wrote to the candidate chosen for the product development position. But other messages require more explanation before getting to the point. Like the refusal messages described in the "In a Nutshell" feature, candidates who are not selected for a job often need information first before the negative news is delivered.

Direct and indirect strategies allow us to communicate clearly and efficiently, with greater attention to the purpose of the message. The **direct communication strategy** allows you to deliver an important point quickly, usually in the beginning of a message. The **indirect communication strategy** delays an important point until you have had a chance to provide explanation. We need both these strategies because the audience is the communicator's first consideration. If the information you will be providing is positive, the receiver will likely want it framed in a clear and straightforward manner. But if the information is negative or unpleasant, the receiver may need you to ease into the main idea of your message by first providing an explanation or some preliminary words that can help to prepare him or her for the news.

Suppose you have requested a refund on a sweater that you received as a gift. If the store gives you the refund, you don't care why; you just take the money. If the store refuses to give you a refund, however, you

direct communication strategy involves stating important points quickly, usually in the beginning of a message.

indirect communication strategy delays important points until after they have been explained.

WORD ON THE WEB

Word on the Web

Why do you have to write letters and memos at all, when there are a variety of free and low-cost documents available on the Internet? The truth is that many of the materials available on the Internet are sufficient. However, most lack the detail and personal attention that a truly effective communication process requires. Take a look at a selection of materials available and try to determine how meaningful they would be to an audience.

- www.homebusinessonline.com
- www.businessnation.com/library/forms/
- www.careerlab.com/letters
- www.101samplebusinessletters.com
- www.money-at-home.com/business.htm
- www.formsquru.com

And just for fun, take a look at some communication bloopers:
- www.business-letters.co.uk/howlers.htm

© Alan Schein Photography/CORBIS

© Lester Lefkowitz/CORBIS

Sometimes the direct approach is best when the message is positive and you want to get straight to the point. However, when the message is negative, the indirect approach may be a better strategy.

generally want to know why. Furthermore, if the store manager bluntly says no to your request without an explanation, you probably won't buy any sweaters at that store in the future.

In other words, if the news is good, the direct strategy is often the best course. If the news is bad, the indirect strategy can work better. Both are efficient ways to communicate a message, and both help to maintain the audience's comfort and goodwill.

Direct Strategy

When Should I Use the Direct Strategy?

Use the direct strategy when the message you are delivering is likely to please your audience, or if the message is neutral.

Positive: Congratulations. Your promotion has been approved by the Human Resources Department. Please contact Linda Garcia at extension 6788 for your new office assignment and other details about your new position. Welcome aboard.

Neutral: Starting March 1, please enter all UPS pickup requests on Form #488. This form will allow our shipping department to plan budgets in greater detail and with greater accuracy.

Whether the news is positive or neutral, the direct strategy states the main idea of the message immediately.

Components of Direct Messages

The main components of direct messages are the main idea; the justification, explanation, and details; and the courtesy close.

Main idea	Good news	The filing cabinet you ordered is on its way.
	Neutral message	Open enrollment month is January.
Justification, explanation, and details	Good news	Your order was shipped 10/31/02 by UPS and should arrive in 3 to 5 days.
	Neutral message	If you would like to change your health care coverage, please visit the benefits office.
Courtesy close	Good news	Thank you for your order.
	Neutral message	For more information call x5555. A benefits agent will be happy to assist you.

Direct, Not Rude

One of the dangers of the direct strategy is bluntness. Although good written and oral business communication style uses a minimal number of words for maximal effect, do not sacrifice politeness and diplomacy. Minimal politeness means saying "please" and "thank you," but a truly effective business communicator remembers this even if the message is something the audience is looking forward to hearing. It should be expressed in terms of the audience's benefits and should use positive expressions ("you will enjoy" rather than negative expressions "you won't be disappointed").

Sometimes you may need to offer criticism of a plan or situation. When this is the case, remember to use empathy. Put yourself in your audience's place: How would you react to a similar criticism? Be honest and clear, but be gentle and understanding when making observations that may offend your audience.

Types of Direct Messages

requests for information or action include the request at the very beginning of the message followed by a detailed explanation of its purpose.

Requests for information or action should include the request at the very beginning of the message. After the request, give a detailed explanation of its purpose. Finish the message with a deadline for response, details for contacting you, and a goodwill statement.

Writing a good direct (not to mention indirect) message requires more than strategy—it also requires clarity. Read the following direct informational e-mail and try to figure out what it means. Then rewrite it with an emphasis on clarity.

To: Full Staff
From: Bill Corey
Subject: Online Expense Report Forms

To clarify, the e-mail sent yesterday referring to the new online expense report forms was only intended to provide information and direction to those employees wanting to get in early on this new technology for those who want to soar with the eagles rather than plod with the cattle.

For those employees not inclined to use the online expense reports yet, please be informed that manually submitted expense reports are still accepted by the A/P Department. Further information will be forthcoming later this year concerning the formal rollout and related training.

As stated in the previous e-mail, the online expense report is now available to all employees (but not required) so those who want to use this application should complete the form "Request for Online Expense Report Access," which you can find in the Online Library under "Forms/Human Resources."

This will give you access to navigate within the online expense report application, where the online expense reports are located.

Sample Request for Information

MEMORANDUM

TO: Jamaal Clark, Marketing Director
FROM: Tammy Jones, Personnel Associate TJ
DATE: January 12, 2003
SUBJECT: Personnel file for Janelle Thompson

Please send the following information via interoffice mail to the Human Resources office:

- Personnel file for Janelle Thompson
- Most recent evaluation form for Ms. Thompson, signed by all concerned parties
- Attendance, vacation, and sick day records for Ms. Thompson

Ms. Thompson has applied for a promotion to Service Coordinator, and Human Resources needs these items before it can make its recommendations to Mrs. Antrim. Please forward these documents to Human Resources by Monday, and contact x5767 if you have any questions. Thank you for your timely response to this request.

claims and positive adjustments also begin immediately with the claim or the requested adjustment followed by support for the claim, explanations, and evidence that prove its validity.

Claims and positive adjustments also begin immediately with the claim or the requested adjustment. Support the claim with explanations and evidence that prove its validity. The close should ask for a response by a particular date and give a confident goodwill message that anticipates a favorable outcome. Be sure to include any supporting documents or enclosures that your audience may need to process your claim. It is vital that you state any claim using positive language. Remember: You want the audience to do as you ask, and you can draw more flies with honey than you can with vinegar.

Sample Requested Adjustment

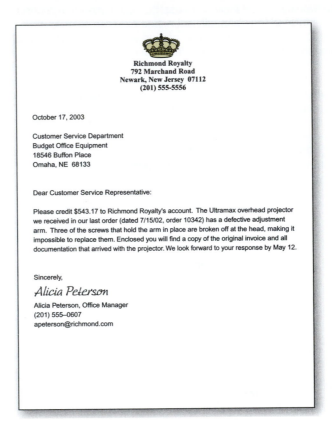

Richmond Royalty
792 Marchand Road
Newark, New Jersey 07112
(201) 555-5556

October 17, 2003

Customer Service Department
Budget Office Equipment
18546 Buffon Place
Omaha, NE 68133

Dear Customer Service Representative:

Please credit $543.17 to Richmond Royalty's account. The Ultramax overhead projector we received in our last order (dated 7/15/02, order 10342) has a defective adjustment arm. Three of the screws that hold the arm in place are broken off at the head, making it impossible to replace them. Enclosed you will find a copy of the original invoice and all documentation that arrived with the projector. We look forward to your response by May 12.

Sincerely,

Alicia Peterson

Alicia Peterson, Office Manager
(201) 555–0607
apeterson@richmond.com

directives and policy statements are messages about company changes that are stated directly, followed by an explanation and reader benefits.

Directives and policy statements that you expect little resistance to can use the direct strategy as well. State the new or changed directive or policy, and then explain in terms of reader benefits the need for the statement. Again, end the message on a positive note that shows appreciation for the consideration of the staff.

MEMORANDUM

TO: Communications department staff
FROM: Linda Peters, Director *LP*
DATE: Supply procedure
SUBJECT: January 12, 2003

When you enter the supply cabinet and notice that we are low on any item, please make a note of it on the new mini dry-erase board installed on the inside door of the cabinet. We all remember our recent envelope fiasco, and to avoid any last-minute (and very expensive) visits to the local stationery store, we have installed the board so Marc will know exactly what to purchase from our online discount distributor. Who knows? Maybe we'll save enough money to buy a new couch for the lounge!

Thanks everybody, for helping out.

Sample Policy Statement

goodwill and social messages recognize the contributions individuals have made to the company and include the main purpose followed by specifics concerning the event or purpose.

Goodwill and social messages recognize the contributions individuals have made to the company and foster positive relationships in the workplace. Such messages include thank-you letters, celebratory messages, and condolences. In all such messages, mention the main purpose at the beginning and move into specifics concerning the event or purpose. The key point in goodwill and social messages is to keep the focus on the audience rather than yourself or your company. End your message with a reassurance of your continued respect for the audience.

CREATIVE

Break into groups with your class colleagues to design three greeting cards (include graphics too, if you like). The cards should be designed for a business to use for thank-you notes, congratulatory purposes, or invitations. (See Chapter 17 for designing visuals.)

CHALLENGE

Sample Goodwill Message

Goodwill and social messages recognize the efforts people have made on behalf of the company and focus praise or attention on them.
© V.C.L./Getty Images

EM Elan Marketing, Inc.
1200 Vineyard Drive
Albany, NY 12205

March 1, 2003

Mary Day, President
Daisy Mae Catering
243 State Street
Albany, NY 12205

Dear Ms. Day:

Thank you for the wonderful job you did last week at our welcome reception for our new partner, the Sunimoto Corporation. Your company, Daisy Mae Catering, provided us with such delicious food (the crab dip was marvelous) and beautiful decorations that we look forward to many more events planned and executed by your fine organization. Please contact us if you ever require a reference. We will certainly contact you the next time we throw a party.

Thank you again for such a terrific experience.

Sincerely,

Ima Eater

Ima Eater
Executive Director

Most *negative* or *"bad news" messages* use the indirect strategy, but in some cases the direct strategy is more appropriate. When you know the audience well, know that your audience prefers things up front, are concerned that the bad news may be missed, or don't expect it to be damaging, write a direct message.

Sample Negative Message

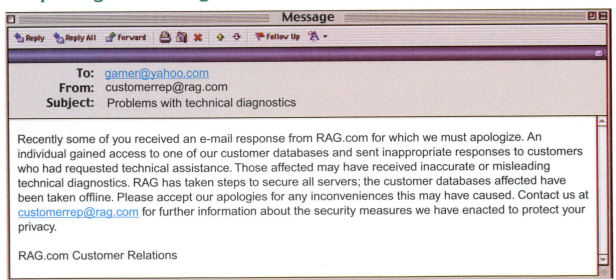

To: gamer@yahoo.com
From: customerrep@rag.com
Subject: Problems with technical diagnostics

Recently some of you received an e-mail response from RAG.com for which we must apologize. An individual gained access to one of our customer databases and sent inappropriate responses to customers who had requested technical assistance. Those affected may have received inaccurate or misleading technical diagnostics. RAG has taken steps to secure all servers; the customer databases affected have been taken offline. Please accept our apologies for any inconveniences this may have caused. Contact us at customerrep@rag.com for further information about the security measures we have enacted to protect your privacy.

RAG.com Customer Relations

Indirect Strategy

When Should I Use the Indirect Strategy?

When you have to refuse or deny a request or send any message that you believe may make your audience uncomfortable or angry, use the indirect strategy. An indirect message allows you to explain the circumstances surrounding the negative news before delivering it. Preparing your readers in advance increases the chance that they will retain goodwill for your company. It also increases the likelihood that they will accept the message, and not drag out an exchange of messages.

Sample Indirect Strategy

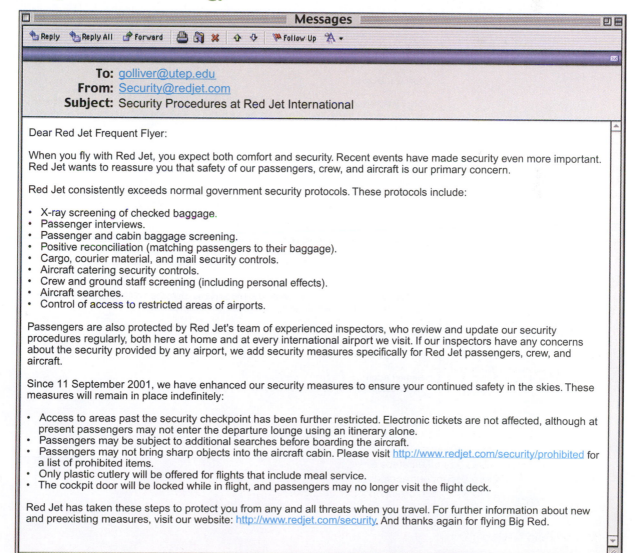

Messages

🔺 Reply   🔺 Reply All   📄 Forward   🖨 📑 ✖ ⬆ ⬇   ⚑ Follow Up   🔤 ▾

To: golliver@utep.edu
From: Security@redjet.com
Subject: Security Procedures at Red Jet International

Dear Red Jet Frequent Flyer:

When you fly with Red Jet, you expect both comfort and security. Recent events have made security even more important. Red Jet wants to reassure you that safety of our passengers, crew, and aircraft is our primary concern.

Red Jet consistently exceeds normal government security protocols. These protocols include:

- X-ray screening of checked baggage.
- Passenger interviews.
- Passenger and cabin baggage screening.
- Positive reconciliation (matching passengers to their baggage).
- Cargo, courier material, and mail security controls.
- Aircraft catering security controls.
- Crew and ground staff screening (including personal effects).
- Aircraft searches.
- Control of access to restricted areas of airports.

Passengers are also protected by Red Jet's team of experienced inspectors, who review and update our security procedures regularly, both here at home and at every international airport we visit. If our inspectors have any concerns about the security provided by any airport, we add security measures specifically for Red Jet passengers, crew, and aircraft.

Since 11 September 2001, we have enhanced our security measures to ensure your continued safety in the skies. These measures will remain in place indefinitely:

- Access to areas past the security checkpoint has been further restricted. Electronic tickets are not affected, although at present passengers may not enter the departure lounge using an itinerary alone.
- Passengers may be subject to additional searches before boarding the aircraft.
- Passengers may not bring sharp objects into the aircraft cabin. Please visit http://www.redjet.com/security/prohibited for a list of prohibited items.
- Only plastic cutlery will be offered for flights that include meal service.
- The cockpit door will be locked while in flight, and passengers may no longer visit the flight deck.

Red Jet has taken these steps to protect you from any and all threats when you travel. For further information about new and preexisting measures, visit our website: http://www.redjet.com/security. And thanks again for flying Big Red.

The indirect strategy also works well for persuasive messages for the same reason. If audience members understand why they should accept your proposal before they hear it, they will be more likely to do what you want. In this case, however, you want to encourage further communication with the audience. For more on persuasion and persuasive messages, see Chapter 6 and the section on proposals in Chapter 10.

Sample Persuasive Message

Monarch Medical Billing Services, Inc.
8989 Old Bookman Road
Boulder, CO 80307

March 5, 2003

Bethany Jackson, Accounts Manager
St. Timothy's Hospital
Boston, MA 02111

Dear Ms. Jackson:

Every hospital requires dedicated personnel: doctors who serve, nurses who care. In addition to the medical staff, every hospital rests on the shoulders of a support staff, whose untiring efforts keep the hospital running. One of the most frustrating and time-consuming tasks for staff members is the billing process. That changes with Monarch Medical Billing Services.

We have the personnel and the systems to conduct your billing process quickly, accurately, and efficiently. Our staff includes insurance specialists, who have unique insight into the workings of the insurance industry. We also employ a battery of talented accountants, who use state-of-the-art technology to ensure prompt assessing of moneys owed and money due. Finally, we have a customer care department that truly cares about the needs of both patients and medical professionals.

Through Monarch Medical, you can reduce administrative problems and increase your bottom line. We'll handle all billing issues, process them, post them, and deposit the total into your accounts, working closely with your own staff. You'll know where you stand when you need to know, and so will your patients.

To find out more about Monarch Medical Billing Services, call us at 1–800–555–6778 or return the enclosed card and we will promptly send an information packet.

Sincerely,

Herbert Acton

Herbert Acton
New Accounts Manager, Monarch Medical Billing Services, Inc.

Enc.

Components of Negative Indirect Messages

1. Begin your indirect message with a **buffer.** Buffers include good news, points of agreement, statements of appreciation, assurance of cooperation, and recognition of the audience's point of view. If you have any good news to share as part of your message, state it right away.

2. Follow the buffer with the **reasons** for the refusal. Reasons may include facts, policies, and reader benefits. Explain the situation as fully as possible, using enough detail to make it clear to your audience.

3. Now, deliver the **bad news.** Bad news should never be stated bluntly and should not be highlighted unless you are concerned that the audience may miss it. In fact, bad news can be implied, especially if the reasons given make it clear that the request is impossible to grant. Otherwise, embed the bad news in the middle of a paragraph or sentence to minimize it.

4. Finish the message with a **positive close** that looks forward to a continuing relationship with the audience. A positive close may contain a goodwill statement or offer alternatives. It may also be an opportunity for resale.

Problems with Negative Indirect Messages

- *Should I apologize?* In some circumstances, as in the message from RAG.com customer relations, an apology may be acceptable, but in most cases a negative message should avoid apologies. When you apologize, you are automatically admitting liability for the problem under discussion. This may lead to further problems down the line, including loss of professional reputation for your company or legal action. Apologize only if directed to by a superior or legal advisor, or if it is company policy to apologize under those specific circumstances.

- *Should I anticipate problems?* It is tempting to encourage goodwill by anticipating other problems a customer or client may have when they lodge complaints. Resist this temptation. By anticipating new problems, you could imply that the problem is more far-reaching than the original complaint.

- *Should I encourage further communication?* Many messages end with a sentence like "If you have any further questions, please contact me at . . ." When designing a negative message, however, you want to explain the situation and forestall further communication on that topic. A better strategy is to end the message with a reassurance to the reader that the problem has been considered carefully and the response you have provided is truly in his or her best interest.

---

buffers are statements added early in a message and include good news, points of agreement, statements of appreciation, assurance of cooperation, and recognition of the audience's point of view.

reasons follow buffers in a message and include facts, policies, and reader benefits.

bad news should never be stated bluntly, can be implied, and should not be highlighted unless you are concerned that the audience may miss it.

positive close follows the main points and reasons offered in a message to provide a goodwill statement or alternatives.

Revise the following memo using the indirect message strategy.

MEMORANDUM

TO: All Staff
FROM: Morris Vanther, Plant Manager
DATE: 7/27/03
SUBJECT: Smoking on the Landing

Please do not smoke on the outside stair landing near Human Resources. There is an air-uptake vent at that location that delivers smoke directly into the building in violation of state smoking laws.

We all know that even secondhand smoke can be harmful. Many of our staff members have said that they are particularly sensitive to cigarette smoke and suffer allergic reactions when exposed to it. Several employees in areas served by the air-uptake vent on the landing have complained of red eyes, runny noses, and sneezing, especially after coffee breaks and lunch hours.

The laws on smoking are clear. Because cigarettes contain so many toxic chemicals, they must be used only in designated areas, such as the rear patio on the ground floor and the parking lot. Anyone found in violation of the law will be subject to a fine levied by the state and disciplinary action by the company.

Other problems to avoid include sounding unsure, sounding selfish, blaming the receiver, and using fillers:

- To avoid *sounding unsure,* do your research before you create your message. Ask questions and check policies before responding. Understanding the situation fully will give you the confident voice you need to relay your message with professional authority.

- Even though the reasons for negative news are sometimes more in the best interests of the business than the audience, *sounding selfish* will do more harm than good. If you frame your message with the company as the most important party, it is more likely to annoy your audience than placate them. Focus on how the reasons you provide are for the recipient's benefit and leave out the sections of policy or procedure that benefit the company alone.

- Never *blame* anyone in a bad news message. While it is important to be empathetic with your audience, blaming an employee or policy will only cause more problems. If you blame another employee you run the risk of being accused of slander, which may have legal repercussions, and if you blame company policy you undermine the company's authority and damage its reputation (not to mention your own).

- Avoid using *fillers.* As we discussed in Chapter 8, the best business writing uses concrete language and employs active, rather than passive, voice. Fillers slow audience reception of a message and may obscure its meaning.

Types of Negative Indirect Messages

Refusals/denials are the most common negative messages that businesses deliver on a regular basis. You cannot always grant a refund to a customer, fill an order, or agree to a plan. Creating a turndown message that the audience will accept is a fundamental part of business communication. Rely on positive language, full explanations, and reader benefits to support refusals and denials.

Collections messages can be tricky to compose because, if there is no response to early indirect notices, your messages must become increasingly direct. Never accuse the audience of anything criminal or negligent. Instead, focus on the real purpose of the message, which is to collect what belongs to the company. Use positive language in early messages and move to neutral language if the collections process continues.

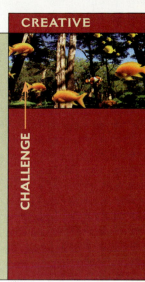

CREATIVE

CHALLENGE

Write four paragraphs representing four separate requests for payment on a credit card bill for $467. The first should be indirect and the last should be direct; the two middle paragraphs should move slowly from indirect to direct approaches. What problems do you encounter as you move from the indirect strategy to the direct strategy? How does your language change? Trade papers with a classmate and comment on one another's successes and failures in the four paragraphs.

refusals/denials are the most common negative messages.

Sample Refusal

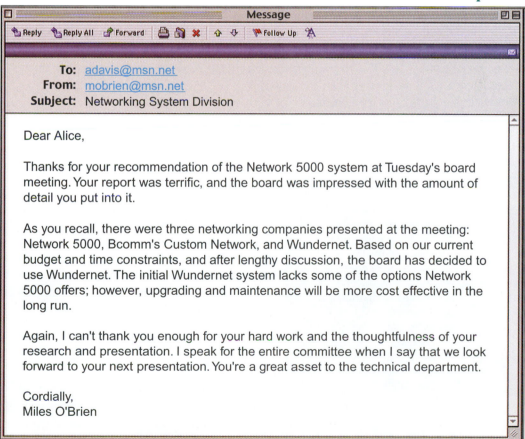

Message

Reply | Reply All | Forward | 🖨 📄 ✖ ⬆ ⬇ | Follow Up

To: adavis@msn.net
From: mobrien@msn.net
Subject: Networking System Division

Dear Alice,

Thanks for your recommendation of the Network 5000 system at Tuesday's board meeting. Your report was terrific, and the board was impressed with the amount of detail you put into it.

As you recall, there were three networking companies presented at the meeting: Network 5000, Bcomm's Custom Network, and Wundernet. Based on our current budget and time constraints, and after lengthy discussion, the board has decided to use Wundernet. The initial Wundernet system lacks some of the options Network 5000 offers; however, upgrading and maintenance will be more cost effective in the long run.

Again, I can't thank you enough for your hard work and the thoughtfulness of your research and presentation. I speak for the entire committee when I say that we look forward to your next presentation. You're a great asset to the technical department.

Cordially,
Miles O'Brien

Sample Collection

Imperial Valley Preowned Auto Sales • 467 Imperial Highway • San Diego, CA 92120 •
www.ivpas.com

Ms. Cherry Aames
2157 Sunnyslope Dr.
San Diego, CA 92127

March 29, 2003

Re: Balance: $6,769.57
    Account: QV9088623

Dear Ms. Aames:

This is a reminder that your payment of $200.00 for your 2000 Acura Integra was overdue
as of February 20, 2003. Please make this payment. Our finance department is available
from 8 A.M. to 9 P.M., Monday through Saturday; please contact us if you need to
restructure your loan or have any problems with repayment. If you have already mailed
your check, thank you for your payment.

Sincerely,

Jack Gatz

Jack Gatz, Accounts Receivable
jgatz@ivpas.com
(415) 555–6782

collections are messages that focus on recovering that which belongs to the company.

social refusals focus on the honor you feel at being offered an invitation to speak or attend an event for which you are unavailable.

Social refusals should reflect the honor you feel at being offered an invitation to speak or attend an event. Invitations are a sign of respect; emphasize your pleasure in your response and, when possible, suggest alternatives. Provide details mentioned in the invitation, such as the full name of the inviting organization, date of the engagement, and topic, to show your audience that you paid serious attention to the invitation.

Rose Heidsel, CPA, Partner
Heidsel, Ross, and Mulroney, Accountants
85 Stillwell Boulevard, Suite 6777
Chicago, IL 60628

John Doggitt, President
Rotary Club
515 Jonesboro Drive
Elmhurst, IL 60126

October 15, 2003

Dear Mr. Doggitt:

Your invitation for me to speak on Community Service Awareness at the annual Elmhurst Rotary Club Holiday Banquet is a great honor. Thank you for thinking of me. I am pleased to know that my commitment to community service has made a difference in our town.

The banquet is planned for December 12, 2003. Unfortunately, I am attending the CPAs of America Convention in Fort Worth, Texas, from December 10 through 15. I am truly disappointed that this conflict in my schedule will keep me from speaking at your event.

If you would permit me to make a suggestion, I know my partner, Derrick Mulroney, is available and would enjoy an opportunity to speak to the Rotarians. Derrick was one of the co-founders of Heidsel, Ross, and Mulroney, and has been active in the Chicago Rotary Club for 15 years. This past year he was chair of a committee that raised more than $350,000 for reading programs in the Chicago Public School System. I think that his story would be perfect for your organization at this very special time of year. He can be contacted at (312) 555–6473.

Wishing you all the best,

Rose Heidsel

Rose Heidsel

Types of Persuasive Indirect Messages

Sales messages are perhaps the most common persuasive messages. These can be very creative, especially in the attention stage of the message. Consider your target audience carefully when planning your sales messages, and tailor the message to match their interests. If you are looking for people to invest in a retirement community, for example, focus on security and comfort to appeal to older consumers.

sales messages are perhaps the most common persuasive messages and can be very creative and appealing.

Sample Sales Message

Green Grove Estates
18 Simplicity Street
Arden, DE 19810
(302) 555–1332

Mr. & Mrs. Evan Wakim
20117 East Post Road
Trenton, NJ 08608

23 September 2003

Dear Mr. & Mrs. Wakim:

Look around yourself right now. What do you see? A comfortable home, pictures of loved ones on the walls, keepsakes from a lifetime of hard work? Now imagine strolling among shady green trees, surrounded by gently rolling hills and the sounds of birds singing. You stop in front of a lovely house, which lies at the edge of a glittering pond of fish. You wonder what's inside that house.

That house is full of pictures of your loved ones on the walls and keepsakes from a lifetime of hard work.

It's your new Green Grove Estates Home.

Green Grove Estates is a new, state-of-the-art secure retirement community, located in the heart of Arden, Delaware. Close to transportation, medical facilities, transportation, and shopping, Green Grove Estates is a gated community where you can meet new people, or just enjoy the quiet beauty of your home and its surroundings.

Every home has been designed with the needs of its residents in mind. Amenities include:

- 24-hour security. Bonded guards protect you and your property, both at the front gate and along the quiet streets of your home.
- Clubhouse. Join your neighbors at the community clubhouse for a meal, or sign up for recreational or educational activities offered throughout the year.
- Wheelchair accessibility. You and your guests can visit any part of the Green Grove community without problems, and your home can also accommodate any special needs necessary.
- Emergency medical care. An on-site nurse is available for any eventuality that may arise.

Green Grove Homes are affordable and available immediately. Financing is available for every situation. Call us today to arrange a visit to your beautiful new home: **(302) 555–1332.**

Sincerely,

Thomas Maggs

Thomas Maggs
Real Estate Agent
Green Grove Estates

Policy and directive changes are often persuasive. If you must change a policy and employees will support the change only if they believe it is for their benefit, a persuasive indirect strategy is far more effective than a direct strategy (which may alienate the employees, since people often resist change). Focus on how the changes will improve the employees' work experience or protect them in the long run.

Sample Policy Directive

> **MEMORANDUM**
>
> **TO:** Blitzfield Mall Merchants
> **FROM:** Blitzfield Mall Security Force
> **DATE:** April 17, 2003
> **SUBJECT:** New Parking Policy
>
> Parking in the mall parking lot has been difficult for us all for the past year. The recent community revitalization project that the city of Blitzfield began last January is bringing in hundreds of new shoppers, but it has led to a serious parking problem. Construction of the new parking facility is complete and it will be opened on May 1. This facility should alleviate some the problems we've encountered.
>
> Blitzfield Mall is reserving this parking structure for merchants and their employees exclusively. Attached to this memo is a parking form. Please enter the names, positions, and phone numbers of all employees on this form and return to the Security Office. Next week, numbered parking stickers will be issued to all employees. These stickers entitle your employees to park in a secure, well-lit place. Because we have reserved the structure for the exclusive use of Blitzfield employees, we cannot allow parking in other areas of the lot. These areas are for customers only, and any stickered car will be towed. For employees who are hesitant to walk through the open areas of the lot to the structure, security will be happy to escort them to their cars. Just call x4567 and ask for Escort Service.
>
> All of us here at Blitzfield Mall Security believe that this policy will create a much more stress free and safe environment. Thank you for your cooperation.

Fund-raising messages need to be crafted carefully because the benefit to the audience from supporting your cause is often intangible. For example, a company would need a clear incentive to donate money to a battered women's shelter. Although it would be doing something good for people in need, the company needs to understand why this project is important enough on both a companywide and community-wide scale to support.

Sample Fund Raising Message

City of Angels Women's Shelter

185 North Alvarado Boulevard
Los Angeles, CA 90016
(213) 555–9254

Imogen Butler, Corporate Giving Manager
Opulate Industries
14266 Industrial Way
Los Angeles, CA 90016

May 18, 2003

Dear Ms. Butler:

Hundreds of women are battered every day. Husbands beat some of these women, boyfriends beat others, but all are in serious danger. Some even die. Many women flee abusive homes with their children, often finding their only refuge in the cold, dirty streets of the city.

These are women who find themselves in impossible situations. When they find themselves homeless, their abilities go to waste. They become targets for increased violence, including robbery and rape. Their children may become gang members, trying to procure some level of safety for themselves and their families.

When these terrible things occur, it is a tragedy for the entire community. Crime increases, along with the security costs for businesses in the area. Property values fall. And the talents of these women go untapped. All because they have nowhere to go when they leave an unsafe home.

What does this have to do with Opulate Industries?

Opulate Industries has a rich history of community involvement. Your interest in the community has led to refurbishing unsafe playgrounds. Your caring has fed the homeless during the holidays. Now you have the opportunity to help the defenseless women in our city.

City of Angels Women's Shelter is currently seeking operating funds to keep its doors open. We are a nonprofit, privately funded organization serving the Los Angeles area. Many companies in our area have already provided funding for our shelter, including Stella's Fashions, Misrahi Custom Metalworks, and Olivares Import/Export. All donations are completely tax deductible.

Help us keep battered women safe and warm, with their children, and with available social services. Their contributions to our community will be immense.

Sincerely,

Lori Stringer

Lori Stringer, Founder and Manager
City of Angels Women's Shelter
(213) 555–8888

Goals of Persuasive Indirect Messages

Goal	Purpose	Example
Generate attention (hook)	Grab the audience's attention; encourage them to listen to the rest.	Would you like to make $1,000 a month from the comfort of your own home?
Arouse interest	Maintain audience's anticipation.	What would you do with an extra $1,000? Take a trip? Buy a new computer? Go on a wild shopping spree?
Build desire	Plant a sense of need in the audience; relate to reader benefits.	Think about it. You could pay off your bills and plan for retirement without leaving the house. And no special training or skills are required!
Push for action	Tell the audience what to do to gain the benefits mentioned earlier.	Just call our toll-free number now to get started on your new career surfing the Web.

STRATEGIES

Strategies

1. Before you write, consider your relationship with your audience. Often you can determine whether you should be direct or indirect in your approach to a message if you understand how your audience perceives you: in a position of authority or as someone making a request.

2. For a really effective message, research your readers at the same time you research your message. If you can communicate with your audience using details that apply to their situation, they will be more likely to accept your message.

3. Check to see whether your message could be misinterpreted. Imagine that you are very angry when you reread the message, or that you are in a hurry. Make sure that the most important points cannot be misunderstood.

4. After your first draft, look carefully at the first paragraph. Do the sentences use concrete language? Do they use active voice? Even in an indirect message, meaningless phrases and "businessese" slow the communication and tend to annoy the audience.

5. Include adequate transitions between paragraphs or sections of the document. It is easy to forget that the message should flow, especially when each section has a particular function.

6. Keep it short. The longer the message, the more opportunities to make a mistake or muddy your meaning.

7. Use only as much detail as necessary. While you want to be sure your readers feel they are getting a satisfactory explanation of events, you don't want to overwhelm them with data that may only serve to confuse them.

8. If you are delivering bad news, state it only once, and state it clearly. Repeating bad news emphasizes the negativity of the message.

9. Focus on what you can do rather than on what you can't do.

10. Remember that what your audience members want and what they need aren't always the same thing. Tell them what they need to know, but make it sound like what they want to hear.

Summary

- Many messages are designed using direct or indirect strategies. The direct strategy delivers the vital points of the communication early in the message. The indirect strategy delivers the vital points of the communication after a delay to explain the reasons for the bad news.

- The goal of both the direct and indirect strategies is to maintain the audience's comfort and goodwill.

- If the message being delivered is something that the audience will appreciate or if it will not have a major impact on the audience, the direct strategy is appropriate.

- The components of the direct strategy are:
  a. Main idea—the purpose of the communication.
  b. Justification, explanation, and details—expansion of the communication.
  c. Courtesy close—a polite ending that invites further interaction.

- Use simple, clear language, but at the same time be polite and diplomatic. Avoid being too blunt.

- The direct strategy is often used for requests for information or action, claims, positive adjustments, directives, policy statements, and goodwill and social messages.

- On occasion the direct strategy is used for negative messages, especially if the audience may miss the bad news otherwise or if it is not directly damaging to the audience.

- If the message being delivered may upset the audience or if persuasion is required before the audience will accept it, the indirect strategy is usually a better design choice.

- The components of negative indirect messages are:
  a. A buffer, which provides good news, points of agreement, and recognition of the audience's position.

b. Reasons for the refusal or request.

c. The refusal or request itself (the bad news).

d. A positive close that looks forward to a continuing relationship with the audience.

- When designing indirect messages, avoid apologizing, anticipating future problems, and encouraging further discussion on the topic. Conduct enough research before composing the message to avoid sounding unsure. Focus on the reasons that are for the audience's benefit to avoid sounding selfish. Above all, don't blame the audience.

- The indirect strategy is usually applied to communications that incorporate refusals, denials, and collections.

- The goals of persuasive indirect messages are to:

a. Get attention with a hook that interests the audience enough to keep it listening to or reading the entire message.

b. Arouse interest, which builds the audience's sense of anticipation.

c. Arouse desire, which creates in the audience a sense of need.

d. Push for action by explaining how the audience can fulfill the need introduced in the desire stage.

- The persuasive indirect strategy is commonly used for sales messages, policy and directive changes, and fund-raising messages.

Business Communication Projects

1. Which strategy, direct or indirect, would be more appropriate for the following communications?

- A memo to all staff members describing new health plan options.

- An e-mail inquiry into the details of a computer warranty.

- A letter thanking a job applicant for his/her interest, although the position has gone to another.

- A letter to a customer regarding two months of missing credit card payments.

- A memo to employees discussing a change in personal holiday time accrual.

2. You own the Gold Nut Café, which has long been a favorite lunch spot for the employees of Metzger Ltd., whose offices are on the fifth floor of the same building. Because they are patrons you have decided to offer Metzger employees a 10 percent discount on all lunch specials starting April 1. To get the discount, employees must show their Metzger ID card when paying the bill. The discount is nontransferable (it is available to Metzger employees only, no guests) and applies only to lunch specials, not other standard menu items. Lunch specials are available from 11 A.M. to 2 P.M.,

Monday through Friday. Write a memo to the management and staff of Metzger informing them of this offer.

3. You work in the credit department of MacGillicuddy's Department Store. A new file has crossed your desk. Christopher Parker has a good credit history at MacGillicuddy's; he has paid at least the minimum on his credit account every month for the last five years. However, recently MacGillicuddy's hasn't received any payment from him at all. The current balance on his card is $2,467, and no new purchases have been made for six months. The monthly interest rate on the card is 15 percent. There is a $25 per month penalty for late or missing payments. If Parker is having trouble making payments he should contact you; maybe you could work out a temporary solution. Still, you must notify him that payments are now past due. Write a series of three letters requesting updated payments on his account. The letters should be polite, but as time progresses each letter should become stronger in tone. If Parker does not pay the bill after three notifications, the matter will be turned over to a collection agency, and his overall credit rating will be damaged.

    - Letter 1—his payments are three months past due (current balance $2,467).
    - Letter 2—his payments are four months past due.
    - Letter 3—his payments are five months past due.

4. The Persimmon Personal Assistant is such a popular PDA that it has been impossible to keep it in stock. You continue to receive requests, however. The manufacturer is out of stock as well; in fact, the current model of the Persimmon is no longer being produced because a newer version will be introduced in two months. If you had to write refusals to the orders you've already received, what strategy would you use for the messages to the following customers? Why would you use that strategy? In groups of three, write explanations for the approaches you would use to write refusals to the following audiences:

    - A friend or someone you know very well.
    - A business acquaintance or regular customer.
    - A total stranger.

5. Compare these two messages:

    a. We cannot process your request for membership until we have received complete contact information. Please confirm your address and work phone number with our Membership Team so we can complete the registration process.

    b. Our Membership Team is ready to welcome you to our exclusive club. To ensure the timely processing of your request for membership we'd like to confirm a couple of items from your application. Please take a few moments out of your busy schedule to let us know what your current address and work phone number are. As soon as we get these minor details out of the way you can start enjoying the benefits of membership.

What are the strengths and weaknesses of these messages? Write a third message that combines the strengths of these two examples and eliminates their weaknesses.

6. Revise the following direct message to reflect greater audience awareness.

A new productivity guideline is being enacted for the benefit of both workers and management. The productivity guideline should bring workers' expectations up to the level of management's standards. In accordance with management's desire to increase productivity by 5 percent by the end of the second fiscal quarter, overtime will be offered to all Level 5 through 8 line workers. Overtime will be granted on a first-come, first-served basis. No worker will be allowed to work more than 80 hours in a single week.

7. A client has made a series of service requests. Some of them you can accommodate, but others you cannot. Ms. Prinn is the manager of an apartment complex that has several vacancies. She would like your company, Fix It Rite, to do some work in these apartments. She is requesting that you change the cupboard doors and countertops in the kitchens of three apartments, retile the bathrooms in two apartments, and paint all four apartments. You can paint the four apartments, but your tiling person is on vacation for two weeks. You have the personnel and materials to install the kitchen cupboards but would have to purchase new countertops if Prinn does not already have them or a vendor for them. Write a letter to Ms. Esther Prinn, Manager, Wellstone Apartments, 245 Westlake Boulevard #1, Los Angeles, CA 90086 that responds to her requests.

8. As a recent graduate from your college, the Young Business Professionals Club has asked you to speak about your academic experience and professional career at its annual awards dinner next month. You'd love to do it, but you'll be out of town on business. You'd like to do it another time, however, especially if the club could give you more notice. Write a social refusal e-mail to the Young Business Professionals Club.

Discussion Questions

1. What is the difference between a message using a direct strategy and one using an indirect strategy?
2. Why are two separate communication strategies necessary?
3. When is a direct strategy appropriate for a message?

4. In what circumstances would it be appropriate to use a direct strategy for a potentially negative message?

5. What are the most common uses of indirect communication strategies?

6. Are there any situations in which a positive message could be delivered using an indirect strategy? Explain.

7. What are the pitfalls common to indirect messages? How can they be avoided?

8. Should you ever apologize in a message?

9. How do persuasive indirect messages differ from negative indirect messages?

10. Which kind of message strategy do you think is more common in the workplace: direct or indirect?

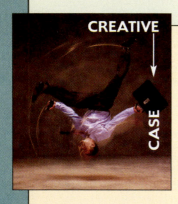

Creative Case

Shooting Gallery Takes a Hit

In January 2001, Canadian software developer and venture firm Itemus acquired Shooting Gallery Inc., a U.S. film and media company, for $56 million dollars. Shooting Gallery was responsible for independent film hits such as the Academy Award winning *Sling Blade* (1996) and Academy Award-nominated *You Can Count on Me* (2000). Shooting Gallery's projected revenue for the year 2000 was $24 million. It also did groundbreaking work in interactive television, digital content development, and digital animation. Itemus believed that with this acquisition it would be able to compete globally with emergent trends on the Internet: broadband and enhanced/interactive television.

Shooting Gallery was best known for its independent films, which were produced on an extremely tight budget. Founded in 1991 with a mere $7,000, Shooting Gallery specialized in developing and distributing unusual, quality films that the traditional Hollywood system ignored. Shooting Gallery also earned the Crain's Small Business Award and the Ernst & Young Entrepreneur of the Year award when it opened the Gun for Hire production facility in New York. In the late 1990s Shooting Gallery built up its Internet and production services divisions.

By September 2001, Itemus had filed for bankruptcy protection. Although Itemus president Jim Tobin cited poor market conditions and bad business decisions, many fingers pointed to Shooting Gallery as the real reason for Itemus's problems. Rather than earning $24 million in revenue in 2000, Shooting Gallery had actually lost $40 million that year. During its brief owner-

"Sling Blade is virtuoso writing, acting and directing."
-*Roger Ebert, Chicago Sun-Times*

Sometimes a hero comes from the most unlikely place.

Sling Blade

THE TRIUMPHANT NEW FILM FROM BILLY BOB THORNTON

© The Everett Collection

ship, Itemus lost more than $70 million on Shooting Gallery–related projects and subsidiaries.

What happened? During Itemus's due diligence process, Shooting Gallery's books were examined carefully and major discrepancies were found. For example, the 1999 Shooting Gallery audit by Reznick, Fedder & Silverman showed that the company had a net loss of $2 million that year. When Itemus audited the same period using Deloitte & Touche, it found that Shooting Gallery had a net loss of $23 million in 1999.

What should Itemus president Jim Tobin tell his shareholders?

Some questions to consider:

1. Which of the details given above would be appropriate to provide to shareholders?

2. Is it appropriate for Itemus to blame Shooting Gallery for the problems?

3. What do the shareholders need to know? What do they want to hear?

4. Should Tobin use a direct or indirect strategy to communicate this bad news?

SOURCES: Naraine, R. (2001). "Shooting Gallery to File Bankruptcy." Retrieved December 18, 2001, from www.internetnews.com/bus_news/article/0,,3_804811,00.html; Saunders, C. (2001). "Itemus to Acquire U. S. Rich Media firm." Retrieved December 18, 2001, from www.internetnews.com/IAR/print/0,,12_500041,00.html.

Chapter 10

chapter 10

The Business of Reports: Informal and Formal Report Writing

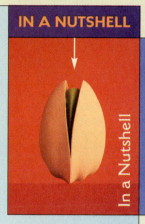

IN A NUTSHELL

In a Nutshell

Because people who become homeless need more permanent shelters than those offered by various charities, an architect in Baltimore decided to take action. He knew that geodesic domes, a cheap, strong, and easy-to-build form of housing, could be built for the homeless in an empty lot. There were several things he had to take into consideration first: a workforce, a designer, a location, materials, cash, and a building permit. People without shelter who were interested in this opportunity could provide the workforce, building their homes with their own hands, and the architect would donate his services as designer and foreperson of the construction site. For the location, materials, and cash, he would have to apply to others for assistance. He went online and looked at various foundations that provided funds for homeless assistance. Government sources, he found, placed many restrictions and conditions on awarded funds, so he chose to look at private foundations instead. When he found a few whose giving patterns matched his needs, he sent proposals to them. He also sent proposals to construction materials companies, encouraging them to donate materials or sell them at cost, noting that they could use the project as a tax deduction. One of his regular contacts believed in his project, too, and provided materials at cost. His contact even offered to help supervise the site. The architect tracked down the owners of three lots that had lain empty for years and put in bids. One of his bids was taken. Now he had everything but the permit. To build this project he would need approval from the city—the last proposal he had to write. By the next winter, a number of homeless Baltimoreans had domed roofs over their heads.

The Business of Reports

From housing projects such as the geodesic dome in Baltimore to educational programs at your college or university, thousands of reports, in a variety of formats, are generated and used to communicate in businesses and organizations throughout the world. Architecture firms such as the one discussed in our "In a Nutshell" feature as well as countless other organizations routinely produce proposals and reports. Without being consciously aware of it, each of us receives and generates some sort of report virtually every day. Common reports include:

- A company's annual report to its stockholders.
- A local school district's quarterly newsletter to residents in the district about the activities in the schools.
- A memo from the human resources office informing employees of a new dental plan.
- Minutes of the last monthly business meeting.
- A sales report listing monthly projections.
- This week's list of top 40 songs.

All of these are reports, which can be a highly effective and compelling form of communication. Preparing reports requires effective writing, analytical, and research skills, which may also include finding and appealing to potential funding sources. This chapter will discuss what reports and proposals are designed to do and strategies to compose and organize them.

What Is a Report?

report an oral presentation or written business document that provides information, requests funding or approval, analyzes company or market data, or makes recommendations for innovation and change.

Business professionals send and receive reports to communicate various company information. A **report** is an oral presentation or written business document that provides information, requests funding or approval, analyzes company or market data, or makes recommendations for innovation and change. The variety, length, and format of reports can range from brief memos and e-mails to volumes of pages. While some reports (for example, sales presentations) are delivered orally, most are written. Written reports are a management tool for both problem solving and decision making. They also provide a permanent record that can be accessed, read, and revised over time.

Styles of Reports

The style of report you use depends on the need for the report and on your audience. Reports are either informal or formal in style. An **informal report** style is more common. Informal reports are usually brief (one to five pages). They use personal pronouns (*I*, *we,* and *you*) and a direct style. They are often presented in memo or letter format. **Formal reports** tend to be longer and are constructed in a prescribed format. They generally use a more impersonal style, avoiding the use of contractions and first- or second-person pronouns. There can be a fine line between a formal and an informal report, depending on its tone, style, and audience. All reports, whether formal or informal, should be grammatically correct, well organized, clear, and interesting to read.

informal reports are usually brief and use personal pronouns (I, we, and you) and a direct style.

formal reports are long and are constructed in a prescribed format.

Purposes of Reports

In general, written and oral reports share information or ideas and offer solutions or options for problem solving and decision making. A report performs one or more of three basic functions: providing information, analyzing data, and persuading an audience.

Provide information	• Managers must stay informed about the status of projects and the operation of the company. The quality and efficiency of the operation is recorded through information on project or task progress, compliance, and even personal expenses. An informational report provides objective statistical data or facts. The writer does not attempt to interpret or draw any conclusions about the information presented.
Analyze data and information	• Analytical reports make sense of the data presented in the context of the situation. For example, an analytical mutual fund report may offer an analysis including percentage of historical return gains and losses, consumer cost of the fund, stocks the fund owns, turnover ratio (how often stocks are traded), and the fund manager's track record. This information is interpreted to determine whether a particular mutual fund is performing well or not. Analytical reports may suggest possible interpretations of information or may offer solutions to problems.
Persuade	• Reports that recommend or call to action usually propose a direction or problem solution and tend to be persuasive messages. Proposals and business plans often try to motivate the audience to do something such as initiate change, expand operations, provide funding, or volunteer support. Persuasive reports interpret data that have been collected and suggest a course of action.

Provide Information

An **informational report** provides objective statistical data or facts. Equipment order, sales figure, or profit information reports are just a few examples. The writer does not attempt to interpret or draw any conclusions about the information presented. For example in July 2001, Yahoo! reported an 87 percent drop in quarterly earnings. Up to that point, Yahoo! provided free Internet services, relying on advertising for 80 percent

informational reports provide objective statistical data or facts. Analysis of the data is usually not included.

of its revenue. The informational report, which Yahoo! produced immediately after the drop in earnings, stated that it was working on joint ventures with companies such as Sony and would begin to offer premium services (GeoCities Pro) for $8.95 a month. This report did not justify the change in business strategy or offer any analysis about the state of Internet advertising. The report merely stated what Yahoo! was going to do.

Similarly, at IBM, CEO Lou Gerstner requires managers to send him periodic activity reports about clients' global services projects, which account for nearly half of the company's revenue growth. The activity reports let Gerstner carefully monitor the progress of customer projects and the development of relationships between IBM employees and their clients. While the reports are purely informational, they help to ensure customer satisfaction.

The following table describes several types of informational reports:

Memos	• Memos are the most common type of report for internal communication in an organization. A memo is written by one employee and transmitted to one or more other employees. Memos are generally brief and are primarily used to convey general information within an organization or a specific department: announcing a new recycling policy, responding to an inquiry, praising a department's performance, or inviting employees to a retirement party, for example.
Progress or interim reports	• Progress reports monitor and describe in narrative form the status of continuing projects or tasks. They tell what work has been accomplished, any delays or problems encountered, and what future activities will be undertaken, including how long these activities will take to complete. Progress reports can be used for an internal audience (for example, reporting progress to management) or an external business audience (a contractor's report to a client on the status of a building project).
Compliance reports	• Compliance reports are used by organizations that work with or are regulated by local, state, or federal government agencies. Governments often require periodic reports that provide specific information and data to prove that the organization doing business with a government agency is conforming to certain standards and regulations. Compliance reports often concern equal employment hiring practices, the number of special populations being served in a community program, occupational safety, or income tax returns.
Annual reports	• Annual reports are a type of compliance report that corporations and many other organizations, including educational institutions and many nonprofits, publish yearly. Annual reports describe the achievements and developments of an organization over the course of a given year. They can also serve as valuable public relations tools for key audiences.
Policy and procedure reports	• Policy and procedure reports communicate broad organizational goals, guidelines, and methods. They outline and explain company policy—such as "All documents for external publication must have the corporate logo and be consistent with the overall mission of the institution." They also set the terms for policies: "Documents must be reviewed by the Office of Public Relations prior to printing and distribution." Finally, they must state the actions necessary to comply with the policy: "All documents must first be approved by the department supervisor, then forwarded with a 'Request for Printing' form to the Office of Public Relations for review."
Minutes	• Minutes are reports that detail the actions and discussions in a business meeting. They serve as the official, often public, record of a meeting. Minutes of a meeting also provide notes on what transpired as a refresher for those in attendance and useful information for those who could not attend.

Sample Annual Report

TRIFOOD GROUP INCORPORATED	1019 MOON DRIVE	FOSTER CITY, CA 94404

January 16, 2001

Ms. Marielena D'Onofrio
Shareholder
1427 State Street
Washington, D.C. 20011

Dear Ms. D'Onofrio:

Subject: Trifood Shareholder's Annual Report, Year End 2000

As you know, the Internet market is wide open, both in terms of risks and opportunities. This year, Trifood's greatest achievement was purchasing DowntownGrocer.com, adding its dedicated customer base and facilities to Trifood's rapidly expanding nationwide presence. However, Trifood faces serious challenges in the coming year. This report will acquaint you with what we are planning for the near future.

This Year's Advances
Trifood exists within a market that changes quickly. In addition to the acquisition of DowntownGrocer, we are currently investing in refinement and modification of computer servers, networks, software, and power sources to maintain our competitive edge in the Internet marketplace. We have also continued to expand our network of warehouses and equipment.

The Picture Right Now
This year, Trifood has incurred $294.7 million in net losses. This includes a restructuring charge of $40.8 million related to the DowntownGrocer purchase. Trifood's facilities are currently operating below their designed capacity. We have adjusted the production capacity of our facilities to suit the market demand in individual areas to reduce waste. Currently, Trifood is unable to issue dividends to shareholders, nor can it assure shareholders that dividends will be paid in the future unless major changes are implemented immediately.

Goals for the Coming Year
We must expand our efforts in other areas to take advantage of the resources we now possess. In order to grow, we must:

- Increase our customer base.
- Execute an effective marketing strategy and strengthen our business plan.
- Improve efficiency and productivity in all facility and delivery operations.
- Attract and retain dedicated employees.

The purchase of DowtownGrocer will assist us in realizing these goals. We are currently incorporating the DowntownGrocer system into our own structure.

Your commitment to Trifood is crucial to its success. All young companies face difficulties in their early years, and we are no exception. We realize that some of the information in this report will cause concern, but would like to assure you that Trifood understands where the problems with our organization lie and is taking steps to address them. Your continued support is invaluable.

Sincerely,

Tanya J. Noonan

Tanya J. Noonan
Chair of the Board of Directors

analytical reports offer interpretations of information or solutions to problems.

justification reports offer support for an action or determine the potential benefit of an action based on a series of reasons.

feasibility study a type of justification report that includes detailed research, analysis, and a judgment on the potential success or failure of an action.

Analyze or Justify

Analytical reports offer interpretations of information or solutions to problems. They provide evidence that supports a decision, action, or problem solution. One example of an analytical report is Active-MEDIA Research's "Real Numbers behind the Online Business-to-Business Industry," which summarizes trends in online business-to-business interactions, provides hard (quantifiable) and soft (anecdotal) data on Internet businesses, and makes projections about how businesses will operate on the Internet in the near future. It not only relates information but also analyzes the state of the industry.

Justification reports offer support for an action or determine the potential benefit of an action based on a series of reasons. They recommend or substantiate changes. A justification report might recommend the purchase of a new software package to improve the company's statistical analysis capability, for example, or a new marketing approach based on recent consumer surveys and sales figures.

In September 1999, the Hotel Employees and Restaurant Employees International Union took over Chicago Local 1, a union representing approximately 14,000 maids, servers, and bartenders in the Chicago area. The international union then had to prepare a report that justified the takeover for a hearing before the Labor Department. In that report, the international union cited Local 1's budget problems, its failure to explain expenditures to the membership and keep accurate records of the membership and dues, and its failure to prepare and file accurate financial reports. The international union had to take over Local 1, the report said, to maintain the respectability of the union as a whole.

A **feasibility study** is a form of justification report that includes detailed research, analysis, and a judgment on the potential success or failure of an action.

CREATIVE

CHALLENGE

You are a human resources manager at a midsize manufacturing company. Overall employee morale is good, but some employees have had problems with management lately. They are complaining that managers don't listen to their suggestions, and that the best jobs always go to the same people. They're beginning to feel that they have no personal investment in the company's development. The vice president for human resources asks you to write a justification report that provides support for the new 360-degree feedback evaluation program your department is scheduled to implement throughout the company. With 360-degree feedback, employees evaluate their supervisors' performance in terms of delegation of task assignments, organization, communication, and overall supervisory skills. Divide into pairs to write this justification report. Include at least three reasons the 360-degree program may prove beneficial. Also include at least one citation in the body of your report from a direct or indirect source.

Sample Justification Report

TEA
Zurich, Switzerland

MEMORANDUM

TO: Jack O'Connor, CEO
FROM: Michelle Encarnacion, David Parnell, and Steve McMath, Policy Analysts
DATE: 03/15/03
SUBJECT: Justification of proposed policy changes

At your request, we have outlined benefits of implementing new policies involving resignation and pension plans to increase employee and investor confidence.

Problem Statement

The problems facing Technical Engineering Associates (TEA) must be addressed if the company wants to regain its once prestigious reputation. Top management resignations, Enron comparisons, and extravagant pension plans have damaged the company image and increased public distrust in what was one of Europe's model businesses. By changing resignation policies and reviewing pension plans, TEA could boost the company image, encourage investments, and define relationships with all levels of employees.

Background

TEA's current stock price has dropped another 7 percent as a result of several top-level resignations within the company. These resignations have contributed to the rise in employee and investor distrust. Some stockholders are liquidating in anticipation of further financial difficulties. Enron comparisons still loom because the current pension plan issues have not been resolved.

Benefits of New Resignation Policy

By implementing a new policy in which resignations must be disclosed to the company at least two weeks in advance for workers, and at least four weeks for middle and upper management, TEA could protect itself from surprise resignations. Proper notification would help the company prepare for the loss of that employee and begin searching for a replacement. A short memo indicating this policy would quickly inform all employees of resignation procedures. All employees will benefit from this policy because it prevents people from having to unexpectedly take on another employee's workload.

Benefits of New Pension Plans

TEA employees should benefit from the company's pension plans. But review of these contracts should commence immediately for TEA to protect itself from bad publicity. Spending nonexistent funds on large pension plans has already hurt TEA's image. By reviewing employees' contracts by department, TEA can demonstrate to its workers and investors that their futures are important to the company, and that all pensions are being monitored and updated. A company accountant could be assigned to review employee pension plans and make sure that the worker and the company agree as to contract issues. Although this could be expensive and time consuming, it would save TEA from another contract dispute. It would also show investors that TEA is keeping track of how funds are being distributed.

Recommendations

By implementing these two policies, TEA will address its problems at the source. Employees will be protected from unnecessary workloads and pension recalls. Investors will feel that the company is planning ahead in terms of fluctuating employee numbers and in the distribution and regulation of company funds. If employees feel that TEA is concerned with their needs as well as the company's, and investors see that TEA is looking at future concerns and remedies, the company will succeed in boosting its image and restoring its reputation.

Sample Feasibility Study

FEASIBILITY OF DAVRON CORP. INVESTING IN TEA

By: Michelle Encarnacion, David Parnell, and Steve McMath

PURPOSE STATEMENT

The purpose of this report is to determine the financial feasibility of investing in the Zurich-based company Technical Engineering Associates (TEA). The report will analyze TEA's current financial stability based on problems associated with executive resignations, excessive pension plans, declining stock prices, and Enron comparisons.

BACKGROUND

In 1988, Swiss-based Technical Services Company joined German-based Engineering Associates in one of Europe's largest mergers (Jones, 2002). Jacques Gaudemir, a Swedish industrialist and TEA's former CEO, was instrumental in founding and launching what would be a multi-million dollar company in 1988 (McBride, 2002). Gaudemir ran this European company like a United States business. All employees were expected to speak English, and all monetary records were in dollars. Following its inception, TEA made a profit for 13 years (Little, 2002). The business goal of TEA is to provide advanced technological products and systems, servicing industrial and commercial companies. By integrating technology and equipment, TEA successfully became a leader in Europe's engineering field (NYSE, 2001). But that prestige has recently come under attack from many angles. TEA's current problems could sink the company.

STOCKS PLUMMETED, GAUDEMIR RESIGNED WITH MILLIONS IN PENSION BENEFITS

In 2001 the company's stocks hit an all-time low of just over $6 a share, compared to almost $19 a share five months earlier (Rosen, 2002). Between 2000 and 2001, TEA laid off nearly 4,000 workers (TEA, 2001). Stock prices for the end of February 2002 are almost exactly where they were at the company's lowest point, October 2001. There are rumors that TEA will be selling part of its Financial Services division in hopes of replenishing funds, but no confirmations have yet been made (Channel 9 News, 2002). Having resigned as CEO at TEA in 1996, Gaudemir remained chairman of the company until the latter part of 2001, when he suddenly resigned from that position as well (Jones, 2002). His resignation occurred only one day after TEA's loss was announced (McBride, 2002). Gaudemir's resignation lowered already sinking TEA stocks by another 7 percent (Jones, 2002).

TEA is trying to collect some of the $69 million Gaudemir received in pension benefits. Gaudemir has still not indicated if he will agree to any return of those funds (Michaels, Morgan, and Hall, 2002). He claims the pension benefits were approved in his contract while the company says they were not (CNN, 2002). Even Gaudemir's successor, Niegel Habel, is being asked to return unspecified amounts of his pension, even though after resigning, he received roughly half of what Gaudemir did (Jones, 2002). The benefits provided to these top executives are not the basis of the financial problems TEA is experiencing. But discrepancies between company profits and pension plans have led many to believe that TEA may be hiding something.

When Gaudemir resigned suddenly during TEA's worst year and still received a considerable pension, stockholders and the public in general began to see eerie similarities between TEA and the U.S. energy giant Enron. The collapse of Enron was the biggest bankruptcy case in U.S. history, leaving many employees with nonexistent retirement funds. Because of the suspicious nature of Gaudemir's resignation and pension benefits, investors have become wary, even though no illegal accounting activities have been reported (Jones, 2002). TEA blames not only Enron comparisons, but also the worldwide economic slowdown for its faltering reputation. Rumored internal investigations have not helped TEA improve its image.

CONCLUSIONS AND RECOMMENDATIONS

Because of the problems TEA is experiencing, investing in this company would be unwise. If the company begins a rigorous change in current policy, the potential for a positive return on investment may improve. By writing new policies concerning resignations and pension plans, TEA could protect itself from future problems. New policies may also strengthen its image as a company that takes care of its employees, instead of giving large pensions but asking for some of them back later. If investors see that TEA is changing policies to meet company needs, the reliability of the company may increase, which will encourage financial support. However, unless these changes are implemented, TEA will not be a positive investment for the Davron Corp.

REFERENCES

BBC News. (2002, February 13). TEA launches pension probe. *BBC News* [Online]. Available: http://news.bbc.co.uk/hi/english/business/newsid_1817000/1817798.stm [2002, February 27].

CNN. (2002, March 3). Former TEA head under fire. *CNN* [Online]. Available: http://europe.cnn.com/2002/BUSINESS/02/26/barnevik/index.html [2002, March 5).

Jones, S. (2002, January 24). TEA: Problems loom at a Swiss giant. *BusinessWeek* [Online]. Available: http://www.businessweek.com/bwdaily/dnflash/feb2002/nf20020214_7463.htm [2002, February 20].

Little, J. (2002, March 9). Engineering giant TEA wants pension benefits back from former bosses. *The Power Marketing Association* [Online]. Available: http://199.97.97.163/IMDS%PMAKRT0%read%/home/content/users/imds/feeds/knightridder.html [2002, March 16].

McBride, S. (2002, March 21). Gaudemir defends TEA pension plan. *MSN Money* [Online]. Available: http://news.moneycentral.msn.com [2002, March 25].

Michaels, T., Morgan, C. and Hall, G. (2002, January 18). Former TEA executive defends payout. *Financial Times* [Online]. Available: http://news.ft.com [2002, March 1].

News9. (2002, February 25). TEA division sales expected soon. *News9.com* [Online]. Available: http://www.news9.co.za/News9/Finance/Companies/0,4186,2-8-24_1149296.00.html [2002, March 2].

Rosen. (2002, April 5). TEA Assoc. The probe in detail. *Rosen* [Online]. Available: http://probe.rosen.com [2002, April 20].

TEA. (2002, January 18). TEA Annual Report 2001. *TEA* [Online]. Available: http://www.tea.com [2002, March 5].

Yahoo! (2002, April 12). TEA profile. *Yahoo! Finance* [Online]. Available: http://biz.yahoo.com/p/a/abb.html [2002, April 20].

Persuade and Propose

persuasive reports
propose, request, or
recommend specific
actions or problem
solutions.

Persuasive reports propose, request, or recommend specific actions or problem solutions. They interpret information and suggest a course of action.

A **business plan** is a comprehensive report that defines and describes all the components of a business, including its feasibility, profitability, and marketing environment. The business plan is designed to persuade potential investors to invest money in the business. Standard business plan formats are available from the Small Business Administration and many local chambers of commerce or other small business organizations. In addition, many software packages are commercially available for constructing a formal business plan.

business plan a
comprehensive report that
defines and describes all
the components of a
business, including its
feasibility, profitability, and
marketing environment.

proposal a persuasive
written report that offers to
provide a service, sell a
product, or provide a
solution to a problem or
need.

A **proposal** is a persuasive written report that offers to provide a service, sell a product, or provide a solution to a problem or need. Whether it is an offer to sell farm equipment, provide estate management services, or establish an inner-city counseling center, a formal proposal is a sales tool. *External proposals* present information, ideas, services, or products and seek to gain acceptance from the targeted business or government audience. *Internal proposals* seek acceptance from an inside authority; you might submit a proposal to create a new public relations initiative to your department manager. In practice, most proposals seek to secure business opportunities and clients. Once accepted, they form the basis of a binding contractual agreement between you and the client. A formal proposal must be well researched, well organized, and persuasively and clearly presented.

Proposals can be subdivided into two categories, solicited and unsolicited.

solicited formal proposals
are submitted at the request
of a potential funder.

funder a business,
government agency, or
private foundation that will
approve or finance a
project.

A **solicited formal proposal** is submitted at the request of a potential funder. A **funder** is a business, government agency, or private foundation that will approve or finance your project. Solicited proposals can be easier to draft because the funder has clearly identified the need or problem to be solved and has stated specific criteria to be met in a formal request

WORD ON THE WEB

Word on the Web

Take a look at the RFPs located at these local, state, and federal government related websites:

- www.state.il.us/agency/DHS/rforproposal_frame.html
- www.co.broward_fl.us/purchasing/bids/bids.htm
- www.epa.gov/otag/rfp.htm
- www.usd381.k13.k5.us/rfpmain.htm
- www.discoveringmontana.com/doa/ppd/ifbrfps/cat10.htm

What similarities do you see in the various requests for proposals? What differences are apparent? How do you account for the differences?

You would like to open your own nightclub. You've found a venue, lined up the graphic artists and printing facilities to produce your advertising materials, contacted the agencies that will provide DJs and security personnel, and contracted with a local grocery warehouse to provide the drinks. Now you just need $140,000 in operating capital to pay for lighting, furniture, and at least 3 bartenders and 10 waitstaff. Of your initial $100,000 in start-up funds, you have $25,000 left in your budget.

Write a business plan or proposal that will entice investors to sponsor your nightclub. Be as specific and detailed as you can. Here are some questions to get you started:

1. What kind of music or entertainment will you provide? What kind of people will be attracted to your club?

2. What inventory of beverages will you stock? Will you serve alcoholic beverages? If so, you'll need a license. From whom will you obtain this license?

3. What equipment will you need to purchase?

4. How will you advertise your club?

5. Where will the business be located? Where will people park, and will they have to pay for parking?

6. How much security do you think you'll need to keep your patrons safe?

7. How many people will you employ? (Don't forget you'll need bartenders, bouncers, and servers.) How much will you pay them? Is there an industry standard for the work your employees will perform?

8. What would the club expenses be for a one-month period?

9. What are the short-term goals for your nightclub?

10. What are the long-term goals?

for proposal (RFP), a request for information (RFI), or a commercial request for proposal (CFP). In some instances, the funder will provide forms or a format to follow, along with criteria for the proposal's contents. It is critical that you follow the directions and instructions outlined in the RFP or CFP exactly when you develop your proposal.

Most organizations and agencies designate a contact person to answer questions and guide you through the proposal application process. It can be very helpful to talk to this representative, if only to establish a personal connection. It is an opportunity to talk with someone from your potential audience who may provide some insight into the organizational culture, even if only by the way he or she treats you on the phone. If a contact person is not designated, you may request an informational interview with the person who is handling the proposal process so you can ask questions about the issues involved and learn about the funder's corporate culture. Many companies that write proposals and provide services also designate a contact person for the funder. At IBM, managing directors serve as the client contact on all major accounts. A managing director helps customers such as Merrill Lynch understand the project process, answers any questions, and handles concerns.

An **unsolicited formal proposal** is drafted and submitted to a government agency, company, or individual without having been requested or invited. Unsolicited proposals can be more difficult to draft because it is up to you as the proposer to identify the need to be met or the problem to be solved. In an unsolicited proposal, it is your responsibility to persuade and compel the reader to embrace your idea and ultimately approve or fund your project or product.

What Are the Differences between Reports and Proposals?

Reports provide information, analysis, or recommendations that can be used to solve problems; monitor or document progress; clarify or implement policies or procedures; and guide change, direction, or decisions. While proposals are a type of report, the difference is that they request funding or acceptance in exchange for work to be performed. While some reports recommend or justify a change or new approach, proposals specifically ask that the business idea, project, or product be accepted. Proposals also ask that the organization or entity that submits the proposal be accepted to perform the proposed work. A proposal is also a promise that may be legally binding, depending on the terms outlined, and if the funding source or business accepts the proposal. For example, if you write a proposal to design and install a computer system for a business and that business accepts your proposal, then you may be legally bound to do what you said you would do. Proposals promise or intend to provide a service in return for acceptance (funding or approval).

Organizing Reports

Organizing a report consists of six basic steps: determining the mission, evaluating the audience, selecting a report structure, establishing the scope of information, assigning tasks when collaborating, and conducting research.

Determine the Mission

Every report has a purpose, and the mission statement spells out that purpose. Depending on whether the report is informational, analytical, or persuasive, your mission statement may take the form of a statement of purpose or a problem statement. In brief informational memos, for example, the mission statement may be in the subject line: "Change in flextime accrual." In a longer, more formal proposal, the mission statement appears at the beginning to tell readers exactly what they will be seeing: "Mandelbrot Inc. is losing $5 million daily because its recent acquisition, Dairy Meats, has been unable to maintain its position in the market."

Ineffective problem/mission statement	Effective problem/mission statement
• Productivity is down because employee morale is low.	• Recent layoffs, forced retirements, and changes in benefits package are damaging employee morale. We estimate that productivity is down 10 percent as a result of the morale problem.
• Changes in the market make this a good time to invest in real estate.	• Real estate is an excellent investment now because interest rates are low and there is an overabundance of affordable housing.
• Meadowvale Health Clinic requires additional funding to maintain its current level of service.	• The patient load at Meadowvale Health Clinic has doubled this past year. To maintain the superior standard of service it has offered in the past, Meadowvale requires $500,000 in additional funds to pay for medications, equipment, and other basic medical supplies.

Evaluate Your Audience

As discussed in Chapter 3, when you plan your message design (in this case your report), you need to consider the audience you are trying to reach. When preparing a proposal, Duitch Franklin & Co., an accounting and consultant firm located in Los Angeles, carefully researches its audience using information brokers and online services such as Dun & Bradstreet to make sure each proposal's goals match those of the intended audience. If you are writing a proposal, there are many directories available through libraries and on the Internet that provide brief profiles of potential funders. One of the most comprehensive directories for the nonprofit sector is *The Foundation Directory*, published annually by The Foundation Center. The Foundation Center also publishes several other directories that target specific types of funding such as operating funds, equipment, capital improvement/building, and higher education, to name only a few.

The table that follows highlights some of the key information you would need to prepare a thorough proposal for a potential fund raiser.

CREATIVE

CHALLENGE

Find a recent posting in the *Federal Register* soliciting proposals for a grant (such as under the Department of Education, Department of Housing and Urban Development, or Department of Commerce). Request an application package by phone or e-mail or download one from the Internet. Prepare an outline for a proposal based on the application requirements, and incorporate the basic components of a formal proposal. (See the strategies section of this chapter for components.)

Funding organization	• Name, address, phone, fax, e-mail, contact person, and website (if available) • Names of primary donors
Type of funder	• Independent foundation or company-sponsored foundation
Financials	• Total assets, total expenditures, and high–low range of awards
Organization purpose and activities	• Education, social services, health
Fields of interest	• People with disabilities, children, arts/culture
Types of support	• Equipment, scholarship funds, program development
Limitations	• Eligibility to apply or geographic limitations
Application information	• Guidelines and requirements • EIN (IRS identification number)
Organization personnel	• Officers and trustees • Number of staff
Funding activity	• Recent grants awarded and amounts (if available)

Once you have researched what information the audience may need, their interests, and their giving patterns, put yourself in their place.

At every stage of the report writing process, be your own worst critic and ask yourself the questions a reader will be asking: "Why should I care about this? What difference is any of this going to make? Why is this information, analysis, action, or plan necessary?" Remember that there may be secondary readers other than the official to whom you submitted the report. Think carefully about any technical, mathematical, or scientific materials you are including, and construct descriptions as simply and clearly as possible. Avoid using insider jargon, slang, or acronyms without explanation. There are cultural issues to consider as well. If the reader is in another country, it's a good idea to learn about the traditional values of that culture and tailor the report to suit those values. Finally, verify the correct name and spelling of the person to whom you are addressing the report. Simple carelessness can turn off a reader before he or she even gets to the second page.

Select a Report Structure

There are several logical ways to organize the body of your report. You may want to use a chronological strategy to trace an issue through a period of time, or you could structure it from a cause-and-effect perspective by describing an action or incident and then explaining its effect. In some cases, you may find a problem and solution structure the most useful for transmitting your message. Other times, you may feel that you want to cover your material in components (for example, by department, by area, or by importance). Choose a structure that will enhance your message and emphasize the report's purpose.

All of the data you have gathered should be described, explained, and interpreted in your own words in the body of the report. Providing a few quotes or paraphrases from authoritative sources can lend credibility to your message. All sources, whether quoted or paraphrased, must be cited. The APA or MLA citation styles are common. Parenthetical citations are most commonly used, but if you have a few brief notes that would detract from the narrative flow of the report, footnotes or endnotes might work better.

Format the Report

The following table highlights three primary report formats: manuscript, memo, and letter:

Manuscript	• Usually used for longer, more formal reports such as proposals and business plans. Formatted in paragraph style with headings and subheadings.
Memo	• Often used for shorter, less formal internal reports such as progress, policy, and analytical reports. This format uses the same sender and receiver headings outlined in Chapter 8 and can also use headings and subheadings in the report body.
Letter	• Primarily used for shorter compliance and persuasive reports for transmittal to an external audience. In a letter format as outlined in Chapter 8, you can use headings and subheadings.

This table outlines a few key points to keep in mind when writing reports:

Use positive language	• When you use negative language, the message you send is negative. This is a real problem when you are trying to write a persuasive report such as a proposal or business plan.
Use appropriate graphics	• A picture really is worth a thousand words, especially in reports. Graphs and charts can make complex data more clear and can help persuade your readers.
Be honest	• Sometimes you might be tempted to ignore certain issues or data that do not support your conclusions, or emphasize sources that are not objective or authoritative, because you want the report to make the greatest impact possible. Resist this temptation. If your audience finds out that you manipulated material or if your outcomes do not match what is already known about the issue, your credibility as a professional will be damaged.

Be original	• Readers don't want a compilation of facts gathered from other sources. They want to see how you put the information together and interpret the data.
Be specific	• Managers complain most about the vagueness of the reports they receive. You want your writing to paint a picture of the situation you are describing, so give enough details to make the picture clear. Rather than simply saying "Our sales are down this quarter," give the whole story. "Our sales are down 10 percent this quarter. This decrease is probably due to three factors: (1) our lead seller retired in April and the position has not yet been filled; (2) our stock was reduced by 15 percent prior to the annual inventory on May 15; and (3) the recent drop in the stock market has made consumers reluctant to purchase new durable goods."

Establish the Scope of Information

The **scope** of the report is the range of issues it addresses. The scope defines for the audience how general or specific your discussion will be and in what context it should be received. Because it is virtually impossible to address every detail of every situation, it is usually wise to focus on one or two major issues. Drawing attention to what you have not included in the body of the report signals to the audience that you haven't forgotten about those issues but that they are not relevant to the discussion at hand.

scope of the report is the range of issues it addresses.

You will need to place certain limitations on what you are writing. It is a good idea to mention those limitations in the body of the report. Some report limitations might include how the data were collected, how time could change certain issues, or aspects of the purpose or problem that are not addressed in the report. There are always limits to researching any issue; more time may be required before conclusions can be reached, or some materials may not be accessible. Warning the audience of the limitations to the data used to write the report gives them a better understanding of the data and more confidence in your conclusions.

Assign Tasks and Collaborate

Often it is necessary to work in a team to construct a report because input and cooperation are needed from multiple departments. There are many benefits to collaborating with others (see Chapter 13). The assortment of ideas, talents, and knowledge that a collection of individuals contributes will result in a better final product because each individual has a different perspective on the issues under consideration. A report can also be completed much more quickly when multiple people work on different aspects of it.

Collaboration works best with clear and open communication among the various members on the team about the goals and objectives for the finished report and a clear understanding of team members' responsibilities toward those goals and objectives. A good way to start is to ask everyone in the team to come up with his or her own conclusions about or solutions to the issues the report will discuss. When you meet with your team members, you can discuss their results and choose the best among them mutually, or you can create a new conclusion or solution from the different options they offered. Break up the work, assigning tasks to team members according to their experience, knowledge, and expertise. Hold regular meetings, with agendas passed out beforehand so everyone will know what to prepare and what to expect from the discussion.

You may choose to develop a *workplan*. In fact, some managers require workplans when assigning work to a team. A workplan generally consists of five parts:

Mission statement	• The statement of purpose or problem statement.
Plan of investigation	• Details regarding how your team will conduct research, what kinds of hard and soft data they intend to use, and what forms of direct and indirect sources will be consulted.
Projection of results	• The conclusion or solution for the report and a determination about what the probable effects will be.
Proposed outline	• A preliminary outline that helps team members focus on their individual tasks and lets the person who assigned the report direct the team toward the questions he or she most wants answered.
Task and assignment schedule	• Spells out to everyone involved in the report process what is expected of team members and when.

When you develop a strategy to write the report, identify the skills and strengths of each team member. If your team includes one individual who is a good writer, you may want to assign the writing to that person. After the first draft is written it should be submitted to all members of the team for review. Then it should be discussed by the group and revised according to the team's recommendations. If each team member writes his or her own section of the report, make sure that a single individual edits the entire text so it is uniform in tone, style, and quality.

Conduct Research and Collect Data

To be effective and credible, any report should have a good foundation of accurate research and data. Reports from organizations often begin by offering broad statements about their performance or success. American Honda Motorcar Co. states on its website, "Historically, Honda has been a leader in fuel efficiency and low-emission technology." To be effective, this kind of statement must have the research and data behind it to support the claim. Honda does support this statement by reporting its ratings in fuel efficiency ratings and low-emission performance, based on Environmental Protection Agency (EPA) analysis. Once you collect data, analyze them as objectively as

One of your team members volunteered to write the workplan for a feasibility report on the purchase of new database software for the company. This is the memo you were given to initial.

MEMORANDUM

TO: Max Well, IT Director
FROM: Sarah Connor, Kyle Reese, and Arnold Schwartz
DATE: December 1, 2002
SUBJECT: Workplan for database software report

Our group will be looking at two database software systems that are commercially available: Filemaker Pro and Microsoft Access.

First we'll look at the features each one has, then we'll look at how well they'll work with our computer system. Finally, we'll analyze the costs required to tailor the database to our needs.

We should be done by February 1, 2003.

What's wrong with this workplan? Revise and add details to make it clear who will be doing what and when.

possible. Then determine how the data relate to your topic and other data you have collected, and how they support your position.

There are two basic types of data to collect when researching your report: hard and soft. Good, comprehensive reports include both types of data to support their cases.

Hard data	• Hard data are quantifiable and specific. They are often presented in the form of statistical information or studies used to support your case.
Soft data	• Soft data are anecdotal, more personal or experiential. They are often presented as "quotable quotes" from experts or satisfied customers.
Direct sources	• Direct sources provide firsthand information, not previously reported elsewhere, based on actual experimentation and results, interviews, or surveys.
Indirect sources	• Indirect sources involve previously reported information, such as statistical reports, documented corporate trends, or reported studies and findings.

Either hard or soft data can come from either direct or indirect sources. For example, a statistical report from the U.S. Department of Labor's Bureau of Labor Statistics on employment projections is hard data that can be retrieved from the Internet, the library, and government publications or other indirect sources. A direct-mail customer survey and its findings are also hard data, but the information comes from a direct source, the customers responding to the survey. An example of soft data from a direct source might be a compelling story that a human services client told you. The story is anecdotal, but the source is direct. Soft data such as feature stories and appropriate quotable quotes from experts can be gathered from indirect sources such as newspapers, magazines, journals, or the Internet.

When InterDigital Communications (IDC) wrote a report on its fourth U.S. residential telecommunications survey, it noted that the data had been gathered through telephone interviews with 1,000 U.S. households in February and March 2000. IDC detailed the exact questions asked and related those questions to the goals it had set: to find out how much people pay for various telephone and Internet connection services and how much they would be willing to pay for those services.

Practice Report Design

Determine the report goal	• Pinpoint the reason you need to communicate. • Consider the potential outcome of the report (such as a solution to a problem, an alternative option for a decision, or information for a question, action, or investment). • Identify goal intention: to provide information, analyze data, or persuade. • Plan for the design by considering length and complexity of information.
Evaluate the audience	• Assess who will read the report. • Determine whether you will be communicating to an internal or external business audience (or both). • Consider what your audience requires, needs, and already knows about the subject. • Use empathy by ascertaining the perspectives and viewpoints of your audience.
Conduct research	• Identify the methods you will use to collect data. • Gather the data and research relevant information. • Focus on the analysis and interpretation of data.
Write the report	• Develop the main ideas. • Develop your argument using reasons that support your recommendations or call to action. • Organize the information logically by introducing the subject, presenting the information, describing the problem, justifying the action or identifying the issue, and then making the recommendation, suggesting the action or providing potential advantages and disadvantages. • Write the message to suit your audience's level of understanding and needs.
Check for design flaws	• Ensure that the information in the report is accurate. • Revise sentences and paragraphs to make sure the writing is logical, clear, and objective. • Look for missing or unnecessary information. • Proofread the document to find grammatical, typographical, or spelling errors. • Format the report according to a prescribed style or use appropriate and attractive page layouts.

Strategies

Formal report writing usually follows a prescribed format that includes introductory, body, and summary elements.

Introductory Materials

1. The *letter or memorandum of transmittal* states the purpose of your proposal and exactly what you are requesting. Letters are usually sent to external contacts (a client or another company), and memos are often used within a company. This document creates a paper trail. It not only notifies the recipient of what he or she is about to read but gives you a chance to gain goodwill. The letter presents the benefits to the reader, provides a contact person and phone/e-mail, thanks the reader for considering your report and, if appropriate, states proactively that you will follow up and look forward to discussing the project further at the reader's convenience. The letter of transmittal is similar in style to the letter accompanying a personal résumé. Keep the tone of your letter respectful and direct. Highlight the features of your organization and/or your proposal that would be of greatest interest to your reader. Remember the letter of transmittal is the first thing a potential funder will read. It should inspire the person to want to read more of your report.

2. Your *cover/title page* identifies the title of the project; the proposing organization's name, address, and phone number; a contact person; the name of the organization and/or individual to whom you are submitting the report; and the date of submission. The cover page is the doorway to the entire report. It should be neat, attractive, inviting, and professional in appearance.

3. The *table of contents* identifies the components of your report in outline form and shows their location in the document. It should reveal an organized path from one component to the next and lay out your report in a logical progression. If using illustrations, include a list of them as well.

4. The *executive summary* is a concise overview of your report, usually one page (the length of the summary may vary depending on the length of the report). The summary identifies you, the problem you are addressing, your objectives, your proposed activities or analysis, and if applicable, the total cost and amount of funding you are requesting. Although it appears in the introductory section of your report, the summary should be written last, after you have developed the other sections and have all your information clearly laid out. The executive summary can be the single most important section of your report because it may be the only part of the report that some busy executives will

read. It must be clear, concise, and interesting enough to make your audience want to read further.

Report Body

The body of the report contains all of the information and analysis you want to deliver to your audience. Each type of report requires different components according to its purpose.

1. The *introduction* provides a context so that your audience will understand the analysis, proposal, or information that is to follow. This is where the mission statement, scope of information, limitations, and methodology of the report are found. The introduction should lead logically into the needs statement or problem statement.

2. In a proposal your *background* section or *problem statement* gives the reason you are seeking funding and the specific need to be met or problem to be solved. It addresses an existing condition or state of being, such as an obsolete facility or poor dental health. The background may also present a historical perspective that illuminates how the problem began. Avoid circular reasoning in your background section. A "lack of" something is not a valid reason for funding a project proposal. You want to demonstrate that the problem or need is supported by statistical evidence, statements from authorities or experts, and input from the potential beneficiaries, if applicable. Address the problem in terms of the beneficiaries. In any type of report, the problem statement addresses a particular situation or state of affairs, such as a high crime rate in a particular neighborhood, decreasing product sales, or changing market trends, and relates it to similar situations, sometimes on a national level. Some reports address both a need and a problem.

3. The *goals* for your proposal or business plan are what you ultimately want to achieve. Your *objectives* state a measurable level of work that will be accomplished within a certain time frame. The steps you take will address the problem or need and achieve stated goals. Be realistic when developing your objectives. Setting measurable levels of work too high or too low can take away from the credibility of your report.

4. In a *task plan*, you specify the tasks that will be performed and the resources needed to achieve your stated objectives as well as the reasons you decided to perform these activities. Establish a time frame for each activity's completion. *Timelines* are useful to demonstrate your task plan chronologically for the reader. Describe any resources, materials, or equipment you will need to perform the tasks, especially if you are including a request for funding for the equipment. Describe specific responsibilities and assigned tasks of any personnel who will be involved in the project. If your report cites data that you have collected through sur-

veys, focus groups, or experiments, detail the *methods* by which you organized these activities. Tell your readers how you selected your survey recipients or focus group members, what questions you asked them, and why. If you are detailing an experiment, explain how it was conducted.

5. An *organization qualifications* section of a proposal describes more fully the qualifications of your organization and demonstrates why your organization is uniquely qualified to accomplish the work. It cites the expertise and credentials of project personnel and provides specific examples of relevant past performance and experience. Note any professional licenses, certifications, special recognition, or awards your organization or staff members have received. (Specific résumés or curriculum vitae can be included in an appendix.)

6. Your *evaluation plan* describes what methods you plan to use to measure the success of your activities. It identifies who will be conducting the evaluation (for example, an outside consultant/expert in the field or an internal research office) and explains why you chose that method and evaluator. The evaluation plan also specifies how the results will be used and distributed.

7. Your *budget* should provide a detailed outline of the specific costs of a report project. Sort applicable costs into relevant categories such as personnel, professional and support staff salaries, employee fringe benefits, travel, supplies and materials, equipment printing and postage, and so on. Round off dollar amounts only to the nearest whole dollar (not to the nearest hundred or thousand dollars). A *budget narrative* justifies the more significant costs in your budget. It might explain why a particular piece of equipment is necessary to the project's success. The more carefully and realistically you plan out your overall project and estimate your budget, the fewer changes will be necessary during implementation.

8. *Solutions, alternatives, or recommendations* for a problem or need can be found in analytical reports and some informational reports. Try to come up with as many solutions as possible (at least three in most cases), and work out the pros and cons of each possibility in detail before you make a final selection. This tells the audience that you have considered a variety of ideas and have made a reasoned, educated selection of options, which enhances your credibility.

Summary/Conclusion

Your summary should briefly review the key points of the report. It revisits the highlights of the report. A good conclusion explains how all its elements work together to make a unique statement. Through support detailed in the body of the report, the conclusion leads the reader to your position or stance.

Notes and References

Any material you use in a report that comes from a source other than yourself must be cited in the body of the report, preferably in parenthetical citations. Complete works cited or bibliographic information must also be included at the end of the report. Business documents usually use APA or MLA citation and reference formats (see appendix—for documentation styles).

Appendixes

Information that does not fit neatly into the body of the report but is necessary or useful for the reader should be attached separately at the end. Appendixes often contain sample documents, spreadsheets, detailed survey materials, and commentary on specific points referred to in the body of the report. Proposal appendixes may also contain annual reports, résumés, names and affiliations of your board of trustees or principal partners (if applicable), letters of support from constituent groups or organizations, and letters of recommendation from former clients. Some proposal funders specify in their RFP or guidelines what they want you to submit as supplemental information. Some request that no additional information be included. If there are no stipulations, use your creativity and discretion in selecting what to include. Make sure your appendix selections are relevant to your report and enhance its significance. If you've held the reader's attention this long, this is your encore, so you want it to be brief but impressive.

Summary

- Reports are used to present information, analyze data and information, and persuade. They often offer solutions or options for problem solving and decision making. Most reports are presented in written form, but some are delivered orally.

- Informal reports are usually short, are in letter, memo, or e-mail form, and use an informal, personal style. Formal reports are longer, use an impersonal style, and must follow a specific format.

- There are three purposes of reports: to provide information (reports that provide facts and figures but do not interpret data or draw conclusions); to analyze and justify (reports that offer the same data as an informational report but also suggest interpretations and solution); and to persuade and propose (reports that encourage the receiver to take a desired action based on the informational and analytical data included).

- To organize a report determine the mission, evaluate your audience, select a report structure, establish the scope of information, assign tasks, and conduct research.

- A formal report has five components: introductory materials, the report body, summary/conclusions, notes and references, and the appendix(es).

Business Communication Projects

1. You are a researcher for a local nonprofit agency that has developed a new program to help at-risk youth in a low-income community stay in school and find employment after school. Research some of the foundation directories available in the library or online, and find five or six potential funders for your agency to approach with a proposal. Look for matching criteria such as fields of interest, types of support, geographic preferences, and eligibility to apply. Prepare a list containing the name, address, phone, website (if applicable), contact person, fields of interest, types of support, and funding ranges of each potential funder to present to your board of directors.

2. Break into pairs with your class colleagues. For this assignment, you and your business partner have an opportunity to purchase a successful bed and breakfast (B&B) in your favorite resort town. You both have degrees in hotel management. You currently work for a major hotel chain, and your partner is the head chef at an upscale local restaurant. This is an opportunity to finally run your own business, but you need startup funding. Prepare an outline for your business plan by using the basic components described in this chapter. Include some research on the B&B industry and the resort town you've selected, and any supporting details you feel would enhance your plan.

3. Write an informational memo to your instructor that compares writing style, content, and layout of annual reports from three different companies in the same or related industries. Include a description of the similarities and differences among these reports.

4. Contact a local foundation or local chapter of a national foundation, and interview its program director (or executive director) about what the organization requires from proposers and what it looks for when considering funding a project. Come to class prepared to discuss your findings with the class. Collectively, your class may then prepare a local directory of foundations based on everyone's interview reports.

5. Develop clear problem statements that explain the scope of each aspect of the following problems:
   - Being chronically late to the office.
   - Stealing office supplies.
   - Surfing the Internet and sending personal e-mail on company time.
   - Hiring friends and relatives.

6. Break into groups of three with your class colleagues. Your team has come up with a proposal for submission to management to supply five small (15 participants) management-training seminars to employees interested in moving up the corporate ladder.

Your job now is to write the task plan and budget for the proposal. Write at least two pages detailing the personnel, costs, materials, locations, and any other items that may be needed to make the seminars possible.

7. Design cover pages for formal reports addressed to the following audiences. Be sure to consider appropriate graphics and color selections in your choices:

   - A graphic arts company report analyzing the creativity of the art department.
   - A justification report examining the impact of employee layoffs.
   - An informational report prepared by the accounting staff providing statistics for the last fiscal year.
   - An Internet start-up company's business plan.
   - An annual report prepared by an oil refinery.

8. The office manager has asked you to prepare an informal report comparing laptop computers with palmtops. She has also asked that you make recommendations about how these technologies can be used and by whom. Do a little research, using both hard and soft data, regarding the advantages and disadvantages of each technology. Then prepare a two-page memo that offers your recommendation for the use of these technologies at the midsized (450-employee) advertising firm where you work.

9. Take a look at one of the websites that provide information about American Psychological Association (APA) citation styles: for example, Purdue University's Online Writing Lab (www.owl.english.purdue.edu/handouts/research/r_apa.html), or the University of Illinois Urbana-Champaign's Writer's Workshop (www.english.uiuc.edu/cws/workshop/bibliography/apa/apamenu.htm). Write a memo to your instructor that explains how to cite the following sources. (Be sure to include examples.)

   - Books.
   - Magazines or newspapers.
   - Websites or other electronic sources.

   Include in your memo citations with and without authors.

10. Break into groups with your class colleagues to find a problem that exists at your school (for example, limited parking). Interview employees in the physical plant or operations department and other people who are affected by the problem and determine its scope. Consider traffic and financial concerns, and then write an analytical report addressed to your dean or school president that describes the problem and provides at least three realistic solutions that could be enacted.

Discussion Questions

1. Why are reports important in the business world?
2. Identify whether the following reports should be formal or informal and explain your choice:
   - A brief justification report to a site supervisor explaining a change in a construction schedule.
   - A 15-page plan for departmental reorganization.
   - A progress report to a funder whose program director you know personally.
   - An e-mail attachment describing a change in overtime policy.
   - American Express's year-end review for stockholders.
3. What are the differences in purpose among informational, analytical, and persuasive reports?
4. Why is it important to describe the scope of a report?
5. How do you develop conclusions or solutions for a report?
6. Discuss examples of hard and soft data and the effective use of each in informational, analytical, and persuasive reports.
7. Why is the executive summary a vital component of a formal report or proposal?
8. Discuss five important reasons you would turn down a proposal if you were a funder, and explain why those reasons are important.
9. In what ways does evaluating your audience affect the tone of your report?
10. How can you project the results of your report in a workplan before you write it?

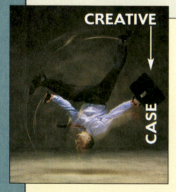

CREATIVE → CASE

Creative Case

Boeing and the Revolt of the Tech Heads

Boeing Aircraft had a problem. Competition from the European company Airbus had cut into its market severely. Traditionally, Boeing focused its business on the production of new planes and research and development (R&D). It built planes to customer specifications using a system that had served it well since 1945. Boeing looked into cutting costs as Airbus plane production began to pose a real threat. It found that the system was losing hundreds of millions of dollars each year. For example, a customer would order a plane at a cost of $10 million. Under the existing production system, it cost $80 million to build a $10 million plane to custom specifications. Obviously, this had to stop. After examining its options, Boeing decided to focus on building only standard planes, updating its production system, limiting customization, and reducing the development of new technology for use in customized planes.

This caused another problem, however. The R&D department, comprising some of the best engineering minds in the United States, was furious that its budget would shrink and its power and contribution to the company would be reduced. It believed that Boeing should maintain the R&D projects at all costs; after all, new engineering theories and technological advances had made Boeing an aviation giant for decades. The engineers were also unhappy about the changes in the production system, which would entail a change in the hardware and software they were accustomed to using. The members of the R&D department faced serious change, and some considered leaving. Boeing had to face either losing enormous amounts of money or losing its valuable R&D staff.

If you had to write a justification report, what would you tell the R&D department?

Some questions to consider:

1. Do you think that the measures Boeing is taking might be temporary, permanent, or a mixture of both?
2. Are there any strategies or incentives that could be employed to keep the R&D department satisfied?
3. What do the R&D people need to know to be able to understand and accept Boeing's changes?
4. How formal would this report need to be? Consider the audience to determine the most appropriate tone and style of language.

SOURCES: Pae, P. (2001). "Airbus Is Rocking Boeing's World." *Los Angeles Times*. Retrieved 2 September 2001: www.latimes.com/technology/business/innovation/la-000008349jul01.story; Reinhardt, A., and S. Browder. (1998). "Boeing: Fly, Damn It, Fly." *Business Week*. Retrieved 2 September 2001: www.businessweek.com/1998/45/los603177.htm.

Chapter 11

Chapter 11

Writing Strategies for Reports and Proposals

In a Nutshell

CyberLab at Indiana University is developing an electronic portfolio system that will allow people to create and display their student, faculty, course, and career portfolios on the Internet. To accomplish this, the CyberLab staff needs to interact with other colleges, universities, and software companies, both for added input on the project and to determine the compatibility of their software with different kinds of networked computer systems. The report the CyberLab writers produced to spread the word about their project had to provide sufficient data to convince potential project participants that their plan was sound and request their assistance in meeting their goals. The "Electronic Portfolios Project @ CyberLab, IUPUI" report accomplishes both tasks by using both direct and indirect strategies in specific sections of the text. The report begins with a direct request for participation. Following this is an indirect description of the research and development methodology, initially focusing on the background research carried out by Indiana University professors over the years before zeroing in on specifics of the design of the new software. This makes the project easier for those not tech-savvy to understand. The report delivers project goals directly, and then moves again into an indirect appeal to the audience, offering them the opportunity to suggest a name for the software. By varying the strategic approach in its report, CyberLab hopes to gain added support for an exciting new product.

Use of Direct and Indirect Strategies in Formal and Informal Reports

Writing an effective report or proposal requires careful selection of the most appropriate strategy. Chapter 9 covered the basic applications of  direct and indirect strategies in common business documents. This chapter refines those strategies and applies them to the purposes of reports and proposals.

The same direct and indirect strategies that apply to the overall construction of a report can also be applied to the specific components of the report. For the purposes of style and maintaining reader interest these strategies can be varied, but some attention must be paid to the strategy applied to each section of the report.

Audience dictates report type. Supervisors and other interested individuals will not require as much contextual information as individuals outside your business.

© Zefa Visual Media–Germany /Index Stock Imagery, Inc.

Consider the Audience to Determine Strategy

Known versus Unknown Audience

In every communication activity, the first thing you must consider is your audience. The audience you are trying to reach will dictate the type of document you need to create. Supervisors, clients, partners, or other interested individuals usually read reports. This audience may already know something about your subject; they may have even assigned it to you. This means that they probably have some knowledge of your topic and the circumstances that surround it. Supervisors or individuals outside your business (such as clients or investors) may read reports or proposals. These individuals may require more contextual information, even if you are responding to an RFP.

Determine the Needed Response

- **Use a direct strategy if you need nothing.**

  If the report is simply delivering information and requires no response from the audience, the direct strategy is usually the best choice. Use this strategy when you do not anticipate resistance from the reader and do not have to persuade the reader to agree with you.

An Unknown Audience   **FIGURE 11.1**

An unknown or external business audience such as clients or investors may need more detail and explanation to understand your report or proposal.

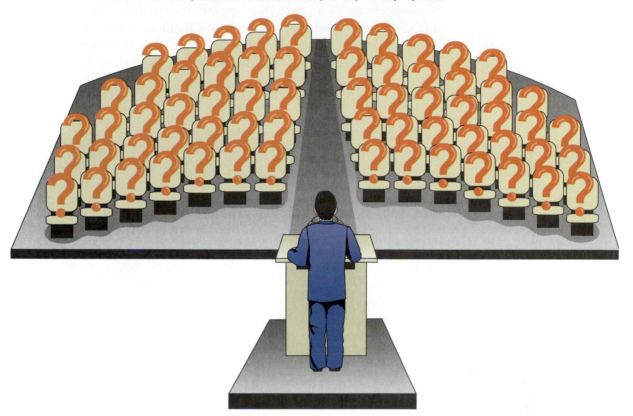

- **Use an indirect strategy if an investment of some kind is required.**

  When the report or proposal requests a response, money, or action from the audience, the indirect strategy is often the best way to go. Use this strategy when you anticipate resistance or must persuade your reader to agree with you.

Types of Reports Connected to Strategy

The purpose of the report also dictates whether you should use a direct or indirect strategy. Informative reports simply relate information about projects or situations, usually without analysis. These reports can be delivered directly. Persuasive documents such as business plans and proposals usually require more explanation and detailed examples. In this case an indirect strategy, which explains the reasoning behind your conclusions, is generally a better approach. In many cases, however, a combination approach may be necessary. When justifying an action or policy or examining the feasibility of a new project, it may be necessary to both inform and persuade at the same time. Some portions of an analytical report may deliver information directly, while the analysis or conclusions that follow may require an indirect approach to ensure that your reader will understand your conclusions or recommendations.

Types of Reports and Strategic Approaches

Informative = direct	• Memos and letters • Progress or interim reports • Compliance reports • Minutes
Persuasive = indirect	• Memos and letters • Proposals • Business plans
Analytical = direct/indirect	• Memos and letters • Policy and procedure reports • Annual reports • Justification reports • Feasibility studies

Following are some sample reports. The sample proposal illustrates an indirect approach. The sample policy report illustrates a direct approach. The justification report combines both approaches.

Sample Proposal

Trifood Group, Inc.

TO: Daniel Nggai, Finance Director

FROM: Kathleen Bitoni, Acquisitions Facilitator *KB*

DATE: February 17, 2001

SUBJECT: Request for Funds to Upgrade DowntownGrocer Facilities

PLAN OF ACTION FOR DOWNTOWNGROCER

Trifood has recently purchased DowntownGrocer (Downtown) as part of our strategic business plan for expansion. Funding is now required to incorporate four of the Downtown facilities into the Trifood network. Our goal is to retrofit all Downtown's facilities to match Trifood operational systems. As you requested in our phone conversation of February 15, this is a brief overview of the retrofit proposal.

DOWNTOWN'S CURRENT OPERATIONS

Downtown currently provides Internet-based grocery services for the Southern California area. It has a well-established customer base and enjoys a high percentage of repeat business. The costs associated with each Downtown facility are approximately $5 million. Facilities rely on manual "pickers," who assemble each order for delivery. The breakeven point for Downtown facilities is 1,500 orders per day. Trifood's plan is to retain and upgrade four of Downtown's main distribution sites.

TRIFOOD'S CURRENT OPERATIONS

Trifood serves the San Francisco Bay area, Sacramento, the Atlanta metro area, and the Chicago metro area. It is in the process of developing an expansive national customer base. The costs associated with each Trifood facility are $25 million. Facilities are based on a highly automated, customized computer system. The breakeven point for Trifood facilities is 4,000 orders per day.

UPGRADES NECESSARY FOR DOWNTOWN

Trifood needs to remodel the existing Downtown facilities to match the operational systems of the larger Trifood facilities. The systems require extensive upgrades because:

• Downtown's facilities are smaller.
• Downtown's facilities use less automated equipment.
• Downtown's computer systems are limited.

Total estimated cost for upgrades to the four Downtown facilities under discussion is $40 million.

RISKS OF DOWNTOWNGROCER EXPANSION

Potential problems we face integrating Downtown into the Trifood network include:

- <u>Disruption of service to current customers</u>. Downtown has a dedicated customer base, with a high percentage of repeat business. Upgrading the Downtown system would take Downtown offline briefly, then direct customers to a new website. Given that online shopping is still in its infancy and customers often have concerns related to reliability and security, disruption of service could alienate some regular patrons.
- <u>Potential failure to meet the breakeven point.</u> Three of the DowntownGrocer facilities are at the breakeven point now; the fourth is making a profit. Trifood has yet to reach its breakeven point. Since the breakeven point for Trifood is more than twice that of Downtown, changing the systems currently in use at Downtown could result in greater losses for Trifood.
- <u>Layoffs of current Downtown employees.</u> Many of Downtown's employees are "pickers," untrained in the technological skills required to run Trifood's automated systems. Upgrading Downtown facilities will result in additional costs of hiring and training additional employees, while laying off key workers who do not possess the skills necessary for Trifood operations.

BENEFITS OF DOWNTOWNGROCER EXPANSION

Although the problems Trifood faces with incorporation of Downtown are important, the benefits of changing the system have a greater potential for success. Benefits include:

- <u>A larger service area</u>. Larger, more sophisticated facilities would allow Trifood to serve a greater number of customers throughout a larger geographical area, which means a potential for larger profits.
- <u>A flexible operational system capable of rapid expansion</u>. Expansion of existing Downtown facilities was not in its original plans. Waiting for demand to expand the system currently in use would be time-consuming and would mean a delay in profits. A system based on the Trifood model would give Downtown facilities a better ability to react to the local market.
- <u>Interactivity with other Trifood facilities</u>. If Downtown facilities match those at existing Trifood sites, the overall operations system will be uniform. If Downtown facilities do not match existing Trifood network, Trifood will face redundant systems that could complicate basic order and supply issues. Downtown sites would have to be run as completely separate entities.

RECOMMENDATIONS FOR DOWNTOWNGROCER INCORPORATION

Upgrading Downtown facilities is costly but essential to create a cohesive single company. The operational shift will cause a temporary disruption to current Downtown customers. On the other hand, it will also bring them greater selection and ease of ordering. The current success of the Downtown locations can be carried over into the Trifood network and expanded using the flexible technological systems currently in use at other Trifood sites. Upgrades could begin as early as March 1, if funding is approved, and completed within a maximum of three months. The first step would be notification of current Downtown customers of the changeover. Customers can be notified by e-mail and announcements on the Downtown site. This can be accomplished within a week.

For more detailed breakdowns of financial elements involved in the Downtown upgrade, please contact me at (415) 555-7895, or <u>kbitoni@trifood.com.</u>

Sample Policy Report

Trifood Group, Inc.

MEMORANDUM

TO: All Delivery Personnel

FROM: Ray Almendariz, Director of Delivery Services *RA*

DATE: January 9, 2001

SUBJECT: Trifood Tipping Policy

Many of you have had questions about Trifood's tipping policy, so I'd like to take a moment to review it with you.

We have many loyal customers who use our service on a regular basis. Some of you are even on a first name basis with the "regulars" on your route. That's terrific; it's exactly the kind of relationship we want to encourage between our drivers and customers.

Customers who are happy with a service usually want to show their approval by tipping the delivery person. If deliveries are made frequently, however, this can lead to an uncomfortable situation. It is expensive for the customer, for one thing. But more importantly, we feel that the relationships we build with our clientele are based on friendship; we are guests in their homes.

You all have business cards with your name, employee number, and contact information for Trifood's customer service department. If customers want to tip you, just give them a card and ask them to call or e-mail customer service with a comment about your work. These comments will go into your personnel file and will count toward employee incentive programs (not to mention your evaluations!).

We have the best delivery team in the industry. Keep up the good work.

Sample Justification Report

Trifood Group, Inc.

TO: Trifood Employees

FROM: Norman Kramden, President *NK*

DATE: September 23, 2002

SUBJECT: Effects of Trifood's Bankruptcy Filing on Employees

OVERVIEW OF THE BANKRUPTCY DECISION

Competition in electronic commerce is fierce. Trifood Group Inc. had an aggressive plan to dominate the online grocery market. We planned to build multiple facilities, each with a complex, automated business system, based on the premise that each facility could be established quickly at the most prudent cost. That plan was ultimately unsuccessful, and we are now faced with the uncomfortable task of filing for bankruptcy. This decision will have an effect on all employees within the next week. Because this action is so drastic, I feel it necessary to explain the reasons behind it.

FACILITY FACTORS

Trifood invested heavily in distribution centers that occupied 350,000 square feet. Most of our competitors' facilities occupy an average of 100,000 to 150,000 square feet of space. These facilities were built to accommodate 8,000 orders per day. The actual customer base utilized only 30 percent of the total capacity. This was short of the breakeven point of 4,000 orders a day.

Anticipating rapid expansion, Trifood entered into long-term lease agreements several years ahead of our need, creating long-term liabilities and leaving expensive equipment in storage. For example, in Kent, Washington, we leased a warehouse and purchased new equipment two years before the facility was to be opened. We also purchased new equipment for preparing meals. When we decided against including prepared food in our online offerings, all of the equipment was auctioned off at a loss. The approximate value of the kitchen items at the Kent facility was estimated at $1.3 million. Recouping these losses is impossible.

FINANCIAL FACTORS

In 1998, Trifood had total expenses of $12.0 million, which included general, administrative, development, and engineering expenses. When we began serving the San Francisco Bay area in 1999, our general and administrative expenses were $92.4 million, and our net losses were $144.5 million. We considered this an acceptable risk, considering the potential of our service. We continued investing in marketing, distribution services, automated equipment, and computer systems: another $453.3 million lost in 2000. We have already incurred net losses of $217 million in the first quarter of 2001. Obviously, we can no longer financially maintain Trifood.

BUSINESS IMPACT

The effects of this decision on employees are twofold. Currently, Trifood is making arrangements to auction off all facilities and equipment to offset as much debt as possible. To maintain these resources until their disposition is resolved, Trifood will retain 600 employees. The remaining 2,000 employees will receive layoff notices later today, effective at the end of the week. I regret that this action is necessary. Trifood employees are among the most dedicated and enthusiastic in the field. I sincerely wish you all the best in your future careers.

Components of Reports and Design Strategy

Executive Summary

As mentioned in Chapter 10, an executive summary is a concise overview of a report. A "sneak peak" at the contents of the report, it is the first, and sometimes only, document the individual screening your report will read. In addition to identifying yourself or your company, the summary also presents the problem you are addressing; your objectives; and your proposed activities, analysis, or conclusions. Because it encapsulates the entire report, it must be written after the report has been completed. The strategy used for constructing the executive summary should reflect the basic strategy used in the original design of the report.

To prepare your executive summary, read the finished draft of the report and highlight its key points. The following table points out typical sources of key points in a report.

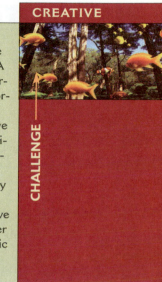

CREATIVE CHALLENGE

Executive summaries are also used in business to summarize lengthy informative articles. A busy executive may need information about a financial opportunity or technological development but may not have time to plow through long articles or documentation. Executive summary to the rescue!

Find a business or technology related article in a magazine and create a one-page executive summary that provides a reader who is unfamiliar with the topic with all the information necessary to understand it.

Headings	The headings of each section of the report indicate major points of discussion.
Topic sentences	The first or second sentence of most paragraphs encapsulates the purpose of the paragraph—its key idea.
Enumerations	Words like "first . . . second . . . third . . ." usually indicate a series of points that support a report's content.
Cause and effect statements	When terms such as "as a result" or "accordingly" appear in a report, the material is usually descriptive of an important result or evaluation.
Essentials	Terms such as "basically," "crucial," and "important" are usually connected to vital information.

Once you have determined what the key points of the report are, organize the resulting information into a draft of the summary. Make sure that the material fits together well. While it is possible to string together sentences lifted from the report to create the summary, a summary constructed in this manner will usually be awkward to read. The sentences and paragraphs need to be connected using the same logic the original report employs. Also, avoid quoting from the report. The goal is to create a new document that flows naturally and is easy to read.

Once you have organized the data in your draft summary, reevaluate the data included and exclude details that are too specific or go beyond the scope of the report. Avoid expressing opinions, inserting new or external data that don't appear in the original report, giving examples, or providing background. Footnotes are unnecessary in the executive summary.

Sample Executive Summary

The New Business Venture Division of Corporate Investments (CI) proposes an investment in the electronic commerce field. Trifood Group Inc. (Trifood) declared bankruptcy on September 19, 2002. Trifood's business was based on sales and delivery of grocery products for profit. This provides CI an opportunity to profit from online grocery services in several key geographical areas previously served by Trifood and DowntownGrocer.

Trifood failed to generate enough revenue to cover general and administrative overhead expenses. Trifood needed to develop a strategic plan that would build a large customer base and reduce operating expenses in order to maintain profitability. Instead, Trifood made huge investments in facilities and equipment in advance of actual sales, projecting further into the future than was fiscally responsible. Many of these resources have never been used. Expansion activities should have remained limited until a reasonable profit level was reached.

CI can learn from these mistakes and provide services similar to those provided by Trifood at a reasonable cost, and with a greater profit margin. Many of the facilities Trifood leased or purchased are currently available at a discount, as is much of the equipment. If CI moves quickly, we can acquire these resources at a 20 percent savings.

Risks to this venture include consumer fears and brick-and-mortar store competition. Many consumers distrust the security of online transactions. Also, shopping online for groceries requires planning ahead rather than simply stopping by the store on the way home for a last-minute item. These are issues that will need to be addressed in a feasibility study.

By purchasing the DowntownGrocer name, the benefits from serving its established customer base can bring in reasonable profits. The positive image of DowntownGrocer establishes a brand recognition that has been proven to be reliable in the past. Buying Trifood's auctioned warehouses, offices, and operating equipment will save CI $200 million in expenses.

Sometimes executive summaries are used to provide executives with information contained in long news articles. This kind of executive summary distills the most important parts of the article and conveys the essence of the data to the audience.

Imagine that you work for a communications company (telephone, electronic media, or anything else you'd like to consider) that is interested in obtaining and using new technology. Look through a technology-oriented publication such as *Wired* or *Technology Today,* and find an article that discusses new advances in communication devices. Write a 250-word executive summary for your supervisor that describes the most important points of the device as represented in the article.

JUMP IN!

Introduction

The introduction of your report or proposal sets the tone for the rest of the document. Decide, based on the audience and purpose of the document, whether you would like to use an informal, conversational tone or a more formal voice, and begin using that tone in the introduction. The introduction also orients your reader, signaling the type of approach and argument you are about to make. The introduction should "hook" the readers, interesting them enough to make them want to read more. Stylistically, the introduction should be engaging and clear.

The introduction also sets up a process that should be continued throughout the document. If you have chosen to develop a theme that will be carried out in the rest of the report, this is where it should begin. You can also introduce key words and concepts that will be repeated elsewhere. You have options available in your introduction, no matter which approach you choose to take with the rest of the report or proposal.

Direct strategy application: Present your context, basic topic, and suggested solutions or responses right away. Preparing the context is important because it shapes the readers' perception of the material that will follow. The amount of context you provide depends on how much you assume your readers will know. The basic topic is a general statement of the problem or issue you will discuss in the remainder of the report. Because you will be developing the nuances of that statement for many pages, your initial statement should be clear, but not specific—you do not need lots of details. By giving the suggested solutions or responses in the introduction, you direct the reader toward the conclusions you have already developed, controlling their perception of both the subject matter and its ultimate resolution.

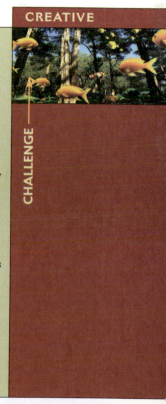

CREATIVE CHALLENGE

Sometimes a theme can be delivered in a document's headings and subheadings. For example, a report titled "An Approaching Storm: Taft, Thomas & Rogers Flooded with Problems" used the following headings for its various sections:

- Before the Storm: A Brief History of TTR
- Lightning Strikes: Jones Burns TTR
- Thunderclouds: The Enron Shadow
- Heavy Downpour: Sinking Stocks
- Stay Indoors: Changing TTR Internally
- Blue Skies Ahead: TTR's Future

After reading over the Trifood proposal used for the examples in this chapter, devise your own series of headers that carry out a similar theme.

direct strategy application presents your context, basic topic, and suggested solutions or responses right away.

261

Example 1a: INTRODUCTION: NEW OPPORTUNITIES FOR IC
Developing the Internet Grocery Market
The New Business Venture Division of Corporate Investments (CI) is seeking $10 million in initial funding for an investment opportunity in the electronic commerce field. Trifood Group Inc. (Trifood) declared bankruptcy on September 19, 2002, which has left a void in online grocery services in several key geographical areas. Trifood's business was based on sales and delivery of grocery products for profit. It is important to review the activities of Trifood to understand the challenges and opportunities that are inherent to this area of electronic commerce businesses.

indirect strategy application presents your context and basic topic, but does not specifically indicate your suggestions or responses. You are not directing the reader toward your results because you want them to be considered a natural outgrowth of your argument.

Indirect strategy application: Present your context and basic topic, but do not specifically indicate your suggestions or responses. You are not directing the reader toward your results because you want them to be considered a natural outgrowth of your argument. Instead, you are creating a story or image that the reader will keep in mind as the report or proposal unfolds.

Example 1b: ANALYSIS: LOOKING AT THE TRIFOOD EXPERIENCE
Exploding Opportunities in the Internet Grocery Market
The electronic commerce field is exploding. Sometimes, the explosion destroys companies unprepared for the volatile nature of the market. Trifood Group Inc. (Trifood) was one of these companies. Trifood declared bankruptcy on September 19, 2002, which has left a void in online grocery services in several key geographical areas. Trifood's business was based on sales and delivery of grocery products for profit. It is important to review the activities of Trifood to understand the challenges and opportunities that are inherent to this area of electronic commerce businesses.

Background

Background can be delivered directly because it sets the stage for your project. Provide details that you can use to analyze your topic in the problem statement. As you prepare the materials you wish to include in the background of your report or proposal, select only the information that is pertinent to your current purpose. Even though you are using a direct approach in this section, it is easy to confuse the reader by providing unnecessary or irrelevant information. Usually, the data you provide here will be tied into other points you make down the road.

You can organize your background several ways. You can choose to take a **chronological approach,** arranging the data according to the order in which they occurred.

chronological approach arranges the data according to the order in which they occurred.

Example 2a: Major Transactions That Led to Trifood's Financial Turmoil:
From June 2000 through August 2001, Trifood opened up large facilities in Sausalito, California (servicing the San Francisco Bay and Sacramento areas), Suwannee, Georgia (servicing the Atlanta metro area), and Carol Stream, Illinois (servicing the Chicago metro area). Each facility was equipped with high-valued customized operating systems for grocery handling processes (SEC, 10-K, year-end December 2001). Trifood also purchased DowntownGrocer Inc. (DowntownGrocer) as part of its

strategic business plan to expand its market. The goal was to retrofit all DowntownGrocer's facilities to match the Trifood operational systems (SEC 10-K report, year-end December 2001).

You may opt to take a **situational approach,** discussing the events from the perspectives of the various influences (departments, individuals) those events had on the current situation.

Example 2b: Trifood's Expansion: Goals without Planning

Trifood's priority was building a complex and expensive operation rather than building its customer base first. In the Registration Statement, Amendment No. 7, dated November 3, 2000, Trifood discloses their plan to build multiple complexes each with a customized business system that is "extremely complex" and based on the premise that each facility can be established quickly, at the most prudent cost. The focus was to provide the most efficient operations possible by setting up these facilities to be highly automated (SEC, Form S-1, November 2000). There is no evidence within the Prospectus that Trifood identified a clear customer base to generate income to support these complex operations and still make a profit.

A **statistical approach,** in which you provide a series of number facts, may be more appropriate if the data you are relating are informational or influence the ultimate goal of the document.

Example 2c: Financial Impact of Trifood's Actions

In 1998, prior to revenue operations, Trifood had total expenses of $12.0 million (Table 1), which included the general and administrative expenses, development and engineering expenses, and other expenses. In the first year of operations, in 1999, Trifood suffered net losses of $144.5 million. Before establishing a solid customer base in the San Francisco Bay area, they expanded into other cities and states. They incurred $92.4 million in general and administrative expenses. After experiencing big losses in 2000, they continued investing in expensive automated equipment and

situational approach
discusses events or situations from the perspectives of certain departments or individuals.

statistical approach
provides a series of number facts, which may be appropriate if the data you are relating are informational or influence the ultimate goal of the document.

Net Losses and Expenses Generated during Years 1998 through 2001 (in Millions)   **TABLE 1**

	2001 (1st Q)	2000	1999	1998	Total
Net sales	$77.2	$178.5	$13.3	$0.00	$269.0
Cost of goods sold	55.6	131.2	11.3	0.00	198.1
Gross profit	**21.7**	**47.2**	**2.0**	**0.00**	**71.0**
General and administrative expenses	88.2	292.3	92.4	8.8	481.7
Development and engineering expenses	6.0	25.5	15.2	3.0	49.8
Other expenses	144.5	182.7	38.9	.2	366.5
Total expenses	**238.6**	**500.5**	**146.5**	**12.0**	**898.0**
Net losses	$(217.0)	$(453.3)	$(144.5)	$(12.0)	$(826.8)

Source: SEC, 10-K report, year-end 2000; and SEC, 10-Q report, month-end March 2001.

TABLE 2

Financial Ratios

	2001 (1st Q)	2000	1999	1998
Debt ratio	7.5%	7.9%	5.1%	N/A
Contribution margin	28.0%	26.5%	15.2%	N/A
Asset turnover ratio	0.060	0.117	0.019	N/A
Return on investment	−16.9%	−29.8%	−19.1%	N/A

computer systems, which created larger losses ($453.3 million), and continued this cycle throughout the company's life (SEC, 10-K report, year-end December 2001).

As shown in Table 2, Trifood suffered a negative return on investment, still continued rapid expansion of a business that was previously established by DowntownGrocer, and made unnecessary investments. Trifood invested large sums of money in marketing, distribution services, equipment, and employees. Marketing expenses for 2000 were $49.1 million compared to $11.7 million in 1999. These expenses include the costs for advertisements, promotions, public relations, and payroll expenses. Because most of their cash came from common stocks, the debt ratios remained low. The asset turnover ratios were extremely low, indicating the company was not utilizing its assets efficiently to generate sales. Contribution margins remained extremely low. This ratio represents the amount of revenue that can be used to cover operating expenses. Trifood chose to ignore all the financial signs of a failing system (SEC, 10-K report, year-end 2000).

Whichever approach or combination of approaches you choose, be sure that the tone matches that of the introduction and the rest of the document.

Problem and Purpose Statements

As discussed in Chapter 10, the problem statement must be very clearly defined. The problem or basic purpose statement in your introduction provides the general concept for your reader, but the problem statement you write after completing the background provides greater detail and clarity. You can also use this section to determine the scope of your document. Recognize that there may be other issues at stake, but explain why you have chosen to focus on the particular issues covered in your document.

Be sure to accompany research and background with your analysis of the problem, even when writing an informational report. Consider not only what the issue is, but also why and how it became an issue and the ramifications of the issue. It is not enough to say, for example, that DeBeers Diamonds is having financial difficulties. You must explain that the company is having trouble because it is facing labor problems and government intervention. Part of your analysis will be set up in the background, but the background is primarily facts. In your problem statement you must explain how those facts relate to underlying issues that your report or proposal will address.

WORD ON THE WEB

Word on the Web

Mixing direct and indirect strategies is not only necessary when writing but is also useful when dealing with problems in the workplace. These websites describe various interpersonal problems in the workplace. In some cases people are being too direct with one another; in other cases they are being too indirect. Can you think of better ways the individuals involved could have interacted?

- www.etiquettehell.com/everydayetiquette/business/ebusiness.htm
- www.bullybusters.org
- www.ivysea.compages/ca1000_2.html

After you think about the options available to the people involved in these situations, you can ask the etiquette experts for their opinion online:

- www.allexperts.com/getExpert.asp?Category=2294

Direct strategy application: Begin the section with a one- or two-sentence statement of the problem or purpose. Analyze the data provided in the background, relating the outcomes of each situation or figure to this initial statement. End the section with a restatement of the problem or topic and how the outcome of your report or proposal will address the issue.

Example 3a: SUMMARY OF PRIMARY ISSUES FOR CI TO CONSIDER
Trifood's Failure versus CI's Success

CI can learn from Trifood's mistakes and could invest in an online grocery business that would be both successful and cost effective. Trifood failed to generate enough revenue to cover the general and administrative overhead expenses and was unable to develop a plan to become profitable. Trifood needed to develop and implement a revised strategic plan that would build a larger customer base and reduce operating expenses in order to maintain profitability. There was a need to identify the market segment best suited for online grocery services in order to increase income. An assessment of the cost of operations was needed, considering both short-term and long-term planning and sensitivity toward cost effectiveness. Expansion activities should have remained limited until a reasonable profit level was attained. With careful forward planning, CI can avoid these mistakes and profit in the online grocery business.

Indirect strategy application: Begin the section with the analysis of the background material. Allow the analysis to lead the reader to your problem or purpose statement. End with a very precise description of the issue to be related.

Example 3b: Lessons for CI in the Internet Market

Trifood Group Inc. failed to generate enough revenue to cover the general and administrative overhead expenses and was unable to develop a plan to become profitable. These actions resulted in Trifood filing for bankruptcy on September 19, 2002. Trifood needed to develop and implement a revised strategic plan that would build a larger customer base and reduce

Graphs and tables are included in documents to illustrate specific points. Whenever a graph or table is included in a report or proposal, it should be explained in the text surrounding it. Take a look at this pie chart. It gives a very clear picture of the overall financial state of Trifood. Write one to two paragraphs that could be included in the Trifood proposal we are looking at that will explain what this pie chart means to the reader.

Financial Scope of Trifood Group Inc.

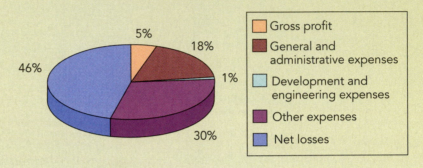

☐	Gross profit
☐	General and administrative expenses
☐	Development and engineering expenses
☐	Other expenses
☐	Net losses

operating expenses in order to maintain profitability. There was a need to identify the market segment best suited for online grocery services in order to increase income. An assessment of the cost of operations was needed, considering both short-term and long-term planning and sensitivity toward cost effectiveness. Expansion activities should have remained limited until a reasonable profit level was attained. With careful forward planning, CI can learn from Trifood's mistakes and could invest in an online grocery business that would be both successful and cost effective.

Goals and Objectives

No matter what strategies have been employed in your report or proposal previously, this section of the report should be delivered using a direct strategy. It is imperative that your audience completely understands the goals of the report. The goals and objectives must also be very specific; any vagueness in their description will lead the audience to believe that you haven't fully analyzed or understood the issue.

Vague goals and objectives	• Revenues must be increased in the next few months. • We should contact new potential vendors to ensure uninterrupted production. • Tensions in the shipping department could be addressed by sensitivity training.
Specific goals and objectives	• Revenues must be increased by 16 percent before July. • Vendors such as Himmelfarb and Brown should be contacted by next week to ensure uninterrupted production. • Tensions in the shipping department stemming from charges of racial discrimination and sexual harassment could be addressed by requiring attendance at sensitivity seminars similar to those offered by Vogt-Fuller Personnel Services.

Example 4: CI's Plans in the Wake of Trifood's Failure in the Internet Grocery Market

The funds required to initiate this project will be approximately $10 million. This amount will establish operations at the proposed sites in California. Execution of this plan needs to be expedited due to the critical time limits. The following activities need consideration:

- The auctions of all Trifood facilities are in progress. To take advantage of the cost savings of procuring equipment, the decision to implement this proposal in the next few days is critical.
- The recent layoff of Trifood personnel will provide a resource of staff members who are trained and experienced, thus reducing start-up time.
- Many of the large grocers have plans to establish online services. To compete within that market segment, online services need to be established within the next month.

Goals and objectives must be specific and direct.
© Charles Mann/CORBIS

Solutions and Recommendations

Because you have built a convincing case for your solution or recommendation in the earlier sections of the report, the final section of your report should be direct. However, you may want to revisit major points noted in the analytical and background sections of the report as you describe your ultimate resolution of the issue. Tie these points directly to the proposed resolution and use them to emphasize the necessity of adopting your ideas.

Example 5a: Request for Consideration
New Venture Proposal

Corporate Investments (CI) should invest in establishing an Internet grocery service. Using data and statistics from the Trifood operations the following actions have been developed and need to be considered:

There are four major areas in California with potential to build a profitable market for this service. It is proposed to open four warehouse locations in San Diego County, Orange County, Los Angeles County, and the San Francisco Bay area. These areas had been previously serviced by Trifood or DowntownGrocer and are not being serviced by a major competitive online grocery service at this time. The DowntownGrocer model of operations should be used for this venture.

These locations have existing facilities previously used by Trifood for the operations of Internet grocery services. Based on the studies of these facilities, the locations have strategic value to ensure that orders can be filled in a timely manner. In addition, the recent layoff of trained personnel will provide a pool of experienced laborers that will not require training.

A thorough marketing study on the customer base of Trifood needs to be performed to develop a strategy to encourage the customers to adopt Corporate Investments' new grocery service and to attract a new customer base in these areas.

Corporate Investments should purchase the rights to use the "DowntownGrocer.com" name. DowntownGrocer had an established following of customers and maintained a high percentage of repeat business. At this time Trifood does not have a positive image due to its failure to serve the acquired DowntownGrocer's customer base in the manner they were accustomed to receiving. DowntownGrocer's established sites in the California community were more efficiently run with less overhead, creating a good image and a recognized brand name.

Warehouse, office, and other operating equipment previously owned by Trifood is currently being auctioned off. It is estimated that the needed equipment to set up the four proposed facilities can be purchased from these auctions at 20 percent of the current market value of each item. This includes the fleet of vans used for delivery. This will allow Corporate Investments to start up each facility with less cash investment compared to the purchasing of new equipment. Careful consideration needs to be given in purchasing equipment that does not require a high level of technical support or is labor intensive.

The cost for establishing each facility is approximately $1 million to $2 million. This estimate is based on the procurement of some of the auctioned equipment of Trifood, the estimated cost of leased property, and the initial cost of setting up each facility. The financial model for personnel will be based on the DowntownGrocer model.

Make your solution or recommendation as detailed as possible. Your audience needs to understand that you have considered all ramifications, good and bad, of the resolution you are offering.

Example 5b: Risk Factors

The competition in this field is extremely high. The large brick-and-mortar supermarkets have a considerable amount of cash flow and already have established brand recognition. There are a few grocers who are beginning to plan online services to the local communities in order to win back consumers who have chosen to use online grocer services. The online grocers that are still operating are located on the East Coast, with a few in Washington and Illinois. The objective will be to offer special services and incentives to consumers that the larger grocers cannot offer. Most large grocers carry either their own brand of products or a limited selection of brand name items. Offering customers the option to special order an item not in stock at no additional cost is an example of a way to gain a competitive edge on the competition.

Most consumers have not gained confidence in online shopping. Some concerns are security and confidentiality issues. Customers may also be reluctant to order online because of the inconvenient delivery time. To change consumer behavior, these issues need to be addressed and resolved.

CREATIVE CHALLENGE

Identify a problem in your school or at your job: a policy, procedure, or current debate that causes friction. Consider at least three possible solutions to this problem, analyzing the risks and benefits from each individual solution. Present your solutions, along with their risks and benefits, to the class, and ask them if they see other risks or benefits you may have missed. As a class, vote on the best solution to your chosen problem.

Benefits

When Trifood first started serving the San Francisco Bay area in 1999, their general and administrative expenses for that year were $92.4 million (SEC, 10K, year-end 2000). In 2000, these same expenses increased 3.2 times. Trifood should have spent at least one-third of this amount for advertising, marketing services, and other professional service to help develop the better business strategies needed to build a larger customer base.

By purchasing the DowntownGrocer name, the benefits from serving its established customer base can bring in reasonable profits. The positive image of DowntownGrocer is a benefit in establishing a brand recognition that has been proven to be reliable in the past. Buying Trifood's auctioned warehouses, offices, and operating equipment will save the start-up company $20 million in expenses.

Conclusion

Most importantly, end your report on a positive note. This is especially important when the message you deliver is negative. Always use positive language and deemphasize the bad news by cushioning it within good or neutral news. For example, if a report discussed the need for layoffs, you would want to avoid mentioning the personal, human aspect of layoffs and focus instead on the necessity for all employees and the good of the company as a whole to reduce costs using the only means available: "Although layoffs are painful, a reduction of 5 percent in the workforce now will increase our cost-to-profit ratio by 25 percent and will make future growth a real possibility."

Example 6: Conclusion: CI in the Brave New Internet World
Finishing Touches for CI's Internet Marketing Plan
While entry into the online grocery market represents risk for CI, it also represents tremendous potential for profit. The potential risks can be minimized if CI learns from the mistakes of Trifood. Careful strategic planning will be critical as will a well thought-out marketing plan. The purchase of the DowntownGrocer name will immediately establish credibility with customers. The purchase of Trifood's warehouses and operating equipment will also help minimize risk by lowering the significant costs to enter this new market for CI.

We have scheduled a meeting on Friday, August 10, to discuss the adoption of this proposal. Your attendance and participation are needed to successfully launch this new venture. It is important that all matters be handled quickly due to time constraints.

Strategies

1. Try writing a report or proposal in chunks, rather than from introduction to solutions. Sometimes it is easier to compose individual sections of text and then link them using transitions.

2. If you are unsure which strategy will work for your purposes, try writing test paragraphs using different strategies. Incorporate the paragraph that best suits the audience you want to reach.

3. When discussing a topic that may irritate the reader, use positive expressions and focus on reader benefits. For example, "Although we have used Gruntick Inc. as our supplier for the last 20 years, it is imperative that we find a new source for raw materials" is likely to produce a negative reaction if the company has otherwise been happy with the services Gruntick has performed. "Finding a new source for raw materials can improve product quality and reduce costs by 12 percent" is far more persuasive (and clear).

4. When possible, examine previous reports and proposals that have been successful with the audience you are addressing. Use a strategic approach similar to that used in those examples.

5. Look for keywords and concepts in the RFP, brochures, or other promotional materials produced by your potential audience that reflect its corporate culture. Incorporate them into your document and strategy; they can help you anticipate resistance.

6. In some cases, you will be asked to revise a report you have written for a different audience. If you are anticipating several audiences from different levels of the company or from outside of the business, consider varying the strategy in key areas to suit the specific audience.

7. Consider the purpose of the report carefully. Sometimes, even in an informative report that requires no investment by the audience, the data you provide may encounter resistance.

8. One of the most convincing elements of any report or proposal is the use of clear, precise data. Supply as many facts and figures as possible, especially for sections in which you anticipate resistance.

9. Use the direct strategy when describing positive aspects of your issue; use the indirect strategy when you need to criticize policies or situations.

10. If the audience anticipates a request, for example, in a proposal, consider using the direct strategy throughout the document.

Summary

- Direct and indirect strategies are useful not only for overall approaches to reports and proposals but also within specific sections of such documents.

- Understanding the audience is a primary concern when developing a report. The choice of strategy depends on the relationship the audience has with the author and/or the data included in the document.

  a. If the contents of the document require nothing from the reader, use the direct approach.

  b. If the contents of the document require an action or investment by the reader, use an indirect approach.

- The strategy used for developing reports and proposals also depends on the type of document being created.
  a. Informative reports, such as compliance reports, meeting minutes, and progress or interim reports, are usually delivered using the direct strategy.
  b. Persuasive documents, such as business plans and proposals, generally require an indirect strategy.
  c. Analytical reports, including justification reports, annual reports, policy and procedure statements, and feasibility studies, often require a combination of direct and indirect strategies.
- The executive summary presents the issue addressed by the report, its objectives, and any proposed activities in a one-page overview (some executive summaries may be longer depending on the length of the report).
- The introduction to the report provides the reader with a context that will help him or her understand the rest of the report. It sets the tone, stylistically and in terms of the argument that follows, for the rest of the document.
  a. A direct introduction states the context, basic topic, and suggested solutions immediately.
  b. An indirect introduction presents the context and basic topic but withholds the suggested solutions or responses until the case can be more fully explained later in the document.
- The background of the report is essential information the reader will need to understand any analysis or conclusions reached later in the document. This material should be delivered directly. Background material can be discussed using a chronological approach, presenting events in the same order in which they originally occurred. The background can also be discussed using a situational approach, which describes events from the perspective of the departments and individuals involved. Finally, the background can be discussed using statistics to describe a situation.
- Problem and topic statements redefine and clarify the specific issue mentioned in the introduction and developed by the background.
  a. To use the direct strategy, begin with the problem statement, followed by the analysis, and end with a description of how the outcome of the report will address the problem.
  b. To use the indirect strategy, begin with the analysis, and then end with a precise problem statement.
- The goals and objectives of the report should be related directly.
- Solutions and recommendations may review key points made earlier in the report but are also delivered directly. They should be as detailed as possible.
- Reports and proposals should always end on a positive note, especially when the recommendations may appear to be negative.

Business Communication Projects

1. You work for a major car manufacturer. One of the lines your company produces has sold poorly for several years, and the Board of Directors has asked you to determine whether the line should be modified or discontinued. The results of your investigation show that the company would be better off if the line were discontinued. Now you must write a report to explain these findings. Consider these potential audiences:

   • Board of directors.

   • Car dealers.

   • Line workers.

   • Consumers.

   • Media.

   Imagine that you will be writing the report in sections, each section tailored to one of these audiences. Create a table in which you describe the strategy you will use in each section for each audience, and explain why you have made that choice.

2. A client has asked you to design a new skateboard. The client has provided strict guidelines regarding the cost, manufacturer, and marketing of the skateboard. As you develop your design, you realize that you can meet the client's cost and marketing requirements, but the chosen manufacturer, Navarro Skateworks, will be unable to build the special components you'd like to include. Bonechillers, another skateboard manufacturer, can. The client has requested a progress report on your project. Write the recommendation section of the report, requesting a change from Navarro Skateworks to Bonechillers and explaining why.

3. Look on the Internet for an online RFP (request for proposal). Create an outline for a proposal that details the strategies you would use in each section to apply for the funds offered.

4. Read the following paragraph carefully:

   Two years ago, Bishop Enterprises expanded its food services division. It acquired the Levy Bagel Company, which had enjoyed a 15 percent annual growth average for the previous five years. This key acquisition was expected to revitalize the Bishop food services. However, when Bishop attempted to change Levy's suppliers to Bishop's usual suppliers, Levy executives complained about the quality of the suppliers' materials. Bishop relented, and determined that although the cost of supplies would be more than 22 percent greater than original plans called for, the extra cost was offset by Levy's annual growth rate. Plans continued to regularize the Levy stores along Bishop restaurant standards and expand the chain. This year's annual report shows that the Levy Bagel chain includes more than 400 stores, 150 added since purchase. Total sales from these stores are 35 percent (1.9 million) lower than projections. Instead of supporting the Bishop food services division, the Levy Bagel chain is quickly draining division resources. Bishop Enterprises should consider a total restructuring of the Levy Bagel Company or sell the company outright.

Is this paragraph targeted at shareholders of Bishop Enterprises or at partners in this firm? Explain, and then revise the paragraph for the *opposite* audience.

5. After watching a presentation by one of your classmates, write a memo report to him or her critiquing his or her performance. Use the direct strategy for sections that describe what was done well and the indirect strategy for sections that describe areas for improvement.

6. Access the report described in the "In a Nutshell" feature for this chapter (http://with.iupui.edu/about.htm). Create a PowerPoint presentation that follows the direct and indirect strategies used in the original report, which Indiana University could use to promote their program.

7. A home television recording service has been ordered by a U.S. court to report the programs being recorded (and possibly pirated). This means that the programs people watch in the privacy of their homes will be noted and reported to a central agency—which may be considered an invasion of their privacy. Currently the service is developing software to protect the anonymity of subscribers in these reports. You have been asked to write a letter to the recording service subscribers explaining this situation. Write this letter, using direct and indirect strategies to explain the court's decision and promote subscriber acceptance of this procedure.

8. A collectible card company planned to produce a new line of cards: Legends of Rock Music. Buyers were excited about the new line, and orders poured in. Initial production runs of the cards came up short and only half of each order could be filled. Worried buyers doubled their renewal orders, expecting that only half of the orders would be filled once again. The second run of the cards, however, met the target, and all orders were filled in total. Now the buyers have too many cards to sell. You work at a collectible card store, and the main office has asked for a report on the Legends collection sales. Legends of Rock Music has sold well, but since the market was flooded with the second run of cards, their value hasn't risen as expected. Write a one-page report that tells the main office that sales are good but values are down, and that also explains the problems with the collectible card company and buyers.

Discussion Questions

1. Why are multiple strategies necessary in some reports and proposals?

2. How does the audience determine the strategic approach used when writing a proposal?

3. In what ways does the purpose of a report determine an effective strategic approach?

4. What is the importance of the executive summary?

5. Why is it necessary to organize background material according to a specific approach (chronological, situational, or statistical)?

6. Why is it necessary to redefine the problem or topic statement mid-report?

7. What is the purpose of using themes or key words throughout a document?

8. What's wrong with a vague objectives statement?

9. Are there any sections of a report or proposal that could employ an indirect approach, even if a direct approach seems to be the best strategy? Explain.

10. How important is a positive ending to an informational report?

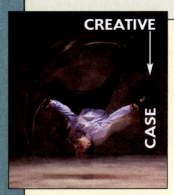

CREATIVE CASE

Creative Case

Buying for Baby on the Internet

In 1994, an entrepreneurial group from Carnegie Mellon University approached Lynne Bingham. Bingham owned a successful children's boutique in Pittsburgh, and the group wanted her to participate in an e-commerce project. They wanted her to put her store on the World Wide Web. She agreed.

Sales were slow in the beginning. It was a full year before someone actually ordered anything from her website. But sales improved eventually, and in 2000 she sold her store to focus on web-based sales. Later, a high-tech company in the Netherlands, Stork Group, paid her a six-figure sum to purchase her site's name. This left Bingham with plenty of capital to work with, but no website.

Initially, Bingham solicited bids for a site design. A site built from the ground up, she found, would probably run her $15,000 to $30,000. She also found Yahoo! shopping. On Yahoo! she could build a site herself using Yahoo!'s templates and reporting tools for inventory and site management for $100 a month. A Yahoo! site would be simpler to build and use but would lack the design options and flexibility a brand new site could offer. She just wasn't sure whether the limited capabilities of the Yahoo! service would meet her goals for growth and development of her company, The Stork Delivers.com.

She chose to use the Yahoo! service. The Yahoo! site generated 50 to 80 sales a month. However, Bingham wanted to improve those sales to 100 per month. She decided to get a web makeover from *BusinessWeek*. The professional web designers *BusinessWeek* contacted made the following observations:

- A small business can't afford to spend too much money on design, but the site must still be sophisticated enough to interest the customer and easy for him or her to use.

- Approximately 90 percent of Bingham's business is from previous customers. This means that once a customer has negotiated her site, he or she is likely to come back. It may also mean that some aspects of the site discourage new customers.

- Most of the products Bingham sells on the site are fairly expensive, ranging from $100 to $4,000. The design of the site she built on Yahoo! could undermine the sense of quality she wanted to convey.

Now the web designers needed to give Bingham their opinion. She could either redesign the Yahoo! site, or she could once again solicit bids for a brand new website.

How should the web designers give Bingham the news?

Some questions to consider:

1. How much control does Bingham want to have over her site? A new site may be more effective in some ways, but she may need assistance to maintain and update it. She can handle the Yahoo! site all by herself.

2. Would the outlay for a new site be cost effective?

3. Are the problems potential new customers are having with the Yahoo! site a result of Bingham's design, or is there a problem with the templates offered by the service?

4. Would a new site have the same access to customers that Yahoo! shopping offers?

SOURCE: Hamilton, J. (2001). "Delivering a More Upscale Look for TheStorkDelivers.com." Business Week Online. Retrieved May 8, 2002: http://www.businessweek.com:/print/technology/content/.../tc20010627362.htm.

Chapter 12

The following themes are explored in this chapter:

MACRO VIEW OF CULTURE
what is culture? / how do we learn culture? / intercultural communication styles

WORKFORCE DIVERSITY
ethnocentrism / race / ethnicity / age / socioeconomics / gender / sexual orientation / physical disabilities

MICRO VIEW OF ORGANIZATIONAL CULTURE
corporate culture

DEEP ORGANIZATIONAL CULTURE
values and beliefs / perspective / attitudes / vision

OBSERVABLE ORGANIZATIONAL CULTURE
norms / rites and rituals / heroes / lore

Culture: Inside and Out

Corporate cultures are changing to meet the demands of new fast-track technologies, new attitudes, and a swift current toward speedy and practically sleepless professional careers. Long, fast workdays are the wave in today's business environment, but not all companies value 10-hour workdays and speed. Some have created corporate environments where fun and the personal needs of employees are priorities. At SAS Institute, a software company, 7,000 employees enjoy seven-hour workdays, lunchtime entertainment, on-site massages, health care, child care, private offices, and a 55,000-square-foot athletic facility, all in a beautiful, campuslike corporate setting. The company believes that valuing employees inspires superior work performance and commitment. SAS also values diversity: 51 percent of its managers are women.

In contrast to this corporate culture, a small, family-owned publishing company requires that employees be at their desks no later than 8:55 A.M. and stay until 5:15 P.M. The corporate belief is that it takes about five minutes for employees to take off their coats, turn on their computers, and get situated before they begin performing their work duties. Similarly, it takes several minutes at the end of the workday to turn off computers and rinse out coffee cups. Therefore, if employees arrive at 8:55 and depart at 5:15, they will not waste company time with morning and evening rituals.

A Macro View of Culture

In virtually any society, *culture* is the most profound unseen force. While there is such a thing as observable culture, which includes such social artifacts as artwork, architecture, highways, and shoes, other aspects of culture are not as tangible. We cannot hold our beliefs and perceptions in our hand for people to see. But cultural values can still be perceived and recognized by people. At the publishing company in the "In a Nutshell" feature, management obviously believed that time spent getting organized at the beginning and end of a workday was unproductive, and this philosophy was enacted through extended work schedules. Corporate cultures also have observable artifacts, such as the athletic facility at SAS, that demonstrate what the company believes in a more obvious way. This chapter will explore both macro (dominant) and micro (corporate) culture and strategies to understand and work effectively within it. Figure 12.1 illustrates a macro view of culture.

We learn culture through interaction with family, friends, and other members of society.
© Chuck Savage/CORBIS

culture is a communally produced and shared model of reality that communicates how people are expected to behave, think, and feel.

What Is Culture?

From a macro perspective, **culture** is a communally produced and shared model of reality that communicates how a group is expected to behave, think, and feel as a society. It characterizes how we live and how we view the world as members of a society. Culture is a collection of socially created meanings, language, values, norms, beliefs, and customs.

Think of your own family structure. What did you learn to consider important and unimportant? How did you learn to communicate verbally and nonverbally? We learn culturally acceptable behaviors by communicating with the people who are closest to us. Culture is a larger version of the small family structure, an organized system that includes the shared meanings, values, and norms that guide our behavior through life.

How Do We Learn Culture?

socialization is learning through a system of shared interaction with other people.

From infancy, we learn a particular way of life through a process of **socialization,** which is learning from human interaction. We learn what we know about the world through a system of shared interaction with other people. We learn to be members of a culture. From generation to generation, a collective social knowledge is shared through both verbal and nonverbal communication. This social

FIGURE 12.1

Macro View of Culture

knowledge helps to shape both our lifestyle and our self-concept (the way we perceive ourselves).

Intercultural Communication Styles

When working with people from other cultures, we sometimes forget that not everyone communicates in the same way we do or values the same things. The following table highlights some differences in communication styles across cultures.

CREATIVE

Think about all the channels of communication through which you first learned how to think and behave in this culture. How did you learn to speak? What specific channels of communication enabled you to learn? Come to class prepared to discuss how we learn culture through interaction with others.

CHALLENGE

Communication	Asian and Middle Eastern Cultures	North American, Swiss, and German Cultures
Direct and indirect	• In some Asian and Middle Eastern cultures people communicate using an indirect style. Verbal statements tend to be reserved and vague, with emphasis on nonverbal behavior, paralinguistic tone, and the physical setting to convey meaning.	• In North America, Switzerland, and Germany direct communication is preferred. Many people from these cultures can be very talkative and value spoken words to convey precise meaning. While nonverbal behaviors and context are important, they are relied on less to convey meaning.

Communication	Asian and Middle Eastern Cultures	North American, Swiss, and German Cultures
Direct and indirect (*continued*)	• In Japanese and some Middle Eastern cultures, a direct style can be considered disrespectful, pushy, embarrassing, and an invasion of privacy.	• People who communicate in an indirect manner can often be viewed as dishonest, devious, or indecisive. For example, as a North American, you may view speaking directly as being honest and straightforward. You may feel that to say exactly what you mean is a sign of decisiveness and sincerity.
Rank, status, and age	• People speak politely and formally when addressing a person who is older or of higher status. • In Japanese culture, communication style and formality change based on the age, rank, and status of the people involved in the exchange. Younger workers defer to older workers, whom they value as more wise and experienced, even if both people hold the same rank. • In Japanese culture, offering opinions without being asked or speaking too casually with someone older or of higher rank may be viewed as disrespectful.	• In the workplace, people sometimes speak informally and offer opinions, even to those of higher rank. However, the level of speech formality can vary depending on the occasion and the people involved in the exchange. • In North America, too much formality may be viewed as unsocial, distanced, detached, or reserved.
Discussion and debate	• In consideration of other peoples' dignity and privacy, open debate is discouraged. Intense discussions about religion, politics, or serious personal problems are considered very personal topics. They are avoided conversations in the workplace. • In Japanese and some Middle Eastern cultures, discussions and differences of opinion might lead to conflict or embarrassment.	• Debates and discussions are encouraged to solve problems and work productively. • In North America, productive conflict and open discussions can be beneficial ways to build stronger relationships and create new directions.
Working together	• In Japanese culture, collaboration means that people work together to reach consensus. Work roles are somewhat less defined and employees often share responsibilities. It is not necessary for superiors to provide explicit direction and explanation of work tasks because subordinates and superiors communicate and often work side by side throughout the process of task achievement. Japanese managers provide only broad direction for assignments and prefer to closely supervise and monitor work performance. • The focus of recognition or credit is on the group and is shared collectively by members. Cooperation with others is necessary to achieve promotion and acceptance. • When Japanese employees work with American managers, they often feel isolated without intensive guidance and supervision.	• In North American culture, work roles are clearly defined by superiors. Employees have specific duties and responsibilities to accomplish independently. • Individual leadership and autonomy is valued, as is recognition of the individual for achievement. • When North American and Japanese people work together, the difference in styles can be frustrating. When working with managers from Japan, North American workers expect clearly defined and detailed assignments that they can perform independently.

A Macro View of Workforce Inclusion and Diversity

In the 21st century, the landscape of business is a **diversity** of workers from many different backgrounds and perspectives. By the year 2008, it is estimated, 70 percent of new workers in the labor market will be women and/or minority members. The range of worker diversity includes race and ethnicity, age, economic level, gender, sexual orientation, and physical disability. Mutual respect and consideration for people and their differences are fundamental for both individuals and the organizations in which they work.

More and more managers are becoming aware of the importance of inclusion for all employees. J. T. Childs, IBM vice president of global workforce diversity, recognizes that if minority customers perceive that a business behaves in a biased or unfair way, or if they do not see people like themselves working at all levels in the business, they will likely do business elsewhere. The loss of minority business for companies can be substantial, since the current total disposable income for African-Americans, Asians, Hispanics, and Native Americans is $1.31 trillion.

Because we learn to view the world from a cultural perspective, sometimes we interpret different behavior, customs, or beliefs as a bit strange. While that perception usually diminishes after we gain more exposure to people from different cultural orientations, sometimes we can destructively perceive differences as unacceptable. **Ethnocentrism,** the belief that our own culture is superior to others, can become a barrier that

diversity involves people from many different backgrounds and perspectives.

ethnocentrism is the belief that one's own culture is superior to others.

Many large corporations have diversity programs that help them select their suppliers. These programs give preference to businesses that are owned and run by minorities, women, and people with disabilities, as long as these businesses can offer competitive services. Some of the supplier diversity policies of large companies can be viewed at these websites:

- Quaker Oats: www.quakeroats.com/about/supplier.html
- Boeing: www.boeing.com/companyoffices/doingbiz/terms/sbsdb
- AT&T: www.att.com/hr/life/eoaa/supplier_diversity.html
- Pillsbury: www.pillsbury.com/about/supplierdiv.asp
- Verizon: www.gte.com/Aboutgte/Organization/Supply/supplierguide/supplierdiver.html
- Sun Microsystems: www.iforce.com/aboutsun/coinfo/diversity/index.html

Take a look at some of these sites. Write an e-mail to your instructor in response to the following questions:

1. How do these programs support diversity in the business world?
2. How specific is each program in its definition of minorities?
3. Would you recommend any adjustments or changes in the policies described at these sites, and what would they be?

WORD ON THE WEB

Word on the Web

race refers to inherited biological characteristics of a group such as skin color, facial features, and other physical variations.

ethnicity refers to ethnic heritage and related cultural characteristics of a given group.

hinders harmony and sabotages productive working relationships. For example, some North American people may believe that Western greetings are more expressive and warm than some Asian and Eastern cultural greetings. Because people from some cultures prefer to bow rather than making physical contact such as shaking hands, North Americans tend to view this custom as somewhat cold and informal.

Race/Ethnicity

Race refers to inherited biological characteristics of a group: skin color, facial features, and other physical variations. In a recent study, 60 percent of minority executives said they had experienced work task discrimination during their careers. While some discriminatory attitudes still linger in the 21st century—including resistance to hiring and mentoring minorities, fewer opportunities for advancement, and less information sharing—many businesses are embracing cultural change. They are becoming more mindful of the value of racial diversity as competition for employees and customers becomes more fierce. In a study of *Fortune* 1000 companies, 91 percent said that diversity initiatives can help maintain a competitive advantage in the market, and 83 percent said diversity programs have improved their overall corporate culture.

Ethnicity refers to cultural characteristics of a given group. An ethnic heritage usually relates to a country of origin (for example, Ireland, Ghana, or Cambodia). Foods, beliefs, clothing, and language may distinguish the culture of a particular ethnic group. Despite the multicultural North American landscape, some ethnic groups still find themselves the brunt of discrimination, rejection, and exclusionary practices.

CREATIVE CHALLENGE

Imagine that the vice president of marketing at your company just distributed a memo asking for feedback about a new department bonus program that rewards individual departments with money and equipment for developing and implementing diversity and inclusion initiatives. These initiatives include recruitment and hiring practices, training seminars, promotion and advancement opportunities, mentoring programs, an inclusive environment at department meetings and social events, community outreach, and celebration of difference activities. Write a memo to the vice president about this bonus program. Include in your memo at least two reasons you think diversity and inclusion programs may enhance employee morale and customer relations.

Nonverbal Cultural Differences

When interacting with people from other cultures, think about how your nonverbal behaviors may affect them.

| Hand gestures | • Hand sign for "OK," characterized by touching the forefinger and thumb together can mean a situation or person is satisfactory in North America.
 • Shaking hands is a greeting in North America. | • In Tunisia the "OK" sign means zero, like a person is nothing. In Greece it is an obscenity.
 • In Turkey men sometimes hold hands as a sign of friendship. The Japanese avoid touching as a greeting, including shaking hands, and prefer the traditional bow. |

Eye contact	• Direct eye contact in North America shows interest and attention.	• In Japan and some other Eastern cultures, direct eye contact can signal disrespect, aggressiveness, or an invasion of privacy.
Physical space	• In North American cultures, standing in close proximity can be uncomfortable because this space is often reserved for intimates.	• In some South American cultures, close physical proximity can show connection and comfort, whether or not the person is an intimate.

Age

Different generations of people have different perspectives based on their historical experiences in the world. From a business perspective, stereotypes about age can damage organizational productivity in at least two ways.

1. When organizations restructure the labor force, older workers sometimes find themselves phased out of their jobs and replaced by younger, cheaper workers. When organizations realize how valuable and knowledgeable the experienced workers were, they have to hire them back as consultants at double their original pay.

2. Younger workers can be blocked from contributing to their full potential because they are not taken seriously or because older subordinates or co-workers resent their authority.

With today's demographic shifting and the struggle to find good workers, companies are making the effort to keep older employees through flexible work programs and incentives. To encourage the 15 percent of its 62,000 employees who are nearing or eligible for retirement, US West, a telecommunications company, offers diversity seminars that focus on working with people of different ages. Interesting work and inclusion strategies can encourage older employees to remain employed, and they can choose to cut back on their hours in a type of "phased retirement."

Socioeconomics

Income, power, and education are some of the distinctions that rank people's cultural status and prestige in American society. Economic issues can affect a person's ability to obtain good health care, education, and professional advancement. Issues sometimes arise in organizations because of perceptions about specific titles or rank. Some people make the mistake of assuming that clerks, secretaries, or administrative assistants are the organization "peons." Often the opposite is true. While these employees may not be highly compensated, many of them possess both power and control in the organization. They often know important information, manage the workflow, and control access to the people they work for. Furthermore, some employees avoid or discourage the development of interpersonal relationships with employees of lower rank than themselves. It's like the old military rule that officers not consort with enlisted personnel. Certainly, antiquated viewpoints are changing, and today, a company manager is just as likely to associate with a clerk as she is with another manager. But some people still believe that title or rank dictates who should associate with whom in the organization.

Gender

Gender roles are learned throughout our cultural life because we are socialized to expect certain behaviors from men and other behaviors from women. While perspectives about role categories are changing, few women are represented in upper-level management. To date, only three women are CEOs in the nation's *Fortune* 500 companies. Resistance to women entering higher levels of management may stem from inaccurate perceptions that women are not assertive enough to manage effectively. Some people believe that early socialization of women toward passivity and accommodation makes them less able to make serious decisions and less likely to influence others when they do. This is a double bind: When a woman behaves according to socialized sex roles (such as nurturing), she may be regarded as ineffectual. But if she demonstrates leadership through more so-called masculine behaviors (such as assertiveness), she may be regarded as pushy, domineering, or headstrong. Not all companies are blind to the talents of women managers and executives. At Nordstrom, a retail clothing chain, 70 percent of the managerial and supervisory positions are held by women; 85 of the company's 120 stores nationwide are headed by women.

Another problem that continues to haunt women is the salary gap. According to the U.S. Census Bureau, women earn, on average, only 74 cents for every dollar men make. Some companies now monitor their compensation methods to narrow the gap and ensure a fair allocation of wages. Despite these efforts, many women still find the road to corporate prominence a monumental challenge.

Gender Differences

Chapter 13 highlights more differences related to gender behavior in the workplace, but we will explore them briefly in the table on the next page.

Sexual Orientation

While gay and lesbian groups have achieved solid progress toward some legal rights and entitlements, many still find barriers in certain professions. Issues about same-sex domestic partner insurance benefits, service in the military, and jobs in education continue to spark controversy. Some gay and lesbian workers feel compelled to hide their

	Women	Men
Communicating professionally	• Engage in more interpersonal conversations and are viewed as superior at building relationships. • Use conversation to achieve or maintain interconnectedness and increase morale. • Tend to use language that is polite in consideration of other people's feelings. • Focus more on the emotional tone in messages. • Use more backchannel communication (feedback) like "yes," "really," and "right" to signal interest and support for a speaker.	• Participate in fewer interpersonal exchanges, but viewed as superior at demonstrating persuasion. • Use conversation to instruct, delegate, and demonstrate control. • Use more concrete and aggressive language. • Tend to focus more on the content of messages. • Nod head more to signal agreement.
Communicating socially	• Tend to talk less in mixed-gender social settings. • Initiate conversation less often. • Yield personal space more often.	• Talk more at mixed-gender social gatherings. • Initiate conversation more frequently. • Tend to invade personal space more often.

preferences to keep their jobs and avoid social judgment. Some report that when they come out, certain co-workers avoid interaction with them or even undermine their work performance.

Physical Disabilities

In business, some of the estimated 17 million working-age Americans with disabilities continue to experience difficulties. Often they are not taken seriously, and their influence and expertise are minimized. Regardless of what health problem they have, some people assume they are mentally retarded or deaf. Too many co-workers respond to people who have physical impairments by shouting, avoiding eye contact, or asking someone else to speak for them.

Some employers fear that workers with disabilities may be absent more often and that accommodating their physical or other needs will be expensive. However, workers with disabilities are often more reliable than other workers, and, in about 85 percent of cases, accommodations for them costs employers under $1,000. Not only is it well worth the investment to take advantage of workers with disabilities and their skills and knowledge, but under the Americans with Disabilities Act, it's the law.

Workers with disabilities are an important part of a diverse workforce.
© Real Life/Getty Images

Practice Diversity

Race and ethnicity	• Avoid racist jokes, descriptions, and words. • Identify or discuss people on the basis of characteristics other than their race, such as "the team member who has the statistics." • Speak clearly and precisely with people from different cultures and ethnic backgrounds. • Do not use slang or ambiguous terms. • Understand that people behave and communicate in varied ways. Use less direct language when communicating with people from Asian and Middle Eastern cultures and avoid discussing personal topics that may embarrass them.
Socioeconomics	• Use respectful terms when addressing employees or co-workers. • Listen to the opinions of all employees and co-workers, regardless of rank. • Use phrases that request rather than command.
Gender	• Use inclusive language such as "his or her" in verbal and written communication. • Use the persons' title for correspondence greetings when you are unable to find the name of the addressee (Dear Service Rep). • Recognize that the management and communication styles of men and women are different and that each has advantages in business contexts.
Sexual orientation	• Don't assume the gender of a colleague's significant other. • Avoid jokes or comments that belittle different lifestyles.
Physical abilities	• Use "people first" language that focuses on the individual and not his or her disability. • Recognize that people who are differently abled live and work productively.

A Micro View of Organizational Culture

corporate culture is the way the organization operates, how it is structured, how members are expected to behave, and what the organization believes is important.

co-cultures like organizations, are smaller groups that exist within the larger culture and have their own values, beliefs, and codes for behavior.

It is as important for you to understand the culture of your company as it is for you to understand the national culture into which you were born. When you walk into an organization, you enter a specific corporate way of life. A **corporate culture** is the way the organization operates, how it is structured, how members are expected to behave, and what the organization believes is important. This culture defines the organization. A micro view of organizational culture is illustrated in Figure 12.2. Organizations are smaller societies, or **co-cultures,** that exist within the larger national culture. These co-cultures have their own values, beliefs, and codes for behavior. Each organization has a unique philosophy and interpretation of organizational life. As an employee, you will need to know what your organization values and what it means to be a member of that corporate group.

Consider two computer service companies with unique corporate cultures. At Abuzz Technologies Inc., an Internet information service owned by New York Times Digital, food, art, hobbies, and community service combine to create a down-to-earth corporate way of

Micro View of Culture   **FIGURE 12.2**

Micro View of Organizational Culture

Microsoft—
Redmond, Washington

Intel—
Santa Clara, California

Walt Disney Corp.—
Burbank, California

Sprint PCS—
Overland Park,
Kansas

Sear's Roebuck—
Chicago, Illinois

New York Stock Exchange—
J.P. Morgan—
American Express—
New York City

Home Depot—
Atlanta, Georgia

Southwest Airlines—
Texas Instruments—
Dallas, Texas

life. Abuzz matches individual and corporate clients with experts and expertise, linking information seekers with information authorities. In Cambridge, Massachusetts, employee artwork, stuffed animals, and cartoons personalize the warm décor of the remodeled factory building that is Abuzz headquarters. Mixing creativity, work, and play, employees meet regularly in the company's spacious kitchen, spend lunch breaks together, or informally gather for Friday afternoon cocktails or dinner at various restaurants. Not only do employees spend time socializing together, but they also volunteer in the community. At elementary schools, they help network computers and build websites. These collaborative activities reinforce the close, comfortable, and playful atmosphere at Abuzz.

At the software giant Microsoft, employees believe that they are extremely different from other people and that the company is extremely different from other companies. Some of the 39,000 computer professionals on staff believe they would not fit in anywhere else. The prevailing perspective is that Microsoft is composed of the chosen smart,

CREATIVE

CHALLENGE

Think about the following questions related to corporate culture:

1. What meanings do the organization members share?
2. What is the corporate philosophy?
3. How do members behave?
4. What is the corporate vision for the future?
5. How important are innovation and change?
6. Are employees allowed to make decisions?
7. How do employees get promoted?
8. How do the members communicate, and who talks to whom?
9. How do the members think?
10. How do the members do things?

Your exploration of both deep and observable corporate culture will help you to answer these questions.

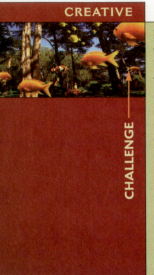

results-oriented, persistent people on whom over 100 million users depend. Microsoft values dedication and attention to detail because it builds character and helps the company succeed. Creativity is sometimes surpassed by the bottom line, which includes shipping out a product that is faster and has fewer bugs than the competition's. Many employees routinely spend hours in meeting after meeting to discuss, evaluate, and work out potential bugs and product improvements. Microsoft's walls in Redmond, Washington, are adorned with paintings by master artists, many of which are loaned to various museums. Work at Microsoft can be life-consuming; many employees eat, play, work, and breathe the company for very long hours each day.

Deep Organizational Culture

deep culture is the organization's identity or personality, what it believes, perceives, and considers important.

A **deep culture** is the organization's identity or personality, what it believes, perceives, and considers important. The elements of deep organizational culture include values, perspective, and vision.

Values and Beliefs

values represent a set of shared principles defining what is important to members of an organization.

beliefs are feelings or opinions about what is right or true.

Values represent a set of shared principles defining what is important to members of an organization. What members affirm as important—right or wrong, good or bad—shapes the core values of an organization. Values encompass basic **beliefs,** the feelings or opinions people hold about what is right or true. For example, some companies believe that employee mistakes are part of the learning experience, while others believe mistakes are detrimental to an employee's success. Beliefs help to shape core values, but are more flexible. Values are strongly held convictions that often come from our dominant culture and can be more difficult to change than beliefs.

Values underscore the standards of the organization and provide a framework for success and achievement. At Alberto-Culver, a personal care and household products manufacturer, employees developed a set of 10 "cultural imperatives" that they live by and can both recite and describe. These cultural imperatives are honesty, ownership, trust, customer orientation, commitment, fun, innovation, risk taking, speed, and teamwork. They inspire and guide employees in accomplishing tasks and provide a framework for what it means to be a member of the Alberto-Culver team.

The values of an organization can determine everything from what is required for promotion to how fairly employees are treated. Corporate values are often communicated to employees and customers through company literature such as bylaws, employee manuals, annual reports, and mission statements. They can also be shared orally, through training initiatives and face-to-face interaction. If an organization's corporate values include total quality and customer service, these values may be found in company policies and/or outlined in the mission statement.

Strong organizational cultures provide values that all members of the organization know and understand. Take, for example, Internet consultant companies such as Scient and Sapient. These new e-business companies have fast cultures. They value speed and innovation on Internet time. Employees must learn to be movers and shakers in an accelerated cultural environment. Because the mission of these companies is to wire their business clients to the Web quickly and efficiently, the culture promotes a no-time-to-lose standard for success. These consulting companies help clients such as Chase Manhattan Bank and iWon.com become faster, more flexible, and cutting-edge 21st-century corporate cultures.

Perspectives and Attitudes

A **perspective** is a particular way of thinking about the world. An organizational perspective is the way members view situations, behaviors, or ideas. Some perspectives are deeply held attitudes that are shared among organizational members. An **attitude** is a learned inclination toward or away from an idea, object, or person. For example, many companies have positive attitudes about collaborative team projects and encourage employees to work together. A given company may have the attitude that management should make all business-related decisions. But, as the business shifts, restructures, and flattens its corporate structure (as many modern businesses do), this attitude may change. At UPS, company policy now encourages employee decision making at all levels in the chain of command because the leaders recognize that employees' perspective on the front lines gives them a better understanding of what changes and decisions are needed. UPS leaders believe that giving rank-and-file employees the authority to make decisions increases customer satisfaction and boosts morale.

perspective is a particular way of thinking about the world.

attitude is a learned inclination toward, or perception of, an idea, object, or person.

Vision

An organization's **vision** is its purpose, mission, and future direction. Corporate visions provide a clear direction for the future and emphasize the importance of reaching company goals. Many corporations' visions include process improvements and innovations, excellence in performance, and success through team building. Like corporate values, visions are presented in company literature and shared at staff meetings, conferences, and company events. At Trilogy, a Texas-based software company, the company vision is communicated through what leaders call a "teachable point of view." Teachable points, which are

vision is an organization's purpose, mission, and future direction.

shared with new employees, describe where the company is going and what steps are needed to get there. Two prime components of Trilogy's vision are innovation through risk and corporate change.

Observable Organizational Culture

observable culture
involves the aspects of culture that can be seen, heard, or directly experienced by people.

Those aspects of culture that can be seen, heard, or directly experienced by people are **observable culture.** Observable culture is rich in symbolism, behaviors, words, stories, and situations that hold specific meaning for members. Observable organizational culture contains various performance interactions that demonstrate how members construct and share reality. These performance interactions include behaviors we can see such as norms, rites and rituals, heroes, and organizational lore.

Norms

norms are a series of behavior codes that guide acceptable conduct.

Norms are a series of behavior codes that guide acceptable conduct in an organization. These normative do's and don'ts reflect corporate values. Often, the corporate codes are similar to those in our society so organization members naturally behave in accordance with them.

Unconscious Norms	Institutional Rules
When corporate expectations for behavior match the dominant cultural expectations, they are unconscious norms. These are common behavioral codes both inside and outside the organization. For example, when you begin working for an organization, there is an unconscious expectation that you will not be physically assaulted on the job—unless you join the ranks at the Worldwide Wrestling Federation.	Some norms are created rules that define specific corporate expectations. These institutional rules are routine behavior codes that you learn when you begin working for a company. For example, some companies allow smoking in designated areas, but others prohibit smoking throughout the professional building and grounds.

Norms can be communicated to members through written materials such as employee handbooks and through interpersonal interactions.

Rites and Rituals

rites and rituals are various activities, ceremonies, and celebrations—particular performance interactions that convey organizational values.

Rites and rituals are various activities, ceremonies, and celebrations— particular performance interactions that convey organizational values. Dramatic performances such as company picnics, employee awards ceremonies, board meetings, Christmas parties, and retirement dinners reinforce what the company believes and encourage employee commitment.

At Alberto-Culver, cultural celebrations include Business Builders Awards, which reward individual employees who work beyond their job requirements and teams whose efforts contribute to the company's revenue growth. Another awards program at Alberto-Culver is the People's Choice Awards, in which employee's vote for other employees who they believe demonstrate dedication and great performance. The company also celebrates individual anniversaries and holds appreciation parties. Valassis, a company that supplies Sunday newspapers with discount circulars, celebrates the achievement of financial goals through stock parties and employee recognition events. The entertainment at these parties can be lavish, including free airplane rides for employees and trips to various amusement parks.

Other company rites and rituals are not for employees only. Medtronic, inventor and manufacturer of the battery-powered pacemaker, invites customers to join events like its annual holiday party. Patients who have lifesaving Medtronic devices implanted in their bodies attend holiday celebrations and offer testimonials to the company and its products. Earl Bakken, cofounder of Medtronic, attends every company event and personally bestows new employees with a special medallion on which the corporate mission is inscribed. The emotional celebrations and events at Medtronic reinforce the belief that the work employees perform is vitally important to doctors and patients all over the world. Of the tens of thousands of employees who work for Medtronic, 94 percent say they feel tremendous pride in their work.

Celebrations and ceremonies reinforce company values and can unite employees as a team.
© Wendy Ashton/Getty Images

Heroes

Heroes are organizational members who best demonstrate and symbolize company values. They are often role models who have achieved success and to whom other members look for leadership. Heroes may be visible CEOs such as Steve Jobs at Apple, founder and chair Bill Gates at Microsoft, or Jack Welch, former CEO of General Electric, but they don't have to be nationally known figures. Ordinary employees can become heroes if they demonstrate solid leadership, achieve success through excellent performance, or exhibit superior motivational skills. Heroes are successful people who personify what the company believes an ideal employee should be.

Lore

Every corporate culture has its own **lore,** stories or legends shared by members that reveal company history, appropriate conduct, and values. Lore provides vivid, dramatic insights into how members believe the organization really works. It is one of the

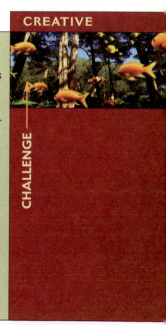

CREATIVE

CHALLENGE

Think about two corporate heroes you know or have learned about through the media such as the late Dave Thomas, founder of Wendy's. You may consider their extracurricular accomplishments, such as Thomas's work on behalf of adoptive children. Draft a two-page memo to your instructor that describes the ways you think these two different heroes represent what the corporate way of life may be like in their organizations. Discuss in your memo whether or not you would want to work for these organizations, based on your perception of the company heroes.

FIGURE 12.3   **Lore**

heroes are organizational members who best demonstrate and symbolize company values.

lore involves stories or legends shared by members that reveal company history, appropriate conduct, and values.

most important ways employees learn the corporate culture and the ropes of corporate life. The oral telling and retelling of stories constitute what employees think is the real deal of organizational life, and the heroes and heroines of lore are the organizational members themselves. Leonard Riggio, CEO at Barnes & Noble, routinely shares with employees stories about his humble beginnings growing up in Brooklyn, New York, to demonstrate the back-to-basics, practical, and resourceful culture the bookstore chain maintains today.

While not all lore is based on absolute truth, most is based on some real event (which is often embellished as time goes on). Members often take a story motif and then tinker with it, adding details to make the story more exciting or tailoring it to fit the situation. Figure 12.3 illustrates the sharing of a story in an organization.

How Lore Works

While stories serve different purposes, two primary functions are to socialize new members and to guide veteran members. As discussed in Chapter 2, informal messages are often transmitted through the grapevine. Lore is informally carried through the grapevine among employees. When you first join an organization, you may hear stories about what happened to other employees that can illustrate how you should approach certain situations. To demonstrate the importance of staff attention to detail, Ray Kroc, founder of McDonald's restaurants, would tell employees about a particular Chicago-area franchise he visited. In this story, Kroc noticed a lot of garbage, like cups and Happy Meal boxes, strewn throughout the shrubs near the parking lot. He pointed out all the garbage in the bushes to the manager. Then Kroc, his driver, and the nervous store manager proceeded to pick up all the trash together.

Themes of Organizational Lore

While employees share numerous unique stories that describe how things work in a company, there are four main themes to lore.

1. **How does the company feel about rule breaking?**

   This type of lore reveals the corporate position on the enforcement of rules. Stories involving rule breaking let employees know whether it will be tolerated or not. They also suggest whether the rules apply to everyone in the organization or some employees are exempt from them. One example of rule-breaking lore involved a young woman serving as a security supervisor at IBM. The story goes that she was responsible for making sure that no one entered a secure area without the proper clearance, a green badge. One day, the chair of the board, Thomas Watson, arrived with some executives to enter the secure area. The security supervisor timidly informed Watson that he did not have the proper clearance badge to enter. Some of the executives began to growl about whether she knew who he was. Suddenly Watson raised his hand to signal quiet, and one of the executives ran off to fetch him a green badge.

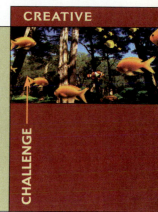

CREATIVE

CHALLENGE

What do you think this story says about the culture at IBM as it relates to rule breaking? Break into groups with your class colleagues to discuss what elements of deep or observable culture are communicated throughout this story.

2. **Is the boss human?**

   Like the story about Ray Kroc, the founder of McDonald's, "is the boss human" lore provides insight into the connection that employees feel with company executives or managers. Employees often determine the culture of the organization by seeing the boss as a symbol. Is the boss down to earth or above it all? A boss who has risen through the ranks inspires vastly different lore from a boss who is hired from outside the organization. Take the story of Charlie Brown, the CEO at Illinois Bell Telephone in the late 1960s. The story holds that during a workers' strike when many company employees were on the picket line, customer phone lines were not being serviced. So Charlie Brown donned work clothes, picked up his tools, and went off to service the lines like any other repairperson.

3. **Will I get fired?**

   This lore involves how the organization deals with fiscal crises. In times of economic and market downturns, organizations handle restructuring or change differently. Some companies issue hundreds of pink slips at a time. Others find alternatives to layoffs. The recent downturn in the economy has created financial difficulty at Motorola. Employees share stories about how to cut costs and save jobs, and, as a result, the company recently directed 17,000 of its employees to take two weeks' vacation to save the company money. Similarly, as a result

Jump In!

JUMP IN! ⟶

Communications Strategies Corp. decided to build on its grapevine to facilitate a knowledge-sharing network, which is a human chain of executives, managers, and line staff at all levels who share information, collaborate, learn, and solve business problems together. The knowledge network would enable employees to gain and give advice, share their expertise, and develop practical solutions to business problems. Communication Strategies Corp. did not want this network to become a formal information system or to be management dominated. The initiative would take advantage of the informal network of employees already in place and offer services to participants, such as materials, data, physical space for meetings, equipment, and even funding for specific projects.

BASIC TENETS FOR THE KNOWLEDGE-SHARING NETWORK

- Interaction builds partnerships in innovation and solutions.
- The knowledge network is an informal strategy for information sharing and problem solving.
- Any employee who wants to participate is welcome.

React to the idea of a grapevine-based knowledge-sharing network by answering the following questions:

1. Would this network need to have clear goals and objectives to be successful?

2. From where or from whom should the goals come?

3. What topics or problems should be addressed? Who would choose them?

4. Would basic situations such as learning new software be included in the discussions?

5. Should a coordinator be appointed to lead network project discussions and solutions?

6. How would solutions or innovations discovered through the network be implemented?

7. How could Communication Strategies Corp. build this knowledge network into the corporate culture? What values do you think would be in keeping with knowledge sharing? What company norms for behavior or rituals would support knowledge sharing?

of the economy and the negative publicity about Ford Explorers equipped with defective tires, Bridgestone/Firestone decreased the workweek from seven to six days at its Illinois plants. While these mandatory vacation days and reduced workweeks may cause some employees distress, the stories focus on the companies' efforts to save jobs.

4. **How does the company deal with obstacles?**

This lore centers on overcoming internal or external obstacles. External obstacles include fire, snow, terrorism, or acts of God. Internal obstacles include technical and scientific mistakes and errors caused by inefficiencies or flawed practices. In most of these stories, obstacles are transformed into a positive outcome for employees and the organization. One example of obstacle lore is the soap story at Procter & Gamble. In 1879, a technician left his soap-mixing machine unattended for more than an hour. When he returned from lunch, he discovered that a good deal of air had been whipped into the mixture, which could have ruined the batch. Despite the mistake, the soap mixture was made into bars. The result was the creation of Ivory, the soap that floats. A similar story is told about Moon's Lakeside restaurant in 1890s Saratoga, New York. The chef was furious that a customer kept sending his fried potatoes back to the kitchen because they were "much too thick." To make a point, the chef angrily sliced the potatoes wafer thin—and the potato chip was born.

Lore passed from employee to employee on the grapevine provides entertaining insights into the corporate way of life. It links employees to the corporate reality and helps them make sense of what situations and events mean. When you hear stories about company employees, you can begin to frame a picture of the prevailing attitudes, traditions, and perceptions they hold.

Practice Organizational Culture

Culture	Communication Response
Values • Customer service	• When discussing customers, avoid using unflattering descriptions or words. • Frame policies using customer-first language. • Explain conflict resolution techniques from a customer perspective.
• Valuing employees	• Avoid terms that demean employees (such as stupid, ridiculous, silly, or obtuse).
Norms and rules • Meeting project deadlines • Observing dress codes	• Discuss project deadlines often. • Use boldface or highlighting for deadline dates on project materials. • Even if a written dress code does not exist, it is advisable to wear clothing similar to company peers'.
Rites and rituals • Company picnics, retirement dinners, events	• Attendance may not be explicitly required, but it is advisable. • Follow behavior patterns of responsible employees.
Company hero • A person who is considered by other employees to be outstanding and who is well known in the company	• Observe this person and focus on his or her nonverbal behavior, clothing, and access to management and other employees. • Listen (when possible and without violating privacy) to this individual's interactions with co-workers, management, and employees. • Ask other employees what characteristics this person has that are outstanding.
Lore • Stories told at meetings, during informal conversations, and on the company grapevine	• Listen carefully to company stories to gain insight about values and norms. • Take mental notes. For example, what rank do the storyteller and the story characters hold in the organization? • Determine the theme of the story being described (like rule breaking or obstacle lore). • Assess the underlying message of the story as it may relate to your own present or future behavior.

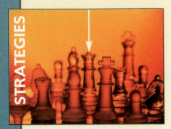

STRATEGIES

Strategies

1. Review your organization's internal company literature, including policy statements, bylaws, employee handbooks, newsletters, and any general memos to staff you can find.

2. Review any available external communication, such as company newsletters, brochures, pamphlets, annual reports, press releases, and advertisements.

3. Attend company functions, outings, and sponsored events.

4. Find a copy of the organization chart to determine staffing patterns and the formal chain of command.

5. Listen carefully to the stories that you hear about employees and the company. Pay attention to who tells the stories and who adds commentary. Assess the meaning of each story as it relates to the context in which you received it.

6. Look for similarities and differences between what the company publicly says is important and what employees relate is important through their stories and interactions.

7. Observe how members behave when they interact in the department offices and in other corporate settings. Notice who talks to whom and who spends lunch or coffee breaks together.

8. Find out which employees receive promotions. Ask how long promoted employees worked in their jobs and what skills they had or what they did that made them good candidates for advancement.

9. Notice how new ideas, advancements in technology, or innovations are handled. Is the company quick to embrace innovation, or does it take time to incorporate change?

10. Before you communicate, make sure you consider the important elements of corporate culture. Be certain that the content of your message is sensitive to the members' corporate values and perspectives.

Summary

SUMMARY

- Culture is shared meaning and a model of reality that outlines how people are expected to think, feel, and act as members of a group. We learn culture through socialization, which is acquired from interactions with group members over time.

- Workforce diversity is the multicultural landscape of corporate America. Its variables include race, ethnicity, age, socioeconomics, gender, sexual preference, and physical disability.

- Organizational culture is a corporate way of life that is derived from the national culture but is a distinct co-culture with its own values, behaviors, and beliefs.

- Deep organizational culture is the soul of what the company values and its vision for the future.

  a. Values are the shared beliefs and principles of the company.

  b. Perspective is the way the members of the company view situations, behaviors, and ideas.

  c. A company's vision is its purpose, mission, and future direction.

- Observable organizational culture is the tangible elements of culture that can be seen or heard. It consists of performance interactions such as norms, rites and rituals, heroes, and lore.

  a. Norms are codes that determine acceptable and unacceptable behavior. Unconscious norms are expected behaviors that we learn from the national culture. Institutional rules are specific codes that guide corporate behavior in routine situations.

  b. Rites and rituals are dramatic cultural performances such as ceremonies, celebrations, and events.

  c. Company heroes are human symbols of what it takes to be a successful employee. They are role models who exhibit leadership, positive influence, and excellent performance.

  d. Organizational lore is stories and legends that travel through the organization on the grapevine. Lore provides cultural insight into what the company values and guides decision making and behavior of both new and veteran employees. The four general themes of organizational lore are, How does the company feel about rule breaking? Is the boss human? Will I get fired? How does the company deal with obstacles?

Business Communication Projects

1. Break into groups with your class colleagues. Discuss the various stories you have heard about the school you are attending. What did the stories make you feel about the school? Are the values that the school publicly espouses in keeping with the stories you heard?

2. Close your eyes and think about the following question: What would the landscape of North American culture be like if we did not have any prejudice or discrimination? Imagine what the culture would look like. Think about how people would interact. Write a short essay that describes what your imagined American culture would be like.

3. Break into groups with your class colleagues and discuss what behaviors you don't like that are sometimes exhibited by your own gender group. In what ways have people used these behaviors to adapt or survive in the culture?

DISCUSSION QUESTIONS

4. Which of the following behaviors reflect unconscious norms? Which reflect institutional rules?

    _____ wearing a tie

    _____ spitting

    _____ substance abuse

    _____ punctuality

    _____ 15-minute coffee break

    _____ required attendance

    _____ theft

5. Ask a family member or friend to relate a story about his or her workplace or the people that work there. Write a memo to your instructor that describes the story and what information you think it conveys about the organization's culture.

6. Based on the chapter description of Ray Kroc's interaction with the manager of the Chicago McDonald's, write a brief summary of his vision for the restaurant chain. Then write about your own experiences with McDonald's, and compare them with the vision summary about Ray Kroc.

7. Nancy Antrim is the quality assurance manager at the steel mill where you work. Through her efforts, your company now does business with four of the aerospace industry's leaders. She has improved her mastery of metallurgical processes with continuing education and spends time mentoring new employees. You have been asked to introduce her and present the employee of the year award to her at the annual board of directors' luncheon. Write a speech in which you describe how she has become a company hero. Be creative and feel free to add any details that you feel are appropriate.

8. Write your own piece of organizational lore describing a supervisor at work or an instructor at school in terms of "is the boss human." Be specific and give examples.

9. You are the organizer of the annual picnic for your company, Tadwell and Binken Stock Inc., a very old, very conservative firm. The employees hold traditional values as important—loyalty, hard work, promoting from within the organization. Reflect on what the rites and rituals of such a company might be. Then devise a series of activities, and plan a schedule of events that you believe would suit Tadwell and Binken's corporate image.

10. Prepare a brief description of your ideal corporate culture and present the description in class.

Discussion Questions

1. How can the 21st-century professional woman overcome the stereotype of nurturer versus domineering?

2. Discuss how values differ from vision.

3. What cultural values are conveyed through corporate dress codes, such as a requirement that male employees wear only blue suits with white shirts?

4. What institutional rules are enforced at the school you attend? (For example, is there a rule governing the auditing of courses?)

5. How can an ordinary employee become a company hero?

6. How do your own cultural experiences affect your performance at work?

7. What do you think the consequences may be for an employee who deviates from the institutional rules?

8. Why is it important to attend formal and informal company functions (parties, picnics, etc.)?

9. What is the purpose of organizational lore?

10. What are some examples of learning about culture through socialization?

Creative Case

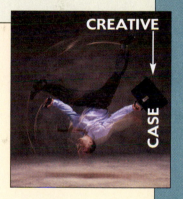

CREATIVE

CASE

Breaking through Barriers

Last year, a Japanese company, Okatami International, bought out the company where you are the warehouse manager, Schusser Fabricators. In the first round of layoffs following the purchase, one of the women who worked for you was let go. While this particular employee had been with the company only three years, she had an impeccable performance record. She was very ambitious, and many insiders believed her ascent up the corporate ladder would be swift. Now some employees speculate that she was fired because Japanese attitudes toward women may not be as liberal as attitudes in the United States and because she used a wheelchair. Of the 39 other employees laid off, 5 were women and 12 were Korean or Latino. Schusser always prided itself on its employment record because the number of excellently qualified women, minorities, and people with disabilities in the company had always been above the industry norm. Now employees are accusing the new management of prejudice and are talking about leaving the company.

You know you need to discuss this problem with the operations supervisor, Myoshi Karahatsu. You also know that, in the past, discussions with him have been difficult because the Japanese communication style is indirect, while the Western style is very direct. In Japanese culture, people are socialized to use a communication style that has been described as resembling an onion: You peel away the layers of meaning until you get to the core message. In other words, it is considered rude and unsophisticated to state a message directly. You should instead hint at your meaning while discussing surrounding issues. Japanese communication also contains formal flattery toward others who are perceived as superiors, as well as exaggerated personal modesty.

This is difficult for individuals who have been socialized according to Western standards, where they are encouraged to get to the point immediately and everyone is assumed to be equal. It doesn't help matters that Karahatsu's English, while grammatically perfect, doesn't include some of the phrases that are used in everyday English—it is necessary to use a simple, clear vocabulary to communicate effectively.

The next round of downsizing layoffs is coming up. What are you going to do?

Some questions to consider:

1. What kind of language will you use to ensure your communication with Karahatsu is clear?
2. How can you hint at something in such a way that the meaning cannot be mistaken?
3. What channel of communication do you think would be most effective to communicate your concerns to Karahatsu? Should you write a memo, send an e-mail, call him, or speak face-to-face?

Writing assignment:

Write two memos to the director of human resources requesting information about how layoff decisions are made and what the diversity policy of Okatami will be at Schusser Fabricators. The first memo should be written using the direct style employed by Western countries. The second memo, however, should be written in a manner that alludes to the questions you have, rather than stating them outright.

SOURCE: Angell, P. and Rizkallah, T. (2002).

Chapter 13

COMMUNICATING INTERPERSONALLY

RELATIONAL COMMUNICATION

do we have a relationship? / why are business relationships important? / types of relationships / how do I influence my relationships? / what are the rules for business relationships? / breaking the rules / cross-cultural rules

COMMUNICATING NONVERBALLY

TYPES OF NONVERBAL BEHAVIOR

kinesics / eye behavior / paralanguage / chronemics / proxemics / haptics / gender differences

COMMUNICATING IN SMALL GROUPS

what is a small group? / what's the difference between small-group and interpersonal communication? / purposes of business groups/teams

THE FOUR C'S OF EFFECTIVE SMALL GROUPS

commitment / cohesion / collaboration / conflict modification strategies

CONFORMITY

LEADERSHIP IN GROUPS AND TEAMS

leadership in meetings / gender differences in meetings

TECHNOLOGY FOR GROUPS AND TEAMS

c-commerce / distance business meetings

chapter 13

Designing Interpersonal and Collaborative Messages

When Lucent Technologies began offering Internet Services, the goal was to move from being the primary source of telephone technology to becoming the primary seller of networking equipment to corporations. The problem was that Cisco Systems historically dominated the networking market. While Cisco prided itself on being able to adjust to customers' demands, Lucent had always relied on its engineers to come up with new technologies and then waited for the customers to come to it. To overcome Cisco's dominance in the networking market, Lucent needed to respond to its customers far more quickly. Lucent also struggled with interpersonal relationship problems, turnover rates, and executive changes that resulted from several acquisitions, including a merger with Ascend Communications. Many high-level employees at both Lucent and Ascend left to start their own companies. How could Lucent retain and reassure the remaining employees? Lucent put Patricia Russo, executive vice president and CEO of Service Provider Networks, on the case. A strong interpersonal communicator and team builder with a history in technology, Russo restructured the business units at Lucent, stressing relationships and small-group interaction. Russo said of Lucent's current staff, "We want them to be professionally challenged and to be able to work in small teams, to feel they have an impact. It's a matter of giving them exciting products and then the access to the tools and resources they need to get the job done." As a result of Russo's strategy, $24 billion of the $38 billion Lucent made in annual sales during the year 2000 came from her teams in the networking project.

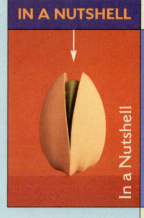

IN A NUTSHELL

In a Nutshell

Communicating Interpersonally

Lucent's Pat Russo knows the value of interpersonal communication and the effectiveness of teamwork to strengthen relationships and cultivate business opportunities. Like Lucent, more and more businesses are discovering that human interaction is as natural and fundamental in our everyday lives as sleeping and breathing. As social creatures, we spend 80 to 90 percent of our time interacting with others, which is why interaction is the center of our personal and professional existence. As discussed in the "In a Nutshell" feature, **interpersonal communication** is interaction between at least two people engaged in the co-creation of a relationship. Interpersonal communication includes patterns of behavior, actions, verbal statements, and events.

> **interpersonal communication** is verbal, nonverbal, and listening interaction between at least two people engaged in the co-creation of a relationship.

This chapter will feature the development of interpersonal relationships, nonverbal behaviors, and working collaboratively in business.

Interpersonal communication operates through both verbal and nonverbal channels. When we interact, we are sending and receiving both verbal and nonverbal messages at the same time. Our conversational interactions convey both content and relationship messages. Verbal messages convey content, and nonverbal messages imply emotional and status clues. Consider the following example, in which a manager conveys both content and relationship messages when she instructs an employee about the schedule for an assignment.

Content message:	"The report must be completed by Monday at 9 A.M."
Relationship message:	I'm the boss and it is my responsibility to determine the deadline for accomplishing work tasks.

Two messages are actually expressed in any given interaction. The content message is stated, and the relationship message is implied through both the nonverbal behaviors demonstrated and the way the message is stated.

Relational Communication

Interpersonal Communication and Relationships

Relationships are established through interpersonal interaction, so communication and relationships are intertwined. A **relationship** is a dynamic system of interaction coordinated through communication between two or more people. Our personal and professional relationships are dynamic systems because they are interdependent, interconnected, and changeable. A relationship is the system in which people interact. Communicators are affected by the verbal and nonverbal behaviors of one another, and their combined interaction produces the relationship. Relationships are always changing because the people involved are always changing.

> **relationship** a dynamic system of interaction coordinated through communication between two or more people.

Why Are Business Relationships Important?

Developing positive relationships with co-workers, vendors, and customers can mean increased productivity and morale, smooth purchase and delivery of services, and heightened customer satisfaction. An employee orientation program developed by Trilogy Software CEO Joe Liemandt, called Triology University, teaches new employees to bond and develop personal relationship networks with other recruits, their teachers, and customers. Like IBM, GE, and Intel, which have similar programs, Liemandt believes that the interpersonal relationships established and nurtured at Trilogy University build leadership skills and foster creative and collaborative business ventures. During the boot-camp orientation, teams of new recruits work together to create business models, marketing plans, and innovative projects. For one such project, CarOrder.Com, a team constructed a website that initiated a relationship between Ford Motors and Trilogy to sell cars over the Internet. Through the close relationships developed by employees and customers at Trilogy University, $100 million in new business has been generated since 1995.

CREATIVE CHALLENGE

List four adjectives or describing words that convey how you perceive or view yourself in a relationship with a particular friend or relative—for example, talkative, understanding, passive. Then list four adjectives or describing words for how you think your relationship partner views you. Compare the two lists. Are there more similarities or differences?

Now ask your friend or relative to list four words that describe how he or she sees you in the relationship. Write a one-page memo to your instructor analyzing why you think the words your relationship partner chose either matched or did not match your own.

Types of Relationships

The patterns of our relationships can establish aspects of relational power, control, and influence. In a **complementary relationship,** communicators engage in contrasting behavior in which one person controls and the other relinquishes control, one is dominant and the other is submissive, one person does most of the talking and the other listens. While professional roles in an organization vary, the traditional relationship between a boss and his or her employee is complementary. When a supervisor directs an employee to do something, the employee usually complies. In Japan, complementary business relationships are customary. Lower-ranking employees treat superiors with deference by tailoring their communication style and messages according to the age, rank, and status of the superior. A younger manager will yield or defer to an older manager even if they hold the same rank.

In **symmetrical relationships,** on the other hand, the individuals involved mirror each other's behavior. Ideally, they mutually respect each

complementary relationship occurs when communicators engage in contrasting behavior in which one person controls and the other relinquishes control.

Some relationships are complementary in nature since one of the communicators talks more while the other listens more.

© Spencer Grant/Photo Edit

JUMP IN! ⟶

You are the regional manager of a large hardware chain. One of your stores has an excellent sales record, completes all corporate-level tasks quickly and accurately, and has produced several wonderful management people. The problem is that the relationship between the current manager and assistant manager is terrible. The manager is new. This is her first store, and the assistant manager has been with the store since its opening five years ago. When the new manager took over, she immediately made several seemingly arbitrary changes that made it difficult for the assistant manager to operate efficiently. The two have argued about everything from merchandise displays to employee schedules ever since, with most of the employees backing the assistant manager. Every week the manager calls you asking for permission to fire her assistant manager. Every week you tell her no because you are aware of the assistant manager's potential; he's a big part of the reason that the store has done so well over the years.

Develop several suggestions you will offer the store manager when you meet with her next week. Detail at least three suggestions about how she can deal with the assistant manager in a more positive and productive manner. Write an e-mail to your instructor that outlines the discussion you will have with the store manager.

symmetrical relationship occurs when the communicators mirror each other's behavior.

other's individuality and position. But symmetrical interpersonal relationships can degenerate into power struggles when the communicators compete for control. When one says, "I'm in charge of the project," and the other replies, "No, I'm in charge!" a struggle for control is sure to follow. Or both can be overly accommodating, as when one employee says, "Do you want to include the direct deposit information with the payroll checks?" and the other responds, "I don't know. What do you want to do?"

Because people and their interactions are not static, no relationship is stuck permanently in either a complementary or a symmetrical arrangement. While many relationships lean toward one side or the other, different contexts, events, and perceptions can temporarily alter the long-term behaviors, roles, and rules in virtually any partnership. Over the course of some partnerships, the ebbs and flows balance out and the participants share control depending on the situation and dynamics involved.

How Do I Influence My Relationships?

Interpersonal interactions are an ongoing sequence of communication events that build on each other, and they can intensify throughout a relationship. As we continually send and receive messages, our behaviors mutually influence each other in an endless feedback loop—a series of interpersonal reactions that spiral around the people communicating. While it may seem as though interpersonal communication is linear (a straight line of back-and-forth messages), the movement of interaction between people is actually circular. Our reactions move round and round in a loop. As the relationship progresses, the interactions accelerate and build momentum in both positive and negative ways. Even as interpersonal relationships in-

To develop your interpersonal business communication skills, there are some websites that can help. You can take an online interpersonal communication skills test at www.queendom.com/tests/relationships/communication skills.htm. If you'd like to read more about interpersonal communication, there is an extensive, well-organized bibliography at www.ib.ohio-state.edu/gateway/bib/interpersonal.html. For general tips on interpersonal communications, visit www.essentialcomm.com/tips and tools/introframeset.html.

WORD ON THE WEB

Word on the Web

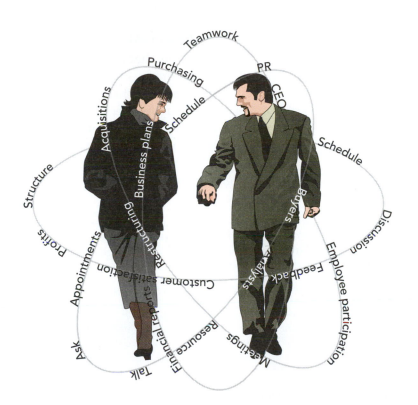

FIGURE 13.1

Endless Feedback Loop

When people interact, they repeatedly send and receive messages. These messages and reactions continually move around and between the communicators.

tensify and accelerate, redesigning our reactions and feedback can change many interactions. While you cannot change another person without his or her consent, you can change yourself. Often we blame others for our behavior. We sometimes believe that we are only reacting to the behavior of our significant other, friends, or co-workers without realizing that they are influenced as much by us as we are by them. We are also mutually influenced by the context that surrounds our experiences. Figure 13.1 illustrates the endless loop of feedback during interaction.

Practice Redesigning Relationships

Talk about the relationship	• Assess the differences in perceptions held about the relationship. • Engage in a dialogue about what aspects of the relationship are unsettling and what you both can do to turn it around.
Negotiate new rules and structure	• Work out a mutually acceptable agreement about how the relationship will be managed and how it will proceed.
Change the context	• Modifying our perceptions or the environment can produce shifts in reactions as well as the relationship.
Change your reaction pattern	• If your reaction has been to criticize someone who annoys you, change your behavior by avoiding negative or critical descriptions about that person. Often a change in our own behavior begins to change not only the reactions and behavior of others but the whole dynamic system.

What Are the Rules for Business Relationships?

Every communication event involves rules that are both cultural and relational. Communication rules are *cultural* because they are typically associated with social norms that determine what behaviors are acceptable and unacceptable. For example, many people follow cultural rules regarding others' privacy by not interrogating individuals they don't know very well. Many of us also comply with the rule of conversational turn taking and yield the floor to give others a chance to talk. Cultural rules for business groups are subdivided into three types: interactive, standard, and role related.

Interactive rules	• Expected communication behaviors performed by members of business groups. They include participating in group discussions, taking turns in conversation, not interrupting speakers, and limiting speaking time when a member has the floor.
Standard rules	• Relate to general conduct, such as punctuality at meetings and performance of required tasks.
Role-related rules	• Spring from specific behaviors that are connected to a given position or role. For example, a project leader may be expected to facilitate group discussions or impose sanctions on members who do not conform to the group rules.

Rules are also *relational* because they are devised and negotiated by the people involved in the interpersonal relationship. We create and agree on a set of verbal and nonverbal behaviors that direct how our communication will flow and determine what is appropriate in a particular situation.

Formal interactions such as those between manager and employee tend to be more rule-involved, less relaxed, and more conventional. However, even those relationships can be informal, depending on the context. At UPS, drivers and other employees meet routinely for lunch or in parks or cafés to interact informally and share information. Similarly, at SAS, a software company, employees of all ranks are encouraged to socialize by playing sports, joining the company choir, and relaxing together.

Breaking the Rules

Breaking the rules can produce varied reactions. In some circumstances, the violation may bring about negative responses. In other situations, a broken rule may be overlooked or ignored. At Cisco Systems, a networking company, the CEO holds "Birthday Breakfasts" each morning during the anniversary month of the company's founding for all 7,000 line staffers. Employees are encouraged to ask even the most sensitive questions about the organization and offer criticism regarding management failings. Traditionally, these kinds of questions and comments are considered taboo in business, but the Cisco Birthday Breakfasts provide a forum for acceptable rule breaking.

Cross-Cultural Rules

In many North American companies, it is acceptable to address superiors informally by their first name. But in most German and Asian companies, specific relational rules prohibit addressing superiors and clients by their first names. Instead, superiors and clients are formally addressed by their surnames: Ms. Habel or Mr. Takahashi, for example. In Sweden, Norway, Israel, and, to some degree, the United States, the emphasis on equality allows employees to openly discuss concerns and frustrations with managers. Employees may also ask direct questions about the reasons for policies and procedures. In Southern Europe, Latin America, Japan, and some other Asian cultures, however, respect for status, position, and age typically prevents employees from openly speaking their minds until they are formally asked for their opinion. Furthermore, in these cultures it is frequently considered disrespectful for subordinates to ask direct questions about policies or procedures.

Communicating Nonverbally

"What you do speaks so loud that I cannot hear what you say," said Ralph Waldo Emerson. Because interpersonal communication involves both verbal and nonverbal communication, we need to focus on behaviors exhibited during our interactions that are specifically nonverbal. **Nonverbal communication** refers to body movements or vocal variations that communicate without words. Nonverbal behavior manages and regulates conversation, displays emotions and feelings, provides feedback, and influences others. Nonverbal behaviors can also communicate to customers. Christian Kar, CEO of Expresso Connection, a chain of drive-through coffee bars, believes nonverbal communication is so important that he includes key principles of body movement in the weeklong training sessions for new hires. During the training, employees learn never to close the drive-through window on customers even if the weather is inclement. Kar believes that nonverbal behaviors can leave a lasting impression on customers and can help build or damage relationships.

nonverbal communication refers to body movements or vocal variations that communicate without words.

What's the Big Deal about Communicating Nonverbally?

Nonverbal communication happens continuously.	• We are constantly sending signals with our body and through our vocal qualities. There is no switch to turn off our nonverbal behavior.
93 percent of our emotional meaning is conveyed through nonverbal communication.	• More of what we feel is communicated nonverbally than any other way. Facial expression and body movement account for 55 percent and vocal characteristics such as tone, pitch, and volume account for 38 percent. Only 7 percent of meaning is conveyed through verbal words alone.
Nonverbal communication can occur unintentionally.	• Sometimes, we are not aware that we are sending nonverbal signals. For example, you may not intend to blush or fidget when you are nervous or uncomfortable or even be aware that you are doing so.
Many nonverbal cues are contextual.	• While some nonverbal behavior is conveyed unconsciously or may have ambiguous meaning, many facial expressions, smiles, nods, postures, and tones of voice match the situation in which they occur.
Nonverbal communication is often more reliable and believable than verbal communication.	• Verbal communication is often convincing or not based on the nonverbal behaviors that accompany the words. For example, if you tell someone that he is "wonderful" but narrow your eyes, frown, stiffen your posture, and say the word sarcastically, what do you think the other person will believe about how you feel?

kinesic behaviors refers to body movements we use to communicate.

eye behavior refers to eye movements that communicate emotions, facilitate and regulate conversation, and monitor reactions.

Types of Nonverbal Communication

The following are six types of nonverbal behavior:

1. **Kinesic behaviors** are the body movements we use to communicate. Kinesic behaviors, such as leaning or pressing your index finger to your lips to signal others to be quiet, can regulate conversation. They can also help us illustrate our verbal points, reduce anxiety, and express emotion.

2. **Eye behavior** can certainly communicate emotions, but it can also facilitate and regulate conversation and monitor others' reactions. Imagine you are at a department meeting during which you are scheduled to present report findings. The department director looks directly at you to signal that it is time for your presentation. While you are presenting, you notice the gaze of your colleagues and determine their level of interest or attention to your message. From a cultural perspective, direct eye contact is important in North America because it can signal interest. But in Japan and some Eastern cultures, direct eye contact can signal aggressiveness, disrespect, or even an invasion of privacy.

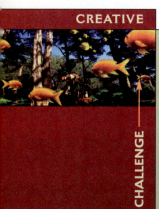

CREATIVE

CHALLENGE

Picture yourself in an elevator facing the other passengers instead of facing the door like everyone else. List all the possible body movements, facial expressions, and eye behaviors that you might observe as a reaction to your out-of-context behavior. Come to class prepared to discuss why and how you think people might respond to your behavior in the elevator.

paralanguage involves vocal sounds other than words. It is _how_ you say something rather than what the words mean.

3. **Paralanguage,** also referred to as vocalics, involves vocal sounds other than words. Paralanguage is about _how_ you say something rather than what the words mean. In our interactions with others, vocal pitch (highness or lowness of tone), speech rate (speed),

volume (loudness), and rhythm (timing and emphasis) can express a variety of different meanings. Suppose that when you present the report to the members of your department, your speech is hesitant, your rate of speech is slow, and you repeatedly use **vocal interferences** such as "um," "er," "uh," and "like, you know" to fill some of the dead air. Your colleagues may interpret this paralanguage as insecurity or limited knowledge of the subject matter.

> **vocal interferences** are paralinguistic sounds such as "um," "er," and "uh," that fill dead air during speech.

4. The study of how people use and perceive time is known as **chronemics.** Time is of great significance in North American culture. In the United States, time equals money, so the focus is on adherence to deadlines, schedules, promptness, and alacrity when making points, all facets of *monochronic time.* From a monochronic time perspective, arriving 10 minutes late to a job interview may convey a message to the employer that the applicant is unreliable or uninterested and may cost the company valuable time. It is not unusual in the United States and England for business meetings to begin exactly at the scheduled time. In Eastern Asia, 20 to 30 minutes early is common. By contrast, in many Latin American and Middle Eastern cultures the focus is on interpersonal relationships and a perception that everything has its own time. In this *polychronic time* orientation, schedules are not strictly observed and expectations about arrival and departure times are less rigid. Being 20 to 30 minutes late is acceptable because the pace is more relaxed.

> **chronemics** is the study of how people use and perceive time.

5. **Proxemics** is the study of our use of space and distance. The following table presents four proxemic zones that characterize the distance North Americans maintain with others. Again, different cultures have different rules about what distances to maintain.

> **proxemics** is the study of how people use space and distance.

Intimate distance	• Ranges from touching to 1½ feet. This distance, also known as a bubble of privacy, is usually reserved for people we enjoy a close interpersonal relationship with, such as significant others, family, children, and some close friends. While in some situations such as a visit to the doctor or a crowded train, concert, or elevator, strangers may encroach on our bubble, it is normally our private distance. Professionally, we rarely invade a co-worker's intimate space unless we are whispering confidential information that could otherwise be overheard.
Personal distance	• Ranges from 1½ to 4 feet. This is a relatively close distance but not intimate. Friends, some co-workers, and even teachers may occupy this space at various times during our interpersonal interactions.
Social distance	• Ranges from 4 to 12 feet. This more formal distance is often occupied by business associates, clients, group members, and people we do not know very well.
Public distance	• Ranges from 12 to 25 feet or more. This very formal distance is maintained by strangers or for public speaking events. Sometimes teachers position themselves in a public distance from students, especially at the beginning of a semester.

Nonverbal touching can communicate a variety of messages, including a formal greeting.
© Michael Newman/Photo Edit

haptics involves touching behaviors.

6. Touching behavior is known as **haptics.** As the most basic form of nonverbal behavior, touch can communicate a wide variety of messages. If you inadvertently bump up against someone at the office, you may apologize and feel a bit embarrassed because you did not intend to touch the person and touch can imply intimacy. While touching is not necessarily intimate, ours is a rather noncontact culture. We tend to avoid them or limit physical exchanges to appropriate contexts. Most business touching consists of formal handshakes, informal pats on the back, and the occasional arm touch when addressing a co-worker in conversation.

While there are differences in the way that men and women communicate, it is important to remember that most of these differences are socially learned behaviors. The following table identifies some primary nonverbal communication differences between men and women.

Nonverbal Behavior	Women	Men	Potential Reasons
Eye contact and gaze	• Tend to make eye contact more frequently during conversation but break eye contact earlier.	• Make eye contact less frequently but maintain gaze longer when they do make eye contact.	Women may avert their gaze because they have learned it is impolite to stare. Men may maintain their gaze to demonstrate power or status.
Facial expressions	• Skilled at sending and interpreting facial expression. Tend to smile more often.	• Maintain more neutral facial expression and smile less often.	Because women are socialized to exhibit greater emotion, they may express themselves and interpret facial behavior somewhat better than do men.
Gestures	• Use fewer and more restrained gestures.	• Use more gestures.	Women may have learned to behave in a less flamboyant, less aggressive manner.
Posture	• Posture is more tense.	• Posture is more relaxed.	Men may feel more confident, in control, and accepted than women.

Behavior	Women	Men	Potential Reasons
Proxemic space	• Approach more closely but prefer side-to-side stance during conversation. • Tend to yield personal space more and are less likely to resist when invaded.	• Prefer more face-to-face frontal stance during conversation. • Tend to invade personal space more (especially women's).	Perhaps a side-by-side stance appears less confrontational and intrusive. It may be more culturally acceptable for a man to invade a woman's space, and women may be less likely to appear aggressive.
Haptics (touch)	• Use touch to signal warmth, comfort, and support. • Touch men less frequently.	• More often use touch to demonstrate control or power or to gain compliance. • Touch women more frequently.	Women may perceive touch as a way to cultivate and maintain interpersonal relationships. Men may perceive touch as a way to maintain control and authority.
Paralanguage	• Use higher pitch, lower volume, faster speech rate, and a more pleasant tone.	• Use louder volume, slower speech rate, and more frequent vocal interferences.	Women may speak faster because they expect to be interrupted and thus hurry to get their point across. Their volume may be lower because they may not want to call attention to themselves or appear aggressive. Men may speak more loudly and harshly to ensure that they are heard or to dominate.

Communicating in Small Groups

Most business professionals spend significant time in problem solving and task management and in project teams and other small groups. These groups shape the way we perceive organizational experience and form the foundation of the corporate way of life.

What Is a Small Group?

A **small group** is composed of two or more interdependent people who are aware of their group membership and who communicate to accomplish common goals. Interdependence means that each group member is connected to and dependent on the other members in the context of the group experience. Group members communicate interpersonally, which means they communicate verbally and nonverbally and exercise listening skills while they interact. A group does not exist unless there is interaction among its members.

small groups are composed of two or more interdependent people who are aware of their group membership and who communicate to accomplish common goals.

What's the Difference between Small-Group and Interpersonal Communication?

Small-group communication is a specific type of interpersonal communication. The core of small-group communication is the interdependence of members and a perception of belonging to the group. Group members are not only interdependent on one another to achieve group goals but aware of their membership in the group. For example, several employees eating lunch in the company cafeteria do not constitute a small group because they are neither dependent on one another to eat their lunch nor necessarily aware of belonging to a group.

Purposes of Business Groups and Teams

In business, groups and teams convene for a variety of purposes, including planning, organizing, negotiating, evaluating, problem solving, research, development, and implementation. The following table lists several types of business groups and teams.

Task force	A temporary group formed to handle a difficult or complex problem or a risky new project.
Quality circles	Special problem-solving groups that convene on a regular basis to develop product, service, or process-quality solutions. Facilitated by a manager, supervisor, or group leader, quality circles are composed of six to eight employees from the same general work unit. Members generate ideas and discuss work-related problems concerning performance, productivity, and quality control.
Steering committee	Groups convened to implement some specific goal, policy, change initiative, or company program. The members of steering committees generally come from different specialties or departments.
Management teams	Responsible for organization mission initiatives. Members plan fiscal, personnel, and program policies and make decisions.
Project teams	Groups of select employees with specialized skills who design, develop, research, coordinate, and evaluate specific company initiatives and programs.
Cross-functional teams	Composed of employees from different functional work areas, such as public relations, finance, and human resources.
Self-managing teams	Groups of employees who, without supervision, plan, manage, analyze, coordinate, and execute task activities. For example, in some hospitals, specialists such as doctors, nurses, social workers, and technicians work together and manage themselves to accomplish complex tasks.
Problem-solving teams	One of the most common business teams. This team is usually convened to gather information, evaluate specific programs or problems, and generate and implement solutions.
Virtual teams	Because saving time and money is important in organizations, meetings are often conducted and sometimes teams are convened through teleconferencing and videoconferencing. Employees who communicate and participate together on projects through e-mail or Web conferences are also virtual teams.

4 C's
ommitment
ollaboration
ohesion
onflict strategies

FIGURE 13.2

The 4 C's of Small Groups

The Four C's of Effective Small Groups

Business groups are often more attractive to people when they perceive that member commitment, cohesion, collaboration, and effective conflict modification strategies exist.

Commitment

Commitment refers to members' consistent participation on group-related tasks, and dedication to maintaining group values and achieving group goals. Committed groups enjoy open and productive communication that includes the contributions and feedback of all members and discourages one individual from dominating the discussion.

Cohesion

Cohesion is the establishment of harmonious and compatible working relationships. Members remain in the group for as long as they are needed and share a powerful interest in the unity of the group.

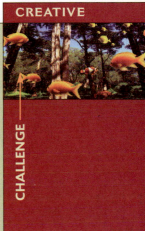

CREATIVE

CHALLENGE

Value management is a strategic process in which a manager encourages common values (beliefs and philosophy) among group members. Break into groups with your class colleagues to discuss whether you think groups that share values are more committed than others. Then list at least three ways that holding similar values can affect communication within the group. Be prepared to share your findings with the rest of the class.

commitment refers to members' consistent participation on group-related tasks, and dedication to maintaining group values and achieving group goals.

cohesion is the establishment of harmonious and compatible working relationships.

WORD ON THE WEB

Word on the Web

One of the things corporations do to improve teamwork skills in their employees is send them to corporate retreats. Some of these retreats include adventure learning, in which team members must survive in the wilderness or complete a scavenger hunt relying only upon one another. To see sample activities, visit these websites:

- www.3simpatico.ca/thetrainingoasis/retreats.htm
- www.tmap.com/updates/activs.html
- www.adventureconsultants.com/adventures.html#
- www.purplemountain.ie/teambuilding.htm
- www.alpine-events.com/team_building/index.html

Come up with your own scenario for an adventure learning experience.

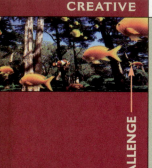

CREATIVE

CHALLENGE

In business, each member of a group often relies directly on other members to complete or begin a task. This is particularly true in service-based industries where the product is the performance of an activity, such as research. Break into groups with your class colleagues and imagine that you are the group leaders of a research project for a client. Your client has asked you to deliver the research report by Friday, but one of your project members has not completed his section of the report. He told you he needs extra time to examine certain data and write an analysis. Knowing the client has little tolerance for reports that are late, would you allow your co-worker to complete the analysis alone and take the heat when you take the report to the client the following Monday? Do you think this would affect future tasks involving that co-worker or the client? What would you do about the work your co-worker has not completed? As a group, write a detailed memo to your instructor that explains how you would like to handle this situation. Then, create a short skit in which you role-play a meeting to discuss and solve the problem.

collaboration occurs when members of a team work together to accomplish a task.

Collaboration

When members of a team work to accomplish a task, they **collaborate.** A shared purpose drives them to act cooperatively to make decisions and achieve goals. Collaboration also involves equality of member expectations regarding group behavior and performance. When business professionals collaborate, they co-create. They communicate openly and share a vision for what they can achieve by working together. The collective efforts of diverse group members can ignite a company's best ideas and strategies. For example, at Lexus, engineers and customers worked collaboratively to improve the 1993 LS 400 car model. More than 100 customer suggestions for improvement were implemented, including bigger tires and a brake indicator that warns drivers about brake-pad wear.

Most effective groups and teams collaborate through the creation of an open atmosphere, dialogue, and brainstorming. Companies such as Johnson & Johnson, Seagate, and Kellogg participate in a collaborative program called DesignShop, created and provided by the M. G. Taylor Corp. DesignShop helps employees from these companies build teams, change their work processes, and develop solutions and creative ideas through dialogue and brainstorming.

Conflict Modification Strategies

Conflict strategies are problem modification techniques that groups can use to resolve disputes. These strategies, detailed in Chapter 14, include identifying, understanding, and transforming perceptions through dialogue.

From your own experience, you know that groups do not suddenly become cohesive and collaborative overnight. People working within groups need to commit themselves to exercise tolerance, use good judgment, listen actively, and move through problems productively. Groups that strive to reach the four C's are not only more rewarding to be a part of, but also more able to realize group goals.

conflict strategies are problem modification techniques that groups use to resolve disputes.

Practice the Four C's

Commitment	• Offer ideas and contribute alternative choices during discussions. • Assist other members to refocus on group goals when discussions become sidetracked. • Reaffirm group goals and values. • Discuss goals in terms of what all members have in common.
Cohesion	• Encourage other members to participate by asking questions and soliciting their opinions. • Smooth ruffled feathers by pointing out the positive aspects of ideas or proposals and any connections you see between opposing points of view. • Respectfully discuss member ideas even if you disagree with them.
Collaboration	• Create an open and informal atmosphere that can facilitate honest discussion, the airing of disagreements or diverse opinions, and the exploration of all sides of an issue. • Brainstorm. Generate as many ideas and solutions as possible that the group can develop and use to accomplish tasks and reach goals. • Offer to assist other members with their tasks. • Stay on schedule with your own assignments, and ask other members to review and comment on your work.
Conflict modification strategies	• Listen actively to the concerns and perspectives of other members. • Refrain from assigning blame for problems. • Accept that different people have different approaches, styles, and views. • Think carefully before presenting your argument and frame your ideas in a nonthreatening way.

Conformity

Conformity is the acceptance of influence and adherence to group rules. As members of an extremely large cultural group, we generally conform to the rules and expectations imposed on us by society. Most of the conforming we do is not difficult or threatening because we have grown up behaving and living in a certain way. Conformity can be productive because it provides a foundation for cohesive, functional business groups. Certainly groups that are cohesive tend to produce more, better, and faster than groups that continually struggle with unproductive conflict.

However, it is also true that overly cohesive or conforming groups can become unproductive, develop unwise ideas, and make ill-advised or uninformed decisions. In instances when **groupthink** emerges, members can neglect relevant news or information if it contradicts what the group already believes. In this case, a bit of dissension and differences of opinion can benefit the group's performance.

conformity is the acceptance of influence and adherence to group rules.

groupthink occurs when members neglect relevant news or information that contradicts what the group already believes.

What are the dangers of groupthink in business? Imagine that you are a team leader who feels like you are doing all the work. Your team is made up of new employees, most of whom are fresh out of college. This project, designing the electrical system for a new high-rise building, could help you all gain a positive reputation within the company and might even get you a promotion if it is handled well. You like your team members and they never argue with you—which is the problem. They wait for your direction and never contribute suggestions or ideas of their own. They automatically accept any suggestion you make. Are they afraid of challenging your authority? Are they unusually uncreative? Either way, you've had enough. This one-sided communication is frustrating for you and probably, you suspect, for the team as well. The project isn't progressing quickly enough for your supervisor and you are exhausted.

Write an e-mail to your team members that encourages them to communicate with you honestly and explains how conformity can endanger projects like your group's.

leadership is the ability to influence people and share a vision that moves projects or the organization forward in a productive and creative way.

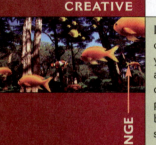

Break into groups with your class colleagues in which one of you plays the part of a manager and the other members play disgruntled employees. The department manager is responsible for ensuring that employees stay informed about new company procedures and requirements. This manager wants the group to discuss ideas for process improvements that will enhance quality and efficiency. To accomplish these tasks, he or she holds weekly staff meetings. The problem is that several of the staffers have complained that the meetings are too long, that they waste time, and that some employees don't participate. In response to these complaints, develop a role-play in which the manager addresses the concerns and collaborates with his or her employees to determine how these weekly meetings should be conducted and how participation will be encouraged.

Leadership in Groups and Teams

Leadership is a combination of the ability to influence people and to see the big picture of how things can work to move a project or the organization forward in a productive and creative way. Strong team and group leaders pay attention to interpersonal interactions and encourage members to perform their best work collaboratively. They motivate people to excel and change. Leaders set the tone for positive influence through dialogue and the open exchange of information between group and team members.

Cynthia Trudell, president of the Saturn division of General Motors, leads through collaboration and team building. She invites each employee to offer ideas and partner with other employees to develop better customer service and performance strategies. At Phonak, a hearing-aid manufacturer, CEO and president Michael Jones encourages collaboration through a no-office-walls leadership approach. An open floor plan with no individual offices allows all employees to communicate and participate freely with each other and breaks down the barriers of traditional hierarchical structures.

Effective leadership involves influencing people's attitudes and behavior. To influence behavior, you must first influence attitudes. A worthy leader will make employees feel valued and provide a supportive environment so that they will want and be able to do their best work. Rather than performing all the work themselves, leaders facilitate the sharing of work, information, and responsibility among all members of the group.

318

While *delegation* (the assignment of work tasks) can be a leadership function, often members share responsibility and select tasks suited to their individual abilities.

Leadership in Meetings

Group leaders typically spend many hours each week in meetings with co-workers, clients, and other business associates. Some professionals complain that group meetings can take a lot of time and accomplish little. Meetings that conclude without concrete actions or strategies to implement can be frustrating.

In business, group and team leaders facilitate meetings by clearly stating group or team goals, what participation will be needed from members, and the time limits for achieving goals. Leaders also create

SOURCE: *Harvard Business Review*, June 2001.

agendas are guidelines for discussion topics and time frames for goal accomplishment during meetings.

agendas for meetings, which means establishing guidelines for discussion topics and time frames for goal accomplishment. Ideally, team or group leaders share the agenda before the meeting so that members can prepare materials and discussion ideas in advance. During the meeting, leaders encourage focused but informal dialogue and brainstorming among members. At the end of the meeting they summarize meeting decisions and steps to be taken to achieve stated goals.

Gender Differences in Meetings

Theorists maintain that men and women sometimes demonstrate different communication styles during meetings. The following table identifies gender differences in meetings.

Women	Men
• Are less likely to interrupt other speakers. If they do interrupt, it is more likely to be another women. • Allow interruption more often than do men.	• Interrupt other speakers more. • Allow others to interrupt less often.
• Are less likely to take the floor to speak during meetings and tend to make points quickly when they do.	• Take the floor more often and hold the floor for longer periods.
• Use tag questions such as "don't you think?" and disclaimers such as "This may sound crazy, but".	• Are more likely to state verbal points concretely and authoritatively.
• Are less confident about building strong arguments.	• Are more verbally aggressive and confident about building arguments.
• Prefer more face-to-face interaction and collaboration.	• Prefer to work independently and collaborate less.

Technology for Groups and Teams

Technology has provided many new virtual teamwork channels to communicate through, including handheld devices, intranets, and instant messaging. Many employees now spend more time interacting while on the road or working at home than ever before.

C-Commerce

c-commerce is technology that allows companies to collaborate with customers, suppliers, and distributors to improve existing products and services and to create new products.

Collaborative commerce, or **c-commerce,** is emerging technology that allows companies such as Caterpiller and Ford to collaborate with customers, suppliers, and distributors to improve existing products and services and to create new products. C-commerce software (for example, PTC, MatrixOne, NexPrise, and Groove Networks) facilitates direct person-to-person computing and communication. Like instant messaging, in which people can exchange written messages in real time (like a chatroom conversation), these software programs let people work together and communicate through their computers at the same time. They also allow people to share files, communicate by

ST Microtronics (STM), a large French–Italian semiconductor company, received an order to design and build microchips that would operate the navigational systems in new Fiats and Peugeots. The car manufacturers needed the chips in a hurry; customers all over the world were asking for the systems. To build the microchips, STM put together a team whose members lived in France, England, Italy, India, and the United States and who specialized in chip design, engineering, fabrication, integration, and quality control, among other things. They communicated through an intranet, e-mail, cell phones, faxes, and teleconferencing.

At first everything was fine. Then the team encountered a problem no one had anticipated. Teams usually operate best when they remain small, but the intranet system made it very easy to keep adding more members to the team. Pretty soon there were so many people interacting on the project that everyone became confused. Lines of communication slowed down and became garbled. The flattened hierarchy of the team ceased to function efficiently.

Imagine that you are the project's coordinator. Design a plan (in a one-page memo with an attached diagram) that retains the flattened hierarchy while organizing a huge number of team members.

voice, participate in virtual conferencing, and work with other members' software programs. C-commerce enables groups and teams to work on projects collaboratively and share information with each other, with clients, and with other business professionals.

Distance Business Meetings

When time and money prohibit a face-to-face business meeting with professionals at different geographic locations, distance conferences bring people together from wherever they are. Teleconferencing, videoconferencing, and Web conferencing offer interactivity among participants and allow for immediate feedback.

1. **Teleconferencing** is the most common type of distance meeting. Each participant can communicate by phone from any location. Advance scheduling and a planned agenda are required for most teleconferences, which means participants must be prepared for the meeting. At EDS, a data system company, employees once behaved very competitively and were individualistic in the way they accomplished tasks. Few employees shared information, and there was no incentive for people to work together. As a result of these working behaviors, EDS started to lose business, and its stock began to decline. The new CEO, Dick Brown, cultivated a collaborative model called "performance call" that encourages dialogue and open discussion among employees. During these performance calls, 100 employees throughout the company participate in a conference call to share information about performance, team initiatives, and disagreements, and they work on these issues collectively.

2. **Videoconferencing** combines both visual and verbal communication so conference participants can see and hear each other at the

teleconferencing is the most common type of distance meeting in which participants communicate by phone from different locations.

videoconferencing combines both visual and verbal communication so conference participants can see and hear each other at the same time by using a video monitor.

321

web conferencing is the use of compact cameras and microphones attached to personal or laptop computers to send and receive audio and video messages transmitted over the Internet.

same time. Participants can view each other on a video monitor and observe nonverbal responses.

3. **Web conferencing** is a developing distance conference technology. Like videoconferences, Web-based conferences offer visual contact and real-time interaction among participants. Compact cameras and microphones attached to personal or laptop computers send and receive audio and video messages. The video images are transmitted over the Internet and displayed on participants' monitors.

The following table highlights the advantages and disadvantages of distance technologies.

	Advantages	Disadvantages
Teleconferencing	• Time and money savings: far-flung employees, colleagues, or clients can communicate, and costly, time-consuming travel can be eliminated. • More employees can be included in the meeting than if extensive travel were necessary.	• Teleconferences lack visual interactivity. You cannot observe nonverbal behaviors, which can make message interpretation more difficult.
Videoconferencing	• It saves time and money. • Videoconferencing comes closest to face-to-face human interaction because participants can see and hear each other.	• Videocameras and conferencing equipment can cost several thousand dollars and require installation and technical user skills. • Coordination of participants can sometimes present difficulties.
Web conferencing	• Web conferences are less expensive than videoconferences to set up. Current software and hardware packages can run as low as $80. • Web conferencing does not require skilled technicians to operate the equipment. • As computers become faster and transmission paths increase, Web conferencing is expected to increase.	• There may be time delays in both visual and audio transmissions, so participants may have to wait several seconds after someone has spoken to receive visual and audio transmissions.

Some companies are finding that, when face-to-face interaction is limited or eliminated, existing relationships may suffer and new relationships can be more difficult to develop. At SEI Investments, a financial services company, the office design of the firm's six buildings facilitates open interpersonal communication. Employees work together in large, windowed rooms without offices or cubicles to divide space. Even the CEO, Al West, works in one of the rooms with other employees. West believes that the open space encourages employees to interact, collaborate, and feel at home. "Nothing beats personal interactions," says John Old of Texaco Oil. Many of the 18,000 employees at Texaco share information, tips, and ideas through technological channels such as the company intranet and a bank of information called "knowledgeMail." But John Old and other Texaco managers encourage these employees to meet face-to-face as well to build trust and reinforce their interpersonal connection.

While it is possible to develop and maintain relationships without face-to-face human interaction, interacting in person from time to time will strengthen the business relationship.

Strategies

1. Observe others' nonverbal behavior during interactions to gauge whether you are receiving a mixed message. If the verbal content conflicts with the nonverbal behaviors, examine the message more closely for meaning beyond the expressed content.

2. Develop relational flexibility. Adapt your interaction style to different contexts and different people. Your ability to assess the situation, audience, and message is central to tailoring your interpersonal behavior appropriately. Use information you have directly observed regarding social skills and your experience with different groups of people to recognize and adjust to different communication rules and relationship partners.

3. Reframe and expand your perception to see situations and relationships in a new way. It is often wise strategically to reframe your mental or emotional perspectives in your dynamic interpersonal relationships. Write about the relationship as if you were another person to gain insight into your own behaviors and those of your relationship partners.

4. In any given interaction, it is a good idea to ask questions and paraphrase other people's verbal messages, especially if you are uncertain about their message meaning.

5. Your descriptive and listening skills will be important. Practice using descriptive language, including examples, when you provide instruction to employees. Actively listen to the concerns and viewpoints of co-workers, superiors, and employees. Be patient in business groups and on teams. Allow others to finish their statements, and avoid considering your response while they are still talking. If you focus your attention on the response you want to offer while others are talking, you will miss some of their message. Take mental or written notes to stay focused on messages, and offer feedback or ask questions when the sender is finished.

6. Use empathy in interpersonal relationships. Be sensitive to the feelings and emotions of others. Body language can provide meaningful clues to the feelings and attitudes of your relationship partners.

7. Modify your own behavior or reactions to change distressing relationships. Be persistent in your efforts; the reactions of your relationship partner will likely change in time.

SUMMARY

8. Discuss the agenda, goals, ideas, and any resources needed with group members before each meeting. Pre-meeting discussions can help leaders organize the agenda better and allow members to come to the meeting prepared.

9. Use clear, down-to-earth language when communicating. Avoid abbreviations and jargon that other group members may not be familiar with. Evaluate each idea or proposal completely as objectively as possible, even if the ideas are opposite your own. Don't suppress any group member's opinions, ideas, or solutions. Remember that when groups become overly cohesive and submit to groupthink, they can make the wrong decisions or miss important opportunities. Encourage follow-up communication when the group is not together to gain more feedback about performance and group decisions.

10. Offer well-constructed and relevant contributions to group discussions to enhance a task goal or build group cooperation. Ask questions and encourage group members to participate with opinions, solutions, and productive criticism. Play devil's advocate in a positive, proactive way to explore alternative viewpoints.

11. Celebrate group successes and accomplishments and encourage recognition of group strengths.

Summary

- Interpersonal communication is the creation of and interaction in a relationship between two or more people. It includes both verbal and nonverbal behaviors. Verbal messages convey message content, and nonverbal behaviors convey relationship messages.

- A relationship is a dynamic system of interaction between two or more people that is coordinated through communication.

- Relationship partners are affected by one another and the context in which the interaction occurs. In a complementary relationship they behave in opposite ways; one partner is dominant and the other more submissive. Partners in a symmetrical relationship tend to behave in similar ways. An endless feedback loop is a spiral of interaction that builds positive or negative momentum as a relationship progresses.

- Communication rules are subdivided into two categories: cultural and relational. Cultural rules are based on societal norms, and relational rules are negotiated by the people involved in the relationship.

- Business relationships tend to be more formal and rule oriented than personal ones, although this varies depending on the company and the context.

- Nonverbal communication is body movements or vocal sounds that carry meaning. Many nonverbal behaviors have multiple meanings. There are six primary types of nonverbal behavior.

  a. Kinesic behaviors are body movements that we use to communicate.

  b. Eye behavior can communicate emotion, regulate conversation, and monitor others' reactions.

  c. Paralanguage refers to vocal sounds other than words and refers to how things are said.

  d. Chronemics is the use and perception of time that communicates messages.

  e. Proxemics is the use of space and distance. Proxemic zones are four ranges of distance that depend on the relationship.

  f. Haptics is touching behavior.

- A small group consists of two or more members who are interdependent, are aware of their group membership, and communicate interpersonally to achieve goals. Small-group communication is a type of interpersonal communication that combines interdependence of members and a perception of belonging to the group. Business groups function for a wide range of purposes and may be task forces, quality circles, steering committees, management teams, project teams, cross-functional teams, self-managing teams, problem-solving teams, or virtual teams.

- The four C's of effective small groups are commitment, cohesion, collaboration, and conflict modification strategies. They involve commitment to the group and its tasks, harmony and interest in group unity, equality of participation and performance expectation, and problem modification skills. Collaboration helps companies achieve business goals that could not be achieved by a single individual. Groups and teams collaborate through the development of an open environment, dialogue, and brainstorming ideas and solutions.

- Conformity is adherence to group rules. Some conformity is good, but too much can lead to groupthink.

- Leadership is the combination of the ability to influence people and the ability to move the project or the organization forward. Effective business leaders encourage collaboration and teamwork to create innovation and to influence behavior and attitudes. Leaders manage the collaborative process during meetings by creating agendas that include open dialogue and member participation.

- Technology has created new channels and changed the way we send and receive messages. Distance technologies that can facilitate communication include c-commerce and teleconference, videoconference, and Web conference systems.

Business Communication Projects

1. Break into groups with your class colleagues and identify at least five nonverbal behaviors, such as thumbs up or thumbs down. Exclude the examples used in the text. Nonverbally demonstrate your examples to the rest of the class and ask them to define what the behaviors mean.

2. List three nonverbal behaviors that you may exhibit with your family (such as kissing a parent good-bye) that you would not practice with a co-worker. In a brief memo to your instructor, describe why these behaviors would be inappropriate in a business context.

3. Etiquette is protocol for socially acceptable and appropriate behavior. Look up *business etiquette* in a book or journal at the library or on the Internet. List three rules of good business etiquette, and discuss whether each is a cultural or a relational rule. Come to class prepared to discuss your findings.

4. Indicate whether the following statements are true or false.

   _____ Interaction is usually affected by changes in the individuals.

   _____ Relationships are dynamic.

   _____ Nonverbal communication is less important than verbal communication.

   _____ People's nonverbal reactions can tell you whether your message is being received as you intend.

5. Imagine that you and a co-worker have had a problem working together in the past. You felt this person followed your lead and waited for you to set direction and determine the approach. In short, you came up with all the ideas. You've just been assigned a project in which you will have to work together again. Break into groups with your classmates and discuss what actions you could take to improve your interpersonal communication with this co-worker and perform the project tasks more collaboratively.

6. Imagine this scenario: You are developing policy for the human resources department at your company. The partner you are working with is a touchy-feely type, always touching your arm during a conversation and resting his hand on your shoulder when the two of you are talking to a third person. You are not comfortable with this invasion of your personal space. Write an e-mail to this person explaining touch in a business context.

7. You are a member of a new program and initiative management team. The team is composed of seven members ranging in age from 27 to 56. Five of the members are male and two are female. Over the course of several months, you notice that the group seems to be ignoring a significant market trend on which other

companies may soon capitalize. Some members discount the trend as a "flash in the pan." You disagree. You suspect that others may also disagree, but nobody wants to appear confrontational. The group has always been highly cohesive, and conformity to group norms and values is high. While you don't want to upset your colleagues, you know that the group may miss a huge opportunity to advance company growth by continuing to ignore this new trend (which can be consumer or technology related). Break into small groups with your class colleagues. Brainstorm what action you could take to initiate discussion about the trend and transform the perspectives of doubting group members, without alienating them or igniting a big conflict.

8. Before class one day, your communication professor mentions that the college tenure committee looks favorably on instructors who participate in student organizations. To seize this opportunity to impress your instructor, write a memo recommending a particular student group. In your memo, explain the group's primary goals and its group dynamics. Be sure to state why you think that your instructor would be perfect for the group.

9. Your message goal is to update team members about a new idea. The five members on your team are located in various geographic areas. Write a memo to your supervisor that explains which distance meeting technology(ies) would best suit your message to these widespread individuals. Include the benefits of each technological channel selected.

10. Break into groups of three with your class colleagues to research recent trends in communication technology online or in periodicals, and answer the following questions: Which types of technology are undergoing important changes? What changes in technology do you feel will have long-lasting effects on business and the collaboration of groups and teams? Explain. Come to class prepared to discuss your findings.

11. The leader of your team, Bill Pretowsky, doesn't let the other team members add their own ideas into the mix. You are working on a corporate restructuring following a merger, which is a complex and delicate operation. Your company wants to retain the most talented people from both companies, but there are political issues that must be taken into account. The rest of the team realizes this, but Bill doesn't let any of you get a word in edgewise. He's more interested in office and equipment assignments to the new employees. Keeping in mind that conflict can be positive, write a one-page memo that includes strategies to make yourself heard.

12. Rochester Fabrication has recently enjoyed unprecedented growth and has added 25 new positions, including yours. Now

the company needs to find a way to get everyone working together smoothly. In a persuasive e-mail to Jane Ellis, vice president of the company, explain how Rochester would benefit by using small-group teams.

13. Look at the following list of employees and put together a team of three people you believe would work well together. Explain in three or more paragraphs why you believe this team will be successful.
    - Rupert Featheringill—sometimes lazy but incredibly creative.
    - Marcia Morningside—quiet, efficient.
    - Baxter Boxer—supervisor's pet.
    - Clara Zenobia—unimaginative but ambitious.
    - Charlie Amaya—enthusiastic, friendly, follows the crowd.
    - Irene Parker—older, experienced, somewhat distant.

14. Make a list of your personal qualities, good and bad. In a letter to your instructor, explain what you could contribute to a teamwork situation and what problems you might have working in a small group. Use your list for reference.

Discussion Questions

1. What nonverbal behaviors are common indicators that communication is breaking down and that the rules need to be renegotiated or redesigned?

2. Why is communication in a business context somewhat impersonal? Are there times when business communication should be more intimate? If so, when?

3. If you wanted to change your relationship with another person, what would you do?

4. Can breaking cultural or relational communication rules improve communication, or does breaking the rules always risk breaking down the communication? Can you think of a situation in which one communicator may wish to break a communication rule? What might be the results?

5. How does understanding interpersonal communication change the way you think about making meaning?

6. Why is nonverbal communication more believable than verbal communication?

7. Why do men and women communicate differently during meetings? Specifically, why do men take the floor to speak more than do women?

8. Why is punctuality or promptness so important in U.S. culture?

9. Can there be any nonverbal communication in a written message? Explain and give examples.

10. Sometimes people in groups and teams behave in ways that most individuals would not. Do you think that a group can change people's values, ethics, and behavior? Why or why not?

11. Are you more committed to the goals of groups you choose (such as social groups, fraternities, political groups), or to groups you must be a part of (business groups and teams, project teams, study groups, class project groups)? Explain.

12. Have you ever left a group before the group's goal was completed? What made you leave? What would have kept you involved?

13. What aspects of channel selection should be considered relative to distance communication?

14. What aspects of team interaction do you believe make the best use of group communication technologies (telephone, video, and Web conference systems)?

15. What qualities make a good team leader? How do you think a team leader should interact with his or her team?

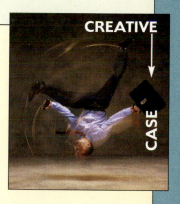

CREATIVE
CASE

Creative Case

What's Your Working Personality?

Many companies use the Meyers-Briggs personality test to determine how well employees will work together. Meyers-Briggs identifies qualities such as assertiveness, compassion, and tolerance, among other things. Using this information, companies can put together more successful teams. Identifying personality traits can also help lessen tensions surrounding corporate mergers and restructuring.

Dr. Pierce J. Howard, research director at the Center for Applied Cognitive Studies in Charlotte, North Carolina, and consultant to major corporations, has identified five basic personality traits (OCEAN) based on the Meyers-Briggs test. Most people have all of these traits to some degree, but some traits are more pronounced than others. When applied, employers try to find where on each scale an individual falls. An employer can then decide whether an applicant's temperament matches the company corporate structure, and if he or she can perform the tasks necessary to excel in the position.

1. O = Openness, Originality
   Low O: pragmatic, conformist, detail oriented; lacks strategic, creative planning skills
   High O: curious, nonconformist, creative; lacks attention to detail

2. C = Conscientiousness, Consolidation
   Low C: flexible, spontaneous, able to multi-task; lacks self-discipline
   High C: disciplined, ambitious, organized; lacks tolerance

3. E = Extroversion
   Low E: solitary, serious, quiet; lacks interpersonal communication skills
   High E: assertive, optimistic, talkative; lacks restraint
4. A = Accommodation
   Low A: guarded, skeptical, independent; lacks flexibility
   High A: cooperative, generous, team player; lacks firmness
5. N = Neuroticism, Negative Emotionality, or Need for Stability
   Low N: calm, reassuring, unstressed; lacks vitality
   High N: excitable, tense, stressed; lacks perspective

If you were to create a successful team, who would you want working with you?

Some points to consider:

1. Where do you fall in the OCEAN scales? Should you lead, or should you follow?
2. Is it necessary to represent all of the traits listed above on a successful team? Why or why not?
3. Are any of these traits more important to corporate success than others? Explain.
4. What traits would be more useful in a strategic planning team? A marketing team? A sales team? Why?

SOURCE: Coplan, J. (2000). "Can Personality Science Improve Your Business I.Q.?" Businessweek Online. Retrieved June 14, 2002: http://www.businessweek.com:/print/smallbiz/content/aug2000/tr000829.htm.

Chapter 14

Chapter 14

The Business of Change and Conflict

Sometimes tradition can make even the best change seem like the worst thing that could ever happen. But sooner or later, change will happen. Even global toy manufacturing company Lego, with its legendary little bricks, has had to face changes in the last several years. When Lego was a young company 70 years ago, the Danish toymaker designed and produced plastic Lego bricks that snapped together and allowed kids to build endless free-form structures from their imaginations. The bricks were sturdy, strong, and simple, reflecting the Lego corporate culture that values the imagination of children and self-directed play. But recently the company's profits began to fall. Between 1997 and 1998, Lego lost millions in sales to more contemporary toys such as Xbox, Sony PlayStation, and a host of other electronic and software games. Children's lives and interests were changing, and technology was broadening the scope of what they considered fun. Suddenly, inevitable change was pounding at Lego's door. While CEO Kjeld Kirk Kristiansen knew his company needed to adapt to a new generation of children's toys, he also needed to preserve the core value of creativity and his Lego bricks. One of the first changes was the introduction of Lego kits such as jungle explorers and dinosaur adventurers, which come complete with step-by-step instructions. Instead of flexible free-form creations that children build from their imagination, these toy kits contain all the Lego pieces necessary to assemble predesigned models. Then came Mindstorms, Lego software that enables kids to use "intelligent bricks" to design their own computer creations. Next came an even bigger change: Lego partnered with Lucasfilm Ltd. to introduce various Star Wars kits that contained not just designs to build but stories. The Star Wars Legos were a huge success for the company. Finally, in the fall of 2001, Lego launched Harry Potter sets that combine recognizable characters and stories. Many of Kristiansen's changes have been met with resistance from Lego employees, who hold fast to company tradition and values. They want to keep the company focused on the traditional little plastic brick. But Legos have changed from their free-form roots and will probably continue to change, at least for as long as kids think Legos are cool.

The Business of Change

Just like the employees at Lego, you can expect to experience or participate in corporate change at some time during your career. As a result of new markets, competition, business mergers, and a focus on quality improvements, change has been a constant in American business since the 1980s. When customer interests and needs change, business must change. As discussed in the "In a Nutshell" feature, Lego updated, redesigned, and created new products to meet customer demands, and those changes were initially met with resistance by some Lego employees who liked the company and its products the way they were. But change is often inevitable and necessary for business to expand and progress into the future.

What Does Change Mean?

change occurs when an organization begins to transform the way work is accomplished—which means a breakdown of business as usual.

From a business perspective, **change** means that an organization begins to transform the way work is accomplished—which means a breakdown of business as usual. Change can involve everything from what products the company manufactures or sells, as it did at Lego, to how they are manufactured and from what services it offers to what job responsibilities are assigned and what procedures are followed. With the rapid changes in our social culture, communication, and information technology, American businesses must be able to adapt to the changing world of business or face an uncertain fate. Companies such as IBM, Xerox, General Electric, Ford, and Harley-Davidson, historically known for their longevity and stability, have experienced tremendous organizational changes and have emerged stronger and smarter competitors.

Who Carries the Flag of Change?

The company CEO and a hand-picked group of change managers usually initiate organizationwide change and design a process for transformation. Middle-level managers and employees are typically called

WORD ON THE WEB

Word on the Web

Take a look at the tips, tricks, and resources that change makers use when they help companies adapt to new conditions:

- www.change-management.org
- www.sci.usda.gov/change_management/customer_service.htm
- www.employee-motivation.net/letter.htm
- www.parshift.com
- www.emeraldinsight.com/jocm.htm

on to perform procedural changes. While many change efforts begin at the top and eventually work their way down to the rank and file, it is often a sound strategic move to include all employees in a major change affecting the organization. Once the need for change has been established, diverse self-managing teams of change makers should be convened. **Change makers,** also called change agents, are people who facilitate the coordination of a change effort. They plan, experiment, communicate, and coach throughout the process of transformation.

Alberto-Culver, a personal care and household products manufacturer, has 70 designated change makers of various ranks throughout the organization. Alberto-Culver change makers are called growth development leaders (GDLs) and are chosen for their strong communication skills. These GDLs mentor other employees through the process of cultural change and address any problems or concerns that arise. They also represent the employees by participating directly with the company executive staff to solve problems and initiate growth.

change makers are people who facilitate the coordination of a change effort.

Why Do Organizations Change?
The following are some of the reasons for organizational change:

- Competition.
- Corporate mergers and acquisitions.

globalization is the manufacture and sale of goods or services to multiple markets around the world.

communication vacuums occur when employees perceive a void in which they are not given adequate information about what is happening in the organization.

- Changing consumer demands.
- Globalization.
- Technology.
- Government regulations and policies.
- Change of management.

Often a crisis of some sort motivates an organization to change. This crisis can take the form of diminishing market shares, competitors in the market, new regulations, court decisions, or legislative actions.

Change can also be initiated without an immediate crisis. Perhaps company leaders detect shifts in consumer demands, or the company is growing or wants to operate in new markets. Today businesses manufacture, offer services, and sell in various countries throughout the world. **Globalization,** the ability to reach multiple markets around the world, creates new competition across national boundaries. Corporate mergers and acquisitions create major internal changes, including personnel, structure, and processes. Changes in executive staff can drive organizationwide changes in values and operating procedures. Often the new leaders have different visions from their predecessors and try to mold the organization to match their philosophy. Finally, new technology has contributed to major transformations involving information sharing, product and service offerings, production processes, and delivery systems.

What Happens When Organizations Change?

During a period of change, employees often become confused and insecure. This is especially evident when the reasons for the change are not explained and when only a handful of top managers are included in the change process. Employees experience great distress when they perceive a **communication vacuum,** a void in which they are not given adequate information about what is happening in the organization. Often employees do not really understand why change is being made and how it will affect them personally. They may also feel they have little opportunity to express their views or contribute to what changes will occur. A communication vacuum is illustrated in Figure 14.1.

Some companies offer vague messages to inform employees that change is imminent but neglect to communicate clearly and consistently about why the change is urgently needed and what it will mean to employees. The result is often a flurry of rumors on the company grapevine, growing anxiety, and even resistance.

FIGURE 14.1

Communication Vacuum

During change, some employees feel like they are in a communication vacuum. It's like being in an isolation booth without information about what's going on in the organization.

The Face of Resistance

Resistance occurs when employees either do nothing to enact the expected changes or actively resist and undermine the change effort. Without knowledge, understanding, and participation, employees are not likely to help the organization to reach its goals. The following four factors contribute to change resistance:

Fear	• Change can produce an emotional upheaval, and one of the most powerful emotions during change is fear. Fear is often a reaction to the unknown. As the old adage goes, "The devil you know is better than the devil you don't." Even when a given change is positive, people may resist what they do not know.
Interruption of routine	• Some employees resist change when they feel their daily work routine is jeopardized. Some habits are hard to break, and change can necessitate job redesign and the formation of new habits. Some employees may feel that new ways of doing things may be difficult to learn, including new technologies to aid work performance.
Loss of faith, trust, and personal investment	• Change threatens the familiar and can compromise employees' faith, trust, and investment in the organization. Trust is often grounded in an ability to count on what will happen next. Accepting change is about adapting to the unpredictable, which is hard for most people to do. Change can produce the unexpected and lead to new ground rules. Some middle managers and employees may believe they will lose pay, status, freedom, or job security.
Feeling that past efforts are meaningless	• Employees may feel as though the contributions they made before the change are now considered worthless by the organization.

At Ford Motors, many internal, cultural, and operational changes were initiated under the leadership of former CEO Jacques Nasser, who spearheaded the development of Web deals (with Microsoft and Yahoo!) and the acquisitions of Hertz Rental Cars, Volvo, and Land Rover. Operational changes during Nasser's tenure included flattening the corporate structure (eliminating layers of management or supervisors), hiring young autoworkers to fill executive posts, and implementing a performance evaluation system that measures employees' performance against the work of other employees. Under the new system, underperformers may not receive bonuses, may be demoted, or may even be terminated. Resistance by veteran managers to Nasser's initiatives became intense. Production during the year 2000 declined by 7 percent, and dozens of Ford's middle managers filed a class action lawsuit charging that the performance evaluation system was unfair and discriminatory.

Reducing Resistance

You can reduce most fear and resistance through productive change communication. Resistance may actually present opportunities dur-

Job #1: News that layoffs may be coming to your company, Alas Inc., has left employees nervous and irritable. As the supervisor, you know not only who will be laid off but also how the selections will be made. Several employees have approached you asking for information regarding who will be kept on the payroll and who will be let go. The tension has caused productivity to decline in your department, so you know you need to address the staff's concerns.

Write a memo to all staffers detailing the position and interests of the company in terms of the layoffs. Explain why the layoffs are necessary, and give a brief description of the criteria that will be used to determine who will be let go.

Job #2: You are an office worker at Alas Inc. The news of layoffs has you terrified. You have a family to feed and bills to pay. When you approached your supervisor to ask for details, he seemed uncomfortable and didn't give you very much information. Then you got a memo from him stating the company's position on layoffs (the memo from Job #1). Now you're upset.

Write a memo to your supervisor, Joe Scattershot, responding to the points he made and identifying your own position and interests in the layoff situation. (See the section in this chapter on "The Real Issues" for descriptions of position and interests).

ing the change process because you can use the feedback received from resisters to modify and improve the process. Trouble can arise when change makers ignore the importance of change communication. They want **employee buy-in,** which is acceptance of and agreement to change. But they may neglect to gain support from the employees who will be expected to implement the changes. For successful change to happen, you need to design appropriate change communication.

> **employee buy-in** is acceptance of and agreement to change.

For example, at the Glendale, California, headquarters of Nestlé USA, a subsidiary of the world's largest food company, change is about integrating e-business into the entire company culture of 17,300-plus employees. To facilitate buy-in, change makers (called e-business catalysts) communicate and work with employees in every division and department to help them develop Web-based strategies and initiatives.

Together, the e-business catalysts and employees create new sites and marketing tactics and use technology to transform the way the 135-year-old food company does business. In another example of how companies can encourage change buy-in, administrators at the Detroit Medical Center persuaded doctors to use a new clinical-information system by asking for their input. The clinical-information system digitizes medical records and allows users to track data over several years. Doctors can access medical information through the system, eliminating the need for paper records and allowing them to coordinate patient care among multiple doctors. To gain buy-in,

CREATIVE

CHALLENGE

Think about how you would react to the following change at your school:

> In a new initiative, the school announced that financial aid for tuition will now be performance based. Every participating student will be required to maintain a 3.0 (out of a possible 4.0) or higher GPA to receive financial aid. Any student whose GPA drops below 3.0 will automatically lose his or her financial aid.

Come to class prepared to discuss what your reaction would be if your school made this change in financial aid.

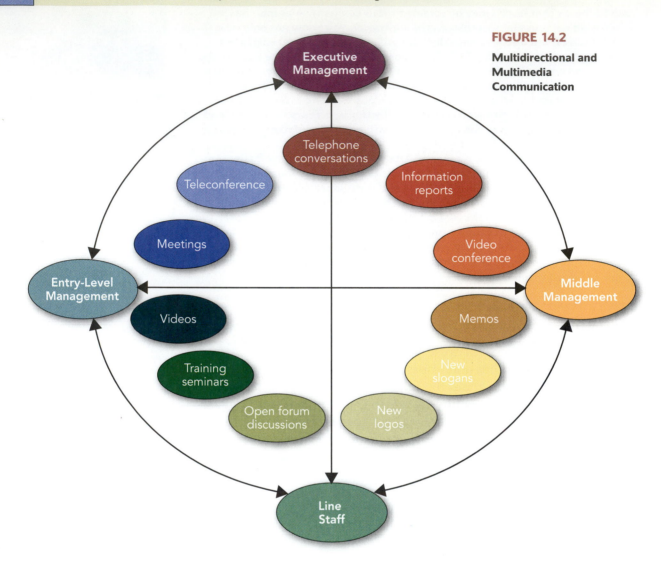

FIGURE 14.2

Multidirectional and Multimedia Communication

doctors were paid for their time while they participated in developing many system features that would help them to deliver better care to their patients.

While some leaders, such as the ones at Nestlé and the Detroit Medical Center, encourage input from employees to facilitate change, many still do not realize the importance of employee buy-in. To increase success, a comprehensive communication change campaign should be created to educate employees and involve them in the process of change development and implementation.

Change Communication

Change communication is both multidirectional and multimedia communication, as illustrated in Figure 14.2.

Multidirectional and Multimedia Communication

Multidirectional and multimedia communication occurs throughout the organization, involves many channels, and should commence from the beginning of the change effort. **Multidirectional communication** is the design of messages that can reach all employees up and down the hierarchy—not only from top managers but also from middle-level supervisors and field employees. **Multimedia communication** is the use of many channels to transmit a message.

The most effective channel for change communication is a face-to-face dialogue during open meetings in which company employees can exchange ideas, ask questions, and make suggestions. The beauty of open communication dialogues is the two-way interaction between people. Issues and interpretations of meaning can be clarified and feedback can be offered. At the Association for Managers of Innovation (AMI), employees from companies such as Kraft Foods, IBM, and Hallmark meet twice per year to participate in an open dialogue about change issues. Participants share ideas about generating innovation, working through transition, and managing immediate change initiatives. Additional channels for communicating change include training seminars, newsletters, videos, and continuous information reports.

multidirectional communication is the design of messages that can reach all employees throughout the organization.

multimedia communication is the use of many channels to transmit a message.

Unintended Messages

Even with the use of more than one channel, many organization change makers do not adequately communicate to employees the reasons for change. The CEO or department manager may announce the change during a large staff meeting and through a companywide memo. Then the appointed change makers will go busily about the business of planning for the change, with little more communication to other staff members. Yet, even when change makers are not communicating, messages are still being received. Employees may interpret the absence of communication as a message that their input is not important—which leads to fear and resistance.

Employees need information and a clear sense of why a change is necessary in order to accept it. Often managers allude to the fact that change is coming but overlook the need to communicate vital information that could convince employees to embrace the change. Some managers hoard information. They think that knowing things their workers don't gives them power. They don't realize that knowledge shared is far more powerful and leads to far greater productivity. Consider the following dialogue between an employee and her manager about an impending procedural change.

CREATIVE

CHALLENGE

Design a strategy to persuade administrators at your school to change the grading system from A through F to Pass/Fail. Write a memo to your instructor in response to the following questions: Who would you choose to become change makers? What reasons would you offer for the change? How would you reduce resistance? How would you communicate your messages about the change and how would you gain support?

PEOPLE AT CROSS-PURPOSES DIALOGUE

Shawnell is one of the clerks in a court system. Her boss, Ricardo, is the court manager. Ricardo just informed Shawnell that she would be trained to operate an electronic recording machine that registers everything that is said during trials.

Shawnell:	I really don't see the feasibility of my learning to monitor and play back the electronic recording machine, since I won't be able to enter and update other data in the back room. If I'm in the courtroom monitoring the recording machine during trials, I can't do my work on the computer.
Ricardo:	There are other things that I can't tell you, but if you knew them, you would understand.
Shawnell:	If I knew more about why you want to do this, it would help.
Ricardo:	All I can say is that this is what we're going to be doing. Unfortunately, I'm not at liberty to tell you more about it.

What Ricardo failed to explain to Shawnell was that the court wanted to replace court stenographers with the recording machines because they could ensure greater accuracy and save the court system money.

Furthermore, Shawnell would be able to perform her other work during the trials because a computer would be in the courtroom for her to use while she monitored the recording machine. Ricardo felt that only court managers needed to know the reasons for the change and that Shawnell should do what she was told without question. If Ricardo had explained the need for the change and the advantages of the new method of reporting trial minutes, Shawnell might have been more willing to accept her new assignment.

Provide Reasons

If you want other people to buy in, you need to design a compelling argument that details the purpose of the change with concrete reasons and advantages. You also need to present information on what your competitors are doing, what your customers want, and what the consequences may be if you don't change. Finally, you need to communicate a vision that describes where the organization will be in the future. From the very beginning of a change initiative, you need to clearly and repeatedly send messages that communicate the purpose, reasons, and vision for the change.

Timing

Messages also need to be conveyed using good timing. Delivering change messages before a holiday or on a Friday is probably not a good idea. While employees need a chance to process the information, they also need an opportunity to talk about the change. Messages delivered right before employees leave the office may delay discussions that can explain the change and calm fears.

Change makers, managers, line supervisors, and employees all need to discuss the change at length before, during, and after the change.

React to the following situation by identifying the problem. At Taylor Jones Consulting, a financial consulting firm, an executive change initiative called for employee experimentation with different methods to solicit new clients. In response, a manager and her staff created an advertisement complete with details about the company's services in the local Yellow Pages. What made this marketing approach different was that the company had previously listed only its name and phone number in the Yellow Pages. Upon publication of the new phone book, the manager enthusiastically presented the ad to the executive staff. Furious, some of the executives reprimanded her for placing an ad like this without their approval. The executives then disseminated a companywide memo that prohibited experimentation without approval.

Come to class prepared to discuss your reaction. If new approaches were called for, why do you think there was such a strong negative response to the new ad the manager and her staff created? What different approaches could the manager have used to persuade these executives to accept and believe in the usefulness of the new ad to reach clients?

Messages presented before the change provide reasons, explanation, expectations, and plan strategies. Messages exchanged during the change can enhance or alter process improvements and experimentation. Finally, messages shared after the change can include feedback, evaluations, and new directions. The more these messages are communicated, the more likely they will get through to employees and the less likely the grapevine will carry fear reports. In the case of change messages, redundancy is a good thing.

At the Milwaukee-based Brady Corp., which manufactures and sells signs and labeling software, company CEO Katherine Hudson characterizes the transformation of employee change resistance to acceptance as going from "no to yo." Inspired by a Brady employee, "no to yo" is a message that is repeated at company meetings, on the floor of the manufacturing plants, and throughout the organization. Hudson says that in the past Brady Corp. had a very conservative corporate culture. Before 1989, policies were so strict that none of the 3,200 Brady employees were allowed to drink coffee at their workstations. Under Hudson's leadership, the culture has changed. It is more collaborative, open, and fun. Policy changes include flextime and the elimination of time cards for workers.

Practice Change Communication Design

Open up the new corporate vision	• Create positive themes and slogans that bring the new change vision to life.
Connect vision to employees	• Tie individual employees' success to the company's success. Personalize the change process so employees know how they can be more productive.

Include new vision in the corporate culture	• Transform familiar and visible company symbols, such as logos, to reflect the new vision. • Create new symbols that can be integrated into the daily work environment. Use computer screensavers, posters, and promotional items to display the new symbols.
Encourage employee role in the vision	• Hold open forums where employees can engage in dialogues.
Reduce vision resistance	• Address fears, company weaknesses, and problems openly and directly with employees before they become grist for the rumor mill.

The Process of Conflict

A natural outgrowth of change is conflict, and workplace conflict is not unusual. Conflict happens because people with different views, styles, backgrounds, and interests work together on a daily basis. We often view conflict as an uncomfortable and confusing struggle that we prefer to avoid. The perceived frustration and discomfort associated with conflict prevent us from seeing its benefits. Positive and productive aspects of conflict include increased understanding of individual or group issues, enhanced innovation, heightened creativity, better ideas, improved relationships, and more useful problem solving. We may also come to understand other people, viewpoints, situations, and ideas better through the process of conflict.

For example, the historic 2000 presidential election involving candidates George W. Bush and Al Gore created a learning opportunity for many Americans. Before November 7, 2000, many people had never considered the various civic, constitutional, and political issues it raised. The conflict between the Republican and Democratic parties during the weeks it took to close that election provided a unique opportunity for exploration of contrasting philosophical perspectives through well-constructed public arguments.

What Is Conflict?

A **conflict** is an event expressed through communication when individuals or groups behave in ways that indicate they have incompatible positions or goals. People usually become aware that a conflict exists when disagreements surface through verbal and nonverbal communication.

Problems can initially seem irreconcilable, but many conflicts can eventually be worked through or

conflict is an event expressed through communication when individuals or groups behave in ways that indicate they have incompatible positions or goals.

CREATIVE

CHALLENGE

A conflict has arisen between a supervisor and his employees about coffee drinking at their workstations. The supervisor tells employees they can no longer drink coffee at their desks because of several stains that have recently appeared on the new office carpeting. But the employees want the freedom to drink their coffee as they work rather than waiting for break time. On the surface, the goals of the supervisor and his employees seem incompatible.

Break into groups with your class colleagues to discuss ideas for a mutually satisfying solution to this problem.

The conflict surrounding the 2000 presidential elections provided many Americans with insight about the political and electoral process.
© AP Photo/Al Behrman

resolved to the satisfaction of all parties. Even before a given conflict becomes overt, interactions between the people involved can become unpredictable, strained, uncertain, and sometimes hostile. Often emotions begin to rise when at least one party feels dissatisfied, disgruntled, offended, or ignored.

Who's Who in Conflict

Disputants are the different parties involved in a conflict. The disputants are the people who believe they have contrasting ideas, goals, or needs. The individuals or groups directly involved in the conflict are the primary disputants. Third parties in the conflict are mediators or negotiators who may intervene to assist the parties to reach accord. In organizations, conflicts can occur among individuals or groups.

An **intragroup conflict** is a problem that occurs within a single group of people. Members of the group may have competing needs or expectations. Intragroup differences can involve values, normative behaviors, business or creative approaches to tasks, power or role expectations, and ineffective communication.

An **intergroup conflict** is a problem that arises between two or more groups. Business departments or units can experience conflict over company resources; turf issues; perceptions about company direction, policies, or goals; and ineffective communication.

The Real Issues

Often, the core of conflict involves our personal needs, fears, and desires. However, the behavior and verbal statements that are conveyed during the initial stages of conflict reflect a position. A **position** is a definitive

disputants are the different parties involved in a conflict.

intragroup conflict is a problem that occurs within a single group of people.

intergroup conflict is a problem that arises between two or more groups.

position a definitive goal or demand advanced by one or both parties that underscores an attitude or disposition.

WORD ON THE WEB

Word on the Web

Take a look at the following websites, which show how mediators solved conflicts in various businesses:

- www.usdoi.gov/crt/ada/mdeiate.htm#anchor68130
- covenor.com/example1.htm
- www.wco.com/-mhsmith/results.html
- www.workplacesolutions.org/resource/success.cfm

Now look at the unsolved case at this website:
- www.sybilevans.com/diversity_learning_center/case_study.htm

HOW WOULD YOU RESOLVE THIS SITUATION IF YOU WERE THE MEDIATOR?

interests are the reasons or motivations underlying a position.

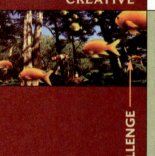

CREATIVE CHALLENGE

There is an ongoing conflict between General Electric and the federal Environmental Protection Agency. PCBs are chemicals that GE released into the Hudson River for some 30 years until 1977, when New York State forbade GE to continue releasing them. In December 2000, the EPA ordered GE to dredge certain portions of the river to remove the contaminants. GE claims that the river has effectively cleaned itself and dredging would bring the contaminants back to the surface and create a bigger problem. It would also cost GE $460 million to complete. To date, the company has spent millions in advertising and lobbying to fight the EPA's order. The state health department warned against eating fish caught from the river because PCBs still contaminate the water.

Research the conflict involving GE and the Environmental Protection Agency. Then break into groups with your class colleagues. Discuss what interests each side of the conflict has and what the potential interests of other people may be, including citizens who live and work by the river. Discuss your conclusions with the rest of the class.

goal or demand advanced by one or both parties that underscores an attitude or disposition. A statement that begins with "I will," "I won't," "I am not," "you are," or "you will" is positional in that the party holds a definite stance or intention on a certain issue. **Interests,** on the other hand, are the reasons or motivations underlying the position. Interests can be basic feelings, needs, or desires that may be fulfilled through the achievement of certain positional goals.

Consider an employee who makes the statement "I want a raise." This statement reflects a position, but the basic interests from which the position springs may include a need to feel safe and financially secure, a desire for increased professional status, a desire for a better standard of living, and a need to enhance self-esteem. The raise may seem like the only way to obtain these personal interests. Very often, people in conflict can imagine only one favorable outcome. But if this employee were to explore other outcomes, such as investing, changing jobs, or working extra hours, she might find that alternative outcomes could satisfy her interests as well as or better than the outcome she originally imagined.

The positions advanced during conflict are often more rigid, aggressive, and polarizing than are the real sources of the problem, the disputants' interests.

Conflict Communication Skills

Several basic communication skills are called on in conflict situations, including active listening, verbal diplomacy, and flexible interpersonal skills.

Listen and Learn

Active listening is an important skill in conflict situations because it enables disputants to learn about the opposing party's needs and feelings and gain their perspective about the problem. Listening also allows for the discovery of new ideas and insights that can help shape the conflict resolution and agreement. When disputants really listen to each other with a willingness to understand, their relationship changes and often deepens, allowing mutual understanding to occur more easily.

Verbal Diplomacy

Speaking diplomatically involves tact and self-control. Framing a message in a way that avoids irritating, threatening, or offending others is a valuable skill in conflict. Diplomacy does not mean glossing over, hiding, or losing the heart of your message. It means designing the message in a less aggressive, antagonistic way. Framing messages using verbal diplomacy makes it possible for you to say exactly what you want without intensifying the problem.

Flexible Interpersonal Style

Flexibility in interpersonal style means the ability to change and adapt verbal and nonverbal behaviors. Flexible interpersonal skills help you communicate appropriately and enhance message fidelity. For example, if someone were expressing heartfelt fears and feelings about an issue, you would not turn your nose up in the air, roll your eyes, and say, "Wah, wah, wah." You manage your nonverbal behaviors and your verbal statements to make sure your communication style is not threatening. Interpersonal flexibility also means that you frame your messages in different ways for different audiences and situations to increase the likelihood that your ideas will be understood.

Types of Conflict

There are four main types of conflict, which can combine in several ways: conflicts in communication, social views, fundamental interests, and business.

Source: Copyright 2002 United Feature Syndicate, Inc.

Randeep and Erin are mechanical engineers: Randeep thinks Erin has unfairly been offered the lead role in a project because she is a "brown-noser." Randeep confronts his supervisor to ask why Erin has been chosen. The supervisor explains that Erin has demonstrated superior leadership skills on other projects and that she has the ability to motivate people. But Randeep argues that he should have been offered the lead role because of his seniority and because he is both more qualified and more knowledgeable than Erin. The supervisor acknowledges Randeep's many skills and confirms that because of his great talents, he will be a very valuable member of the team. Randeep is dissatisfied with his supervisor's position and decides later to prove his boss wrong by challenging Erin at every opportunity when the project team meets. He believes that when Erin's incompetence is revealed through his challenges, his supervisor will have no alternative but to concede that she was the wrong choice for project leader.

Imagine that you are Randeep's and Erin's supervisor. You know that Randeep is unhappy about being passed over as team leader and are concerned that he may not fully support Erin's decisions regarding team assignments and assessment. Randeep is a very valuable member of your staff. He has strengths that Erin lacks and will need to make the project a success.

Erin	Randeep
• Well-spoken	• More experience
• Good organization skills	• Attention to detail
• Creative ideas	• Pragmatic applications

You still believe you made the right choice for team leader, but you want Randeep to understand how important he is, not only to the team but also to your company. Break into pairs with your class colleagues to develop a role-play. In your role-play, develop the conversation you would have with Randeep to highlight his strengths while also providing suggestions about what he can do to improve his chances to become team leader on the next project.

Communication Conflicts

Communication conflicts arise as a result of interpreted meaning (sarcasm; indirect language; different interpretations of rules, facts, or ideas; and miscommunication), styles of communication, and behaviors. Communication conflicts can occur when the meaning of a message is ambiguous or the communication styles of the people involved are very different.

Social View Conflicts

Social view conflicts concern basic values; beliefs; moral, ethical, or philosophical perspectives; and world views. They arise because people view the world and situations differently, and their distinct behaviors, practices, and approaches reflect these differences.

Fundamental Interest Conflicts

Fundamental interest conflicts comprise emotions, needs, self-defense, ego-centered interests, and expectations. Disputants in fundamental interest conflicts usually identify very personally with their position and tend to feel threatened in some way.

Business Conflicts

Business conflicts tend to combine all the types of conflict, including personality clashes, disagreements about how to interpret tasks or procedures, power and decision making, resource competition and entitlements, and turf issues. Business conflicts often occur because people (and companies) compete for resources, power, and control.

Traditional Conflict Strategies

Traditional conflict strategies focus on a desired outcome, such as a settlement. They are tailored to achieve a lasting resolution. In most traditional strategies, some form of negotiation is the primary way to resolve conflict.

Negotiation is a give-and-take technique to achieve accord. Opposing parties discuss and analyze the problem and begin a process of compromise or the offering of proposals and counterproposals. Different forms of negotiation are used depending on the conflict and the parties involved.

negotiation is a give-and-take technique to achieve accord through a process of compromise or the offering of proposals and counterproposals.

Positional bargaining	As a structured form of negotiation, bargaining focuses on specific issues or problems. Disputants compete with each other by haggling and providing demands and counterdemands, promises, persuasion, and even threats until an agreement can be reached. Negotiating the price of office supplies with a product vendor is a simple example of bargaining.
Mediation	Mediation is a form of negotiation that uses a neutral third party to assist the disputants in problem solving and settlement. The mediator typically facilitates and coordinates the negotiation process and pushes for resolution. Mediators assist parties by • facilitating the exchange of information; • pinpointing the cause of the problem; • developing alternative solutions; • helping the disputants to weigh alternatives; and/or • crafting a settlement that is acceptable to both parties. Neither party is required to accept the agreement reached through mediation.
Conflict management	Conflict management essentially involves a manager who controls the conflict process, including the disputants' behavior and the establishment of problem solving procedures. A conflict manager determines how the conflict will be resolved. He or she sets the ground rules for behavior during negotiation and the pace of the proceedings.
Arbitration	When conflicting parties seem deadlocked or have reached an impasse, an arbitrator is a neutral third party who resolves the dispute by rendering a decision that the disputants are required to accept.

Transformative Communication in Conflict

In business as in life, the dynamics of conflict are always changing. The parties, problems, relationships, and events continue to change throughout the process of conflict. However, change does not necessarily mean resolution. No matter which traditional strategy is used or what outcome is achieved, the disputants may still come back to conflict. If the parties involved and the way we perceive conflict remain unchanged, then the conditions for conflict will continue. Conflict is often viewed as a contest with the deeply held goal being to win. **Transformative communication** focuses on interaction and relationship building by reframing the terms and concepts of conflict rather than focusing on a finish line. The conflict process may not finish. The parties may not win or lose, but they may be transformed.

Dialogue Transformation Strategy

Dialogue transformation is a relationship–dialogue process that can be used to modify differences and disputes. Transformation also involves increasing the disputants' understanding by expressing emotions and shifting perceptions of the other parties, their interests, and the disputed issues.

At Pharmacia, a pharmaceutical company, a team of scientists, clinicians, and marketing professionals was created to collectively develop a new antibiotic drug to better treat multiple infections. Pharmacia encouraged the collaborative working model by linking team members' monetary compensation to the speed, efficiency, and profit of the products they created together. Because these scientists, clinicians, and marketing specialists tended to have different approaches to accomplishing tasks and different communication styles, conflicts arose as they worked together. The group decided to use open dialogues as a strategy to air differences and to gain a better understanding about each other while maintaining their focus to create a superior medication. The result of the team's collaborative dialogue was Zyvox, a hugely successful antibiotic drug that none of the team members could have produced acting alone.

Through dialogue, personal perceptions can be recast, a higher understanding can be achieved, and even the organizational system in which the disputants operate can be transformed. The stages of dialogue transformation are exploring interests and emotions, reframing and replacing expectations, and finally converting and resolving conflict.

Explore Interests and Emotions

During conflict, it is often difficult for us to assess accurately where the other party is coming from. We make assumptions regarding the opposing party's motives and expectations, but our assumptions may be

---

transformative communication focuses on interaction and relationship building by reframing the terms and concepts of conflict.

dialogue transformation is a relationship–dialogue process that can be used to modify differences and disputes.

wrong. We think we know what the opposing side wants, but we don't understand the underlying reasons for their position. At this stage of the conflict, disputants are encouraged to share and explore their honest emotions about the conflict, any stereotypes they hold about others, and the interests or reasons behind their positions. The emphasis is on acknowledging anger, fear, and resentment.

A mediator or even a psychologist can facilitate this stage of the process if the disputants believe the conflict may escalate during the exchange. The purpose of this dialogue is to build trust in the relationship and to enhance the disputants' insight and understanding of the other party from a human perspective.

Reframe and Replace Expectations

At this stage in the dialogue, disputants jointly begin the process of recasting the terms and meanings of various words, concepts, and ideas embroiled in the conflict. For example, if the conflict includes terms that trigger hostility, such as "gross mismanagement," the disputants can replace them with less provocative words. When words, phrases, or concepts are modified, perspectives begin to change, casting the attached meanings in a different light. Reframing also allows the disputants to concentrate on the other side's interests rather than their positions. Interests are usually easier to work with than the more rigid positions advanced by disputants.

Convert and Resolve the Conflict

Conflict conversion incorporates the process of reframing and changing the conflict into a more manageable, flexible situation. At this stage of the dialogue, parties further explore their feelings about the conflict and specific interests, using the reframed terms. Then the parties jointly brainstorm and develop alternative solutions that fairly meet each side's interests. Finally, conflict conversion allows disputants to refocus on the issues and collaboratively move the discussion toward mutually agreed-upon solutions.

Practicing Dialogue Transformation

Exploring interests and emotions	• Listen actively. • Avoid interrupting the other party. • Focus on understanding the other side's point of view. • Openly discuss your feelings and assumptions. • Identify and share your interests. • Focus on the problem or issues and not the other party. • Avoid personal attacks. • Understand that people communicate from their emotions, including fear, anger, and distrust.

Reframing and replacing expectations	• Discuss points of disagreement. • Brainstorm for alternative words and terms. • Develop a wide range of options. • Jointly create shared meanings for new words and terms. • Focus on working with interests rather than with positions.
Converting and resolving	• Focus on exploring areas of common ground rather than on persuading. • Share your resources to enhance the process. • Avoid ultimatums that have an "or else" requirement. • Avoid threatening verbal or nonverbal communication. • Narrow issues down and reframe terms or concepts about the conflict. • Collaborate with the other side to develop solutions that are mutually acceptable, using the new words and terms.

STRATEGIES

Strategies

1. Design change communication that states a clear purpose and details why the change is urgent. Specifically justify the need for change and the consequences if the change is not enacted. Build an argument with evidence that clearly shows the need for and the advantages of the change. Describe what aspects of the business will change. Discuss particular procedural and policy changes that should be developed. Design a clear, visionary message that explains what can be accomplished and what is likely to happen as an outcome of the change.

2. Initiate change communication on all fronts. Create self-managing and interdisciplinary teams as active partners in the change process. Encourage participation from diverse segments of the organization. Make sure that each department and each unit understands the change messages. Send these messages consistently and through various channels of communication. Hold open forums for employee dialogue where information, ideas, and innovations can be exchanged.

3. Empower employees and support experimentation. Remove barriers to change by providing support and facilitating dialogues. People do not respond positively to orders that require them to change without their input or opinion. They often need to be encouraged, given sound information, guided to reach their own conclusions, and allowed to respond. Employees who have information and support for experimentation will more readily rise to the challenge of change.

4. Reduce resistance with the following five tactics.
   • All employees should be provided with an understanding of the importance of change, the process, and any standards for measuring performance success.

- Messages should be clear and transmitted repetitively, with a specific focus on how the change will affect people personally.
- Employees should be encouraged to participate in change development and implementation.
- Managers and supervisors should provide support for innovation and experimentation.
- Open dialogues should be facilitated among change makers, managers, supervisors, and employees.

5. Celebrate victories. Collaborative change happens slowly, and disruptions in daily operations and workflow can produce anxiety and decrease enthusiasm. Recognizing and rewarding small victories throughout the change process can renew momentum.

6. Recognize and avoid ego involvement that can escalate conflict and minimize others' perspectives. Avoid interrupting other people in discussions, and check yourself for ego-based messages such as "You don't know what you're talking about!" Look at it from the other person's perspective: He or she believes he/she does know what he/she is talking about, and he/she also likely feels, as you do, that his/her position is justified.

7. It is especially important to recognize that an individual or group position in conflict may be quite different from the underlying interests or reasons for that position. It is much easier to work with interests than with hard-and-fast positions. Remember that your assumptions about the other party's motives or reasons for disagreeing with you may be wrong. Knowing the other side's position is not enough to fully understand the problem and the people involved. If you have only half the information you need, you can't reach an acceptable solution. You need to learn about their interests (why they want what they want) and how they perceive you and the problem. Identify and examine your own interests in the conflict. If you really want to resolve the problem, then you need to be willing to talk honestly about why you hold a certain position and how you feel about the problem.

8. Listening and diplomacy skills are fundamental in modifying conflict. Listen actively to learn and understand, not only about the problem but also about other people and their points of view. Frame your messages diplomatically to avoid offending others.

9. The act of simply reframing words or phrases and changing their meanings may not solve the conflict. But this process can help reduce hostility by taking the sting out of words that trigger negative emotions. It can also strengthen relationships because the parties work together collaboratively to recast terms.

10. Avoid passing judgment or blaming the other party. Adversarial or finger-pointing messages only intensify the problem and can

further polarize everyone involved. The dialogue you jointly create and participate in must allow everyone involved the freedom to express her or his feelings and opinions without fear of judgmental feedback or attitudes.

11. Don't try to persuade the other side to accept a solution that is not really reasonable for them. Even if they agree, the problem will likely resurface because the solution wasn't fair to begin with. Through dialogue, workable solutions can be found that meet the needs and interests of all the parties involved in the conflict. Dialogue is "how to" reach an agreement. Dialogue means that you suspend your own beliefs when listening to the views of others to understand them. It also means that you listen for areas of agreement or common interest and share your own ideas and feelings openly.

Summary

- Organizational change means modifying the way the company conducts business and performs work tasks. Change makers are employees of any rank who work in teams to plan and coordinate organizational change.

- Major reasons organizations change include increased competition, mergers, changing consumer trends, expanding markets, new technology, government regulations, and executive transitions.

- Change can upset the status quo, which can affect every aspect of the company. It can make people confused and apprehensive, especially if they are unclear about the reasons for the change and how it will affect them. A communication vacuum happens when information about the change is not shared with employees. Without the facts, people may imagine the worst-case scenario.

- Resistance means that acting in opposition, employees of various ranks may ignore or attempt to block the change effort. Resistance reactions stem from emotional factors including fear, love of routine, perceptions of loss or betrayal, and the assumption that one's efforts are being devalued.

- Change communication can reduce resistance through multidirectional messages and multimedia communication. The more messages you send and the more channels you use to send them, the better.

- As an outgrowth of change, conflict is an event expressed through communication that motivates individuals or groups to behave in ways that suggest incompatible goals.

- Disputants are the parties engaged in conflict. Third parties or mediators are individuals who intervene to facilitate and coordinate the conflict process. An intragroup conflict involves a disagreement among members of the same group. Intergroup conflict refers to disagreements between different groups.

- Disputants often hold a particular position (a stance involving their attitude and behavior). For example, you may hold the position that you dislike public speaking. An interest is the reason or motivation for your position (how you feel, what you need, or what you want). If your position is that you dislike public speaking, your basic interests may be that you don't want to feel rejected or embarrassed.

- Conflict communication skills include active listening, verbal diplomacy, and interpersonal flexibility.

- There are four general types of conflict: communication, social view, fundamental interest, and business conflicts.

- Traditional conflict resolution strategies involve negotiation, which is the analysis and discussion of a problem that includes a process of compromise and trading offers and counteroffers. Negotiation strategies include positional bargaining, mediation, conflict management, and arbitration.

- Transformative communication is a process of dialogue that emphasizes exploring the parties' interests and emotions, reframing conflict and the corresponding terms and concepts, and building relationships between parties to achieve conflict conversion.

Business Communication Projects

1. In a one-page memo to your instructor, identify three channels of communication you would use to communicate organizational change, and explain the benefits of each channel.

2. Positive communication is an important part of change communication. Which of the following sentences would result in a positive response from employees? Why?
   - "The company will make several changes in administrative practices over the next year." Or "Within one year, this administration promises the development of new procedures that will benefit the entire organization. These procedures involve the following . . ."
   - "The company is increasing spending by $3 million for technology to automate production." Or "An investment of $3 million in automation technology will increase the growth potential of our firm and provide new advancement potential for employees."

3. In a company newsletter, the CEO says only, ". . . decisions are now being made that will dramatically alter the future of our organization . . ." Explain what is wrong with this statement.

4. Your professor just announced that she is changing the grading policy for the course, but she failed to explain exactly how grades

will be computed. Since the beginning of the semester, you have been a borderline B/C student. You are not sure whether the change will drive your grade up or down. Write a letter to the professor explaining how you feel about her announcement and requesting clarification of the new grading policy.

5. Find a recent article in a business periodical on the Internet that announces a company change initiative. Write a memo to your instructor evaluating the announcement. Be sure to use the concepts presented in this chapter to form your arguments.

6. A corporate CEO has hired you as a communication consultant for a business change effort. Write the CEO a letter in which you describe a change communication strategy that needs to be enacted throughout the process.

7. When you decided to form your own website directory for disk jockeys in your local community, it met with great success. DJs from the surrounding area all paid $9.95 a month, grateful for the exposure your site provided them. Last year another website was created featuring not only a directory but also a ratings page where people who have used the DJs can comment on the service they received. Your site has suffered in comparison. You know you have to make some changes to compete. Write a one-page plan that details components you can add to your website to not only compete but beat the competition.

8. You are the group leader of an ongoing company project. Reviewing the work produced by a member of your group, you notice a number of careless mistakes, including grammatical and typographical errors. Although the substance of this person's work is generally good, he is consistently sloppy about grammar. You have mentioned that his work needs to improve, but the problems have not been corrected. You know from past encounters and observations that this employee is very sensitive to criticism and tends to become defensive. Break into groups with your class colleagues. Design two different role-play situations involving this fundamental interest conflict between the group leader and the group member whose work is not up to par. Approach one of the role-play scenarios using a traditional resolution method, such as conflict management. In the second role-play focus on dialogue transformation strategy. Remember the leader's goal is to encourage better work performance from the group member. Present your role-plays to the rest of the class.

9. You are asked to mediate a conflict between a supervisor and an employee in another department of the company. The problem involves a performance evaluation in which the supervisor rated the employee's work unsatisfactory. The employee believes the unfavorable evaluation is the result of a personality clash. During your

initial meeting with the disputants, you quickly learn that there really is a personality clash between them. They become angry and their exchange becomes increasingly disturbing and hostile. In an effort to help the disputants communicate and interact more productively, you suggest that all three of you come up with basic ground rules for the process, including definitions of what behavior is acceptable and what is unacceptable. Make a list of at least six such behaviors. Then prepare a two-page plan for your role in mediating this conflict that outlines how you will help the parties identify their interests and interact together constructively.

10. The last time you shopped at MacGregor's department store you were ignored by the salespeople. This isn't unusual, but in this case you were shopping for a new stereo system and were prepared to spend a lot of money. You needed to ask questions, but no one seemed interested in helping you. In response, you've written a rough draft of a letter to the general manager of MacGregor's:

> To Whom It May Concern,
>
> I'll never darken your doorstep again. I went to your store on January 30 ready to buy a new stereo system to hook up to my TV in preparation for Super Bowl Sunday but was unable to get any of your lazy employees to help me. I took my business to Chaucer's Stereo City instead and will continue to do so until you guys get your act together.

You realize after writing this letter that it's not likely to get you what you want. Reframe the letter to make a positive response more likely.

11. You are the assistant director of the human resources department. The director of human resources has never gotten along with the director of the accounting department. In fact, at the last board meeting the two got into a screaming fight over changes in paycheck disbursal for new employees. Obviously, their personal dislike of one another has gone too far. Write a memo to Howard Taft, the CEO of Dewey, Robham, and Howe, describing the effects this conflict has on the staffs of the accounting and human resources departments.

Discussion Questions

1. Why do you think some companies and business leaders delay or skimp on messages to their employees about change?

2. In change communication, what do you think is the audience's (employees') primary concern?

3. What are the primary goals of change messages? What are the secondary goals?

4. Most often a company CEO, president, or owner is the sender of change messages. What other message sources can and should be used? Why should other sources be used?

5. Can resistance be positive? Why or why not?

6. Why are change makers useful in the process of change?

7. In what ways can change communication encourage employee participation?

8. How is conflict positive, and what are some of the benefits to the parties involved?

9. Which conflict do you think is more difficult to transform, intragroup or intergroup? Are both about the same level of difficulty?

10. How can changing or reframing words or terms help in the conflict process?

11. Can you think of any type of conflict for which the dialogue transformation strategy may not work to help disputants bridge their differences? What about the conflict between GE and the Environmental Protection Agency or Microsoft versus the United States?

12. Why is it important to determine the interests and positions of the people involved in conflict?

13. Do you believe that people are always consciously aware of their interests and positions while involved in a conflict? Why or why not?

14. Why is listening so important in conflict situations?

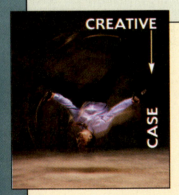

CREATIVE

CASE

Creative Case

Is Amtrak Leaving the Station?

Many businesspeople travel by train to work both morning and night. The ride gives them a chance to relax or prepare for a busy workday. Congress created Amtrak in 1970 to preserve passenger train service in a dwindling rail transportation market. Amtrak is a for-profit government corporation that has access rights to tracks owned by freight companies and passenger train priority over freight trains. More than 30 years and $22 billion later, Amtrak is in trouble. In June 2001 Amtrak mortgaged one of its most famous assets, New York's Penn Station, to raise $300 million for operating costs. Congress projects that it will cost another $20 billion to repair and maintain train tracks over the next 20 years.

In 1997 the Amtrak Reform Council (ARC), an independent bipartisan federal commission, was convened to make recommendations to help Amtrak become self-sufficient and to submit a plan to Congress for a nationalized rail passenger system if Amtrak was unable to reach self-sufficiency. The ARC submitted a plan to Amtrak in

March 2001 that recommended a split into two separate entities: a nonprofit, government-run corporation that would maintain the stations, tracks, and related facilities and a private corporation that would run the train service. This move would flatten the organizational hierarchy and provide the funds for maintaining rail facilities from a government trust.

This proposal has met resistance from Amtrak employees. Amtrak president and CEO George Warrington believes the plan moves away from the ARC's original mission—to make Amtrak more businesslike and less dependent on government funding. Labor unions are also opposing the change, believing that the ARC hasn't fully considered the realistic outcomes of such a split. They would prefer the ARC to call on Congress to fully fund Amtrak train services.

Amtrak is on the brink of going under. Should it accept the change or fight?

Write a letter to Amtrak CEO George Warrington urging him to back one option.

1. Accept the ARC's proposed changes. Use the principles for making people comfortable with change to explain how he can reassure Amtrack employees and the labor unions that this change will beneficial for employees and customers.

or

2. Fight for a new proposal that will make Amtrak more profitable. Use the principles for change to explain how the ARC can be persuaded to change its mind about Amtrak's possibilities and how those possibilities can create a stronger corporate/governmental company.

Sources: Amtrak Reform Council (2001). Retrieved September 10, 2001: www.amtrakreformcouncil.gov; Ognanovich, N. (2001) Amtrak Reform Council Restructuring to Separate Train Operations, Infrastructure. Government Employee Relations Report, 39, p. 1904. Retrieved September 10, 2001: subscript.bna.com/SAMPLES/ger.nsf.

Chapter 15

The following themes are explored in this chapter:

CREATING A CAREER

examine goals and interests / find out more / create an inventory of skills and abilities / take a temporary job

DESIGNING RÉSUMÉS

RÉSUMÉ FORMATS

chronological / functional / targeted / integrated / scannable

SAMPLE RÉSUMÉS

RÉSUMÉ INGREDIENTS

identification / education / accomplishments / capabilities / professional experience / references / problems

DESIGNING COVER LETTERS

what cover letters accomplish / types of cover letters

FINDING A JOB

Creating a Career
and Designing Résumés

Lupe Valdez is about to graduate from college with a degree in business, and she would like to find a job that will allow her to travel. She is fascinated by the performing arts, attends plays and concerts, and is involved in community theater projects. During school, she was active in the International Club, serving as the student liaison to foreign students, helping them with their visa paperwork and immigration issues when necessary. Her work experience as a receptionist and administrative assistant at the Automobile Club has acquainted her with worldwide travel opportunities and problems. She would like to work in an international field but would also like to work within her academic concentration: human resources.

One day while surfing the Net, Lupe comes across the Cirque du Soleil website. Based in Montreal, Canada, Cirque du Soleil is a unique international circus. Instead of the traditional animal acts and clowns, Cirque du Soleil consists entirely of human performers who create strange, beautiful, and often provocative stage shows using highly creative costuming and set design. The performers are incredible acrobats, magicians, and dancers. Their performances often baffle their audiences, prompting the response, "How did they do that?"

Lupe is thrilled when she finds a posting for a human resources technician on Cirque du Soleil's employment page. The job requires the technician to handle travel-related documents for performers, including immigration forms, letters, and applications. It also requires standard human resources training, two years of related administrative experience, and good interpersonal skills. Lupe knows she meets all the requirements.

She decides to prepare a résumé specifically for this job. She creates a list of her experiences and education, emphasizing the specific items that directly address the human resources technician requirements. When she considers how to organize her résumé, she chooses an integrated résumé design because that will allow her to highlight both her education and her unusual experience with immigration matters. She checks the résumé carefully for correctness and readability—she wants to impress Cirque du Soleil with its professional appearance. She then carefully crafts a solicited cover letter that shows Cirque du Soleil what she is capable of beyond what is listed in her résumé. A few days after she mails the résumé, she prepares to follow up with a telephone call.

IN A NUTSHELL

In a Nutshell

Creating a Career

Lupe is excited about the prospect of a new job at Cirque du Soleil. But if she is hired, she may not stay with this international circus forever.

Fifty years ago, many people selected a specific kind of work and stayed with it for their entire career. Even if the field, job, or company turned out to be unsatisfactory, the promise of career-long job security held many people in less-than-favorable jobs throughout their working lives. Today, shifts in organizational structures, employment trends, and technology have increased the frequency with which people change jobs, employers, and even careers. The key to choosing a career that will satisfy you begins with discovering what work you really enjoy. Like Lupe, you may find a job that appeals to you through an advertisement or posting. High salaries, good benefits, and even job security can initially be very appealing aspects of a job but they may never be enough if you dislike the work, company, or people. As discussed in the "In a Nutshell" feature, creating a career is a process of determining the right field and the type of job you want, identifying your skills and abilities, researching companies, and designing an effective résumé.

Creating a career means selecting the right field and matching your skills to the job you want and will enjoy.
© Rob Crandall/The Image Works

A Career-Finding Strategy

Examine Your Professional Goals and Interests

Choosing a job that's right for you involves an intrapersonal analysis of your professional aspirations, needs, and interests. Before you begin job hunting and even before you prepare a solid résumé, you need to consider the type of job you really want in a field that matches your values, skills, and qualifications. To begin self-examination, think about the courses you have taken that interested you. Often, interest in a career or type of work evolves from learning about the field and its

many subjects. You should also consider any internship, volunteer project, or job you liked performing, which can help you focus on a particular field. Once you identify the kind of work that interests you, think about the career fields that are growing; the geographic areas of the country that appeal to you; salaries; travel opportunities; and the visions, values, and standards of various industries. Stephen Roulac, CEO of the California-based consulting firm Roulac Group Inc., says, "People are choosing more purposefully where they want to live, and then they are looking for a job. In the future, companies that aren't in the right place may have to move." Roulac believes that to live in an area of choice, people will often change careers or establish independent consulting businesses.

Find Out More

To gain a better understanding and more insight about the job market and the fields that interest you, plan to look for information that can help you choose a career direction and get the job you want.

shadowing a business professional means to spend time watching him or her perform in the work environment.

Visit the campus career counseling center or placement office.	• Career counselors are trained to help you assess your skills and talents and match them with career choices. Sometimes career counselors use personality tests along with your feedback and school records as indicators of your potential. They may also help you to identify what courses and qualifications you will need to get the job you want.
Check out employment planning and job listing websites on the Internet.	• There are numerous websites that offer skill assessments, job listings, and company profiles and descriptions that can provide you with valuable information.
Network with professionals in the fields that interest you.	• Talk to business professionals who can shed light on the industry, the company culture, and the responsibilities involved with specific jobs. You can also **shadow** a business professional, which means to spend time watching him or her perform in the work environment. Shadowing can allow you to see firsthand what a typical workday is like and explore what your mentor likes and dislikes about the job.
Take a part-time or freelance job in the field.	• During the summer months or while you are in school, you can work part-time or perform freelance work for an employer you want to learn about. With a foot already in the door, you can establish yourself as an asset to the company and more easily move into job openings.
Read trade journals.	• You can find insights about employment, industry attitudes, and directions in trade journals.
Review classified ads in newspapers.	• The classified ads can provide information about what jobs are most available and the requirements for employment in the fields you are thinking about. While the classifieds are not necessarily the most effective way to actually land a job, you can gain some good information about the preponderance of different types of jobs.
Write exploratory letters to companies.	• Compose a letter that asks for an informational interview and include your résumé. In addition to providing insight about the company, exploratory meetings can sometimes lead to job opportunities.

Create a Professional Inventory of Skills and Abilities

Once you determine the career you want, you need to pinpoint and assess your most marketable skills. Create a list of all the skills you possess that you think potential employers may want. These skills can be personal or professional and can come from your participation in school activities, social clubs, and volunteer or internship work as well as your job history. Consider skills ranging from oral and written communication, interpersonal interaction, second languages, and visual illustration to problem solving, management and supervision, leadership, and computer proficiency.

Once you have listed your many skills, compare them with the requirements for the job you are seeking. Several of the skills you have listed may complement the position you want. Most businesses look for a solid fit between an applicant and the position. Job seekers and employers alike are looking for long-term relationships, says Jay Sidhu, CEO of Sovereign Bancorp. He believes that applicants want a secure business to work for and employers want a steady candidate whose talent and skills match the organization's needs. Tony Zhang, CEO of AskMeFinance, an online financial information company, agrees. Zhang looks for people who will fit well into his Boston-based organization. "New companies operate under extreme pressure, so your team really has to work well together. And a big part of making sure that a new executive succeeds is making sure that there's a good fit," he says.

At Mattel, the Los Angeles–based toymaker, new CEO Robert Eckert wanted to hire a few people with whom he had worked at another company. But Mattel's veteran VP of human resources, Alan Kaye, believed that one of the candidates would not be a good match with Mattel's corporate culture. While Eckert disagreed with this assessment, he agreed not to hire the candidate. Later, after learning more about the Mattel culture, Eckert realized that Kaye had been right and the candidate didn't share the company's cultural priorities.

If your skills or goals don't seem to match the job you want, consider pursuing a different, more realistic position. Or you might focus your energies on taking additional courses, attending seminars, or working as a volunteer in the field to develop relevant abilities.

After you identify four or five of your skills that match the job, develop brief statements that describe what you accomplished by using them. Use action words as you write these passages to present each skill in terms of an outcome or a result. These vignettes can be featured in a bulleted list under an accomplishment or skills heading in your résumé or cover letter.

CREATIVE CHALLENGE

Write two brief paragraphs that describe your strengths, skills, and accomplishments. Compare the skills and strengths you describe with a job ad you find in the newspaper or on the Internet. Then bring your paragraphs to class. Break into groups with your class colleagues and use the paragraphs to develop bulleted statements that relate to the advertised job.

Take a Temporary Job

Short-term jobs can provide valuable experience you can use on your résumé. They can also help you determine the kind of work you want to do. Many temporary agencies, such as Manpower and Snelling Personnel Services, link job applicants with employers. Since 90 percent of businesses hire temporary workers to fill full- and part-time vacancies, a temp job may be a good opportunity to work in an interesting field.

Designing Your Résumé

A **résumé** is a written marketing tool that briefly summarizes your skills, abilities, education, and experience for a potential employer. Your résumé is a written representation of you and the skills you have to offer. It tells employers why they should hire you. A résumé should "sell" you quickly, since employers may spend only seconds reviewing the document.

The primary purpose of a résumé is to get you an interview with an employer. A well-prepared, quality résumé can inspire a hiring official to select you over several hundred other applicants for a job interview. Résumés are also designed to highlight your credentials, including work experience, education, and any training that matches the requirements for a specific job. Employers often use résumés to screen out applicants by scanning for key words that meet the specifications they are seeking. Résumés that don't contain those key words get tossed quickly. Résumés that quickly and effectively demonstrate beneficial results are also likely to get noticed. A résumé that outlines proactive and positive achievements such as "increased company revenues," "designed successful marketing strategies," or "streamlined procedures" tells an employer what to expect from you. Finally, employers use résumés to assess an applicant's overall professionalism and neatness. A quality document that is neat, well constructed, and error free can demonstrate how well you plan, design, organize, and write.

résumé a written marketing tool that briefly summarizes your skills, abilities, education, and experience for a potential employer.

A quality résumé that is written and prepared well can get you an interview for the job you want.
© Diaphor Agency/Index Stock Imagery, Inc.

Résumé Formats

The best format for your résumé depends on your career goals and your relevant experience. Because there are so many fields, jobs, and employers, it is difficult to design a one-type-fits-all résumé. You'll be better off developing a customized résumé for the job you want. The best résumé presents your skills and talents in an attractive and easy-to-read format. Consider the format that most effectively suits your goals and qualifications and the position for which you are applying.

Chronological Résumés

chronological résumé a traditional format organized by positions held, starting with the most recent.

The most common and traditional format for résumés is the **chronological résumé.** It is organized by positions held, starting with the most recent. This style presents your work experience in a reverse timeline that begins with your current job and moves back in time to your earliest positions. Your job titles, duties, and education and their associated dates should appear in this order. Often called a tombstone résumé, a chronological format is a logical choice for job seekers who have solid work experience in a given field.

Functional Résumés

functional résumé presents relevant skills and achievements in categories rather than under job titles. It does not require dates of employment or titles.

A **functional résumé** allows you to present relevant skills and achievements in categories rather than under job titles. Because it does not require dates of employment or titles, the functional résumé is particularly useful for individuals who have little job experience, gaps or breaks in employment continuity, or a change in career fields.

One drawback to the functional style is that some employers may not approve of the absence of specific job titles they can use to compare duties performed. Even if you list similar skills and capabilities in functional categories, some employers may not make the connection to the job for which you are applying. Another drawback is that employers may wonder if the lack of dates for given jobs is designed to hide something.

Targeted Résumés

targeted résumé a customized format tailored to a precise career field or job. It contains only the content that applies to a set of job requirements.

A customized format tailored to a precise career field or job is a **targeted résumé.** It contains only the content that applies to a set of job requirements. This style is effective for candidates who have narrowed their career search to very specific jobs, companies, or fields.

Integrated Résumés

integrated résumé includes aspects of all the other formats.

Aspects of all the other styles are combined in an **integrated résumé.** This format may include an employment and education chronology together with various skills grouped into certain categories. It is helpful for job seekers who have just graduated, are changing careers, or have spotted work histories or employment gaps. This style gives potential employers chronological titles, dates, and duties, but also highlights the areas of strength that may not be demonstrated adequately through the positions you have held.

Scannable Résumés

A **scannable résumé** is formatted in plain text for electronic scanning systems. Many organizations use scanning and processing systems to manage the high volume of résumés they receive. Scanning systems enter paper résumé information into databases that can be searched to match applicants with job requirements. Scanned résumés are searched by key words that hiring managers specify as relevant to a given job. The content of a scannable résumé does not need to be vastly different than the content of a traditional hard-copy, mailed version. You don't have to spend a great deal of time rewriting your résumé, but you do need to reformat and modify the layout.

Here are some tips for designing scannable résumés:

- Use common type fonts such as Helvetica, Times Roman, or New Century School Book.
- Avoid text enhancements such as boldface, italics, and underlining.
- Use a 12- or 14-point type size.
- Don't justify the right margin.
- Use asterisks, dashes, or hyphens (half dashes) instead of bullets.
- Avoid boxes and borders.
- Use standard white paper and black ink.
- For copies, use a laser printer.
- Send only one scannable résumé.
- Use white space to separate categories.
- Use capital letters for headings.
- Don't fold or staple.
- Keep length to one page.

Elaborate font styles and design layouts don't scan well. Keep your scannable résumé plain and simple to avoid complications that could prevent if from being read properly. Because key words are searched to determine selection, it is a good idea to use nouns and adjectives rather than action verbs because scanning systems sometimes won't process verbs. To increase the chances that your résumé will be selected, list key words that match the job description at the beginning of your résumé.

Table 15.1 lists some examples of key nouns and adjectives for scannable résumés.

scannable résumé
formatted in plain text for electronic scanning systems.

bilingual	innovation
collaboration	leadership
communication skills	management
creative	motivation
dedication	organization
flexible	teamwork

TABLE 15.1

Scannable Words

Sample Résumés

Figure 15.1 is a chronological résumé for a student who will graduate with a bachelor's degree in business administration. This student is seeking to move up from primarily administrative and clerical jobs to a position in management. While she has some relevant project management experience to list on her résumé, she emphasizes her management and administrative skills through relevant courses and through her accomplishments. Figures 15.2 through 15.5 are functional, targeted, integrated, and scannable résumés.

FIGURE 15.1

Chronological Résumé Format

Indicate date that degree will be completed.

List courses related to the position you are seeking.

Use bullets to identify accomplishments.

Capabilities demonstrate skills you want to highlight.

Boldface job titles and bullet major duties.

Use dates to indicate time spent in positions.

M. Chris Forget

33 Sunset Drive   (518) 555-3101
Waterford, New York 12188   E-mail: forgch@rpi.edu

EDUCATION
B.S. in Business Administration, Siena College
Loudonville, NY, anticipated May 2004
GPA: 3.5/4.0
Courses relevant to major:

Microsoft Excel	Organization and Management
Programming and Logic	Business Communication
Micro and Macro Economics	Financial Accounting
Business Law I and II	Managerial Accounting

ACCOMPLISHMENTS
- Development and management of outreach and educational programs
- Coordination of annual and special events
- Editor of two quarterly e-newsletters with readership of 2,500
- Liaison to various agencies, manufacturers, and utility companies to facilitate fund raising
- Creation of database system for the immediate retrieval of all statistical and narrative information

MANAGEMENT CAPABILITIES
- Management of various programs and projects
- Management of workshops
- Development and management of database systems
- Special events planning and organizing
- Liaison to investors and business community

EXPERIENCE
Education Program Coordinator, RPI, School of Architecture, Lighting Research Center, Troy, NY
October 1997 – Present
- Manage graduate and outreach education programs
- Design and develop new programs
- Coordinate staff, faculty, and student workshops and meetings
- Plan and coordinate annual and special events, including the recruitment of keynote speakers
- Write speech content based on relevant trends and market data
- Liaison to business community and other investors
- Supervise alumni, staff, and student program database
- Edit quarterly e-newsletters for staff, faculty, and investors
- Write monthly progress reports for current sponsored projects
- Design and administer survey instruments, compile data, and compose research reports
- Write, edit, and format grant proposals

Administrative Assistant, Cotler Architecture & Planning, PC, Latham, NY
September 1994 – September 1997
- Prepared memos and correspondence for principal architect and staff
- Prepared proposals and maintained the billing schedule for all projects
- Coordinated project schedules and organized weekly project meetings to track project progress

Merchandising/Administrative Assistant, SYSCO Foods, Inc., Albany, NY
July 1991 – September 1994
- Prepared various memos and correspondence for vice president of merchandising and marketing
- Coordinated weekly meetings and travel arrangements for vice president and staff
- Charge of accounts payable and receivable
- Wrote and designed promotional flyers, daily commodity pricing for customer and sales distribution

COMPUTER SKILLS
- Proficient in Microsoft Office 2000, Windows 98, WordPerfect 6.1, QuattroPro 6.0

FIGURE 15.2

Functional Résumé Format

KAREN HABEL

• 72 Doorstown Blvd • Latham, New York 12110 • (518) 555-9292

EDUCATION

Bachelor of Arts in Communication, May 2001
State University of New York at Plattsburgh, Plattsburgh, New York
GPA: 3.6/4.0
International Studies Program: Ealing College of Higher Education
London, England, Fall semester 1999

Relevant Coursework:

- Interpersonal and Relational Communication
- Media Planning
- Public Relations Writing
- Public Speaking and Performance
- Electronic Media Management
- Editing and Graphic Design
- Mass Communication
- Media Production
- Group Communication and Facilitation
- Intercultural Communication
- Principles of Advertising
- Newswriting

COMMUNICATION SKILLS

- Wrote training manual for new real estate associates
- Wrote copy and developed magazine advertising campaign for Chamber of Commerce
- Wrote, produced, and directed promotional videotape for university energy efficiency program
- On-camera television ad talent for local furniture company
* Liaison to business community
- Developed and delivered several oral presentations involving local business development

COMPUTER SKILLS

- Proficient in most PC and Macintosh applications.
- Microsoft Office 2000   • Microsoft Windows 98   • Adobe PageMaker   • Adobe Illustrator
- QuarkXpress   • WordPerfect

ACTIVITIES AND HONORS

- Dean's list, four consecutive semesters
- Public Relations Club
- Election Day election inspector for the past five years
- Volunteer for Equinox Program for Youth
- Century 21 Home Towne Properties, Rookie of the Year Award, 1999, and Winners Circle Award, 2000

EXPERIENCE

Century 21 Home Towne Properties, Plattsburgh, New York
March 1999 – Present
Licensed Independent Real Estate Associate
- Reach daily, weekly, and monthly sales goals
- Apply motivation and communication principles to achieve sales goals
- Develop sales and customer outreach strategies
- Wrote training manual for new real estate associates

Plattsburgh Chamber of Commerce, Plattsburgh, New York
Fall and Spring Semesters 2001
Intern
- Wrote and designed magazine advertising campaign
- Prepared and delivered comprehensive local business development presentations for a variety of audiences

---

List courses that demonstrate competence in the field where you are seeking employment.

Group career and other experiences into categories that emphasize relevant skills and strengths.

Downplay scant work history by placing it at the end of your résumé.

FIGURE 15.3

Targeted Résumé Format.

List academic activities that are tailored to the field.

Use a special heading to highlight work experience that matches the job or field.

Limit experience listed to a specific job or career field.

Other related academic activities and skills can be listed at the end of your résumé.

CHRISTOPHER J. BRANTIGAN

70 Springfield ◆ Voorheesville, NY 12118 ◆ (518) 555-2963 ◆ cbrantigan@yahoo.com

EDUCATION

JOINT DEGREE PROGRAM (JD/MBA)
Albany Law School of Union University, Albany, NY
Juris Doctor Candidate, May 2004
Activities: *Executive Editor for Lead Articles*, ALBANY LAW REVIEW

Union College, Graduate Management Institute, Schenectady, NY
Masters in Business Administration Candidate, June 2004

Union College, Schenectady, NY
Bachelor of Arts in Economics, June 1998
Honors: Dean's List, 1997–1998
Activities: *Vice President of Administration*, Student Government Association, 1996–1997
President, Student Government Association, 1997–1998
President, Inter-Fraternal Council, 1997–1998
Employment: 25-30 hours per week during academic year, 1995–1998

LEGAL EXPERIENCE

Wilson, Elser, Moskowitz, Edelman and Dicker, LLP, Albany, NY
Law Clerk, May 2001–present
- Conduct legal research and draft memos for health law department
- Attend legislative sessions and committee meetings
- Coordinate joint efforts with lobbyists to research and draft legislation to be introduced by members of either house of the legislature

New York State Supreme Court, Albany Law School Clinical Legal Studies Program
Judicial Intern, The Honorable Joseph C. Teresi, August 2000–May 2001
- Performed legal research and drafted memoranda for judge's review
- Observed all phases of trial preparation, including conferences and court proceedings
- Participated in dialogue with judge regarding decisions and opinions

New York State Executive Department Division of the Budget, Albany, NY
Graduate Intern, June 2000–December 2000
- Developed budget for NYS Temporary Commission of Investigation in conjunction with commission's needs and Division of the Budget's guidelines for overall agency spending
- Monitored commission's expenditures and revenues to ensure compliance with state financial plan
- Reviewed legislative initiatives and proposals affecting commission's policies and spending
- Drafted legislation in regard to newly proposed state appropriations

New York State Legislative Bill Drafting Commission, Albany, NY
Legal Assistant, June 1999–May 2000
- Conducted research and examination of proposed legislation upon the request of a member or committee of either house of the legislature
- Edited all bills, documents, and amendments to ensure correct recitation of the law

ACITIVITIES/SKILLS

- *Alumni Council Representative*, Union College, 1998–2003
- *Student Member*, NYS Bar Association, 1998–present
- *Marketing Representative*, Bar-Bri Bar Review, 1998–present
- *Volunteer*, Peer Advisory Program, 1999-present
- *Vice-Chair*, Economics of Tort & Insurance Law Practice Committee, American Bar Association, 2000–2001
- Computer proficiency: LEXUS-NEXIS, Westlaw, LRS, Microsoft Office 2000, Corel Suite, Front Page, JMP & Internet

ROBYN E. AURELIA
34 Bristow Street, Saugus, Massachusetts 01906
(781) 555-4942
E-mail: r_aurelia@yahoo.com

ACCOMPLISHMENTS

- Created national advertising and promotional campaign
- Wrote copy and designed successful national ads
- Wrote comprehensive company marketing and public relations plans
- Designed company web page that generated an average of 1,000 hits per day
- Wrote and edited company newsletter with readership of nearly 10,000
- Company fund raising liaison to business community

MARKETING SKILLS

- Designed and streamlined customer financial services
- Researched and analyzed market trends and consumer service utilization patterns
- Created innovative customer service financial incentive program

PUBLIC RELATIONS SKILLS

- Transformed company image, which established a solid company competitive advantage
- Managed multimedia relations
- Wrote, designed, and edited various advertising and public relations presentations materials
- Developed and delivered educational and public relations presentations

COMPUTER CAPABILITIES

- Microsoft Word   • Microsoft Excel   • Adobe PageMaker   • Adobe Illustrator
- Microsoft PowerPoint   • Goldmine

EXPERIENCE

Investors Capital Corporation, Lynnfield, Massachusetts   April 2000 – Present
Marketing/Communications/Public Relations Manager

Responsibilities
- Develop and execute marketing, communications, and public relations plans and budgets
- Write and edit all internal and external communications and field support tools
- Handle media relations, including press releases, interviews, and public appearances
- Primary media contact for newspaper, magazine, radio, and TV

Accomplishments
- Created corporate identity, strategy, and unique selling proposition for new public company
- Developed national advertising campaign

Excelsior Credit Union, Albany, New York   January 1999 – April 2000
Marketing Director

Responsibilities
- Oversaw daily operations of the marketing department
- Developed and maintained the credit union marketing and public relations plans
- Created copy and design ads for journals, program books, and directories
- Supervised the design, development, and maintenance of the credit union website
- Implemented new services to meet customer financial needs

Accomplishments
- Designed national ad campaign
- Created successful marketing and PR strategies to promote services and improve customer relations
- Designed web page that reached 1,000 customers daily

March 1996 – December 1998
Membership Coordinator/Marketing Specialist

Responsibilities
- Wrote, designed, and edited newsletters, service materials, forms, and promotional letters
- Researched product or service enhancements to provide quality member service
- Liaison to sponsor companies and prospective companies

EDUCATION

State University of New York College at Brockport, New York
Bachelor of Science, Business Administration, May 1995
Concentration: Marketing
GPA: 3.7/4.0

FIGURE 15.4

Integrated Résumé Format

Bullet information in categories.

Group related experience and skills in categories.

List job experience from most recent first as you would using a chronological format.

Separate responsibilities and accomplishments for each position.

Place your education at the end of the résumé if it is not directly applicable to the position or if your experience is stronger.

FIGURE 15.5

Scannable Résumé Format

Use key words that match the job description or listing.

Use a single- rather than a two-column format.

Use asterisks or hyphens rather than bullets for lists.

Use white space so scanner can identify and read separate categories.

If you indent, use the space bar rather than tabs.

Avoid the use of bold, italic, or underlining when formatting the résumé.

Mark Chamberlain

28 Eaton Road
Delmar, NY 12054
(518) 555-1322
E-mail: chambm@earthlink.com

Key words: budgets, sales management, market research and analysis, interpersonal communication, innovation, dedication, motivation, teamwork.

ACCOMPLISHMENTS

Marketing and Sales
* Increased department annual sales revenues by over 30%
* Increased company customer base by 15% through comprehensive market analysis
* Designed various pricing policies that established a company competitive advantage
* Reduced sales department annual operating expenses by 20%
* Increased employee productivity through training, mentoring, and daily evaluations

Management
* Employee supervision and management
* Administration of department operations and budgets
* Program development and analysis
* Training development and evaluation
* Liaison to consumers, vendors, subcontractors, and executive management

EXPERIENCE

Davies Office Refurbishing, Inc., Albany, NY
(1999 – Present)
Service Manager
* Manage operation of service department
* Develop marketing strategies
* Supervise 5 staff professionals
* Administer department budget
* Manage personnel hiring, scheduling, and project assignments
* Develop new department tracking procedures

Business Environments by Ras, Albany, NY
(1996 – 1999)
Operations and Sales Manager
* Managed department sales and day-to-day operations
* Supervised 13 staff professionals
* Coordinated customer service projects
* Oversaw personnel administration
* Developed pricing strategies
* Created new administration policies and procedures
* Administered department annual budget
* Increased annual sales by over 30%
* Increased department revenues to $122 K
* Reduced department operating expenses by 20%
* Managed marketing and research projects
* Expanded client base by over 15%

COMPUTER SKILLS
Windows 98, Microsoft Word 98, Excel 97, ACT

EDUCATION
A.S. in Business Administration, May 2001
Hudson Valley Community College, Troy, NY
GPA: 3.8/4.0

You are the hiring manager for Ginn's Gym Equipment, a company that supplies athletic equipment to professional gyms and health centers. You are currently looking for someone to design and produce new marketing campaigns. This entry-level position requires an individual who can create visual and/or media ad campaigns while keeping a close eye on the bottom line. Professional experience is important, but not as important as adaptability; after all, you sell your products to companies that have very different attitudes toward gym equipment. Gyms are mostly interested in developing clients' bodies, while health centers use the equipment for physical rehabilitation. You have received the sample résumés in Figures 15.1 through 15.5. Mr. Ginn has asked you to provide a written comparison of the applicants for him to review. Examine the contents of each résumé carefully, identifying the qualities you feel would be most beneficial for your company and purpose. Then write one paragraph on each applicant, stating his or her strengths or weaknesses. Create a table that directly compares the applicants for Mr. Ginn to use in his evaluation.

Résumé Ingredients

The ingredients of your résumé should be organized depending on the format you choose and the education and experience requirements for the kind of work you want. Among the ingredients are your identification heading, education, accomplishments, capabilities, and professional experience.

Identification

An **identification** is a heading centered on top of the first page that includes your full name, home address, telephone number, and e-mail address. Your name should be presented in bold, in a type size one point larger than the text. Centered under your name, include your permanent address and your telephone number (with area code). Put your e-mail address on the same line as your telephone number or on a separate line, centered and spaced appropriately.

identification a heading centered on top of the first page of a résumé that includes your full name, home address, telephone number, and e-mail address.

Education

You want to lead with your strengths. If your **education** is your most important asset, lead with this information. If your education is not relevant to the position you are seeking or if your skills and achievements are stronger, then you may want to place education at the end of your résumé. When you describe your education, list the name and address of the school, degree earned, major, date your degree was completed or is anticipated, and your grade point average (GPA). You may spell out the degree (bachelor of science) or abbreviate (BS). You can also include any relevant seminars attended; professional training received; and certificates, scholarships, or honors earned.

education includes academic degrees earned, major field of study, date your degree was completed or is anticipated, and your grade point average (GPA).

You can present your education in one of the following ways:

Bachelor of Science, Business Administration, May 2002
State University of New York at Albany, Albany, New York
Honors: President's List, Spring 2002
GPA: 3.3 / 4.0

BS in Radio, Television and Film, December 2002
S. I. Newhouse School of Communication, Syracuse University, Syracuse, NY
GPA: 3.5 / 4.0

A.S. in Marketing, May 1999
Hudson Valley Community College, Troy, NY
Honors: Dean's List, Spring 1999
GPA: 3.8 / 4.0

Ithaca College, Ithaca, New York
Master of Science, Corporate Communication, June 2002
Honors: Phi Kappa Phi

You can also list honors, awards, and activities under a separate heading, especially if they are numerous.

Accomplishments

accomplishment
something you have achieved or produced by using your talent and skills.

An **accomplishment** is something you have achieved or produced by using your talent and skills. Everyone has accomplishments, but some of them may not be obvious. Think of the work you have completed at school, in clubs, in your community, on the job, during an internship, or through self-employment. There are probably numerous achievements in your background that can highlight your abilities. Accomplishments don't need to be monumental to have produced some beneficial results. For example, if during your work experience you saved, managed, or made money for your company, found new clients, coordinated project or team efforts, supervised or trained employees, located or obtained resources, organized events, or produced documents, you have accomplished a great deal.

Once you think of experiences that can be used as accomplishments, frame the message in a clear, concise, and positive way. Quantify your accomplishments with specific numbers if possible.

Accomplishments	Framing Accomplishments for Your Résumé
• Saved the marketing department $5,000 out of the $25,000 allocated for equipment by changing product and service providers	• Reduced marketing department operating expenses by 20 percent
• Added 12 new clients to the 30 we already had for the last sales quarter	• Expanded quarterly client base by 40 percent

Accomplishments	Framing Accomplishments for Your Résumé
• Three full-time and six part-time employees currently report to me and I coordinate their activities	• Supervise nine staff professionals
• I oversee a $5.5 million department annual budget and determine expenditures	• Administer $5.5 million annual department budget
• Wrote and produced a videotape shown to entry-level retail employees that instructs them how to deal with difficult clients. Now the company uses the tape for all new hires.	• Wrote and produced customer service training videotape presented to all new company employees

capabilities are the abilities you possess, such as communication skills, computer proficiency, and second languages.

professional experience includes full-time, part-time, volunteer, internship, and self-employment experience.

references are people who know you personally, your work, and your talents and who will recommend you for employment.

Capabilities

The abilities you possess, such as communication skills, are **capabilities.** This section lets recruiters and employers know what you can do for them. If you use a targeted or functional résumé style, you might label this section specifically to match the job (marketing skills, public relations, managerial experience). Generally, capabilities are areas of competence involving computer proficiency, second languages, verbal and interpersonal communication, and management. Whether you use "capabilities" or another headline, your individual strengths and competencies will dictate the title and the content of this category.

Professional Experience

If relevant to the position you want, full-time, part-time, volunteer, internship, and self-employment **professional experience** should all be included on your résumé. If you use a functional format, group experiences together according to category. For a chronological format, list the most recent experiences first and then move backward in time to include earlier work that is applicable to the position you are seeking. This section should also list the names and addresses of employers, dates of employment, and the official or working titles you held.

When you prepare your résumé, use action verbs to describe your skills and abilities. A list of action verbs appears in Table 15.2.

CREATIVE

CHALLENGE

Rewrite the following sentences using action verbs to tighten the language and eliminating personal pronouns and grammatical errors.

- I was responsible for researching and writing grant proposals.
- As an administrative assistant, I filed documents in alphabetical order and separated priority files into their own category.
- Online video editing experience for training and promotional videotape presentations.
- I looked at customer buying patterns and other trends and assisted in the writing of a marketing strategy.

TABLE 15.2   **Action Verbs**

administered	delivered	facilitated	increased	motivated	researched
analyzed	demonstrated	financed	initiated	navigated	reviewed
applied	designed	fixed	instructed	negotiated	revised
arranged	developed	formulated	integrated	operated	scheduled
assembled	directed	founded	invented	organized	shot
assessed	drafted	generated	investigated	performed	sold
audited	documented	guided	laid out	planned	spoke
budgeted	edited	handled	lectured	prepared	supervised
built	eliminated	headed	led	produced	tested
communicated	engineered	hired	maintained	programmed	trained
compiled	established	identified	managed	reduced	transmitted
conducted	evaluated	implemented	mediated	repaired	utilized
coordinated	expanded	improved	merged	reported	wrote

References

References are people who know you personally. They know your work and your talents and will recommend you for employment in a

"Your references checked out. Now let's see how well you can think on your feet."

Source: From Harvard Business Review 2001 July-Aug Edition.

complimentary way. The people you select as references should be familiar with your academic or professional strengths, abilities, and potential. Prepare a list of references on a separate sheet of paper rather than including it in your résumé. In general, it is not necessary to include references or the line "References available upon request." For most employers, it is a given that you will furnish a list of references when you are invited to interview for the job. Employers usually don't check references until after you interview.

Who can you use as references? Consider current or former professors, supervisors or employers, and colleagues or mentors who know your academic or professional work. References should also be effective communicators and, ideally, have a good reputation in the community. Keep your references strictly professional by excluding friends and relatives from your list. Ask each person for permission to use him or her as a reference. Show your résumé to those willing to talk about you with potential employers. Discuss any points or attributes you would like them to share.

Your reference list should be formatted to match your résumé. It should include at least three, and no more than six, people who can testify positively about your academic or professional work. Include the name, title, organization, address, and phone number of each reference.

The Problems with Résumés

The following résumé mistakes can prevent you from being interviewed and from getting the job you want.

The résumé does not identify accomplishments or achievements.	• Résumés that do not demonstrate what you can do for potential employers will probably not get you an interview. Listing accomplishments lets you showcase your talents and skills in a results-oriented way.
The résumé contains falsehoods and lies.	• Stated qualifications that are overly embellished or outright falsehoods can really get you into trouble. Either the employer will recognize immediately that the information is far-fetched, or the company may hire you and then discover the truth later on and fire you. A résumé is like a letter of intent that promises you have earned the credentials you say you have and you can perform the work you say you can. So it is important that you present your skills, achievements, and education honestly. But you don't have to express the information in a boring or ho-hum manner. You can skillfully frame the message in a positive, engaging way while remaining forthright and honorable.
The résumé is long and wordy.	• Long-winded, wordy sentences and paragraphs that endlessly explain your responsibilities will not likely be read. Employers spend only a brief time reviewing your résumé, so you need to highlight only the most relevant and interesting information using brief, bulleted sentences. Your résumé should not exceed one page.

The résumé exceeds the need to know.	• Recruiters and employers don't need to know every detail of your work duties and professional experience. They also don't need to know your height, weight, bowling league, and favorite color. Some information is illegal for employers to ask and is definitely unnecessary in your résumé, such as your marital status, age, race, and any disability.
The résumé is scattered, jumbled, and hodgepodge.	• Résumés that arbitrarily list unrelated jobs in different fields can make you look disorganized, unfocused, and sloppy. If you have diverse experiences, select the most relevant jobs to write about or create specific categories in which you can include the information in an organized manner.
The résumé contains typos, poor grammar, and misspellings.	• Résumés that contain errors are likely to be "circular filed" (i.e., thrown away). If you neglect to thoroughly proofread your résumé for mistakes, you may appear careless and inattentive to potential employers. Search your résumé relentlessly for design flaws including typographical, grammatical, and spelling errors.
The résumé uses "I," "me," and "my."	• Avoid personal pronouns when you write your résumé. Write "complete responsibility for . . ." instead of "I was completely responsible for . . ."
The résumé shows obvious employment gaps.	• There are numerous reasons a candidate may have a block of time spent unemployed (attendance at school, professional training, having a baby, raising a family, or caring for an ill family member). To avoid obvious gaps in chronology use a functional format. You can also chunk jobs and timeframes together by describing the work performed during the 1980s or 1990s. This way you provide a timeframe for employers to reference without specific dates of employment for each position held. If you feel you absolutely need to discuss the gap, you may include a brief explanation in your cover letter. Be prepared to explain any gaps in your work history during the interview.

Designing Cover Letters

cover letter a brief and persuasive application document that accompanies your résumé.

A **cover letter** is a brief and persuasive application document that accompanies your résumé. While the résumé summarizes your work history and skills, the cover letter offers a brief but valuable first impression of you as a job candidate. A good cover letter can make the difference between whether a hiring manager will fully consider your résumé or not. A well-written cover letter can gain an employer's interest and compel him or her to read your résumé more thoroughly and consider it more seriously.

What Cover Letters Accomplish

A well-crafted cover letter can convince a hiring manager to read your résumé and can get you an interview. Your résumé describes what you *have* done; the cover letter is an opportunity to describe what you *can* do. Many managers believe the cover letter is as important as your résumé, so it is vital that you spend time customizing your letter to meet the specific needs of the company and the job. To gain the attention of a hiring manager, a good cover letter should accomplish the following goals:

Distinguish you from other applicants	• Ideally, your cover letter should distinguish you from other candidates by providing information about your unique experiences, coursework, language skills, knowledge, or areas of strength that will benefit the organization.
Illustrate your knowledge of and interest in the company	• Demonstrate your knowledge about and interest in the company by incorporating company information such as specific products, initiatives, or projects into your letter. To integrate the project or task effectively, tailor the letter to reveal how one or more of your skills complements it.
Identify how your key skills and work experience can benefit the company and meet the requirements of the job	• Without restating points from your résumé verbatim, briefly highlight two to four key strengths you possess that specifically match the job for which you are applying.
Demonstrate your ability to express yourself as a business communicator	• A well-crafted and tailored letter can show off your skills as a competent business communicator. Be sure to describe specific communication assets you possess as well.

Types of Cover Letters

Cover letters are written either in response to solicitations for applications or to explore opportunities.

Solicited applications are sent in reply to requests for résumés involving open positions announced through internal organization job postings or external ads in newspapers, trade journals, and Internet postings. When you reply to a job announcement, find out the name and title of the hiring manager. You can call the organization directly and request the name (be sure to get the correct spelling), title, and address. Use the hiring manager's surname in your letter salutation: Dear Mr. Miller or Dear Ms. Jones. In the first paragraph, specify how you learned about the position, give the job title, and state that you are applying for it. For example, if you are responding to an ad in the newspaper, you may say, "I am responding to your advertisement in Sunday's *Times Union* and applying for the position of Accountant." If you learned about the position through an internal posting or an employee, say so in your letter: "Tiera

solicited applications are sent in reply to requests for résumés involving open positions.

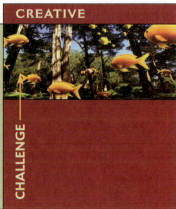

CREATIVE

CHALLENGE

Research companies in your area (you may find information at your campus career center or at the local chamber of commerce) and select one that interests you. Call the company and find out the name of a hiring manager in the department where you would like to work. Then draft a cover letter requesting an informational interview.

FIGURE 15.6

Sample Solicited Cover Letter

First paragraph identifies how you learned about the position and states that you are applying for the job.

Duties and skills that match the job description can be bulleted.

A proactive closing paragraph indicates that you will be following up to gain an interview.

Jean Rodriguez
645 Cortland Street
Phoenix, AZ 85045
(480) 555-5249

April 31, 2003

Mr. John Hope
Director of Human Resources
Elan Marketing
2505 Baseline Avenue
Phoenix, AZ 85045

Dear Mr. Hope:

In response to your advertisement in Sunday's edition of the *Arizona Republic*, I am enclosing my résumé for your consideration, and applying for the position of Marketing/Publications Manager.

Since 1996, I have been working in publication development market research and promotion. Your ad mentioned experience in "writing promotional materials and advertising copy." Last year, I developed a nationwide marketing campaign for Blue White Design's new product line that included newspaper and television ads, brochures, and sales letters.

As a marketer at Blue White Designs, I routinely perform the following activities:

• Write copy; lay out and design publications

• Write marketing plans

• Manage trade and sales promotion

• Use desktop publishing software (Microsoft PowerPoint, Adobe PageMaker, Illustrator, and Photoshop)

• Develop public presentations and trade shows

An undergraduate degree in marketing, combined with extensive experience in publications development and promotion, enables me to provide Elan Marketing with superior marketing and management skills. I would appreciate the opportunity to show you how I can contribute to the success of Elan Marketing's many writing and promotional missions.

I will call next week to schedule an interview at your earliest convenience. Thank you for your consideration.

Sincerely,

Jean Rodriguez

Jean Rodriguez

Enclosure: Résumé

Aurelia of your human resources department suggested that I contact you about the vacant administrative assistant position in your office." Customize your letter to the company and the position announced. Use the language provided in the announcement to describe your strengths and parallel skills. In your closing paragraph, ask for an opportunity to interview. A solicited cover letter is illustrated in Figure 15.6.

Exploring opportunities involves selecting a company and preparing a letter to request an informational meeting. If you don't know whether or not a company is hiring, you can design a letter that expresses your interest in the company and asks for an opportunity to

exploring opportunities
involves selecting a company and preparing a letter to request an informational meeting.

Nola Deway
1755 North Greenbush Avenue
Los Angeles, CA 90089
(213) 555-7891

May 5, 2003

Paige Lennox
Human Resources Director
Jordan Marketing Research, Inc.
2525 Techdale Drive
Industry, CA 91508

Dear Ms. Lennox:

Sunday's *Los Angeles Times* reported that Jordan Marketing Research plans to extend its services overseas, effectively doubling its clientele and capitalizing on the European Free Trade agreement. Since this exciting expansion may open up new opportunities in market analysis, I'd like to become part of the Jordan team that *BusinessWeek* has called the "most innovative group in America today." I can offer you the following qualifications:

- Two years' experience as an intern at Zyco Marketing. As an intern, I designed and facilitated focus groups examining products like the Firefly nightlight (recently praised by *Parents* magazine for its safety features) and Moxie Cola.
- Bachelor's degree in marketing, minor in graphics arts, with honors. I graduated fourth in a class of 300.
- Fluency in French and Italian. My senior honors thesis was a comparison of marketing techniques in France and Italy. It included interviews and analysis of marketing texts in the original languages.

More of my related skills and experiences are detailed in the enclosed résumé. If you're looking for an energetic self-starter who has creative ideas and the know-how to put them into action, I am eager to meet with you to discuss what I can contribute to Jordan's continued success and to learn more about the company. I will call next week to schedule an informational meeting at your convenience. Thank you for your consideration.

Sincerely,

Nola Deway

Nola Deway

Enclosure: Résumé

FIGURE 15.7

Sample Exploring Opportunities Cover Letter

First paragraph demonstrates knowledge of the company.

Bullets highlight the most applicable qualities listed in the résumé.

The close mentions résumé and initiates follow-up.

schedule an informational meeting. When you prepare a letter to explore opportunities, indicate that you are interested in and have knowledge of the company but that you want to learn more. You can also mention that you are attaching your résumé for the reader's review and for discussion. Follow up your letter by calling the company to schedule a date and time for the meeting. Informational meetings demonstrate your interest in the company and can provide a hiring manager with an opportunity to meet you in person. Often companies can create jobs for people who have impressed them. They can also keep you in mind the next time a position opens up. Figure 15.7 illustrates an exploring opportunities cover letter.

networking means identifying and contacting people you know who can help you find a job or who may refer you to someone who can help.

Finding a Job

After you have determined the field and the type of position you want, it is time to find an acceptable job. Searching for the right job requires both time and a lot of focused energy. To market yourself effectively, you'll need to accomplish the job search activities outlined below.

Network	• Many positions are not advertised or posted because applicants who know someone in the organization fill them. Often employers feel that employees located through referral from the "hidden job market" are preferable to unknown applicants. So it is vitally important that you tap your personal network of people who can assist your job search. **Networking** means identifying and contacting people you know who can help you find a job or who may refer you to someone who can help. Your personal network may consist of family, friends, co-workers, vendors, professors, and business associates. Tell them you are actively seeking a job and what work you are interested in doing. Ask your personal contacts if they know about any positions or any organizations that are hiring, and ask them to keep you in mind if they do learn about job openings. Also ask them for the names of people they know who may be hiring or who may further assist you with your search. Send each of your contacts a copy of your résumé, and write a brief letter of thanks to let them know you appreciate their assistance.
Make an employers list	• Create a list of all the companies for which you may want to work. To develop a desirable company list, research companies to find such information as the number of employees, location of headquarters and any branch offices, the goods or services they offer, their business philosophy, and their financial stability. Your can find company information in *Standard and Poor's Register of Corporations, Directors, and Executives*, or read industry trade journals and business magazines and publications such as *Fast Company, Forbes, BusinessWeek, Fortune, Harvard Business Review, The New York Times*, and *The Wall Street Journal.* Visit the library, log on to websites such as webfeet.com and jobvault.com, or ask current or former employees for a profile of their company. Your college placement office may also have local company descriptions and profiles you can use.
Write exploratory letters to companies on your list	• Prepare letters that request informational meetings with potential employers. Ask for an opportunity to meet with them to learn more about the company. Exploratory meetings can increase your chances of landing a job because they offer an opportunity to interact directly with employers.
Attend job fairs	• Read the local newspaper or contact your campus career counseling or placement office to find out about job fairs. Arrive early, dress appropriately, and visit each booth. Bring copies of your résumé with you to distribute to potential employers.
Search the Internet	• You can search the Internet for job listings and post your résumé on job boards at sites such as Headhunter.net. Thousands of jobs are listed on the Internet, and many companies have their own websites that contain various job postings.
Websites for job listings and job fairs	• www.joblistings.com • www.jobhunt.org • www.monster.com • www.career.com • www.joblynx.com • www.hotjobs.com • www.jobtrak.com • www.usajobs.opm.gov (U.S. Office of Personnel Management for federal government jobs)

Hiring managers often complain about two things in cover letters: that they describe responsibilities rather than achievements and that they are too boastful. While employers are looking for experience and confidence in the applicants they interview, they also want to see honesty and potential. Revise the following letter with that in mind.

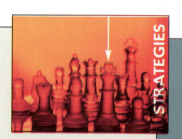

Dear Mr. Eugene Maltz:

You can stop your search for a distribution supervisor because here I am! Fresh out of college, I am ready to take your company to new heights.

My education makes me the perfect candidate for the position you advertised in the *Weekly* (9/28/2002). My business course GPA was 3.75, well above the university average of 2.6. As president of the College Business Council, I organized and administered the annual fundraiser, which garnered over $6,000 for various educational and charitable projects. I was also in charge of scheduling and resource planning for the business school's award-winning tutoring service.

I don't have much practical experience in the field, but so what? I learn quickly and am eager to begin my professional career with your wonderful company. So give me a call soon. Who knows how much longer a great catch like me will be on the market?

Hoping to talk soon,

Josh Davis

Josh Davis

P.S. My résumé is enclosed.

Strategies

1. Write your résumé beginning with your strongest abilities and skills. If you have limited work experience, use a functional résumé format and highlight your abilities under accomplishments or other headings. If your education is your greatest strength, list it first.

2. Make sure your résumé is clear and concise. Employers are not interested in every little detail about your experience, so just highlight the most relevant aspects of your work history. You can offer more details and explanations during the interview.

3. Use bullets to present duties or skills information under headings. Employers appreciate bulleted lists because they are easier to read than long paragraphs of narrative.

4. Use action words to describe skills and responsibilities.

5. Employers want to know what you can do for them, so when possible, present results-oriented information with figures and percentages.

6. Adapt the language of your résumé to the company or industry. When appropriate, use jargon or phrases that match the field or job. Adapting to the language of the job description is also very important. When you compose your cover letter, be sure to directly discuss the requirements outlined in the posting or ad.

7. Design an attractive document for employers to read. Leave white space between headings. Use 11- or 12-point type and a readable font. Print your résumé on high-quality, plain white or ivory bond paper.

8. It is acceptable to list temporary or seasonal jobs on your résumé, especially if they are relevant to the job you are seeking or if you have meager work experience.

9. Your résumé should be no longer than two pages (one page is better) and your cover letter no longer than a page.

10. You can place a working title in parentheses under your official job title, especially if the work you actually perform is not clear from or equivalent to the official title you hold. Sometimes working titles can give employers a better idea of your job duties.

Summary

- Finding the right career involves examining your professional goals and interests. To explore your interests, visit the campus career center or placement office; log on to employment planning and job websites; talk to businesspeople; take a part-time job; or read trade journals, periodicals, and the want ads.

- To determine your most marketable skills, compile a list of all your skills and then match them with the kind of position you want. Look beyond work experiences to school activities, social clubs, and volunteer or internship experiences to cultivate valuable business skills that may appeal to a variety of potential employers.

- A résumé is a written document that briefly summarizes your skills, education, and work history for employers. Its primary purpose is to capture the interest of employers so they invite you for a job interview.

- Different résumé formats allow job seekers to present their skills and work experiences in the most appropriate and appealing way possible depending on their goals, abilities, and career field. Formats include chronological, functional, targeted, integrated, and scannable résumés.

- Fundamental résumé ingredients include an identification (your name, address, phone number, and e-mail address), schools attended and degrees earned, relevant accomplishments, capabilities and skills, and your work experience.

- References are people who know you, are familiar with your academic or professional abilities, and can recommend you for employment. Reference lists contain three to six people and should be presented separately from your résumé.

- The most common résumé problems involve the absence of viable accomplishments, inaccurate information, long-winded sentences or paragraphs, unnecessary information, disorganized information, typos and misspellings, use of personal pronouns, and employment gaps.

- Cover letters are brief, persuasive documents that accompany and introduce your résumé. Well-written cover letters can convince employers to read your résumé more closely. They can distinguish you from other job candidates, confirm your knowledge of the company, highlight your most important skills, and demonstrate your competence as a business communicator. Solicited cover letters accompany résumés that have been requested by an organization that has announced a particular job opening. Cover letters that explore opportunities are designed to gain an informational meeting with a desirable company.

- Once you have designed a solid résumé, you need to find the right job. Job hunting involves such self-marketing activities as networking; selecting, researching, and writing to attractive employers; attending job fairs; checking out job-listing websites; and pounding the pavement for employment.

Business Communication Projects

1. Interview a business professional regarding the changes he or she has experienced in the job market. Before the interview prepare a list of questions similar to these:
   - When did you begin to work?
   - What kind of work did you start out doing?
   - How did you get your first job? Subsequent jobs?
   - What did you do to prepare for your job search?
   - How much did your education help you in your early career? What kind of things did you learn on the job?
   - Did you make a major career change at any point? Why? How?
   - On average, how long did you spend at each position over the course of your career?
   - How do you feel about the job market today?

Write a memo to your instructor detailing what aspects of the professional's comments and insights may be helpful for you in your job search.

2. Make a list of courses you like and those you dislike. Examine this list carefully. Do you see any trends? Do you favor creativity or logical thinking? Do you enjoy writing more than mathematics? What kinds of jobs do you think would fit with your preferences? Look in the newspaper or on the Internet for jobs that would fit.

3. Research a company that interests you. Look at corporate profiles to learn more about potential employers. You can select specific companies to target. Create a list of the job search parameters that you think would be appropriate to gain a job in the company you chose. Usually the company website home page contains links to employment information or opportunities within the company. Corporate profile websites include the following:

   • www.corporateinformation.com
   • www.profiles.wisi.com (Wright's Investors' Service)
   • www.hoovweb.hoovers.com (Hoover's Online)
   • www.nonprofitcareer.com (Nonprofit Career Network)
   • www.forbes.com

4. Select the résumé format that would work best for each of the following candidates:

   • New graduate with a bachelor's degree in accounting. This candidate has very little job experience. The only position she has held is as an assistant manager at Pizza Hut for three years. She takes customer orders, supervises waitstaff, handles inventory, and closes the business in the evening. She has also developed select marketing and display promotions for the restaurant. The job this candidate is seeking is in the field of banking.

   • New graduate with an associate's degree in computer network engineering. This job seeker has certification in Microsoft Windows 2000 Network and Operating Systems and Microsoft Windows 2000 Professional and Server and was an intern at Earthlink, an Internet service provider for one year. Before the internship, he was employed as a data processor at a local insurance company for six years. The position he is currently seeking is as a systems analyst.

   Write two paragraphs that describe why the résumé formats you selected would work best for these job seekers.

5. Develop a strategy to find a job. Prepare a list that describes 5 to 10 steps that you will take to seek employment. Write a memo to your instructor that explains the strategy and why you think it will help you land a job.

6. Using the strengths and skills you described for the creative challenge on page 364, write a bulleted list of at least three accomplishments you can use for your résumé. Then craft a second heading that highlights specific capabilities or skills, such as "managerial skills," "writing skills," or "computer proficiency." Write at least four bulleted statements to use under the heading you develop.

7. Missie Miller graduated from high school and then worked for several years at a CD factory. At this job she worked on the production line ensuring product quality standards, a highly specialized task that required a great deal of concentration. Working in this industry sparked an interest in emerging technologies, which she has maintained and developed on her own for the last decade. A few years ago she left the job to have a baby. Then she decided to go back to school to get her bachelor's degree in information technology. Her time in school has been well spent: She earned several grants and scholarships for her innovative work in IT. Now she is six months away from graduation and is preparing her résumé. She has a five-year employment hole in her experience. She asks you for suggestions about how to address this problem. Write two paragraphs that detail what she can do to fill the employment hole (in addition to her choice of résumé formats).

8. Who will you ask to be your references? Create a list of suitable individuals. Identify what areas of your personality and expertise they can attest to: academic performance, professional ability, and so on. Approach at least six people and ask them if they are willing to be your references. Then compile a reference list that includes their names, positions, and complete contact information.

Discussion Questions

1. What is the best résumé format to use if you have little job experience or significant time gaps between jobs?

2. Discuss the primary differences between a scannable résumé and a traditional format.

3. Do you think well-crafted résumés are the primary determinants that hiring managers use when selecting candidates for a job? If not, explain what résumés can do and what you think actually convinces a manager to select an applicant.

4. Can you use a targeted résumé format if your education is not specific to the job you are seeking?

5. Why do some hiring managers disapprove of functional résumés that do not include job titles or dates?

6. Why is it important to include key words on a scannable résumé?

7. Should applicants with a lot of job experience stick to a chrono-logical résumé format?

8. What would a hiring manager think if he or she received a résumé cover letter that was unsigned?

9. What kinds of details should you include in an exploring opportunities cover letter? Why?

10. Is it appropriate to submit your cover letter and résumé via e-mail? Explain.

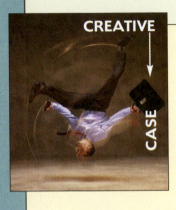

CREATIVE → CASE

Creative Case

Generation X Looks for a Job

According to *BusinessWeek Online,* today's younger job seekers rely less on networking to find positions than on job recruiting services and employment announcements. A survey on outplacement conducted by Drake Beam Morin showed that Generation Xers (people born between 1965 and 1981) are far less aggressive than baby boomers (those born between 1946 and 1964) when looking for work. Instead of creating their own opportunities like the boomers, Gen Xers rely on existing job opportunities.

The survey was given to 15,800 executives, professionals, and managers who had used DBM's career development services during the year 2000. The results showed that 36 percent of Gen Xers used networking contacts to find work or develop opportunities, as opposed to 46 percent of boomers and 51 percent of older workers. Gen Xers are most likely to find work through job postings: 19 percent, compared to 13 percent of boomers and 12 percent of mature workers. Gen Xers also look to corporate headhunters and recruiters more often (18 percent) than their older counterparts (boomers, 13 percent; mature workers, 8 percent).

What does this mean for someone entering the job market now? Is networking becoming an unimportant tool in the job search process? Not at all, according to DBM's Greg Pettenon, managing consultant for the Deerfield, Illinois, office. In a fluctuating job market networking is becoming even more important to the search for the ideal career. Networking allows individuals to develop positions that reflect their abilities and aspirations instead of fitting into a ready-made job. Pettenon says, "By networking, you are telling the employer what you want before the opportunity presents itself . . . If you respond to an ad, there is going to be a remote possibility that the job is going to be exactly what you are looking for. If Gen Xers don't take ownership over their careers, they will be looking for something that isn't there."

How should Gen Xers develop their networking skills?

Some questions to consider:

1. Why do Gen Xers seem to use networking less often than other groups?

2. Why do other groups rely so heavily on networking, especially since networking wasn't taught in business schools when they were young as it is today?

3. What are the benefits of networking for new job seekers?

4. How important is networking in the overall job search process?

Source: Wahlgren, E. (2001). "For Gen X, It's Schmooze or Lose." *Businessweek Online*, Retrieved December 14, 2001: www.businessweek.com/careers/content/aug2001/ca20010828_696.htm.

Chapter 16

chapter 16

Interviewing to Get the Job

Regina Delmar, an MBA student at the Wharton School of Business, was preparing for internship interviews with a variety of investment and banking firms. She had done her research using Wharton's facilities and had landed four interviews. She had practiced her interviewing skills in mock interviews and considered a variety of actual and hypothetical business cases. Still, she approached the interviews with a mixture of fear, anxiety, and dread. The greatest concern centered on the interviewers themselves: some would focus on technical financial knowledge, others would be more interested in determining whether her personality would match the company. Anticipating this, Delmar reviewed notes from her finance and accounting courses. She rehearsed her answers to questions that might be raised about her academic and professional decisions. She also considered carefully why she was seeking the positions she had applied for at the interviewing companies. After she completed all four interviews, Delmar was notified within two days of each company's interest in her. She also received an invitation from her first choice, Merrill Lynch, to their New York offices for a "sell day," which allowed her to meet the people she would work with and gain a general feel for the corporate culture of the company. They made an internship offer, and she accepted. The following summer, Delmar began her internship with Merrill Lynch.

IN A NUTSHELL

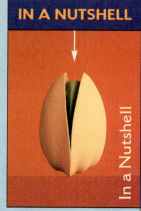

In a Nutshell

The Employment Interview

Few interviews in your life will be as important as an employment interview, so you may feel nervous, anxious, or intimidated. The key to handling virtually any anxiety-provoking communication is practice and preparation. Like Regina, preparing to interview through role-play and writing answers to potential interview questions on paper can make a big difference. While the fear associated with being interviewed may never completely go away, you can reduce it by knowing what to expect and how to get ready to secure the job you want. The internship interviews mentioned in the "In a Nutshell" feature are em-

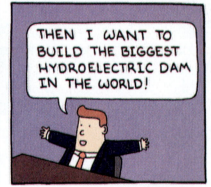

Source: Copyright 1998 United Feature Syndicate, Inc.

ployment interviews because whether the employee is paid or not, employers still look for skill, ability, and personality compatibility between you and the company.

An **employment interview** involves the interpersonal communication exchange between a potential employer and a job applicant who both consider an employment match during a formal business meeting.

The Process

While every organization approaches the recruiting and interview process a bit differently, there are some traditional methods. For example, many large organizations often conduct several rounds of interviews before selecting a candidate and offering a job.

In some instances, a screening interview is conducted to eliminate unsuitable or unqualified applicants. In fact, much of the hiring process involves the elimination of job seekers. At Microsoft Corporation, the interview process called an "interview loop" tests job applicant's survival skills. To weed out applicants, Microsoft interviewers ask candidates brain-teasing questions such as "How many piano tuners are there in the world?" Or "Given a gold bar that can be cut exactly twice and a contractor who must be paid one-seventh of a gold

employment interview
the interpersonal communication exchange between a potential employer and a job applicant.

During a panel interview, it is common to feel excited or nervous. Use this energy to focus on and answer each question carefully and positively.
© Michael Newman/Photo Edit

bar a day for seven days, what do you do?" Microsoft believes that probing questions like these can test a job candidate's ability to analyze and evaluate information, come up with alternatives, and determine the best choice. Given the difficulty of responding correctly to interview loop questions, those Microsoft employees who manage to get hired are considered highly analytical and quick on their feet.

After the initial screening (which may occur over the phone, on campus, or during an in-person meeting), selected candidates are invited to participate in a second round of interviews. One individual or a panel of people may conduct this interview.

It's Just You and Me

one-on-one interviews occur when a single company hiring representative conducts the interview with you alone.

During a **one-on-one interview,** a company human resource representative, hiring manager, or position supervisor will conduct the interview with you alone. This individual will discuss your qualifications and ask specific questions to glean information about your background, experience, and attitude.

The Gang's All Here

panel interviews occur when various people (including supervisors, managers, and colleagues or contemporaries) interview you at once.

While the one-on-one interview is still the most common, more and more organizations are conducting **panel interviews** in which various people (including supervisors, managers, and colleagues or contemporaries) interview you at once. At MTW Corp., a Web-based software and consulting firm, candidates are first screened through telephone interviews before being flown to the company's headquarters in Mission Woods near Kansas City, Kansas. If a job candidate qualifies, he or she will meet with at least five members of the company for an interview. Usually, two members of the panel are senior managers who provide applicants with a personal perspective on the long-range opportunities for advancement available at the company.

In the event you face a panel or committee of interviewers, remain calm, pay attention, and stay focused. Use your energy and adrenaline to your advantage. Field each question individually at your own pace and respond as positively and honestly as you can. The interviewers will be evaluating your speaking and listening communication skills, your attitude, and your ability to think clearly under pressure.

The Difference between Traditional and Behavioral Interviews

behavioral interviews rely on actual performance or situation-based questioning and require specific examples of past performance.

Traditional employment interviews often approach questioning in a way that elicits descriptions of what skills applicants think they possess and how they may react in hypothetical situations. **Behavioral interviews** use techniques that rely on actual performance or situation-based questioning and require specific examples of what applicants actually did in the past. Supporters of the behavioral approach believe this style of questioning is a better predictor of an applicant's real skills and abilities.

Jump In!

← **JUMP IN!**

Behavioral interviews often involve questions like "How do you deal with an angry customer?" and "Describe a situation when you made a mistake at your previous job." When an interviewer uses behavioral interviewing techniques he or she is trying to determine what real knowledge, skills, and behaviors you possess, like assertiveness, commitment, and the ability to deal with ambiguity. Such questions should be answered truthfully; be sure to take the opportunity at the end of each answer to explain what you learned from the experience.

When faced with challenging questions, the best strategy is to consider possible answers beforehand and rehearse them. Consider the following questions and write specific, detailed answers for each:

1. What is the worst mistake you've ever made on the job?
2. Describe the most uncomfortable interaction you've ever had with a co-worker.
3. What do you do when your schedule is suddenly interrupted?
4. Describe a situation where your work or an idea was criticized.

For example, in a behavioral interview, you may be asked to describe a specific conflict situation you experienced and what you actually did to resolve or handle it. Many behavioral interview questions involve conflict resolution, decision making, leadership, managerial skills, teamwork, and interpersonal communication. It is a good idea to think ahead of time about real situations from your professional or academic career that you can use to answer any behavioral questions an interviewer may ask.

What Are the Goals of an Employment Interview?

Both you and the interviewer have goals for the interview. Keeping the interviewer's goals in mind can help you achieve your own.

Interviewer goals	One of the primary goals is to gather relevant information regarding a specific topic for subsequent evaluation and use. In an employment interview, an interviewer's goals may include gathering information to • assess a match between the applicant's qualifications and the requirements for the position; • evaluate the applicant's personality, attitude, disposition, team skills, and general ability to fit in with other employees; • determine the applicant's motivation, communication skills, and dependability; and • orient the applicant to the job requirements and background of the organization.
Your goals	Your primary goals are to provide information and convey the kind of enthusiasm and can-do attitude that get the job. You'll want to • provide positive, relevant professional and skill-based information; • behave in a polite and professional manner; • articulately respond to questions; • learn more about the organization and the position; • determine a match between you and the organization and position; • learn about the opportunities for advancement and growth; and • assess whether the job will be rewarding and enjoyable.

What to Expect from Start to Finish

While all interview situations can be handled somewhat differently, the stages of interviews normally consist of an opening or introduction, a body, and a closing.

Opening	The initial greeting and get-acquainted stage of an interview is when the interviewer gains the first and perhaps strongest impression of you. It is also during the opening stage that the interviewer may begin to provide you with an overview of the interview and hiring process and a description of the company and the position. Because the opening is your chance to make a good impression, pay attention to the interviewer's nonverbal behaviors and verbal descriptions. Use the information to tailor your statements about yourself and your abilities.
Body	The body generally comprises the longest part of the interview and involves numerous questions and answers. It is during this stage that you can discuss and showcase your qualifications and match your skills to the position. Be aware that you can also ask questions at this stage, including those that relate to the company's expectations of employees.
Closing	The end of the interview may last only a few minutes, but it is a good opportunity for you to close on a positive note. At this stage, you can clear up any misconceptions or transform any reservations that the interviewer may have about your qualifications or ability to perform the job. The interviewer may indicate what is likely to happen next in the hiring process such as, "We'll be conducting our remaining interviews until Wednesday. The second round of selected interviews will probably start the following week. We will be in touch by Friday to let you know." If the interviewer does not offer information about what happens next, you can politely ask when a decision will likely be made. Finally, when the interviewer verbally or nonverbally signals that the interview is over (by stating, "I think we have everything we need now" or by standing up), follow his or her lead. When the interviewer stands up, stand up yourself and express your interest in the organization and the position. Remember to thank the interviewer by name.

Getting Ready

Identify at least three or four major strengths that you possess related to a specific job or field. To identify your strengths, you need to think carefully about your skills and talents. You may be good at organizing and coordinating projects and people, or you may possess solid supervisory, sales, accounting, or writing skills. Once you have identified these strengths, you need to pinpoint examples of work you have accomplished that demonstrate your strengths. Then focus on those strengths and corresponding accomplishments that show what you can do in the position for which you are applying.

CREATIVE

CHALLENGE

List at least three strengths that you possess from your professional or academic experiences. Then write a paragraph or two about each strength. Highlight specific examples and use action words such as "I coordinated," "I developed," or "I increased. . ."

Do Your Homework on the Company

Before the interview, you should learn about the company to which you are applying. Gather basic information about the following:

- Number of employees.
- Company products or services.

- Location of the home office and any branch offices.
- Competitors and customers.
- Mission, goals, and philosophy.
- Market share.
- Structure of the company, including divisions, departments, and units.

To gather information on a specific company, log on to its website or call the company communication or public relations office to obtain annual reports, brochures, and newsletters. You can also look for company information through the chamber of commerce and college placement office, and you can talk to current or former employees.

What to Wear

Before the interview, investigate what the company's employees typically wear, especially those with job titles similar to the one you're applying for. But even if employees normally dress in a casual fashion, it is not advisable for you to dress casually for the interview.

1. Wear a well-pressed, conservative dark suit.
2. Wear sensible, polished shoes that match the outfit.
3. Wear a conservative hairstyle.
4. Avoid excessive or flashy jewelry and downplay makeup.
5. Avoid tight or form-fitting clothing.
6. Go light on the cologne or aftershave.

What to Do

Basically, you want to be prepared and considerate during your employment interview. The following table highlights several important aspects of good interview behavior.

Before you interview, find out about the company. The information you gather can help you prepare responses to potential questions and demonstrate your knowledge of and interest in the company.
© Charles Gupton Photography/CORBIS

Arrival time	• Arrive 5 to 10 minutes early. Research in advance the interview site and how long it takes to get there. You can call the receptionist to get exact directions and make a trial run a day or two before the interview date. Give yourself plenty of time to get there.
Upon arrival	• When you arrive, be polite to the receptionist or anyone you meet while waiting for the interview. • Be courteous and wait to be invited into the interviewer's office or meeting room.
The greeting	• When the interviewer greets you, make eye contact, smile, introduce yourself, and firmly (but not aggressively) shake hands.
In the meeting room	• Wait to take a seat until you are invited to do so.
During the interview	• Act naturally and be yourself during the interview. Putting on airs or playing a certain role is hard to pull off and can leave a false or negative impression on the interviewer. Maintain poise, good posture, and eye contact. Avoid nervous adaptive behaviors like hair or jewelry twisting or foot tapping. • Listen actively to the interviewer. Focus on and retain what is said, and observe the interviewer's nonverbal behaviors to gain insight about meaning and intention. • Don't interrupt the interviewer. Wait for him or her to finish questions or comments before responding. • Don't smoke, even if the interviewer smokes during the interview.

What to Bring

Bring at least two copies of your résumé, a small notepad and pen to take notes, a list of your references, and a list of questions you may want to ask. You may also bring a portfolio of your work or writing samples, designs, or illustrations that demonstrate your skills. Carry a briefcase, not a backpack or book bag, for your interview materials.

Websites for interviewing techniques, phone interviews, appropriate behavior, salary negotiation, and success dress	• www.geocities.com/optimabiz/interv.html • www.collegegrad.com • www.wetfeet.com

Questions and More Questions

While many of the questions asked during interviews are standard, the style of question can vary, depending on the situation, position, and interview technique. As presented in the following table, questions can be closed, open-ended, hypothetical, loaded, or behavior-based.

Closed questions	• Generally, when an interviewer asks a closed question, he or she wants a certain response, and there are not many responses to choose from. Closed questions permit only a narrow range of response possibilities such as yes or no. Examples: "Are you able to handle quick turnaround writing assignments?" "Do you prefer large or small organizational work environments?" This type of questioning offers little latitude for reply.
Open-ended questions	• As a less directive form of inquiry, open-ended questions encourage a broader and more thoughtful response. In this case, rather than ask if you can work well under pressure, the interviewer may ask, "How do you work when you are under the gun? Tell me what that is like for you." Open-ended questions give you more room to share your experience and perspective.
Hypothetical questions	• Hypothetical questions assess what you would do in a specific situation. An interviewer may ask, "If you get this position, what would you do if you had three priority projects due the same day and you knew you couldn't complete them all in time?" While hypothetical questions can provide the interviewer with some insight into your reaction in a specific situation, the response may or may not reflect how you would really behave in that situation.
Loaded questions	• Loaded questions put you on the spot by inquiring about something negative. For example, an interviewer may ask, "Why were you fired from your last job?"
Behavior-based questions	• Behavior-based questions determine your actual performance in specific past situations. These questions require real examples of experiences from your professional or academic career.

The Usual Questions

Interviewers ask numerous questions during an interview to gather more information about you than your résumé provides. It is a good idea to prepare and practice your responses to the following commonly asked interview questions.

1. **Tell us about you.**

   Often the first question an interviewer asks involves a brief description of you. In response, you want to describe your primary strengths and accomplishments in under two minutes. Most **you-oriented questions** focus on your educational background and relevant training.

   • What can you tell me about yourself?
   • What was your major in college, and what drew you to this field?
   • Why did you choose the college or university you attended?
   • Did you intern or serve as a volunteer for any agencies or companies? What was that experience like?

   you-oriented questions focus on your educational background and relevant training.

2. **Tell us about us.**

   Questions about the company are **company questions,** which usually aim to assess whether you have done your homework and why you want to be hired. Your responses can reveal your level of interest in the organization and your enthusiasm about the job.

   company questions are about the company or organization to which you are applying for work.

Provide several realistic reasons why you want to work for the company and why the job appeals to you.

- How did you learn about this job?
- What do you know about our company?
- Why are you interested in this position and our company?

3. **Tell us about your professional experience.**

Experience questions revolve around qualifications and serve to further determine whether you match the job. Your responses can crystallize your strengths, skills, and achievements for the interviewer. Use the opportunity to stress your experience, abilities, and knowledge as they relate to the mission of the organization and the position. Include any performances that highlight your problem-solving, decision-making, leadership, motivation, communication, and task accomplishment skills.

- In what ways are you a good candidate for this position?
- What are your major strengths?
- What are your best professional or scholastic achievements?
- What specific skills and talents will you bring to this position?
- What aspects of your former jobs did you like the most? The least?
- How do you demonstrate initiative? What motivates you?
- Describe what features of a job would be ideal for you.

experience questions revolve around your qualifications and skills to further determine whether you match the job.

CREATIVE

CHALLENGE

Develop brief (one- to two-minute) specific responses to the following questions:

- Can you tell me a little about yourself?
- Why should we hire you for this position?
- Describe a conflict situation you have been involved in. How did you handle it?
- Can you tell me about an experience you've had as a group leader? In what ways did you exercise leadership?
- If you got this position, how long would you expect to stay?
- What are your expectations about promotion?

Practice your responses in a mock interview with a classmate. Have someone videotape the interview if possible. Be prepared to answer questions and receive feedback from your class colleagues.

4. **Tell us about your communication and interpersonal skill.**

Generally, **questions about teamwork** involve your leadership ability and your interactions with others to help assess how you will fit in and work with colleagues. Your responses should reflect a positive attitude and the ability to get along with co-workers, subordinates, and superiors.

- Are you a team player, and do you work well with others?
- What would your co-workers say about your interpersonal skills? Your subordinates? Your supervisors?
- Do you see yourself as a leader? What would you say are your best leadership skills?
- What are your strongest communication skills?
- How do you handle criticism?

questions about teamwork involve your leadership ability and your interactions with others.

5. **Tell us about your future plans.**

   Essentially, **future questions** focus on your future career goals, your ambitions, and what you want to achieve in the long term. Your responses should emphasize opportunities for growth as a professional or tasks you look forward to performing in the field rather than on job titles ("I want to be CEO"). Describe realistically the areas of performance where you can improve and excel as a professional.

   - Where do you see yourself in five years?
   - Do you plan on furthering your education, such as graduate school?
   - Do you plan to stay in the same field?
   - If you get this job, how long would you plan on staying?
   - When would you be available to start the job?

   > **future questions** focus on your future career goals, your ambitions, and what you want to achieve in the long term.

6. **Tell us about your weaknesses.**

   Often interviewers hone in on some weak area discovered on your résumé by posing a **weakness** or loaded question to see how you will react. Plan to discuss and explain weak areas in your résumé—such as **job hopping** (moving from job to job in a short time period), gaps between jobs, and why you want a different job. A good strategy for responding to loaded questions is to focus on the positive. If the interviewer asks you about a weakness, you can reveal a weakness that has been improved, such as a software program you lacked proficiency in and took a course to learn. You can also focus on a weak area that is unrelated to the job at hand, such as cold sales calls or illustration. Questions about numerous positions or job hopping can also have positive explanations. If asked, "Why did you job hop?" you can reply that several opportunities arose that offered you career growth or advancement. Don't condemn or blame any organization you have worked for in the past. Focus instead on the positive and productive opportunities you have had to learn, grow, and improve.

   > **weakness questions** focus on a weak area discovered on your résumé.

   > **job hopping** means moving from job to job in a short time period.

   - From your résumé, it appears you've held a number of jobs. Why did you leave these jobs?
   - What are your professional weaknesses?
   - Why do you want to leave your current job?
   - Describe the worst mistake you have made during your career.

7. **Tell us what you want to know.**

   When the interviewer asks for **your questions,** take the opportunity to ask appropriate questions about the organization or position. It is not just the employer who makes an assessment about suitability. You need to decide if the job and company are right for you, since you will be investing a good deal of time and energy in them. At E*Trade, an online brokerage firm, CEO Christos Cotsakos believes that answers applicants receive to questions about the company often determine whether they will take the job or not. During an interview, a particular job applicant, who was concerned about the stability of the company,

   > **your questions** are what you want to know about the company or position.

asked Cotsakos, "How do I know that you are smart enough not to screw this up?" While shocked by the question, Cotsakos believes pointed questions like this one about the company's future are appropriate. He maintains that people are entitled to feel secure about the company's business strategy and that it is managed effectively.

While it is important to learn about a company's future potential, you need to use tact when asking company officials questions. Questions should be framed so that they are not offensive or threatening. Asking questions about the company's future plans can provide valuable information. Further, since interviewers may view applicants as uninterested if they don't ask questions, it is a good idea to compose a brief list of relevant questions to ask.

- Do you have any questions about the position or the company?

What You Should Ask

There are many good questions you can ask during the interview.

- What are the day-to-day duties of the position?
- How are employees evaluated?
- Does the company offer training programs?
- Who would I report to?
- Does the organization support employees' continuing education?
- What are the opportunities for advancement from this job?
- Why did the last person to hold this position leave?
- How would you describe the company philosophy regarding employees and customers?
- Does the company culture encourage innovation and procedural experimentation?
- What would you say is this company's competitive advantage?

Avoid asking questions about salary and benefits until you've been offered the job.

Practice Interviewing

Speech	• Speak in an enthusiastic, informative, and professional style. • Rehearse stating your primary strengths and associated performances and accomplishments.
Paralanguage	• Practice speaking confidently and eliminating vocal interferences such as "um," "ah," and "you know." • Practice varying your vocal tone and rate. Use voice inflections.
Homework	• Refer to company literature to demonstrate knowledge of the company. • Frame your responses to commonly asked questions using the information you have gathered about the company.
No blame	• Don't play the blame game. If you say your former job was awful or your boss was a jerk, the interviewer will wonder how much you contributed to the problem. Stay positive and focus on how your experiences have helped you to grow.

The Salary Question

While it is advisable to delay or avoid salary discussions until after an offer has been made, an interviewer may ask you directly about your salary requirements. Sometimes, employers use responses about salary to weed out applicants whose expectations are too high. To avoid salary-oriented questions, you can say, "While salary is certainly important, my primary interest is securing a job I enjoy. I am open to negotiation." If the interviewer presses you for a figure, you can begin by offering a range, such as "between $35,000 and $46,000." (See the section in this chapter on "Negotiating the Position Package" for salary range sources.)

Illegal or Unethical Questions

Some interview questions are illegal under federal law, and still others are unethical for an interviewer to ask. Nevertheless, some inexperienced or unsophisticated interviewers may allude to or directly ask you illegal questions. How (or whether) you respond to these questions depends on several factors, including your desire for the job and the interviewer's probable intention. While you do not have to answer any question you feel is unethical or inappropriate, there are strategies you can use to deflect the question or focus on the underlying issue. For example, if an interviewer asks if you are married or plan to have children you might say, "I'm not sure I understand how my plans for a family will affect my ability to perform in the position." Or you might focus on the actual issue that may underlie the question: "I think you may be wondering about my availability to travel. . ."

Examples of Illegal or Unethical Questions

- Are you married? What is your maiden name? Do you go by Ms. or Mrs.? Are you divorced or separated? You're single, right?

- How old are you? When were you born? (Asking if you are over 18 is legal.)

- Do you have children? How old are your kids? Will you need child care? Planning on starting a family soon?

- Do you own your own home? Does anyone live with you? Are any of the people who live in your house dependents?

- Do you have a religious preference? What religious holidays do you celebrate? Do you celebrate Hanukkah? What church do you attend? Are you Catholic?

- Have you ever been arrested? Have you ever participated in any illegal activities? (It is legal to ask if you have been convicted of a felony.)

- How much do you weigh? Is your whole family short? Are you a natural blonde?

- Are you of mixed race? What is your ethnic background? You're Irish, aren't you? Were your parents born in the United States?

- Have you ever been involved in or party to any legal actions? Any lawsuits? Any bankruptcies?

- Do you have any physical disabilities? Have you ever received workers' compensation benefits? Are you healthy?

What Happens Next

Job hunters sometimes fail to recognize the importance of following up their communication with potential employers after the interview. Employers appreciate an applicant's good manners and sincere desire to work as a member of the corporate team. In some instances, a decision about two equally qualified candidates could hinge on the follow-up efforts made. Right after the interview, while it's still fresh in your mind, take as many notes as you can about what was discussed, the interviewer's name and title, where the interview was held, and any other relevant details. Your notes will be useful when you place a follow-up call or write a thank-you letter—which you should do the day of or the day after the interview.

Follow-Up Calls

It is acceptable to follow up after the interview with a phone call to the interviewer. The purpose of this call is to ask if any additional materials or information are needed, dispel any negative misconceptions, and stress the positive aspects of your experience and your enthusiasm about the job. Keep the phone call brief and to the point.

Thank-You Letters

Expressing your appreciation for the interviewer's hospitality and time is both polite and smart. It demonstrates your genuine interest in the position and reminds the interviewer of you.

Thank-you letters can accomplish the following goals:

- Express appreciation for the interview opportunity.
- Refer to the position for which you are applying.
- Clarify or correct any negative impressions about your qualifications, abilities, or attitude.
- Emphasize your strong points and suitability for the job.
- Show enthusiasm and interest in the position and the organization's mission.
- Politely refer to an upcoming interview or the status of your application.

FIGURE 16.1

Sample Thank-You Letter

Jennifer McCabe
6 Meadow Drive
Albany, NY 12203
(518) 555-2525

January 10, 2003

Elizabeth T. Jones
Executive Director
American Theater Arts Associates
13 In View Avenue
Albany, NY 12205

Dear Ms. Jones:

Thank you for the opportunity to interview yesterday for the position of Public Relations and Promotion Director.

I was impressed not only by the important work that American Theater Arts Associates is doing on behalf of New York's theater, but also by the warmth and professionalism of both you and your staff.

I especially enjoyed learning about the proposed campaign to promote special theater events in this area. I appreciate you taking the time to discuss some of the grassroots campaign strategies with me. After our discussion, I am more convinced than ever that my writing, audiovisual, and promotional skills can help to advance theater arts in the capital district.

It was a great pleasure to meet you. I am eager to assist you with American Theater Arts Associates' many public relations and promotional missions in the future. In the meantime, you can contact me at (518) 555-2525 if you need additional information to support my application.

Thank you for your consideration. I look forward to hearing from you soon.

Sincerely,

Jennifer McCabe

Jennifer McCabe

Express appreciation for the interview and specify the position.

Relate enthusiasm and interest in the position, people, and details discussed about the work.

Reinforce your qualifications to perform the job.

Offer to provide supporting information.

Graciously thank the reader and close on a hopeful note.

Make sure you proofread your thank-you letter thoroughly to avoid typographical or grammatical errors and misspellings. A sample thank-you letter is illustrated in Figure 16.1.

What If the Employer Doesn't Contact You?

Sometimes after the interview, employers become bogged down with work and fail to respond by the date promised. It is acceptable to send a letter of inquiry if you do not receive word from the employer by two weeks after the promised notification date as illustrated in Figure 16.2.

FIGURE 16.2

Sample Letter of Inquiry

Gerald Good, Esq.
14 Brookedge Road
Guilderland, PA 46206
(717) 555-6337

January 14, 2003

Edward Lewis, Esq.
Lewis and Brown
Attorneys At Law
612 N. Main Street
Guilderland, PA 46206

Dear Mr. Lewis:

During my interview for the position of Associate on December 3, 2002, you indicated that you would notify me about the status of my application by January 3, 2003. Since I am very interested in the position and excited to join your team, I am inquiring about whether you and Mr. Brown have reached a decision.

If you need more information or have any questions about my qualifications, feel free to call me at (717) 555-6337. I would also be happy to submit further documentation to support my application.

Thank you for your consideration and your anticipated response.

Sincerely,

Gerald Good, Esq.

Gerald Good, Esq.

Introductory paragraph should specify the position and the purpose of your correspondence.

Offer more information that may help the reader make a decision.

Thank the reader in advance for the response to your inquiry.

Negotiating the Position Package

While it is a good idea to delay salary discussions until after a job is offered, negotiating for monetary compensation and other benefits is usually acceptable and often expected. To negotiate effectively you must know the going salary rate for the job you are seeking. To determine an appropriate salary range, you need to know the industry standard for this job. You can find salary information from work associates who hold similar positions, college placement offices, professional trade journals, the *American Almanac of Jobs and Salaries,* and the *Occupational Outlook Handbook.* You can also search online at www.daytonwallis.com/cx-geop.htm for standard salary ranges for many jobs.

It is important to investigate the benefits package the company offers and weigh it against the offer you receive. If the employer is inflexible about starting salary, you can negotiate for more benefits. The following table outlines some of the benefits and compensation packages that can be negotiated:

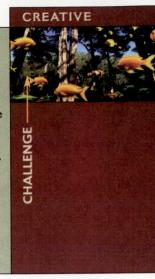

CREATIVE

CHALLENGE

Research salary ranges for the jobs you are most interested in. Then imagine that a company has offered you a position. You really want the job, but the salary is about $2,000 below the industry standard. You schedule a meeting for the following day to negotiate the terms of the offer. Prepare a plan to negotiate the salary using actual information you have gathered. Include what you plan to say, what exactly you will negotiate for, and any arguments you will use to support your request.

Insurance	• Medical insurance (with or without dental and eye care coverage) • Life insurance • Disability insurance
Additional compensation	• Stock options • 401(k) or other pension plans (be sure to ask about vesting terms) • Profit sharing • Year-end or signing bonus
Continuing education benefits	• Tuition reimbursement • Training programs and seminars
Vacation, holiday leave, and flextime	• Additional vacation or personal leave days • Flexible schedule or work hours
Performance-based review	• Percentage of salary increase after two or six months

Accepting a Position

Whether the offer is presented at the interview or weeks later, it is a good idea to request time for consideration. It is also wise to ask that the offer be committed to writing so that you have confirmation of important agreed-upon terms. Once you have reviewed the offer and decided to accept it, respond promptly with a letter of acceptance as illustrated in Figure 16.3.

FIGURE 16.3

Sample Acceptance Letter

Directly state your acceptance and include position title.

Indicate the employment start date and express appreciation for the opportunity.

John D. Bloomenfeld
80 Radnor Avenue
Croton-on-Hudson, NY 10520
(914) 555-4334

January 20, 2003

Dr. James P. Myhalyk
567 Southport Street
Croton-on-Hudson, NY 10520

Dear Dr. Myhalyk:

I am happy to accept the position of senior caseworker at the Croton Mental Health Clinic. I have enclosed my completed employment forms for your files.

As agreed, I will plan on a February 1 start date. I am excited about joining your staff, and I want to thank you for the opportunity to serve in this position.

Sincerely,

John D. Bloomenfeld

John D. Bloomenfeld

Enclosure: Employment forms

React to this letter written by an applicant who is declining a job offer. Because the letter may come as a disappointment to the reader, how would you frame the message better? Would you include more positive information about the position, company, or interview experience? Do you think you should include a reason for declining, such as something about the other job that was accepted?

Rewrite this letter to reflect how you think a turndown message should be designed.

Veronica Rivers
310 Mt. Bore Street
Pine City, NY 12906
607-555-3222

January 10, 2003

Ms. Lorraine Peck
Arnot Ogden Hospital
44 Roe Avenue
Elmira, NY 12903

Dear Ms. Peck:

I received your letter offering me the position of assistant manager in your billing department.

I am flattered that you selected me. However, I have accepted a position at another hospital. I thank you for the time you spent with me. I wish you well in your search to fill the position.

Yours,

Veronica Rivers

Veronica Rivers

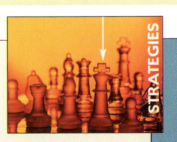

Strategies

1. Plan for and rehearse both verbal responses to commonly asked questions and nonverbal behaviors with friends or relatives. Remember that winging an interview can decrease your chances of getting the job. Applicants who are unprepared can easily be caught off guard by probing interviewer questions that require specific examples. Further, they may answer questions awkwardly or inaccurately if they have not planned in detail what to say.

2. Identify and develop a body of professional strengths and skills that you possess. Match and apply those skills with real experiences you have had to use as examples during the interview.

3. Slow the pace during an interview involving a panel or committee of people. Panel interviews can feel overwhelming, so take time to answer each question thoroughly and remain focused.

4. Research the companies for which you want to work. Make sure you are armed with adequate information about the company's structure, competitors, products, and goals before the interview. Use the information during the interview to demonstrate your interest in and knowledge of the company.

5. Dress appropriately for the interview, even if employees wear casual attire. Wear conservative, professional clothing that signals to the employer that you know the difference between a formal interview and a day at the beach.

6. Be yourself during the interview. There is no point in pretending to be someone else. Let the interviewer see your genuine goodness, quality, professionalism, and confidence. At the same time, show courtesy, respect, and manners. Chewing gum, slouching, looking sloppy, avoiding eye contact, or interrupting the speaker may leave a particularly unfavorable impression. Use good judgment.

7. Practicing active listening skills can help you understand and interpret what the interviewer is looking for and what aspects of your qualifications or personality he or she is interested in. When you listen carefully, you can better determine what direction to take with your responses and how to frame your messages.

8. Be honest when answering interview questions. Find ways to convey the message that you are a self-starter, disciplined, hard working, dedicated, organized, cooperative, and dependable. Frame responses to loaded questions in positive ways, such as describing mistakes as opportunities for learning and growth. Never lie to interviewers.

9. If you are asked an illegal or unethical question, you may choose not to answer or you can assess the reason behind the question and address it. For example, if an interviewer asks you if you're healthy, you may determine that what they may really want to know is if you will call in sick a lot or take a good deal of personal time. You might address the issue by saying, "I accrued some sick and personal days in previous jobs, but I maintained a solid attendance record."

10. Make sure you ask questions during the interview, since it is a great opportunity for you to assess whether the job, people, and company are right for you. Try not to let your eagerness for cash outweigh your better judgment about the fit between you and the job. Sometimes a job that offers less money than others turns out to provide greater opportunities for professional growth and, more importantly, personal satisfaction.

11. Write a thank-you letter or place a follow-up call on the day of the interview or the next day at the latest. Express your appreciation

for the interview opportunity and convey your enthusiasm about the position for which you have applied.

12. Accept or decline any job offer promptly and cordially.

Summary

- An employment interview is an exchange of communication between an employer and a job applicant for the purpose of considering an employment match. One company representative or a panel of people can conduct interviews. Behavioral interviews focus on performance-based questioning that requires specific examples of behavior from the applicant's real-world experience.

- Interviews consist of an opening (during which time pleasantries and information about the company are shared), a body (which usually consists of sequential questions and answers), and a closing.

- Preparing for the interview is critical. You want to respond to questions effectively and present your qualifications in a professional, enthusiastic manner. Identify major skill strengths and examples, collect company information, select appropriate business attire, and practice professional and courteous behavior.

- Question styles include closed, open ended, hypothetical, loaded, and behavior-based. Common topics are educational experience, company or industry information, professional experience, interpersonal communication, future plans, weaknesses, and salary requirements. Prepare for the interview by rehearsing answers to the usual questions.

- Following up with employers through letters of thanks and phone calls can make a big difference and improve your chances of getting the job. If you are not contacted by the date specified by the employer, you may write a letter to inquire about the status of your application.

- Salary and benefit packages should be discussed once a job offer has been made. You must know the standard salary range for the position you are seeking to negotiate effectively.

- When you are offered a job, try to get it in writing so that you can better determine whether the offer is acceptable to you. Once you decide to accept a job, send a letter confirming your acceptance.

Business Communication Projects

1. Break into groups of three. Discuss and select at least six interview questions from the chapter, including one illegal or unethical question. Conduct three interview role-play scenarios using the six selected questions. Take turns playing the roles of

the job applicant and the two panel interviewers. Brainstorm for positions for which each of you will apply. Interviewers should take notes and be prepared to offer the applicant helpful suggestions and a productive critique.

2. List the weaknesses that potential employers may identify from your résumé and associated questions they may ask. Examples of weaknesses are gaps in your work history, job hopping, or being fired from a job. Then develop responses that explain or minimize your weaknesses. Practice your responses with a friend or relative in a mock interview situation.

3. Contact the human resources office at a local company, and schedule a phone call with someone who conducts employment interviews. Prepare a list of seven or eight questions to ask about interviews and job hunting. For example:

   - What personality traits do they look for in an applicant?
   - How do they structure the interview process?
   - What behaviors by applicants do they think make a good impression?
   - What advice do they have for job seekers?

   Write a memo to your instructor that describes the information you gathered during the call.

4. Prepare a list of five questions you would want to ask of companies where you'd like to work in the future. Research four companies that interest you. Develop a written profile of each company. From the information you collected, answer your five questions. If you can't find written information that answers your questions, try contacting the company or an employee directly. Be prepared to present your findings to the class.

5. Imagine that you have interviewed with a company you are interested in working for. Write a thank-you, inquiry, and acceptance letter to the interviewer.

6. In some cases, businesses actually interview candidates via conference calls, video conferencing, or e-mail questionnaires. In these cases the interviewee does not have the opportunity to see and interact with the interviewer personally. Think carefully about how body language and other visual clues affect our perception of messages. How likely would it be to misinterpret a question or comment made by either the interviewer or interviewee? Write a brief e-mail memo to your instructor that describes how you could avoid such misinterpretations in a technology-assisted interview, and give examples.

7. You can learn from other people's mistakes. Start collecting "interview nightmare" stories from friends, family, co-workers, and

the Internet. What kinds of mistakes have people made? How could they have been avoided? Did those mistakes have an effect on whether or not the applicant got the job? Create a PowerPoint presentation that illustrates the mistakes and their results and present it to the class.

8. Plan your appearance for a job interview. Consider the corporate cultures of the various businesses listed below. Then determine what you would wear to an interview at these businesses, and explain in a memo to your instructor (perhaps illustrated with photographs of yourself in the outfits) why that apparel would be appropriate:

- A dot-com startup.
- An established financial institution.
- A clerical position in a music company.
- A small export–import business.
- A medical institution.

Discussion Questions

1. Are behavioral interview techniques better than traditional techniques for predicting an applicant's actual behavior or attitude? Why?

2. Why should an applicant ask about timelines for further interviews or decisions about the position if the interviewer does not offer the information?

3. Why should you learn as much about the organization as possible before accepting a position? If the salary is good, what else matters?

4. Answer the following question from an interviewer's perspective: If two applicants are both equally qualified for a position, what factors may tip the scale?

5. Why do you think interviewers appreciate applicants who have done their homework about the company?

6. What information can you learn by actively listening to the interviewer? How can the information be helpful to you?

7. Why is waiting for a day or two to accept a job offer a good idea?

8. What questions should an applicant ask regarding benefits after a job offer has been made?

9. How does a panel interview differ from a one-on-one interview?

10. How can honesty be combined with positivism when answering difficult interview questions?

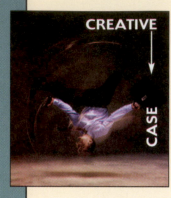

CREATIVE → CASE

Creative Case

Microsoft's Puzzle Interviews

You never know what you're going to be asked in a job interview. Some companies, such as Microsoft and several Wall Street firms, occasionally use logic problems as interview questions. These problems are not obviously business-related. Examples include:

• Calculate the number of degrees between the hour hand and the minute hand of a clock that reads 3:15.

• You have two containers. One holds five gallons; the other holds three. How can you put exactly four gallons of water in the five-gallon container?

• You wake up during a power outage. You have 12 black socks and 8 navy blue socks. How many socks do you have to put on before you can be sure you are wearing a matching pair?

• You are on your way to Truthtown. You come to a fork in the road: One path leads to Truthtown, where everyone tells the truth, the other leads to Liartown, where everyone lies. There is a man at the fork in the road who is from one of these towns, but you don't know which one. You can ask him one question to help you find your way—what question do you ask?

• How many gas stations are there in the United States?

Microsoft pioneered this technique. In an effort to find people who are "smarter" than the rest, Microsoft uses logic and mathematical puzzles as questions. If an applicant can solve these puzzles during the interview process, it is believed that he or she will fit into the corporate culture Microsoft has created. In part, puzzles like this replicate the software designing process: Take a problem that seems to have no clear solution or is very complicated and clarify it.

How effective are logic problems to determine a job applicant's ability?

Some questions to consider:

1. What exactly is being tested when an applicant is given a question like the ones listed above?

2. Are these questions a fair assessment of an individual's abilities?

3. Is the ability to answer these puzzles really a measure of one's intelligence?

4. How would you answer a question like this if it were asked of you during an interview?

Source: Kane, K. (1995). "The Riddle of Job Interviews." *Fast Company.* Retrieved December 15, 2001: http://www.fastcompany.com/online/ol/jobint.html.

Chapter 17

Chapter 17

Creativity and Visual Design

An advertising company gained a valuable new client: a company that made brass fittings used in home remodeling and decoration—doorknobs, doorknockers, hinges, drawer pulls, etc. The only requirement that the client had for advertisements was that it didn't feature anything as mundane as a picture of a doorknob. Since most advertisements for brass fittings were placed in "women's" magazines (which run home decoration stories on a regular basis) and trade journals, the client wanted something chic and new that would appeal to both audiences. The advertising company put its best team on the project but was horrified when the team came back with the new artwork: a picture of a manicured hand on an ornate doorknob. The client wasn't amused either. The client told the team that its position was based on knowledge of other advertisements in the field, which always gave pictures of products but provided no sense of elegance and style. The team responded that they believed that the hand on the doorknob would add an air of mystery: what was behind the door? They also told the client that there were two versions of the picture: a man's hand would be featured in the women's magazines' ads and a woman's hand would be used for the trade journals. This would also add a minor sensual appeal. The client listened carefully and decided that there was some sense in what the advertising team was saying. However, the client still wanted more than a hand on a doorknob. The advertising team understood the client's complaint. Perhaps they needed to come up with something more obviously eye-catching. The client gave them another week. When they met again, the team produced an image of a handsome man in formal wear with his hand on a doorknob, just beginning to open a door. Inside the room one could see the barest glimpse of a beautiful woman in a long dress. "This will be the advertisement for the women's magazine. What do you think?" "Yes!" said the client. "Now that's a doorknob I would buy!"

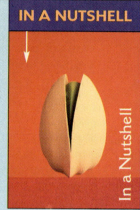

IN A NUTSHELL

In a Nutshell

Designing Messages with Visuals

Visual images enhance the many different messages that business communicators design and disseminate. As the advertising team in the "In a Nutshell" feature discovered, not all images are appropriate or appealing for every message or audience. The brass fitting company wanted an image for their advertisements that would be uncommon but elegant, while still illustrating what the company sells. They wanted customers (viewers) to be enticed and impressed. After the advertising team fully understood what the client wanted to say visually, the right images were designed for the advertisements.

Visual designs can be used effectively in oral presentations, training sessions, web pages, reports, proposals, and many other channels of business communication. More often than not, people can interpret patterns and comparisons from visual depictions of information or numeric data more easily than they can from verbal speech or written text. Visual images often clarify or simplify the meaning of complex concepts, helping the audience to better understand complicated ideas, facts, and relationships. Visual designs can emphasize key points and make messages more exciting, vivid, and memorable than words alone. Visual images can also condense lengthy messages because pictures, diagrams, or photographs can often tell a story in a shorter, simpler, more manageable way.

visual design is the process of generating and structuring messages using drawings, photos, and other graphics.

What Is Visual Design?

Visual design is the process of generating and structuring messages using visual elements and channels. Good visual designs are rooted in the message you want to convey, so you must match your message goal with your purpose for using the visual image. The primary purpose of any visual image is to communicate a message, but what do you want the visual message to accomplish? You can use visual images to stimulate audience interest, increase understanding and clarity, summarize or condense, and strengthen persuasive messages.

At Mullen/Long Haymes Carr, a North Carolina advertising agency, artist Stephen Hendee uses lines, colors, and geometric shapes to stimulate employee inspiration and creativity. Hendee designed the agency's conference room using saturated colors and geometric shapes and lines to transform both the space and the employees' frame of mind. He believes that physical space can revitalize and energize the mind, body, and spirit to foster improved creativity, brainstorming, and problem solving.

When you create visuals, consider which visual channels and elements can best help you to achieve

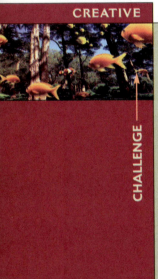

CREATIVE

CHALLENGE

Visual channels include drawings, photographs, and graphics that are used to clarify or develop the meaning of accompanying text. However, visual channels often go beyond pictures. Take a look at a business magazine. Examine the quality of the paper stock, the layout of the text, the fonts used, and any of the other physical attributes of the magazine. In a one-page memo addressed to your instructor, describe how these elements contribute to creating the "look" of the magazine. Describe who the magazine's audience is and how these elements might appeal to this audience.

The conference room artist Stephen Hendee created at Mullen/Long Haymes Carr Advertising uses several visual elements to stimulate creative thinking.
© Photo by Bob Hiemstra

your message goals. **Visual channels** include all visual imagery—such as drawings, photos, and graphics—that can be incorporated into a business message. All visual images can communicate, but you need to select the best channel to reach your audience and convey your message. Some visual channels look appealing but do not adequately present the information you want the audience to know and understand. Good visual designs combine the verbal message with the appropriate visual channel and the right **visual elements,** including lines, shapes, colors, and text.

visual channels include all visual imagery—such as drawings, photos, and graphics—that can be incorporated into a business message.

visual elements include lines, shapes, colors, and text.

How Do I Choose Visual Channels?

The first step in selecting a visual channel is to consider all the information you want to share with your audience. As you review the information, think about what concepts, ideas, or topics may be too complicated or difficult to present verbally through speech or writing. Then determine what aspects of the information may be simplified, clarified, or condensed with visuals. Consider what points from your message you most want to accentuate; building emphasis is another good reason to use visual images. Once you have decided what information is best presented pictorially, you need to assess what channel can convey the information most effectively and economically in the context you plan to communicate.

When you select visual channels for business presentations or documents, you need to match the goal of your message with the purpose of the visual image. For example, if your message goal is to present this year's earnings from the sale of several products, you could use a pie chart to demonstrate the breakdown per product. In this case, the goal of the message is to inform the audience about how each product compares to the company's overall revenue, and the purpose of the visual is to enhance viewer understanding of the financial information. A pie chart is the most effective channel because it compares portions to a whole. The following table shows ways to match messages and visual goals with visual channels.

Message and Visual Goal	Visual Channel
• Demonstrate how a relative portion compares to the whole	• Pie chart
• Show relationships, similarities, or different pieces of information, objects, or ideas	• Bar or line chart
• Demonstrate geographic area distance or proximity	• Map
• Depict the progress or status of information or events over time	• Line chart
• Present a realistic image of an event, place, or person to which your audience can relate	• Photograph
• Rank the importance or size of an idea, event, or object	• Bar chart
• Present specific numeric information or brief comparative text	• Table
• Chart the duration of scheduled activities for a project or task	• Gantt chart

Basic Design Principles

There are several elements you must consider in developing any visual message. Among them are contrast, balance, rhythm, and unity. One way to synthesize all these elements is to use the grid approach.

WORD ON THE WEB

Web pages use the same visual design principles as business documents and presentations. Visuals are perhaps even more important on a web page because the format, purpose, and audience of most web pages are different from those of other business documents. There are hundreds of sources on the Internet that provide useful ideas for designing web pages; these are just a few:

- http://www.wpdfd.com/index.htm
- http://www.dsiegel.com/tips/
- http://www.info.med.yale.edu/caim/manual/contents.html
- http://www.werbach.com/web/page_design.html
- http://www.sev.com.au/webzone/design.asp

After looking at some of these web page design sites, try designing your own web page. You can do this in Microsoft Word if you do not have access to another web page program.

Designing with a Grid Approach

To design effective visuals, use your creative skills and your knowledge about the audience to achieve message goals. Good visuals are designed with the whole image that you want to present in mind. While all the individual visual elements are important, appropriate organization of the whole design is key. A grid approach lets you visualize and organize balanced and unified elements throughout the design. Visual elements are selected to work together and to stimulate viewers in the way you intend.

The **grid approach** uses an invisible grid system (see Figure 17.1) to organize the placement of visual elements on a page or within a graphic design frame. Horizontal and vertical lines are used in various combinations to create square and rectangular shapes and spaces in which visual elements can be placed. Grids enable you to determine the space around or between elements you will use and the width of certain items. If you think of a grid with horizontal and vertical lines when you conceptualize and select visual elements, you can more easily create a design that is balanced, in proportion, and visually pleasing.

Artists such as Leonardo da Vinci and numerous architects throughout history used visible and invisible grids to outline, plot, and ensure

grid approach organizes the placement of visual elements on a page or within a graphic design frame.

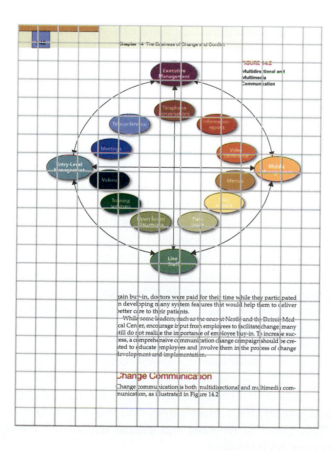

FIGURE 17.1

The Grid Approach as applied to page 340.

their designs were in proportion. The grid is like an artist's canvas on which visual design elements are planned, organized, and positioned. To create a grid, you can format through margins or by using rulers from both sides of the page.

contrast is the varied level of difference and emphasis among visual symbols, shapes, colors, or tones.

Contrast is the varied level of difference and emphasis among visual symbols, shapes, colors, or tones. Depending on your message goals, you may choose to use high-contrast or low-contrast elements. For example, if you use high-contrast shapes (such as squares and circles) or colors (such as purple and yellow) together in the same visual image, you may create tension in the viewer. This tension may stimulate the viewer to perceive the image with excitement and enthusiasm or irritation and uneasiness. On the other hand, low-contrast complementary colors such as blue and green or smooth round shapes that are similar may stimulate a calm, conventional, and relaxed viewer reaction. Often contrast is used to make the overall design effect more or less dramatic. Contrast contains the visual factors that cause dark objects to appear closer than light objects and light objects to appear even lighter against dark backgrounds.

balance is symmetry, or an equal distribution of weight within the frame of the design.

Balance is symmetry, or an equal distribution of weight within the frame of the design. A balanced design places visual elements in equal distance and weight distribution between horizontal and vertical axes. The use of white space also helps to balance elements and achieve symmetry. Not all designs are symmetrical; like high-contrast symbols or colors, asymmetrical designs can stimulate viewer tension. For example, think of the balanced scales of justice symbol. If one side was heavier than the other, the scales would be uneven, or asymmetrical. While balanced designs are more common in business documents and presentations, sometimes you want the emotional reaction that asymmetry evokes. Symmetry is easier to create, but asymmetry can be perceived as more intriguing, hold the viewer's interest, and be perceived as more inviting and active. Symmetrical layouts often appear to be more static or stationary, while asymmetrical designs appear to be more dynamic and mobile. Figure 17.2 illustrates symmetry.

rhythm refers to the positioning of elements that allows the viewer's eyes to gaze at certain aspects of the design before others.

Rhythm refers to the positioning of elements that allows the viewer's eyes to gaze at certain aspects of the design before others. The placement and the size of elements can lead the movement of the viewer's eyes along an invisible path from one element to the next. Rhythm can be facilitated through contrast, white space, the use of lines, and even size. For example, imagine a page in a newsletter that has a large dominant photograph positioned in the middle of the design frame (page). Your eyes will probably focus on the photo first and then move to other elements, such as the text and the caption.

The number of visual elements can also contribute to rhythm. If a design has relatively few elements, the viewer's eyes will not need to move very much to absorb the whole design. But if the design contains numerous elements, the viewer's eyes will move from one element to another. This rapid movement can create tension as the eyes dart around to view each element.

FIGURE 17.2
Symmetry Example

unity involves choosing visual elements that belong together and are similar, are in close proximity, or are pointed in the same direction.

Unity involves choosing visual elements that belong together and are similar, are in close proximity, or point in the same direction. The words, images, and graphics in a given design should all convey a united tone or theme. All of the visual elements in a design need to work together to communicate the same message. Grouping elements together, repetition, and the use of a grid can help to create unity. In some documents (reports, proposals, or newsletters) grids can enable you to position repeating visual elements in the same place on each page. For example, you could incorporate the company logo on each page of a document or use the same typeface and color for headings, which would demonstrate unity of visual elements.

CREATIVE CHALLENGE

Find a visual newspaper or magazine ad, and examine it for contrast, balance, rhythm, and unity. Write a memo to your instructor that describes the contrasting use of colors and shapes and the symmetry, rhythm of positioning, and unity of the visual elements in the ad design. Include in the memo a brief discussion of what you think the message communicates to viewers and whether the designers' intention matches the message conveyed.

Through **proportion,** which is the relative size of an element based on importance, a design may place a dominant visual element in the center of the frame, but other secondary elements presented in the design should be consistent and compatible to maintain unity. If the elements in a design are not familiar, consistent, or in some other way linked, the viewer may become distracted by all the different elements rather than focusing on the message meaning.

proportion is the relative size of an element based on importance.

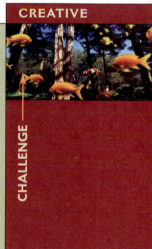

Using Color

There are seven million colors that can be distinguished by the human eye. Most of these colors are variations of the primary colors red, blue, and green with yellow, black, and white. There are three essential characteristics of color that communication designers need to understand: (1) **Hue** refers generally to the individual colors of the white light spectrum, such as red, green, and blue, and to the differences between shades. (2) **Saturation** involves the concentration of color purity and richness. (3) **Brightness** is associated with the degree of intensity and brilliance of a color as it reflects the light. Bright colors tend to stimulate viewer's attention. For the purpose of visual design, we can separate color into three categories: warm, cool, and neutral. Warm colors include various shades of red, orange, and yellow. Cool colors refer to the spectrum of blue, green, and violet shades, while neutral colors usually include black, white, and gray; subtle shades of beige and blue-gray can also be considered quite neutral.

At Lear Corporation, a manufacturer of automobile seating and interior design, designers, sculptors, and animators all work collaboratively inside the company's Reality Center to create and build car interiors and vehicles using visual technologies such as CAD software in a virtual-reality environment. The colors in the company's Reality Center are neutral shades of black, white, and gray, producing an atmosphere that feels like a different world. The neutral colors of the room and furniture provide the backdrop for the many colors of the vehicle interiors projected on a 20-foot wide screen. Viewers can perceive neutral colors as dull if used alone without other tones. Without the large screen in the Reality Center that displays the colorful designs, Lear employees could feel uneasy or listless working in a black, white, and gray room. But as background, neutral colors provide a perfect showcase for the brilliance of other colors.

Viewers often associate colors with different moods and emotions, such as "seeing red" for anger or "feeling blue" for melancholy. The type of mood that is stimulated may come from the individual's own personal or cultural experience, and, in this way, people perceive color very differently. While the color purple can be associated with royalty or spirituality in some cultures, it is associated with death in Brazil. Furthermore, different professionals have various interpretations of color based on associations to their work (e.g., red for financial difficulty). But from a design perspective and depending on your particular audience, visually stimulating and energetic colors tend to be bright yellow and red. These colors can easily spark feelings of excitement in viewers. Blues, greens, and light pastel colors tend to foster feelings of relaxation. Calm and neutral colors serve as a background for highlighted warm and cool colors. Elements in your design can be accentuated or deemphasized, depending on color. For example, if you want to highlight bars, lines, or objects you can use bright yellow or blue with a neutral background. To deemphasize objects or diminish the impact of bad news, you may use dark shades such as navy, maroon, or brown.

hue refers to the individual colors of the white light spectrum and to the differences between shades.

saturation involves the concentration of color purity and richness.

brightness is associated with the degree of intensity and brilliance of a color as it reflects the light.

Using Shapes

A **shape** is any form or design with height and width. Depending on the message and the elements you choose, various shapes may be used. Shapes can frame designs or other elements, guide the eye, organize, and symbolize visual designs. The three basic types of shapes in visual design include geometric, natural, and abstract. *Geometric shapes* include the three basics: a square, circle, and triangle. These shapes are often used to frame the design or form the structure in charts, graphs, or boxed information in documents or as display on slides and posters. *Natural shapes* are found in the natural world or constructed from ideas. Rolling hills, the leaves on trees, billowy clouds, or a person's face form natural shapes. Sometimes natural shapes can form a fluid frame for elements in a design and can depict a more emotional, creative, or flowing tone. *Abstract shapes* are often culturally specific symbols such as company logos or icons that communicate visual messages. **Icons** are abstract shapes created to look like the object they represent. Icons, like the handicapped parking sign or the gender-defined drawings of little people on restroom doors or even the checkered black and white racing flag, represent abstract shapes.

shape refers to any form or design with height and width.

icons are abstract shapes created to look like the object they represent.

Infographics

Infographics are informational or explanatory graphic images. The design elements of the infographic you choose depend not only on the goal of your message but also on the type of information you want to convey. There are two primary types of information used for infographics: quantitative and qualitative.

Quantitative

Quantitative infographics are visual designs that present numerical or statistical information in a condensed visual format such as tables, charts, and graphs. When designing quantitative infographics to be used in business presentations or written documents, remember to visualize a grid as the foundation of your design. Use the grid to position visual elements like lines and bars, which represent numbers or information for measurement or comparison. The grid is framed by a **plot area,** which is designated by two axes: the horizontal (X) axis and the vertical (Y) axis. The X-axis extends from left to right, and the Y-axis extends from bottom to top. **Titles** are used at the top of the chart or graph and on both axes to identify the comparison or measurement you want to demonstrate and to identify the chart categories. **Labels,** which are words or figures that accompany the chart categories, identify the items along the chart or graph axes. Titles and labels help to interpret the visual for your viewers. As a rule, avoid presenting too much information in simple charts and graphs. The presentation of one basic relationship, comparison, or measurement topic is usually enough for these designs. A grid plot area is illustrated in Figure 17.3.

quantitative infographics are visual designs that present numerical or statistical information in a condensed visual format.

plot area refers to a portion of a grid designated by two axes: the horizontal (X) axis and the vertical (Y) axis.

titles are used at the top of the chart or graph and on both axes to identify the comparison or measurement and to identify the chart categories.

labels are words or figures that accompany the chart categories to identify the items along the chart or graph axes.

FIGURE 17.3

Quantitative Infographics Grid

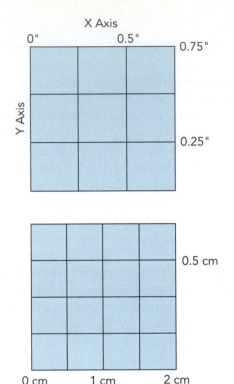

FIGURE 17.4

Sample Table

(X AXIS)

	Title	Title	Title	Title	Title	Title	Title
Title							
Title							
Title							
Title							
Title							
Title							
Title							

(Y AXIS)

Source of table data (if applicable):

1. Tables.

tables are square or rectangular in design and are used to present specific figures or narrative data.

Tables are square or rectangular in design and are used to present specific figures. (Tables may also be used for brief narrative data.) Tables use columns (categories) and rows to separate the items (numbers and other information) for comparison. Usually, the items are presented in logical order as illustrated in Figure 17.4.

2. Line and area charts.

The **line chart** is the most commonly used and is considered the easiest to understand. Line charts are used to show trends, increases or decreases in quantities or events over time, and comparisons and relationships among numbers. The line that represents information should be thick enough to differentiate it from the lines of the chart grid and the design frame. If two or more lines are used to depict different items, they may be differentiated by color and labeled. Avoid using more than four lines on the chart, since too many lines may confuse viewers.

An **area chart** is a more dramatic version of a line chart. It also presents data with a line extending across a grid, but the area under the line is shaded to the baseline below. The area chart is useful in presenting information about an individual set of data depicted by a single line. Line and area charts are illustrated in Figure 17.5.

3. Pie charts.

Pie charts are circular in design and demonstrate the relationship or distribution of parts, or slices (items), to the whole. Pie charts are used to compare one to seven slices, which are usually labeled as percentages or shares of the total pie (100 percent). Too many slices of a visual pie can be very difficult for viewers to read. The slices are normally labeled outside or adjacent to the circle so they look less crowded. Pie charts are usually read in a clockwise direction, so choose the most appropriate slices for a rhythm that leads the viewer's eyes to move in that direction. Flat and three-dimensional pie charts are illustrated in Figure 17.6.

4. Bar graphs.

Bar graphs, also known as bar charts, present shaded rectangles (bars) side by side for visual comparison as illustrated in Figure 17.7. Bar charts can effectively demonstrate changes in two or more items—including relationships, comparisons, trends, or events—at a specific point in time. The rectangular bars represent items such as

line chart shows trends, increases or decreases in quantities or events over time, and comparisons and relationships among numbers.

area chart a more dramatic version of a line chart because the area under the line is shaded to the baseline below.

pie charts are circular in design and demonstrate the relationship or distribution of parts, or slices (items), to the whole

bar graphs present shaded rectangles (bars) side by side for visual comparison.

FIGURE 17.5

Line and Area Charts

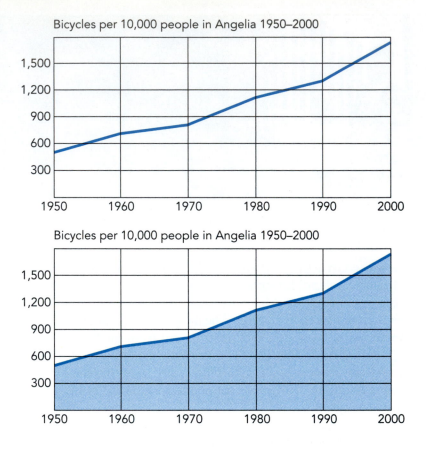

Bicycles per 10,000 people in Angelia 1950–2000

Bicycles per 10,000 people in Angelia 1950–2000

percentages, numerical data, or time frames and are positioned on a grid either horizontally or vertically. Horizontal designs allow for longer bars that may be needed for certain comparisons. Labels representing time frames or quantities should be placed outside the chart on both the horizontal and vertical axes. While differing in length and color (sometimes contrasting) to show comparison, the bars should be unified by being the same width and balanced by being an equal distance apart.

5. **Pictograms.**

pictograms use graphic symbols to represent items for measurement or comparison.

Pictograms are very similar to bar graphs except they use graphic symbols rather than bars to represent items for measurement or comparison. The graphic symbols chosen for a pictogram should be simple, identifiable, and related to the measured or compared items. For example, many pictographs use little people symbols, when what is being measured is numbers of people. Two types of pictograms are illustrated in Figure 17.8.

6. **Gantt chart.**

Gantt charts use bars on a grid, but Gantt chart bars exclusively represent scheduled lengths of time (days, months, or years) for the performance of activities on a particular project.

Like bar graphs, **Gantt charts** use bars on a grid. The difference is that the Gantt chart bars exclusively represent scheduled lengths of time (days, months, or years) for the performance of activities on a

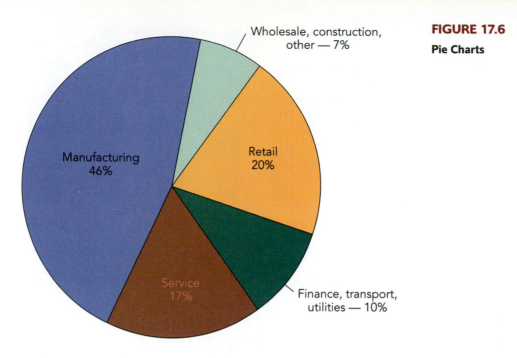

FIGURE 17.6

Pie Charts

Liabilities and Net Assets

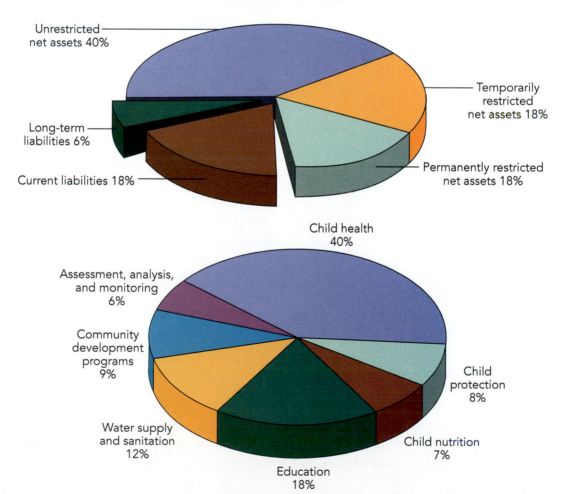

FIGURE 17.7

Bar Graph

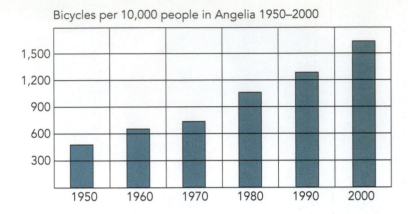

Bicycles per 10,000 people in Angelia 1950–2000

FIGURE 17.8

Pictogram

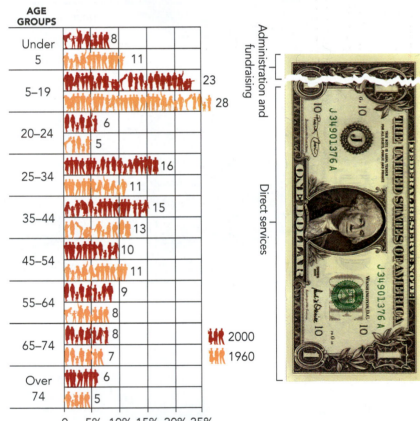

County Population Distribution by Age Group, 1960–2000

particular project. Sometimes proposals include a Gantt chart to visually present time frames for project performance. The bars on Gantt charts do not need to connect to either axis because their starting points may be positioned in various locations on the grid as illustrated in Figure 17.9.

The choice of quantitative graphic style can affect the viewer's perception of the data you're providing. To understand how the style of the chart or table influences the viewer's perception, create a series of quantitative visual graphics using the following table. Create separate graphics for all of the channels available: a line and area chart, a pie chart, a bar graph, and a pictogram.

JUMP IN!

"Lifestyle" mutual fund portfolios and allocation of resources

	U.S. Equities (%)	Cash (%)	Bonds (%)	International Equities (%)
Wealth builder	45	35	10	10
Preretirement	40	30	20	10
Retirement	50	25	20	5

SOURCE: http://www.forbes.com/personalfinance/2002/02/19/0219adviser.html

FIGURE 17.9

Comprehensive Plan Schedule

Gantt Chart

Task Name	1999			2002		
	Oct	Nov	Dec	Jan	Feb	Mar
Volume I						
Document						
Review/revisions						
Print						
Distribute						
Volume II						
Collect baseline information						
Generate section/committee document						
Generate committee executive summary						
Integrate committee documents into Volume II						
Generate Volume II executive summary						
Review/revisions						
Print						
Distribute						

Qualitative

Qualitative infographics include narrative or conceptual information presented using appealing visual formats like flow charts, maps, photos, drawings, and diagrams.

1. **Flow charts.**

   Flow charts use boxes with arrows or lines to connect them. They usually demonstrate the relationships between and sequencing of procedures, processes, and people as illustrated in Figure 17.10. The

qualitative infographics include narrative or conceptual information presented using appealing visual formats.

flow charts use boxes with arrows or lines to connect them.

431

FIGURE 17.10

Flow Chart

1. Goal statement
2. Objectives
3. Methods
4. Activities

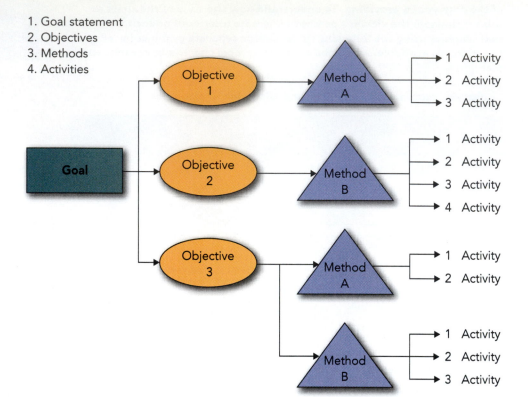

organizational chart depicts the chain of company command from top to bottom.

pert chart refers to a type of flow chart that outlines a process.

maps are used to present geographic locations, proximity, or distance.

photography is the process of capturing permanent images on film for eventual processing and printing onto special paper.

most common type of flow chart is an **organizational chart** that depicts the chain of command from top to bottom and relationships among divisions, departments, and positions in a company. Another type of flow chart is the **pert chart,** which outlines a process, such as the steps involved in manufacturing a particular product.

2. **Maps.**

Maps are used to present geographic locations, proximity, or the distance of select pathways, roadways, counties, states, or countries. Different areas can be distinguished by color, and a brief narrative can explain the location where an event has occurred. Sometimes, numeric or statistical information accompanies a map. You may use maps to visually show the location of a company's plants or branch offices, the various cities or states in which your company conducts business, or new areas for marketing development efforts. A six-county map is illustrated in Figure 17.11.

3. **Photographs.**

Originally called heliography, **photography** is the process of capturing permanent images on film for eventual processing and printing onto special paper. Photographic images are realistic representations of the physical world: people, places, and events. Most viewers find photos more believable than drawings or illustrations. Although perspective, lighting, camera angles, and cropping can manipulate images, most people perceive photos as true to life and authentic.

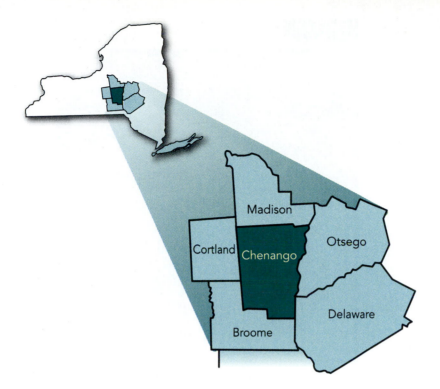

FIGURE 17.11

Sample Map

4. Drawings and diagrams.

Drawings are hand-produced lines using ink, pen, or pencil to represent images on paper. Drawings often can present the fine details of an object better than other representations, like photos. Further, drawings can be rendered of ideas not yet materialized (which obviously can't be photographed). **Diagrams** are a type of drawing used for visual description that explain how a process or procedure works or show the details of how a product or machine is produced, assembled, or used. Diagrams allow viewers to understand complicated processes that could be difficult to explain with words.

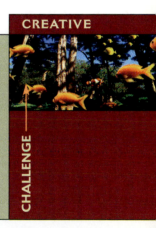

CREATIVE

Break into groups of five with your class colleagues to design an organizational chart. Each of you is a department director. Decide the type of organization, tasks, and positions. Include the titles of all employees in your chart design.

CHALLENGE

drawings are hand-produced lines using ink, pen, or pencil to represent images on paper.

diagrams are a type of drawing used for visual description that explain how a process, procedure, or product works or is used.

Developing Visuals

Many infographics used for business presentations, reports, and other documents are designed using computer graphic software programs. Programs such as Microsoft Excel, QuattroPro, and Harvard ChartXL allow users to plot pie charts, line charts, and bar graphs and attach text and titles. Many programs contain set formats and graphics that can be effective in presentations and written documents, and most programs allow users to integrate or import visuals

HERMAN®

by Jim Unger

5-3   © Jim Unger/dist. by United Media, 2002

**"I don't suppose you remembered
to put up my painting?!"**

Source: Copyright 2002 Jim Unger/United Media.

into word-processing files. Most of these software programs offer instruction or user tips through "wizards" or help functions that facilitate the design process.

Word-processing programs allow you to make and change text. You can type in sentences and paragraphs, change the order of words, delete them, or change the way they look when printed on paper. Most commercially available programs allow you to import visual images as well. Both Microsoft Word and WordPerfect let you add graphics to pages of text. Word-processing programs are used in business to create letters, memos, reports, proposals, magazine articles, simple ads, tables, newsletters, legal documents, faxes, and many other forms of printed text-based communication. Most word-processing programs have **templates,** which are predesigned models or sample layouts of business memos, résumés, reports, and letters. The benefit of a template is that you can create a professional-looking page without needing to format the page yourself. However, some templates for memos and letters do not use correct standard formatting rules and need to be modified.

While word processing is sufficient for many memos, reports, and correspondence, more sophisticated or graphics-rich documents require desktop publishing programs.

templates are predesigned models or sample layouts of business memos, résumés, reports, and letters.

Jump In!

← **JUMP IN!**

Desktop publishing programs	Visual designs such as flow charts, drawings, diagrams, and photographs can be created or integrated using various desktop publishing programs, including QuarkXPress; CorelDRAW; and Adobe PageMaker, Illustrator, and Photoshop. Graphic software programs allow designers to create graphic images and lay out text, graphics, and photographs. Even Microsoft Word enables users to create simple tables with narrative or numeric information that can be developed within a text document or copied and pasted from a separate file.
Presentation programs	Presentation programs are specialized graphics programs such as Microsoft PowerPoint that help you create a layout of information in the form of slides that are similar to single frames from slide projectors, overhead transparencies, or filmstrips. These slides can be printed into a written document, e-mailed or placed on a web page for your audience to review, or displayed on a monitor or projection screen as part of a formal business presentation. PowerPoint can incorporate files you create in Microsoft Word or Excel for use during your presentation. Like PowerPoint, other presentation programs, including Adobe Persuasion or Macromedia Director, can offer visual effects, animation, photos, graphics, video, and sound. The important thing to remember when creating a presentation is simplicity. Each slide should contain one important idea that is expressed in a very concrete manner. For written or bulleted text, short statements are best and may be followed up with visuals that can provide more explanation or detail.

Integrating Visuals

Integrating visuals into business documents and presentations involves determining the size, visibility, and placement of visual elements, choosing colors and shapes, numbering and labeling tables and figures, and citing the sources of data.

Size, Visibility, and Placement

Depending on the volume and complexity of the information you want to convey, the size of your visual will vary. Don't cram visual elements and information into a frame that is inadequately sized because the visual will appear cluttered. Viewers may also find it difficult to read or interpret.

The size of your visual will vary depending on the size of your audience. If you plan to display a visual during a presentation, make sure it is visible to everyone in your audience. Some visuals may need to be enlarged or positioned in a location to allow everyone to see them. To determine visibility, visit the site at which you will be speaking and check visuals from the perspective of the audience.

If you plan to use a visual image during an oral presentation, introduce it in the speech by providing the audience with an introduction, interpretation, or summary of what they will see, what it means, and why it is important. Describe the purpose of the visual for your viewers and what it is intended to demonstrate. Introducing a visual and providing some explanation does not mean that you should repeat all the information presented in the visual. Because some visual images are not necessarily self-explanatory, viewers may not reach the conclusions you do without some direction.

If your visual will appear in a written document, it should be placed as close to the description in the text as possible. While it is important to introduce a visual before it appears in written text, the size may determine placement. Depending on size, it should be positioned immediately following or on either side of the written text description. Often, text can wrap around images on a page. **Runaround** refers to text that wraps around a visual image. If the image is too large to fit adequately on the same page as the description, you should place it on the next page, or if appropriate, in the appendix. Refer to the visual in the text description and lead the viewer to the page where it is located.

runaround refers to text that wraps around a visual image.

Numbers, Labels, and Titles

For written documents, each visual needs to be numbered in consecutive order. Numbering allows you to refer to visuals and allows viewers to locate them. Visuals are labeled using two general categories: figures and tables. Figures are distinguished from tables in that all other visuals including charts, graphs, and diagrams are labeled as figures. Tables are grouped and labeled separately from figures. For example, if your document contained two bar graphs, three tables, one pie chart, and a diagram, the corresponding labels and numbers would appear as Figure 1, Figure 2, Table 1, Table 2, Table 3, Figure 3, and Figure 4, respectively. If you are using visuals in oral presentations, you may omit the numbers, but use a title for each visual that specifically describes the visual. For example, during your presentation you may refer the audience to a table entitled "Project Budget Expenditures for the First Two Quarters of 2003." This title should lead your viewers to an understanding of what you want to emphasize in the visual. Visuals in documents also need concise but descriptive titles. Titles should provide viewers with the content of the visual in a clear and concise way. Titles should be placed above visuals in a slightly larger font size than labels and numbers. This allows viewers to conceptualize what the visual represents and why it is important.

Give Credit Where It's Due

Just as you would cite the source of written information in a bibliography, references, or works cited, you must also indicate the source of your visuals. Citing the source means that you give the person, group, or entity credit for creating the design or researching and collecting the data used in your visual. To cite the source of a visual, you simply include "Source: *The Wall Street Journal*" at the bottom of the design frame. If you or someone on your work team created the design and collected the information, then you need not cite the source or you may refer to the source simply as "primary." To cite the source during an oral presentation, you may refer to the source name in your verbal speech or display the name under the visual as you would in a written document.

Strategies

1. Select visuals that can make complicated ideas easier for your audience to grasp. Remember that the right visuals can simplify and condense difficult or wordy ideas and concepts. Numeric information is especially difficult for some people to interpret without a visual aid.

2. Maintain unity in your design. Avoid designing visuals that are overwhelming or cluttered; they are likely to distract or confuse viewers. Too many items, colors, or inconsistent elements can draw attention away from you or the message. Clip art may be visually pleasing decoration, but it doesn't always add to your message design. Use visual elements sparingly and only when they contribute to the message you want to convey.

3. Keep visual designs simple. Focus on presenting one major idea for each visual. But do not provide a visual for every idea. If your readers constantly need to refer to visual after visual, or you introduce dozens of them during a presentation, the audience will be overwhelmed—or worse, annoyed by unnecessary, time-consuming, excess information. Remember that visuals do not replace words. They should enhance your message, but they are not a substitute for it.

4. If you use visuals during a business presentation, make sure each image is visible to everyone in your audience. There is nothing more frustrating than having to struggle to view visual materials. Your audience may perceive such flaws in your presentation as a signal that you lack credibility as a speaker—exactly what you want to avoid.

5. During presentations, focus on the audience, not the visuals. Audience members may lose interest or become distracted if you talk to the visuals instead of them.

6. If you are using visual aids such as PowerPoint, visit the room in which you will be speaking to check the placement of electrical outlets, light levels, glare from the sun, equipment, and visibility. Practice using the equipment and presenting visual aids.

7. Timing is key for using visuals. Present visual images at the most appropriate times when relevant ideas arise in your message.

8. Explain and briefly describe your visuals. Don't assume that viewers will automatically understand their meaning or importance. Guide their interpretation of the visuals you use.

9. Make certain your visual designs represent accurate and unbiased information. They should present a realistic picture of events, relationships, or comparisons. When you create visual images you need to be wary of any information that may be embellished, distorted, or misleading. It would be unethical to modify or omit information from a bar graph, line chart, or pie to oversimplify a relationship or reflect data more persuasive of your argument.

Summary

- Visual design is the process of structuring messages by using visual elements. The purpose of visuals is to communicate messages. Good visual designs match the message goal with the purpose for using the visual—for example, to increase understanding or interest and to clarify, simplify, or summarize ideas.

- Choosing the right visual channel involves identifying which information can most effectively be presented graphically. Visuals can clarify, condense, or emphasize information. Matching the goal of your message with the purpose of the visual will help you to pinpoint the best channel to use.

- Basic principles of visual design include the grid approach, which can help you to determine the placement of visual elements on a page or within a graphic design frame. The basic principles also include contrast, balance, rhythm, and unity.
  a. Contrast is the varied emphasis among visual symbols, shapes, colors, or tones.
  b. Balance involves the equal distribution of weight of visual elements in the design.
  c. Rhythm is the strategic placement of visual elements to direct the viewer's gaze from element to element.
  d. Unity is the use of visual elements that belong together and are similar, in close proximity, or pointed in the same direction.

- Infographics are informational or explanatory graphic images. Designing infographics includes determining the size, visibility, and placement of visual elements; choosing colors and shapes; numbering and labeling tables and figures; and citing the sources of data. Two types of information are used in infographics: quantitative and qualitative.
  a. Quantitative infographics use numerical or statistical information in condensed visual formats such as tables, charts, and graphs.

    b. Qualitative infographics present text or narrative information in visual formats, including flow charts, maps, photos, drawings, and diagrams.

- There are many word-processing programs that let you add graphics. Most have templates you can follow. Presentation programs are specialized graphic programs that let you lay out text and visuals as slides.

Business Communication Projects

1. Select a visual channel not discussed in this chapter (perhaps videotapes, flip charts, or overhead transparencies). Evaluate how the visual may be used effectively. Come to class prepared to present your visual and describe its advantages and disadvantages.

2. Find a written vignette from a newspaper, journal, or magazine containing statistical or narrative information that could be presented visually. Choose the most appropriate design and create the visual using the information you gathered. Come to class prepared to present your visual. Be sure to introduce and explain it adequately to the class, and offer at least two reasons the visual you chose conveys the information better than spoken or written words could alone.

3. Select an appropriate visual to graphically present the information in each of the following:
   - An increase in the speed of the Intel microprocessing chip over the last four years.
   - A comparison of TV network ratings (percentage share of viewers) for the 9 P.M. timeslot for the month of November.
   - Changes in consumer buying patterns in the United States, France, Germany, and Japan this year.
   - A breakdown of which consumers use satellite, cable modem, DSL modem, or dial-up modem to gain access to the Internet.
   - A comparison of this year's minivan sales among three big auto manufacturers.
   - Top 10 cities in the United States hiring the most computer networking engineers.

   Design one of the visuals you selected using the information provided.

4. The company you work for, Excelsior Temporaries, is located on the 23rd floor of a high-rise office building. Employees are concerned about their safety in the case of fire or other disaster: How will they get out of the building? The Board of Directors asked you to look into various escape alternatives, and you have found information on skyscraper parachutes. Research skyscraper parachutes (here's a website to get you started: http://abcnews.go.com/sections/GMA/GoodMorningAmerica/GMA011106_HunterParachutes.html#),

look for appropriate visual aids that use any of the channels described in this chapter, and create a PowerPoint presentation to deliver to the Excelsior Board of Directors.

5. Hobler Hamburgers, a fast-food restaurant, has employed you to create advertising for their new Hot & Tasty Chicken Fingers. They have identified two demographic groups as their primary targets for this product: children (ages 5 to 12) and single working people (ages 25 to 40). Create two one-page advertisements for Hobler Hamburgers' Hot & Tasty Chicken Fingers, paying special attention to the colors and visual style that will appeal to these very different audiences.

6. Break into groups with your class colleagues to create a brief report (one to two pages) that describes a health or safety process that businesses should be aware of: CPR procedures, artificial respiration, disposal of hazardous medical waste, natural disaster protocols, etc. Find or create six infographics to illustrate this process, and incorporate them into your report with appropriate numbering and captions. Make sure that all six infographics have complementary styles (unity) and use size effectively.

7. Don's Market is having a Fourth of July sale. Specially priced items include hotdogs ($2.15 per package), hamburger ($3.29 per pound), buns ($1.50 per half dozen), potato salad ($3.79 per pound), corn on the cob (two ears for $1.00), and watermelon (19¢ a pound). Create a grid-based layout for a one-page advertisement that emphasizes the best deals. Include both graphics and text.

8. Break into groups with your class colleagues to create a PowerPoint presentation for Tuff Stuff Trucking, comparing year-end data from last year with year-end data from this year. Use separate slides for each category, incorporate graphs to clarify data that require it, and include other visual aids to create a graphically unified presentation.

Category	Last Year	This Year
Number of operational trucks	7	7
Miles traveled	15,029	17,258
Number of full-time drivers	12	10
Tonnage	450,000	510,000
Products shipped	Chemicals (nonhazardous) Livestock feed Fertilizer	Chemicals (hazardous) Chemicals (nonhazardous) Livestock feed Fertilizer
Gross profit	$4,110,150	$5,000,897
Taxes, licenses, insurance, fees, and salaries	$2,432,001	$2,372,090
Net profit	$1,678,149	$2,628,807

Discussion Questions

1. In what ways could the design of a visual distract or confuse viewers? In what ways could the presentation of the visual distract viewers?

2. Why is it necessary to introduce visuals and provide some interpretation for viewers? In what ways does this strategy share basic business communication concepts described in earlier chapters?

3. Why is it important for business professionals to understand the design and use of visuals in reports, proposals, and presentations?

4. Why are contrast, balance, rhythm, and unity important components of visual design?

5. What is the difference between qualitative and quantitative visuals? Consider content and purpose as well as design principles.

6. Templates allow you to create professional looking pages without formatting the page yourself. Are there any potential drawbacks to templates? What are they?

7. Why is timing a key issue in visual design? What is its role in a PowerPoint presentation?

8. In what situations is the grid approach advisable? When is it not advisable to use the grid approach?

9. Do visual design principles apply to text documents such as letters or memos that have no pictures, tables, or graphs in them? Explain.

10. Why do asymmetrical layouts appear more mobile and dynamic?

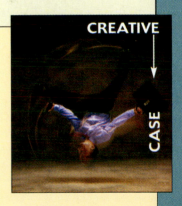

Creative Case

Feng Shui in the Office

Feng Shui is a Chinese philosophy that dictates the ergonomic design of an environment. It incorporates contrast, balance, rhythm, and unity. This includes the arrangement of furniture and fixtures, the use and placement of decoration, and the use of color to encourage a healthy flow of spiritual energy called "chi." A living space designed using Feng Shui principles is purported to bring health, comfort, happiness, and success to those who dwell there. Office spaces designed using these principles are supposed to result in increased sales, happier clients, higher productivity, and higher employee retention. Companies that have used Feng Shui in their office spaces include Citibank, Chase Asia, the Morgan Bank, Rothschilds, and *The Wall Street Journal*.

Lange Productions is a multimedia production company in Hollywood, California. Employees there complained to management that they felt stressed at work due to the heavy workload. Rob Shaffner wanted to make the office space more pleasant for employees, so he approached Life Design, a Feng Shui–based interior design company. Constance Whitelaw of Life Design looked at the Lange facilities and determined that the primary problems were the colors in the office. Heavy, dark brown beams over the employees' desks were oppressive, and the walls were a boring shade of blue-gray. Constance painted the overhead beams a lighter shade, and then used pastel colors in the individual cubicles. She also incorporated yellow accents and encouraged Shaffner to put up bright artwork on the walls and place silk flowers around the room. Employees soon reported improved moods.

Speculate on how Constance's use of color in the Lange Productions office used contrast, balance, rhythm, and unity. Then take a trip to an office near you: a school departmental office, a back office at a store, or a traditional office. (Even the most haphazardly organized office will yield results.) Look for the basic design principles at work—how the furniture is arranged and what colors are predominant. Also consider the purpose of the office (public or private) and the type of work completed in it.

How could the office space you are examining be improved using basic design principles?

Some questions to consider:

1. How important is mobility in this office space? Do people need to move around freely, or is the area largely static?

2. How formal is the office area? What colors would be most appropriate given the status of the occupants and the type of work they do?

3. What kinds of equipment and furniture are used in the office? How do they influence the way the office "feels?"

4. How extensive would your redesigning effort be? What kinds of little changes would make a difference? How effective would huge changes (like remodeling) be?

Sources: Feng Shui Advisors. (1999). "Feng Shui and Retail Stores." Retrieved May 8, 2002: http://www.168fengshui.com/Articles/retail.htm; Life Design. (2000). "Testimonials." Retrieved May 15, 2002: http://www.lifedesignworks.com/generic.html;$sessionid$ TOGZNQQAATYFWGIHUUUTIWYZA451PXO?PID=4.

Grammar and Punctuation

Grammar and mechanics are integral parts of effective communication. This summary of basic grammar is provided as a guide for student reference.

Sentences

Nouns

Nouns identify or name people, places, things, ideas, or actions. They have many functions.

Subject
1. *Nancy* was the special guest at the party.
2. The *trainees* wanted to leave class early.
3. The *discussion* continued.
4. How many *assignments* have been completed?

Subject complement (names or identifies the subject)
1. My co-worker's *name* is *Jamaal*.
2. *Dinah* is the law *professor*.

Direct object
1. The tourists saw the white *alligator*.
2. The car's owner had lost his *key*.

Indirect object
1. Carlos gave the director a *mike*.
2. The travelers bought souvenirs for all their *friends*.

Object of preposition (indicates direction or relation)
1. Richard pointed *at the doorway*.
2. *At the sound of the bell*, all students returned to classes.

Object complement (completes meaning of the object it follows)
1. Chancellor O'Brien appointed Lydia associate *vice-chancellor*.
2. The symphony made Rebecca Reeve *director*.

Pronouns

Pronouns serve the same function as nouns. They may be subjects, objects, complements, and objects of prepositions. Pronouns may refer to nouns and can appear in the same positions as nouns in a sentence.

Personal pronouns (refer to specific persons, animals, or objects)
1. I, me, my, mine
2. we, us, our, ours
3. you, your, yours
4. he, him, his, she, her, hers, it, its
5. they, them, their, theirs

Reflexive pronouns (refer to person or thing already mentioned in a clause)
1. myself, ourselves
2. yourself, yourselves
3. herself, himself
4. itself, themselves

Demonstrative pronouns (point to something)
1. this, that
2. these, those

Relative pronouns (link relative and main clauses)
1. who, whom, whose, whoever, whomever
2. that, which

Interrogative pronouns (as questions)
1. who, whom, whose
2. which, what, whatever

Adjectives

Adjectives modify nouns and pronouns.
1. She wore a *red* dress.
2. John always has the *wildest* ideas for a *class* project.

Predicate (a kind of complement)
1. Suzanne sounded *happier.*
2. Caroline and Thomas were *elected.*

Articles (always come before a noun or pronoun)
1. The customer had *a* large order.
2. The laundry was finished in *an* hour.
3. Will *the* program last long?

Verbs

A verb is a word or group of words that expresses an action, a state of being, or an assertion. The verb is the heart of a sentence. Without a verb, there is only a sentence fragment.

One word

1. statement—The manager *speaks* quickly.

2. question—*Will* José attend?

3. command—*Call* immediately.

Two or more connected words

1. The children *will attend* regularly.

2. The children *have been attending* regularly.

3. The children *should have been attending* regularly.

Separated words

1. Christa *could* almost certainly *write* a novel.

2. It *will* in all likelihood *storm* next week.

Combined with *not* or a contraction of *not*

1. He *will not* be able to *attend* the conference.

2. The speaker *didn't finish*.

Adverbs

Adverbs modify a verb, adjective, or another adverb.

Modifying a verb

1. Bruce walked *carefully* down the steps.

2. Woody *heartily* endorsed the proposal.

Modifying an adjective

1. Though *slightly* overweight, he ran quickly.

2. She was *very* smart.

Modifying an adverb

1. The runner walked *very rapidly* to his starting point.

2. This train rides *exceedingly rough*.

Transitive Verb

Transitive verbs transfer an action from the actor to the receiver.

1. Debra *drove* the car.

2. Ron *had remembered* all the details.

Intransitive Verbs

Intransitive verbs make an assertion about the subject but do not extend the action to an object or receiver.

1. Debra *drove* dangerously.

2. Ron *had remembered* again.

Linking Verbs

A linking verb conveys no action. It is a sign of identification that connects the subject with a word or phrase that comes after it and completes its meaning. Linking verbs include forms of the verb *be* (am, is, was, and were), seem, appear, become, and verbs relating to the senses (taste, look, feel, sound, and smell).

1. Ludmilla *is* a computer specialist.
2. Fireproof file cabinets *are* the best.
3. The meeting *sounds* exciting.
4. That brochure *looks* professional.

Verbals

Verbals are participles, infinitives, prepositions, and gerunds derived from verbs. They are not verbs because they cannot serve as the heart of a sentence. Verbals are in phrases and clauses.

Participle (also called verbal adjective)
1. The woman *taking notes* is the assistant director.
2. *Speaking at a slow pace,* the speaker was easily understood.

Infinitive (verbs preceded by "to")
1. *To walk three miles,* you must first practice.
2. Sean chooses *to play soccer.*

Preposition (shows relationship between a noun or pronoun and something else)
1. You'll find the money *under the paper.*
2. *On the bus,* the consulting team discussed what happened.

Gerund (verbal noun)
1. Nathan enjoys *telecommuting.*
2. *Keying* data is Joanne's specialty.

Conjunctions

Conjunctions are used to connect words, sentence parts, or sentences. Two sentences that are joined are called *clauses.*

Coordinating conjunctions (and, but, for, nor, or, so, yet)
1. Her favorite speakers are Robert *and* Lorraine.
2. The surveyors stopped *and* questioned each client.
3. You can find the pen on the desk *or* on the counter.
4. The driver was conscious *but* disoriented.
5. The final outcome was desirable, *yet* many participants never finished the program.

Correlative conjunctions (either . . . or, neither . . . nor, both . . . and, not only . . . but also)

1. She used *both* oil *and* water paints.

2. *Either* you finish your work today, *or* you will have to come in on Saturday.

Relative pronouns as conjunctions (who, whom, whose, which, that)

1. Dylan was the dog *that* won everyone's heart.

2. Glen is the carpenter *who* can completely transform the kitchen.

Interrogative pronouns as conjunctions (who, whom, whose, what, where, when, why, how)

1. She asked me, "*When* are you coming for a visit?"

2. Janice asked Paul *why* he is always late.

Phrases

Phrases are groups of related words that contain a subject but typically no predicate.

Verb phrases

1. He *walked.*

2. She *could not run.*

3. He *could not walk very fast.*

Noun phrases

1. *Jason* speaks clearly.

2. *A 20-year-old college junior* ran the anchor leg for *his alma mater.*

3. *Telling jokes* is Marc's specialty.

Participle phrases

1. *Speaking softly,* Lisa explained the danger of getting sunburned.

2. *Excited,* the scout troop left on its mountain hike.

Prepositional phrases

1. *When the storm was over,* we could see all the damage.

2. She bought five rocking chairs *at the festival.*

Phrases within phrases

1. *The managers with the most experience* will receive a free vacation.

2. *Most houses on our street* are painted white.

Clauses

Clauses are groups of related words that contain a subject and verb.

Independent clauses (can stand alone as a sentence)

1. *The contractor was hired* for remodeling the offices.

2. And then *a contractor was hired* for remodeling the building.

3. Next, *an architect was hired* for remodeling the entire block.

Dependent clauses (subordinate and relative)

Subordinate (begin with subordinating conjunction like *after, although, as, as if, as though, because, before, except that, even though, if, since, so that, than, that, until, unless, when, whenever, where, whereas, wherever*)

1. *Although the game was over,* several players remained on the field.

2. She received the recognition *because she saved the child's life.*

Relative (begin with a relative pronoun like *who* or *that*)

1. They know *who wrote the threatening letter.*

2. The bid *that was accepted* was from a local contractor.

Transitional Words and Phrases

Transitional words and phrases allow you to move smoothly and coherently from one sentence to another, one paragraph to another, and one section to another. Use transitional words frequently enough to make your message cohesive.

Words that express time relationships (after, again, during, every time, first, next, second, the next day, then, while)

Words that express spatial relationships (behind, in back of, inside, on the left side, on top, over, under)

Words that express relationships of likeness or similarity (also, comparable, either . . . or, likewise, neither . . . nor, similarly)

Words that express relationships or dissimilarity (but, however, in comparison, conversely, despite, nevertheless, in contrast, on the other hand, rather, unlike)

Words that express causal relationships or a result (as a result, because, consequently, hence, therefore, thus)

Words that signal an example or illustration is to follow (as, for example, for instance, namely, first, next, second, then)

Basic Sentence Patterns

The basic sentence pattern is a subject and verb. However, as shown in the various examples of the different parts of grammar, a good sentence can range from the simple to the complex.

Subject and Verb Agreement

The subject and its verb must agree in number. For example, a singular subject requires a singular verb and a plural subject requires a plural verb. Singular verbs are generally marked with an "s" or "es." The plural nouns usually have an "s" or "es."

Singular verbs

1. The owner *works.*

2. Her assistant *flies.*

Plural nouns

1. The *owners* work.

2. Her assistants *fly*.

A pronoun and its antecedent must also agree in number and in person. (The antecedent is the noun, pronoun, or noun phrase to which the pronoun refers.)

1. *Melissa* completed all *her* assignments.

2. The *children* asked *their* questions.

3. *I* found *my* wallet.

A pronoun and its antecedent must also agree in gender (male, female, or neutral). Many people now prefer using the masculine and feminine pronouns together whenever the gender of the antecedent is unknown.

1. *Each* member cast *his or her* vote.

2. *Each* member cast *his/her* vote.

3. *Members* cast *their* votes.

Numbers

Whether to use figures or spell out numbers varies among writers. However, writers tend to **spell out numbers that require only one or two words and use figures for other numbers.**

1. The theater was completed in *twenty* years.

2. John has saved *four thousand* dollars.

3. Mary won the election by *2,153* votes.

4. The building they destroyed was *158* years old.

Another guide for writing numbers is to **spell out numbers from one to ten and use figures for any number over ten. If a sentence contains a series of numbers less than and greater than ten, write all numbers in the same format.**

1. *Seven* of the crew members were involved in the incident.

2. When the play was over, *two* of the actors signed autographs.

3. More than *25* people signed the list.

4. We need *105* hot dogs for the picnic.

5. The office will need *eight, ten,* or *twelve* tables.

6. Certificates will be awarded to *45* community leaders, *12* university officials, and *7* junior achievers.

Figures in Dates

The letters *st, nd, rd,* and *th* should not be added to the day of the month.

1. The meeting is scheduled for *May 5, 2003.*

2. The performances concluded on *June 8.*

3. Thursday, *November 1,* was Jack's birthday.

Figures in Street Numbers, Book Pages, Decimals and Percentages, and Hour of Day

1. She lives at *4807 Franklin Avenue.*

2. His address is *144 Fourth Street.*

3. A reference is on *page 72.*

4. The yellow poster is *.38 of an inch* wide.

5. The city will receive *15 percent* of the profits from the sale.

6. A flight is due at *9:45 P.M.*

Figures in Series

Be consistent in spelling out or using figures. Ordinarily, you use figures for a series of numbers.

1. Rick's office was *50* feet long and *25* feet wide.

2. Her salary increased from *$1,800* to *$2,000* per month, but her monthly expenses increased from *$800* to *$1,200.*

Figures at the Beginning of a Sentence

In most cases, you should spell out any numeral at the beginning of a sentence. If possible, you may want to restructure the sentence.

1. *Forty-three* students passed the exam.

2. *One hundred and seventy-five* business executives are members of this club.

3. This club includes *175* business executives.

Numbers Spelled Out and in Parentheses

The custom of spelling out a number and repeating it in parentheses is generally reserved for legal and commercial writing. Generally, a letter or memo will not repeat a number. Smaller numbers (such as one to ten) typically are not repeated as much as larger numbers.

1. Enclosed is my payment of two hundred and fifty-one *(251)* dollars.

2. The total cost of the property is one million dollars *($1,000,000).*

Punctuation

Punctuation is used to clarify meaning. Punctuation is communicated through space on the page (e.g., margins, paragraphs, at the end of a sentence), uppercase letters, and special marks (e.g., comma, hyphen). A punctuation mark serves the same purpose in writing that a pause or gesture does in a speech.

Sentence Punctuation

Period (used to mark the end of a sentence that is a statement or a command)

1. It has rained every day.
2. Amy wondered what kind of gifts she would get for her birthday.

A period can also be used to end a sentence before a second sentence starting with a coordinating conjunction if you want to cause a sharp break for emphasis.

1. She wanted to go to the conference. However, she didn't want to go with Sheila.
2. She wanted to go to the conference; however, she didn't want to go with Sheila.

Question mark (used at the end of sentences that ask a direct question)

1. Is the meeting tomorrow?
2. He asked, "Is the meeting tomorrow?"

Question marks can also be used after one word or phrase, as in a conversation.

1. "Janice told me that Kathy and Dave are engaged."
2. "Really?"
3. "But the wedding is supposed to be in Paris."
4. "Why?"

Exclamation mark (used for emphasis, surprise, or strong emotion)

1. Yeah!
2. Bill is such a loudmouth!
3. Watch out for the car!

Comma

Main clauses joined by one of the coordinating conjunctions

1. Mr. Thomason's garden has yielded many delicious vegetables, but only the tomatoes survived this year.
2. Ten auto dealerships lined the highway, and Benson owned nine of them.

Introductory clauses preceding the main clause

1. Although I have been teaching for five years, I am still an assistant professor.
2. Generally speaking, the older teachers have more accumulated sick leave.
3. Because she was willing to help, Shanteesha received a citation.
4. Yes, everyone gave a donation to the charity.

Items in a series (comma before the conjunction is sometimes omitted)

1. Her favorite colors are red, white, and blue.
2. He wore a blue shirt, black slacks, green socks, and brown shoes.
3. The horse ran out of the barn, across the field, and into the forest.

Nonrestrictive clauses and other parenthetical elements

1. "The game is over," he said.
2. "Your main problem," she said, "is your attitude."
3. Clyde's jet boat, parked in the garage, is royal blue and white.
4. Lori, the hostess, is extremely friendly.

Items in titles, dates, and addresses

1. My co-workers include James Logan, Ph.D., and Dinah Payne, Esq.
2. The speakers were Bill Eckert, Jr., Jaime Rush, and Jim Stone.
3. On August 9, 2001, the O'Connors got married.
4. The winter conference is scheduled for December 2003.
5. David moved to 4051 Campo Street, Albany, NY 12208, two months ago.
6. The 2002 ABC Convention was held in Cincinnati, Ohio, at the Hyatt Regency.

Semicolon (used like a comma when it separates elements within a sentence and like a period when it separates independent clauses)

Separating independent clauses

1. Tim began his training this week; other team members had been training for the past three weeks.
2. Pet Perfect Veterinary Clinic has been sheltering animals for 25 years; it is the oldest clinic in Sacramento.

Long clauses and clauses containing commas

1. Students were instructed to bring pencils, paper, and crayons for the class assignment; the teacher would bring the scissors.
2. The student assistants wanted more flexible hours; however, with the reduction of teachers, the grading load was excessive.
3. Sharon played the piano; Joe, the clarinet; Bill, the trumpet; and Joyce, the violin.

Colon

Between independent clauses

1. The accident caused major damage to the car: the radiator was cracked, the front bumper was destroyed, and the headlight was broken.
2. Mary Lee will always remember what the teacher said: "You are the only one who got an A!"

Before lists

1. The majority of his order was personal care items: soap, shampoo, conditioner, and aftershave.
2. Once the order was complete, she still had to perform more tasks: check for duplicates, combine products to make cases, and check the number of items ordered.

Other uses (in a title, to separate hours and minutes, and in Bible citations)

1. Alfonzo gave a book report on *Free Enterprise: How to Start a Business of Your Own.*
2. Erin's plane left Atlanta at 7:30 A.M. and should arrive in New Orleans at 1:05 P.M.
3. The pastor reminded the youngsters to read Isaiah 2:1–5 and John 3:16 before the next service.

Dashes and parentheses

Sometimes dashes are used like commas and parentheses and sometimes they are used like colons. A dash is used to set off elements within a sentence. A hyphen is used to break words at the end of a line or to join compound words. When you want to deemphasize nonrestrictive modifiers, use parentheses.

Hyphens (use the hyphen key with no space before or after)

1. Stacey received the first-place trophy.
2. Brooke realized she had a one-of-a-kind end table.
3. Anyone living in a large city, such as Chicago, knows that transportation can be a challenge.
4. Nancy wanted to re-cover the sofa.
5. J. Alice Jones is the governor-elect.

Dashes (strike the hyphen key twice with no space before or after)

1. When words or phrases are combined into clauses and sentences, the inflections of nouns, verbs, and pronouns must all be consistent—that is, in agreement with one another.
2. You should assemble the documentation for your paper—at least in preliminary form—no later than when you complete your first draft.

Parentheses

1. Her coat (a hand-me-down from her sister) was bright blue.
2. The CDPHP (Capital District Physician's Health Plan) has many members.

Apostrophes

An apostrophe may be used to form a contraction, show possession, or form a plural.

Contraction

1. After paying all the bills, Jack and Pam couldn't afford to eat out.
2. Abramson's the best school.
3. It's the only solution to our problem.
4. They've agreed to attend the function.

Possession

1. Susan's business was growing at a rapid pace.
2. The road was as crooked as a dog's hind leg.
3. Amy was looking for a children's book.
4. Adam was the child's teacher.
5. There goes the Joneses' daughter.
6. Please use the women's dressing room.
7. The family's home was destroyed.
8. All the families' homes were painted the same color.

Plural

1. The patterns come in 8's or 10's.
2. Only 37 students received their MBA's.
3. Five students were awarded their GED's.

Underlining and italics

Use an underline or italics for the titles of newspapers, magazines, books, pamphlets, and everything that is published as a separate work. Use quotation marks for parts of the larger work.

1. <u>The Times Union</u>   *The Times Union*
2. <u>Fortune</u>   *Fortune*
3. <u>Crime and Punishment</u>   *Crime and Punishment*
4. <u>Understanding Your Environment</u>   *Understanding Your Environment*

Other media (films, television and radio programs, works of art, major musical works, and record albums, cassettes, or CDs) are also underlined or italicized.

Well-known vehicles—ships, aircraft, trains, and race cars—should also be underlined or italicized.

Foreign words and phrases are also underlined or italicized.

Use an underline or italics for emphasis.

1. The end result is <u>total</u> freedom.
2. I will *not* vote for Tony.

Quotation marks

Use quotation marks when quoting words from another source or to show parts of published books and music.
Periods and commas *always* go before the closing quotation mark.
1. Kim heard Kevin say, "That's it."
2. "No," she said, "children under five are not allowed."

Colons and semicolons *always* go outside quotation marks.

1. "Come one, come all"; was this statement attributed to a circus act?
2. "Only authorized personnel allowed": does this mean adults, too?

Other punctuation marks are placed inside or outside the quotation mark, depending upon whether they are a part of the quoted material.

1. "Do I have to take a bath?" Liza asked.
2. Did Liza ask, "Do I have to take a bath"?
3. "Don't take that report!" shouted Steve.
4. The security guard yelled, "Stop, or I'll shoot!"

Single quotation marks set off quotations within quotations.

1. The leader said, "Scouts, do not shout 'I know' until you have the complete answer."
2. "One of the contestants told the audience, 'I will win' before the game even began," said Marilyn.

Ellipses and brackets

Both are used when a writer alters quoted material for some reason.

Ellipses (made with three spaced periods) show that something has been omitted.

1. "Each author needs to prepare any questions . . . if appropriate."
2. The authors were told to "prepare any questions they want to discuss during the conference call. . . ."

Brackets show an inserted editorial comment.

1. According to the sign, "All children [not adults] are admitted free."
2. Once the decision was made, they [Josh and Barbara] bought their tickets.

Capitalization

Sentences and titles

The first word of each sentence and the beginning word of each line of poetry begin with a capital letter.

A full sentence that follows a colon may begin with a capital letter—especially if you want to show emphasis.

1. Pay attention to these directions: First you clean the desk; then you paint it.
2. He was careful to make the following point: Most of you are un-educated on the latest office technology.

Always capitalize the personal pronoun *I*.

1. Somehow, I always arrive late for the meeting.
2. How could I tell them that I forgot the deposit?

Proper nouns (names of persons, places, organizations, and groups)
1. Several of the participants went shopping at The Commons.
2. Susan, Yuriy, and I went to the convention.

3. Over 400 attended the Association for Business Communication Conference this year.

4. The company's retreat will be in Spartanburg, South Carolina, next year.

All capital letters may be used for titles of newspapers, magazines, books, pamphlets, and everything that is published as a separate work (or underlines or italics may be used).

THE TIMES UNION

FORTUNE

CRIME AND PUNISHMENT

UNDERSTANDING YOUR ENVIRONMENT

Abbreviations

Titles and forms of address (almost always used in front of a name)

1. Mr., Ms., Dr., Prof., St., Hon., and Gen.

Do not abbreviate the words *company, corporation,* or *incorporated* or use an ampersand (&) unless the official company title is written that way.

Acronyms are words that have been made out of abbreviations (NATO, OSHA, SIDS, etc.).

Spelling Guidelines

Misspelled and misused words can cause problems for the writer. However, following some basic spelling guidelines will help you determine the correct spelling and usage of words.

Routine Spelling Patterns

ie and *ei*

If the vowel rhymes with *be,* write *i* before *e* except after *c.*

ie:

believe	pierce
chief	relief
field	thief
grief	wield
niece	yield

ei:

ceiling	perceive
conceit	receive
conceive	receipt
deceive	

ie exceptions:

financier	glacier

ei exceptions:

caffeine	protein
either	seize
leisure	weird
neither	

If the vowel sounds rhyme with *say,* write *e* before *i.*

beige	sleigh
eight	veil
freight	vein
neighbor	weigh
reign	

If the vowel sounds are neither *ee* nor *ay,* the *e* comes before the *i.*

ei:

counterfeit	heifer
fahrenheit	height
forfeit	heir
foreign	stein

Exceptions:

friend	mischief

Final *e* before a Suffix

Before adding a suffix that begins with a vowel, drop the final silent *e.*
Keep the *e* when the suffix begins with a consonant.

excite	exciting, excitable	excitement
guide	guidance, guided	guidebook
like	likable, liking (likeable is also acceptable)	likely
probable	probably	
love	loving, lovable	lovely
use	usable, usually	useful

The final *e* may also be dropped with suffixes *-dom, -ful, -ly, -ment,*
and *-y.*

wise	wisdom
awe	awful
due	duly
true	truly
whole	wholly
argue	argument
judge	judgment
acknowledge	acknowledgment

If the preceding consonant is a soft *c* or *g* (sounds like "s" or "j"), the *e* is usually kept; a silent *e* is usually dropped before *i*.

change	changeable	changing
notice	noticeable	noticing
revenge	vengeance	revenging
advantage	advantageous	
courage	courageous	
marriage	marriageable	
outrage	outrageous	
service	serviceable	servicing

Some other words retain the *e* before a vowel.

acre	acreage
dye	dyeing (die/dying)
here	herein
hoe	hoeing
line	lineage
mile	mileage
shoe	shoeing
singe	singeing
there	therein

Changing *y* to *i*

When a word ends in a consonant followed by *y*, change the *y* to *i* before adding a suffix beginning with any letter *except i*.

apply	applied	applying
carry	carried, carries	carrying
cry	cried, cries	crying
defy	defiance	defying
forty	fortieth	
happy	happiness	
lovely	lovelier, loveliest	
ninety	ninetieth	
party	parties, partied	partying
study	studies, studied	studying

If the vowel precedes the *y*, keep it.

day	days
dismay	dismayed
joy	joyful
lay	layperson
pay	payment
play	player

Exceptions that keep the *y*:

baby	babyhood
lady	ladylike
shy	shyness

Doubling Final Consonants

If the final consonant follows a single vowel, double the final consonant before adding a suffix.

drag	dragged
hid	hidden
kid	kidded, kidding
sit	sitting
wrap	wrapped, wrapping

If the final consonant ends on an accented syllable, double the final consonant before adding a suffix.

abhor	abhorred
admit	admitted
begin	beginning
occur	occurring
regret	regrettable

When more than one vowel precedes the final consonant, do not double the consonant.

appear	appeared
rain	raining
feed	feeding
kneel	kneeling

When the last syllable is not accented, do not double the consonant.

consider	considered
reckon	reckoned

Exception: benefit, benefited, or benefitted

The accent shifts in some words when a suffix is added.

confer	conferring	conference
defer	deferred	deference
infer	inferring	inference
prefer	preferring	preference
refer	referring	reference

When a word ends in two consonants, the last consonant should not be doubled.

insist	insistent
turn	turned, turning

Exception: question, questionnaire

Doubled Letters with Prefixes and Suffixes

When a prefix ends in the same letter the word begins with, or if a suffix begins with the same letter the word ends with, do not drop one of the doubled letters.

bookkeeper	preeminent
cleanness	unnecessary
dissatisfied	woolly
misspelled	

-able and -ible Suffixes

If the root of a word is itself an independent word or complete except for the dropped final *e,* the suffix will usually be spelled with *-able.*

acceptable	believable
comfortable	likable
profitable	sizable
taxable	

Some words use the *-able* suffix because they were originally independent words before the final syllable was dropped.

irritate	irritable
separate	separable (inseparable)
tolerate	tolerable (intolerable)

If the root of a word does not exist as an independent word, the ending is usually *-ible.*

compatible	edible
credible	visible

Exception: capable

If the root word ends in a double consonant that includes at least one *s* or is pronounced like "s," the ending is usually *-ible* (even if the double consonant is followed by a silent *e* that is dropped).

collapse	collapsible
defense	defensible
response	responsible
resist	resistible
admiss	admissible
permiss	permissible
transmiss	transmissible
flex	flexible

Some words are exceptions to all *-able* and *-ible* patterns.

gullible	durable
discernible	flammable
formidable	

Distinguishing *-ally* and *-ly*

The *-ly* suffix is usually added to adjectives to form adverbs.

fair	fairly
usual	usually
swift	swiftly
sincere	sincerely

The *-ally* suffix is usually added to adjectives ending in *ic* to form adverbs.

academic	academically
basic	basically
scientific	scientifically

Exception: public, publicly

Plural and Present-Tense *s* and *es* Endings

The ending for plural nouns and the third-person singular present tense of the verb is usually *s*.

table	tables
cookie	cookies
speak	he speaks
move	he moves

Add an *es* to a noun or verb that ends in *ch, s, sh, x,* or *z* when the *s* ending would be difficult to pronounce.

church	churches
kiss	kisses
wish	wishes
box	boxes
buzz	buzzes
latch	she latches
pass	he passes
fish	she fishes
fix	she fixes

Words that end in *o* are made plural by adding *s* or *es*.

auto	autos
memo	memos
piano	pianos
buffalo	buffaloes
echo	echoes
hero	heroes
mosquito	mosquitoes
potato	potatoes
tomato	tomatoes

veto	vetoes	
motto	mottos	mottoes
no	nos	noes
zero	zeros	zeroes

Frequently Confused Words (homonyms)

accept	verb—to take
except	verb—to leave out
access	noun—a way in
excess	noun—too much
addition	noun—increase
edition	noun—issue of a book
adapt	verb—to adjust
adept	adjective—skilled
adopt	verb—to take as one's own
advice	noun—guidance
advise	verb—to guide
affect	verb—to influence; noun—an emotion
effect	verb—to bring about; noun—result
aid	noun—help
aide	noun—helper, assistant
aisle	noun—a space between rows
isle	noun—island
alley	noun—a back street
ally	noun—a supporter
allude	verb—to refer
elude	verb—to avoid
allusion	noun—reference
illusion	noun—mistaken belief
already	adverb—previously
all ready	pronoun/adverb—everyone prepared
altar	noun—table, place of sacrifice
alter	verb—to change
altogether	adverb—completely
all together	pronoun/adverb—everyone (or everything) in one place
angel	noun—supernatural messenger
angle	noun—corner
appraise	verb—to determine the worth of
apprise	verb—to inform
arc	noun—curve

ark	noun—boat
ascent	noun—rise
assent	noun—agreement; verb—to agree
assistance	noun—help
assistants	noun—helpers (plural of *assistant*)
bazaar	noun—fair
bizarre	adjective—strange
bare	adjective—naked
bear	noun—animal; verb—to carry
birth	noun—to be born
berth	noun—sleeping place
board	noun—piece of wood; noun—food (as in *room and board*)
bored	adjective—uninterested
born	adjective—alive
borne	adjective/verb—carried
breath	noun—air taken in through the lungs
breathe	verb—to take in air
canvas	noun—cloth
canvass	verb—to poll
capital	adjective—uppercase or major
	noun—top of an architectural column
	noun—wealth, net worth
	noun—major city or seat of government
capitol	noun—building that houses a state or national government
censor	verb—to not allow
censure	noun—condemnation; verb—to criticize
choose	verb—to pick
chose	verb—picked, past tense of *choose*
cite	verb—to acknowledge or point out
site	noun—a place; verb—to locate
sight	noun—ability to see
coarse	adjective—not fine
course	noun—path or unit of study; verb—to move swiftly through
complement	noun—completer; verb—to provide balance
compliment	noun—flattery; verb—to flatter
conscience	noun—inner sense of right and wrong
conscious	adjective—aware
corps	noun—military group

corpse	noun—dead body
council	noun—legislative body
counsel	noun—advice; verb—advise or give advice
dam	noun—barrier to hold back water
damn	verb—to consign to hell
defer	verb—to put off
differ	verb—to disagree
deference	noun—respect, yielding
difference	noun—lack of similarity
descent	noun—the way downward
dissent	noun—disagreement
desert	verb—to leave; noun—dry land
dessert	noun—sweet course at the end of a meal
device	noun—a machine or implement for getting something done
devise	verb—to create or think up
dully	adverb—in a boring manner
duly	adverb—in a proper manner
dyeing	verb—coloring
dying	verb—losing life
envelop	verb—to enclose
envelope	noun—enclosure for a letter
fair	adjective—objective or pale
fare	noun—food or entrance money
formerly	adverb—before
formally	adverb—not casually
forth	adjective—forward, ahead
fourth	adjective—the number four item
gorilla	noun—jungle animal
guerilla	noun—soldier who surprises enemy
gild	verb—to cover with gold
guild	noun—organization of craftspeople
hear	verb—listen and understand
here	adverb—in this place
heard	verb—past tense of *hear*
herd	noun—group of animals
hole	noun—gap
whole	adjective—in one piece
holy	adjective—sacred
wholly	adjective—completely

incidence	noun—frequency of an occurrence
incidents	noun—occurrences or happenings
its	pronoun—possessive of *it*
it's	pronoun/verb—contraction of *it is*
later	adverb—after a while
latter	adjective—last mentioned
lead	noun—metal
led	verb—past tense of *lead* (meaning "to guide")
lesson	noun—something to learn
lessen	verb—to cause to be less
lightning	noun—electricity caused by a storm
lightening	verb—making lighter
lose	verb—to misplace
loose	adjective—not tight
maybe	adverb—perhaps
may be	verb—might be
miner	noun—one who works in a mine
minor	adjective—small or insignificant; noun—someone underage
moral	adjective—good; noun—lesson
morale	noun—state of mind
passed	verb—past tense of *pass*
past	adjective—previous
patience	noun—quality of being patient
patients	noun—persons undergoing treatment
peace	noun—absence of war
piece	noun—part or section
personal	adjective—intimate
personnel	noun—employees; adjective—pertaining to employees
plain	adjective—without decoration
plane	noun—surface or aircraft; verb—to shave off wood
precede	verb—to go before
proceed	verb—to continue
presence	noun—state of being present
presents	noun—gifts
principle	noun—moral conviction
principal	adjective—major; noun—head of a school
prophecy	noun—prediction
prophesy	verb—to make a prediction

purpose	noun—aim
propose	verb—to suggest
quiet	adjective—silent
quit	verb—to stop
quite	adverb—very
respectfully	adverb—with respect
respectively	adverb—in the order given
right	adjective—correct
rite	noun—ceremony
stationary	adjective—not moving
stationery	noun—paper for writing letters
statue	noun—sculpture
stature	noun—height or influence
statute	noun—law
straight	adjective—without curves
strait	noun—narrow passage, especially in water
taut	adjective—tight
taught	verb—past tense of *teach*
taunt	verb—to tease
than	preposition—besides; conjunction—as
then	adverb—at that time
their	pronoun—possessive form of *they*
there	adverb—in that place
they're	pronoun/verb—contraction of *they are*
through	preposition—in and out; adjective—finished
thru	informal preposition—not preferred usage
thorough	adjective—complete
to	preposition—toward
too	adjective or adverb—also
two	adjective—one plus one
track	noun—course or road
tract	noun—pamphlet
weather	noun—atmospheric conditions
whether	conjunction—if
wear	verb—to have clothes on
were	verb—past tense of *be*
we're	pronoun/verb—contraction of *we are*
where	adverb or conjunction—in what place
who's	pronoun/verb—contraction of *who is*
whose	pronoun—possessive form of *who*

your   pronoun—possessive form of *you*
you're   pronoun/verb—contraction of *you are*

Frequently Misspelled Words

Some of the most frequently misspelled words (notice that some are also frequently confused words) follow:

1. accommodate	35. interest	68. professor
2. achievement	36. its (it's)	69. prominent
3. acquire	37. led	70. pursue
4. all right	38. lose	71. quiet
5. among	39. losing	72. receive
6. apparent	40. marriage	73. receiving
7. arguing	41. mere	74. recommend
8. argument	42. necessary	75. referring
9. belief	43. occasion	76. repetition
10. believe	44. occurred	77. rhythm
11. beneficial	45. occurrence	78. sense
12. benefited	46. occurring	79. separate
13. category	47. opinion	80. separation
14. coming	48. opportunity	81. shining
15. comparative	49. paid	82. similar
16. conscious	50. particular	83. studying
17. controversial	51. performance	84. succeed
18. controversy	52. personal	85. succession
19. definite	53. personnel	86. surprise
20. definitely	54. possession	87. technique
21. definition	55. possible	88. than
22. describe	56. practical	89. their
23. description	57. precede	90. then
24. disastrous	58. prejudice	91. there
25. effect	59. prepare	92. they're
26. embarrass	60. prevalent	93. thorough
27. environment	61. principal	94. to, too, two
28. exaggerate	62. principle	95. transferred
29. existence	63. privilege	96. unnecessary
30. existent	64. probably	97. villain
31. experience	65. procedure	98. woman
32. explanation	66. proceed	99. write
33. fascinate	67. profession	100. writing
34. height		

Basic Word Division Guides

The following guidelines for word division are among the most widely accepted.

1. Sometimes the most acceptable point for dividing a word is a matter of opinion; however, enough of the word should appear on the first line to identify the entire word. The division should allow for a significant part of the word to appear on each line. An important factor to consider is the word pronunciation.

2. Divide words only between syllables. Words with only one syllable (such as *pulled, front,* and *fused*) should not be divided.

3. When dividing a word, put at least two letters on the first line (*interest*, not *i-tinerary*) and put at least three letters on the second line (*greet-ing*, not *great-er*). Even though it is acceptable to have two letters at the beginning of the word division, it is not preferred.

4. Never divide a word of five or fewer letters (such as *diet, depot,* and *lemon*). Avoid dividing words of six letters, too. Six-letter words such as *dismal* (*dis-mal*) and *girdle* (*gir-dle*) look better undivided.

5. If adding a suffix to a word generates a double consonant, divide the word between the two consonants (for example, *clip-ping*, not *clipp-ing; control-ling*, not *controll-ing;* and *tag-ging*, not *tagg-ing*). But if the root word ends in a double consonant, divide the word between the root word and the suffix (for example, *roll-ing*, not *rolling; recess-ing*, not *reces-sing;* and *thrill-ing*, not *thril-ling*).

6. Divide compound words that do not contain hyphens between the elements of the compound (for example, *key-punching*, not *keypunching*). If the compound word has a hyphen, divide only at the point of the existing hyphen (for example, *self-reliance*, not *self-reli-ance*).

7. Single-vowel syllables within a word should be written with the first part of the word (for example, *formu-late*, not *form-ulate*). The exceptions to the general rule are:

   a. Join a single-vowel syllable to the last part of the word if the word ends in a two-letter syllable (for example, *ingenu-ity* and *normal-ity*).

   b. Join single-vowel syllables *a, i,* or *u* to the final syllables *ble, bly, cle,* or *cal* (for example, *expand-able, invari-ably, chron-icle,* and *iron-ical*).

8. Divide a name, date, or address at the logical point for readability:
   Name:
   Ms. Caroline/Gardner, not Ms./Caroline Gardner
   Jack/O'Connor, Ph.D, not Jack O'Connor/Ph.D
   Date:
   February 14,/20xx not February/14, 20xx
   Address (divide between the city and state):
   New Orleans,/LA 70148, not New Orleans, LA/70148

9. Refrain from dividing figures, abbreviations, and signs representing words or abbreviations:

   Figures:

   $600,000, not $600,/000

   Abbreviations:

   CDPHP, Not CDP/HP

   Signs representing words or abbreviations:

   #66866, not #/66866; 11 in., not 11/in.

10. Minimize word division. Avoid dividing words at the end of more than two consecutive lines. In addition, avoid dividing the last word of a paragraph or page.

Proofreader's Marks

Some of the most frequently used proofreader's marks are shown in Figure A.1. Proofreader's marks are standardized symbols used for text editing. These marks identify changes needed before the final copy is printed, and they guide the person editing the document by indicating the corrections, deletions, and additions. It may be helpful to use a different color of ink (red or green rather than blue or black) so the marks can more easily be seen. For more examples and details concerning these English grammar and related concepts, consult a dictionary and/or an English handbook.

FIGURE A.1

**Frequently Used
Proofreader Marks**

add/insert space	The computer operator was extremely efficient.
align type	Pens 3 doz. Pencils 5 doz.
capitalize	Bill caldwell teaches the law class.
change copy as indicated	Monday your office will be painted.
close up	Too many space s can cause problems.
delete	Our consulting firmm is busy.
delete and close up	There was an error in document transmisssion.
double-space	Sincerely yours DS DOBE INTERNATIONAL
ignore the correction	In the ~~international~~ market, distribution is the key.
insert apostrophe	The position is for Don's marketing assistant.
insert comma	Lena Mary Lee's mother, is a design specialist.
insert period	You should remember that everyone has a dream
lower	Accounting Trainee
lowercase	Remembering All Names can be difficult.
move copy as indicated	Changes will be made after the order is received.
move right	Once the changes have been made, we can leave.
move left	What are advantages of the change?
new paragraph	¶ First, you must be willing to help others.
quadruple-space	Yours truly QS Betsy Short
raise	February 14, 20 - -
single-space	Dr. Homer Watts SS Veterinarian
spell out	SP ⑩ trainees will attend the workshop.
transpose	At times, your moves mind faster than your fingres.
triple-space	Subject: How to Create Wealth TS A dynamic seminar on creating wealth for you and your entire family. . .
underline	Who Stole the American Dream sold out!

Formatting and Documenting Business Documents

Just as your appearance is important to consider when going on an interview, the appearance or "packaging" of business documents is also important. Since business correspondence may be the only contact you have with your customers and clients, it is imperative that a document's appearance makes a positive impression. Appearance characteristics often go unnoticed unless "noise" attracts the reader's attention. Noise might consist of inferior paper quality; ineffective stationery design; or typing, formatting and documenting errors. To help prevent inaccurate typing and formatting and documenting errors, we will study the guidelines to follow when formatting and documenting business documents.

Formatting Business Documents

The following formatting guidelines should be followed when preparing business letters, memorandums, and reports.

Letters

The generally accepted guidelines to follow when preparing business letters involve letter styles, letter punctuation styles, letter placement, and letter parts.

Letter Styles

Letters can be arranged in four format styles—the block style, the modified block style with block paragraphs, the modified block style with indented paragraphs, and the simplified style.

- The block letter style is popular in businesses because it saves typing time. In the block letter style, all paragraphs begin at the left margin (see Exhibit B.1).

- In the modified block letter styles, the dateline, the complimentary close, and the signature block begin at the center of the writing line (between the left and right margins). The *modified block style with block paragraphs* (see Exhibit B.2) begins all other lines at the left margin, whereas the *modified block style with indented paragraphs* (see Exhibit B.3) begins all other lines at the left margin except that each paragraph is indented five spaces (or one-half inch with proportional fonts).

Appendix B

EXHIBIT B.1

**Block Letter Style with
Mixed Punctuation**

January 1, 2003

Ms. Tiffany Luse, Office Manager
Thompson and Council, Inc.
1350 First Avenue
Boston, MA 02129

Dear Ms. Luse:

SUBJECT: BLOCK LETTER STYLE USE

As shown in this letter, the full block letter style is quite simple to
follow and has become one of the most widely used letter-style
arrangements.

Time is saved since standard default word-processing format
settings are used and tab keystrokes are eliminated. The paragraphs
are blocked and begin at the left margin. Also, the date, inside
address, salutation, and closing lines all begin at the left margin.

Another time-saving feature, as illustrated in this letter, that can be used
with the block letter style is mixed punctuation. When using mixed
punctuation, use a colon after the recipient's name and after the close.

Since the block letter style is a widely adopted letter style, its usage
will convey a modern and attractive appearance while saving time
and money. I heartily recommend this style as being the most
suitable style for your office needs.

Sincerely,

Tracy N. Johnston

Tracy N. Johnston
President

- As in the block style, all lines of the letter in the **simplified letter style** (see Exhibit B.4) begin at the left margin. However, two letter parts—the salutation and complimentary close—are omitted from the simplified style, and one letter part—the subject line—is *always* included. The subject line is usually typed in all capital letters for emphasis and always omits the word *SUBJECT.*

Letter Punctuation Styles

The punctuation styles that can be used in the block and modified block styles are the open and mixed styles. When using the open punctuation style, punctuation is omitted after the salutation and complimentary close (see again Exhibit B.2). Mixed punctuation, the most

March 15, 2003

Latisha Harris, Coordinator
Twin City Supply Company
P O Box 1560
Cincinnati OH 45238

Dear Ms. Harris

The modified block letter style has traditionally been a popular letter style and has some distinctive features as shown in this example.

The date, complimentary close, and signature block, including the company name (if used), writer's/sender's name, and writer's/sender's identification, begin at the horizontal center of the page. Place these letter parts at the center point by tabbing to this position.

All other letter parts are placed at the left margin. The modified block style may be typed with blocked paragraphs, as shown in this letter, or with indented paragraphs. This letter has open punctuation. When using open punctuation, no punctuation is placed after the salutation and close.

Both of the modified block letter styles have traditionally been popular in formatting business letters.

Sincerely

SMITH & LYONS, INCORPORATED

Brandon E. Luse

Brandon E. Luse, Director

Enclosure

EXHIBIT B.2

Modified Block Style with Blocked Paragraphs and Open Punctuation

commonly used punctuation style, requires a colon after the salutation and a comma after the complimentary close (see Exhibits B.1 and B.3). Since the salutation and complimentary close are omitted from the simplified style (see Exhibit B.4), you need not be concerned about the punctuation style with this letter style.

Letter Placement

The goal of letter placement is the creation of a visually appealing impression. Traditionally, the length of a letter determined where a letter was placed on a page to achieve a "picture-frame image" (making use of the margin's white space to achieve a picture-frame effect). Today, because of the increased emphasis on efficiency and the use of

EXHIBIT B.3

**Modified Block Style with
Indented Paragraphs**

June 24, 2003
1333 Evers Avenue
Redlands, CA 92373

Ms. Amy Pulliam, Owner
Pulliam Enterprises
5670 First Street
Hinsdale, Il 60521

Dear Ms. Pulliam:

As shown in this example, a popular letter style is the modified block with indented paragraphs.

In both modified block styles, the date, complimentary close, and signature block are begun at the horizontal center of the page. However, as illustrated here, the paragraphs may be indented five spaces or 1/2 inch. All other letter parts are placed at the left margin.

Traditionally, this letter style has been quite popular, and it continues to be used by many businesses.

Sincerely,

E. L. Walton

Mr. E. L. Walton

word-processing software, most businesses use the margins set by default by the software. Generally, typed business letters have at least 1- to 1.25-inch side and bottom margins.

Because letterhead stationery is normally used in preparing business letters, the date is usually placed two to three lines below the letterhead; however, for shorter letters, the date could be placed up to six lines below the letterhead. If letterhead stationery is not used, the top margin is usually one to two inches, depending on the length of the letter. The "center page" feature on word-processing software can also be used to vertically center the letter.

August 5, 2003

Ms. Pat Neffenger
Office Manager
SQL Office Products
650 North Street
Fullerton, CA 92631-6111

SIMPLIFIED BLOCK LETTER STYLE FORMAT

The simplified block letter style is quite different from the traditional block and modified block letter styles. Since it was designed to improve keying efficiency and remove outdated salutations and complimentary closings, it has become a popular letter style.

When using the simplified block style, all letter parts and paragraphs begin at the left margin. The inside address may be keyed in the traditional style of lowercase with initial caps, or it may be keyed in ALL CAPS with no punctuation to show through a window envelope. The signature block may also be keyed in all caps.

The three main differences between this style and traditional styles are

1. The salutation is omitted.

2. The complimentary close is omitted.

3. A subject line is always included without including the word *subject*. The subject line is usually keyed in ALL CAPS for emphasis.

Although the salutation is omitted, if you would like to personalize your letter, you may begin the letter with the reader's name.

Because this letter style is so simple to use, many companies have adopted it as their standardized letter format.

Gary Luse

GARY LUSE, TRAINING SUPERVISOR

Letter Parts

As shown in Exhibit B.5, some letter parts are required and should always be included in business letters, while other letter parts are optional. Required and optional letter parts are discussed next in the order in which they are placed in a business letter. In this discussion, required letter parts are boldfaced and elective letter parts are italicized.

- **Letterhead or return address.** Either the letterhead or return address is a required letter part since they contain information about how to contact the writer if needed. Letterhead stationery provides the company's name, address, telephone number, e-mail address, and other descriptive company information. If letterhead stationery is not

	Required Letter Parts	Elective Letter Parts
Heading:	Letterhead or return address data	Mailing/special notations Second-page heading
Opening:	Inside address Salutation (not used in simplified)	Attention line
Body:	Message	Subject/reference line (required in simplified)
Closing:	Complimentary close (not used in simplified) Signature block: —Writer's/sender's name —Writer's/sender"s identification	Company name Reference notation Enclosure notation Copy notation Postscript

used, as when writing a personal business letter (see Exhibit B.6), the writer should include his or her address immediately preceding the date. A technique growing in popularity is the insertion of the telephone number after the address and before the date. Of course, if you are using word-processing software and have a laser printer, you could create your own personal, professional-looking letterhead.

- **Date.** The date on which a letter is typed is a required letter part and should be typed in the order of month (spelled out), day (written in figures and followed by a comma), and year (complete year written in figures). If mailing letters to companies outside the United States or the U.S. military, you may follow their practice of placing the date in the order of day, month, and year. The date is typed at the left margin in the block and simplified styles but at the center point in the modified block letter styles. As discussed earlier, the date is usually typed two or three lines below the letterhead. If letterhead stationery is not used, the date is typed on the line after the city, state, and zip code of the return address.

- *Mailing/special notations.* Mailing or special notations are elective letter parts and are used if a letter is to be mailed or delivered in some method other than first-class mail or is special in some other way (such as personal or confidential). Besides keying this notation on the envelope, you should also type this information on the letter since envelopes are often discarded. The notation should be typed in all capital letters and either placed a double space after the date or centered between the date and the inside address. Examples of special business letter mailing or delivery notations are SPECIAL DELIVERY, REGISTERED, CERTIFIED, FEDERAL EXPRESS, and FAX: (include fax number). Examples of special personal notations are PERSONAL, CONFIDENTIAL, PLEASE FORWARD, and HOLD FOR ARRIVAL.

P.O. Box 123, NLU
Monroe, LA 71209
June 4, 2003

Mr. John Brown, Manager
XYZ Corporation
1650 Logstram Road
Monroe, LA 71203

Dear Mr. Brown:

Here is an example of the format you should use when writing a personal business letter.

You should use plain paper when writing a personal business letter, not company letterhead. Examples of this type of letter are when you want to write a letter to ask about home insurance, to make a complaint about some matter, to inquire about land for sale, or to seek employment.

A personal business letter requires a return address block consisting of the street or post office box number; city, state, zip; and the date. With the zip code, the state is written with a two-letter abbreviation in ALL CAPS with no period following.

The inclusion of the return address block is the only format difference between the personal business letter and the letter format of any other business letter. Therefore, after typing the return address block, you would type the inside address, salutation, body, complimentary close, and typed signature line. Of course, if additional letter parts are needed, you can include them.

Please use this format when writing personal business letters.

Sincerely,

S. Aulds

Susan Aulds

- *Attention line.* Another elective letter part is the attention line. When a letter is written to a company but the sender feels it should be routed to a particular person or supervisor, then an attention line is included as the first line in the inside address. An attention line signifies that the letter pertains to company business. The sender prefers that the individual listed or the person holding the position listed in the attention line deal with the letter's contents. Since the letter is still being written to a company, as indicated in the inside address, the salutation should agree with the inside address (the company) rather than the attention line. If used, the attention line is the first line in the inside address and is keyed in four lines below the date or two lines below the mailing/special notation.

EXHIBIT B.7

Mailing Information

Line 1	Recipient's name and job title or attention line
Line 2	Recipient's job title (if not included on Line 1)
Line 3	Recipient's department (if needed)
Line 4	Organization's name
Line 5	Delivery address
Line 6	City, state, and zip code
Line 7	Name of country if being sent abroad (if used, one of the above lines should be omitted)

- **Inside address.** The inside address, a required letter part, provides essential delivery information by indicating the complete mailing address of the person to whom the letter is going. The inside address should consist of only three to six lines of delivery information; the length of each line should not extend past the center point of the paper. The order in which the recipient's mailing information should be presented, from smallest delivery unit to largest delivery unit, is shown in Exhibit B.7.

  If the sender knows the name of the person who should handle the letter, then the recipient's name (including a courtesy title, first name or initials, and last name) is placed on the first line of the inside address. The recipient's job title can be included on either the first line (preceded by a comma to separate name and job title) or the second. Line length and appearance determine where the job title should be located. If other descriptive recipient information is presented, such as a recipient's department, it appears next. The company for which the recipient works would be the next delivery unit listed. On the next line, the business mailing address is included; the last line contains the city, state (using two-letter abbreviation in all caps), and zip code. The name of a country is used only if a letter is being mailed abroad.

  If a letter is being sent to a company rather than to an individual, a specific recipient's name and job title are omitted or an attention line is included. The attention line can be directed to a position (such as Attention Director of Marketing) or a department (such as Attention Marketing Department).

  In the past, the inside address was typed using initial caps (upper/lowercase). Today, because so many companies use window envelopes and/or mail merge capabilities of word-processing software, the inside address may be typed following the U.S. Postal Service's envelope addressing requirements (to be discussed shortly)—that is, in all caps with no punctuation. This way, a sender can fold the letter so that the inside address shows through the window envelope. If mail merge is used, the inside address could be keyed in all caps with no punctuation so that only one secondary merge file/document would have to be keyed and used.

- **Salutation.** The salutation, a required letter part in the block and modified block letter styles (omitted in simplified style), is typed at the left margin a double space below the inside address and is determined by information provided in the inside address. If the business letter is written to a specific person, that person's last name is placed in the salutation preceded by the word "Dear" and a courtesy title (Mr. or Ms.): for example, "Dear Ms. Jones." If the sender is on a first-name basis with the recipient, a first name may be used: for example, "Dear Joe."

  A salutation may also address a position, such as "Dear Customer Service Representative."

- *Subject/reference line.* A subject/reference line is always used in the simplified letter style but is an elective letter part for the block and modified block letter styles. The subject line, placed a double space below the salutation (at the left margin or centered, depending on letter style), is used to let the reader know what the letter is about or to make filing easier. The word "Subject" or the abbreviation "Re:" may or may not precede the subject information; however, these words are never used in the simplified letter style. The subject line may be placed in all caps or underscored for emphasis. When using the simplified style, the subject line is always typed in all caps.

  The two kinds of subject lines are topical and informative subject lines. A topical subject line includes a couple of words about the subject matter of the letter—it is more general in nature and is normally used for indirect messages to avoid presenting the negative purpose of the letter. It is also used as a guide for filing. An informative subject line actually states the main point of the business letter. Since the reader can immediately grasp the meaning of the message, an informative subject line is often used with a direct message. A subject line should contain no more than five to six words—it is not a sentence.

- **Message.** The message of the letter is a required element and is separated from the preceding letter part by a double space. The message is single-spaced with a double space between paragraphs. The paragraphs begin at the left margin in all letter styles except the modified block with indented paragraphs, in which the paragraphs are indented five spaces or one-half inch.

- **Complimentary close.** The complimentary close, a required letter part in all of the letter styles except the simplified style, is typed a double space below the last line of the message. If one of the modified block letter styles is used, the complimentary close begins at the center point. The most popular closing used is "Sincerely."

- **Signature block.** The signature block designates whom the letter is from and is a required letter part in all letter styles. The writer's/sender's name and title are required letter parts, whereas the company name is an elective letter part. The signature block is usually placed at the left margin, but it would begin at the center when a modified block letter style is used.

—*Company name.* The company name may be included for legal reasons to indicate the letter represents the views of the entire company—not just the sender's. It may also be used if the sender is not using letterhead stationery or if the company being represented has a different name from the one on the letterhead stationery (for example, if it is a subsidiary company). It can also be used simply to reinforce the company's name. If used, the company name is typed in all capital letters a double space below the complimentary close.

—**Writer's/sender's name.** Usually, the letter writer's name appears in this part. However, since many individuals rely on subordinates or specialists to write letters for them, the writer's (or sender's) name may be included. The writer's/sender's name, a required letter part, is typed four lines below the company's name (if used) or the complimentary close to allow adequate space for the writer's/sender's signature.

If someone else signs the letter for the sender, that individual should include his or her initials under the sender's replicated signature.

—**Writer's/sender's identification.** The writer's/sender's identification includes the job title of the sender. The job title can be placed on a separate line under the writer's/sender's name or on the same line as the sender's name (preceded by a comma), depending on line length and appearance.

- *Reference notation.* Traditionally, the reference notation contained only the initials of the typist and was called "reference initials." Now the reference notation can contain any information that can be used to determine who wrote the letter, who typed the letter, what file name the letter is saved under, and where the letter is maintained. The reference notation is typed at the left margin a double space below the writer's/sender's identification.

Generally, who typed the letter is always contained in the reference notation and is signified by that individual's initials in lowercase: for example, "dl" or "dwl." If the sender of the letter differs from the letter writer, then the letter writer's initials are placed in the reference notation line in all caps along with the typist's initials; for example, "JR/dl," "JWR/dwl," "JR:dwl," or "JWR:dl." Two or three initials can be used, depending on the company's accepted practice.

Many individuals save their documents on CDs or networks. To help an individual quickly find where a letter is stored, the letter's file name and location may be included in the reference notation. For example, if a letter is stored under the file name "jrltr1," the reference notation may be "dl/jrltr1." If the letter is stored on a network, the reference notation may be "dl/f;\luse\jrltr1."

- *Enclosure notation.* If additional information or material is being enclosed with or attached to the letter, an enclosure notation is used. The enclosure notation is typed at the left margin a double space below the last included letter part. If more than one enclosure is included, you should always either list the enclosures or indicate the number of enclosures. Some acceptable enclosure styles from which to choose are

Enclosure	Enclosures
Enclosures: 2	Enc. or Encs.
Enclosures: Order form	2 Enclosures Attachment
Preaddressed envelope	

- *Copy notation.* If copies of a letter are to be sent to other individuals, a copy notation may be placed at the left margin a double space below the enclosure notation or the last included letter part. While "cc" stands for "courtesy copy," you should be aware that using "cc" when sending a copy might be thought to be out of date. Other abbreviations that may be used are "c" for "copy" and "pc" for "photocopy." The individual(s) or department(s) that are to receive the copy are keyed in after the copy notation abbreviation; for example:

cc Mr. James Smith	pc: Legal Department
Copies to: Jane Brown	c Dr. Frank Gilsby
Clint Black	

If the writer wants to send a copy of the letter to someone without the recipient's knowledge, a blind copy notation is used. The blind copy notation is the last letter part and is typed only on the file copy and that of the individual receiving the blind letter copy. The abbreviations "bc" for "blind copy," "bpc" for "blind photocopy," or "bcc" for "blind courtesy copy" are typed on the letter in the same manner copy notations are typed.

- *Second-page heading.* If a letter consists of more than one page, a second-page heading should be used in case the pages are separated. To whom the letter is addressed, the page number, and the date are typed one inch from the top; two or three empty lines should follow this information. Two acceptable styles are the block/vertical style used with the block style:

Jane Smith
Page 2
June 19, 2003

and the horizontal style used with the modified block style:

XYZ Corporation	2	June 19, 2003

Envelopes

The way in which an envelope is prepared is dictated by the United States Postal Service. To expedite the sorting and delivery of mail, the

EXHIBIT B.8   **U.S. Postal Service Envelope Formatting Guidelines**

Address placement
(not drawn to scale)

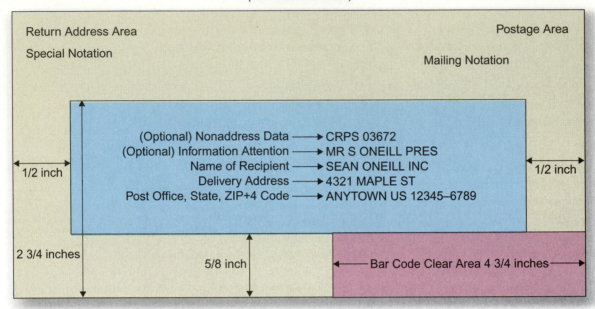

Postal Service uses optical character readers. So that an envelope can be properly read and sorted by this advanced equipment, you should take care to follow the U.S. Postal Service's envelope formatting guidelines, as illustrated in Exhibit B.8. Note the following specific points related to envelope preparation:

1. The information contained in the envelope address should be identical to that in the inside address. As discussed, this information is entered in the order of smallest delivery unit to largest; for example:

   Line 1—Recipient's name and job title, attention line, or other non-address information

   Line 2—Recipient's job title (if not included on Line 1)

   Line 3—Recipient's department

   Line 4—Organization's name

   Line 5—Delivery address

   Line 6—City, state, and zip code

   Line 7—Name of country (if letter is being sent abroad)

   The envelope address should contain between three and six lines of information.

2. The envelope address should be single-spaced in all capital letters with no punctuation (except for the hyphen in the nine-digit zip code).

3. The two-letter state abbreviation (see Exhibit B.9 for state abbreviations) should be used, followed by the zip code. Using the expanded

EXHIBIT B.9

Two-Letter State and Territory Abbreviations

Alabama	AL	Montana	MT
Alaska	AK	Nebraska	NE
Arizona	AZ	Nevada	NV
Arkansas	AR	New Hampshire	NH
American Samoa	AS	New Jersey	NJ
California	CA	New Mexico	NM
Colorado	CO	New York	NY
Connecticut	CT	North Carolina	NC
Delaware	DE	North Dakota	ND
District of Columbia	DC	Northern Mariana Islands	MP
Federated States of Micronesia	FM	Ohio	OH
Florida	FL	Oklahoma	OK
Georgia	GA	Oregon	OR
Guam	GU	Palau	PW
Hawaii	HI	Pennsylvania	PA
Idaho	ID	Puerto Rico	PR
Illinois	IL	Rhode Island	RI
Indiana	IN	South Carolina	SC
Iowa	IA	South Dakota	SD
Kansas	KS	Tennessee	TN
Kentucky	KY	Texas	TX
Louisiana	LA	Utah	UT
Maine	ME	Vermont	VT
Marshall Islands	MH	Virginia	VA
Maryland	MD	Virgin Islands	VI
Massachusetts	MA	Washington	WA
Michigan	MI	West Virginia	WV
Minnesota	MN	Wisconsin	WI
Mississippi	MS	Wyoming	WY
Missouri	MO		

Directional Abbreviations			
North	N	Northeast	NE
East	E	Southeast	SE
South	S	Southwest	SW
West	W	Northwest	NW

nine-digit zip code should allow for faster processing, directing, and delivery of the correspondence. One or two spaces should be placed between the state and zip code.

4. Special notations, such as PERSONAL or CONFIDENTIAL, are placed a double space below the return address, typed in all caps or underlined.

5. Mailing notations, such as CERTIFIED or SPECIAL DELIVERY, are placed a double space below the stamp position, typed in all caps or underlined.

6. Nothing should ever be typed in the bar code area, which is the lower 5/8 inch margin of the envelope.

Memorandums

The memorandum is an internal channel of communication between and among organizational members. Memorandums can be arranged in two styles—the traditional style and the simplified (or modern) style. The difference between these two styles is discussed next, followed by formatting guidelines that can be applied in preparing either style.

Traditional Memorandum Style

The traditional memorandum style utilizes four headings—TO, FROM, DATE, and SUBJECT. To the right of these headings are listed whom the memo is to, whom the memo is from, what date the memo was typed, and what the subject is.

To expedite the preparation of memorandums, most businesses have a stock of preprinted forms containing these headings. As seen in Exhibit B.10, to type such a memorandum, you would simply space two times after the SUBJECT heading (the longest guide word followed by a colon) and begin typing.

Simplified Memorandum Style

Because it improves the productivity and efficiency of producing memorandums on computer systems, the simplified memorandum style is growing in popularity. The simplified memorandum style includes the heading information found in the traditional memorandum style but omits the headings (see Exhibit B.11).

In typing a simplified memorandum, the following guidelines should be followed:

- After keying in the date, return four times.

- Key in the name (and title if needed) of the person to whom the memorandum is going. Return two times.

- Key in the subject line in all caps. Return two times.

- Key in the message. Return two times.

- Key in the sender's name and title (if needed).

MEMORANDUM

TO: Terri Smith, Sales Division Employee

FROM: Fran Jones, Office Manager   *FJ*

DATE: July 26, 2003

SUBJECT: TRADITIONAL MEMORANDUM STYLE

The traditional memorandum style is still used extensively in many businesses. The traditional style, as illustrated in this example, is set up in a fairly standardized way by including the four headings, "To," "From," "Date," and "Subject." Additional headings, such as a department or branch name, may be included.

Courtesy titles such as Mr. and Ms. are omitted unless you would normally use the title when addressing the individual in person. Job titles are optional. A sender may place his or her initials after the typed signature in the "From" line; or if the memorandum contains unusual information, a sender may sign his or her name at the bottom.

Typically, one-inch margins are used when following this style. If preprinted forms are used, heading entries should be aligned two spaces after the longest heading. If needed, any of the letter parts, such as enclosure notations, reference notations, and copy notations, can be used.

This information should help you type your memos in an expeditious manner.

This style closely resembles the simplified letter style and is a simple, time-saving style to prepare.

General Memorandum Format Guidelines

Whether the traditional or simplified style is used, some general format guidelines can be followed when preparing a memorandum.

- One-inch margins are used around the message.

- The "Memorandum" heading may be centered one or two inches from the top of the page. However, many memorandum preparers use a memorandum "macro" header (see Exhibit B.12) when using word-processing software.

EXHIBIT B.11

Simplified Memorandum Style

August 25, 2003

BUSN 305 Students

MODERN FORMAT FOR INFORMAL MEMO

The informal memo format has been changed to improve productivity and efficiency of producing printed work on computer systems. The following guides should be followed when setting up memos to reflect a modern appearance.
1) Omit the standard memo headings of TO, FROM, DATE, and SUBJECT.
2) Use a block format. Do not indent paragraphs or center the subject line.
3) After keying in the date, return four times.
4) Key the name and, if given, the title of the receiver. Return two times, making a double space.
5) Key the subject line in ALL CAPS (omit the heading SUBJECT). Return twice.
6) Key the message. Return four times.
7) Key the sender's name and title, if given. Return twice.
8) Key the document code as illustrated at the bottom of this document. Document codes usually include the operator's name or initials and the diskette label if a diskette is the storage medium.
9) If enclosures or photocopies (pc) or courtesy copies (cc) are noted, key that notation.

After you use this format, I'm sure you will see that this format is quite efficient and readable.

Jason Clark

Jason Clark

Associate Professor

dl/BUSN305

pc J. Rettenmayer

- All lines of the memorandum begin at the left margin.
- Use titles when keying in whom the memo is going to or coming from.
- The text of the memorandum begins a double space after the subject line or after the last heading information presented.
- The message should be single-spaced, with a double space between paragraphs.
- Enclosure notations, reference notations, and copy notations are used in the same manner as in preparing letters (see the previous discussion).

Sample A

Interdepartmental Memorandum
Computer and Office Information Systems

Sample B

Intradepartmental Memorandum
Computer and Office Information Systems

Sample C

Computer and Office Information Systems Department
Memorandum

- Second-page headings are used in multiple-page memorandums as in letters (see the previous discussion). A memorandum second-page heading includes whom the memorandum is to, the page number, and the date.

- The sender signs the memorandum using his or her initials, first name, or complete name. If the traditional style is used, the sender usually places his or her initials after the name in the "From" section. However, some companies prefer the sender's complete name be signed at the bottom of the memorandum. Signing the complete name at the bottom of the memorandum also indicates the message is extraordinary or nonroutine. If using the simplified

EXHIBIT B.13   **Business Report Margins (in inches)**

Head	Head	Head	Head	Head	Head	Head	Head	Head	Head	Head	Head	Head
First page or major page divisions	2	1	1	1	2	1	1.5	1	2.5	1	1	1
All other pages	1	1	1	1	1	1	1.5	1	1.5	1	1	1

EXHIBIT B.14   **Business Report Pagination**

Report Section/Page	Position	Style	Position	Style	Position	Style
Prefatory Parts—						
First page or major page divisions	Bottom	Lowercase Roman numeral	Bottom	Lowercase Roman numeral	Bottom	Lowercase Roman numeral
All other pages	Top	Lowercase Roman numeral	Top	Lowercase Roman numeral	Top	Lowercase Roman numeral
Text and Supplementary Parts—						
First page	Optional or bottom	Arabic numeral	Optional or bottom	Arabic numeral	Optional or bottom	Arabic numeral
Major page divisions	Bottom		Bottom		Bottom	
All other pages	Top	Arabic numeral	Top	Arabic numeral	Top	Arabic numeral

style, the sender would place the initials, first name, or complete name above the typed name at the bottom (as in a letter).

Frequently, internal memorandums are sent in specially prepared, reusable envelopes that contain space for listing the recipient's name and department. When using this type of envelope, simply cross out the name of the previous recipient and write in the current recipient. When using a regular envelope, you should type "COMPANY MAIL" or "INTEROFFICE MAIL" in the stamp position to ensure the memorandum is not inadvertently mailed. Then type the recipient's name and department in the address location.

Reports

Just as the appearance of a letter is important, the appearance or "packaging" of a report is also important and can have a great impact on the reader's acceptance of it. Therefore, care should be taken in the formatting of margins, pagination, spacing, indentions, and headings.

Margins

The margins used in a report are contingent upon how the report will be bound, as shown in Exhibit B.13. Generally, the margins are one inch unless the page is a major page division or the report is bound at the top or left. In these instances, extra spacing is added—an extra one inch is added to the top margin for major page divisions, and an extra one-half inch is added to the top or left margins for binding.

Although the bottom margin for report styles is one inch, if a complete page is not needed to present the material in a division of a report, a wider margin will occur. A wider bottom margin may also occur because headings should not be found at the bottom of a page by themselves and at least two lines of a paragraph should be placed at the bottom and the top of a page.

Pagination

Many variations of the placement of report page numbers exist. The most prevalent pagination placements and styles are shown in Exhibit B.14. Page numbers of all first pages or major divisions are placed one inch from the bottom of the paper and are centered between the left and right margins. The page numbers for all other pages are placed one inch from the top at the right margin. As shown in Exhibit B.14, prefatory pages are numbered using lowercase Roman numerals such as i, ii, iii, and iv; text and supplementary pages are numbered consecutively using Arabic numerals such as 1, 2, 3, and 4.

Although every page found in the report is counted as a page, every page is not always numbered. For example, the first page of the report body need not have the number "1" typed on it because the numbering of the first page is optional. Also, the title page is counted as page "i," but this identification should not appear on the title page.

Spacing and Indentions

Generally, business reports are double-spaced to make them easier to read. If a report is double-spaced, the paragraphs typically are indented five spaces or one-half inch. If a report is single-spaced rather than double-spaced, paragraphs begin at the left margin and text is single-spaced, with double spaces between paragraphs.

Headings

Headings should be used in the body of a report as well as in other business documents to aid the reader in understanding the document's contents. Generally, one to five heading levels are used, as seen in Exhibit B.15. All of these heading levels do not have to be used within a document or used in the order presented. For example, if a document you are preparing has three heading levels, you may choose Level 1, Level 2, and Level 4 heads; for a two-level heading document, you may choose Level 2 and Level 4 heads. The heading levels you choose are contingent upon stipulated format requirements or the customary format used by your company or audience.

Do, however, ensure that same-level headings are typed in the same manner. For example, if the report objective is typed as a side heading under "Introduction," then all other same-level headings found under "Introduction" should also be typed as side headings.

Following these formatting guidelines will enable you to concentrate on the *contents* of the document rather than its appearance.

Level one: CENTERED UPPERCASE HEADING

Level two: Centered Uppercase and Lowercase Heading

Level three: Centered, Underlined, Uppercase,
                                and Lowercase Heading

Level four: Flush Left, Underlined, Uppercase, and Lowercase Side
                     Heading

Level five: Indented, underlined, lowercase paragraph
                       heading ending with a period.

For example:
                     SHOULD STERLING CORPORATION OFFER A
                              MENTORING PROGRAM?
                                     Introduction
                                       Objective

        Problem
        Purpose
        Methodology
              Secondary research.
              Primary research.

Documenting Business Documents

The documentation of sources used in preparing a business document is imperative for achieving validity and credibility. All sources, whether quoted directly or paraphrased, should be documented. (If information presented within a business document is general knowledge, it need not be documented.) By documenting where information was obtained, you accomplish five goals:

1. You give credit where credit is due.

2. Your statements are supported, adding credibility to your report.

3. The reader can easily find a source if additional information is needed.

4. You adhere to copyright laws.

5. You are protected against accusations of plagiarism.

An important point about fair use should be noted. Even if information used in a business document is adequately documented, the fair use doctrine prohibits you from using someone else's work if your use of that work unfairly prevents the author from benefiting. For example, if you photocopy pages of material from a book and distribute them to employees—even though you thoroughly documented where you obtained the information—you may be depriving the author of the opportunity to sell the book to these people. Therefore, before using a reproduction of an extended amount of another's copyrighted work, you should write the author and receive permission.

Writers utilize various documentation methods to indicate which sources were used in preparing a business document. Traditionally, the footnote form of documentation was used. When using this form, full bibliographic information is placed at the bottom of the page on which the source is presented, preceded by consecutively numbered superscript Arabic numerals. Today, however, this documentation form is preferred primarily in the humanities.

The preferred documentation method in the social and natural sciences (including business) is the parenthetical form. This method uses parenthetical notes throughout the text to refer the reader to a list of sources (the bibliography or references section) at the end of the document. Superscript numbers or symbols (such as an asterisk) are used by the writer to make supplementary or explanatory notes. These notes may be comments about a source or the text or references to another section in the report. Since the parenthetical documentation method is the preferred method in business, the two most popular styles—the APA (American Psychological Association) and the MLA (Modern Language Association) styles—are discussed next.

The APA and MLA documentation styles use abbreviated bibliographical citations set off from the rest of the text by parentheses. The elements usually included in parentheses are the author's last name, the date of the source, and/or the page of the source. If any of the required citation elements are stated in a sentence, they may be omitted from the parentheses. If two or more sources are cited in the same set of parentheses, they should be listed alphabetically and separated by a semicolon.

To avoid interrupting the reading flow of the document, parenthetical citations should be placed wherever a natural pause would occur or as near as possible to the information they document. Additionally, the parenthetical reference should precede the punctuation mark that concludes the sentence, clause, or phrase that contains the borrowed material.

APA Citation Method

The APA citation method is often commonly referred to as the author–date or author–year citation method. The basic elements of the APA parenthetical citation method are the author's last name and the year of publication. The page number is also included if the reference directly quotes a source or refers to a specific source passage. All of these citation elements are separated by commas.

Once the author and publication year have been introduced, subsequent references to a source *within the same paragraph* need not include a parenthetical reference to the year of publication. APA citation guidelines for special situations follow (American Psychological Association, 2001):

1. If a source has multiple authors, use the word "and" to join the names when included within the text; use an ampersand (&) to join the names in a parenthetical citation and source list (bibliography). For example, *in text* use—"Angell and Butler (2002) showed. . ."; *in parentheses*—"(Angell & Butler, 2002)."

2. If a source has two authors, the last names of both authors should always be cited; for example, "(Angell & Butler, 2002)."

3. If a source has three to five authors, all of the authors should be cited the first time the source is documented in the text; subsequent citations of the source need only include the first author's name followed by "et al." (a Latin term meaning "and others"). For example, use "(Habel, Jones, Angell, & Butler, 2002)"—first citing; "(Habel et al., 2002)"—subsequent citings. If a citation has six or more authors, you should list only the first author's name, followed by "et al."

4. If a source has no author, the first few words of the first element listed in the bibliography should be used in the author's place. Typically, this will consist of the title of an article, book, periodical, or brochure. Quotation marks should be placed around article and chapter titles; an underline should be placed under book, periodical, or brochure titles.

5. If a source has an anonymous author, the word "Anonymous" should be used in place of an author name in the parenthetical citation and the list of sources.

6. If more than one source by the same author with the same publication date is used, the parenthetical citation should also include a suffix (such as a, b, c) after the year: for example, "(Jones, 2003a)" and "(Jones, 2003b)." This suffix would also be used in the list of sources.

7. If a quotation from a source you have not read is included in your text, enclose the author and year of the source you cited in parentheses preceded by "cited in." Generally, reference is made to the original author within the text: for example, "Smith's study (cited in Reed, 2002). . ."

8. When directly quoting a source or when referring to a specific part of a source, the page number should always be included: for example, "(Jones, 2003, p. 44)."

9. If a source is an organization or government agency that uses an abbreviation, the full name of the organization should be used in

the citation followed by the abbreviation in brackets. Subsequent citations use only the abbreviation. For example, write "(New York State Department of Transportation [NYS DOT], 2002)." In later citations when the same organization is referenced, use "(NYS DOT, 2002)."

10. If a source is electronic (online periodical, nonperiodical Web document or chapter), the author–date format should be used for citation in text and in parentheses.

When using the APA citation method, the list of sources is referred to as "References" or "Bibliography." A reference list includes only the sources cited in the business document, whereas a bibliography includes sources cited in addition to sources for background or further reading.

MLA Citation Method

The basic elements of the MLA parenthetical citation method are the author's last name and the page number of the material used in the source (no comma between author and page number): for example, "(Smith 15)." However, if an author's name has recently been cited, only the page number needs to appear in parentheses. Once another author is used, the writer would again include the author and page number. Guidelines for special situations expressed by The Modern Language Association of America (Gibaldi, 1999) follow:

1. If a source has two or three authors, the last name of each should be used: for example, "(Angell and Butler 20)" or "(Habel, Jones, and Myers 35)."

2. If a source has more than three authors, the first author's name is followed by "et al.": "(Williams et al. 200)."

3. If no author is given, the first bibliographic entry for that source would be used in the author's place.

4. If a source has an anonymous author, the word "Anonymous" *should not be used* in the parenthetical citation or list of sources—it is simply omitted. The first important bibliographic entry item is cited parenthetically and in the source list.

5. If a list of works includes more than one source by the same author, the parenthetical citation should also include a shortened title of the second bibliographic entry, placed between the author and page number and preceded by a comma: for example, "(Jones, *Managerial Communication* 75)."

6. If more than one page number is used, a hyphen indicates continuous pages were used and a comma indicates separate pages were used. For example, "(Jones 75–76)" indicates continuous pages; "(Jones 75, 80)" indicates separate pages.

7. If a quotation from a source you have not read is included in the text, enclose the author and page number of the source you cited in parentheses, preceded by "qtd. in": "(qtd. in Jones 75)."

8. If a source is an organization or government agency, use the organization name in text with the page number in parentheses or use a shortened title in the parentheses with the page number. For example, write "The New York State Department of Health maintains that . . . (62)" or "(NYS DOH 62)."

9. If a source is electronic, the same rules apply for citing print sources in text and in parentheses; use both the author's name and page number.

When using the MLA citation method, the list of sources is referred to as "Works Cited" and includes *only* the sources used in the business document. A "Works Consulted" section may be included instead of or in addition to the "Works Cited." It contains sources cited as well as other background sources.

List of Sources

So that the reader can see a complete listing of the sources used in preparing a business document, a list of sources should be included at the end of the document. As stated earlier, the APA style requires either a "References" section, which includes only the sources cited, or a "Bibliography" section, which includes sources cited as well as background sources. The MLA style requires a "Works Cited" section, which includes only those sources cited within the document, or a "Works Consulted" section, which includes background sources. Whichever style is used, the sources are listed alphabetically, and the second and subsequent lines of a citation are indented five spaces. The trend today is to double-space citations. Additionally, if the source list is lengthy, subheadings denoting the type of research method or type of publications used may be listed; for example, "Articles," "Books," "Interviews."

Sufficient bibliographic information should be listed so that the reader can locate the source if desired. Usually, the following elements are placed in the source listing: author, title, and publication data; however, the order of information and the use of capitalization and quotation marks differ in the APA and MLA styles. Examples of the APA and MLA bibliography styles follow.

The APA and MLA styles differ in the method used to cite books, periodicals, and electronic sources.

Pamphlets and government publications are documented in the same manner as books; however, if the writer of a government publication is not known, the government agency should be cited as the author—the larger government body should be stated first, followed by the agency name.

APA

Book

Fisher, A. B., & Adams, K. L. (1994). *Interpersonal communication* (2nd ed.). New York: McGraw-Hill.

Neuliep, J. W. (1996). *Human communication theory.* MA: Allyn & Bacon.

Government agency or corporate publication

Bank of Albany. (2002). *How sweep accounts work.* New York: Author.

U.S. Department of Labor, Bureau of Labor Statistics. (2000). *Producer price indexes.* Washington, DC: U.S. Government Printing Office.

Periodical

Prusak, L., & Cohen, D. (2001). How to invest in social capital. *Harvard Business Review,* 79, 86–93.

Sebenius, J. K. (2002). The hidden challenge of cross-border negotiations. *Harvard Business Review,* 80, 76–85.

Newspaper article

Jones, L. (2001, April 5). Taking the town. *The Times Record,* pp. A3, A12.

Electronic source

When citing periodicals or documents in text from an online source, direct the reader to the document you are citing rather than to the site or home page. For example, "(Jones, 2000, p. 32)." In the reference or bibliography section provide the author, date of publication, title of document (titles of books and journals in italics), volume and/or issue numbers, date of retrieval, and the current URL (Internet address). For an online article that is based on a printed source, include [electronic version] in brackets rather than the URL.

Nonperiodical document

Jones, L. (2001 July). *Leadership capital.* Retrieved September 5, 2002, from *http://www.leader.usc.edu/cap/text.htm.*

Online periodical that also appears in a printed journal

Jones, L., Butler, J., & Winston, A. (2001). Making money in these times [electronic version]. *Journal of Money,* 5, 201–203.

Online only journal article

Jones, L. (2002, April 7). More money. *Journal of Money,* 2(2). Retrieved November 10, 2002, from http://journal.mmo.org/money/volume2/mon001a.html.

MLA

Book

Fisher, Aubrey, and Katherine Adams. *Interpersonal Communication* (2nd ed.). New York: McGraw-Hill, 1994.

Neuliep, James. (1996). *Human Communication Theory.* MA: Allyn & Bacon, 1996.

Government agency or corporate publication

Bank of Albany. *How Sweep Accounts Work.* New York: Bank of Albany, 2002.

U.S. Department of Labor, Bureau of Labor statistics. *Producer Price Indexes.* Washington, DC: U.S. Government Printing Office, 2000.

<u>Periodical</u>

Prusak, Laurence, and Don Cohen. "How to Invest in Social Capital." *Harvard Business Review,* 79 (2001): 86–93.

Sebenius, James. "The Hidden Challenge of Cross-Border Negotiations." *Harvard Business Review,* 80 (2002): 76–85.

<u>Newspaper article</u>

Jones, Linda A. "Taking the Town." *The Times Record,* 5 Apr. 2001: A3.

<u>Electronic source</u>

In the works cited section provide the author, title of document (use quotation marks for article titles and underline book titles), volume number and issue, date of publication, total number of paragraphs or pages, date of retrieval, and the current URL (an Internet address). Place the URL in <angle brackets>.

<u>Nonperiodical document-</u>

Jones, Linda. *Leadership Capital.* New York, 2001. 5 Sept. 2002 *<http://www.leader.usc.edu/cap/text.htm>.*

<u>Online periodicals-</u>

Jones, Linda, and Joanne Butler. "Buying Power." *Journal of Money* 5.3 (2001): 31 pars. 6 Feb. 2002 *<http://www.journal.mmo.org/make/ current.issue/005c.html>.*

Both the APA and MLA styles are simpler documenting methods than the traditional footnote method and, as previously mentioned, either is acceptable in preparing a business document. When documenting citations in a report or other business document, you should choose only one of these citation methods and use it exclusively throughout your report.

References

Chapter 1

1. Andersen, P. A. "When One Cannot Not Communicate: A Challenge to Motley's Traditional Communication Postulates." *Communication Studies 42* (1991), pp. 309–25.

2. Barker, L. L. *Communication* 4th ed. Englewood Cliffs, NJ: Prentice-Hall, 1987.

3. Clevenger, Jr., T. "Can One Not Communicate? A Conflict of Models." *Communication Studies* 42, no. 4, (1991), pp. 340–353.

4. Daniels, C. "This Man Wants to Help You. Seriously." *Fortune* 142, no. 1 (2000), pp. 327–30.

5. Goleman, D.; R. Boyatzis; and A. Mckee. "Primal Leadership: The Hidden Driver of Great Performance." *Harvard Business Review* 79, no. 11 (2001), pp. 42–51.

6. Goss, B. *Communication in Everyday Life.* Belmont, CA: Wadsworth, 1983.

7. Gouran, D. S.; W. E. Wiethoff; and J. A. Doelger. *Mastering Communication,* 2nd ed. Needham Heights, MA: Allyn and Bacon, 1994.

8. Grossmann, J. "The Idea Guru." *Inc.* 23, no. 6 (2001), pp. 32–41.

9. Fisher, B. A. *Perspectives on Human Communication.* New York: MacMillian, 1978.

10. Hammonds, K. H. "Continental's Turnaround Pilot." *Fast Company,* December 2001, pp. 96–101.

11. "Michael Porter's Big Ideas." *Fast Company,* March 2001, pp. 150–55.

12. Infante, D. A.; A. S. Rancer; and D. F. Womack. *Building Communication Theory,* 2nd ed. Prospect Heights, IL: Waveland Press, 1993.

13. Krapels, R. H., B. D. Davis. "Communication Training in Two Companies." *Business Communication Quarterly* 63, no. 3 (2000), pp. 104–10.

14. Muoio, A. "NCR's Speed Demons." *Fast Company,* February 2001, pp. 50–52.

15. Roberts, C. V., and K. W. Watson, eds. *Intrapersonal Communication Processes: Original Essays.* New Orleans, LA: Spectra, 1989.

16. Salter, C. "Attention, Class! 16 Ways to Be a Smarter Teacher." *Fast Company,* December 2001, pp. 114–26.

17. Shedletsky, L. *Meaning and Mind: An Intrapersonal Approach to Human Communication.* Bloomington, IN: ERIC Clearinghouse on Reading and Communication Skills, 1989.

18. Walt Disney World College Program, Disney Worldwide Services, Inc., Lake Buena Vista, FL www.wdwcollegeprogram.com.

19. Zellner, Wendy. "How Well Does Wal-Mart Travel?" *Business Week Online,* September 3, 2001. Retrieved August 27, 2002: www.businessweek.com:/print/magazine/content.

Chapter 2

1. Barker, L. L. *Communication,* 3rd ed. Englewood Cliffs, NJ: Prentice-Hall, 1984.

2. Boyle, M. "How to Cut Perks without Killing Morale." *Fortune* 143, no 4 (2001), pp. 241–44.

3. Brown, J. S., and E. S. Gray. "The People Are the Company." *Fast Company,* November 1995, p. 78.

4. Dahle, C. "Is the Internet Second Nature?" *Fast Company,* July 2001, pp. 145–50.

5. Fisher, B. A. *Perspectives on Human Communication.* New York: Macmillian, 1978.

6. Foltz, R. *Inside Organizational Communication.* New York: Longman, 1981.

7. Gimein, M. "Smart Is Not Enough." *Fortune* 143, no. 1 (2001), pp. 124–36.

8. Glater, J. "Andersen Auditor Testifies Policy Entailed Shredding." *The New York Times,* May 22, 2002.

9. Glater, J. "Prosecutors Use Notes to Bolster Case against Andersen." *The New York Times,* May 21, 2002.

10. Goldhaber, G. M. *Organizational Communication.* Madison, WI: Brown & Benchmark, 1993.

11. Gross, N., August 28, 2000. "Mining a Company's Mother Lode of Talent." *Business Week Online.* Retrieved July 31, 2001: www.businessweek.com:/print/magazine/content.

12. Herbold, R. J. "Inside Microsoft: Balancing Creativity and Discipline." *Harvard Business Review.* Vol. 80, no. 1, 2002, pp. 73–79.

13. Katz, D., and R. Kahn. *The Social Psychology of Organizations.* New York: John Wiley & Sons, 1966.

14. Littlejohn, S. W. *Theories of Human Communication.* Belmont, CA: Wadsworth, 1999.

15. Meyer, C. "The Second Generation of Speed." *Harvard Business Review,* 79, no. 4 (2001), pp. 24–25.

16. Mochari, I. "In a Former Life." *Inc.* 23, no. 10 (2001), p. 84.

17. O'Connor, J. R. "Serial Transmission of Information: A Study of the Grapevine." *Journal of Applied Communication Research* 5 (1977), pp. 61–72.

18. Overholt, A. "Intel's Got (Too Much) Mail." *Fast Company,* March 2001, pp. 56–58.

19. Putnam, L., and M. Pacanowsky, eds. *Communication and Organizations: An Interpretive Approach.* Beverly Hills, CA: Sage, 1983.

20. Seglin, J. L. "The Righteous Stuff: Reviewing Your Boss." *Fortune* 143, no. 12 (2001), p. 248.

21. Shockley-Zalabac, P. *Fundamentals of Organizational Communication: Knowledge, Sensitivity, Skills, Values.* New York: Longman, 1991.

22. Singer, T. "Can Business Still Save the World?" *Inc.,* April, 2001 pp. 58–72.

23. Torriero, E. A. "Shredding Catchphrase at Issue." *Chicago Tribune,* May 22, 2002.

24. Welles, E. O. "Great Expectations." *Inc,* 23, no. 3 (2001), pp. 68–74.

Chapter 3

1. Altheide, D. L. *Media Power.* Newbury Park, CA: Sage, 1985.

2. Barron, K. "Toy Story." *Forbes,* 165, no. 14 (2000), pp. 140–44.

3. Bettinghaus, E. P., and M. J. Cody. *Persuasive Communication,* 5th ed. Fort Worth, TX: Harcourt Brace, 1994.

4. Bunn, A. "Call of the Wired." *Brills Content* 3, no. 5 (2000), pp. 64–65.

5. Burrows, P. "Technology on Tap." *Business Week,* (2000), pp. 74–84.

6. Champion, D. "Mastering the Value Chain." *Harvard Business Review,* 79, no. 6 (2001), pp. 109–14.

7. Chase, R. B., and S. Dasu. "Want to Perfect Your Company's Service? Use Behavioral Science." *Harvard Business Review,* 79, no. 6 (2001), pp. 79–84.

8. Fleming, M., and L. Levie. *Instructional Message Design.* Englewood Cliffs, NJ: Educational Technology Publications, 1978.

9. Gagne, R. M.; L. J. Briggs; and W. W. Wagner. *Principals of Instructional Design.* Fort Worth, TX: Hartcourt Brace, 1992.

10. Gayeski, D. Personal communication, April 20, 2000.

11. Gingold, D. "Keeping Your Edge." *Fortune,* 143, no. 12 (2001), pp. s2–s17.

12. Goffman E. *The Presentation of Self in Everyday Life.* New York: Doubleday, 1959.

13. Hybels, S., and R. L. Weaver II. *Communicating Effectively,* 5th ed. Boston, MA: McGraw-Hill, 1998.

14. Kemp, J. E.; G. R. Morrison; and S. M. Ross. *Designing Effective Instruction,* 2nd ed. Upper Saddle River, NJ: Prentice Hall, 1998.

15. Kirsner, S. "How to Stay on the Move When the World Is Slowing Down." *Fast Company,* (July 2001), pp. 113–21.

16. McCroskey, J. C., and T. Young. "Ethos and Credibility: The Construct and Its Measurement after Three Decades." *Central States Speech Journal* 32 (1981), pp. 24–34.

17. McQuail, D. *Mass Communication Theory: An Introduction,* 2nd ed. London: Sage, 1987.

18. Rogers, E. M. *Diffusion of Innovations.* New York: Free Press, 1983.

19. Rosenbloom, J. "Midnight Express." *Inc.* 23, no. 10 (2001), pp. 76–79.

20. Varchaver, N. "A Geek Tragedy." *Fortune,* 142, no. 1 (2000), pp. 42–43.

21. Windahl, S.; B. Signitzer, and J. T. Olson. *Using Communication Theory: An Introduction to Planned Communication.* London: Sage, 1995.

Chapter 4

1. Barker, L. L. *Communication.* Englewood Cliffs, NJ: Prentice Hall, 1984.

2. Barker, L.; K. J. Wahlers, and K. W. Watson. *Groups in Process: An Introduction to Small Group Communication.* 6th ed. Needham Heights, MA: Allyn & Bacon, 1995.

3. Charan, R. "Conquering a Culture of Indecision." *Harvard Business Review,* 79, no. 4 (2001), pp. 75–82.

4. Daniels, C. "The Plane Truth about Lucent." *Fortune,* 143, no. 12 (2001), p. 252.

5. _____. "How to Goof Off at Your Next Meeting." *Fortune,* 142, no. 10 (2000), pp. 289–90.

6. Floyd, J. *Listening: A Practical Approach.* Glenview, IL: Scott, Foreman, 1985.

7. Gallagher, P. "How Can You Be a Great Leader? "*Success* 48, no. 3 (2001), p. 33.

8. Goss, B. *Communication in Everyday Life.* Belmont, CA: Wadsworth, 1983.

9. Hybels, S., and R. L. Weaver. *Communicating Effectively.* 5th ed. Boston, MA: McGraw-Hill, 1998.

10. Montgomery, R. *Listening Made Easy.* New York: Amacon, 1981.

11. Mornell, P. "The Sounds of Silence." *Inc.,* February 2001, pp. 117–18.

12. Nichols, M. P. *The Lost Art of Listening.* New York: Guilford Press, 1995.

13. Shockley-Zalabak, P. *Fundamentals of Organizational Communication: Knowledge, Sensitivity, Skills, Values.* New York: Longman, 1991.

14. Stewart, J., and C. Logan. "Empathetic and Dialogic Listening." In *Bridges Not Walls,* 7th ed., ed. J. Stewart. Boston, MA: McGraw-Hill, 1999.

15. Tannen, D. *That's Not What I Meant.* New York: Ballantine Books, 1986.

16. _____. *You Just Don't Understand.* New York: Ballantine Books, 1990.

17. Tichy, N. M. "No Ordinary Boot Camp." *Harvard Business Review* 79, 4 (2001), pp. 63–70.

18. Ulwick, A. W. "Turn Customer Input into Innovation." *Harvard Business Review 80,* no. 1 (2002).

Chapter 5

1. Brigham, J. C. *Social Psychology.* Glenview, IL: Scott, Foresman, 1986.

2. Bruner, J. *Acts of Meaning.* Cambridge, MA: Harvard University Press, 1990.

3. Eco, U. *A Theory of Semiotics.* Bloomington, IN: Indiana University Press, 1976.

4. Einhart, N. "Job Titles of the Future." *Fast Company,* April 2001, p. 66.

5. Foss, S. K.; K. A. Foss; and R. Trapp. *Contemporary Perspectives on Rhetoric.* Prospect Heights, IL: Waveland Press, 1985.

6. Frankl, V. E. *Man's Search for Meaning.* New York: Simon & Schuster, 1963.

7. _____. *The Will to Meaning: Foundations and Applications of Logotherapy.* New York: Penguin Books, 1988.

8. Herndon, S. Personal communication, April 4, 2000.

9. Laing, R. D. *Self and Others.* London: Travistock, 1969.

10. _____. *Knots.* London: Travistock, 1971.

11. Lavin-Bernick, C. "When Your Culture Needs a Makeover." *Harvard Business Review* 79, no. 6 (2001), pp. 53–61.

12. Lester. R. L.; M. J. Piore; and K. M. Malek. "Interpretive Management: What General Managers Can Learn from Design." *Harvard Business Review* 76, no. 2 (1998), pp. 86–96.

13. Littlejohn, S. W. *Theories of Human Communication,* 4th ed., Belmont, CA: Wadsworth, 1992.

14. Manis, J. G. and B. N. Meltzer, eds. *Symbolic Interaction.* Boston, MA: Allyn & Bacon, 1978.

15. Mead, G. H. *Mind, Self, & Society.* Chicago: University of Chicago Press, 1934.

16. Moore, P. L. "GE Embraces the Paperless Office." *Business Week,* 2001, p. 10.

17. Moore, P. "Demand Rises for Simpler Documents." *Business Journal.* Retrieved online 3 June, 2002, www.denverbizjournals.com.

18. Neuliep, J. W. *Human Communication Theory.* Needham Heights, MA: Allyn & Bacon, 1996.

19. Powers, V. J. "Speaking the Language of Business at Dow: Marketing Communications Translates Value to Dollars." *Excellence in Practice* 4 (1998), pp. 1–8.

20. Prusak, L., and D. Cohen. "How to Invest in Social Capital." *Harvard Business Review* 79, no. 6 (2001), pp. 86–93.

21. Redding, W. C. *The Corporate Manager's Guide to Better Communication.* Glenview, IL: Scott, Foresman, 1984.

22. Shedletsky, L. *Meaning and Mind: An Intrapersonal Approach to Human Communication.* Bloomington, IN: ERIC Clearinghouse on Reading and Communication Skills, 1989.

23. Tannen. D. *You Just Don't Understand.* New York: Ballantine Books, 1990.

24. _____. *That's Not What I Meant.* New York: Ballantine Books, 1986.

25. Thibaut, J. W., and H. H. Kelly. *The Social Psychology of Groups.* New York: Wiley, 1959.

26. Watzlawick, P.; J. H. Beavin; and D. D. Jackson. *Pragmatics of Human Communication: A Study of Interactional Patterns, Pathologies and Paradoxes.* New York: Norton, 1967.

27. Windahl, S.; B. Signitzer; and J. T. Olson. *Using Communication Theory.* Thousand Oaks, CA: Sage, 1992.

28. Zellner, Wendy. "How Well Does Wal-Mart Travel?" *BusinessWeek* Online. Retrieved August 27, 2001: www.businessweek.com:/print/magazine/content.

Chapter 6

1. Barker, L. L. *Communication.* 3rd ed.. Englewood Cliffs: Prentice-Hall, 1984.

2. Foss, S. K.; K. A. Foss; and R. Trapp, eds. *Contemporary Perspectives on Rhetoric.* 2nd ed. Prospect Heights, IL: Waveland Press, 1991.

3. Griffin, E. A. *A First Look at Communication Theory.* New York: McGraw Hill, 1994.

4. Gouran, D. S.; W. E. Wiethoff; and J. A. Doelger. *Mastering Communication,* 2nd ed. Needham Heights, MA: Allyn & Bacon., 1994.

5. Infante, D. A.; A. S. Rancer; and D. F. Womack. *Building Communication Theory.* 2nd ed. Prospect Heights, IL: Waveland Press, 1993.

6. Lucaites, J. L.; C. M. Condit; and S. Caudill, eds. *Contemporary Rhetorical Theory.* New York: Guildford Press, 1999.

7. McCroskey, J. C. "Oral Communication Apprehension: A Summary of Recent Theory and Research." *Human Communication Research* 4 (1977), pp. 78–93.

8 Mornell, P. "The Sounds of Silence." *Inc,* vol. 23, no. 2 (2001), pp. 117–18.

9. Morton, O. "Shadow Science." *Wired* 9, no. 6 (June 2001), pp. 163–69.

10. Richmond, V. P., and J. C. McCroskey. "Willingness to Communicate and Dysfunctional Communication Processes." In *Intrapersonal Communication Processes: Original Essays,* eds. C. V. Roberts and K. W. Watson. New Orleans, LA: Spectra, 1989.

Chapter 7

1. Adler, R. B., and J. M. Elmhorst. *Communicating at Work: Principles and Practices for Business and the Professions.* New York: McGraw-Hill, 1999.

2. Bailey, E. P. *Writing and Speaking at Work: A Practical Guide for Business Communication.* Upper Saddle River, NJ: Prentice Hall, 1999.

3. Barker, L. L. *Communication.* Englewood Cliffs, NJ: Prentice Hall, 1984.

4. Conger, J. A. "The Necessary Art of Persuasion." *Harvard Business Review* 75 (1998), pp. 82–95.

5. Cooper, L. *The Rhetoric of Aristotle.* Englewood Cliffs, NJ: Prentice Hall, 1932.

6. Daniels, C. "This Man Wants to Help You: Seriously." *Fortune* 142, no. 1 (2000), pp. 327–30.

7. Doelger, J. A.; D. S. Gouran; and W. E. Wiethoof. *Mastering Communication.* Needham Heights, MA: Allyn & Bacon, 1994.

8. Gregory, J. M. *The Seven Laws of Teaching.* Grand Rapids, MI: Baker Books, 1997.

9. Greene, M., and J. G. Ripley. *Communicating for Future Business Professionals.* Upper Saddle River, NJ: Prentice Hall, 1998.

10. Grossmann, J. "The Idea Guru." *Inc.* 23, no. 6 (May 2001), pp. 32–41.

11. Gouran, D. S., W. E. Wiethoof; and J. A. Doelger. *Mastering Communication.* 2nd ed. Needham Heights, MA: Allyn & Bacon, 1994.

12. Hybels, S., and R. L. Weaver II. *Communicating Effectively.* Boston, MA: McGraw-Hill, 1998.

13. Lavin Bernick, C. "When Your Culture Needs a Makeover." *Harvard Business Review* 79, no. 6 (2001), pp. 53–62.

14. Morgan, N. "The Kinesthetic Speaker: Putting Action into Words." *Harvard Business Review* 79, no. 4 (2001), pp. 113–20.

15. Nice, S. E. *Speaking for Impact: Connecting with Every Audience.* Needham Heights, MA: Allyn & Bacon, 1998.

16. O'Hair, D., and R. Stewart. *Public Speaking: Challenges and Choices.* New York: Bedford/St. Martin's, 1999.

17. Tichy, N. M. "No Ordinary Boot Camp." *Harvard Business Review* 79, no. 4 (2001), pp. 63–70.

18. "PacifiCare Health Systems Announces Exit from Ohio and Kentucky Markets." Retrieved online (June 14, 2000), www.pacificare.com/corporate/ news/pressrel/.

Chapter 8

1. Abromowitz, R. "Everything Ventured, Everything Lost." *Los Angeles Times,* September 23, 2001, p. F8.

2. BigBooster.com. "A Tribute to Warren Buffet. Hall of Financial Giants" (2001). Retrieved: September 26, 2001, www.bigbooster.com/tribute/warren_ buffet.html.

3. Buffet, W. "Chairman's Letter." Berkshire Hathaway Inc. 2000 annual report (2000). Retrieved: September 26, 2001, www.berkshirehathaway.com/200ar/ 2000letter.html.

4. Chase, M., and S. Trupp. *Office Emails That Really Click.* Newport, RI: Aegis Publishing Group, Ltd., 2000.

5. Cohen, A. "Worker Watchers." *Fortune,* May 14, 2001, pp. 70–80.

6. Dembling, S. "E-Mail Minefield." *Sky,* October 2000, p. 116.

7. Fisher, A. "Ask Annie: Readers Weigh in on Letter Writing and Raising Kids." *Fortune,* October 30, 2000, p. 300.

8. Furfaro, D. "Finch Pruyn Alerts Strikers." *Times Union,* September 19, 2001, p. E4.

9. Hamilton, J. O. "Like It or Not, You've Got Mail: E-mail Brings Convenience—But at What Cost?" *BusinessWeek Online,* October 4, 1999. Retrieved: September 21, 2001, www.businessweek.com/ 1999/99_40/b3649026.htm.

10. Headlam, B. "How to E-Mail Like a C.E.O." *New York Times Magazine,* April 8, 2001, pp. 6–7.

11. Hyman, J. "Companies Take a Hard Line against Nasty Worker E-Mail." *Washington Times*, September 18, 2000, p. D9.

12. Messmer, M. "Enhancing Your Writing Skills." *Strategic Finance* 82, no. 7 (January 2001), p. 8.

13. Naraine, R. "Shooting Gallery to File Bankruptcy." (19, July 2001). Retrieved December 18, 2001, from www.internetnews.com/bus_news/article/0,,3_804811,00.html.

14. Reuters News Service. "Compaq Flees PC Price Wars for Higher Ground—Memo." Forbes.com, June 25, 2001. Retrieved: September 21, 2001.

15. Seglin, J. "Attention, E-Mail Snoops." *Fortune*, May 14, 2001, p. 254.

16. Whelan, J. *E-Mail: Getting Moving with Digital Communication.* London: Pearson Education Limited, 2000.

17. Wingfield, N. "Concerned Employers Are Sending a Stern Message to Workers These Days: Sending the Wrong Kind of E-Mail Can Get You Fired." *The Wall Street Journal,* December 2, 1999, p. B, 8:4.

Chapter 9

1. Abromowitz, R. "Everything Ventured, Everything Lost." *Los Angeles Times*, September 23, 2001. Retrieved through Proquest, December 18, 2001.

2. EARepBackflash. "Inappropriate Email Responses." Electronic Arts Majestic Message Board, October 29, 2001. Retrieved November 1, 2001, www.majestic.com (no longer in service).

3. Naraine, R. "Shooting Gallery to File Bankruptcy," July 19, 2001. Retrieved December 18, 2001, www.internetnews.com/bus-news/article/0,,3_804811,00.html.

4. "Sample Collection Letters." *Business Owner's Toolkit*, 2002. Retrieved June 20, 2002, www.toolkit.cch.com/tools/letter_m.asp.

5. Saunders, C. "Itemus to Acquire U.S. Rich Media Firm," 2001. Retrieved December 18, 2001, www.internetnews.com/IAR/print/0,,12_500041,00.html.

6. "Uncertain Future for Film Company." Retrieved December 18, 2001, BBC News Online www.news.bbc.co.uk/low/English/entertainment/film/newsid_1431000/1431788.stm.

Chapter 10

1. ActiveMEDIA Research. "Real Numbers behind the Online Business-to-Business Industry," 2000. Retrieved August 14, 2001: www.info-edge-asap.com/info/com.infoedge_articles_7457.html?se+ink.

2. Buchman, M. L. "The Fine Art of a One Page Proposal." *Journal of Systems Management* 44, no. 2 (1993), pp. 28–32.

3. Chairez, B. C. "Tackling Business Proposals." *Dallas Business Journal* 19, no. 12 (1995), p. B6.

4. Couch, T., and Knack, R. "Get That Grant: How to Write a Winning Proposal." *Planning* 62, no. 12 (1996), pp. 17–20.

5. Dickinson, M. "The Secrets of Their Success." *The Grantsmanship Center Magazine*, 1998. Retrieved May 17, 2001. Available: www.tgci.com/publications/98fall/SecretsToSuccess.html.

6. Economist Intelligence Unit eBusiness Forum. "US: Yahoo! Aims to Cash in on Freeloaders," August 31, 2001. Retrieved September 1, 2001: www.ebusinessforum.com/index.asp?doc_id=4393.

7. Fulscher, R. J. "A No-Fail Recipe: Winning Business Proposals." *Journal of Property Management* 61, no. 1 (1996). pp. 62–67.

8. Gillie, J. "Boeing Jets Get in Line Assembly." *News Tribune*, August 26, 2001, p. D1.

9. Holmes, S. "Boeing Goes Lean." *BusinessWeek Online*, June 4, 2001. Retrieved September 2, 2001: www.businessweek.com/magazine/content/01_23/b3735098.htm.

10. InterDigital Communications Corporation. "Homeward Bound: 2000 U.S. Residential Telecommunications Survey," 2000. Retrieved August 14, 2001: www.marketresearch.com/product/display.asp?productid=270979.

11. Jablonsky, J. "Teaching the Complexity of Business Proposals." *Business Communication Quarterly* 62, no. 3 (1999), pp. 108–12.

12. Kiritz, N. J. "Hard Data/Soft Data: How They Help You Build Strong Proposals." *The Grantsmanship Center Magazine*, 1997. Retrieved May 15, 2001. Available: www.tgci.com/publications/97winter/hardsoft.htm.

13. Koudsi, S. "Remedies for an Economic Hangover." *Fortune* 143, no. 14 (2001), pp. 130–40.

14. Knowles, F. "Hotel Union to Hold Hearings on Takeover Justification." *Chicago Sun-Times*, March 13, 2001. Retrieved August 14, 2001: www.suntimes.com/output/business/hotel13.html.

15. Miner J. T., and L. E. Miner. *A Guide to Proposal Planning and Writing.* The Oryx Press, 2000. Retrieved January 1, 2001: www.oryxpress.com/miner.htm.

16. Murphy, N. R. "The ABCs of Grant Writing or 'Always Be Certain.' " *Fund Raising Management* 30, no. 6 (1999), pp. 30–32.

17. Nassutti, C. "Art and Science of Proposals (Business Proposals)." *Outlook* 61, no. 3 (1993), pp. 18–22.

18. Pae, P. "Airbus Is Rocking Boeing's World." *Los Angeles Times*, January 28, 2001. Retrieved September 2, 2001: www.latimes.com/technology/business/innovation/la-000008349jul01.story.

19. Reinhardt, A., and S. Browder. "Boeing: Fly, Damn It, Fly." *BusinessWeek*, November 8, 1998. Retrieved September 2, 2001: www.businessweek.com/1998/45/bs603177.htm.

20. Worth, C. "How to Use Plain English Writing Annual Reports." *Washington Business Journal* 18, no. 40 (2000), p. 48.

Chapter 11

1. Cato, S. "Getting Better All the Time." *Chief Executive (U.S.)* (November 2000), p. 42. Retrieved February 15, 2001 from Business and Company ASAP.

2. Cook, J.; M. Leff; and D. Richman. "Webvan Founder Borders Unloaded Block of Share." Bell & Howell Information Service, July 11, 2001.

3. "Electronics Portfolios Project @CyberLab," Indiana University Purdue University at Indianapolis, 2000. Retrieved May 20, 2002: www.with.iupui.edu/about.htm.

4. Encarnacion, M.; S. McMath; and D. Parnell. "An Approaching Storm: ABB Flooded with Problems." Student paper for Dr. T. Rizkallah. California State University, Fullerton, March 15, 2002.

5. Grant, D. A. "Webvan Bags Kent Move—E-Grocer to Sublease Site, Auction Equipment." *South County Journal*, May 22, 2001. Retrieved July 29, 2001: www.msnbc.com/local.scj/a54532.asp.

6. Green, F. "HomeGrocer's Big Orange Peach Is Being Tossed." Bell & Howell Information Service, December 13, 2000.

7. Hamilton, J. "Delivering a more upscale look for The Stork Delivers.com." *BusinessWeek Online*, June 27, 2001. Retrieved May 8, 2002: www.businessweek.com:/print/technology/content/.../tc20010627_362.htm?mainwindow.

8. Himelstein, L. "Webvan Left the Basics on the Shelf [Analysis and Commentary]." *BusinessWeek,* July 2001, p. 43.

9. Mangalindan, M. "Webvan Shuts Down Operations, Will Seek Chapter 11 Protection." *The Wall Street Journal*, 2001.

10. Monroe, E., and H. Patel. "Proposal Group Project on Webvan Group, Inc. (Webvan)." Student paper for Dr. T. Rizkallah. California State University, Fullerton, 2001.

11. News Factor Network "With Webvan Gone, Where Will Online Shoppers Turn?" 2001. Retrieved July 22, 2001: www.dailynews.yahoo.com/h/nf/20010710/tc/11884_1.html.

12. Otterbourg, R. "Annual Report Copy: Banishing the Boredom." *Public Relations Journal* 46, no. 7, (July 1990), pp. 21–23.

13. Securities and Exchange Commission. "Form 10-K, Webvan Group, Inc., Annual Report for the Fiscal Year Ended December 31, 2000, April 2, 2000. Retrieved July 22, 2001: www.sec.gov/Archives/edgar/data/1092657/000101287001001485/0001012870-01-001485-0001.txt.

14. Securities and Exchange Commission. "Form 10-Q, Webvan Group, Inc., Quarterly Report for the Quarter Ended March 31, 2001," May 5, 2001. Retrieved July 22, 2001: www.sec.gov/Archives/edgar/data/1092657/000101287001500862/d10q.txt.

15. Securities and Exchange Commission. "Form S-1, Webvan Group, Inc., Registration Statement, November 3, 1999." Retrieved July 22, 2001: www.sec.gov/Archives/edgar/data/1092657/0000891618-99-00.

16. Sharp, R. "Popular Financial Reports for Citizens." *CPA Journal* 68, no. 3 (March 1998), pp. 34–39.

Chapter 12

1. Boorstin, J. "You Didn't Want to Work Friday Anyway." *Fortune* 143, no. 10 (2001), p. 252.

2. Childs, J. T. "Looking Back: 1996–2001." *Fast Company* March 2001, p. 89.

3. Conlin, M., and K. Moore. "Dr. Goodnight's Company Town." *BusinessWeek,* 2000, pp. 192–202.

4. Daniels, C. "How the Workplace Was Won." *Fortune* 143, no. 1 (2001), pp. 140–68.

5. Deal, T., and A. Kennedy. *Corporate Cultures: The Rites and Rituals of Corporate Life.* Reading, MA: Addison-Wesley, 1982.

6. Deetz, S. A.; S. J. Tracy; and J. L. Simpson. *Leading Organizations through Transition: Communication and Cultural Change.* Thousand Oaks, CA: Sage, 2000.

7. Dennehy, R. "The Executive as Storyteller." *Management Review* 88, no. 3 (1999), pp. 40–43.

8. Griffin, E. A. *A First Look at Communication Theory.* New York, NY: McGraw-Hill, 1994.

9. Geertz, C. *The Interpretation of Culture.* New York: Basic Books, 1973.

10. Gimein, M. "Smart Is Not Enough." *Fortune* 143, no. 1 (2001), pp. 124–36.

11. Gingold, D. "Keeping Your Edge: Managing a Diverse Corporate Culture." *Fortune* 143, no. 12 (2001), pp. s2–s17.

12. Goldhaber, G. M. *Organizational Communication.* Madison, WI: Brown and Benchmark, 1993.

13. Gudykunst, W. B., and S. Ting-Toomey. *Culture and Interpersonal Communication Theory.* Newbury Park, CA: Sage, 1988.

14. Hall, E. T. *Beyond Culture.* New York: Anchor, 1976.

15. _____. *The Hidden Dimension.* New York: Doubleday, 1966.

16. Henslin, J. M. *Essentials of Sociology: A Down to Earth Approach.* Boston, MA: Allyn and Bacon, 1996.

17. Korn/Ferry International and Columbia University Graduate School of Business. In *BusinessWeek* (2000), p. 16.

18. Lavin-Bernick, C. "When Your Culture Needs a Makeover." *Harvard Business Review* 79, no. 6 (2001), pp. 53–62.

19. Littlejohn, S. W. *Theories of Human Communication.* Belmont, Ca: Wadsworth, 1999.

20. Lundberg, and J. Martin, eds. *Reframing Organizational Culture.* Newbury Park, CA: Sage, 1991.

21. Marcus, M. B. "Workouts at Work Can Sweeten Long Days, But Don't Cut Loose on the Boss." *U.S. News and World Report* 128, no. 24 (2000), p. 57.

22. Moss Kanter, R. "A More Perfect Union." *Inc.* 23, no. 2 (2001), pp. 93–98.

23. Pacanowsky, M. E., and N. O'Donnell-Trujillo. "Organizational Communication as Cultural Performance," *Communication Monographs* 50, (1983), pp. 127–47.

24. _____. "Communication and Organizational Cultures." *Western Journal of Speech Communication* 46 (1982), pp. 115–30.

25. Powers, V. J. "Xerox Creates a Knowledge-Sharing Culture through Grassroots Efforts." *Knowledge Management in Practice* 18 (1999), pp. 1–4.

26. Prusak, L., and D. Cohen. "How to Invest in Social Capital." *Harvard Business Review* 79, no. 6, (2001), pp. 86–93.

27. Rogers, E. M. *Diffusion of Innovations.* 3rd ed. New York, NY: Free Press, 1983.

28. Roy, J. Personal communication. May 2, 2000.

29. Schein, E. *Organizational Culture and Leadership.* 2nd ed. San Francisco, CA: Jossey-Bass, 1992.

30. Schisgall, O. *Eyes on Tomorrow.* Chicago: J. G. Furgeson, 1981.

31. Sherrid, P. "Retired? Fine. Now Get Back to Work." *U.S. News & World Report* 128, no. 22 (2000), pp. 64–72.

32. Shockley-Zalabak, P. *Fundamentals of Organizational Communication: Knowledge, Sensitivity, Skills, Values.* New York: Longman, 1991.

33. Stepanek, M. "Clash of the E-Consultants." *BusinessWeek* (2000), pp. 123–24.

34. Tichy, N. M. "No Ordinary Boot Camp." *Harvard Business Review* 79, no. 4 (2001), pp. 63–70.

35. Wallace, E. L., and M. D. Taylor. *Coping with Cultural and Racial Diversity in Urban America.* New York: Praeger, 1990.

36. Wheelan, S. A. *Group Processes: A Development Perspective.* Boston, MA: Allyn and Bacon, 1994.

37. Whitford, D. "A Human Place to Work." *Fortune* 142, no. 1 (2001), pp. 108–20.

38. Winston, M. A. Personal communication, June 23, 2000.

Chapter 13

1. Barker, E. "High-Test Education." *Inc.* 23, no. 10 (2001), pp. 81–82.

2. Beebe, S. A.; S. J. Beebe; and M. V. Redmond. *Interpersonal Communication: Relating to Others.* Needham Heights, MA: Allyn and Bacon, 1996.

3. Berger, C. R. *Self-Conception and Social Information Processing.* In *Personality and Interpersonal Communication*, eds. J. C. McCroskey and J. A. Daly, Newbury Park, CA: Sage, 1987.

4. Boyle, M. "How the Workplace Was Won." *Fortune* 143, no. 1 (2001), pp. 140–68.

5. Breen, B. "Jazzed about Work." *Fast Company*, May 2001, pp. 194–99.

6. Burgoon, J. K., and T. Saine. *The Unspoken Dialogue: An Introduction to Nonverbal Communication.* Boston, MA: Houghton Mifflin, 1978.

7. Charan, R. "Conquering a Culture of Indecision." *Harvard Business Review* 79, no. 4 (2001), pp. 75–82.

8. Coplan, J. "Can Personality Science Improve Your Business I.Q.?" *BusinessWeek Online.* Retrieved June 14, 2002: August 29, 2000. www.businessweek.com:/print/smallbiz/content/aug2000/tr000829.htm?mainwindow.

9. Curry, P. "Lend Me Your Ear." *iSource Business*, May 2001, pp. 85–90.

10. Duck, S. W. *Understanding Relationships.* New York: Guilford Press, 1991.

11. Duck, S. W., and D. E. Miell. "Towards an Understanding of Relationship Development and Breakdown." In *The Social Dimension: European Perspectives on Social Psychology*, eds. H. Tajfel, C. Fraser, and J. Jasper. Cambridge, MA: Cambridge University Press, 1984.

12. Ekman, P., and W. V. Friesen. "The Repertoire of Nonverbal Behavior: Categories, Origins Usage and Coding." *Semiotica* 1 (1969), pp. 49–98.

13. Ekman, P., ed. *Emotion in the Human Face*. 2nd ed. New York: Cambridge, 1982.

14. Ekman, P., and W. V. Friesen. *Unmasking the Face*. Englewood Cliffs, NJ: Prentice-Hall, 1975.

15. Ellis, J. "Groove Makes It Possible to Light Up the Edge." *Fast Company* May 2001, pp. 96–101.

16. Fisher, A. B., and K. L. Adams. *Interpersonal Communication*. 2nd ed. New York: McGraw-Hill, 1994.

17. Gallagher, P. "Drive the Vision." *Success* 48, no. 3 (2001), pp. 32–33.

18. Germer, E. "Not Just for Kicks." *Fast Company,* March 2001, pp. 70.

19. Goldberg, M. "Cisco's Most Important Meal of the Day." *Fast Company* 13 (Feb 1998), p. 56.

20. Goss, B. *Communication in Everyday Life*. Belmont, CA: Wadsworth, 1983.

21. Hall, A. D., and R. E. Fagen. "Definition of a System." In *Modern Systems Research for the Behavioral Scientist*. ed. W. Buckley. Chicago: Aldine, 1968.

22. Hall, E. T. *The Hidden Dimension*. New York: Doubleday, 1966.

23. Harrington, A. "I'll Take That Pitch with a Dash of Politesse." *Fortune* 141, no. 12 (2000), pp. 334–36.

24. Hotch, R. "Put the Quality in Equality." *Success* 48, no. 3 (2001), p. 30.

25. Hofman, M. "Lost in the Translation." *Inc.* 22, no. 6 (2000), pp. 161–162.

26. Infante, D. A.; A. S. Rancer; and D. F. Womack. *Building Communication Theory*. 2nd ed. Prospect Heights, IL: Waveland Press, 1993.

27. Katzenbach, J., and Smith, D. "Virtual Teaming." *Forbes Global,* May 21, 2001. Retrieved September 20, 2001: www.forbes.com/best/2001/0521/048.html.

28. Kodama, D. "Tooling Up for Collaboration." *eCommerce Business,* 2001, pp. 5–10.

29. Knapp, M. L. *Nonverbal Communication in Human Interaction*. 2nd ed. New York: Holt, Rinehart & Winston, 1978.

30. Knapp, M. L. *Essentials of Nonverbal Communication*. New York: Holt, Rinehart & Winston, 1980.

31. _____. *Interpersonal Communication and Human Relationships*. Boston, MA: Allyn & Bacon, 1984.

32. Knapp, M. L., and A. L. Vangelisti. *Interpersonal Communication and Human Relationships*. 2nd ed. Boston, MA: Allyn & Bacon, 1992.

33. McGarvey, J.; T. Steinert-Threlkeld; and C. Wilson. "What's Ailing Lucent?" *Interactive Week,* February 21, 2000. Retrieved September 21, 2000: www.zdnet.com/zdnn/stories/news/0,4586,2444 141–2,00.html.

34. Mehrabian, A. *Silent Messages: Implicit Communication of Emotion and Attitudes*. Belmont, CA: Wadsworth, 1971.

35. _____. *Silent Messages: Implicit Communication of Emotion and Attitudes*. 2nd ed. Belmont, CA: Wadsworth, 1981.

36. Mosvick, R. K., and R. B. Nelson. *We've Got to Start Meeting Like This*. Glenview, IL: Scott, Foresman, 1987.

37. Odomirok, P. W. "The Power of Collaborative Purpose." *Industrial Management* 43, no. 1 (2001), p. 28.

38. Prusak, L., and D. Cohen. "How to Invest in Social Capital." *Harvard Business Review* 79, no. 6 (2001), pp. 86–93.

39. Reese, A. K. "The Collaborative Question." *isource Business,* May 2001, pp. 71–76.

40. Spiegel, R. *Next-Gen B2B: Collaboration*. *eCommerce Business,* 2001, pp. 1–5.

41. Schrage, M. "I'll Have the Pasta Primavera, with a Side of Strategy." *Fortune* 143, no. 1 (2001), p. 194.

42. Shinal, J. "Turning a Big Ship." *Forbes.com,* November 19, 1999. Retrieved September 20, 2000: www.forbes.com/1999/11/19/feat.html.

43. Siekman, P. "Seagate's Three-day Revolution." *Fortune* 43, no. 4 (2001), pp. 210A–210H.

44. Tichy, N. M. "No Ordinary Boot Camp." *Harvard Business Review* 79, no. 4 (2001), pp. 63–70.

45. Verderber, R. F., and K. S. Verderber. *Inter-Act: Using Interpersonal Communication Skills*. 7th ed. Belmont, CA: Wadsworth, 1995.

46. Warner, F. "He Drills for Knowledge." *Fast Company,* September 2001, pp. 186–91.

47. Westgeest, A., and B. Alves. "Make Your Meetings Matter." *Association Management* 53, no. I (2001), p. 121.

48. Wilmont, W. W. "Communication Spirals, Paradoxes, and Conundrums." In *Bridges Not Walls,* 7th ed., ed. J. Stewart. Boston, MA: McGraw-Hill, 1999.

49. _____. *Relational Communication*. New York: McGraw-Hill, 1995.

Chapter 14

1. Amtrak Reform Council (2001). Retrieved September 10, 2001: www.amtrakreformcouncil.gov.

2. Augustine, N. R. "Reshaping an Industry: Lockheed Martin's Survival Story." In *Harvard Business Review on Change.* Boston: Harvard Business School Press, 1998.

3. Barker, L. L. *Communication.* Englewood Cliffs, NJ: Prentice-Hall, 1984.

4. Bauman, R. P. "Five Requisites for Implementing Change." In *Navigating Change,* eds. D. C. Hambrick; D. A. Nadler; and M. L. Tushman. Boston: Harvard Business School Press, 1998.

5. Breen, B. "Change Is Sweet." *Fast Company,* June 2001, pp. 169–76.

6. Charan, R. "Conquering a Culture of Indecision." *Harvard Business Review,* 79, no. 4 (2001), pp. 75–82.

7. Deetz, S. A.; S. J. Tracy; and J. L. Simpson. *Leading Organizations through Transition.* Thousand Oaks, CA: Sage, 2000.

8. DeVoe, D. "Don't Let Conflict Get You off Course." *InfoWorld* 21, no. 32 (1999), p. 69.

9. Duck, J. D. "Managing Change: The Art of Balancing." In *Harvard Business Review on Change.* Boston: Harvard Business School Press, 1998.

10. Fisher, R.; W. Ury; and B. Patton. *Getting to Yes: Negotiating Agreement Without Giving In.* 2nd ed. New York: Penguin, 1991.

11. Fishman, C. "Why Can't Lego Click?" *Fast Company,* September 2001, pp. 145–57.

12. Gerard, G., and L. Teurfs. "Dialogue and Organizational Transformation." In *Community Spirit: Renewing Spirit and Learning in Business,* ed. G. Kazimierz. San Francisco, CA: New Leaders Press, 1995.

13. Goldhaber, G. M. *Organizational Communication.* Madison, WI: Brown and Benchmark, 1993.

14. Goss, T.; R. Pascale; and A. Athos. "The Reinvention Roller Coaster: Risking the Present for a Powerful Future." In *Harvard Business Review on Change.* Boston: Harvard Business School Press, 1998.

15. Hall, A. D., and R. E. Fagen. "Definition of a System." In *Modern Systems Research for the Behavioral Scientist* ed. W. Buckley. Chicago: Aldine, 1968.

16. Hamada, K. "Digital R$_x$." *Fast Company,* May 2001, pp. 183–91.

17. Henderson, R. "Managing Innovation in the Information Age." *Harvard Business Review,* 1994, pp. 100–5.

18. Houghton, J. R. "Corporate Transformation and Senior Leadership." In *Navigating Change,* eds. D. C. Hambrick; D. A. Nadler; and M. L. Tushman. Boston: Harvard Business School Press, 1998.

19. Hudson, K. "Transforming a Conservative Company One Laugh at a Time." *Harvard Business Review* 79, no. 7 (2001), pp. 45–53.

20. Jones-Yang, D. "Why Gates Is Smiling." *U.S. News & World Report* 130 no. 9 (2001), pp. 38–40.

21. Klein, S. M. "A Management Communication Strategy for Change." *Journal of Organizational Change Management* 2, no. 9 (1996), pp. 32–46.

22. Kotter, J. P. *Leading Change: Why Transformation Efforts Fail.* Boston: Harvard Business School Press, 1998.

23. Lavin-Bernick, C. "When Your Culture Needs a Makeover." *Harvard Business Review* 79, no. 6 (2001), pp. 53–62.

24. Lawrence, D. M. "Leading Discontinuous Change: Ten Lessons from the Battlefront." In *Navigating Change,* eds. D. C. Hambrick; D. A. Nadler; and M. L. Tushman. Boston: Harvard Business School Press, 1998.

25. Lederach, J. P. *Preparing for Peace: Conflict Transformation Across Cultures.* Syracuse, NY: Syracuse University Press, 1995.

26. _____. "Director's Circle." *Conciliation Quarterly* 8, no. 3 (1989), pp. 12–14.

27. Martin, R. "Changing the Mind of the Corporation." In *Harvard Business Review on Change.* Boston: Harvard Business School Press, 1998.

28. Moore, C. *The Mediation Process: Practical Strategies for Resolving Conflict.* 2nd ed. San Francisco: Jossey-Bass, 1996.

29. Mornell, P. "Nothing Endures but Change." *Inc.* 22, no. 10 (2000), p. 131.

30. Montgomery, P. "Tearing Down the Walls: Andreessen Discusses Mozilla." *PC Week,* 2000. Retrieved online July 28, 2000: www.zdnet.com/eweek/news/0316/18emarka.html.

31. Muoio, A. "Beg, Borrow, Stimulate." *Fast Company,* February 2001, p. 68.

32. Muller, J. "Ford: Why It's Worse Than You Think." *BusinessWeek,* 2001, pp. 80–89.

33. Ognanovich, N. "Amtrak Reform Council Restructuring to Separate Train Operations, Infrastructure." Government Employee Relations Report, 39, March 27, 2001, p. 1904. Retrieved September 10, 2001: www.subscript.bna.com/SAMPLES/ger.nsf.

34. Pearce, W. B., and Littlejohn, S. W. *Moral Conflict.* Thousand Oaks, CA: Sage, 1997.

35. Pruitt, D. "Strategic Choice in Negotiation." In *Theory and Practice,* eds. J. W. Breslin and J. Z. Rubin. Cambridge, MA: The Program on Negotiation at Harvard Law School, 1991.

36. Rogers, E. M. *Diffusion of Innovations.* 2nd ed. New York: Free Press, 1983.

37. Sebenius, J. K. "Six Habits of Merely Effective Negotiators." *Harvard Business Review* 79, no. 4 (2001), pp. 87–95.

38. Serwer, A. "A Rare Skeptic Takes on the Cult of GE." *Fortune,* 2001.

39. Shockley-Zalabak, P. *Fundamentals of Organizational Communication: Knowledge, Sensitivity, Skills, Values.* New York: Longman, 1991.

40. St. Pierre, N. "How to Get Amtrak on the Right Track." *BusinessWeek* online, June 28, 2001. Retrieved July 19, 2001: www.businessweek.com:/ bwdaily/dnflash/jun2001/nf20010628_026.htm.

41. Strebel, P. "Why Do Employees Resist Change?" In *Harvard Business Review on Change.* Boston: Harvard Business School Press, 1998.

42. Von Bertalanffy, L. *General Systems Theory: Foundations, Development, Applications.* New York, NY: Braziller, 1968.

43. Wehr, P. "Conflict Mapping," 2000. Cited online: www.colorado.edu/conflict/peace/treatment/ cmap.htm.

44. Winslade, J., and Monk, G. *Narrative Mediation.* San Francisco, CA: Jossey-Bass, 2000.

45. Wetlaufer, S. "Driving Change: An Interview with Ford Motor Company's Jacques Nasser." *Harvard Business Review,* 1999, pp. 77–88.

Chapter 15

1. Allen, J. G. *Jeff Allen's Best: The Résumé.* New York: Wiley, 1990.

2. Bernasek, A. "Help Wanted. Really." *Fortune* 143, no. 5 (2001), pp. 118–20.

3. Cirque du Soleil "Join Cirque—Offstage," 2002. Retrieved February 2, 2002: www.cirquedusoleil.com/ CirqueDuSoleil/en/jobs/offstage/current/IHQ_H um_Res_Tec.htm.

4. Enelow, W. S. "What Do Employers Really Want in a Résumé?" *JobWeb,* 2001. Retrieved January 25, 2001: www.jobweb.com/catapult/enelow-r.html.

5. Hammonds, K. H. "How Do You Structure Success?" *Fast Company,* April 2001, p. 58.

6. Kurlantzick, J. "A Temporary Boom in the Job Market." *U.S. News & World Report* 130, no. 11 (2001), p. 40.

7. Newfield, P. "The Netiquette of Internet Communications." *Career Bytes,* 2001. Retrieved January 25, 2001: www.headhunter.net/JobSeeker/ CareerBytes/hints0599.htm.

8. Parker, Y. *Ready-to-Go-Résumés.* Ten Speed Press, 1995.

9. Wahlgren, E. "For Gen X, It's Schmooze or Lose." *Business Week Online,* August 28, 2001. Retrieved December 14, 2001: www.businessweek.com/ careers/content/aug2001/ca20010828_696.htm.

10. Walsh R. D. "Job-Search Guidance from an Executive Recruiter." Career Journal from *The Wall Street Journal,* 2001. Retrieved January 25, 2001: www.careerjournal.com/recruiters/workexec/ 19971231walsh.html

11. Wellner, A. "Your Space Is the Place." *Fast Company,* May 2001, p. 60.

Chapter 16

1. Allen, J. G. *Jeff Allen's Best: Get the Interview.* New York: Wiley, 1990.

2. Barker, L. L. *Communication,* 3rd ed. Englewood Cliffs, NJ: Prentice-Hall, 1984.

3. Bolles, R. N. *What Color Is Your Parachute? A Practical Guide for Job-Hunters and Career Changes.* Berkeley, CA: Ten Speed Press, 2000.

4. Fry, R. *Your First Interview.* Hawthorne, NJ: The Career Press, 1991.

5. Gimein, M. "Smart Is Not Enough." *Fortune* 143, no. 1, (2001), pp. 124–136.

6. Kane, K. "The Riddle of Job Interviews." *Fast Company,* November 1995. Retrieved December 15, 2001: www.fastcompany.com/online/01/jobint.html.

7. Medley, A. H. *Sweaty Palms: The Neglected Art of Being Interviewed.* Berkeley, CA: Ten Speed Press, 1993.

8. Messmer, M. "Best Impression: Interview to Get the Job" 2000. Retrieved from www.headhunter.net/ jobseeker/careerbytes/hints0500.htm.

9. Moock Jr., R. T. *Get That Interview! The Indispensable Guide for College Grads.* Hauppauge, NY: Barron's, 1996.

10. Stimac, D. J. "Winning Career Strategies." Retrieved from www.careermag.com/newsarts/ interviewing/1050.html.

11. Useem, J. "Dot-coms: What Have We Learned?" *Fortune,* 142, 10 (2000), pp. 104.

12. Virtue, A. "Navigating the Internship Interviewing Process." *BusinessWeek,* February 1, 1999. Retrieved December 7, 2001: www.businessweek.com/ bschools/content/mbajournal/98seg6/alex6.htm.

13. Welles, E. O. "Great Expectations." *Inc.* 23, no. 3 (March 2001), pp. 68–74.

14. Wilson, G. L., and H. L. Goodall. *Interviewing in Context.* New York: McGraw-Hill, 1991.

Chapter 17

1. Ashford, J. "Graphics: Building Extraordinary Charts and Graphs." *Macworld*, 1998. Retrieved from www.macworld.com.

2. Broekhuizen, R. *Graphic Communications*, 4th ed. New York: Glencoe, 1995.

3. Feng Shui Advisors. "Feng Shui and Retail Stores," 1999. Retrieved May 8, 2002: www.168fengshui.com/Articles/retail.htm.

4. Howard Bear, J. "Grids: Order Out of Chaos." Retrieved from www.desktoppub.about.com.

5. Lester, P. M. *Visual Communication: Images with Messages*. Belmont, CA: Wadsworth, 1995.

6. Life Design. "Testimonials," 2000. Retrieved May 15, 2002: www.lifedesignworks.com/generic.html;$sessionid$TQGZNQQAAATYFWGI HUUUTIWYZA4S1PX0?pid=4.

7. Schrage, M. "Beyond Babble: Why the Babble Below Will Matter Less." *Fortune* 143, no. 6, 2001, p. 214.

8. Schwartz, B. "Off the Walls." *Fast Company*, 2001, p. x.

9. Sullivan, M. "No Fuss No-Loads." *Forbes Online*, February 19, 2002. Retrieved May 8, 2002: www.forbes.com/personalfinance/2002/02/19/0219adviser.html.

10. Warner, F. "Lear Won't Take a Back Seat." *Fast Company*, June 2001, p. 179–85.

11. Williams, R. *The Non-Designers Design Book*. Berkeley, CA: Peachpit Press, 1994.

Appendix A

1. Gefvert, Constant J. *The Confident Writer*, 2nd ed. (New York: W. W. Norton & Company, 1988), pp. 428–49.

2. Hacker, Diana, The Bedford Handbook, 5th ed. (Boston: BedfordBooks, 1998).

3. Perry, Devern J. and Silverthorn J. E., *Word Division Manual*, 3rd ed. (Cincinnati, OH: South-Western Publishing Company, 1984), pp. v–vi.

4. Troyka, Lynn Ouitman, *Simon & Schuster Handbook for Writers*, 3rd ed. (Englewood Cliffs, NJ: Prentice Hall, 1993).

Appendix B

1. American Psychological Association. (2001). Publication Manual of the American Psychological Association (5th ed.). Washington: APA. www.apastyle.org.

2. Gibaldi, J. (1999). MLA Handbook for Writers of Research Papers (5th ed.). New York: MLA. www.mla.org.

Index